Lecture Notes in Artificial Intelligence 8684

Subseries of Lecture Notes in Computer Science

T0213845

Christian Freksa   Bernhard Nebel
Mary Hegarty   Thomas Barkowsky (Eds.)

Spatial Cognition IX

International Conference, Spatial Cognition 2014
Bremen, Germany, September 15-19, 2014
Proceedings

 Springer

Volume Editors

Christian Freksa
Universität Bremen
Enrique-Schmidt-Str. 5, 28359 Bremen, Germany
E-mail: freksa@sfbtr8.uni-bremen.de

Bernhard Nebel
Universität Freiburg
Georges-Köhler-Allee 52, 79110 Freiburg, Germany
E-mail: nebel@informatik.uni-freiburg.de

Mary Hegarty
University of California
Santa Barbara, CA 93106, USA
E-mail: hegarty@psych.ucsb.edu

Thomas Barkowsky
Universität Bremen
Enrique-Schmidt-Str. 5, 28359 Bremen, Germany
E-mail: barkowsky@sfbtr8.uni-bremen.de

ISSN 0302-9743   e-ISSN 1611-3349
ISBN 978-3-319-11214-5   e-ISBN 978-3-319-11215-2
DOI 10.1007/978-3-319-11215-2
Springer Cham Heidelberg New York Dordrecht London

Library of Congress Control Number: 2014947471

LNCS Sublibrary: SL 7 – Artificial Intelligence

© Springer International Publishing Switzerland 2014

Typesetting: Camera-ready by author, data conversion by Scientific Publishing Services, Chennai, India

Printed on acid-free paper

Springer is part of Springer Science+Business Media (www.springer.com)

Preface

This is volume nine in a series of proceeding volumes dedicated to basic research in the interdisciplinary research area of spatial cognition. This research investigates relations between the physical spatial world on one hand and the mental world of humans, other species, and artificial agents, on the other hand. Cognitive agents – natural or artificial – make extensive use of spatial and temporal information about their environment and about their relation to the environment in order to move around, to behave intelligently, and to make decisions in the pursuit of their goals. More specifically, cognitive agents use topological, orientation, and distance information for navigating in space and for communicating about space.

From a cognitive point of view, a central question is how our minds represent and process spatial information. When designing representation systems for spatial information, usability will be increased if the external and internal forms of representation and processing are well aligned. This requires a thorough understanding of the roles of external spatial structures and how they are represented by natural cognitive agents. This volume comprises research contributions to the more specific topics of spatial memory, spatial language and communication about spatial environments, wayfinding and navigation, computational models of spatial capabilities, spatial knowledge processing with diagrams and maps, technical approaches to intelligent behavior in space, and spatial ability in humans.

Today, spatial cognition is an established research area that investigates a multitude of phenomena in a variety of domains on many different levels of abstraction involving several disciplines with their specific methodologies. One of today's challenges is to teach the different perspectives on spatial thinking in an integrated way such that the next generation of spatial cognition researchers develop a deep understanding of structural, perceptual, representational, computational, action-related, behavioral, linguistic, and philosophical aspects of spatial cognitive processing. To communicate these perspectives across disciplinary boundaries, 73 researchers from 12 countries contributed their work to the Spatial Cognition 2014 conference in Bremen. In a rigorous peer-review process, 27 original key papers were selected for single-track oral presentations, which are published in this volume. Each paper was reviewed and elaborately commented on by at least three Program Committee members.

In addition, 59 contributions were selected for poster presentation and discussion at the conference. The conference also featured three invited keynote lectures providing three different perspectives on spatial cognition: Ranxiao Frances Wang from the University of Illinois elaborated on the differentiation of various spatial reference frames to structure spatial knowledge; Stephan Winter from the University of Melbourne provided a critical perspective on intelligent spatial information systems and how they might better support human users; and Stefano Mancuso from the University of Florence provided a botanical perspective on spatial cognition from his research on plant intelligence.

Once again, this year's conference was co-sponsored by the Transregional Collaborative Research Center SFB/TR 8 Spatial Cognition (Bremen and Freiburg) and the Spatial Intelligence and Learning Center (Philadelphia and Chicago) with funding for student participation through the National Science Foundation SAVI Thematic Network in Spatial Cognition and the German Research Foundation funding. It was co-organized by the UC Santa Barbara Center for Spatial Studies. This conference brought together researchers from these centers and from other spatial cognition research labs around the world.

Spatial Cognition 2014 took place at the University of Bremen site of the Transregional Collaborative Research Center SFB/TR 8 Spatial Cognition. The conference program also featured tutorials on the sketch understanding system CogSketch and on information visualization for innovating research methods, as well as workshops on design cognition and behavior and on indoor wayfinding assistance. The conference was collocated with the final colloquium of the SFB/TR 8, which reaches the end of its 12 year German Research Foundation center funding.

Many people contributed to the success of Spatial Cognition 2014. First of all, we thank the authors for carefully preparing excellent contributions and we thank the members of the Program Committee for carefully reviewing and elaborately commenting on this work. Thorough reviews by peers are one of the most important sources of feedback to the authors that connects them to still unknown territory and that helps them to improve their work and to secure a high quality of scientific publications.

We thank Kenneth D. Forbus, Maria Chang, and Andrew Lovett, as well as Tomi Kauppinen and Willem van Hage for offering tutorials, and Beatrix Emo, Kinda Al Sayed, and Tasos Varoudis, as well as Falko Schmid and Christoph Stahl for organizing workshops. We thank the members of our support staff, namely, Gracia Kranz, Alexander Mittelstorb, Evgenia Sazonkina, Susanne Schwarze, and Dagmar Sonntag for professionally arranging many details too numerous to mention.

We thank the German Research Foundation and the National Science Foundation and their program directors Bettina Zirpel, Gerit Sonntag, and Soo-Siang Lim for continued support of our research and for encouragement to enhance our international research collaborations. Finally, we thank Alfred Hofmann and his staff at Springer for their continuing support of our book series.

September 2014

Christian Freksa
Bernhard Nebel
Mary Hegarty
Thomas Barkowsky

Organization

Program Chairs

Christian Freksa   University of Bremen, Germany
Bernhard Nebel   University of Freiburg, Germany
Mary Hegarty   UC Santa Barbara, USA
Thomas Barkowsky   University of Bremen, Germany

Publication Chair

Kai-Florian Richter   University of Zurich, Switzerland

Workshop Chair

Maria Vasardani   University of Melbourne, Australia

Tutorial Chair

Victor Schinazi   ETH Zurich, Switzerland

Sponsorship Chair

Tomi Kauppinen   Aalto University, Finland

Program Committee

Elena Andonova	Anjan Chatterjee	Carola Eschenbach
Marios Avraamides	Christophe Claramunt	Sara Irina Fabrikant
Anna Belardinelli	Ruth Conroy Dalton	Paolo Fogliaroni
Michela Bertolotto	Michel Denis	Kenneth Forbus
Mehul Bhatt	Matt Duckham	Antony Galton
Stefano Borgo	Frank Dylla	Dedre Gentner
Martin Butz	Max Egenhofer	Nicholas Giudice
B. Chandrasekaran	Russell Epstein	Klaus Gramann

Christopher Habel

Stephen Hirtle

Christoph Hölscher

Toru Ishikawa

Petra Jansen

Gabriele Janzen

Tomi Kauppinen

Alexander Klippel

Antonio Krüger

Werner Kuhn

Antonio Lieto

Gérard Ligozat

Andrew Lovett

Hanspeter Mallot

Mark May

Tobias Meilinger

Stefan Münzer

Bernd Neumann

Nora Newcombe

Eric Pederson

Fiora Pirri

Albert Postma

Marco Ragni

Martin Raubal

Terry Regier

Kai-Florian Richter

Roy Ruddle

Holger Schultheis

Angela Schwering

Thomas Shipley

Cyrill Stachniss

Andrew Stull

Holly Taylor

Thora Tenbrink

Sabine Timpf

Barbara Tversky

Florian Twaroch

Maria Vasardani

Jan Oliver Wallgrün

Frances Wang

Jan Wiener

Katharine Willis

Stephan Winter

Stefan Wölfl

Thomas Wolbers

Diedrich Wolter

Constanze Vorwerg

Wai Yeap

Table of Contents

Spatial Memory

Language and Communication

Wayfinding and Navigation

Computational Models

Diagrams and Maps

Technical Approaches

Spatial Ability

Spatial Updating in Narratives

Adamantini Hatzipanayioti, Alexia Galati, and Marios Avraamides

Department of Psychology, University of Cyprus, Cyprus
{chatzipanagioti.adamantini,galati.alexia,mariosav}@ucy.ac.cy

Abstract. Across two experiments we investigated spatial updating in environments encoded through narratives. In Experiment 1, in which participants were given visualization instructions to imagine the protagonist's movement, they formed an initial representation during learning but did not update it during subsequent described movement. In Experiment 2, in which participants were instructed to physically move in space towards the directions of the described objects prior to testing, there was evidence for spatial updating. Overall, findings indicate that physical movement can cause participants to link a spatial representation of a remote environment to a sensorimotor framework and update the locations of remote objects while they move.

Keywords: Spatial updating, narratives, sensorimotor interference, transient representations, reading comprehension.

1   Introduction

1.1   Egocentric Updating of Spatial Relations

Many of our daily tasks rely on the on-line processing of spatial information. For instance, navigating in an unfamiliar environment requires considering either continuously or at frequent temporal intervals where we are and how we are oriented relative to the locations of landmarks, the origin of travel, the goal destination etc. Previous studies have established that people are capable of keeping track of the changing spatial relations between their body and the main objects of the environment without much effort even when movement takes place without vision (Farell & Thomson, 1999; Rieser, 1989; Wang & Spelke, 2000). The mechanism that allows people to continuously monitor egocentric relations is commonly referred to in the literature as spatial (or egocentric) updating.

Studies investigating spatial updating typically require participants to memorize the location of one or more objects and then point to them from an initial standpoint, as well as from novel standpoints. Novel standpoints can be adopted either by physical or imagined movement, consisting of rotation, translation, or a combination of the two. Converging findings indicate faster and more accurate performance when pointing from the learning standpoint or from novel standpoints adopted through physical movement compared to standpoints adopted through imagined movement (e.g., Presson & Montello, 1994; Rieser, Guth, & Hill, 1986). A popular explanation

C. Freksa et al. (Eds.): Spatial Cognition 2014, LNAI 8684, pp. 1–13, 2014.

for these findings is that the idiothetic cues (i.e., proprioceptive information and vestibular signals), which are present during physical locomotion, are necessary for effortless updating (Rieser, 1989). Another explanation is that imagined movement leads to sensorimotor interference from the automatically-activated physical codes that signify self-to-object relations; these codes must be suppressed in order to compute the location of an object from an imagined perspective (May, 2004).

1.2   Representational Systems of Spatial Memory and Updating

Successful spatial updating during movement without visual cues relies on people maintaining accurate spatial representations. Thus, several studies have focused on the organizational structure of the spatial representations that support updating. A few accounts have emerged. Mou, McNamara, Valiquette and Rump (2004) posited that maintaining and updating spatial information involves two memory systems: an egocentric system storing self-to-object relations that are updated when the observer moves, and an allocentric system that codes object-to-object relations that remain stable during movement.

Participants in the study of Mou et al. (2004) studied a layout of objects from one standpoint and then performed Judgments of Relative Direction (JRDs) after moving to a novel standpoint. The researchers manipulated independently: (1) the angle between the learning perspective and the imagined perspective adopted during a JRD (e.g., "Imagine standing at x, facing y, point to z" where x, y, and z are objects from the layout) task and (2) the angle between the participant's actual orientation and the imagined perspective adopted for the JRD task. Two independent alignment effects were observed. First, performance was superior when the imagined perspective matched the orientation of the learning perspective; this is now a well-established effect indicating that memories are maintained from a preferred direction (see McNamara, 2003, and Galati & Avraamides, 2013, for a discussion of how the preferred orientation is selected). Second, in line with typical findings from spatial updating studies, performance was better for imagined perspectives aligned with the participant's physical orientation at test (Kelly, Avraamides & Loomis, 2007). Based on these findings Mou et al. (2004) argued that in addition to storing object-to-object locations in an orientation-dependent representation, people code self-to-object relations in a representation that gets updated with movement.

Similarly, Waller and Hodgson (2006) argued for a transient memory system in which egocentric relations are kept with high precision but decay rapidly in the absence of perceptual support, and an enduring system in which information is maintained for prolonged intervals but in a coarser manner than the transient system.

More recently, Avraamides and Kelly (2008) proposed that spatial updating relies on an egocentric sensorimotor system that represents the self-to-object relations for the main objects in one's immediate environment. In this proposal, in line with May's (2004) explanation, the automatic activation of the sensorimotor system may cause interference to an allocentric system that people must use in order to compute a response from an imagined standpoint. Another consequence of this proposal is that interference is absent when reasoning about remote environments, since distal locations are not maintained within a sensorimotor framework.

These theories of spatial memory, which posit separate systems for egocentric and allocentric storage, imply that egocentric updating relies on the sensorimotor system and can thus only take place when reasoning about immediate spatial locations, insofar as self-to-object relations are maintained in sensorimotor, transient representations.

Empirical support for this prediction comes from a study by Kelly, Avraamides and Loomis (2007), who examined spatial reasoning in immediate and remote virtual environments. In one experiment, participants studied and committed to memory a layout of objects placed around them within a virtual room. Half of the participants remained in the same room for testing whereas the other half walked out of the virtual room and assumed a position in the center of an adjacent virtual room. In both testing conditions participants rotated 90° to their left or right, adopting a physical orientation that was offset from the orientation they had during learning. While at this testing orientation, participants were asked to point to the memorized objects from various imagined perspectives by responding to perspective taking (JRD) trials of the form 'imagine facing x, point to z', with x and z being objects from the layout. For testing in both the same and the adjacent room, performance was better for imagined perspectives aligned with the participants' initial learning orientation than other orientations, in line with proposals that spatial memories are orientation dependent (e.g., Mou & McNamara, 2002). Additionally, when participants were tested in the same room, but not in the adjacent room, performance was also better for the imagined perspective aligned with the orientation participants occupied during testing. The selective influence of the participants' orientation at testing was taken to indicate that participants updated their orientation relative to the memorized objects when rotating from their initial perspective in the immediate environment, but not the remote environment. This is consistent with two-system accounts of memory that consider egocentric updating to operate on representations within a sensorimotor system–representations that are most readily available for spatial relations in immediate environments.

1.3 Spatial Updating in Remote Environments

Although studies suggest that effortless updating may be limited to reasoning about immediate locations, there is some evidence that it can occur under certain circumstances in remote environments as well (Kelly et al., 2007; Rieser, Garing & Young, 1994). Specifically, when people represent their physical movement relative to a remote environment, they can successfully update their orientation relative to remote locations.

For example, in one study, Rieser et al. (1994) asked young children and their parents, while at their homes, to imagine being in the classroom and to point to classroom objects from two perspectives: first from the children's seat and then from the teacher's seat in the classroom. In one condition, participants imagined walking from the children's seat to the teacher's seat. In another condition, they physically walked the path they were imagining. Parents and children who carried out physical movement towards the teacher's seat showed similar performance in terms of accuracy and response latency suggesting that they could update their position in the remote environment, whereas when they had only imagined the movement, parents were more accurate than children. Overall, these findings indicate that physical movement coupled with instructions to visualize a remote environment can enable effortless updating.

One possible explanation for how people update remote locations is that, by following the visualization instructions and performing compatible physical or imagined movements, they can link the remote environment to their sensorimotor framework and update the distal locations as if they were immediate. The proposal that visualization instructions can recruit the sensorimotor system, even with respect to a remote environment, is broadly compatible with the embodied cognition view that sensorimotor representations can be reenacted "offline", even when reasoning is decoupled from the immediate environment (e.g., Simmons, et. al, 2003; Wilson, 2002)

Further support for the proposal that visualization can facilitate spatial updating comes from an experiment conducted by Kelly et al. (2007; Experiment 3). Using the layout and the procedure of the experiment described earlier (with testing in the immediate or adjacent virtual room), in this experiment, participants in the different room condition received instructions to imagine the objects of the layout as being around them while standing in the center of the testing room. Following these visualization instructions, participants physically rotated 90° to the left or right and carried out a series of pointing trials from imagined perspectives. Compared to when rotation was not accompanied by visualization instructions, when physical rotation was coupled with visualization instructions, participants pointed faster and more accurately from the imagined perspective that was aligned with their orientation at testing than the perspective opposite to it. This, so called, *sensorimotor alignment effect* suggests that, despite rotating with respect to a remote environment, participants could still update egocentric relations.

Altogether, a confluence of findings suggests that spatial updating operates on spatial relations maintained in a transient system of spatial memory and thus occurs effortlessly in immediate environments. Although spatial relations about remote environments are not maintained in such a system and are thus not updated by default, providing visualization instructions that link the remote objects to a sensorimotor framework can cause updating with physical movement.

1.4   Functional Equivalence of Representations Derived from Perception and Language

In addition to vision, people encode spatial information in memory through other sensory modalities, such as touch and audition, and through symbolic modes of representation, such as language. One proposal is that the spatial representations derived from different modalities are functionally equivalent (Avraamides, Mello, & Greenauer, 2013; Bryant, 1997; Giudice, Betty, & Loomis, 2011; Loomis, Klatzky,

Avraamides, Lippa & Golledge, 2007). This claim stems from the hypothesis that once the spatial representation is formed, it is no longer dependent on the modality from which it was encoded but is instead dependent on the properties of the representation (Loomis & Klatzky, 2007). A prediction that follows is that if spatial updating occurs in environments experienced perceptually, it should also take place in environments encoded through indirect inputs, such as language.

Avraamides, Loomis, Klatzky and Golledge (2004) examined the possibility of functional equivalence by having participants memorize objects that were either encoded visually or through verbal descriptions (e.g., "there is a ball at 3 o'clock, 6 feet away from you"). Then, participants had to reproduce from memory the relative direction of pairs of objects by rotating a rod. Results showed that participants' accuracy was comparable whether the objects were encoded visually or verbally (Experiment 3), suggesting that the representations derived from the two modalities were functionally equivalent.

Other studies (e.g. Klatzky, Lippa, Loomis & Golledge, 2002) provide support for functional equivalence by demonstrating that despite the inherent differences between language and vision (e.g., serial vs. near-simultaneous encoding, slower encoding with language than vision), representations derived from the two modalities support in the same manner the execution of spatial tasks (for a review see Loomis et al, 2007, Avraamides et al., 2013, and Loomis, Klatzky & Giudice, 2013).

However, studies demonstrating that language supports representations that are functional equivalent with vision, have involved primarily short descriptions for the locations of objects. In addition, in many cases (e.g., Avraamides et al., 2004) these objects were described at locations within environments that were previously experienced visually. Thus, it is not yet clear whether object locations in environments that are in their entirety constructed through descriptions are represented and updated the same way as object locations that are encoded directly through visual perception. Here, we investigate spatial updating for locations encoded from narratives. Narratives typically describe fictitious environments that are remote to the reader; that is, they refer to environments that differ from those in which readers are physically present while reading the text.

1.5 Spatial Relations in Narratives

When reading narratives people construct mental representations of the state of affairs described in the text. These representations, retaining the semantic content or gist of sentences, are known as situation models (Kintsch, 1998) or mental models (Johnson-Laird, 1983). Several aspects of the situation can be included in these models, including spatial, temporal, causal, motivational, protagonist-related and object-related information, which readers monitor during comprehension (e.g., Zwaan, 2004; Zwaan, Langston, & Graesser, 1995). Relevant to our enterprise here, readers monitor the protagonist's location and perspective in space and time in an effort to organize information in a coherent spatio-temporal framework (Zwaan & Radvansky, 1998). A potential mechanism implicated in this monitoring is that readers simulate perceptually what is being described in text by activating their own motor and perceptual experience. In support of this potential mechanism are findings showing that described actions interfere with real actions, such that the execution of a manual response interferes with the processing of an action described in the text (Glenberg & Kaschak, 2002).

If readers of narratives indeed activate motor-related processes when interpreting described movements, this sensorimotor simulation during reading may result in the same effortless updating of spatial relations as that effected by physical movement in immediate environments or visualization in remote environments. That is, with narratives, it is possible that even imagined movement within the described environment could lead to successful spatial updating. The experiment reported next examines this possibility with narratives that involve described protagonist rotations.

2   Imagined Movements in Narratives

2.1   Experiment 1

In order to examine whether readers automatically update the protagonist's orientation within a situation model, we investigated readers' spatial judgments when, prior to testing, the protagonist is described to rotate from an initial orientation to adopt a novel orientation. The paradigm used was adapted from the one used by Kelly et al. (2007), such that in the present experiment (1) the environment and the objects to be memorized were described rather than presented visually, and (2) participants did not carry out any physical movement but rather imagined the protagonist's movement and change in orientation prior to testing. If readers simulate the change in protagonists' orientation in space by activating motor processes in imagined movements then imagined movements should suffice for updating spatial relations in a narrative. In this case, and as long as readers have updated their situation model following the protagonists' described rotation, performance should be particularly good when responding from imagined perspectives aligned with the final orientation of the protagonist.

Participants were presented with narratives that described a protagonist in a fictitious environment (a hotel lobby, a court room, an opera house, and a construction site), each of the 4 environments presented as a different block. The stories in the narratives were loosely based on those used by Franklin and Tversky (1990). Each narrative comprised a series of short segments of text that included information about the geometry of the described environments and the placement of critical objects in them. Four objects were positioned at canonical orientations (front, back, right and left) and 4 additional objects at diagonal orientations in the corners of the environment. Participants were instructed to imagine being at the protagonist's position and to create a vivid mental image about the described environment. First, participants read an initial segment of text that described the protagonist entering a room through the door, walking to its center, and adopting an *initial orientation* facing towards a starting object; the door that was then behind the protagonist served as an additional object of the layout. Then, participants read a second segment of text in which the protagonist was described to rotate 90° either to the left or to the right to inspect another object. Participants read additional text that provided information about all remaining objects (one object at their back and four in the corners of the room) from this orientation (hereafter referred to as the *description orientation*). Finally, participants read a description of a sudden event (e.g., a loud noise or a telephone ringing) that caused the protagonist to turn 180° to face the opposite direction from the description orientation. After the protagonist was described to adopt this new orientation (referred to as the *updated orientation*), participants read instructions to create a mental image of the described environment from this orientation.

Following this learning phase and after memorizing the positions of all objects participants carried out a series of perspective taking trials, with the use of a joystick, in which they responded to auditory statements (delivered through headphones) of the form 'imagine facing x, point to z' with x and z being objects from the narrative. Objects at canonical orientations served as facing objects to establish imagined perspectives, whereas those in the corners served as the targets to which participants pointed. Participants remained oriented towards the same physical orientation (aligned with the initial orientation of the protagonist[1]) throughout learning and testing. As narratives used the pronoun "you" we assume that participants mapped the initial orientation of the narrative to this physical orientation

2.2 Results

Pointing error and latency were analyzed as a function of the imagined perspective participants had to adopt on a given trial. Since the results for accuracy and latency converged, we present only the analyses on latency data for the sake of brevity.

As shown in Figure 1, participants were faster to point to targets when the imagined perspective adopted was aligned with the protagonist's initial orientation. Performance did not differ between imagined perspectives aligned with the description orientation and the updated orientation.

Thus, participants' performance suggested that they organized their memory around the protagonist's initial orientation in the narrative and did not update spatial relations when the protagonist rotated to new orientations. This finding is compatible with proposals that support that people maintain spatial layouts in orientation-dependent memories based on a variety of cues available at encoding (e.g., symmetry of the layout, structure of the general space, instructions, observation standpoint, etc.) and refrain from changing the preferred orientation of their memories unless additional cues provide a substantial benefit for re-interpreting the layout (Mou & McNamara, 2002).

---

[1] As narratives used the pronoun "you" to describe the position of the protagonist in the environment, we assume that participants mapped the initial orientation of the narrative to this physical orientation.

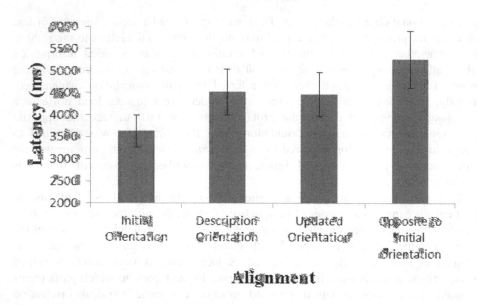

Fig. 1. Average latency as a function of imagined perspective. Error bars represent standard errors of the mean

Thus, in this context, instructions to vividly represent the environment and to imagine the protagonist's movement may have not been sufficient to reorganize the reader's initial representation of the described environment. This is compatible with claims that remote environments (including described ones) are not updated effortlessly with either physical or imagined movement (Avraamides & Kelly, 2008).

Overall, the findings of Experiment 1 indicate that, as with perceptual environments, imagined movement does not readily result in spatial updating.

3   Physical Rotation with Narratives

In the experiment described in previous section, simply imagining the protagonist's movement did not enable readers to successfully update their spatial representations. This is in line with previous findings that imagined movement in environments encoded perceptually is not sufficient for spatial updating (e.g., Rieser et al., 1994). These findings clarify that even if readers simulate the described movement, recruiting motor processes, this simulation does not lead to effortless and automatic spatial updating. The question that arises is whether updating in narratives *could* occur if the described movement is accompanied by the reader's physical movement.

A study from our laboratory (Avraamides, Galati, Pazzaglia, Meneghetti & Denis, 2013) investigated this possibility. In that study, participants read several narratives that described protagonists rotating in fictitious environments in order to inspect objects placed around them. When the protagonist was described to rotate to a different orientation, participants physically rotated to a direction that was either congruent or incongruent with the protagonist's rotation (Experiment 4). Despite this manipulation, performance in perspective-taking pointing judgments showed neither facilitation nor interference from the participant's physical orientation (whether congruent or incongruent). Instead, performance was best from the orientation in which object locations were encoded in memory, consistent with the findings presented in the previous section. The lack of influence of physical rotation suggests that people can easily suppress any sensorimotor information stemming from their physical movement when reasoning about an environment that is completely detached from their sensorimotor framework, such as an environment in a narrative world.

The results of Avraamides et al. (2013) indicate that even physical rotations, intended to link the participants' sensorimotor system to the protagonist's movement in the narrative environment, fail to result in successful spatial updating. These findings are at odds with those from studies with perceptual environments showing that physical movement coupled with visualization instructions may lead to the effortless updating of remote environments and, thus, a sensorimotor alignment effect. However, methodological differences across experiments could potentially account for the discrepancy between results. One difference is that participants in Avraamides et al. (2013) executed physical rotations by turning the swivel chair they sat on to a new orientation, whereas in the studies of Kelly et al. (2007) and Rieser et al. (1994) participants carried out extensive physical walking. It could be that the stronger idiothetic cues that are present in physical walking are necessary for updating. To examine this, we conducted another experiment in which participants (1) physically walked during the encoding of objects in a narrative, and (2) physically rotated, while standing, to adopt a new orientation just prior to testing.

4   Extensive Physical Movement in Narratives

4.1   Experiment 2

To further examine whether more involved movement *can*, in fact, give rise to a sensorimotor alignment effect and facilitate the updating of spatial representations acquired through narratives, we conducted an experiment that recruited extended physical walk. Previous studies have shown that visualization instructions and physical walk in space (Kelly et al., 2007; Rieser et al., 1994) can indeed result in spatial updating in remote environments–at least for remote environments encoded perceptually. The question is whether the same occurs for environments encoded through narratives.

In this experiment, participants were presented with a single narrative that provided a detailed description about the geometry of a store. The geometry involved 4 objects that were located at canonical orientations and 4 additional objects that were located at diagonal orientations. Participants had to memorize the position of all objects during the learning phase and then proceed to the testing phase, which involved carrying out pointing judgments with eyes open or closed. Manipulating visual access during testing aimed at investigating whether visual input influences the presence of sensorimotor interference by providing perceptual markers for the discrepancy between the actual and imagined facing direction. Participants initially stood with their backs next to one of the laboratory walls and were told that it represented the entrance of a clothing store, while the other walls of the laboratory mapped to those of the described environment. Then participants were given a printed version of the narrative to read and were instructed to move in the laboratory reproducing the movement of the protagonist in the description as they read it. The description had participants walk to the center of the room and adopt an initial facing orientation ($0°$). Next, they walked to the far end of the room towards an object described as being directly in front of them. Then, participants followed the described movements in the narrative and moved within the room to "view" or "interact with" described objects that were present at both the four canonical (i.e., near the center of each wall) and diagonal (i.e., in the corners of the store) directions. At two occasions in the description, these movements took participants back to the center of the room. At all other instances, participants walked directly from one object to the other. After memorizing the locations of all objects, participants were instructed to return to the center and face the $0°$ orientation and, from there, visualize the environment in the narrative. Just prior to testing participants were asked to physically rotate $90°$ to their right. After adopting this testing orientation, they were seated and carried out perspective-taking trials just like in Experiment 1 (i.e., they responded to statements of the form 'imagine facing x, point to z'), using a joystick that was placed in front of them. This final rotation was not linked explicitly to any described protagonist rotation.

4.2   Results

Following Kelly et al. (2007), we computed the presence of (1) an *encoding alignment effect* by subtracting the latency for responding from the initial learning orientation from the latency of responding from a baseline perspective that was opposite to the testing orientation, and (2) a *sensorimotor alignment* effect by subtracting the latency of pointing from an imagined perspective aligned with the testing orientation from the latency of responding from the baseline perspective. A significant encoding alignment effect would indicate that participants created an orientation-dependent memory at the time of encoding as claimed by McNamara and colleagues (e.g., Mou & McNamara, 2002). A significant sensorimotor alignment effect would show that participants updated the representation of the environment described in the narrative when they physically rotated to the testing perspective.

As shown in Figure 2, both alignment effects were present regardless of whether participants carried out testing with their eyes open or closed. Notably, both effects were greater when responding with eyes open. If visual access enhanced sensorimotor facilitation/interference by providing participants with a perceptual marker for their facing direction, this could explain the larger sensorimotor effect in the eyes open condition. However, this explanation cannot account for the larger encoding alignment effect. An alternative possibility is that the optic array introduced noise on the execution of mental transformations, making it harder for participants in the eyes open condition to adopt and maintain imagined perspectives other than the preferred orientation and their physical perspective at testing. Another possibility is that the available visual information made it difficult for these participants to feel as present in the remote environment as participants in the eyes closed condition.

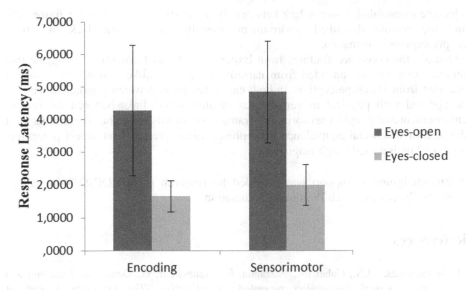

Fig. 2. Encoding alignment and sensorimotor alignment effects for response latency in Experiment 1. Error bars represent standard errors.

These results extend the findings of studies showing that extended physical movement (Rieser et al., 1994) and visualization (Kelly et al., 2007) can update spatial relations within remote environments encoded perceptually, by demonstrating that extended physical movement is effective for updating remote environments acquired through narratives as well. Whereas mere rotation or visualization on their own may be ineffective for updating spatial relations in described environments, more involved movement, like walking, can help participants link their sensorimotor framework to the remote environment (Avraamides & Kelly, 2008; May, 2004) and update it more successfully as they simulate the protagonist's changes in orientation.

5   Conclusion

The results from the two experiments reported here extend our understanding of how spatial updating takes place in remote environments and inform theories of spatial memory.

Specifically, Experiment 1 shows that despite evidence that text comprehension can have an embodied basis, with readers recruiting motor processes when reading about movement in narratives, such imagined movement does not necessarily result in the effortless updating of spatial relations. Findings from Experiment 2 indicate that updating of remote environments described in narratives can nevertheless take place, provided that the remote environment is linked efficiently to the reader's sensorimotor framework. Carrying out extensive movement towards imagined objects during learning seems to be sufficient in establishing this link. The findings from Experiment 2 contrast with those of Avraamides et al. (2013) who failed to observe any sensorimotor facilitation or interference stemming from physical rotation. Our conjecture is that the physical rotations performed while seating in a chair were not adequate to establish a strong link between the participants' sensorimotor framework and the remote described environment, possibly due to the lack of strong proprioceptive information.

Overall, the combined findings from Experiment 1 and Experiment 2 suggest that remote environments encoded from narratives are not unlike remote environments encoded from visual perception. In both cases, relations between remote objects can be updated with physical movement that creates strong links between the remote environment and people's sensorimotor framework. In this sense, our findings support the idea of functional equivalence for representations created from direct perceptual input and indirectly through language.

Acknowledgments. Support was provided by research grant KOINΩ/0609(BE)/15 from the Cyprus Research Promotion Foundation.

References

1. Avraamides, M.N., Galati, A., Pazzaglia, F., Meneghetti, C., Denis, M.: Encoding and updating spatial information presented in narratives. The Quarterly Journal of Experimental Psychology 66, 642–670 (2013)
2. Avraamides, M.N., Kelly, J.W.: Multiple systems of spatial memory and action. Cognitive Processing 9, 93–106 (2008)
3. Avraamides, M.N., Loomis, J.M., Klatzky, R.L., Golledge, R.G.: Functional equivalence of spatial representations derived from vision and language: Evidence from allocentric judgments. Journal of Experimental Psychology: Learning, Memory, and Cognition 30, 804–814 (2004)
4. Avraamides, M.N., Mello, C., Greenauer, N.: Spatial representations for de-scribed and perceived locations. In: Tenbrink, T., Wiener, J., Claramunt, C. (eds.) Representing Space in Cognition: Behaviour, Language, and Formal Models, pp. 27–41. Oxford University Press (2013)
5. Bryant, D.: Representing space in language and perception. Mind & Language 12, 239–264 (1997)
6. Farrell, J.J., Thomson, J.A.: On-line updating of spatial information during loco-motion without vision. Journal of Motor Behavior 31, 37–53 (1999)
7. Franklin, N., Tversky, B.: Searching imagined environments. Journal of Experimental Psychology: General 119, 63–76 (1990)
8. Galati, A., Avraamides, M.N.: Flexible spatial perspective-taking: Conversational partners weigh multiple cues in collaborative tasks. Frontiers in Human Neuroscience (2013), doi:10.3389/fnhum.2013.00618
9. Giudice, N.A., Betty, M.R., Loomis, J.M.: Functional equivalence of spatial images from touch and vision: evidence from spatial updating in blind and sighted individuals. Journal of Experimental Psychology: Learning, Memory, and Cognition 37, 621–634 (2011)
10. Glenberg, A.M., Kaschak, M.P.: Grounding language in action. Psychonomic Bulletin & Review 9, 558–565 (2002)
11. Johnson- Laird, P.N.: Mental models: Towards a cognitive science of language, in-terference, and consciousness. Cambridge University Press, Cambridge (1983)
12. Kelly, J.W., Avraamides, M.N., Loomis, J.M.: Sensorimotor alignment effects in the learning Environment and in novel Environments. Journal of Experimental Psychology: Learning, Memory and Cognition 33, 1092–1107 (2007)

13. Kintsch, W.: Comprehension: A paradigm for cognition. University Press, Cambridge (1998)
14. Klatzky, R.L., Lippa, Y., Loomis, J.M., Golledge, R.G.: Learning directions of objects specified by vision, spatial audition, or auditory spatial language. Learning & Memory 9, 364–367 (2002)
15. Loomis, J.M., Klatzky, R.L.: Functional equivalence of spatial representations from vision, touch and hearing: Relevance for sensory substitution. In: Rieser, J.J., Ashmead, D.H., Ebner, F.F., Corn, A.L. (eds.) Blindness and Brain Plasticity in Navigation and Object Perception, pp. 155–184. Lawrence Erlbaum Associates, New York (2007)
16. Loomis, J.M., Klatzky, R.L., Avraamides, M.N., Lippa, Y., Golledge, R.G.: Functional equivalence of spatial images produced by perception and spatial language. In: Mast, F., Jäncke, L. (eds.) Spatial Processing in Navigation, Imagery, and Perception, pp. 29–48. Springer, New York (2007)
17. Loomis, J.M., Klatzky, R.L., Giudice, N.A.: Representing 3D space in working memory: Spatial images from vision, touch, hearing, and language. In: Lacey, S., Lawson, R. (eds.) Multisensory Imagery: Theory & Applications, pp. 131–156. Springer, New York (2013)
18. May, M.: Imaginal perspective switches in remembered environments: Transformation versus interference accounts. Cognitive Psychology 48, 163–206 (2004)
19. Mou, W., McNamara, T.P.: Intrinsic frames of reference in spatial memory. Journal of Experimental Psychology: Learning, Memory and Cognition 28(1), 162–170 (2002)
20. Mou, W., McNamara, T.P., Valiquette, C.M., Rump, B.: Allocentric and egocentric updating of spatial memories. Journal of Experimental Psychology: Learning, Memory and Cognition 30, 142–157 (2004)
21. Presson, C.C., Montello, D.R.: Updating after rotational and translational body movements: Coordinate structure of perspective space. Perception 23, 1447–1455 (1994)
22. Rieser, J.J.: Access to knowledge of spatial structure at novel points of observation. Journal of Experimental Psychology: Learning, Memory, & Cognition 15, 1157–1165 (1989)
23. Rieser, J.J., Garing, A.E., Young, M.E.: Imagery, action, and young children's spatial orientation. It's not being there that counts, it's what one has in mind. Child Development 65, 1262–1278 (1994)
24. Rieser, J.J., Guth, D.A., Hill, E.W.: Sensitivity to perspective structure while walking without vision. Perception 15, 173–188 (1986)
25. Simmons, W.K., Pecher, D., Hamann, S.B., Zeelenberg, R., Barsalou, L.W.: fMRI evidence for modality-specific processing of conceptual knowledge on six modalities. Paper presented at the meeting of the Society for Cognitive Neuroscience, New York, NY (2003)
26. Waller, D., Hodgson, E.: Transient and enduring spatial representations under disorientation and self-motion. Journal of Experimental Psychology: Learning, Memory & Cognition 32, 867–882 (2006)
27. Wang, R.F., Spelke, E.S.: Updating egocentric representations in human navigation. Cognition 77, 215–250 (2000)
28. Wilson, M.: Six views of embodied cognition. Psychonomic Bulletin and Review 9, 625–636 (2002)
29. Zwaan, R.A., Langston, M.C., Graesser, A.C.: The construction of situation models in narrative comprehension: An event-indexing model. Psychological Science 6, 292–297 (1995)
30. Zwaan, R.A., Radvansky, G.A.: Situation models in language comprehension and memory. Psychological Bulletin 123, 162–185 (1998)

Effects of Global and Local Processing on Visuospatial Working Memory

Holly A. Taylor[1], Ayanna K. Thomas[1], Caterina Artuso[2], and Caroline Eastman[1]

[1] Department of Psychology, Tufts University,
490 Boston Ave., Medford, MA 02155, USA
holly.taylor@tufts.edu, ayanna.thomas@tufts.edu,
eastman.caroline@gmail.com
[2] Brain and Behavioral Science Department, University of Pavia,
Piazza Botta 6, 27100 Pavia, Italy
caterina.artuso@unipv.it

Abstract. If you want to find something, you need to know what you are looking for and where it was last located. Successful visuospatial working memory (VSWM) requires that a stimulus identity be combined with information about its location. How identity and location information interact during binding presents an interesting question because of 1) asymmetries in cognitive demands required by location and identity processing and 2) the fact that the two types of information are processed in different neural streams. The current studies explore how global and local processing approaches impact binding in VSWM. Experiment 1 explores effects of global spatial organization. Experiment 2 induces local processing demands through memory updating. Results show better location memory with both global and local processing, but also suggest that the processing focus (global or local) affects the interaction of location and identity processing in VSWM.

Keywords: visuospatial working memory, location-identity binding, configural processing, memory updating, local/global processing.

1 Introduction

You have recently moved to a new town and feel you have a basic idea of local businesses locations. When you do misremember, you notice two different problems. In one case, you remember, for example, that there was a business on the south end of Barrett Rd., but cannot remember what type. In other words, you remembered a location, but cannot remember the business identity (identity memory failure). In the other case, you remember having seen a Thai restaurant, but cannot remember where (location memory failure). Both errors represent a failure to bind identity and location information. What might affect the likelihood of these error types? In line with this example, the present work explores how factors contributing to global versus local processing affect visuospatial working memory (VSWM), including location memory, identity memory, and location-identity binding.

C. Freksa et al. (Eds.): Spatial Cognition 2014, LNAI 8684, pp. 14–29, 2014.
© Springer International Publishing Switzerland 2014

1.1   Visuospatial Working Memory

VSWM involves memory for object identity, location and their combination (binding). Identity memory first relies on object recognition, a ventral stream process [1, 2]. Location can be coded on either a fine-grained, individual basis, giving exact position and/or at a categorical level, designating position relative to a larger context and thus offering a more global sense of position [e.g., 3, 4, 5]. Location memory involves the "where" or dorsal stream [2], although some research also suggests a role for ventral areas [1]. Although identity and location processing alone are important in establishing memory representations, binding the two is crucial for successful VSWM. Through binding, identity and location become integrated and represented as a single unit [6].

How identity and location information interact during binding presents an interesting question for a number of reasons. Identity and location processing involve different neural circuits. As discussed above, location processing engages the ventral stream and identity processing the dorsal stream. Additionally, attentional demands for processing these two information types may differ. Some researchers have argued that location processing is automatic [7]. However, because factors such as practice, intention to learn, strategic processing, and age influence spatial memory, automaticity has been called into question [8, 9]. Our earlier work [10] suggests less effortful, or partially automatic [11], processing of location information.

The role of identity memory in VSWM has received much less attention. Taken alone identity memory has similar characteristics to verbal working memory (VWM), particularly for name-able or verbally processed items [12]. An important point for the current work emerging from the VWM literature is that maintenance of information is effortful. Recent debates on working memory capacity suggest a low capacity of 4 items without strategic processing or rehearsal [13, 14] and the classic 7 plus or minus 2 items with rehearsal or strategic processing [15].

When considering VSWM components, asymmetries emerge. Notably, research suggests that position processing proceeds with limited effort [10, 16], whereas identity processing ("what") requires central effort [16, 17]. This asymmetry has implications for identity-location binding. The reduced effort of location processing should give it precedence in memory. However, characteristics of the information being processed as well as processing goals may shift around the weighting of the VSWM components. The present work explores stimulus characteristics that encourage global processing (Experiment 1) and task goals requiring local processing (Experiment 2) and their effects on VSWM.

1.2   Local Versus Global Processing

Visual scenes and individual stimuli involve details that form a whole when related together. In processing this information, one can focus on the details (local processing) or on how the details fit together (global processing). Navon [18] proposed a *global dominance hypothesis* or *global precedence*, with faster processing and reduced interference for a global interpretation of his letter stimuli. More recently, Förster and colleagues [19, 20] suggest malleability in global and local processing. In Förster's GLOMO[sys] model, he suggests that real-world factors (e.g., arousal; [21]) affect global versus local perceptual and conceptual processing and that the processing approach can carry over across tasks and modalities. Förster [22] suggests that global or local processing should be conceptualized as a cognitive approach, i.e. a content-free way of perceiving the world that can be applied across perceptual and conceptual modalities.

In terms of a cognitive approach, why would global processing be dominant? One answer emerges from the cognitive literature. Global precedence emerges across cognitive processes to help us to manage information overload. For example, we tend to generalize instances into categories based on commonalities and use those categories to interpret new instances. In other words, global processing organizes information into manageable and informative units.

Viewed this way, VSWM, and its components, should show global precedence. There is some indication that location memory does. Spatial correspondence studies suggest that people consider individual locations within an organized structure (see [23] for a review). Similarly, when locations can be grouped into spatial categories, memory appears biased toward the spatial category as evidenced by under-estimation of distances within a category and over-estimation across categories [e.g., 24, 25, 26]. Further, configural changes disrupt location processing in VSWM [27]. Global/relational processing via semantic categories suggests that the identity aspect of VSWM also shows global precedence. Evidence of category use shows lower accuracy and longer reaction time for within- compared to across-category responses [28]. Further, when individual items all relate to a single strong associate, that associate is remembered as having been presented when it was not [false memory; 29] and is remembered at an even higher rate when it was presented [30]. However, global precedence can only emerge in VSWM if the information being processed can be conceived as having hierarchical structure. For location information, items forming some kind of configuration would accomplish this; for identities, different semantic categories would need to be distinguished.

Individual differences may guide tendencies to process locally or globally. Global precedence appears to increase with age. With spatial arrays, children seem to individuate elements, although they will use a meaningful organization [23, 31]. Adults readily extract and advantageously use perceptual and conceptual organizing information [29, 32]. Older adults tend to over-rely on semantic organizing information, which can, in some cases, increase false memory [33]. Habitual processing approaches also play a role. With environment learning, Pazzaglia and De Beni [34] find individual differences in habitual spatial processing that map onto local versus global processing. They identify three spatial processing styles for environments, *landmark, route,* and *survey. Landmark* processing has the most local focus while *survey* processing takes the most global, configural approach.

1.3   Previous Work

Our previous work [10] explored VSWM, separating location, identity, and binding of the two. Participants studied 5x5 grids containing between 2 to 5 shapes. Immediately after test, they made a Judgment of Learning (JOL) and then completed one of three *yes/no* recognition test trials (assessing identity, location, or both identity and location). In Experiment 1, participants knew whether they would be tested on location, identity, or both, so could separate them and strategically encode. In Experiment 2, the test type could not be predicted, so separation of the elements only occurred at retrieval.

The results provided insights into VSWM. First, cognitive load, as operationalized by the number of objects in the array, differentially affected the memory types. Identity memory accuracy decreased as load increased, as did combined object/identity memory. Location memory accuracy, in contrast, decreased from 2 to 3 objects, but then remained relatively stable. We interpreted the lack of sensitivity to array size as indicating that learning location information was less cognitively demanding than identity or combination information. Alternatively, it could suggest that location information is processed first, as differences between location and identity memory were more pronounced when participants had less time to study the array ([10] Experiment 1b).

The lack of sensitivity to array size for location information had one interesting exception [10]. Location accuracy decreased from 2 to 3 objects, but then remained stable. The decrease from 2 to 3 objects likely reflects cognitive load. What might explain the stability with 3 or more objects? Three or more objects form a configuration; two objects only ever form a line. Thus, with 3 or more objects, participants may adopt global, configural processing to strategically remember locations. This may be akin to global precedence [18], showing configural processing when possible. The first study in the present work will further explore configural processing in VSWM.

2   Experiment 1: Location-Identity Binding with Spatial Organization

Within VSWM, location processing appears to be less cognitively demanding than identity processing. When items in a spatial array can be processed configurally, array size has a negligible effect on location memory [10]. Spatial configural processing occurs even when the objects do not form identifiable configurations [25]. In our earlier work, we randomly located objects within a 5x5 grid. Experiment 1 makes configural processing more obvious by using easily identifiable configurations. The study compares VSWM components with 2-object arrays, which do not form a configuration, to 5-object arrays with either a recognizable configuration (organized) or an emergent one based on random object placement (unorganized). We predict that the affordance for location processing provided by the organized configuration will aid location memory and also negatively impact identity memory. The spatial configuration chunks location memory, improving memory for those locations. However, a good Gestalt form appears to impair visual target detection [35], suggesting that the global configuration draws attention from local object processing. This prediction is also consistent with more general models of comprehension [36].

2.1   Method

Participants. Eighteen Tufts undergraduates (aged 18 to 24) participated in exchange for partial course credit.

Design. The experiment used a 3(Array Type: *2-object, 5-object Unorganized, 5-object Organized*) X 3(Question Type: *Identity, Location, Combination*) within-participant design.

Materials. Stimuli consisted of 5 x 5 grids containing either two or five objects. Objects consisted of twenty simple shapes. When the grid contained 5 objects, they were arranged in either an organized manner (i.e., analogous to the construction of Navon [18] figures) with objects placed in adjacent grid cells and together forming a larger recognizable shape such as an L, square, V, or T or in an unorganized manner (i.e., random placement with no consistently recognized structure). See Fig. 1 for sample grids. A total of 108 grids were used, 36 of each of the three types. Across trials, both the object shown and location it occupied on the grid were relatively equally balanced.

Fig. 1. Example of a 2-object, a 5-object unorganized, and a 5-object organized grid

Procedure. The Tufts University Social, Educational and Behavioral Research (SBER) IRB approved all procedures. Experiment instructions informed participants that they would "be presented with a series of displays containing various shapes in various locations within a grid." The experiment was presented on an Apple™ computer running SuperLab (version 4.0; Cedrus Corporation). At the beginning of each block, participants were told to attend either to object shapes, locations, or both shapes and locations for a later test. Following instructions, participants completed three practice trials (one from each question type – identity, location, and combined identity and location).

Experimental trials consisted of a 3-part procedure involving studying a grid, then rating their learning of the grid, and finally completing a *yes-no* recognition question. Each trial began with a 500ms central fixation cross, followed by a study grid for 1500ms. A mask and a central fixation cross then replaced the grid for 500ms. Participants then provided a Judgment of Learning (JOL) regarding the likelihood they would be able to recognize, depending on block, either object identity, location, or identity and location. Participants recorded JOLs using a Likert scale ranging from 0 (*not likely at all to recognize*) to 9 (*extremely likely to recognize*). Finally, participants responded to the grid's corresponding *yes-no* forced choice recognition probe (which assessed either identity, location, or both) by pressing either the yes ("c") or no ("m") key.

Recognition probes had 1/3 of the questions paired with previously presented stimuli (correct) and 2/3 of the questions were paired with stimuli not previously presented (incorrect lures). This ratio was used to provide a greater proportion of incorrect lure trials for analysis without also engendering a response bias. The 36 object-identity questions presented a single object and asked, "Was this shape presented in the previous grid?" The 36 location questions presented a blank grid with one square shaded red and asked, "Was an object presented in this location in the previous grid?" Finally, the 36 combination identity-location questions presented a single object within a grid and asked, "Was this shape presented in this location in the previous grid?" With our design, participants could commit only one type of error on identity or the location trials (correct recognition or not), but could commit one of three types of errors when recalling combined identity-location information. Specifically, they could recall a new (incorrect) identity in an old (correct) location, an old (correct) identity in a new (incorrect) location, and finally, a new (incorrect) identity in a new (incorrect) location. At the end of the experiment, participants filled out a general demographic questionnaire.

2.2   Results

With the present paper's focus on VSWM, we present only the memory, and not the metacognitive data here. All p-values reported were less than 0.05 unless otherwise stated. Recognition hits and false alarms were examined separately. To begin, we compared memory for location and identity to examine how spatial organization affected memory for each VSWM element. A 3(Array Type: 2-object, 5-object organized, 5-object unorganized) X 2(Element: Identity, Location) within-subjects ANOVA performed on hit proportions found a main effect of Array Type, $F(2, 34) = 31.06$, $\eta_p^2 = .65$. In addition, the interaction between Array Type and Element was significant, $F(2, 34) = 8.09$, $\eta_p^2 = .32$. Memory for location was better than memory for identity with spatially organized grids, $t(17) = 3.23$, $d = 1.16$ (See Fig. 2). There were no other significant differences between location and identity memory.

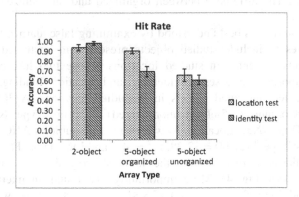

Fig. 2. Experiment 1 hit rate showing better location memory for organized grids

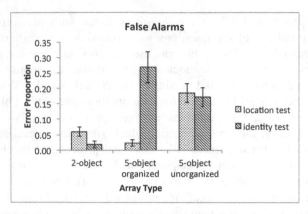

Fig. 3. False alarm rate showing high identity false alarms for organized grids

A similar analysis on false alarm proportions also yielded a main effect of Array Type, $F(2, 34) = 28.53$, $\eta_p^2 = .63$, and an interaction between Array Type and Element, $F(2, 34) = 16.98$, $\eta_p^2 = .50$. As Fig. 3 illustrates, participants more often false alarmed to location than identity lures when arrays consisted of two objects. This difference was marginally significant after Bonferroni correction, $t(17) = 2.30$, $p = .04$. In contrast, participants false alarmed more often to identity lures as compared to location lures with 5-oject organized arrays, $t(17) = 4.55$, $d = 1.57$. False alarm responding did not differ when arrays were unorganized.

With combination trials, analyzed separately, we examined how spatial organization affected identity-location binding. As with the previous analysis, hits and false alarms were analyzed separately. For hit proportions, we found an effect of Array Type, $F(2, 34) = 28.69$, $\eta_p^2 = .63$. Hit proportions were highest when participants studied 2-object grids ($M = .89$). There was a dramatic hit-rate drop with 5-object organized ($M = .57$) and 5-object unorganized ($M = .44$) grids. Planned comparisons revealed differences between 2-object and 5-object organized arrays, $t(17) = 4.57$, $d = 1.41$, and between 2-object and 5-object unorganized arrays, $t(17) = 10.32$, $d = 2.78$. The difference between organized and unorganized arrays did not reach significance.

Memory integration is best understood by examining false alarms. In this study we constructed lures to include studied objects presented in unstudied locations, and unstudied objects presented in studied locations. These two lure conditions were particularly important in assessing identity and location binding. A third lure condition presented unstudied objects in unstudied locations. A 3(Array Type: 2-object, 5-object organized, 5-object unorganized) X 3(Lure Type: New Object/Old Location, Old Object/New Location, New/New) within-subjects ANOVA found main effects of Array Type, $F(2, 34) = 12.28$, $\eta_p^2 = .42$, and Lure Type, $F(2, 34) = 5.06$, $\eta_p^2 = .23$. False alarms were lowest for the smallest array size and were lowest with New/New lures (see Fig. 4). More importantly, we found an interaction between Array Type and Lure Type, $F(4, 68) = 3.81$, $\eta_p^2 = .18$. As we were particularly interested in memory integration, we conducted a follow-up 3(Array Type: 2-object,

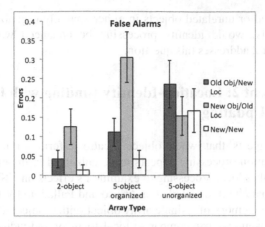

Fig. 4. Experiment 1 false alarm rates to different lure types with combination location-identity memory

5-object organized, 5-object unorganized) X 2(Lure Type: New Object/Old Location, Old Object/New Location) ANOVA. Again, the interaction between Array Type and Lure Type was significant, $F(2, 34) = 4.62$, $\eta_p^2 = .21$. Planned comparisons revealed that when participants studied 5-object organized grids, they had more difficulty rejecting an unstudied object in a studied location (M = .31) as compared to a studied object in an unstudied location (M = .11), $t(17) = 2.43$, d = .89.

2.3   Discussion

We found that spatial organization impacted VSWM, such that when presented with spatially organized grids participants were better able to recognize previously presented location, rejecting location lures. This was particularly pronounced on combination trials in which participants had to remember both location and identity information. Under these conditions, participants made significantly more errors remembering object identity as opposed to location.   These data suggest a prioritization of location information over identity information. Whether this priority involves less effortful or earlier processing of location information remains an open question.

The false-alarm results provided the most insight into how spatial organization affected location-identity binding. Notable in these results is that participants false-alarmed to identity information at a much higher rate with 5-object organized than with 5-object unorganized grids. With 5-object unorganized grids, they false-alarmed roughly equivalently to location and identity information. This is consistent with false alarm pattern for 5-object arrays in other, unpublished data from our labs [37]. Thus, spatial organization increases processing of location information in VSWM to the detriment of identity information.

Would identity processing be enhanced if it had a global structure and location did not? Current work in our labs is addressing this question, using a similar paradigm. In this new work, global structure for identity is defined through semantic categories. It pits a global focus for location against one for identity by presenting either semantically related or unrelated objects in either spatially organized or unorganized grids. Alternatively, would identity processing be enhanced with a greater local focus? Experiment 2 addresses this question.

3   Experiment 2: Location-Identity Binding with Local Focus through Updating

Experiment 1 suggests that when object locations form an interpretable global configuration, location processing appears to be enhanced at the expense of identity. Experiment 2 invokes local processing to examine its effects on VSWM. To do so, we used an updating paradigm modeled after Artuso and Palladino [38]. In this paradigm, participants update memory of a single array object (either object identity, location, or both). With this design, we can compare a local focus on individual component parts of VSWM and to a focus on their combination. We predict that a local focus will enhance processing on the focused information. To limit configural processing, here we use 3x3 grids with 3 objects.

3.1   Method

Participants. Thirty-four Tufts University undergraduates, ranging in age from 18 to 23, participated in exchange for monetary compensation.

Design. The experiment design involved a 2(Semantic Relatedness: related, unrelated) x 4(Updating Type: Identity, Location, Combination, Nothing) x 2(Test Type: Identity, Location) mixed-factor design. Semantic relatedness served as a between-participant factor and Updated Information and Test Type served as within-participant factors.

Materials
Study Materials. The stimuli consisted of 432 3x3 grids containing three object pictures, drawn from Snodgrass and Vanderwart [39]. We used 70 pictures, 10 each from 7 semantic categories: animals, tools, clothes, transportation, fruit, furniture, and body parts. In half of the grids, objects were semantically related and in the other half they were unrelated. Pictures placement in grids was random, but followed overall constraints, including 1) using each object and grid location relatively equally (20 to 25 times) across the stimuli and 2) any two objects or any two locations could not be used within the same grid more than 5 times.

Each study grid had associated updating grids, which related to the study grid in one of four ways. For an identity update, one of the object identities changed. If a semantically related grid, the new identity belonged to the same semantic category (e.g., if the study grid had a *cat, tiger, dog*, the identity change grid might have *cat, elephant, dog*). For semantically unrelated grids, the new object belonged to a different semantic category than the replaced object (e.g. if they studied *cat, arm, banana*, the updated grid might have *cat, arm, dress*). For a location update, object identities remained constant, but one object changed location, appearing in one of the six open locations. For a combination update, both an object identity and its location changed. The identity change depended on whether the objects were semantically related, as described above. Finally, for "nothing" updates, the grid was identical to the study grid.

Test Materials. The experiment involved location and identity tests. *Identity tests* used the object pictures, presented individually. For a given trial, the picture either corresponded to one in the most recently studied (updated) grid (*old*), had occurred in the first-studied, but not in the updated grid (*intrusion*) or was not studied in the trial (*new*). New items matched the semantic category for semantically organized grids and came from a different category for semantically unrelated grids. *Location tests* involved a 3x3 grid with one of the squares colored red. As with the pictures for the identity test, the designated location was either one most recently studied (*old*), had been originally studied, but then updated (*intrusion*), or was an unstudied location (*new*). For both test types, 50% test items were old, requiring a *yes* response and the other 50% required a *no* response (equally divided between intrusion and new information).

Procedure. Tufts University SBER IRB approved all procedures. Participants were randomly assigned to study semantically related or semantically unrelated grids. To start, participants read instructions about the experimental procedures, presented on the computer screen. The experiment was presented on an Apple™ computer running SuperLab (version 4.0, Cedrus Corporation).

Each trial involved a self-paced sequence of grid study, grid updating, and immediate forced recognition test. The sequence unfolded as follows. For grid study, a grid appeared on the screen. The participant studied and then hit the space bar to proceed. Average study time was 3.30 seconds. Next a single dot appeared in the center of the screen. Average "remember" time was 3.30 seconds. The dot signalled participants to imagine the grid they had just studied. When finished imagining, they pressed the space bar to continue. Next came the updating phase. Participants viewed one of the associated grids that was either the same as in the study phase (nothing updated) or had been changed in one of three ways (identity, location, combination). Then the single dot again appeared, signalling the participant to imagine the updated grid (or the same grid if nothing had changed). Average "remember" time was 5.70 seconds. After pressing the space bar, the test phase ensued. Participants received either an identity or location test, matching those used in Experiment 1. After responding, the next trial began. Trial order was randomized across participants and the test type was counterbalanced across trials. Participants could not anticipate the test type on a given trial. We recorded study time for each step of the study and updating procedures and recognition accuracy.

3.2   Results

For the memory test participants designated whether the presented information had been studied in the most recent, i.e. updated, grid. Half of the time, the test item came from the updated grid (*hits*) and half of the time it did not (*correct rejection*). There were two types of correct rejections. *Intrusions* involved information that had been originally studied, but then updated and *new, unstudied* information had not appeared earlier in the trial. Because these item types have differential implications for memory and intrusions only occur when the test type matches the information updated, we analyzed the item types separately. Analyses for both Hits and Correct Rejection of New Items used a 4(updated information: identity, location, combination, nothing) x 2(test type: identity, location) x 2(semantic relatedness: related, unrelated) mixed-factor ANOVA. Updated information and test type served as within-participant variables and semantic relatedness as a between-participant variable.

Hits. Participants had a higher hit rate for location ($M = 0.92$) compared to identity information ($M = 0.87$), $F(1,31) = 11.72$, $\eta_p^2 = .27$. Test type also interacted with the information updated, $F(3, 93) = 2.83$, $\eta_p^2 = .08$. Participants more accurately identified updated locations than updated identities, when no updating was required or when they had updated identities alone or identities and locations in combination. A different pattern emerged when they updated location information. After updating a location, participants recognized updated identities and locations equally well (see Fig. 5).

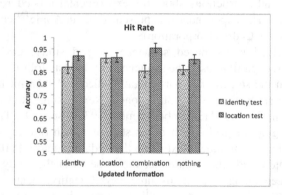

Fig. 5. Experiment 2 hit rates as a function of updated information

Correct Rejection – New Items. Participants correctly rejected new locations ($M = 0.93$), not originally studied or updated in the grid, more accurately than new identities ($M = 0.91$), $F(1,31) = 4.55$, $\eta_p^2 = .13$. Test type also interacted with the information updated, $F(3, 93) = 2.98$, $\eta_p^2 = .09$. Participants more accurately rejected new locations compared to new identities after updating identity or location information. In contrast, if they updated both identity and location, they more accurately rejected new identities. If they did not need to update, they rejected new identity and location information equally well (see Fig. 6).

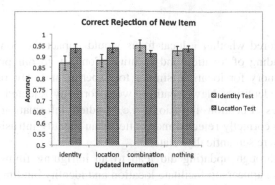

Fig. 6. Experiment 2 correct rejections of new information as a function of updated information

Intrusions. Intrusions occurred when participants indicated that information from the first study grid, was included in a second, updated grid. Thus, the analysis involved a 2(amount updated: one aspect, both aspects) x 2(test type: identity, location) x 2(semantic relatedness: related, unrelated) mixed-factor ANOVA with amount updated and test type as within-participant variables and semantic relatedness as a between-participant variable.

Results showed a three-way interaction between amount updated, test type, and semantic relatedness, $F(1,31) = 4.49$, $\eta_p^2 = .13$. With semantically unrelated information, participants rejected identity and location intrusions at roughly equal rates, regardless of whether they had updated one aspect of the information or both. With semantically related information, participants more accurately rejected location than identity intrusions, whether they had updated one aspect or both, but more so if they had only updated one (see Fig. 7).

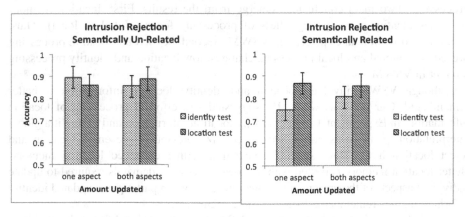

Fig. 7. Experiment 2 correct rejection of intrusions, i.e. previously studied but then updated information.

3.3   Discussion

Experiment 2 explored whether a local focus would impact the constituent parts of VSWM or the binding of location and identity. Contrary to our prediction, results showed better memory for location, similar to Experiment 1. Hit rate for locations exceeded that for identities. New locations were correctly rejected at a higher rate than new identities. Location intrusions, i.e. studied information that had been updated, were also correctly rejected more often than identity intrusions, particularly when the objects were semantically related.

A local focus through updating did lead to an intriguing finding. Focusing on location information appears to facilitate location and identity binding. Notably, when participants updated location information, their hit rate for location and identity information was equivalent. This contrasts with all other updating conditions (identity, both location and identity, or nothing). In all of these cases, hit rate for location exceeded that for identity. One interpretation for this finding is that focusing on location information, which is less effortful to process, leaves open cognitive resources for further processing object identity and binding it with that location. Although the case where nothing needs updating requires few cognitive resources, it does not also promote a local focus on any particular grid items.

4   Conclusions: Effects of Global and Local Processing on VSWM

The present work explored how global (Experiment 1) and local (Experiment 2) processing affect the components of and binding within VSWM. Experiment 1 induced global location processing by organizing locations into an interpretable whole [18]. Experiment 2 used task demands inherent in memory updating to promote local processing. Two main conclusions emerge from the results. First, location memory surpasses identity memory, regardless of processing focus (global or local). Thus, location information takes priority in VSWM. Second, beyond the location processing precedence, global and local processing changes how location and identity processing interact in VSWM.

Although VSWM involves location and identity, location information is better remembered. Our previous work [10] suggested less effortful processing of location information. In Experiment 1, by organizing location information and giving it a global interpretation, participants could better recognize previously presented location and reject location lures. Thus, spatial organization further enhanced location memory. Better location memory persisted with the local processing demands required to update individual aspects of the presented information. Even when participants updated identity information, they remembered locations more accurately.

A global or local focus does impact VSWM; the global or local focus changed how location and identity information interacted. While a global focus on location information improved location memory, it impaired identity memory, with strikingly higher identity false alarms when arrays were spatially organized. Whether this global processing effect is limited to the less cognitively demanding location processing or more generally to global processing is the focus of our current work. The effects of local processing do seem specific to the less demanding location processing. The results suggest an interesting notion for location-identity binding. Although we predicted improved memory for the aspect of focus, we found that when participants updated location information, identity memory improved. This suggests that focusing on less cognitively demanding location information facilitated binding of identity information. A similar focus on identity information did not impact either identity or location memory.

In sum, the components of VSWM, identity and location, have asymmetric processing demands, which impact how they interact during binding. The current studies, which manipulate global and local processing, further highlight these aysmmetries. Location appears less cognitive demanding and consequently is better remembered and can be further improved with spatial organization. Counterintuitively, focusing locally on location information improves identity memory and may aid binding in a way that a concomitant focus on identity information does not. This suggests that difficulties in binding location-identity information may result from difficulties processing or differentiating identity information.

Acknowledgments. We thank Michelle Dorfman for her data collection assistance and Thora Tenbrink for comments on a draft of this work. Funding by the NRSDEC U.S. Army Natick Soldier Research, Development, & Engineering Center, Cognitive Science division, is appreciated.

References

1. Milner, A.D., Goodale, M.A.: The visual brain in action. Oxford University Press, Oxford, England (1995)
2. Ungerleider, L.G., Mishkin, M.: The cortical visual system. In: Ingle, D.J., Goodale, M.A., Mansfield, R.J.W. (eds.) Analysis of Visual Behavior, pp. 549–586. MIT Press, Cambridge (1982)
3. Huttenlocher, J., et al.: Spatial categories and the estimation of location. Cognition 93, 75–97 (2004)
4. Postma, A., Kessels, R.P.C., Van Asselen, M.: The neuropsychology of object location memory. In: Allen, G. (ed.) Remembering Where: Advances in Understanding Spatial Memory, pp. 143–162. Lawrence Erlbaum Associates, Mahwah (2004)
5. Postma, A., Kessels, R.P.C., Van Asselen, M.: How the brain remembers and forgets where things are: The neurocognition of object-location memory. Neuroscience & Biobehavioral Reviews 32(8), 1339–1345 (2008)
6. Landau, B., Jackendoff, R.: "What" and "where" in spatial language and spatial cognition. Behavioral and Brain Sciences 16(2), 216–265 (1993)
7. Hasher, L., Zacks, R.T.: Automatic and effortful processes in memory. Journal of Experimental Psychology: General 108, 356–388 (1979)
8. Light, L.L., Zelinski, E.M.: Memory for spatial information in young and old adults. Developmental Psychology 19, 901–906 (1983)

9. Naveh-Benjamin, M.: Coding of spatial location information: An automatic process? Journal of Experimental Psychology: Learning, Memory, & Cognition 13, 595–605 (1987)
10. Thomas, A.K., et al.: Metacognitive monitoring in visuospatial working memory. Psychology and Aging 27(4), 1099–1110 (2012)
11. Caldwell, J.L., Masson, M.E.: Conscious and unconscious influences of memory for object location. Memory & Cognition 29, 285–295 (2001)
12. Pezdek, K., Evans, G.W.: Visual and verbal memory for objects and their spatial locations. Journal of Experimental Psychology: Human Learning and Memory 5(4), 360–373 (1979)
13. Cowan, N.: The magical number 4 in short-term memory: A reconsideration of mental storage capacity. Behavioral Brain Sciences 24, 87–185 (2000)
14. Jonides, J., et al.: The mind and brain of short-term memory. Annual Review of Psychology 59, 193–224 (2008)
15. Miller, G.A.: The magical number seven, plus or minus two: Some limits on our capacity for processing information. Psychological Review 63, 81–97 (1956)
16. Creem-Regehr, S.H.: Remembering spatial location: The role of physical movement in egocentric updating. In: Allen, G. (ed.) Remembering Where: Advances in Understanding Spatial Memory, pp. 163–189. Lawrence Erlbaum Associates, Mahwah (2004)
17. Pezdek, K.: Memory for items and their spatial locations by young and eldery adults. Developmental Psychology 19(6), 895–900 (1983)
18. Navon, D.: Forest before trees: The precedence of global features in visual perception. Cognitive Psychology 9(3), 353–383 (1977)
19. Förster, J.: GLOMOsys. Current Directions in Psychological Science 21(2), 15–19 (2012)
20. Förster, J., Dannenberg, L.: GLOMOsys: A systems account of global versus local processing. Psychological Inquiry 21(3), 175–197 (2010)
21. Brunyé, T.T., et al.: Emotional state and local versus global spatial memory. Acta Psychologica 130(2), 138–146 (2009)
22. Förster, J.: Local and global cross-modal influences between vision and hearing, tasting, smelling, and touching. Journal of Experimental Psychology: General 140(3), 364–389 (2011)
23. Uttal, D.H., Chiong, C.: Seeing space in more than one way: The development of children's use of higher-order patterns to solve spatial problems. In: Allen, G. (ed.) Remembering Where, pp. 125–142. Lawrence Erlbaum Associates, Mahwah (2003)
24. Maddox, K.B., et al.: Social influences on spatial memory. Memory & Cognition 36(3), 479–494 (2008)
25. McNamara, T.P., Hardy, J.K., Hirtley, S.C.: Subjective hierarchies in spatial memory. Journal of Experimental Psychology: Learning, Memory, & Cognition 15(2), 211–227 (1989)
26. Stevens, A., Coupe, P.: Distortions in judged spatial relations. Cognitive Psycholgy 10(4), 422–437 (1978)
27. Jiang, Y., Olson, I.R., Chun, M.M.: Organization of visual short-term memory. Journal of Experimental Psychology: Learning, Memory, & Cognition 26(3), 683–702 (2000)
28. Grill-Spector, K., Kanwisher, N.: Visual recognition: As soon as you know it is there, you know what it is. Psychological Science 16(2), 152–160 (2005)
29. Roediger, H.L., McDermott, K.B.: Creating false memories: Remembering words not presented in lists. Journal of Experimental Psychology: Learning, Memory, & Cognition 24(4), 803–814 (1995)
30. Miller, M.B., Wolford, G.L.: Theoretical commentary: The role of criterion shift in false memory. Psychological Review 106(2), 398–405 (1999)

31. Clements-Stephens, A.M., Shelton, A.L.: Go figure: Individuation vs. configuration in processing spatial arrays. Journal of Vision, 13(9), 65 (2013)
32. Rock, I., Palmer, S.: The legacy of Gestalt psychology. Scientific American 263(6), 48–61 (1990)
33. Thomas, A.K., Sommers, M.S.: Attention to item-specific processing eliminates age effects in false memories. Journal of Memory & Language 52(1), 71–86 (2005)
34. Pazzaglia, G., De Beni, R.: Strategies of processing spatial information in survey and landmark-centred individuals. European Journal of Cognitive Psychology 13(4), 493–508 (2001)
35. Banks, W.P., Prinzmetal, W.: Configurational effects in visual information processing. Perception & Psychophysics 19(4), 361–367 (1976)
36. Kintsch, W.: Comprehension: A paradigm for cognition. Cambridge University Press, Cambridge (1998)
37. Thomas, A.K., Taylor, H.A., Bonura, B.M.: Disentangling location and identity information in VSWM binding, Tufts University (2014)
38. Artuso, C., Palladino, P.: Content-context binding in verbal working memory updating: On-line and off-line effects. Acta Psychologica 136, 363–369 (2011)
39. Snodgrass, J.G., Vanderwart, M.: A standardized set of 260 pictures: Norms for name agreement, image agreement, familiarity, and visual complexity. Journal of Experimental Psychology: Human Learning and Memory 6(2), 174–215 (1980)

Environment Learning from Spatial Descriptions: The Role of Perspective and Spatial Abilities in Young and Older Adults

Chiara Meneghetti, Erika Borella, Veronica Muffato,
Francesca Pazzaglia, and Rossana De Beni

Department of General Psychology, University of Padova, Italy
chiara.meneghetti@unipd.it

Abstract. The present study investigated age-related differences between young and older adults deriving mental representations from survey and route descriptions, and the involvement of spatial skills in their representation. A sample of 34 young (aged 20-30), 34 middle-aged (50-60) and 32 older (61-80) adults listened to survey and route descriptions of an environment and their recall was tested with a free recall task, a verification test, and a map drawing task; several spatial measures were also administered. The results showed that: i) middle-aged and older adults performed worse than young adults in all recall tasks; ii) all participants formed a perspective-dependent mental representation after learning a route description, but not after learning a survey description (as shown by the verification test); iii) age and spatial abilities predicted recall performance (in relation to type of task and the perspective learnt). Overall, spatial perspective and spatial skills influence the construction of environment representations in young, middle-aged and older adults.

Keywords: Spatial descriptions, Spatial abilities, Spatial self-assessments, Age-related differences, Aging.

1 Introduction

Knowledge of an environment can be learned directly (from sensorimotor experience) or indirectly, such as from maps, virtual displays [1,2 for a review], or descriptions [3 for a review]). The latter occurs in many real-life situations, such as when people unfamiliar with a place (e.g. someone visiting Bremen in Germany for the first time) read a description of how to reach a place of interest (to go from the train station to the historical city center, for instance) in a guidebook. When people read or hear descriptions of environments, they mentally represent them as resembling the state of affairs in the outside world [4], creating a so-called mental model, and this representation preserves its spatial properties [5].

Spatial descriptions typically convey environment information from one of two perspectives, i.e. route or survey, or a combination of the two [5]. Route descriptions represent a space from an egocentric perspective (a path view) and use an intrinsic

C. Freksa et al. (Eds.): Spatial Cognition 2014, LNAI 8684, pp. 30–45, 2014.

frame of reference ("to your left", "behind you", etc.), while survey descriptions represent a space from an allocentric perspective (a bird's-eye view) and use an extrinsic frame of reference (like cardinal points).

There has been lengthy debate on the perspective (in)dependence of spatial mental representations derived from survey or route descriptions. Several studies found that mental representations became abstract, incorporating multiple views [5, 6], while others reported that they maintained the perspective encoded [7, 8, 9]. The typical finding in favor of perspective independence is that individuals asked to read a route or survey description and then say whether sentences testing spatial relations from survey and route perspectives are true or false (a task typically used to test mental models [5]) were equally accurate in verifying inferential sentences from both perspectives, irrespective of the one used in the description [5, 6]. In contrast, a finding that supports perspective dependence is that participants answer more accurately for sentences expressed from the same perspective as the one learned [7, 8, 9]. Research has now identified some factors that modulate perspective (in)dependence, some external like the number of times a text is read (perspective independence is reached after extended reading [6]), the type of recall task (survey descriptions are associated with a better performance in comparing distances between landmarks [10]), others internal, i.e. individual factors capable of modulating the formation of perspective (in)dependent mental models, such as gender (females are more perspective-dependent than males [8, 9]) and spatial competences.

Individual differences in spatial competences and their role in spatial representation have been analyzed in terms of: i) spatial cognitive abilities, distinguishing [11] between spatial perception (i.e. spatial relationships with respect to which way a person's body is facing), spatial visualization (making multistep manipulations of complex stimuli; as measured with the Minnesota Paper Form Board – MPFB [12]), and mental rotation (rotating 3D stimuli; as measured in the Mental Rotations Test –MRT [13]); ii) visuospatial working memory (VSWM), i.e. the ability to retain and process spatial information [14]; and iii) self-assessed preferences for orientation and way-finding in an environment [15].

Concerning spatial abilities, when it comes to memorizing survey descriptions, individuals with strong spatial abilities (as measured with the MPFB [7] or MRT [16]) have a better recall (in verification test and map drawing task, for instance) than those with weaker spatial abilities. But the difference in their performance becomes negligible when route descriptions are memorized (and tested using various tasks). In some studies, like those focusing on VSWM [17], individuals with a high spatial span recalled a route text better than those with a low spatial span [18], while other studies found no difference between individuals with high and low spatial abilities (measured with the MPFB [7] or MRT [14]). Meneghetti, Pazzaglia and De Beni [19] recently analyzed individual spatial differences in spatial descriptions in terms of perspective-taking, a spatial ability that involves having to imagine adopting different positions from the observer's view, which can be measured using the Object Perspective Test (OPT [20, 21]). They found that, after learning survey and route descriptions, spatial recall performance correlated with MRT and OPT scores, and sense of direction self-assessments, but the OPT was the best predictor of spatial recall performance.

Spatial self-assessments influence environment learning (together with spatial abilities [1]), even when information is acquired from spatial descriptions [9]. For instance, Meneghetti et al. [9] found that individuals who reported preferring an extrinsic frame of reference to orient themselves (i.e. survey preference mode) formed more perspective-independent mental representations than people without this preference. The former were equally accurate in judging true/false sentences from both types of perspective, irrespective of the perspective learnt, but their preference for a survey recall format emerged from their better map-drawing performance.

Overall, these results indicate that spatial abilities – i.e. spatial visualization, mental rotation and perspective taking (measured with the MPFB, MRT and OPT, for instance) – VSWM, and spatial self-assessments are all relevant factors to take into account when analyzing the individual spatial skills needed to form good mental representations from spatial descriptions. It is worth noting that the role of such abilities may change, depending on the type of description (survey vs. route perspective) and the type of recall task (e.g. verification test or map drawing task).

Another important variable that may influence people's mental representations and spatial resources is age. People's ability to form mental representations of spatial settings as they grow older is a topic of increasing interest [22, 23] because it is crucial to their autonomy in everyday activities (e.g. reaching destinations). Analyzing age-related changes in this ability could also reveal whether certain environment learning skills are more or less sensitive to aging [24, 25]. More specifically, the question of how spatial representations formed from descriptions change with aging is particularly intriguing for several reasons. For a start, spatial descriptions are a particular case in which spatial information is expressed verbally and, since verbal skills such as vocabulary and text comprehension relate to crystallized abilities [26], and are consequently less sensitive to aging (whereas spatial skills like environment learning from visual input [22, 23, 27] are more liable to decline with age), it may be that using a verbal format to convey environment information would enable older adults to form more adequate mental representations of environments. The literature on aging that explores mental models derived from spatial descriptions shows that spatial features such as the layout of spatial locations and their relationships [28], and the effects of spatial distance [29] are maintained with aging. Although no studies involving older adults have investigated the role of spatial perspective directly, some data obtained with descriptions that presented spatial relations between objects with no reference to the person's point of view (resembling a survey perspective [28]), or referring to the person's movements [29]) showed that older adults did just as well as young adults in recall tasks (verification of spatial sentences, or recognition of elements in a layout [28]). No studies have focused as yet on the differences between young and older adults' mental representations derived from spatial descriptions presented from a survey or route perspective, and this was the first aim of the present study.

There is some initial evidence of the involvement of spatial competences (recorded in terms of VSWM, spatial abilities and spatial self-assessments) in elderly people's environment learning abilities. The few studies examining the relationship between age, spatial competences and environment learning [30, 31] indicate that the influence of age on environment learning performance is mediated by people's spatial competences. In a study across the adult lifespan, for instance, Meneghetti et al. [31] showed that both spatial self-assessments (a factor concerning sense of direction and pleasure in visiting new places) and spatial abilities (measured with the MRT and OPT) mediate the relationship between age and environment orientation performance. Studies conducted with spatial descriptions found that older adults' spatial recall performance related to their working memory (WM) and spatial abilities (tested with the MRT, for instance) [32], but no research has simultaneously examined the involvement of different spatial competences in sustaining young and older adults' spatial representations acquired from survey and route descriptions. This was the second aim of the present study.

This study thus aimed to assess: 1) age-related differences, comparing young with middle-aged and older adults, in mental representations derived from survey and route descriptions, exploring their perspective (in)dependence; and 2) to what extent this representation is sustained by spatial competences. A middle-aged adult group was included because spatial learning from visual input is liable to decline early [33], [25] so worsening spatial mental representations derived from spatial descriptions might be detectable already in middle age too.

A sample of young, middle-aged and older adults completed a series of objective spatial tasks measuring spatial abilities and self-assessments. Then they listened to survey and route descriptions. Their recall of the descriptions was measured with a verification test (using filler, paraphrased and survey or route inference sentences, as in mental model studies [5]), and free recall and map drawing tasks (both sensitive measures used to test mental representation [14]).

Regarding the first aim (age-related differences in mental representations derived from survey and route descriptions), we expected the young and old groups to reveal either a similar recall performance (as suggested by studies on older adults [28]), or a worse performance in the older adults, given their poor performance in environment learning from visual inputs (e.g. maps [32], or navigation [23]), which prompt the formation of mental representations with some features resembling those formed from spatial descriptions [3]. Given the known early decline in spatial learning skills in the middle-aged [25], [33], we tested whether they resembled the older adults in terms of spatial recall performance. We also examined whether our results suggested a perspective dependence (as shown in [8, 9]) or independence [as in 5, 6]. The latter type of result might also relate to the type of recall measure used, so we aimed to see whether older (and middle-aged) adults had difficulty in switching perspective (as moving from egocentric to allocentric information [34, 35]); or whether they found it difficult to form mental representations with spatial features [22], irrespective of the type of recall task used.

Regarding our second aim (age-related differences in mental representations derived from survey and route descriptions in relation to spatial competences), we assumed that spatial competences related to spatial recall accuracy in young and in middle-aged and older adults (as suggested by other studies on age-related differences [30, 31]). We also explored the different role of spatial competences as a function of the perspective learnt (survey vs. route), and of the tasks used to test spatial recall.

Indeed, certain spatial abilities, VSWM, and possibly spatial self-assessments too (as studied in young adults [9], [14]), would be more strongly involved in tasks requiring an active reproduction of the information memorized (free recall and map drawing) than in the verification test.

2   Method

2.1   Participants

The study involved 34 young adults (17 females, age range 20-30), 34 middle-aged adults (18 females, age range 50-60) and 32 older adults (16 females, age range 61-80) and, within each group, all the various ages were fairly equally represented (see mean ages in Table 1). They were all native Italian speakers, healthy and living independently, and they all volunteered for the study. The groups differed in years of formal education, $F(2,99) = 20.04$, $\eta^2 = .29$, $p < .001$, young adults having had more schooling than the others (all groups had attended school for at least 13 years). The adequate cognitive functioning of our participants (particularly for the middle-aged and older groups) was tested by administering the Vocabulary test of Wechsler Adult Intelligence Scale - Revised (WAIS–R) and Reading Comprehension tasks (RCT; [36]), which showed no differences between the three age groups ($F < 1$; $F = 2.04$ $p = .14$). All participants reached the cutoff for their age in the WM tasks (backward digit span and Corsi blocks; see description below [37]), though the middle-aged and older adults fared worse than the young adults -$F(2, 97) = 7.03/9.92$ $p < .001$- (see Table 1).

Table 1. Means (M) and standard deviations (SD) for demographic variables by age group

	Young adults		Middle-aged		Old adults	
	M	SD	M	SD	M	SD
Age	25.12	1.90	53.74	3.09	67.94	5.49
Years of education	16.91	2.73	13.12	2.83	13.47	2.59
Vocabulary (WAIS–R)	47.91	6.70	44.76	6.50	47.16	6.90
Reading comprehension task (RCT)	8.76	1.23	8.06	1.67	8.03	1.77
Backward digit span	5.38	0.95	4.76	1.10	4.50	0.88
Backward Corsi blocks	6.00	1.18	4.91	1.24	4.88	1.10

2.2   Materials

Experimental Tasks

Spatial texts. Four descriptions of two fictitious outdoor environments were used (a tourist center and a holiday farm, adapted from [9]), two from a route and two from a survey perspective. Both descriptions contained 14 landmarks and were of similar length (between 302 and 309 words). In the survey version, the description first outlined the layout of the environment, then defined the relationship between landmarks using canonical terms ("north", "south-east"). In the route version, a person imagined walking along a route and the landmarks' position was presented as seen by the person using egocentric terms ("left", "right") (see Table 2). Each description was recorded in an MP3 file lasting 3 minutes.

Verification test. Thirty-two true/false sentences were used (half of them true, adapted from [9]) for each spatial text, i.e. 8 filler sentences on non-spatial information, 8 paraphrased sentences drawn from the description learnt, 8 route and 8 survey inferential sentences on spatial relations between landmarks not mentioned explicitly (the number of sentences in each category was consistent with previous studies [5, 6]; see Table 2).

Table 2. Examples of route and survey descriptions and verification test (tourist center)

Route description	Survey description
"[…] Go straight ahead and you will soon see the tennis courts, which are used for a number of local competitions, on your left at the end of the oak wood. Keep going as the road bends slightly to the right and, beyond the bend, you will see the hills on your left, which surround the whole area."	"[…] a dense oak wood, famous for its many centuries-old trees, stretches from north to south. This dense oak wood extends to the south as far as the tennis courts. At the southernmost tip of the lake there are hills stretching from east to west across the whole area of the tourist center."

Verification test sentences	Example
Filler	The tennis courts are used for a number of local competitions.
Paraphrased for route texts	You will find the hills on your left beyond the bend.
Paraphrased for survey texts	The hills stretch from east to west across the area of the tourist center.
Route inference	Going towards the hills, you will find the oak wood on your right.
Survey inference	The tennis courts are to the south of the hills.

Spatial Measures

Working memory tasks. The Backward Corsi blocks task [17] and the Backward digit span task [37] involve repeating in reverse order increasingly long sequences of blocks/numbers presented by the experimenter. The final score is the longest correctly-repeated sequence.

Spatial objective tasks. Short (s) versions of the following tried and tested spatial tasks [24] were used: Embedded Figures Test (sEFT; adapted from [38]), Minnesota Paper Form Board (sMPFB; adapted from [12]), Mental Rotations Test (sMRT; adapted from [13]), Object Perspective Test (sOPT; adapted from [21], for the psychometric features see [24, 25]). The sEFT (10 items) involves finding simple elements (listed separately) embedded in a complex overall figure. In the sMPFB (16 items) respondents choose a figure (from among five options) obtainable by arranging a set of fragments. The sMRT (10 items) requires the identification of two 3D cube-objects that match a target object in a rotated position. The sOPT (6 items) involves imagining standing at one object in a configuration, facing another, and pointing in the direction of a third; the answer is given by drawing an arrow from the center towards the edge of a circle. All these short spatial tasks have a time limit of five minutes. The number of correct answers (for the sEFT, sMPFB and sMRT) and the absolute degrees of error (for the sOPT) were considered as dependent variables.

Sense of Direction and Spatial Representation questionnaire (SDSR [15]). This comprises 11 items measuring general sense of direction, knowledge and use of cardinal points, and preference for survey, route or landmark-centered representations (see psychometric features in [24, 25]). All scores (using Likert scale 1 "not at all" -5 "very much") were added together (found to be a sensitive method in older adults [25]) and the total score was considered as a dependent variable.

2.3   Procedure

Participants were tested individually in two sessions lasting an hour each. In the first, participants completed the Vocabulary test and RCT, then performed the spatial measures (presented in balanced order across participants). In the second, they listened twice (for six minutes in all) to a description from one perspective (survey or route; the type of perspective combined with a given type of environment was balanced across participants), then they performed the following, in the same order as listed: the free recall test (orally reporting everything they could remember about the environment), the verification test (on filler, paraphrased, route inference or survey inference sentences, presented in random order), and the map-drawing task (depicting the layout and the location of the landmarks)1. Then participants heard the description from the other perspective twice and performed the recall tasks.

3   Results

3.1   Scoring

In the verification test, one point was awarded for each correct answer for each type of sentence (maximum score: 8). For the free recall and map drawing tasks, we examined first whether landmarks were recalled, irrespective of their position (obtaining a 'landmarks mentioned' score, one point for each landmark), and then whether landmarks were located correctly ('landmark location' score), a measure used to test the spatial features of the participants' mental representations [14]; in this latter case, in free recall a point was awarded for each landmark verbally reported in the correct position relative to others nearby (e.g. the tennis court is on the left of the path and at the edge of the oak wood; see Table 2). In map drawing, a point was awarded for each landmark written or drawn in the correct position on the map in relation to others nearby (e.g. the tennis court was drawn to the bottom right of the sheet of paper and the oak wood was further to the right). No points were awarded for wrong or partly wrong information. The scores awarded by two independent judges correlated closely ($r = .98$, $r = 93$; $p < .001$), so the analyses were run on the scores awarded by the first judge.

3.2   Age-related Differences in Mental Representations Derived from Survey and Route Descriptions (Aim 1)

Verification Test. A 3 (Age: young vs. middle-aged vs. old adults) as a between-participants factor – x 2 (Type of description: route vs. survey) x 4 (Type of sentence: filler vs. paraphrased vs. route inference vs. survey inference) as within-participant

---

[1] Map drawing was chosen as the final task to avoid the visual layout influencing the free recall and verification test. The free recall and verification tests assessed verbal recall (the first without and the second with anchoring information).

factors, mixed ANOVA was carried out. The results showed the following main effects: Age, $F(2, 97) = 12.27$, $\eta_p^2 = .20$, $p < .001$ – where young adults performed significantly better than the middle-aged ($p < .01$) or older adults ($p < .001$), while the latter two were similar ($p = .29$; see Table 3); Type of sentence, $F(3, 97) = 60.83$, $\eta_p^2 = .39$, $p < .001$ – where accuracy was similar for filler sentences ($M = 6.85$, $SD = 1.14$) and paraphrased ones ($M = 7.03$, $SD = 1.04$, $p = .32$), and higher for both ($p < .001$) than for route ($M = 5.62$, $SD = 1.42$) or survey sentences ($M = 5.36$, $SD = 1.95$), and the latter two were similar ($p = .17$). Only the Type of description x Type of sentence interaction was significant, $F(3, 97) = 7.30$, $\eta_p^2 = .07$, $p < .001$ (see Table 3). The comparisons within each type of description (using Bonferroni's correction, differences where $p \leq .001$ were considered significant) showed that: in route descriptions, accuracy was similar for filler and paraphrased sentences ($p = .96$), and higher than for route or survey inference sentences ($p < .001$), and responses were more accurate for route inference sentences than for survey inference sentences ($p < .001$); in survey descriptions, accuracy was the same for filler and paraphrased sentences ($p = .73$) and higher ($p < .001$) than for route or survey inference sentences; the latter two did not differ ($p = 1.00$). The comparisons between survey and route descriptions showed that survey inference sentences were answered more accurately for survey than for route descriptions ($p < .01$), and there was no difference in the proportion of correct answers concerning filler, paraphrased and route inference sentences between the route and survey descriptions were found ($p > .63$).

To clarify the role of age in relation to Type of description and Type of sentence, the older adults were divided into 60-69 year-olds (n = 22) and 70-80 year-olds (n = 12)[2]. The 2 (Age) x 2 (Type of description) x 4 (Type of sentence) mixed ANOVA showed a significant Age x Type of sentence interaction, $F(3, 96) = 2.68$, $\eta_p^2 = .08$, $p = .05$. Further comparisons showed that 70-80 year-olds performed worse with survey sentences ($M = 3.96$, $SD = 1.26$) than with route sentences ($M = 5.29$, $SD = 0.81$; $p < .001$), while the 60-69 year-olds' performance did not differ between survey ($M = 4.71$, $SD = 1.61$) and route sentences ($M = 4.68$, $SD = 1.60$; $p = .54$). Both older adult subgroups performed better with filler and paraphrased sentences than with inferential ones (no differences in sentence accuracy were found between the two subgroups, $F < 1$ to $F = 1.90$ $p = .12$).

Free Recall and Map-Drawing. Preliminary it was ascertained the recall of landmarks (independently of the location reported): all participants recalled most of the landmarks (in free recall and map drawing young adults mentioned 90% of the landmarks, the middle-aged 73%, and the older adults 70%). The 3 (Age) x 2 (Type of description) mixed ANOVA on the scores for landmarks correctly located showed only a main effect of Age for both free recall, $F(2, 97) = 45.98$, $\eta_p^2 = .49$, $p < .001$, and map drawing, $F(2, 97) = 35.48$, $\eta_p^2 = .42$, $p < .001$: young adults performed better ($p < .001$) than the middle-aged or older adults, with no difference between the latter two ($p > .35$; see Table 3). In free recall, all participants used language expressions consistent with the perspective learnt. The lower scores obtained by the middle-aged and older adults were due to mistakes in positioning the landmarks. The analyses on the 60-69 and 70-80 year-old subgroups showed no significant differences between the two ($F_s < 1$).

---

[2] This procedure was suggested by the Reviewer 4 of the paper

Table 3. Means (*M*) and standard deviations (*SD*) for accuracy in the verification test (by Type of sentence, Type of description, and Age), free recall and map drawing (by Type of description and Age)

Type of recall task	Type of description	Type of sentence	Young adults M	SD	Middle -aged M	SD	Old adults M	SD	Total M	SD
Verification test	Route	Filler	6.94	1.04	6.47	1.19	6.41	1.43	6.61	1.24
		Paraphrased	7.15	1.02	6.26	1.31	5.69	1.45	6.38	1.39
		Route inference	5.65	1.61	5.35	1.43	5.06	1.37	5.36	1.48
		Survey inference	4.97	2.01	4.56	2.03	3.94	1.63	4.50	1.93
	Survey	Filler	6.76	1.23	6.56	0.99	6.41	1.24	6.58	1.16
		Paraphrased	6.91	1.06	6.03	1.53	6.13	1.41	6.36	1.39
		Route inference	5.59	1.23	4.88	1.65	4.72	1.44	5.07	1.49
		Survey inference	5.74	1.88	5.24	1.65	4.72	1.33	5.24	1.68
	Total		6.21	1.39	5.67	1.47	5.38	1.41		
Free recall			10.77	2.62	5.81	2.75	4.73	2.86		
Map drawing			9.66	2.84	5.13	2.77	4.36	2.74		

3.3   Age-Related Differences in Mental Representations Derived from Survey and Route Descriptions in Relation to Spatial Competences (Aim 2)

Correlations. Correlations between all variables (only inferential sentences were considered for their role in testing spatial mental models [5]) showed that Age correlated negatively with WM (Backward digit span and Corsi blocks tests), with all the spatial objectives tasks (but not with the SDSR), and with all the recall tasks (except for the route and survey inference sentences in the route descriptions and the route inference sentences in the survey descriptions). The correlations between spatial measures and recall tasks showed that: i) accuracy in free recall and map drawing, in either route or survey description conditions (which correlated quite closely with one another), correlated strongly with WM and all objective spatial tasks. In contrast, true/false sentences, which correlated modestly within each other, did not correlate significantly with spatial objective tasks, the SDSR or WM tasks (see Table 4).

Regression Analyses. Hierarchical regression analyses were run to estimate the percentage of variance explained by age, processing resources (WM), spatial abilities and self-assessments for route and survey descriptions in map drawing, free recall and the verification test (distinguishing between the survey and route inference sentences). The order in which the variables were entered, based on their theoretical importance judging from the literature, was: Age (Step 1), WM (Step 2) as a basic cognitive ability [31], Spatial abilities (Step 3) as higher cognitive abilities [25], and spatial self-assessments (Step 4). Cook's distance was computed to check for outliers on the criterion and predictor variables (Cook's distance >1), and the variance inflation factor values and tolerance criterion showed no significant multicollinearity.

Map drawing. The predictors explained 38% of the overall variance for route descriptions and 45% for survey ones. For both types of description, when age was entered in the regression, it accounted for a significant part of the variance (route: 27%; survey: 34%); in subsequent steps, for both route and survey descriptions the spatial objective tasks explained another 7% and 9% of the variance, respectively. In the final step, Age ($\beta = -.52$, $p < .0001$) and the sOPT ($\beta = -.26$, $p < .05$)

Table 1. Correlations between age and the measures of interest

	1	2	3	4	5	6	7	8	9	10	11	12	13	14
1. Age	1.00													
2. WM	-0.41**	1.00												
3. sEFT	-0.34**	0.52**	1.00											
4. sMPFB	-0.50**	0.30**	0.29**	1.00										
5. sMRT	-0.44**	0.38**	0.45**	0.31**	1.00									
6. sOPT	0.39**	-0.43**	-0.63**	-0.30**	-0.45**	1.00								
7. SDSR	0.10	-0.02	-0.17	0.03	0.05	-0.11	1.00							
8. Route D. - Free recall	-0.59**	0.26**	0.31**	0.42**	0.40**	-0.36**	0.20	1.00						
9. Route D. – Map drawing	-0.53**	0.33**	0.27**	0.37**	0.39**	-0.43**	0.13	0.74**	1.00					
10. Route D. - Route inference sentence	-0.13	0.08	0.16	0.01	0.12	-0.16	0.01	0.35**	0.45**	1.00				
11. Route D. - Survey inference sentence	-0.21	0.24	0.05	0.08	-0.02	-0.14	-0.07	-0.03	0.20	0.30**	1.00			
12. Survey D. - Free recall	-0.69**	0.32**	0.33**	0.39**	0.39**	-0.45**	0.07	0.72**	0.64**	0.24	0.06	1.00		
13. Survey D. - Map drawing	-0.59**	0.37**	0.41**	0.36**	0.41**	-0.52**	0.02	0.56**	0.62**	0.27**	0.10	0.80**	1.00	
14. Survey D. - Route inference sentence	-0.21	0.13	0.26	0.02	0.12	-0.15	-0.11	0.27**	0.31**	0.43**	0.27**	0.33**	0.30**	1.00
15. Survey D. - Survey inference sentence	-0.29**	0.11	0.06	0.21	0.01	-0.08	-0.12	0.12	0.29**	0.14	0.32**	0.30**	0.32**	0.25

Note (for Tables 4 and 5). N = 100, only $p < .01$ was considered significant (**); WM: working memory; the mean z score was calculated for the Backward digit span and Corsi blocks tests); sEFT: short Embedded Figure Test; sMPFB: short Minnesota Paper Form Board; sMRT: short Mental Rotations Test; sOPT: short Object Perspective Test; SDSR: Sense of Direction and Spatial Representation scale; D: Descriptions.

significant predictors for both route and survey descriptions, Age (β = -.58, p < .0001) and sOPT (β = -.27, p < .05).

Free recall task. The predictors explained 44% of the overall variance in the route description condition and 53% in the survey one. In both types of description, age accounted for a significant part of the variance (route: 34%; survey: 47%). In subsequent steps, spatial self-assessments explained another 5% of the variance for route descriptions, and spatial objective tasks another 5% for survey descriptions. In the last step, the only significant predictors were: Age (β = -.58, p < .0001) and SDSR (β = .24, p < .01) for route descriptions; and Age (β = -.69, p < .0001) and sOPT (β = -.20, p < .05) for survey descriptions.

Verification test. For route descriptions and route inference sentences the model explained 5% of the overall variance; for the other conditions (route descriptions - survey inference sentences, survey descriptions - route inference sentences, route descriptions - survey inference sentences), the predictors explained 14%, 14% and 12% of the overall variance, respectively. Age accounted for a significant part of the variance (4% for route descriptions - survey inference sentences; 4% for survey descriptions - route inference sentences; 9% for survey descriptions - survey inference sentences). Any additional variance for the route descriptions - survey inference sentences, and survey descriptions - survey inference sentences was explained by the other measures in subsequent steps, and Age was the only significant predictor in the final step (route descriptions - survey inference sentences β = -.20, p < .05; survey descriptions - survey inference sentences β = -.30, p < .0001). For the survey descriptions - route inference sentences condition, the spatial objective tasks explained another 10% of the variance in subsequent steps; in the final step, Age (β = -.20, p < .05) and sEFT (β = .38, p < .001) were the only significant predictors (see Table 5).

Table 5. Hierarchical regression analyses with age and measures of interest for map drawing, free recall and verification test by type of description (route vs. survey)

Type of description	Predictors	Map drawing ΔR^2	β	Free recall ΔR^2	β	Route inference sentences ΔR^2	β	Survey inference sentences ΔR^2	β
Route	Age	.27***	-.52***	.34***	-.58***	.02	-.12	.04***	-.20*
	WM task	.02	.14	.001	.03	.00	.04	.03	.20^
	Spatial objective tasks	.07*		.05		.02		.06	
	sEFT		-.15		.02		.11		-.06
	sMPFB		.11		.16		-.05		-.19
	sOPT		-.26*		-.07		-.07		-.09
	sMRT		.13		.11		.03		-.19
	Spatial self-assessments	.01				.01		.01	
	SDSR	.01	.12	.05*	.24**		.04		-.07
	Total R^2	**.38**		**.44**		**.05**		**.14**	
Survey	Age	.34***	-.58***	.47**	-.69***	.04*	-.20*	.09**	-.30***
	WM task	.02	.16	.001	.05	.00	.07	.00	-.02
	Spatial objective tasks	.09*		.05*		.10*		.02	
	sEFT		.03		-.03		.38*		.01
	sMPFB		.07		.12		.18		-.10
	sOPT		-.27*		-.20*		.10		-.03
	sMRT		.07		.02		-.02		-.15
	Spatial self-assessments	.01		.001		.00		.00	
	SDSR		.03		.10		-.02		-.06
	Total R^2	**.45**		**.53**		**.14**		**.12**	

4   Discussion and Conclusions

The present study aimed to investigate age-related differences in young, middle-aged and older adults' mental spatial representations derived from learning environments described from a survey or a route perspective. In particular, we explored age-related differences in perspective (in)dependence, and to what extent mental representations are sustained by spatial competences, in relation to the type of description and the type of recall task used. Previous studies had indicated that: i) spatial representation in young adults may [6] or may not [8] be perspective-independent, and individual differences (in spatial competences, for instance) can influence the final features of the representation [9]; ii) older adults retain the ability to form mental models from spatial descriptions [28] though studies using visual input found older adults impaired in forming environment representations [22]. No studies had investigated whether older adults (and the middle-aged too, since spatial learning abilities decline early across the adult lifespan [33]) are susceptible to a perspective (in)dependence effect, and whether their mental representations are sustained by spatial competences.

Concerning the age-related differences for survey and route descriptions (Aim 1), our results showed that middle-aged and older adults performed less well than young adults in all recall tasks (free recall, verification test and map drawing). Our findings contrast with previous studies showing no age-related differences (young vs. older adults) in the recall of spatial descriptions [28], but said studies did not examine mental representations derived from survey and route descriptions. Our results are consistent, on the other hand, with findings obtained using visual inputs (maps and navigation tools) showing that older adults were more impaired than younger ones [22]. This suggests that mental representations derived from spatial descriptions have spatial features to a similar extent to those formed from visual input [3].

The verification test results specifically showed that mental representations derived from route descriptions are perspective-dependent, while those derived from survey descriptions are perspective-independent. Indeed, after learning route descriptions, participants gave answers that were more accurate for route inference than for survey inference sentences, whereas, after learning survey descriptions, they showed a similar performance in survey and route inference sentences (though they performed better with survey inference sentences after hearing a survey description than after hearing a route description). These results indicate that mental representations are perspective-dependent when derived from route descriptions, and perspective-independent after learning survey descriptions. These findings are consistent with studies showing that route descriptions require more extensive learning to generate perspective independence properties [6], and the strong support of cognitive resources [14], [39], while it was easier to generate perspective-independent mental models after learning survey descriptions.

Although this result at least partially confirms previous findings in young adults, it is novel as regards the age-related differences: all age groups had a similar pattern of performance when the types of sentence and perspective were analyzed (although middle-aged and older adults were generally less accurate than younger ones).

Taken together the results of all recall tasks indicated that middle-aged and older adults generally had more difficulty in forming spatial mental representations derived from spatial descriptions. Their performance was worse in all recall tests, i.e. tasks preserving the same format and based on active reproduction (free recall), or on identifying true/false spatial relations (verification test), or involving a change of format and based on active reproduction (map drawing). Our results thus support the assumption of a general difficulty in managing spatial information [22] to correctly locate landmarks and infer spatial relations, not only in people over 60, but even in those over 50 (as suggested by studies using visual input [25], [33]). This decline in spatial description learning ability – judging from our results, at least - was not attributable to difficulties in switching, for instance, from an egocentric to an allocentric view [34,35], but to a more general difficulty in forming mental representations with spatial features. Our comparison between 60-69 year-olds and 70-80 year-olds brought out the type of difficulty encountered with aging: the old-old performed worse with survey sentences than with route sentences (whatever the type of description learnt). Although further studies are needed to confirm it, this result suggests that the old-old are impaired in their ability to manage allocentric information, i.e. to form a survey representation (a finer level of environment representation according to Siegel & White [40]), as seen in studies on age-related differences using visual input [22], [27]. On the other hand, aging has a less severe effect on people's ability to manage egocentric information (as seen from the person's point of view), which is more commonly needed to process environment information in everyday situations.

Concerning how age-related differences in coping with survey and route descriptions were influenced by spatial competences (Aim 2), the correlations and regression analyses showed that the spatial competences (assessed using different measures) play a part in supporting spatial text recall accuracy – also depending on the type of recall task used and the type of perspective learnt. Our results indicate that age and spatial competences have a stronger influence on active recall tasks (map drawing and free recall) than on tasks that involve judging the truthfulness of sentences (verification test). This is consistent with studies on young adults showing a clear involvement of cognitive and spatial resources in tasks requiring an active reproduction of the information memorized [14], [39]. Accuracy in active recall tasks was found to correlate with WM and with objective measures of spatial abilities (while the verification test correlated only modestly with these measures of individual differences). Regression analyses showed, however, that only one spatial task – the sOPT – significantly predicted survey and route description recall (as shown with map drawing for both types of description, and with free recall for survey descriptions). The sOPT assesses the ability to adopt an imaginary perspective misaligned with the observer's view, which is plausibly involved in learning route descriptions since the listeners' view changes as they move along their imaginary path (and this was only detected with the map drawing task). At the same time, the sOPT proved the best predictor of survey description learning (as tested with map drawing and free recall): although this type of description does not entail a change in the person's imaginary point of view, the sequence in which the spatial information is presented may induce listeners to imagine moving and changing their perspective, so their perspective-taking ability sustains their recall of a survey description. This interpretation is an intriguing possibility, but further studies will be needed to better elucidate the strategies used by participants in recall tasks. Although the role of perspective-taking proved important in supporting mental representations derived from survey and route descriptions, it should be noted that performance in the sOPT correlated with the scores obtained in tasks measuring other spatial skills, so these resources must have some aspects in common [25]. Performance in free recall after hearing a route description was also predicted by spatial self-assessments on sense of direction, confirming the relationship between self-assessments and environment description learning [9]. In the verification test, the contribution of the predictors was minimal and age accounted for most of the variance (it was only after learning survey descriptions and saying whether route inference sentences were true or false that an additional variance was accounted for by the sEFT).

On the whole, our results suggest that similar underlying cognitive mechanisms are at work across the age groups examined when mental representations are derived from survey and route descriptions. Spatial abilities, particularly in perspective-taking, have an important role in sustaining the active reproduction of memorized spatial information in any age group, so spatial competences are needed to support the construction of a reliable mental representation of an environment not only in the young, but also in middle-aged and older adults [31].

Our results seem interesting, but further studies will need to better elucidate how the ability to generate representations from spatial descriptions develops across the adult lifespan. Future research should pay attention to several aspects, such as: age range (preferably considering evenly-distributed samples ranging from 20 to 80 years old); type of input (other types of environment); types of recall task (e.g. using sensitive measures to identify the type of difficulty encountered in spatial learning); and the order of their presentation (to avoid effects of one task on another).

In conclusion, our results suggest that: i) middle-aged and older adults both find it more difficult (than younger adults) to recall environment descriptions conveyed from route or survey perspectives; ii) all age groups are equally liable to a perspective independence effect (after learning from survey descriptions, at least); and iii) spatial competences sustain mental representations derived from spatial descriptions based on both route and survey perspectives (especially when active recall tasks are used).

References

1. Hegarty, M., Montello, D.R., Richardson, A.E., Ishikawa, T., Lovelace, K.: Spatial Ability at Different Scales: Individual Differences in Aptitude-Test Performance and Spatial-Layout Learning. Intelligence 34, 151–176 (2006)
2. Montello, D.R., Waller, D., Hegarty, M., Richardson, A.E.: Spatial Memory of Real Environments, Virtual Environments, and Maps. In: Allen, G. (ed.) Human Spatial Memory: Remembering Where, pp. 251–285. Lawrence Erlbaum Associates, Mahwah (2004)
3. Gyselinck, V., Meneghetti, C.: The Role of Spatial Working Memory in Understanding Verbal Descriptions: A Window onto the Interaction Between Verbal and Spatial Processing. In: Vandienrendonck, A., Szmalec, A. (eds.) Spatial Working Memory, pp. 159–180. Psychology Press (2011)

4. Johnson-Laird, P.N.: Mental Models: Towards a Cognitive Science of Language, Inference and Consciousness. Harvard University Press, Cambridge (1983)
5. Taylor, H.A., Tversky, B.: Spatial Mental Models Derived from Survey and Route Descriptions. Journal of Memory and Language 31, 261–292 (1992)
6. Brunye, T.T., Taylor, H.A.: Extended Experience Benefits Spatial Mental Model Development With Route But Not Survey Descriptions. Acta Psychologica 127, 340–354 (2008)
7. Bosco, A., Filomena, S., Sardone, L., Scalisi, T.G., Longoni, A.M.: Spatial Models Derived From Verbal Descriptions of Fictitious Environments: The Influence of Study Time and the Individual Differences in Visuospatial Ability. Psychologische Beitrage 38, 451–464 (1996)
8. Perrig, W., Kintsch, W.: Propositional And Situational Representations of Text. Journal of Memory and Language 24, 503–518 (1985)
9. Meneghetti, C., Pazzaglia, F., De Beni, R.: Spatial Mental Representations Derived From Survey and Route Descriptions: When Individuals Prefer Extrinsic Frame of Reference. Learning and Individual Differences 21, 150–157 (2011)
10. Noordzij, M.L., Postma, A.: Categorical and Metric Distance Information in Mental Representations Derived From Route and Survey Descriptions. Psychological Research 69, 221–232 (2005)
11. Linn, M.C., Petersen, A.C.: Emergence and Characterization of Sex Differences in Spatial Ability: A Meta-Analysis. Child Development 56, 1479–1498 (1985)
12. Likert, R., Quasha, W.H.: Revised Minnesota Paper Form Board. Psychological Corporation, New York (1941)
13. Vandenberg, S.G., Kuse, A.R.: Mental Rotations, a Group Test of 3-Dimensional Spatial Visualization. Perceptual and Motor Skills 47, 599–604 (1978)
14. Meneghetti, C., Gyselinck, V., Pazzaglia, F., De Beni, R.: Individual Differences in Spatial Text Processing: High Spatial Ability Can Compensate For Spatial Working Memory Interference. Learning and Individual Differences 19, 577–589 (2009)
15. Pazzaglia, F., Cornoldi, C., De Beni, R.: Differenze Individuali nella Rappresentazione Dello Spazio: Presentazione di un Questionario Autovalutativo (Individual Differences in Representation of Space: Presentation of a Questionnaire). Giornale Italiano di Psicologia 3, 627–650 (2000)
16. Pazzaglia, F.: Text and Picture Integration in Comprehending and Memorizing Spatial Descriptions. In: Rouet, J.F., Lowe, R., Schnotz, W. (eds.) Understanding Multimedia Documents, pp. 43–59. Springer, NYC, US (2008)
17. Corsi, P.M.: Human Memory and the Medial Temporal Region of the Brain. Unpublished doctoral dissertation, McGill University, Montreal (1972)
18. Pazzaglia, F., Cornoldi, C.: The Role of Distinct Components of Visuo-Spatial Working Memory in the Processing of Texts. Memory 7, 19–41 (1999)
19. Meneghetti, C., Pazzaglia, F., De Beni, R.: Mental Representations Derived from Spatial Descriptions: The Influence of Orientation Specificity and Visuospatial abilities. Psychological Research (in press)
20. Kozhevnikov, M., Hegarty, M.: A Dissociation Between Object-Manipulation Spatial Ability and Spatial Orientation Ability. Memory and Cognition 29, 745–756 (2001)
21. Hegarty, M., Waller, D.: A Dissociation Between Mental Rotation and Perspective - Taking Spatial Abilities. Intelligence 32, 175–191 (2004)
22. Klencklen, G., Despre's, O., Dufour, A.: What do we know about aging and spatial cognition? Reviews and perspectives. Aging Research Reviews 11, 23–135 (2012)

23. Moffat, S.D.: Aging and spatial navigation: what do we know and where do we go? Neuropsychology Review 19, 478–489 (2009)
24. De Beni, R., Meneghetti, C., Fiore, F., Gava, L., Borella, E.: Batteria Visuo-spaziale. Strumenti per la valutazione delle abilità visuo-spaziali nell'arco di vita adulta (Visuo-spatial Battery: Istrument for assessing visuo-spatial abilities across adult life span). Hogrefe, Firenze (2014)
25. Borella, E., Meneghetti, C., Ronconi, L., De Beni, R.: Visuo-spatial Abilities Across the Life Span. Developmental Psychology (2013)
26. Craik, F.I.M., Salthouse, T.A. (eds.): Handbook of Aging and Cognition, 3rd edn. Psychology Press, New York (2008)
27. Head, D., Isom, M.: Age effects on wayfinding and route learning skills. Behavioural Brain Research 209, 49–58 (2010)
28. Copeland, D.E., Radvansky, G.A.: Aging and Integrating Spatial Mental Models. Psychology Aging 22, 569–579 (2007)
29. Radvansky, G.A., Copeland, D.E., Berish, D.E., Dijkstra, K.: Aging and Situation Model Updating. Aging, Neuropsychology, Cognition 10, 158–166 (2003)
30. Kirasic, K.C.: Age Differences in Adults' Spatial Abilities, Learning Environmental Layout, and Wayfinding Behaviour. Spatial Cognition and Computation 2, 117–134 (2000)
31. Meneghetti, C., Borella, E., Pastore, M., De Beni, R.: The Role of Spatial Abilities and Self-Assessments in Cardinal Point Orientation Across the Lifespan. Learning and Individual Differences (accepted), doi: 10.1016/j.lindif.2014.07.006
32. Meneghetti, C., Borella, E., Gyselinck, V., De Beni, R.: Age-differences in Environment Route Learning: The Role of Input and Recall-Test Modalities in Young and Older Adults. Learning and Individual Differences 22, 884–890 (2012)
33. Gyselinck, V., Meneghetti, C., Bormetti, M., Orriols, E., Piolino, P., De Beni, R.: Considering Spatial Ability in Virtual Route Learning in Early Aging. Cognitive processing 14, 309–316 (2013)
34. Harris, M.A., Wolbers, T.: How age-related strategy switching deficits affect wayfinding in complex environments. Neurobiology of Aging 35, 1095–1102 (2014)
35. Harris, M.A., Wiener, J.M., Wolbers, T.: Aging specifically impairs switching to an allocentric navigational strategy. Frontiers in Aging Neuroscience 4, 29–29 (2012)
36. Wechsler, D.: Wechsler Adult Intelligence Scale, rev. edn. Psychological Corporation, New York (1981)
37. De Beni, R., Borella, E., Carretti, B., Marigo, C., Nava, L.A.: BAC. Portfolio per la Valutazione del Benessere e Delle Abilità Cognitive Nell'età Adulta e Avanzata (The Assesment of Well-Being and Cognitive Abilities in Adulthood and Aging). Giunti OS, Firenze (2008)
38. Oltman, P.K., Raskin, E., Witkin, H.A.: Group Embedded Figures Test. Consulting Psychologists Press, Palo Alto (1971)
39. Gyselinck, V., De Beni, R., Pazzaglia, F., Meneghetti, C., Mondoloni, A.: Working Memory Components and Imagery Instructions in the Elaboration of a Spatial Mental Model. Psychological Research 71, 373–382 (2007)
40. Siegel, A.W., White, S.H.: The development of spatial representations of large-scale environments. In: Reese, H.W. (ed.) Advances in Child Development and Behavior, vol. 10, pp. 9–55. Academic Press, New York (1975)

Alignment Effects and Allocentric-Headings within a Relative Heading Task

Heather Burte and Mary Hegarty

Department of Psychological & Brain Sciences, University of California, Santa Barbara, USA
{heather.burte,mary.hegarty}@psych.ucsb.edu

Abstract. Human navigational abilities likely depend on the accuracy of coding one's location and facing direction, either real or imagined. The ability to compare one's current facing direction to a photograph's facing direction was assessed using the Allocentric-Heading Recall task (Sholl et al., 2006). The angular difference between the facing directions (or allocentric-headings) produced an alignment effect, such that trials were easiest when the facing directions were aligned but hardest when contra-aligned. In the present study, a Relative Heading task was used to determine if the original alignment effect was due to the comparison of allocentric-headings or was due to interference from sensorimotor cues. To accomplish this, participants compared text or photographed headings and responded with a directional button-press. Failure to replicate the alignment effect suggested that inference from sensorimotor cues contributed to the original effect. Thus, directional comparisons are impacted by an individual's location and heading within an environment.

Keywords: Spatial cognition, alignment effect, allocentric-heading.

1 Introduction

When planning routes or giving verbal directions within a familiar environment, we often have to imagine being at a location and in an orientation that are different from our physical location and orientation. In these situations, spatial judgments (such as, pointing to a destination in the environment) can be impacted by at least two factors: the facing direction from which you learned the environment and your physical facing direction when pointing. The deviation between the imagined perspective and the two other facing directions contributes to systematic differences in pointing accuracy, or *alignment effects*. Imagined facing directions that are aligned with either the learning direction or one's physical facing direction produce more accurate pointing than counter-aligned facing directions [1]. In previous research, these alignments effects have been documented for pointing accuracy, based upon *egocentric-headings*, that is directions towards objects or locations that are made relative to the body [2]. However, it is unclear if these alignment effects also exist for *allocentric-headings*, or headings relative to fixed directions within the environment, such as cardinal directions [2]. The purpose of this paper is to investigate whether the alignment effects found for egocentric-headings also exist for allocentric-headings.

C. Freksa et al. (Eds.): Spatial Cognition 2014, LNAI 8684, pp. 46–61, 2014.
© Springer International Publishing Switzerland 2014

1.1   Allocentric-Heading Recall Task

The Allocentric-Heading Recall task [3] was developed to investigate the ability to effectively code and compare allocentric-headings. This task required the comparison of a participant's physical facing direction in a known environment (a college campus) to a photograph's facing direction (i.e., the perspective of the photographer when taking the photograph). The photographs were taken of prominent building facades on a campus that was familiar to participants. Both the photograph's and the participant's facing directions matched the four cardinal directions. Participants were oriented to the environment by looking out a window, so that they had a strong sense of their alignment within the environment. On each trial, participants determined the heading of a photograph and rotated in their chair to reproduce that heading. For example, if the participant was seated facing north, and was shown a south-facing photograph, the correct answer would be to turn 180°.

One of the major findings from the Allocentric-Heading Recall task was an alignment effect [3], such that accuracy decreased with increasing deviation between the participant's physical facing direction and the photograph's facing direction (Fig. 1). This effect has been replicated in another study on different campus [4]. In these studies, the deviation between facing directions was referred to as a *heading disparity* [3]. It was proposed that heading disparities resulted in an alignment effect because of the properties of a hypothesized human head-direction system [3]. Which was assumed to operate similarly to the head-direction system found in rats [5]. The alignment effect was assumed to be caused by interfering head-direction and other bodily signals, or *sensorimotor cues*. According to this account, when individuals are oriented to an environment, their head-direction cells fire with respect to their physical facing direction. When individuals then view a photograph of a familiar location, they recall memories of when they visited and viewed the location, from the orientation shown in the picture. Those memories are associated with head-direction signals that match the picture's orientation. The head-direction signals from the participant's physical facing direction are assumed to interfere with the recalled head-direction signals from the photograph's facing direction, and this interference results in lower accuracy rates, especially for headings that differed by 180°.

While the alignment effect was predicted a priori [3], based on the functioning of rat head-direction cells, it is unclear if the effect is solely due to interference from sensorimotor cues. For example, it is possible that comparing two allocentric-headings is more computationally difficult with increasing deviation between the headings, regardless of sensorimotor cues. Thus, sensorimotor interference and angular disparity effects might be confounded within the Allocentric-Heading Recall task. In order to determine the mechanism driving the alignment effect, we developed the Relative Heading task. In this task, participants determine the allocentric-headings of photographs, like the Allocentric-Heading Recall task, but this task lacks the requirement to be physically oriented to the environment. This allows for the effects of sensorimotor interference to be separated from effects of angular disparity, in order to reveal the cause of the alignment effect.

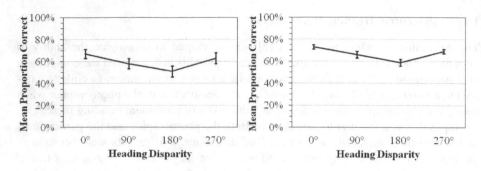

Fig. 1. Accuracy across heading disparities as found by Sholl et al. [3] (left) and as found by Burte and Hegarty [4] (right) with error bars indicating the standard error of the mean.

1.2   Alignment Effects for Egocentric-Headings

While the current experiments investigate the nature of an alignment effect for allo-centric-headings, the majority of the literature on alignment effects involves egocen-tric-headings. We first briefly review the literature on egocentric-headings and then consider possible causes of the alignment effects found within the Allocentric-Heading Recall task.

First, a *memory alignment effect* [1] is often found in Judgments of Relative Direc-tion (or JRD), which is a perspective-taking task. In this task, people typically learn an environment from one or more directions and later have to imagine standing at a particular location, facing an object, and they point towards another object. Pointing is most accurate when the individual imagines facing the direction from which the envi-ronment was learned [6,7]. This alignment effect is due to the egocentric experience of facing a particular direction during learning, which sets the facing direction during learning as the preferred direction in memory [8,9].

In contrast, the *sensorimotor alignment effect* [1] is found when environmental learning is followed by spatial updating. Spatial updating tasks typically involve learning the location of objects in a room, moving to another location and/or facing direction, followed by blindfolded pointing. In these tasks, pointing is more accurate from an orientation that corresponds to individual's physical orientation after move-ment [10,11]. This alignment effect is due to sensorimotor cues facilitating pointing accuracy when the imagined orientation is the same as the individual's physical orien-tation, and sensorimotor cues interfering with pointing when counter-aligned [10,11].

Two hypotheses account for the difficulty individuals experience in taking new perspectives [12]. First, the *mental transformation hypothesis* states that imagined changes in location and/or facing direction result in errors because the individual must update their relationship to target objects, after the imagined rotation or translation. In contrast, the *sensorimotor interference hypothesis* states that imagined changes in location and/or facing direction result in errors because the individual must suppress bodily senses, or sensorimotor cues, that conflict with imagining a new location and/or facing direction.

The sensorimotor interference hypothesis is similar to the explanation we proposed for the alignment effect in the Allocentric-Heading Recall task, as both hypotheses posit that an alignment effect is due to interference from sensorimotor cues. In the case of the Allocentric-Heading Recall task, the interference from sensorimotor cues is due to changes in facing direction. The combination of these two hypotheses suggests that an individual's physical location might impact not only egocentric-headings, but also allocentric-headings.

While the physical location and facing direction of the individual is essential for the computation of egocentric-headings, allocentric-headings are fixed to the external environment, and therefore the physical location and orientation of the participant is unnecessary for their computation. As such, it would make sense that the comparison of allocentric-headings would be equally accurate, regardless of the facing direction of the participant. However, our explanation of the alignment effect suggests that when an individual is nested within and oriented to an environment, their facing direction impacts their judgments of allocentric-headings – whether the task requires the use of their physical facing direction or not. Understanding the extent to which an individual's physical location and facing direction impacts their spatial understanding of an environment could provide insights into navigational abilities, and may aid in the understanding of individual differences in navigational abilities, more generally.

1.3   Alignment Effects due to the Structure of the Environment

In addition to memory and sensorimotor alignment effects, alignment effects have also been found to result from the structure of the environment. For example, alignment effects arise from sensitivity to the salient reference system within the environment [7] [9], alignment towards intrinsic axes of objects [8] [13], and intrinsic reference systems based on collections of objects [14]. In the current experiments, performance on the Relative Heading task will also be assessed with respect to the salient reference system of the environment – the cardinal directions.

Previous experiments, using the Allocentric-heading Recall task on the UCSB campus, have revealed increased accuracy for physical facing directions towards the mountains (north) and Isla Vista (west) [4] [15]. These results indicated that environmental features, which correspond with the salient reference system, can facilitate the comparison of allocentric-headings. The current experiments will investigate similar effects, using the Relative-Heading task on the UCSB campus.

1.4   Individual Differences in the Allocentric-Heading Recall Task

Another key finding from the Allocentric-Heading Recall task was that individual differences in task performance were strongly correlated with self-reported sense-of-direction [3], as assessed by the Santa Barbara Sense-of-Direction (SBSOD) scale [16]. Burte and Hegarty [4] [15] found significant but weaker correlations between these measures. If the current experiments replicate a significant correlation between accuracy and SBSOD scores, that result would provide evidence that Relative Heading task reflects some sources of individual differences found within the original task.

1.5   Alignment Effects within the Relative Heading task

The Relative Heading task consists of comparing two allocentric-headings that do not match the participant's physical facing direction. To ensure that participants' sensorimotor cues were uninformative for the task, participants lay on their backs and compared the headings of photographs, which were taken from a standing position. In addition, all participants were tested in a window-less room and some participants were disorientated, to disrupt orientation to the outside environment.

In the first experiment, the Relative Heading task was used to determine if orientation via a photograph could produce the alignment effect. In this experiment, participants viewed two photographs: an orienting photograph that provides an initial heading, and a target photograph that provides a target heading. Participants compared the headings and produced a directional response. For this experiment, replicating the alignment effect would provide evidence that this effect is not specific to situations in which people are physically oriented to an environment. In contrast, failing to replicate the alignment effect would suggest that the effect requires the participant to have sensorimotor awareness of their physical orientation to the environment.

In the second experiment, the Relative Heading task was modified to determine if orienting headings, which lacked a specific location, could produce the alignment effect. This was accomplished by providing an orienting heading via text, which referred to large-scale referents [15], and by providing a target heading via a photograph. Replicating the alignment effect would provide evidence that sensorimotor interference is not critical to the presence of an alignment effect. In contrast, failure to replicate the alignment effect would provide evidence that sensorimotor cues, from being oriented within the environment, are necessary to produce the alignment effect.

2   Experiment 1

The goal of Experiment 1 was to examine whether an alignment effect was observed when sensorimotor cues were made uninformative to the task, by having participants lay on their backs in a windowless room. Photographs of orienting headings were used to determine if photographs could elicit a sense of orientation.

2.1   Methods

Participants. Forty undergraduate students (15 males and 25 females) completed the experiment. Participants were required to have spent at least two quarters on campus.

Design. The methodology was both experimental and correlational. The independent variables were the orienting and target headings (within subjects). The dependent variables were accuracy and decision latency, which were correlated with SOD.

Materials. The experiment took place in a laboratory aligned with the main axes of the campus and with the cardinal directions. The laboratory lacked windows and was located on the second floor of a building, which also lacked visual access to the outside environment. Introductory tasks were given in a large room, in which the participants sat facing north. However, the Relative Heading task was completed in a smaller adjacent room. Participants lay down under an apparatus that held a laptop at a 45-degree angle above their heads, with their feet facing west. Participants responded using four directional buttons.

The materials included four orienting photographs and forty target photographs of the UCSB campus, each taken facing a cardinal direction (10 per direction). The orienting photographs were used to indicate an initial orientation, from which to make the comparison between headings. The orienting photographs were taken along the two main pathways through campus, providing wide views of campus and distal cues, such as the nearby mountains. In contrast, the target photographs were taken of the facades of familiar campus buildings, were focused views of that building, and did not include distal cues. Both sets of photographs were taken around noon on a sunny day, were not cropped or edited, and were taken from a standing position (Fig. 2).

Procedure. Participants completed a demographics questionnaire (gender, age, quarters spent on campus), the SBSOD, and then rated their familiarity with the 40-target photograph locations on a 7-point Likert scale (1 = "very familiar" and 7 = "not at all familiar). To ensure that participants were familiar with the heading of the target photographs, the experimenter also asked each participant to name the building in each target photograph, and to provide the name and direction towards two nearby buildings. The experimenter provided feedback, but most participants responded correctly.

The Relative Heading task started with instructions, four practice trials with feedback from the experimenter, and eight practice trials with feedback from the computer. Half of the participants received additional practice tasks to teach the fundamentals of the Relative Heading task. These practice tasks used photographs of the experiment room to train participants on the meaning of allocentric-headings, and on how to compare allocentric-headings. These additional practice tasks contained ten trials with feedback, and were given before the training of the Relative Heading task started.

The Relative Heading task consisted of 80 trials without feedback. Individual trials required determining a target photograph's heading (or facing direction), relative to an orienting heading (or initial facing direction). On each trial, participants first viewed an orienting heading (via a wide view photograph of a campus path) followed by a target heading (via a focused view photograph of a campus building), then the participant determined the relative heading between the orienting and target photographs, and indicated the relative heading by pressing a button on a button-box (Fig. 2). Since the photographs were taken facing cardinal directions, that there were four possible responses: no difference between the orienting and target heading (represented by a forward arrow), the target heading is 90-degrees to the right of the orienting stimulus (right), the target heading is 180-degrees from the orienting stimulus (down arrow), or the target is 90-degrees to the left of the orienting stimulus (left).

Each of the four orienting photographs was paired with twenty target photographs (five facing each direction). In this way, each target photograph was presented twice during the task. Trials were blocked by the orienting photograph used, such that participants first completed twenty trials with a north-facing orienting photograph, followed by twenty trials with a south-facing orienting photograph, and so forth. Participants were randomly assigned to different block orders, using a Latin Square design.

In order to indicate to participants when a switch in orienting photographs was to occur, participants viewed a slide with text indicating the switch for 10 seconds, and orienting photographs were viewed for 5 seconds. The target photographs were viewed for a maximum of 10 seconds and the next trial started after the participant's response. Time to respond (or decision latency) was calculated as the time from when the target stimulus was presented to the time the participant responded.

Fig. 2. An orienting photograph facing north (left) and target photograph facing east (right) from Experiment 1. The correct response would be to press the right arrow button.

2.2   Results

Overall Accuracy and Decision Latency. Mean accuracy was 51% (SD = 24%), ranging from 13% to 95%, and mean correct decision latency was 4.5 seconds (SD = 1.4 s), ranging from 1.4 to 7.4 seconds. Correct decision latency outliers were recoded to 2.5 SD above the mean. None of the following significantly influenced task accuracy: including or excluding additional practice tasks, $t(38) = -.74$, $p = .47$; the order of orienting headings, $F(3, 36) = 2.11$, $p = .12$; or, gender, $t(38) = -1.60$, $p = .88$.

None of the following significantly influenced correct decision latency: the order of orienting headings, $F(3, 36) = 1.43$, $p = .25$; or, gender, $t(38) = -.55$, $p = .59$. Including or excluding additional practice tasks did produce significant differences in decision latency, $t(38) = 2.04$, $p < .05$, as participants who completed the additional practice tasks ($M = 4.1$ s) were significantly faster than participants who did not complete the additional practice tasks ($M = 5.0$ s).

Alignment Effect. Heading disparity was the angular clockwise difference between the heading of the orienting and target photographs. To determine if the relative heading between the photographs resulted in an alignment effect, we first examined the effects of heading disparity on accuracy. A one-way ANOVA indicated a significant effect of heading disparity, $F(3, 117) = 14.52$, $p < .001$ (Fig. 3). Least Squares

Difference (LSD) post-hoc tests revealed that participants were less accurate for the 180° heading disparity (M = 43%), compared to all other heading disparities. This finding is consistent with the predicted alignment effect. However, participants were also less accurate when orienting and target stimuli had the same heading (M = 50%), than for disparities of 90° (M = 56%) and 270° (M = 56%) heading disparities, contrary to the predicted alignment effect.

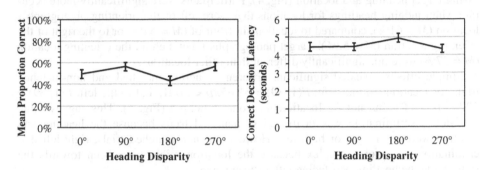

Fig. 3. Accuracy (left) and correct decision latency (right) across heading disparity with error bars indicating the standard error of the mean

A one-way ANOVA comparing correct decision latency indicated a significant effect of heading disparity, $F(3, 117) = 11.70, p < .001$ (Fig. 3). Participants took significantly more time when the orienting and target stimuli differed by 180° (M = 4.9 s) compared to 0° (M = 4.4 s), 90° (M = 4.5 s), and 270° (M = 4.3 s).

Both the accuracy and decision latency results indicated a detrimental effect on performance when the stimuli differed by 180°, which is consistent with the predicted alignment effect. However, the lack of enhanced performance when the stimuli faced the same direction (facilitation effect) does not match the predicted alignment effect.

Error Analysis. Previous studies using the Allocentric-Heading Recall task revealed a common confusion amongst participants, such that participants tended to confuse the direction towards the location depicted in the photograph, with the photograph's heading [4] [15]. For example, if the photograph's location is physically in front of the participant, but the photograph was taking facing towards the participant's right, the correct answer is to press the right arrow. In this case, the typical error is to incorrectly respond with the forward arrow, indicating the direction towards the photographed location. It is likely that this error results from the need to first identify the location of the photograph, before the heading can be determined.

We now consider whether these typical errors were made in the Relative Heading task. Within this task, there are trials in which the target heading and the direction towards the target location matched, whereas in other trials the heading did not match the direction. If participants were confusing target heading with target location, they should be less accurate during mismatched trials. To investigate this possibility, the UCSB campus was divided into quadrants: in front of, to the right or left, and behind each of the orienting photographs. The four orienting photographs were taken at separate locations, so quadrants were created for each orienting photograph. A 2 (matched, mismatched) by 4 quadrants ANOVA indicated a significant main effect of matching, $F(1, 39) = 39.16$, $p < .001$, a significant main effect of quadrant, $F(3, 117) = 2.96$, $p < .05$, and a significant interaction, $F(3, 117) = 11.38$, $p < .001$. LSD post-hoc tests revealed that matched trials ($M = 65\%$) resulted in significantly higher accuracy than non-matched trials ($M = 47\%$), suggesting that some participants were confusing target heading and location (Fig. 4). Participants were significantly more accurate when judging headings for locations that were left of the orienting photograph's location ($M = 61\%$), compared to locations in front of ($M = 54\%$) or to the right of the orienting location ($M = 52\%$). Target photographs taken behind the orienting location ($M = 57\%$) were not significantly different than other locations.

Simple effects revealed significant differences across matched and non-matched trials for locations to the right, $F(1, 39) = 51.65$, $p < .001$, and to the left, $F(1, 39) = 30.58$, $p < .001$, but not for locations in front or behind (Fig. 4). This suggests that right-left discrimination was facilitated in matched trials because the heading and location were both right or both left. However in non-matched trials, right-left discrimination was more complex because the location might have been towards the right while the heading was facing left, or vise versa.

Alignment Effect for Non-matched Trials. Given that some participants incorrectly responded with the location towards the target instead of the target's heading, matched trials were removed from the heading disparity analysis, and the effects of heading disparity were reanalyzed for non-matched trials alone. A one-way ANOVA for accuracy across heading disparities revealed a significant effect, $F(3, 117) = 11.38$, $p < .001$ (Fig. 4). LSD post-hoc tests revealed that heading disparities of 90° ($M = 55\%$) and 270° ($M = 51\%$) were more accurate than 0° ($M = 44\%$) and 180° ($M = 41\%$), replicating the effects found in accuracy across all trials.

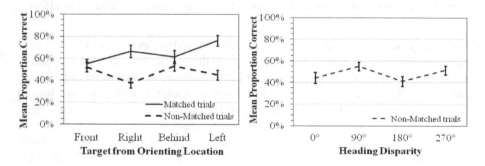

Fig. 4. Accuracy rates across directions towards the target, from the orienting location, for matched and non-matched trials (left). Accuracy rates across heading disparities for non-matched trials (right). Error bars indicate the standard error of the mean.

Sense-of-Direction. The mean score on the SBSOD was 4.2 ($SD = 0.8$), with scores ranging from 3.5 to 5.3 (on a scale of 1 to 7 where higher scores indicate a better sense-of-direction). SBSOD scores did not significantly correlate with accuracy, $r(38)$ = -.14, p = .39, or with correct decision latency, $r(38)$ = -.20, p = .21.

Alignment Effects due to the Structure of the Environment. One-way ANOVAs comparing accuracy and correct decision latency across orienting headings (North, South, East, West) revealed non-significant effects for accuracy, $F(3, 117)$ = 1.30, p = .28, and for decision latency, $F(3, 117)$ = 1.67, p = .17. This result indicates that the direction of the orienting heading does not influence task performance.

However, a one-way ANOVA indicated a significant effect of target heading (North, South, East, West) on accuracy, $F(3, 177)$ = 6.06, $p < .01$, such that participants were more accurate in deciding relative heading for target stimuli that faced north (M = 56%) or west (M = 55%), and less accurate for target stimuli that faced east (M = 46%) or south (M = 48%). A one-way ANOVA also indicated a significant effect of target heading on decision latency, $F(3, 177)$ = 10.00, $p < .001$, such that participants took significantly less time to decide relative heading for target stimuli that faced north (M = 4.2s) compared to target stimuli that faced east (M = 4.7s), south (M = 4.6s), or west (M = 4.7s) based on LSD post-hoc tests. In sum, north-facing photographs resulted in the greatest accuracy and the lowest decision latencies.

Differences in accuracy and decision latency, across target headings, might have been due to familiarity differences with the target photographs. A one-way ANOVA comparing familiarity across target headings revealed a significant effect, $F(3,117)$ = 4.09, $p < .01$. LSD post-hoc tests revealed that north (M = 2.4 / 7) and east-facing photographs (M = 2.5 / 7) were rated as significantly less familiar than south-facing photographs (M = 2.0 / 7). North-facing photographs were also significantly less familiar than west-facing photographs (M = 2.1 / 7). In sum, higher accuracy and shorter decision latencies for north photographs were not likely due to familiarity, because participants rated north photographs as less familiar than south and west photographs.

2.3   Discussion

Multiple measures indicated that participants struggled with the Relative Heading task: accuracy rates were low, correct decision latencies ranged greatly across participants, and participants confused the direction towards the target location with the photograph's heading. This confusion led to higher accuracy rates when the target location and facing direction were confounded (matched trials) compared to when they were not confounded (unmatched trials). Perhaps due to participant confusion, the pattern of accuracy across heading disparities did not resemble the previously found alignment effect [3] [4]. In the current experiment, accuracy and correct decision latency analyses revealed a detrimental effect when the orienting and target headings differed by 180°, as predicted. However, participants were less accurate at 0° than at 90° and 270°, contrary to the predicted facilitation effect.

It is unclear whether this failure to replicate the alignment effect was due to the difficulty of comparing headings given by photographs, or if it was due to the reduced influence of sensorimotor signals. Participants were more accurate with targets located in front or behind the orienting photograph, on non-matched trials. This suggests that they were able to imagine themselves at the orienting photograph and their task performance was impacted by that imagined body location. This result is consistent with previous research showing that space around the body is divided into head/feet, front/back, and right/left dimensions, with front/back decisions being made faster than right/left decisions [17]. Given that a similar pattern was found in the accuracy data, it is likely that participants overcame the influence of lying on their backs.

Previous studies found a significant correlation between sense-of-direction and overall task performance on the Allocentric-Heading Recall task [3] [4] [15]. However, the correlation between SBSOD scores and performance on the Relative Heading task was not significant. This might be due to a restriction in the range of SBSOD scores in the current experiment, or it might reflect differences between the tasks, such as the fact that participants were not physically oriented to the environment, and therefore did not have to suppress sensorimotor cues from their current orientation.

With respect to alignment effects based on the structure of the environment, the current experiment did not find an alignment effect for orienting headings, but did find one for target headings. Target photographs that faced north and west were the most accurate; however, south target photographs were rated as the most familiar. Thus, it is likely that environmental features, rather than familiarity, leads to these differences. The mountain range to the north is visible across campus and the neighborhood to the west is home for most undergraduates. These environmental features are likely major points-of-reference.

3   Experiment 2

The results of Experiment 1 indicated that some participants have a tendency to confuse the target photograph's heading with the direction towards the target photograph. To eliminate this confusion, in Experiment 2, the orienting heading was changed to text instructions, which specified only an orientation to imagine. This change ensured that participants had an orienting heading (but not an orienting location) to compare to the target photograph. The text instructed participants to imagine facing one of four large-scale spatial referents surrounding the UCSB campus, namely the mountains (north), Goleta Beach (east), the lagoon (south), and Isla Vista (west). These spatial referents were used because some participants indicated that they used these referents in a previous study [15]. To further ensure that sensorimotor cues were uninformative, half of the participants were disoriented before they completed the Relative Heading task, while the other half were not disoriented. This allowed the impact of disorientation to be compared.

Several smaller changes were also made to the Relative Heading task for the second experiment. To improve participant understanding of the task and to boost overall accuracy, instructions and practice tasks were improved. In addition, some participants mentioned using shadows to determine photograph headings, but since the photographs differed in the time of day that they were taken, shadows did not provide consistent heading information. To eliminate this strategy, all photographs were retaken on a cloudy day.

3.1   Methods

Participants. Thirty-six undergraduate students (12 males and 24 females) completed the experiment. Participants spent at least two quarters on campus.

Design. The methodology was both experimental and correlational. The independent variables were the orienting and target headings (within subjects). The dependent variables were accuracy and decision latency, which were correlated with SOD.

Materials. The materials were identical to those used in Experiment 1, except that the initial headings used to orient the participant were written instructions to imagine facing one of four large-scale spatial referents and the target photographs were retaken around noon on a cloudy day, to eliminate visible shadows.

Procedure. The timing within the Relative Heading task changed, such that the slide indicating a switch in orienting headings was viewed for 10 seconds, the orienting heading stimuli were viewed for 5 seconds, and the target heading stimuli were viewed for 7 seconds. The next trial started after the 7 seconds elapsed. Time to respond (or decision latency) was the time between the presentation of a target stimulus and the participant's response. No other changes were made to the procedure.

3.2   Results

Overall Accuracy and Decision Latency. Accuracy was much higher, with a mean accuracy of 81% ($SD = 18\%$) that ranged from 36% to 100%, and correct decision latency was lower, with a mean of 3.6 seconds ($SD = 700$ ms) that ranged from 2.5 to 5.0 seconds. Correct decision latency outliers were recoded to 2.5 SD above the mean. None of the following significantly influenced task accuracy: additional disorientation with a wheelchair, $t(34) = -.98$, $p = .34$; or, orienting heading order, $F(3, 32) = .62$, $p = .61$. Males were marginally more accurate than females, $t(34) = -1.80$, $p = .08$.

None of the following significantly influenced correct decision latency: orienting heading order, $F(3, 32) = .45$, $p = .72$; or, gender, $t(34) = -.19$, $p = .85$. Being disoriented in a wheelchair resulted in significantly different decision latencies, $t(34) = 3.47$, $p < .01$, such that participants who were not disoriented ($M = 3.9$ s) took significantly more time than those who were disoriented ($M = 3.2$ s).

Alignment Effect. A one-way ANOVA comparing accuracy across heading disparities indicated a non-significant effect, $F(3, 105) = 1.09$, $p = .36$ (Fig. 5). Participants were equally accurate for heading disparities of 0° ($M = 82\%$), 90° ($M = 80\%$), 180° ($M = 83\%$), and 270° ($M = 80\%$). In contrast, a one-way ANOVA comparing correct decision latencies indicated a significant effect of heading disparity, $F(3, 105) = 2.91$, $p < .05$ (Fig. 5). LSD post-hoc tests revealed that participants took significantly more time when the heading disparity was 180° ($M = 3.8$ s), compared to 90° ($M = 3.5$ s). Heading disparities of 0° ($M = 3.5$ s) and 270° ($M = 3.6$ s) did not differ significantly from other heading disparities.

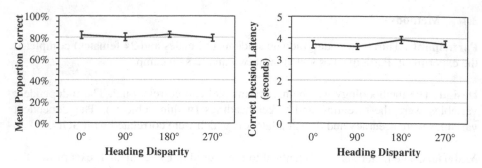

Fig. 5. Accuracy (left) and decision latency (right) across heading disparity with error bars indicating the standard error of the mean

Sense-of-Direction. Mean SBSOD scores were 4.6 (SD = 1.1) and ranged from 2.4 to 6.8. SBSOD scores were significantly correlated with accuracy, $r(34)$ = .57, p < .001, such that participants with better sense-of-direction were more accurate. SBSOD scores were not significantly correlated with decision latency, $r(34)$ = -.19, p = .27.

Alignment Effects due to the Structure of the Environment. A one-way ANOVA comparing accuracy across orienting headings (North, South, East, West) was significant, $F(3, 105)$ = 7.08, p < .001, such that north (M = 84%) and west (M = 86%) orienting heading trials were significantly more accurate than those for east (M = 78%) and south (M = 77%). A one-way ANOVA comparing correct decision latencies across orienting headings was not significant, $F(3, 105)$ = 1.05, p = .37.

A one-way ANOVA comparing accuracy across target heading (North, South, East, West) was significant, $F(3, 105)$ = 4.88, p < .01. Participants were significantly less accurate in deciding relative heading for target stimuli that faced east (M = 77%) than for target stimuli that faced north (M = 84%), south (M = 80%), or west (M = 84%) based on LSD post-hoc tests. A one-way ANOVA comparing decision latencies across target heading was also significant, $F(3, 105)$ = 7.18, p < .001. Correct decision latencies were significantly longer for deciding relative heading for target stimuli that faced east (M = 3.8s) than for target stimuli that faced north (M = 3.5s), south (M = 3.6s), or west (M = 3.5s). Both of these results indicated that participants struggled with east-facing target stimuli.

As in Experiment 1, we examined whether differences in accuracy and decision latency were due to familiarity differences with the target photographs. A one-way ANOVA comparing familiarity across target headings revealed a significant effect, $F(3,105)$ = 3.61, p < .05. LSD post-hoc tests revealed that north (M = 1.7 /7) and east photographs (M = 1.7 /7) were significantly less familiar than west photographs (M = 1.4 /7). South photographs (M = 1.5 /7) were not significantly different than other photographs. Poor performance on east-facing photographs was likely due to low familiarity. However, lower familiarity with north-facing photographs did not led to reduced accuracy rates or shorter decision latencies for those photographs.

3.3   Discussion

Participants were generally highly accurate, quick to respond, and decision latencies did not show large individual differences. The changes in the instructions, practice tasks, and the use of verbally specified imagined orienting headings appeared to have made the task more understandable to participants. Disorienting participants did not lead to changes in accuracy rates, but did reduce decision latencies. Lying down in a windowless room likely produced a sufficient disconnect from the environment that accuracy rates were not influenced by physical orientation. However, being disoriented might have facilitated this disconnect, resulting in reduced decision times.

Critically, accuracy did not differ across heading disparities, suggesting that the alignment effect found by Sholl et al [3] was no longer present, when the need to suppress sensorimotor cues (from one's physical facing direction in the environment) was reduced. This failure to replicate the alignment effect was not likely due to participant misunderstandings, because participants were highly accurate in the task. This result suggests that the alignment effect in the Allocentric-Heading Recall task was due to the suppression of sensorimotor cues and not due to computational complexity resulting from angular disparity between the two headings.

In contrast with the lack of an alignment effect within the accuracy data, a partial detrimental effect was found in the decision latency data. Trials with heading disparities of 180° took significantly longer than 90°, indicating that comparing headings might require more time as the difference between the headings increases.

Once again, we assessed if changes made to the Relative Heading task altered the previously found relationship between accuracy and SOD. We replicated a strong correlation between SOD and overall performance, suggesting that the Relative Heading task seems to measure similar individual differences as the Allocentric-Heading Recall task. This result suggests that the correlation between accuracy and SOD is not necessarily due to individual differences in suppression of sensorimotor cues, but is due to other aspects of the ability to compare allocentric-headings.

With respect to alignment effects based on the structure of the environment, participants were more accurate with orienting headings that faced north and west. This finding might be due to increased familiarity thinking about campus locations related to the mountains (north) and Isla Vista (west). In contrast, target headings revealed slightly different effect: low performance for only east headings, and high familiarity for only west headings. It is possible that high performance with west headings was due to high familiarity, and high performance with north headings was due to experience with north-facing maps. However, the consistent result across orienting and target headings is that east stimuli were challenging for participants. After both experiments, some participants expressed unfamiliarity with thinking about facing east (Goleta Beach) and with pictures that faced east. Difficulty with east-facing headings and photographs might be due to the inherent structure of the UCSB campus.

4   General Discussion

The Allocentric-Heading Recall task was developed to assess the functioning of a hypothesized human head-direction cell system and typically demonstrates an alignment effect [3]. It was unclear from previous research whether this alignment effect was due to sensorimotor interference, or was a function of the angular disparity between the two headings being compared. We modified the properties of the Allocentric-Heading Recall task so that sensorimotor cues were uninformative and irrelevant to the task. We referred to this new task as the Relative Heading task.

The Relative Heading task requires participants to determine the difference between an orienting and target heading – neither of which was their sensorimotor heading. When the orienting heading was specified by a photograph (in Experiment 1), the results suggested that participants imagined standing at the orienting photograph's location, and confused the direction towards the photograph's location with the photograph's heading. Possibly for these reasons, the alignment effect found in the first experiment did not fully match the alignment effect found within the Allocentric-Heading Recall task. As such, it was unclear how to interpret the results.

In order to prevent participant misunderstandings, text was used to specify the orienting heading in Experiment 2, which freed participants from imagining standing at a specific location. Under these circumstances, there was no alignment effect in accuracy, suggesting that angular disparity between the two headings, on its own, does not produce an alignment effect. This suggests that the alignment effect in the Allocentric-Heading Recall task [3] [4] was due to interference from sensorimotor cues and not angular disparity.

Experiments on the nature of spatial memory have revealed alignment effects in tasks, such as pointing, that rely on egocentric-headings. These alignment effects have revealed that perspectives during learning, perspectives during testing, and perspectives aligned with the intrinsic structure of the environment produce greater pointing accuracy. The current experiments, combined with previous research [3][4], have provided evidence that perspectives during testing and perspectives aligned with the environment also produce similar alignment effects for allocentric-headings. It appears that when individuals arc nested within and oriented to an environment, sensorimotor cues of facing direction can affect imagined headings in the environment, even when those headings are relative to allocentric cues.

Acknowledgements. We would like to thank Chelsea Lonergan and Nahal Heydari for their assistance with these experiments. This research was supported by the Institute for Collaborative Biotechnologies.

References

1. Kelly, J.W., Avraamides, M.N., Loomis, J.M.: Sensorimotor alignment effects in the learning environment and in novel environments. Journal of Experimental Psychology: Learning, Memory, and Cognition 33, 1092–1107 (2007)
2. Klatzky, R.L.: Allocentric and egocentric spatial representations: Definitions, distinctions, and interconnections. In: Freksa, C., Habel, C., Wender, K.F. (eds.) Spatial Cognition 1998. LNCS (LNAI), vol. 1404, pp. 1–17. Springer, Heidelberg (1998)

3. Sholl, M.J., Kenny, R.J., DellaPorta, K.A.: Allocentric-heading recall and its relation to self-reported sense-of-direction. Journal of Experimental Psychology: Learning, Memory, and Cognition 32, 516–533 (2006)
4. Burte, H., Hegarty, M.: Revisiting the relationship between allocentric-heading recall and self-reported sense-of-direction. In: Miyake, N., Peebles, D., Cooper, R.P. (eds.) Proceedings of the 34th Annual Conference of the Cognitive Science Society, pp. 162–167. Cognitive Science Society (2012)
5. Ranck Jr., J.B.: Head-direction cells in the deep cell layers of dorsal presubiculum in freely moving rats. Society of Neuroscience Abstracts 10, 599 (1984)
6. Shelton, A.L., Mcnamara, T.P.: Multiple views of spatial memory. Psychonomic Bulletin & Review 4, 102–106 (1997)
7. Shelton, A.L., McNamara, T.P.: Systems of spatial reference in human memory. Cognitive Psychology 43, 274–310 (2001)
8. Mou, W., McNamara, T.P.: Intrinsic frames of reference in spatial memory. Journal of Experimental Psychology: Learning, Memory, and Cognition 28, 162–170 (2002)
9. McNamara, T.P.: How are the locations of objects in the environment represented in memory? In: Freksa, C., Brauer, W., Habel, C., Wender, K.F. (eds.) Spatial Cognition III. LNCS (LNAI), vol. 2685, pp. 174–191. Springer, Heidelberg (2003)
10. Mou, W., Zhao, M., McNamara, T.P.: Layout geometry in the selection of intrinsic frames of reference from multiple viewpoints. Journal of Experimental Psychology: Learning, Memory, and Cognition 33, 145–154 (2003)
11. Waller, D., Montello, D.R., Richardson, A.E., Hegarty, M.: Orientation specificity and spatial updating of memories for layouts. Journal of Experimental Psychology: Learning, Memory, and Cognition 28, 1051–1063 (2002)
12. May, M.: Imaginal perspective switches in remembered environments: Transformation versus interference accounts. Cognitive Psychology 48, 163–206 (2004)
13. Mou, W., McNamara, T.P., Valiquette, C.M., Rump, B.: Allocentric and egocentric updating of spatial memories. Journal of Experimental Psychology: Learning, Memory, and Cognition 30, 142–157 (2004)
14. Mou, W., Liu, X., McNamara, T.P.: Layout geometry in encoding and retrieval of spatial memory. Journal of Experimental Psychology: Human perception and performance 35, 83–93 (2009)
15. Burte, H., Hegarty, M.: Individual and strategy differences in an allocentric-heading recall task. In: Knauff, M., Pauen, M., Sebanz, N., Wachsmuth, I. (eds.) Proceedings of the 35th Annual Conference of the Cognitive Science Society, pp. 1958–1963. Cognitive Science Society (2013)
16. Hegarty, M., Richardson, A.E., Montello, D.R., Lovelace, K., Subbiah, I.: Development of a self-report measure of environmental spatial ability. Intelligence 30, 425–447 (2002)
17. Franklin, N., Tversky, B.: Searching imagined environments. Journal of Experimental Psychology: General 119, 63–76 (1990)

On Egocentric and Allocentric Maps

Wai Kiang Yeap

Auckland University of Technology, Centre for AI Research, New Zealand

Abstract. The question as to whether spatial information is coded using an egocentric or an allocentric frame of reference has led to three prominent but competing models of spatial cognition being proposed. In this paper, these models are reviewed on theoretical rather than empirical grounds and are shown to be similar. While using these two different frames of reference produce equivalent maps, the action guiding property of egocentric maps means that these maps are best computed at the perceptual-motor level and the ease of updating an allocentric map means that these maps are best computed for representing the larger environment. However, the latter is simply too empowering and is not suitable as a "map in the head". Based on a recent computational theory of perceptual mapping, we suggest an alternative – an allocentric trace of local environments visited rather than an allocentric map of the physical environment itself. Such a trace is egocentric and transient and has both a spatial and a temporal aspect. It provides a rich input that will allow different species to learn a different enduring representation of its environment, each tailored to their own needs for survival.

Keywords: Computational theories, spatial cognition, egocentric, allocentric.

1 Introduction

A significant question underlying human spatial cognition research is the way in which spatial information is encoded in memory. In particular, researchers are concerned whether such information is encoded using an egocentric frame of reference or an allocentric frame of reference. The former encodes information with respect to the position of the viewer and the latter does not. Given that vision delivers us an egocentric description of what is out there, many argue that what is computed initially, via the integration of such views, is an egocentric map. However, the spatial co-ordinates of the objects in such a map require continuous updating as one moves and as the map grows in size, such updating would deem to be too daunting. Consequently, many researchers (e.g. Burgess, 2006) argue that information in it would, at some stage, be transferred into an enduring allocentric map. Such a dual representation theory of spatial cognition is popular among researchers interested in spatial cognition (Burgess, 2006; Gallistel, 1990; Waller & Hodgson, 2006).

One example of such a dual model is Sholl's (2001) model. She argues that while there exist many different egocentric representations at the perceptual-motor level, there should nonetheless be an independent self-reference system at the representation

C. Freksa et al. (Eds.): Spatial Cognition 2014, LNAI 8684, pp. 62–75, 2014.

level that allows one to create egocentric maps either from information derived at the perceptual level or from information retrieved from one's cognitive map (Tolman, 1948). The former is used to maintain a perspective view of things in one's immediate surroundings, and the latter to create different perspectives on the remembered spatial arrangements of objects. The map computed using such a self-reference system codes self-to-object spatial relations in body-centered co-ordinates, using the body axes of front-back, left-right, and up-down. By incorporating McNaughton, Chen and Markus's (1991) animal model of sense direction, Sholl discusses how such a representational self-reference system would enable one to track one's movement in the physical space, thereby allowing one to create an egocentric map while exploring a new environment. As its content is transient, information in it would, at some stage, be transformed to become part of one's cognitive map. One's cognitive map codes object-to-object spatial relations and is thus an allocentric representation. Henceforth, I will refer to any such map, computed at the interface between perception and cognition, as a perceptual map (see Fig. 1).

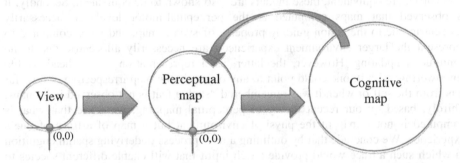

Fig. 1. Sholl's model: The dot with a cross represents the viewer's position and orientation in the map. Both the view and the perceptual map are egocentric representations and one's cognitive map is an allocentric representation.

Despite wide acceptance, the dual representation theory has been challenged recently. For example, questions were raised as to whether animals other than humans have an allocentric cognitive map (Benhamou, 1996; Bennett, 1996; Mackintosh, 2002). A key argument against the idea is that many of these experiments supporting its presence could possibly be explained without postulating the presence of such a map-like representation. More recently, Wang and Spelke (2002) further postulated that even humans do not compute their allocentric map directly from perception; rather, they learn it using symbolic reasoning. In short, an allocentric map is not computed at all. This is a radical departure and many researchers have argued against it (Burgess, 2006; Waller & Hodgson, 2006). Interestingly, McNamara and his colleagues (2003) propose a model that computes only allocentric maps and not egocentric maps. The debate rages on over the issue: do we compute an egocentric map or an allocentric map or both (Galati, Pelle, Berthoz & Committeri, 2010, Pecchia & Vallortigara, 2010).

We developed a recent computational theory of perceptual mapping (Yeap, 2011) which shows that one's perceptual map is updated only with views that denote local environments visited rather with every successive view. To update the perceptual map with such a view, the viewer's position in the perceptual map is first triangulated using some landmark objects tracked across views. Then, the incoming egocentric view is transformed to become part of an allocentric description of the environment in the perceptual map. However, one significant step, during updates, is that there is no integration of what is in the incoming view with what is in the perceptual map. Information in the perceptual map occupying the same mental space as the incoming view is simply deleted. Consequently, the resulting map is an allocentric description of a trace of local environments visited rather than a map of the physical environment itself. Using this theory, this paper presents a fresh new perspective on the egocentric versus allocentric debate.

Firstly, the three existing models, Sholl's (2001), McNamara et al.'s (2003) and Wang and Spelke's (2002), are reviewed and compared on theoretical rather than empirical grounds. Based on the fact that these two representations, egocentric and allocentric, are equivalent, these models are also shown to be equivalent. Secondly, it is observed that maps computed at the perceptual-motor level are necessarily egocentric due to the action guiding property of such a map, and maps computed to represent the larger environment experienced are necessarily allocentric due to no continuous updating. However, the latter, as a representation in our head, is too empowering; with it, one could point to any object in the map irrespective of how far it is from the self or when it was remembered. Such a feat is not observed in humans. Thirdly, based on our recent theory of perceptual mapping, we argue that what is computed is not a map of the physical environment but a map of a trace of one's experience. We conclude that by outlining a new process underlying spatial cognition in which such a trace would provide a rich input that will enable different species to learn a different enduring representation of its environment, each tailored to their own needs for survival.

2   A Tale of Two Models

Using a disorientation paradigm, Wang and Spelke (2000) investigated whether humans' ability to track their movements in the environment is done by updating their allocentric position in an enduring allocentric cognitive map or by the use of an egocentric map. They find evidence in support of the latter and together with other research on spatial cognition (see Wang & Spelke, 2002), they propose a model of human spatial cognition where three separate representations are computed: an egocentric perceptual map, the geometrical shape of local environments, and view-specific representations of places (see Fig. 2). They argue that given these representations are found in non-human species, just not the enduring allocentric cognitive map, it is unnecessary to propose that humans compute their enduring allocentric map at the perceptual level. The latter, they claim, would require a significant shift in navigation strategy from non-humans to humans and it comes about through our cognitive ability to reason about space symbolically rather than a change in our navigation strategy.

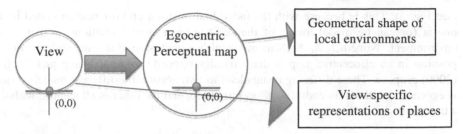

Fig. 2. Wang and Spelke's model: No allocentric map is computed

Using a perspective-taking paradigm, McNamara et al.'s findings initially supported the idea that an egocentric map is remembered (e.g. Diwadkar & McNamara, 1997). However, they later found conflicting evidence and proposed a model whereby what is remembered is a description of the spatial layout of objects using some intrinsic frame of reference (McNamara, 2003; McNamara, Rump, & Werner, 2003; Mou & McNamara, 2002; Mou, McNamara, Valiquette, & Rump, 2004; Shelton & McNamara, 2001). The intrinsic frame of reference is derived from an observer's point of view or from the spatial layout of objects in view or from the environment structure itself. They argue that such a map is not updated with subsequent views of the same environment unless the new view offers a better description such as being less obstructed or aligned with more salient axes in the environment.

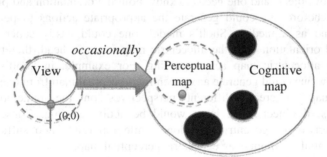

Fig. 3. McNamara et al.'s model: Individual allocentric maps are remembered (denoted by circles inside the cognitive map), and the most recent one (the dashed circle) includes the allocentric position of the self (indicated by a dot). The dashed circle superposed on the view indicates limited egocentric updating of a few objects that have moved out of view.

One's cognitive map, according to their model, is thus a collection of these allocentric maps; each with its own heading. There is no intermediate representation. Egocentric updating occurs only at the perceptual-motor level and no independent egocentric map is computed. In order to orient oneself, one's position and orientation are coded and updated inside the current allocentric map. While they claim that such updating treats the individual like any other object in the environment (see also Rump & McNamara, 2007; Zhang, Mou, & McNamara, 2011), its presence in the current allocentric map means that the current map functions effectively as a perceptual map (see Fig. 3). This is because with the individual position and orientation coded in it, one is (or can be made) aware of the self-to-object spatial relations in that local environment. Nonetheless, McNamara et al.'s conclusion that one updates one's position in an allocentric map is diametrically opposite to what Wang and Spelke (2000) propose. These differing results lead to two apparently different models – one is egocentric without an enduring allocentric map, and the other is allocentric without a transient egocentric map.

3   Egocentric or Allocentric – What Matters?

It is interesting that three different models are proposed, egocentric-only, allocentric-only, and combined, despite the fact that these representations are equivalent, mathematically. By equivalent, it is meant that one could easily transform from one such map to the other with no loss of information. Thus, having one of them means you can create an equivalent map using the alternative frame of reference. If so, are these models distinct?

Some researchers argue that the egocentric representation is not a special case of its allocentric equivalent whereby it differs only by where the center of the co-ordinates is positioned. This is because the former is action guiding (Campbell, 1994; Evans, 1982; Briscoe, 2009; Grush, 2000). In a strict sense, an allocentric representation of space is not action guiding. This is because it holds only locational information of objects and one needs to know both the orientation and position of the viewer in it before one could generate the appropriate actions to perform a task. However, and as argued in Sholl's model, one could easily superimpose one's position and orientation onto the allocentric map in one's head, thereby making (a part of) the allocentric map action guiding. For example, in Sholl's model, she discusses how one could generate an egocentric perceptual map from one's allocentric cognitive map to create different perspectives on the remembered spatial arrangements of objects. The latter would be action guiding. Consequently, this unique property of an egocentric map alone, while important, is not sufficient to argue that it is essential to compute an egocentric perceptual map.

In Sholl's model, an egocentric map is computed to track one's movement while exploring a new environment and subsequently, the map is transformed and updated as part of its enduring allocentric map. Again, this is not essential, as robotics researchers have shown how one could compute an allocentric map while simultaneously tracking one's position in it. They refer to this problem as SLAM, simultaneous localization and mapping (see some of these works in Jefferies and Yeap, 2008). However, doing so would have the advantage of creating a map that is also immediately action guiding. Given that many different egocentric maps are created at the perceptual-motor level for performing various immediate tasks (Paillard, 1991; Sholl, 2001), it is likely that we compute first an egocentric map and later, transform the information in it to a more enduring allocentric map. However, the two maps are then not distinct; the egocentric map is simply a transient subset of the allocentric map.

In McNamara et al.'s model, only allocentric maps are computed but in the current allocentric map, one's position and orientation are also coded and updated. This means that the current allocentric map can be readily transformed into an egocentric map, and in this sense, their current allocentric map is equivalent to Sholl's egocentric perceptual map. One interesting difference though is that the allocentric maps in their model are not updated with subsequent views of the same environment. As noted, this is also an important step in our model. However, in their model, nothing is said about what happens when new objects come into view or when the next allocentric map is created. Given that one's position and orientation are tracked continuously, these individual allocentric maps are spatially connected and together they should form a global map, despite the fact that each allocentric map has its own intrinsic frame of reference. Otherwise, one would not be able to orient oneself in the environment or to move from one allocentric map to another. If so, the two models, Sholl's and McNamara et al.'s, are equivalent; they both compute an equivalent representation of one's local environment and combine them to form a global map of the environment traversed.

In Wang and Spelke's model, three representations are computed, namely, a transient egocentric map, the geometrical shape of local environments and view-specific representations of places, but not an allocentric map. Since the latter two representations are used as special navigation aids, we will consider first the role of the egocentric map in Wang and Spelke's model. As noted, computing an egocentric map is equivalent to computing an allocentric map except that as the map grows bigger, it would be daunting to maintain (Burgess, 2006). Putting this disadvantage aside, their model is thus equivalent to the other two models; the information in the egocentric map is simply never transformed into an allocentric map. However, Wang and Spelke stress in their model that the egocentric map is a transient map. If so, information in it will disappear and that part of the map will be lost. While they suggest that humans could use their symbolic capacities to create an allocentric map out of these initial representations, their claim is based on observing that there is little evidence that non-human species compute such a map. Logically then, non-human species will eventually have little memory of where they have been in their environment unless they also compute a more enduring representation out of their egocentric map. While what is computed depends on the needs of the individual species and that some would require only computing simple representations that are not map-like, it should nonetheless be straightforward, given their equivalence, to remember a part of the egocentric map as an enduring allocentric map. If so, the claim that there is little evidence that non-human species compute an allocentric map is both puzzling and inconsistent with their model.

Contrary to Wang and Spelke's claim, the two other representations computed in their model, namely, the geometrical shape of local environments and view-specific representations of places, are direct evidence that allocentric maps are computed in non-human species. Any view-specific representation, once remembered, becomes an allocentric representation since the viewer is no longer position at the center of that co-ordinate system. The geometrical shape of a room is an allocentric map; it can be derived from transforming the boundary surfaces in one's egocentric map into an allocentric map. As McNamara et al. noted, the allocentric maps computed in their model could, depending on the intrinsic frame of reference used, capture either the geometrical shape or view-specific representation of local environments as described in Wang and Spelke's model (Mou et al., 2004; Mou, McNamara Rump & Xiao, 2006). Recent studies of wild primates gathering food in the wild provide further evidence that these primates require some form of an allocentric map to plan their foraging journeys over large distances and in a goal-directed manner (e.g. Noser & Byrne, 2007; Normand & Boesch, 2009). Thus, contrary to Wang and Spelke's (2002) argument, the fact that such representations are already found in lower species such as ants and bees might well argue that developing an allocentric map for the *larger* environment at the perceptual level has always been part of the evolutionary process. However, if so, why does the idea of computing an allocentric map remain controversial and in particular, why would Wang and Spelke argue against it despite having them in their model?

4   What Kind of a (Allocentric) Map Do We Compute?

Over the past 20 years, robotics researchers have been studying a similar process of computing an allocentric map from integrating successive views. They implement the process on wheeled robots and despite using sensors (usually a laser and an odometer) with much less distortions than, say, human vision (Glennerster, Hansard & Fitzgibbon, 2009), they show that the map computed is seriously distorted if the errors from the sensors are not corrected. Fig. 4 shows how distorted the map is when sensor errors are not corrected. While robotics researchers show the problem can be solved on the fly (i.e. doing simultaneous localization and mapping), using some probabilistic error-correction algorithms (Durrant-Whyte & Bailey, 2006), it does mean that the map produced is either precise or distorted. That is, either you correct the errors sufficiently and obtain a precise map or the errors will accumulate and your map will become too distorted. An example of a precise map computed using one of these algorithms for the same environment is shown in Fig. 5. It is not possible to compute a partially distorted map that is useful for navigation and especially with a

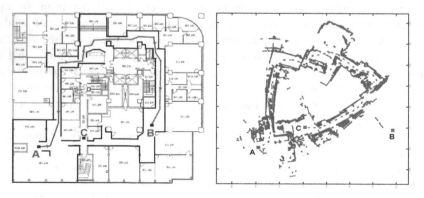

Fig. 4. A distorted map produced by the robot without serious attempt to correct sensor errors: (left) the test environment, and (right) the map produced when the robot reaches point B in the environment.

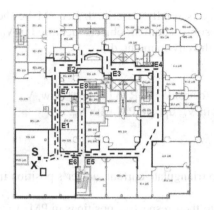 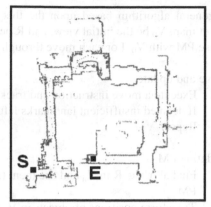

Fig. 5. An accurate map (right) produced using Carmen mapping which uses Monte Carlo Localization based on particle filters and scan matching techniques (Thrun et al. 2001)

highly illusory visual system such as ours (Hurlbert, 1994; Snowden, 1999). Yet, our ability to point to unseen places often impresses upon us that our map, even though distorted, is still reasonably accurate and useful (Ishikawa & Montello, 2006). Nature must have found a different solution in dealing with the errors present in our sensors – by computing a different kind of map.

We recently developed a computational theory of perceptual mapping which argues that a view makes explicit not just what and where things are but also an environment that affords venturing into (Yeap, 2011). Remembering a view thus provides one with a map of the local environment that one could explore. By assuming that the physical environment one lives in is stable, the map does not need to be updated as one moves in its bounded space. New objects might come into view but the local environment itself remains unchanged until one is at its edge and about to move out of it. At this point, a new view is remembered. By describing the new view in the perceptual map using the same co-ordinate system of the previous view remembered, one gets a map of the larger environment. However, as we noted in McNamara's model, without continuous updating of the map with successive views, how can such views (i.e. local environments) be combined to form a global metric map?

A solution to this problem is proposed by observing that one could triangulate one's position in the map if one recognizes some of the objects in the map in the current view. Thus, instead of the traditional approach of tracking one's position in space and updating the map with every successive view, one tracks familiar objects in successive views. These objects are those seen earlier, in the view remembered, and their positions in the map are thus known. With them in sight, one can triangulate one's approximate position in the map and this will enable one to describe the current view in the perceptual map using the same co-ordinate system of the remembered views. These objects thus function as landmarks in the current local environment and if none of them is in view, one is deemed "lost". As such, one remembers a new view prior to all the landmarks disappearing from view. One's perceptual map is thus a collection of such views, described using a single allocentric frame of reference.

A general algorithm based upon the theory is briefly described. Let PM be the transient map, V_0 be the initial view, and R be some landmark objects identified in V_0. Initialise PM with V_0. For each move through the environment, do:

Move and update:
1. Execute a move instruction and track for some $r \in R$ in the new view, V_n.
2. If deemed insufficient landmarks left in V_n, update PM with V_n.
3. Repeat.

Updating PM
4. Find all r's $\in R$ in V_n and use them to triangulate current viewer's position in PM.
5. Transform positions of objects in V_n to their respective positions in PM.
6. Delete all surfaces in PM that lie inside the space occupied by the incoming view.
7. Add the transformed objects of V_n to PM
8. Identify objects in V_n that are suitable for tracking and replace R with these objects.

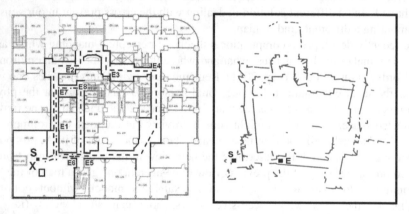

Fig. 6. A perceptual map computed according to our theory of perceptual mapping: (left) the test environment, and (right) the map produced

The theory was tested with an implementation on a mobile robot equipped with a laser sensor and an odometer (Yeap, Hossain & Brunner, 2011). Fig. 6 shows an example of a perceptual map computed by our robot. Information in it is coded using a global allocentric co-ordinate system. While the display shows the position of individual surfaces, surfaces from the same view are marked as such.

According to the theory, what is remembered in the perceptual map are local environments and not individual surfaces Consequently, when a view is remembered, individual objects in it are not matched with individual objects in the map. Instead, any object in the map found lying within the same mental space for the incoming local environment is deleted (see step 6 of the algorithm). Note that due to distortions, these objects may or may not belong to the same part of the environment. Thus, it is possible that some relevant parts of the trace are wiped out and/or some obsolete parts remain in the perceptual map. This contrasts with the traditional approach (as realized in traditional robot mapping) whereby the focus is on updating every individual object perceived from one view to the next and also when one is re-visiting a familiar part of the environment; the result of which is a precise and complete map.

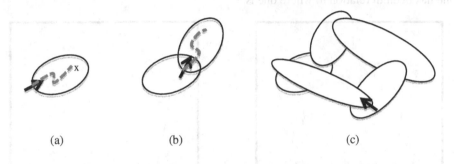

(a)   (b)   (c)

Fig. 7. A transient allocentric perceptual map: (a) the map is updated with a view and no further updating as one moves within its bounded space (dashed line indicates the path). At the end of the path, the viewer is about to move out of the bounded space. It triangulates its position in the map (marked x) but due to errors, its position is not exactly on the path; (b) a new view is added at point x and part of view 1 is deleted; (c) a fifth view is added which also requires wiping out part of view 1.

Fig. 7 shows, diagrammatically, how the perceptual map is updated and what is computed in it is a trace of local environments visited. Since information in it is described using an allocentric frame of system, one is able to point to some earlier parts of the environment visited. This is particularly true if there is little overlap of local environments (see Fig. 6 – the map computed is not as distorted as that shown in Fig. 4). However, information further away from where one is or information perceived much earlier could become unreliable, not only because of distortions due to sensor errors but also because of unexpected changes in the physical world. Thus, unlike the traditional allocentric map we discussed earlier, it is not over-empowering. In fact, information in it needs to be interpreted with care since the map is transient and has both a spatial and a temporal aspect.

The head of the trace is the current local environment and where the viewer is positioned. It keeps changing as one moves from one local environment to another. In this sense, the perceptual map is said to be egocentric, despite having an allocentric frame of reference. Fig. 8 highlights the subtle interpretive differences between an allocentric map and an allocentric trace map that is also egocentric. In Fig. 8a, the map produced is plotted with the center of the co-ordinate system positioned at the start of the journey. In this map, one interprets the viewer as not being positioned correctly and consequently, the map is described as distorted. The emphasis in constructing such a map is on how accurate it is and whether one could close the loop when one returns to a familiar place. In Fig. 8b, the map produced is plotted with the center of the co-ordinate system positioned at the end of the journey (i.e. where one is). In this map, the viewer's position and the spatial layout of the current local environment are most accurate but the position of other information becomes increasingly less certain as one moves back to the start of the journey. For example, the first corridor traversed is now no longer correctly positioned with respect to the viewer. The emphasis in constructing the trace is to focus on capturing the most recent description of the local environment that one is in and some memory of where one has been in relation to where one is.

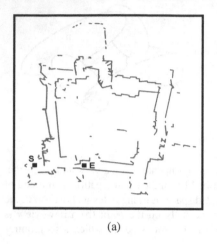 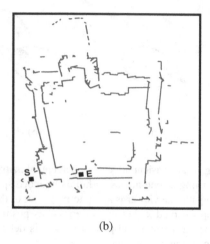

(a)   (b)

Fig. 8. Interpreting the content of one's perceptual map: (a) oriented from the robot's starting position, and (b) oriented from where the robot is

5   Final Remarks

The nature of cognitive maps in both humans and animals has long been the subject of investigations since Tolman (1948) first coined the term. Despite the huge interests, the notion of a cognitive map remains vague and controversial (Bennet, 1996). Many researchers have attempted to define what it is and while it is clear that the term is meant to refer to one's representation of one's environment, what is unclear is its map-like property that supposedly distinguishes it from other known knowledge of one's environment. Rightly so, Wang and Spelke (2002) rejected that we compute an allocentric map as a cognitive map that is precise and complete (or in their words, an internalized form of the kind of geographic maps humans create for navigation (p. 376)). Such a map is too empowering. We suggested an alternative, a map of a trace of local environments visited rather than a map of the physical environment itself.

By describing a process that remembers views as individual allocentric maps and no updating while moving in them, McNamara et al.'s model came close to what we described here. While we argue that their model is similar to Sholl's model, it is important to stress that our argument is based on the assumption that their individual allocentric maps are combined into a map of the physical environment. They have, in fact, left this as an open question in their model; presumably, their experimental findings were inadequate for them to draw a conclusion. It is hoped that our new model is insightful for them and others to design further experiments to unravel the mystery of the process underlying spatial cognition. In turn, these findings could help us to advance our computational model. For example, McNamara et al. also argue that the intrinsic frame of reference for each local environment does not need to be always derived from an observer's point of view. One could use, for example, the spatial layout of objects in view. Future implementations of the theory could investigate this possibility.

We conclude by outlining a process for spatial cognition that incorporates the computation of our proposed perceptual map (see Fig. 9). At the perceptual level, and like Sholl's model, one computes different representations using an egocentric co-ordinate system. These representations are used to perform various tasks as noted in Sholl's model. In addition to these representations, one also computes an egocentric trace of local environments visited at the perceptual level. Such a trace map provides an input rich enough for learning different representations of one's environment. For example, from it, one could abstract a vector map, a route map, a network of landmarks, or a hierarchy of place representations, all depending on the needs of the individual species. For an example of how a hierarchy of place representations can be formed, see Hossain and Yeap (2013).

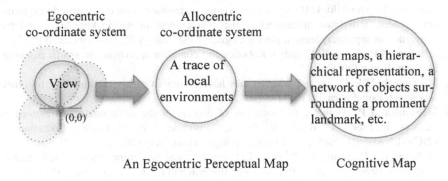

Egocentric co-ordinate system   Allocentric co-ordinate system

View   (0,0)

A trace of local environments

route maps, a hierarchical representation, a network of objects surrounding a prominent landmark, etc.

An Egocentric Perceptual Map   Cognitive Map

Fig. 9. A tentative process supporting spatial cognition

Acknowledgments. Special thanks to my student, Md. Hossain, for his assistance in implementing the theory and generating the robot maps, and to two anonymous reviewers and Prof. Christian Freksa for their comments on an earlier draft.

References

1. Benhamou, S.: No evidence for cognitive mapping in rats. Animal Behavior 52, 201–212 (1996)
2. Bennett, A.T.D.: Do animals have cognitive maps? The Journal of Experimental Biology 199, 219–224 (1996)
3. Briscoe, R.: Egocentric spatial representation in action and perception. Philosophy and Phenomenological Research 79(2), 423–460 (2009)

4. Burgess, N.: Spatial memory: How egocentric and allocentric combine. Trends in Cognitive Sciences 10, 551–557 (2006)
5. Campbell, J.: Past, space and time. MIT Press, Cambridge (1994)
6. Diwadkar, V.A., McNamara, T.P.: Viewpoint dependence in scene recognition. Psychological Science 8, 302–307 (1997)
7. Durrant-Whyte, H., Bailey, T.: Simultaneous Localization and Mapping (SLAM): Part I. IEEE Robotics & Automation Magazine 13(2), 99–110 (2006)
8. Evans, G.: The varieties of reference. Oxford University Press, Oxford (1982)
9. Glennerster, A., Hansard, M.E., Fitzgibbon, A.W.: View-based approaches to spatial representation in human vision. In: Cremers, D., Rosenhahn, B., Yuille, A.L., Schmidt, F.R. (eds.) Statistical and Geometrical Approaches to Visual Motion Analysis. LNCS, vol. 5604, pp. 193–208. Springer, Heidelberg (2009)
10. Galati, G., Pelle, G., Berthoz, A., Committeri, G.: Multiple reference frames used by the human brain for spatial perception and memory. Experimental Brain Research 206(2), 109–120 (2010)
11. Gallistel, C.R.: The organization of learning. MIT Press, Cambridge (1990)
12. Grush, R.: Self, world and space: The meaning and mechanisms of ego- and allocentric spatial representation. Brain and Mind 1(1), 59–92 (2000)
13. Hurlbert, A.C.: Knowing is seeing. Current Biology 4, 423–426 (1994)
14. Hossain, M.Z., Yeap, W.K.: How Albot1 computes its topological-metric map. Procedia – Social and Behavioral Sciences 97, 553–560 (2013)
15. Ishikawa, T., Montello, D.R.: Spatial knowledge acquisition from direct experience in the environment: Individual differences in the development of metric knowledge and the integration of separately learned places. Cognitive Psychology 52, 93–129 (2006)
16. Jefferies, M.E., Yeap, W.K. (eds.): Robotics and cognitive approaches to spatial mapping. Springer, Berlin (2008)
17. Mackintosh, N.J.: Do not ask whether they have a cognitive map, but how they find their way about. Psicologica 23, 165–185 (2002)
18. McNamara, T.P.: How are the locations of objects in the environment represented in memory? In: Freksa, C., Brauer, W., Habel, C., Wender, K.F. (eds.) Spatial Cognition III. LNCS (LNAI), vol. 2685, pp. 174–191. Springer, Heidelberg (2003)
19. McNamara, T.P., Rump, B., Werner, S.: Egocentric and geocentric frames of reference in memory of large-scale space. Psychonomic Bulletin and Review 10(3), 589–595 (2003)
20. McNaughton, B.L., Chen, L.L., Markus, E.J.: "Dead reckoning," landmark learning, and the sense of direction: A neurophysiological and computational hypothesis. Journal of Cognitive Neuroscience 3, 190–202 (1991)
21. Mou, W., McNamara, T.P.: Intrinsic frames of reference in spatial memory. Journal of Experimental Psychology: Learning, Memory and Cognition 28, 162–170 (2002)
22. Mou, W., McNamara, T.P., Rump, B., Xiao, C.: Roles of egocentric and allocentric spatial representations in locomotion and reorientation. Journal of Experimental Psychology: Learning, Memory and Cognition 12(6), 1274–1290 (2006)
23. Mou, W., McNamara, T.P., Valiquette, C.M., Rump, B.: Allocentric and egocentric updating of spatial memories. Journal of Experimental Psychology: Learning, Memory and Cognition 30(1), 142–157 (2004)
24. Normand, E., Boesch, C.: Sophisticated Euclidean maps in forest chimpanzees. Animal Behaviour 77, 1195–1201 (2009)
25. Noser, R., Byrne, R.W.: Travel routes and planning of visits to out-of-sight resources in wild chacma baboons, Papio ursinus. Animal Behaviour 73, 257–266 (2007)

26. Paillard, J.: Motor and representational framing of space. In: Paillard, J. (ed.) Brain and Space, pp. 163–182. Oxford University Press, Oxford (1991)
27. Pecchia, T., Vallortigara, G.: View-based strategy for reorientation by geometry. The Journal of Experimental Biology 213, 2987–2996 (2010)
28. Rump, B., McNamara, T.P.: Updating in models of spatial memory. In: Barkowsky, T., Knauff, M., Ligozat, G., Montello, D.R. (eds.) Spatial Cognition 2007. LNCS (LNAI), vol. 4387, pp. 249–269. Springer, Heidelberg (2007)
29. Shelton, A.L., McNamara, T.P.: Systems of spatial reference in human memory. Cognitive Psychology 43, 274–310 (2001)
30. Sholl, M.J.: The role of a self-reference system in spatial navigation. In: Montello, D.R. (ed.) COSIT 2001. LNCS, vol. 2205, pp. 217–232. Springer, Heidelberg (2001)
31. Snowden, R.J.: Visual perception: Here's mud in your mind's eye. Current Biology 9, R336-R337 (1999)
32. Thrun, S., Fox, D., Burgard, W., Dellaert, F.: Robust Monte Carlo Localization for Mobile Robots. Artificial Intelligence 128(1-2), 99–141 (2001)
33. Tolman, E.C.: Cognitive maps in rats and men. Psychological Review 55, 189–208 (1948)
34. Waller, D., Hodgson, E.: Transient and enduring spatial representations under disorientation and self-rotation. Journal of Experimental Psychology: Learning, Memory, & Cognition 32, 867–882 (2006)
35. Wang, R.F., Spelke, E.S.: Updating egocentric representations in human navigation. Cognition 77, 215–250 (2000)
36. Wang, R.F., Spelke, E.S.: Human spatial representation: Insights from animals. Trends in Cognitive Sciences 6(9), 376–382 (2002)
37. Yeap, W.K.: A computational theory of perceptual mapping. In: Proceedings of the Cognitive Science Conference, Boston, USA, pp. 429–434 (2011)
38. Yeap, W.K., Hossain, M.Z., Brunner, T.: On the implementation of a theory of perceptual mapping. In: Proceedings of the Australasian Conference on Artificial Intelligence, Perth, Australia, pp. 739–748 (2011)
39. Zhang, H., Mou, W., McNamara, T.P.: Spatial updating according to a fixed reference direction of a briefly viewed layout. Cognition 119, 419–429 (2011)

Attentional Distribution and Spatial Language

Thomas Kluth and Holger Schultheis

Cognitive Systems, Universität Bremen,
Enrique-Schmidt-Str. 5, 28359 Bremen, Germany
{kluth,schulth}@cs.uni-bremen.de

Abstract. Whether visual spatial attention can be split to several discontinuous locations concurrently is still an open and intensely debated question. We address this question in the domain of spatial language use by comparing two existing and three newly proposed computational models. All models are assessed regarding their ability to account for human acceptability ratings for how well a given spatial term describes the spatial arrangement of two functionally related objects. One of the existing models assumes that taking the functional relations into account involves split attention. All new models incorporate functional relations without assuming split attention. Our simulations suggest that not assuming split attention is more appropriate for taking the functional relations into account than assuming split attention. At the same time, the simulations raise doubt as to whether any of the models appropriately captures the impact of functional relations on spatial language use.

1 Introduction

Visual spatial attention allows selectively focusing on certain regions of perceivable space such that information processing in the attended regions is enhanced. According to two influential theories, the selective focus of visual spatial attention can be likened to a spotlight [1] or a zoom lens [2]. These conceptualizations highlight a number of important properties associated with attention: (a) enhanced processing is restricted to circumscribed regions in space; (b) processing enhancements are highest at the focal point of attention and gradually decrease with distance from this focus point; and (c) the size of the attended region is not fixed, but can be adjusted based on task demands. Both theories also assume that the attentional focus is unitary in the sense that it comprises a single focal point (perhaps with a graded surrounding) that cannot be split to several discontinuous locations in space. Under this assumption, attentional distribution is uni-focal with the mode coinciding with the focal point of the attentional "spotlight".

Whether attentional distribution is in fact uni-focal or whether it may be multi-focal (i.e., divided attention to several discontinuous locations concurrently) remains a controversial issue. While earlier studies mainly yielded evidence supporting uni-focal attentional distribution [3] there are now many studies that claim to show the existence of multi-focal attentional distribution

C. Freksa et al. (Eds.): Spatial Cognition 2014, LNAI 8684, pp. 76–91, 2014.

(e.g., [4,5]). However, methodological complications render it difficult to interpret the results of these studies leading a recent review on divided attention to conclude that decisive evidence in favor of multi-focal attentional distribution still remains to be provided [6].

Producing and comprehending spatial utterances such as "The cups are on the shelf *above* the sideboard" is tightly related to the workings of visual spatial attention [7]: For example, attention is required to identify the objects (shelf and sideboard) that are related in the utterance [8] and also to apprehend the spatial relation between the related objects [9]. In accord with this importance, visual spatial attention plays a key role in a seminal computational cognitive model of processes involved in spatial language use. This model, called *attentional vector-sum* (AVS) model [10], computes acceptability ratings for how well a given spatial term such as *above* describes the spatial arrangement between two objects. In the light of evidence that functional relations between objects impact spatial language use [11,12], [13] proposed an extension of the AVS, henceforth called *functional* AVS (fAVS), that allows the computation of the acceptability ratings to be influenced by functional object relations.

Apart from its merit for our understanding of spatial language use, the fAVS is also of interest for our understanding of visual spatial attention more generally, because the mechanisms realized in the fAVS assume a multi-focal attentional distribution. Against the background of the existing debate in the visual spatial attention literature it is not immediately clear whether such an assumption is justified. On the other hand, if multi-focal attentional distribution is found to be a crucial component of a functional extension of the AVS, this would lend further support to the idea that visual spatial attention can be distributed multimodally. In this paper we investigate the role of multi-focal attentional distribution in the fAVS. We propose a number of alternative functional extensions of the AVS that employ uni-focal attentional distributions and compare all models' ability to account for pertinent empirical data. In doing so, we not only examine the role of attentional distribution in the AVS, but also provide the first quantitative assessment of the fAVS.

2   Models

As in the utterance "The cups are on the shelf *above* the sideboard" spatial terms such as *above* are often used to indicate where to look for a certain object (called *trajector*) in relation to another object (called *landmark*). Determining how well a given spatial term matches the spatial relation between trajector and landmark is an important step in producing / comprehending spatial utterances [14] and all models considered in our simulations address this step. Put differently, the models determine how acceptable a given spatial term is to describe the spatial relation between landmark and trajector.

The considered models are the AVS, the fAVS, and three functional extensions of the AVS that employ a uni-focal distribution of attention. All five models are described in more detail in the remainder of this section.

2.1 AVS

The AVS-model takes a landmark-object, a trajector position and a spatial preposition (e.g., *above*) as input. Its output consists of an acceptance rating on a given scale. If AVS returns a low rating, the spatial term *above* is not considered to adequately describe the spatial relation between landmark and trajector. On the other hand, if the rating is high, the AVS predicts that most observers accept *above* as an appropriate description of the scene.

The rating is computed from two main sources: A height component and an angular component. The height component produces a value between 0 and 1 depending on the height relation between the trajector and the top-side of the landmark. The higher the trajector is compared to the top-side of the landmark, the higher the height component will be.

To compute the angular component, an attentional focus f is defined. Its center is the vertically aligned point on top of the landmark. In case the trajector is not vertically aligned with the landmark, the attentional focus lies at the point that is closest to being so, i.e., the closest edge of the landmark. Fig. 1 shows an example landmark, trajector and the corresponding attentional focus as assumed in the AVS.

Every point i of the landmark gets an amount of attention a_i. The attention is highest in the attentional focus f and decreases exponentially with increasing distance from f. A vector v_i is rooted at every landmark point i, pointing to trajector t. The length of each v_i is weighted by the amount of attention a_i at landmark point i. Fig. 2 visualizes this process with the same example trajector t as in Fig. 1.

All these vectors are summed up to create a single vector that is compared to a reference vector. In case of *above* the reference vector is a vector aligned with the upright vertical. The angular deviation between the vector sum and the reference vector determines the angular component: The higher the deviation, the lower the angular component will be. To arrive at a final value for the acceptance rating, the height value and the angular value are multiplied. For example, the trajector used in Figs. 1 and 2 would result in an acceptance rating of 6.46 where 1 is the lowest rating and 7 is the highest rating.

The different functional extensions of the AVS differ only in how the angular component is computed. Computation of the height component is the same as in the AVS for all functional extensions discussed here.

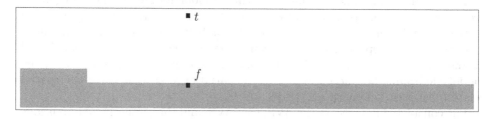

Fig. 1. An example landmark (toothbrush) with trajector t and resulting focus f

Fig. 2. An example trajector t and resulting vectors v_i weighted by attention a_i

2.2 fAVS

The AVS has been shown to successfully account for human acceptability ratings across a wide range of spatial arrangements and object shapes [10]. However, in its original formulation, the AVS does not take into account possible functional relationships between the related objects. Therefore [13] proposed the fAVS as a functional extension to the AVS. The idea behind the fAVS is that a functional part attracts more attention such that the amount of attention at every point lying in the functional part is increased:

$$
A_i = \begin{cases} a_i \cdot (1 + \varphi) & \text{if } i \text{ lies in functional part} \\ a_i & \text{else} \end{cases} \tag{1}
$$

Here, a_i denotes the amount of attention at point i, as defined in the AVS and φ is a free parameter. In the fAVS A_i is used instead of a_i to weight each vector v_i.

In [13] three values for φ were suggested:

$\varphi = 2$ strong functional interaction between landmark and trajector
$\varphi = 1$ weak functional interaction between landmark and trajector
$\varphi = 0$ no functional interaction (i.e., AVS)

The fAVS has the flexibility to behave like the AVS with $\varphi = 0$ – i.e., every point i of the landmark gets the amount of attention a_i as defined in the AVS model. However, if $\varphi > 0$ the else condition of (1) is needed, because only the functional part of the landmark receives a higher amount of attention.

Attentional Distribution. Fig. 3 shows an exemplary attentional distribution as assumed by the fAVS. It can be seen that the fAVS leads to a bi-focal attentional distribution if f does not lie in the functional part, since the functional part receives more attention than its surroundings.

Fig. 3. Bi-focal attentional distribution when using the AVS extension proposed by [13]. Trajector is assumed to be a toothpaste tube and is positioned at the yellow dot. Toothbrush bristles are defined as functional part. Brighter color means higher amount of attention. Borders of landmark are colored black.

Accordingly, the mechanisms realized in the fAVS amount to the assumption that humans are able to divide their visual spatial attention.[1] As available empirical evidence does not unequivocally support whether or not this is possible (see [6]), we subsequently present three different functional extensions of the AVS that do not assume a multi-focal attentional distribution.

2.3   Alternative Functional Extensions for AVS

In this section we present three alternative functional extensions to the AVS. In the first two extensions the location of the attentional focus is changed, in the last extension an attentional switch is proposed. Note that for all extensions the key idea – functional parts attract attention – stays the same, but that there is no assumption of divided visual spatial attention.

Focus only at Functional Part. This extension changes the location of the focus point: The focus always lies on the functional part. The way the focus point is chosen is very similar to the AVS. The only change is that the top of the functional part is used instead of the whole top of the landmark. Note that, although the focus always lies on the functional part, the whole landmark gets considered to compute the angular component. Fig. 4 shows an exemplary resulting focus point. This extension is not able to gradually account for the strength of the functional relationship between landmark and trajector (cf. the φ parameter in the fAVS).

---

[1] One may speculate whether the workings of the fAVS could also be interpreted as a formalization of sequential attention shifts instead of instantiating a concurrent multi-focal attentional distribution. However, since nothing in the original formulation of the (f)AVS alludes to such attention shifts, an interpretation in terms of multi-focal attention seems appropriate. Furthermore, as our simulations show, explicitly including attention shifts into the AVS leads to significantly different performance of the resulting model.

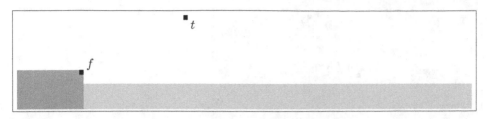

Fig. 4. An example trajector t and its resulting focus f using the *focus only at function* extension. The functional part is colored in dark gray. Trajector is assumed to be a toothpaste tube.

Move Focus. In this extension the location of the attentional focus f, that is, the point with the highest amount of attention, is changed. In the original model, the attentional focus f is the point, which is vertically aligned with the landmark (or closest to being so). This extension also starts with this focus point, but adds another step. The focus is moved into the direction of the functional part. The farther away the focus is from the functional part, the more it moves toward the functional part.

To compute the new focus the leftmost and rightmost point on the functional top are used, where the functional top is defined as all points in the functional part where one cannot find a point with the same x-value but a higher y-value. More precisely, the new focus mf is derived from the original focus f, the leftmost point on top of the functional part ltf or the rightmost point on top of the functional part rtf as follows:

$$mf = \begin{cases} f + w \cdot \overrightarrow{f, ltf} & \text{if } f \text{ is to the left of the functional part} \\ f + w \cdot \overrightarrow{f, rtf} & \text{if } f \text{ is to the right of the functional part} \\ f & \text{if } f \text{ lies in the functional part} \end{cases} \quad (2)$$

The parameter w controls the functional strength and is defined as $w = \frac{\varphi}{2}$ to obtain values for φ that are comparable with the values proposed in [13], see Section 2.2. If $\varphi = 0$, this extension behaves like the AVS (no functional interaction) and if $\varphi = 2$, this extension behaves like the *focus only at function* extension.

Fig. 5 shows the focus point mf of the same example trajector t used to illustrate the mechanisms of the AVS, using $w = 0.5$ (i.e., $\varphi = 1$). Note that with this extension the location of the focus point may not lie inside the landmark, as can be seen in Fig. 5.

Attentional Switch. In this last alternative extension an attentional switch is assumed to operate when the landmark contains functional parts. First the attentional focus lies on the functional part of the landmark and then the landmark is attended as if it had no functional part. More precisely, the extension consists of the following steps:

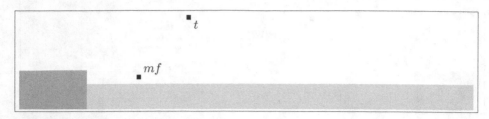

Fig. 5. An example trajector t and its resulting focus mf using the *move focus* extension. The functional part is colored in dark gray. Trajector is assumed to be a toothpaste tube.

1. One vector-sum is computed as in the AVS, but with the focus f_1 chosen like in the *focus only at function* extension (i.e., the focus lies on the functional part).
2. A second vector-sum is computed, but this time the attentional focus f_2 is the one from the AVS, that is, the landmark is handled as if it were not containing any functional part.
3. The deviation from upright vertical (in the case of *above*) is measured for both vectors.
4. Both deviations are combined to get a final value for the angular component. Here, w controls again for the functional strength between landmark and trajector:

$$angle = \frac{w \cdot funcDev + geomDev}{w + 1} \tag{3}$$

Once more, the parameter w is defined as $w = \frac{\varphi}{2}$ to obtain comparable values for φ. If $\varphi = 0$ this extension is the same as AVS – i.e., equivalent to no functional interaction. If $\varphi = 2$ function and geometry both play an equal role. For values between 0 and 2 the functional strength is weighted accordingly.

Fig. 6 shows the two vectors as defined in step 1 (left vector) and step 2 (right vector) in light gray. The vector drawn in solid black is the vector with the average deviation from upright vertical, as stated in step 4, using $w = 1$ (i.e., $\varphi = 2$). However, note that, to avoid visual clutter, the starting points and lengths of the vectors have been modified.

3   Model Comparison

Two questions seem of prime importance regarding our inquiry into attentional distribution and spatial language use. The first question is whether any of the functional extensions is able to better account for functional effects in human spatial language use than the other extensions. If, for example, the fAVS would outperform the other extensions this would lend support to the idea that visual spatial attention can be multimodally distributed. The second question is whether any of the four functional extensions is able to better account for functional effects in human spatial language use than the AVS. If, for example, the

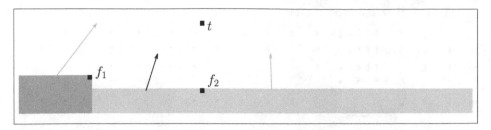

Fig. 6. An example trajector t, two foci f_1 and f_2 and the resulting vectors according to the *attentional switch* extension. The functional part is colored in dark gray. Trajector is assumed to be a toothpaste tube.

AVS would perform as well as or better than the functional extensions, this would raise doubt whether the extensions appropriately capture the impact of functional relationships between landmark and trajector.

To provide a first answer to these questions, we assessed the ability of the AVS and its four extensions to simulate human acceptability ratings from two empirical studies that employed functionally related landmark and trajector objects.

In the following we will first describe in more detail the data and method used for model assessment. Then we will present and discuss the results of the model assessment.

3.1   Data and Method

To compare the AVS and its four extensions we used data from [12, experiment 2] and [15][2]. For both data sets the experimental setup was the following: Participants were shown a landmark and a trajector at different positions around the landmark. For each trajector (shown at a specific position), participants had to rate the appropriateness of the sentence "The [trajector] is [spatial-preposition] the [landmark]" on a scale from 1 to 7, with 1 being lowest acceptance and 7 highest acceptance.

Carlson-Radvansky et al. Fig. 7(a) shows the landmark and trajector positions used in [12, experiment 2], Fig. 7(b) shows the schematized landmark used in our simulations. As can be seen in Fig. 7(a), experimental conditions manipulated the location of the functional part of the landmark (i.e., the coin slot) to investigate how the location impacts acceptability ratings. For each of the 3 slot positions ratings were obtained for all 58 trajector positions from each participant. The considered spatial term was *above*.

Hörberg. In [15] experiments are presented that investigated the swedish spatial prepositions *ovanför, över, nevanför* and *under* (corresponding to the english

---

[2] We thank Thomas Hörberg for sharing his data.

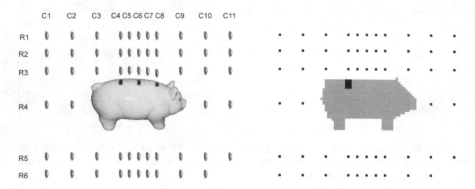

(a) Landmark, trajector positions and functional parts used in [12]. In the experiment only one coin and slot were shown at the same time. (reproduced from [12, p. 519]. Copyright © 1999 American Psychological Society. Reprinted by permission of SAGE Publications.)

(b) Schematized piggy bank with slot in the back and trajector positions used in the simulations.

Fig. 7. Landmarks and trajector positions for [12] data

prepositions *above, over, below* and *under*) with respect to their acceptability when influenced by a functional relationship between landmark and trajector. As the AVS simulations in [10] and Experiment 2 in [12] only consider *above*, we restricted our simulations to the corresponding swedish preposition *ovanför*.

The functional interaction between landmark and trajector in [15] is divided in two types: *center-of-mass aligned* and *center-of-mass deviant* interactions. For functional interactions of the first type the center of mass of the trajector needs to be above the landmark in a strict geometric way (e.g., coin over piggy bank, see Fig. 8(a)). For *center-of-mass deviant* interactions the center of mass of the trajector is either to the left or to the right of the landmark (e.g, ketchup bottle over hot dog or Fig. 8(c)).

To evaluate the AVS and its extensions with both types of functional interaction, we chose one landmark-trajector pair for each type, shown together with their corresponding polygons used for simulation in Fig. 8. The piggy bank with its trajector (a coin) is an example of a *center-of-mass aligned* functional interaction, the petrol can with its trajector (a gas pump handle) is an example of a *center-of-mass deviant* interaction. The functional part of most of the other landmarks used in [15] spanned the whole top of the landmark – we did not use these landmarks, because all AVS extensions would have behaved the same for such landmark objects.

Every landmark was tested with a prototypical trajector (e.g., coffee mug and a sugar cube) and a non-prototypical trajector (e.g., coffee mug and an ice cube). Our simulations focus on prototypical trajectors.

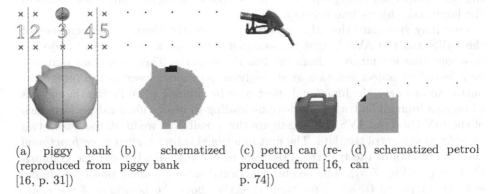

(a) piggy bank (b) schematized (reproduced from piggy bank [16, p. 31])

(c) petrol can (reproduced from [16, p. 74])

(d) schematized petrol can

Fig. 8. (a) and (c): Landmarks and trajector positions used in [15]. (Reprinted by permission of Thomas Hörberg.) (b) and (d): Schematized landmarks and trajector positions used for simulations. Functional parts are colored in black.

Since the AVS represents trajectors only as a point, but the trajectors were quite big objects in the experiments, we had to decide, which trajector positions to use in the simulation. We used the center of mass of the coin trajectors for the data from both [15] and [12]. This seems reasonable, because a coin is a small trajector and the functional interaction shown in Fig. 8(a) and Fig. 7 are *center-of-mass aligned* interactions. Fig. 8(c) shows an example of *center-of-mass deviant* functional interaction. We decided to use the positions of the functionally important parts of the trajector (i.e., the bottom right of the gas pump handle in Fig. 8(c)) as trajector positions in the simulation and not the center of mass positions.

Method. The AVS and its extensions were implemented in C++.[3] Each of the models was fit to three different data sets: (i) ratings for all three slot positions in [12, Experiment 2]; (ii) ratings for the piggy bank landmark in [15]; and (iii) ratings for the petrol can landmark in [15]. Using the RMSE of model ratings and empirical ratings as the criterion function, all models were fit using a variant of the Metropolis algorithm [17]. The RMSE that resulted from fitting the models was used as a measure for the *Goodness of Fit* (GOF) of the model to the data.

3.2 Results: Goodness of Fit

All model variations are able to tightly fit the first data set as can be seen in Fig. 9(a). However, in comparison, the *focus only at function* extension is the worst. The extensions *attentional switch* and *move focus* result in neither the best nor the worst fit. The fAVS-model fits the data best, but interestingly,

---

[3] The sourcecode can be found at https://bitbucket.org/kluth/avs.

the AVS-model fits nearly equally well – without taking any functional parts of the landmark objects into account.

One may speculate that the reason for the nearly identical performance of the fAVS and the AVS is that the complete data set includes many trajector positions that are far away from the functional parts. These positions may not be affected by object function as strongly as positions closer to the functional parts. Accordingly, the functional effect may be clouded when fitting the models to ratings from all 58 trajector positions leading to nearly identical performance of the fAVS and the AVS. To investigate this possibility, we fit all models to two *functional subsets* of the data. The first functional subset (called *large functional subset*) consists of the trajector positions in the rows R1-R3 and the columns C2-C10 (see Fig. 7(a)). The second functional subset (called *small functional subset*) comprised trajector positions directly above the positions of the slots, i.e., rows R1-R3 in columns C4, C6 and C8 (see Fig. 7(a)).

All models except *focus only at function* achieve closer and nearly similar fits to the large functional subset (Fig. 9(b)). The GOF achieved by the models on the small functional subset is different from the GOFs on both the complete set of trajector positions and the large functional subset, as can be seen from Fig. 9(c). All models are able to fit even closer to the small functional subset (cf. magnitude of the RMSE). Interestingly, the models with rather bad GOFs for all trajector positions or the large fuctional subset (i.e., *attentional switch* and especially *focus only at function*) achieve the best GOFs for the small functional subset.

The GOF results for the second data set (piggy bank from [15]) and the third data set (petrol can) are depicted in Fig. 10(a) and Fig. 10(b), respectively. The pattern of results are very similar to the results for the first data set: All models are able to closely fit the data, the (f)AVS and *move focus* fit best, and the rest of our proposed alternative extensions result in comparably bad fits, especially the *focus only at function extension*. Note, however, that the fits for the petrol can are generally worse than those achieved on the other two data sets. This may be due to the simplification of the trajector and the *center-of-mass deviant* functional interaction. Since the data sets in [15] are considerably smaller than the data set from [12], it did not seem reasonable to further reduce the number of data points by employing a functional subset.

In sum, across all three data sets, the *focus only at function* extension proposed in this article result in relatively bad GOF-values, except for the small functional subset. The fAVS, the AVS, and the two other proposed extensions perform similarly well.

3.3   Results: Simple Hold-Out

As outlined by [18] a good fit is necessary but not sufficient for a "good" model. If the compared models are of different complexity, more complex models may achieve better GOF values solely by virtue of their complexity and not because they provide a better explanation for the observed data [19]. Against this background, it is worthwhile to ask to what extent the obtained GOF results

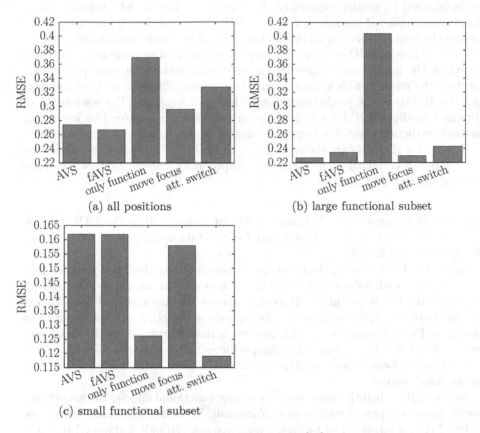

Fig. 9. GOF results for [12]

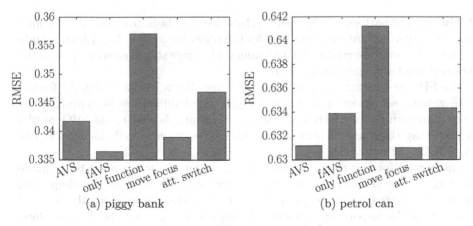

Fig. 10. GOF results for [15]

are influenced by model complexity. To investigate the models' behavior more closely, we employed the *simple hold-out* (SHO) method, which was found to be among the best performing methods that control for model complexity [20].

The key idea of SHO is to use only a part of the data to estimate parameters (or: train the model) and to predict the remaining data with these parameters (or: test the model). This is done several times using different splits of the data and the RMSE of the prediction is saved for each iteration. The median of all obtained prediction RMSEs is used as an evaluation measure: The lower this median prediction error, the better the model is able to account for the data.

Results for the SHO are shown in Figs. 11 and 12. The shown error bars are the bootstrap standard error estimates computed as stated in [21, p. 47] using 100,000 bootstrap samples.

Carlson-Radvansky et al. Simple hold-out results mirror the GOF results, both for all positions (Fig. 11(a)) and for the functional subsets of positions (Figs. 11(b) and 11(c)).

As for the GOF results, the difference between the models' performance patterns on the small subset versus the other two sets seems noteworthy. On all positions and the large subset all models except the *focus only at function* extension perform similarly while the *focus only at function* extension performs clearly and significantly worse. This pattern is nearly inverted for the small subset: the *focus only at function* extension performs better than the AVS, the fAVS, and the *move focus* extension. The *attentional switch* extension performs best on the small subset.

Accordingly, when the data contains strong functional effects, the *attentional switch* extension provides the best explanation. When the functional effects are embedded in a larger set of ratings, which are not strongly influenced by functional relations, the AVS performs as well as and sometimes even better than all of its functional variants.

Hörberg. The pattern of SHO results is less clear for the data from [15]. Although the relative performance of the models for the piggy bank data (Fig. 12(a)) is quite similar to the one observed with GOF values, the large standard errors render the obtained SHO differences inconclusive.

The SHO results for the petrol can data are shown in Fig. 12(b). As for the GOF results, all models have comparatively great difficulties in capturing the petrol can ratings. In contrast to the GOF results, however, the SHO results suggest that there are no substantial differences in how well the models can account for the petrol can data.

The reason for this might be the simplification of the trajector to a simple point in all tested models. This provides further evidence that the shape and the functional parts of the trajector are more important than currently assumed in the AVS. An important step towards improving the AVS should, therefore, consist of a better implementation of how shape and functional parts of the trajector are taken into account (see also discussion in [15]).

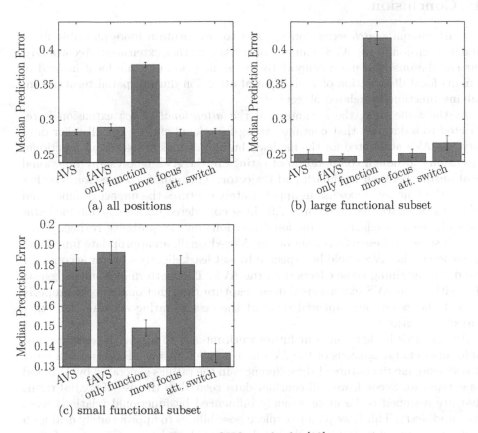

Fig. 11. SHO results for [12]

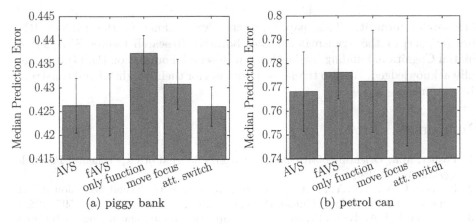

Fig. 12. SHO results for [15]

4 Conclusion

The *attentional switch* extension appears to constitute a more plausible functional extension of the AVS than any of the three other extensions. Accordingly, our simulations lend more support to the assumption of a uni-focal instead of a multi-focal distribution of visual spatial attention during spatial term use involving functionally related objects.

At the same time, the advantage of the *attentional switch* extension is restricted to a data set that contains strong functional effects. For all other data sets, the AVS accounted for the modeled human ratings as well as all functional extensions, although computation of ratings in the AVS ignores any functional relationship between landmark and trajector. This calls into question whether any of the functional extensions appropriately captures the impact of functional relations on spatial language use. All three considered data sets contained statistically reliable effects of functional relations on acceptability ratings. Even though some of these effects may be considered small, an appropriate functional extension of the AVS would be expected to – at least slightly – better account for the data containing these effects than the AVS. This pattern of results suggests that either the AVS extensions did not capture the functional effects properly or that the extensions captured them at the cost of rating accuracy for other trajector positions.

Against this background, our future work intends to further investigate possible functional extensions of the AVS in a number of ways. First, we will more closely examine the nature of the differences in the ratings generated by AVS and its extensions. Second, we will consider data related to the use of spatial terms that are assumed to be more strongly influenced by functional relations (e.g., *over* and *över*). Third, we plan to explore possibilities to appropriately deal with spatially extended trajectors such that differences found between *center-of-mass aligned* and *center-of-mass deviant* relations can be captured. Ultimately, this work is aimed at devising a refined version of the (f)AVS.

Acknowledgement. This paper presents work done in the project R1-[ImageSpace] of the Transregional Collaborative Research Center SFB/TR 8 Spatial Cognition. Funding by the German Research Foundation (DFG) is gratefully acknowledged. We also thank the reviewers for their insightful and constructive comments.

References

1. Posner, M.I.: Orienting of attention. Quarterly Journal of Experimental Psychology 32, 3–25 (1980)
2. Eriksen, C.W., Yeh, Y.Y.: Allocation of attention in the visual field. Journal of Experimental Psychology: Human Perception and Performance 11, 583–597 (1985)
3. McCormick, P.A., Klein, R., Johnston, S.: Splitting versus sharing focal attention: Comment on Castiello and Umilta. Journal of Experimental Psychology: Human Perception and Performance 24, 350–357 (1992, 1998)

4. Yap, J.Y., Lim, S.W.H.: Media multitasking predicts unitary versus splitting visual focal attention. Journal of Cognitive Psychology 25, 889–902 (2013)
5. Eimer, M., Grubert, A.: Spatial attention can be allocated rapidly and in parallel to new visual objects. Current Biology 24, 193–198 (2014)
6. Jans, B., Peters, J.C., De Weerd, P.: Visual Spatial Attention to Multiple Locations at Once: The Jury Is Still Out. Psychological Review 117(2), 637–684 (2010)
7. Carlson, L.A., Logan, G.D.: Attention and spatial language. In: Itti, L., Rees, G., Tsotsos, J. (eds.) Neurobiology of Attention, pp. 330–336. Elsevier, San Diego (2005)
8. Carlson, L.A., Logan, G.D.: Using spatial terms to select an object. Memory & Cognition 29, 883–892 (2001)
9. Franconeri, S.L., Scimeca, J.M., Roth, J.C., Helseth, S.A., Kahn, L.E.: Flexible visual processing of spatial relationships. Cognition 122, 210–227 (2012)
10. Regier, T., Carlson, L.A.: Grounding Spatial Language in Perception: An Empirical and Computational Investigation. Journal of Experimental Psychology: General 130(2), 273–298 (2001)
11. Coventry, K.R., Garrod, S.C.: Saying, seeing, and acting: The psychological semantics of spatial prepositions. Psychology Press, New York (2004)
12. Carlson-Radvansky, L.A., Covey, E.S., Lattanzi, K.M.: "What" Effects on "Where": Functional Influences on Spatial Relations. Psychological Science 10(6), 516–521 (1999)
13. Carlson, L.A., Regier, T., Lopez, W., Corrigan, B.: Attention Unites Form and Function in Spatial Language. Spatial Cognition & Computation 6(4), 295–308 (2006)
14. Logan, G.D., Sadler, D.D.: A computational analysis of the apprehension of spatial relations. In: Bloom, P., Peterson, M., Garrett, M., Nadel, L. (eds.) Language and Space, pp. 493–529. M.I.T. Press, MA (1996)
15. Hörberg, T.: Influences of Form and Function on the Acceptability of Projective Prepositions in Swedish. Spatial Cognition & Computation 8(3), 193–218 (2008)
16. Hörberg, T.: Influences of Form and Function on Spatial Relations: Establishing functional and geometric influences on projective prepositions in Swedish. Magister thesis, Stockholm University (2006)
17. Metropolis, N., Rosenbluth, A.W., Rosenbluth, M.N., Teller, A.H., Teller, E.: Equation of state calculations by fast computing machines. The Journal of Chemical Physics 21(6), 1087–1092 (1953)
18. Roberts, S., Pashler, H.: How persuasive is a good fit? A comment on theory testing. Psychological Review 107(2), 358–367 (2000)
19. Pitt, M.A., Myung, I.J.: When a good fit can be bad. Trends in Cognitive Sciences 6(10), 421–425 (2002)
20. Schultheis, H., Singhaniya, A., Chaplot, D.S.: Comparing Model Comparison Methods. In: Proceedings of the 35th Annual Conference of the Cognitive Science Society (2013)
21. Efron, B., Tibshirani, R.J.: An Introduction to the Bootstrap. Chapman & Hall, New York (1993)

Boundaries and Prototypes
in Categorizing Direction

Vivien Mast[1], Diedrich Wolter[2], Alexander Klippel[3],
Jan Oliver Wallgrün[3], and Thora Tenbrink[1,4]

[1] I5-[DiaSpace], SFB/TR 8 Spatial Cognition, University of Bremen, Germany
viv@informatik.uni-bremen.de
[2] Smart Environments, University of Bamberg, Germany
diedrich.wolter@uni-bamberg.de
[3] GeoVISTA Center, Department of Geography,
The Pennsylvania State University, USA
{klippel,wallgrun}@psu.edu
[4] School of Linguistics and English Language, Bangor University, Wales, UK
t.tenbrink@bangor.ac.uk

Abstract. Projective terms such as *left, right, front, back* are conceptually interesting due to their flexibility of contextual usage and their central relevance to human spatial cognition. Their default acceptability areas are well known, with prototypical axes representing their most central usage and decreasing acceptability away from the axes. Previous research has shown these axes to be *boundaries* in certain non-linguistic tasks, indicating an inverse relationship between linguistic and non-linguistic direction concepts under specific circumstances. Given this striking mismatch, our study asks how such inverse non-linguistic concepts are represented in language, as well as how people describe their categorization. Our findings highlight two distinct grouping strategies reminiscent of theories of human categorization: prototype based or boundary based. These lead to different linguistic as well as non-linguistic patterns.

1 Introduction

Imagine you want to divide a circle into four segments, on a piece of paper. A natural solution would be to cut it into *quadrants* using a vertical and a horizontal stroke of the pen. This segmentation is easy to do and to think about, but surprisingly hard to put into words. Simple direction concepts such as *left* and *right* just do not fit very well. However, other ways of categorizing space—for example, based on these simple direction concepts—may serve as natural solutions in other contexts. In this paper, we ask how people categorize direction and how they verbalize these categories, relevant to long-standing debates about human categorization and the relationship between language and thought.

Categorization has been a topic of central interest in psychology and linguistics for many decades (e.g., Smith and Medin, 1981; Taylor, 1989). In the 1970ies, a major paradigm shift led away from previous assumptions that humans distinguish members from non-members of a category by means of essential features

C. Freksa et al. (Eds.): Spatial Cognition 2014, LNAI 8684, pp. 92–107, 2014.

(*boundary*-based categorization). Categories are now typically seen as characterized by an idealization of what a perfect member would be, with membership
depending on overall perceived similarity to this *prototype* (Mervis and Rosch,
1981).

In much of the earlier research on categorization, linguistic expressions and
non-linguistic concepts were not distinguished very clearly. However, in a different strand of research, the linguistic relativism debate initiated by Whorf (1956)
is aimed at determining the extent and directionality of correspondences between
language and thought (Bierwisch and Schreuder, 1992; Levinson et al., 2002; Li
and Gleitman, 2002). With respect to spatial directions, this relationship has
been subject to debate, as we will outline next.

2   Spatial Relations and Their Categorization

It is uncontroversial that the use of projective terms such as *left, front, above*
relies heavily on prototypical axes: turning *right* invokes a prototypical 90° angle
from a view direction just as well as reference to an object *on your right* does
(Tenbrink, 2011), with various linguistic effects when the relevant direction de-
parts from the prototypical axis (Gapp, 1995; Logan and Sadler, 1996; Tenbrink,
2007; Zimmer et al., 1998). While systematic differences emerge depending on
the task setting (Vorwerg and Tenbrink, 2007), in particular between dynamic
and static uses of projective terms (Herzog, 1995; Hickmann and Hendriks, 2006),
existing research shows a stable *prototype* effect amongst a broad range of tasks.

Regarding the relation to non-linguistic categories, however, the picture is less
clear. While Hayward and Tarr (1995) claim that both verbal and non-verbal
categories have the same prototype structure, there is compelling evidence that
linguistic prototypes for horizontal and vertical directions can correspond to
boundaries in non-linguistic categorization (Crawford et al., 2000; Huttenlocher
et al., 1991; Klippel and Montello, 2007). This may be due to differences in the
specific task and analysis procedures. Hayward and Tarr (1995) showed participants images with configurations of schematic objects. Participants replicated
the position of the locatum on a sheet of paper showing only the relatum, or
judged the similarity of two consecutively shown configurations. In both tasks,
accuracy was greatest when the locatum was on a perpendicular axis. From
this, Hayward and Tarr (1995) conclude that verbal and non-verbal categories
have the same prototype structure. In contrast, Crawford et al. (2000) and Huttenlocher et al. (1991) presented experiments addressing estimation bias effects
in memory tasks. Studies in a large range of domains have demonstrated that
humans show an estimation bias away from category boundaries towards prototypes in memory reproduction tasks (Crawford et al., 2000), a fact which can
be exploited for analyzing the conceptual structure of human categories. When
reproducing the position of a dot in a circle (Huttenlocher et al., 1991), or of
a dot in relation to a schematic image of a television (Crawford et al., 2000),
participants showed an angular bias of the reproduction towards the center of
quadrants, away from the perpendicular axes. Linguistic ratings on the same
stimuli, however, show the typical prototype effect. Thus, Crawford et al. (2000)

conclude that the perpendicular axes play the role of prototypes for linguistic categories while they serve as boundaries for non-linguistic categories.

Further evidence supporting this surprising claim was subsequently obtained by Klippel and Montello (2007), who found that linguistic awareness influences categorization of turn direction concepts in a similar way. Participants were presented with depictions of turns of different angles and asked to group them into categories based on similarity – first without, then with the knowledge that they would later be asked to label the groups linguistically. Klippel and Montello (2007) identified the items which were most consistently categorized together using a cluster analysis. Without verbal task awareness, the aggregated categories of all participants had the perpendicular right and left axes as boundaries. When participants were aware of the verbal task, the aggregated categories had the perpendicular axes in their center, suggesting a prototype structure.

These findings are highly relevant for both of the debates mentioned above. With respect to the controversy on linguistic relativism, the findings suggest that language and cognition may sometimes diverge. On the other hand, the debate on boundary vs. prototype based categorization may have to be addressed separately for linguistic as opposed to non-linguistic categories.

These findings are furthermore relevant when considering the discrepancy between concept-based knowledge representation approaches such as spatial calculi and psycholinguistic research. Spatial calculi typically treat projective terms as crisp, mutually exclusive categories that allow for feasible reasoning processes (Renz and Nebel, 2007), contrasting with the psycholinguistic findings on gradedness of spatial concepts. Shedding light on these issues may improve the further development of separate, but interconnected conceptual vs. linguistic ontologies (Bateman et al., 2007) by gaining a better understanding of how a cognitively adequate mapping between the different ontologies may be achieved.

To our knowledge, only Klippel and Montello (2007) have used a grouping task for a non-linguistic categorization assessment of spatial directions. Although their analysis reveals a difference between linguistic and non-linguistic grouping patterns similar to the results by Crawford et al. (2000), Klippel and Montello (2007) do not assess the role the axes played in the participants' conceptualizations of the groups. Also, they address (dynamic) turn direction concepts rather than (static) spatial relationships. With respect to the spatial relation between two locations, the nature of the relationship between linguistic and non-linguistic categories has only been tested on memory tasks.

Moreover, the task settings so far have all been based on schematic depictions, with dots and lines representing spatial directions. Real world relationships between objects are far more complex, often involving extended shapes and functional relationships that lead to distinct effects on verbalization (Carlson and van der Zee, 2005; Zwarts, 2003). It is unknown, so far, if more realistic scenes would lead to similar categorization patterns as found in the abstract settings.

Finally, although a range of findings exist with respect to the verbalization of non-prototypical spatial relationships, no studies so far have addressed systematically just how non-linguistic categories that do not directly correspond to linguistic categories are referred to in language. How will the quadrants in a segmented circle be described? While previous findings show that non-typical spatial relationships lead to more complex spatial expressions (Tenbrink, 2007; Zimmer et al., 1998), these only concern individual relations and do not yield predictions as to how a category might be referred to that encompasses a range of spatial relationships grouped together. Identifying systematic patterns in such references will shed more light on the relation between linguistic and non-linguistic spatial direction concepts. For this purpose, we combine the category construction paradigm using the CatScan tool (Klippel et al., 2013) with Cognitive Discourse Analysis (CODA, Tenbrink, in press) by eliciting unconstrained verbalizations in carefully constrained settings, and analyzing the linguistic data systematically with respect to relevant linguistic features. This concerns not only directly elicited labels for categories but also explicit metacognitive statements about how the grouping was performed, so as to shed more light on principles that participants draw upon for the non-linguistic categorization task.

In a nutshell, our study asks (1) whether spatial relationships between objects shown in a realistic scene will be grouped according to known linguistic principles or in other ways, (2) what kinds of linguistic labels are used for categories that were identified non-linguistically, and (3) what kinds of principles people draw upon and verbalize when asked about the non-linguistic grouping task.

3   Our Study: Linguistic and Non-linguistic Categorization of Spatial Relations

We examine the non-linguistic categorization of spatial relations and its interrelation with verbal expression, employing a framework we previously developed for analysis of humans' intuitive spatio-temporal concepts (Klippel et al., 2013). The central component is CatScan, a software we designed to administer category construction experiments (Medin et al., 1987) in which the participant has to sort icons into groups (Figure 1). Neither the groups nor their number are predetermined and the participant is instructed to group the icons based on how similar they are (details in Section 3.3). The software is designed to be compatible with the Amazon Mechanical Turk (AMT)[1] crowdsourcing environment. By employing AMT, the challenge of recruiting an adequate participant pool is reduced significantly. AMT has gained widespread recognition in the scientific community with its demonstrated reliability, efficiency, and comparability with lab experiments. Additionally, research on the demographics of AMT workers has shown that general population characteristics are better reflected compared to classic on-campus lab experiments (Ross et al., 2010).

In our studies, a reference object R and a target object T were positioned on a table. Since we were aiming for realistic scenarios, scenes were shown either in a photograph, or in a rendered image of a 3d scene model. R and T were either a blue and a yellow ball, respectively, or two mugs of different colors, yielding three different conditions. Figure 2 shows the three types of stimuli used in the study.

---

[1] https://www.mturk.com/mturk/

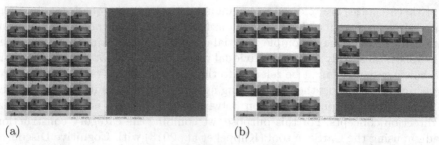

Fig. 1. (a) Screenshot of the CatScan interface at the beginning of the main study. (b) Screenshot of the interface of an ongoing mock-up trial.

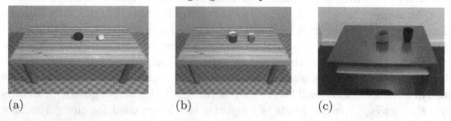

(a)   (b)   (c)

Fig. 2. (a) Yellow and blue ball in 3d model rendering. (b) Red and blue mug in 3d model rendering. (c) Black and blue mug in photograph.

3.1 Stimuli

For each condition (balls/mugs in model, mugs in photograph), 80 images were created. The model-based images were rendered using POV-ray[2]. The photographs were created by manipulating a physical scene and taking images of different configurations of reference object R and target object T while keeping all camera settings identical. In all images, R was a blue object (mug or ball, accordingly), while T had different colors (yellow ball, red mug, black mug). All mugs were displayed without a handle to avoid effects of handle position. Both objects were placed on a table. The table was placed in the scene such that the camera was oriented towards the center of the table surface, looking down onto the table. As Figure 2 shows, the different types of stimuli were presented from the same perspective horizontally. The camera was always positioned in front of the table with a 90° angle. Vertical camera position and field of view were slightly varied. R (blue mug/ball) was placed exactly in the center of the table surface. T (yellow ball, red mug, black mug) was placed onto the table with equal distance to R in all images of the same image type. The angle increases in steps of 4.5°.

The effects of differences in stimulus presentation will be subject to further study, but are of no relevance for the work presented here. Thus, all three conditions are analyzed jointly for current purposes.

---

[2] http://www.povray.org/

3.2   Participants

We recruited 59 participants using AMT. Of these participants, 16 were excluded based on responses to the follow-up verbal task: We excluded participants who reported that they grouped the images based on criteria other than direction (e.g. distance or randomly) or whose category descriptions were inconsistent with the labels such that they indicated contradictory directions. We also excluded participants who created several categories for exactly the same direction and participants who provided incomplete systems, for example using seven cardinal directions S, SW, W, NW, N, NE, E, but lacking SE. Although the latter may in fact be a legitimate non-linguistic grouping, inspection of the individual cases showed that most of these cases were signs of carelessness or difficulty with the task. In order to be consistent, we removed all participants with incomplete systems. Of the remaining 43 participants, 21 were female and 22 male. The average age was 33.07 (maximum age: 60, minimum age: 19).

3.3   Procedure

Individual studies were posted to AMT's webpage. AMT workers were given a unique participant number and instructed to download and run CatScan. Participants were required to enter their demographic information (age, gender, native language, and educational background) and read the study instructions which introduced the basics of the study. To ensure that the participants read and understood the instructions, they were only allowed to proceed after a certain time and had to answer a question about the instructions. In a warm-up task, participants were then acquainted with the interface and the idea of category construction by sorting animals into groups. In the main study, all 80 images were initially displayed in the left panel on the screen. Participants had to sort the images into categories they created on the right panel of the screen (see Figure 1 for a mock-up trial). Once all images were sorted into the categories, participants had to do a follow-up task in which they were presented with the groups they created, one group at a time, and asked to provide a short label (no more than five words) and a detailed description providing reasons for their categories. In addition, they had to select the most representative image for every group they had created. Upon the completion of the second part, CatScan generated a zip file that participants then had to upload to AMT. The zip file contained log files, grouping results, and linguistic descriptions.

4   Results

4.1   Analysis of Segmentation Types

Based on the verbal labels and descriptions provided by the participants, we annotated the groups created for basic segmentation types: we annotated whether participants divided the relations into four cones, four quadrants, eight cones, or segmented directions in some other way. In two cases, participants did not provide descriptive labels (e.g. numbering categories). For those participants, the detailed descriptions were considered for this analysis. In the following, we describe the different segmentation types and give examples for each type.

We counted as *4-cone segmentation* all cases where directions were split into exactly four groups, typically labeled with simple linguistic direction terms coinciding with the four prototypical axes of 0°, 90°,180° and 270°. Example 1 shows a typical set of labels for participants using this segmentation. A *4-quadrant segmentation* was identified when exactly four categories with labels using combined linguistic direction terms were created, as in Example 2. An *8-cone segmentation* was identified when exactly 8 categories with labels using simple and combined linguistic direction terms were created, as in Example 3.

(1) *South* **vs.** *West* **vs.** *East* **vs.** *North* (P 12100022)

(2) *Upper Left Quadrant* **vs.** *Upper Right Quadrant* **vs.** *Lower Left Quadrant* **vs.** *Lower Right Quadrant* (P 12020036)

(3) *In Front* **vs.** *In Back* **vs.** *To the Left* **vs.** *To the Right* **vs.** *Diagonal Back Right* **vs.** *Diagonal Front Right* **vs.** *Diagonal Back Left* **vs.** *Diagonal Front Left* (P 12100009)

Finally, all cases that did not match any of the segmentation types described above were counted as *Other*. These were half plane-based segmentations, segmentations that conflated opposite directions into one category, and full clock segmentations creating 12 categories according to the hour positions of the clock.

We compared the results of this verbal-label based analysis to a clustering of the non-verbal segmentation behavior in order to verify whether these were indeed coherent segmentation types. Similarity values for each pair of participants were derived by summing up over the pairs of icons that were placed in the same group by one but not the other participant. Ward's method was then used to cluster participants based on these similarity values. Table 1 shows the relationship between segmentation types identified on the basis of verbal as opposed to non-verbal (clustering) data. When two clusters are assumed, all quadrant segmentations fall neatly into one cluster, while all 4-cone segmentations fall into the other cluster. The 8-cone segmentations are divided between both clusters. Finer segmentation with 4 clusters separates the 4-cone segmentations from the 8-cone segmentations, and yields a separate cluster of 3 segmentations annotated as *Other*. Even when allowing a larger number of clusters, the four deviant 8-cone segmentations remain in one category with with the 4-quadrant segmentations. Closer inspection of individual participants' data showed that this was due to them not being true cone segmentations, but rather form a separate segmentation type: an extension of 4-quadrant segmentations with additional narrow categories for each boundary axis between quadrants. Thus, these four cases will be subsumed under the category *Other* in the following tables.

In summary, we verified three major segmentation types, 4-cluster, 4-cone, and 8-cone through combining linguistic and non-linguistic analysis. The large proportion of segmentations subsumed under *Other* shows that there is great variability with respect to segmentation types. For the remainder of this paper, our discussion mainly focuses on the 26 participants who conformed to one of the main patterns, since these are theoretically the most interesting. The fact that there are further possibilities and a wide range of individual creativity does not call the existence of the main types into question. Further analysis of the less frequent segmentation types would be highly interesting in order to gain insights into the full range of possibilities of human category formation. As this would require further data in order to obtain a sufficient number of cases for each of the respective categories, it is left for future research.

Table 1. Correspondence of segmentation types derived from analysis of verbal data with clusters of similar participant behaviour from the grouping task.

	2 Clusters		3 Clusters		4 Clusters	
	1	2	1 2	3	1 2 3	4
4C	0	9	0 9	0	0 0 9	0
4Q	11	0	11 0	0	11 0 0	0
8C	4	6	4 6	0	4 6 0	0
Other	7	6	4 6	3	4 4 2	3

4.2   Analysis of Verbalization Types

In order to determine how the identified segmentation types relate to linguistic categories, we annotated which system of direction terms was used in the category labels. Four main verbalization types were identified: *horizontal projective terms* describing lateral and frontal (i.e., horizontal) axes on a plane (Example 4), *vertical projective terms* denoting vertical relationships (Example 5), *clock terms* which use the hour or minute hand of a clock (Example 6), and *cardinal directions*, i.e., compass terms (Example 7). Other terms, such as angles or mixed verbalizations, were categorized as *Other*.

(4)   *to the right of the blue mug* **vs.** *in front of the blue mug* **vs.** *to the left of the blue mug* **vs.** *behind the blue mug* (P 12040018)

(5)   *To the left* **vs.** *Right side* **vs.** *Bottom group* **vs.** *Top group* (P 12100013)

(6)   *12:00 to 2:59* **vs.** *3:00 to 5:59* **vs.** *6:00 to 8:59* **vs.** *9:00 to 11:59* (P 12090003)

(7)   *South* **vs.** *West* **vs.** *East* **vs.** *North* (P 12100022)

Table 2 shows the number of participants using the different types of verbalization by segmentation type. Standard projective terms are more frequent than other systems. Overall, the results show that preferences for different segmentation strategies are fairly evenly distributed. However, projective terms are particularly frequent in the *Other* category, indicating that they are flexibly applicable to many different segmentation types.

Accordingly, there is no one-to-one correspondence between segmentation types and verbalizations. The two most frequent types, 4-cone and 4-quadrant, occur with all major verbalization types, and the 6 instances of 8-cone segmentation occur with all verbalization types except for clock verbalization.

Table 2. Frequency of the different verbalization types by segmentation type

	4 Cones	4 Quadrants	8 Cones	Other	Total
Horizontal Proj.	3	4	2	7	16
Vertical Proj.	1	2	1	6	10
Clock	2	2	0	1	5
Cardinal	3	1	3	0	7
Other	0	2	0	3	5
Total	9	11	6	17	43

4.3   Verbal Analysis of Category Structure

Going beyond the category labels, we performed an analysis of the verbal descriptions participants gave to clarify the rationale behind their categorization decisions. We analyzed these metacognitive statements for content and linguistic markers indicating prototype versus boundary conceptualization. As Tenbrink (in press) argues, language provides humans with a network of options, allowing them to refer to a given situation in one of several possible ways. While speakers may not even be aware of those choices, they give an insight into the underlying conceptual perspective (Schober, 1998). For example, referring to the same spatial configuration as either "the blue cup is in the bottom-left quadrant" or "the blue cup is to the south-west of the red cup" construes the cup as being contained in a region in the first case, while it is construed as being positioned in a certain direction in the second case. Each kind of expression highlights a different aspect of the situation, thus allowing the conclusion that this aspect is relevant to the way the speaker perceives the situation.

In our analysis, in order to avoid distortions due to different verbosity or repetitiveness of answers, we did not count individual occurrences of markers, but rather the number of participants who used a type of marker at least once.

Markers of Boundary-Based Conceptualization. We identified the following markers for boundary-based conceptualization in the data:

Dividing: On the content level, many participants explicitly mentioned dividing space into quadrants or segments (see Example 8). This is a very clear indicator for boundary-based conceptualization. We counted all participants as explicitly mentioning a dividing strategy if they at least once used a verb with the semantics of dividing (divide/ split/ segment/ separate) in relation to the space around the reference object (8a) or the spatial relations (8b).

Boundaries: Some participants made this even more explicit by mentioning specific boundary lines, angles or positions (see Example 9). We counted participants as explicitly mentioning boundaries if they at least once used a *between* relationship to explain which images were put in a category (9a), or if they mentioned drawing imaginary boundary lines (9b), or when they described specific spatial positions or angles serving as an excluding criterion (9c) for the category.

Containment: Finally, a linguistic marker of boundary-based conceptualization was describing the location of the target as a containment relation with respect to a region (see example 10) using prepositions such as *in* (10a), *within* (10b), or *on* (10c) and a region term such as *area* (10c) or *quadrant* (10a). While a containment relation does not per se exclude prototypes or vague boundaries, we consider it to be indicative of boundary conceptualization, as it constitutes the alternative to a projective relation which emphasizes the aspect of directionality, as usually depicted by an arrow, and consistently shows prototype effects (Crawford et al., 2000; Gapp, 1995; Hayward and Tarr, 1995; Huttenlocher et al., 1991; Vorwerg and Tenbrink, 2007; Zimmer et al., 1998). The containment relation, on the other hand, emphasizes the aspect of containment in a region, and thus de-emphasizes any gradual differences within the region.

(8)   Explicit mention of dividing into quadrants/segments

    a. *I divided the area into a quadrant plane* (P 12080029)

    b. *using the blue ball as the center, I divided them into quarters (like the hours on a clock face).* (P 12020022)

(9)   Mentioning of boundaries

    a. *They were all between 3:00 and 6:00* (P 12020022)

    b. *I made an imaginary line on the table both along the length and width going through the blue mug and then asked whether or not it would be in the furthest left quadrant.* (P 12080018)

    c. *Whenever the yellow ball was below the blue ball and less than 45° to either side I considered it to be on the bottom.* (P 12020023)

(10)   Containment relation

    a. *The yellow balls are in the northwest quadrant of the table with regards to blue being the center.* (P 12020026)

    b. *with the blue mug as the 0 on the coordinate axis.,All of the black mugs were within the bottom right quadrant of the coordinate planes in relation to the blue mug.* (P 12080005)

    c. *Red cup is located on the area I called lower right quadrent.* (P 12040016)

Markers of Prototype-Based Conceptualization. We identified the following markers of prototype-based conceptualization in the data:

Direction: We counted participants as explicitly mentioning direction if they either mentioned direction as a categorization criterion (Example 11a), or used the term "direction" to explicitly mark the spatial relation between the target object T and the reference object R as a direction (Example 11b).

Projection: While boundary conceptualization is characterized by containment relations (see above), prototype conceptualization is characterized by projective relations. We counted participants as using projective relations if they expressed a projective relation between T and R at least once. We did not consider relations between an area and R, only those which located the target object T itself. In the data, projective relations were mainly realized as prepositions or preposition groups (Example 12).

Vagueness: While boundary-based concepts tend to be crisp, prototype-based concepts are by definition vague. This can be expressed by vagueness markers such as *mostly, roughly,* or *approximately* (Example 13). This was scored if participants used a vagueness marker to modify the location of T at least once, either by directly modifying a projective term (13a) with T as the locatum, or by elaborating on such a relation using a vagueness marker (13b) or a vague exclusion criterion (13c). In contrast to the exclusion criteria which are defining for boundary-based conceptualization, vague exclusion criteria do not specify a concrete line or angle or point. Rather, they specify some criterion which is vaguely tied to a direction or distance relation to an environmental feature.

Comparatives: Another way to indicate vagueness of boundaries is to use comparatives and superlatives when describing the location of T (Example 14), for example by saying that it is *closest to* a certain prototype, or *closer to* it than to another (14a), or by using an environmental feature to serve as a prototype, and using relative closeness to this feature to define directions (14b).

(11) Direction

    a. *I decided to group by direction.* (P 12020030)

    b. *Any yellow ball that was facing the North East direction away from the blue ball was considered for this group.* (P 12020024)

(12) Projective relations

    a. *Above the blue mug slightly angled* (P 12080020)

    b. *If the black mug was almost straight to the left of the blue mug* (P 12080012)

(13) Vagueness

    a. *any picture where the black mug was in approximately a west, west-southwest, or west-northwest position (P 15998256)*

    b. *Above the blue mug slightly angled* (P 12080020)

    c. *I chose icons that had the black mug to the right of the blue mug, but not too far up or down* (P 12080025)

(14) Comparatives

    a. *I picked the mugs in this group that were the westernmost mugs in relation to the blue mug.* (P 12080008)

    b. *the black mug was closer to the front of the desk* (P 12090005)

Table 3 shows the total number of participants using either no markers at all, or at least one marker of boundary and/or prototype conceptualizations in their detailed category descriptions in relation to the segmentation types. As the table shows, almost all participants used markers of at least one of the conceptualizations (41 out of 43). All participants who segmented according to quadrants used boundary markers, while only few of them used prototype markers. Conversely, participants who used cone segmentation predominantly used prototype

Table 3. Number of participants using markers of boundary and/or prototype conceptualization in their group descriptions, grouped by segmentation types.

	4 Cones	4 Quadrants	8 Cones	Other	Total
none	0	0	0	2	2
prototype	4	0	6	11	21
boundary	1	8	0	1	10
both	4	3	0	3	10
Total	9	11	6	17	43

Table 4. Usage of the different markers of prototype and boundary-based conceptualization in their group descriptions by segmentation types. Each participant may have used none, one, or several types of markers, therefore column-totals do not represent number of participants.

	4 Cones	4 Quadrants	8 Cones	Other	Total
divide	2	2	0	1	5
boundaries	2	4	0	3	9
containment	2	9	0	3	14
Total Boundary	6	15	0	7	28
direction	0	0	1	2	3
projection	6	3	6	12	27
vagueness	4	0	5	8	17
comparative	0	1	1	3	5
Total Prototype	10	4	13	25	52

markers, a tendency which is more strongly expressed for the 8-cone segmentation which co-occurs only with prototype markers. For the 4-cone segmentation, either prototype or a mix of prototype and boundary markers were found, while one participant used boundary markers only. Although these are clear tendencies, the results show that there is no strict one-to-one correspondence of prototype vs. boundary conceptualization to segmentation type: in all segmentation types except for the 8-cone segmentation, there are participants who used markers of both conceptualizations.

Table 4 shows a more detailed view of the occurrence of markers of prototype- and boundary-based conceptualization with the different segmentation types. The clearest indicators of prototype-based conceptualization are vagueness and projective terms, while comparatives and explicit mention of direction play virtually no role due to their rare occurrence. Quadrant-based segmentation coincided with some projective relations and one comparative, but none of the other features. The most dominant indicator of a quadrant segmentation is the use of a containment relation to describe the location of the target object. This marker only co-occurred very rarely with cone-based segmentation. The explicit mention of boundaries was only slightly more frequent for quadrant segmentation than for the other types, and explicit mention of dividing lines was fairly infrequent overall, and also not limited to quadrant-based segmentation.

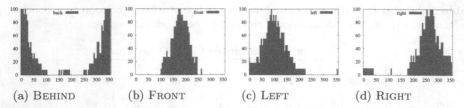

Fig. 3. Structure of simple term categories. X-axis represents angles starting with 0 at prototypical BEHIND, and increasing counter-clockwise. Y-axis represents percentage of occurring groups of the respective category containing the image with that angle.

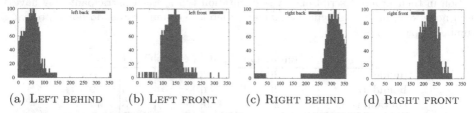

Fig. 4. Relative frequency of occurrence of each angle in complex term categories

4.4   Visual Analysis of Category Structure

Based on the analysis of verbalization types, we conclude that different types of direction terms such as *left,right,front,back* or *north,south,east,west* do not correspond to different segmentation types. On the other hand, the analysis of markers for conceptualizations suggests that the central axes—0°, 90°, 180° and 270°—play a crucial role for both quadrant and cone segmentation. To further verify this claim, we combined data from all types of direction terms across all types of segmentation and compared the angular spread of those categories which are expressed by simple direction terms such as *left* or *west* (simple term categories) with that of categories which are expressed by complex direction terms such as *left-front* or *southwest* (complex term categories). For the sake of simplicity, we named the directions according to horizontal projective terms, though we use small caps spelling to indicate that these are the underlying (linguistic) concepts, and not the actual verbalizations.

Figure 3 shows that for simple term concepts, there is a small frequency peak around the established prototypes of 0°, 90°, 180° and 270°, and gradually decreasing frequency of inclusion with further distance from the prototype. The extremes of all concepts except for FRONT lie about 200° apart, confirming the large variance of boundaries. FRONT shows the same overall pattern, although its maximal range is slightly narrower than that of the other concepts. This indicates that participants associated a wide variety of non-linguistic categories with simple term linguistic concepts, all centered around the prototype, but varying in extension depending on the segmentation strategy used.

On the other hand, the complex term concepts show little boundary variation (Figure 4) with a high plateau and a steep drop approximately at the central axes, supporting the assumption that those combined term concepts are mostly defined by their boundaries, and therefore cannot be appropriately used for many different segmentation strategies. The variation within the plateau is most probably due to the influence of the 8-cone segmentation, which seems to use additional intermediate prototypes.

5   Discussion and Conclusion

We have presented a category construction study in which participants sorted images of object configurations into groups of similar spatial relationships. Our findings reveal that the available space was segmented mostly into either four cones, four quadrants, or eight cones. These segments did not correspond directly to any specific types of verbal labels (horizontal or vertical projective, clock-based, cardinal) that participants assigned to their categories; in that sense, no simple one-to-one correspondence between linguistic and non-linguistic categories could be found. However, only four-cone segments were represented by simple terms such as *left* or *north*, reflecting the fact that four basic spatial directions can easily be expressed in language (e.g., using sets such as *left, right, front, behind* or the compass terms). Other concepts that do not directly correspond to this kind of linguistic set, such as a more fine-grained segmentation of space (into 8 cones) or a quadrant-based segmentation, require more complex spatial descriptions. This matches well with the literature on complex and non-standard spatial relationships (Vorwerg, 2003; Zimmer et al., 1998).

More surprisingly, our linguistic analysis of metacognitive strategy verbalizations revealed that the different segmentation types related to fundamentally distinct categorization concepts. Cone-based segmentation was associated with *prototypes*, and quadrant-based segmentation with *boundaries*. Linguistically, prototype-based categories were almost exclusively verbalized as a *projective* relation between two objects, while boundary-based categories were mostly verbalized as a *containment* relation between object and a region. The visual analysis of grouping patterns confirmed the existence of these two distinct types of categorization in simple vs. combined linguistic term concepts. Both were dominated by the four major axes of 0°, 90°, 180°, and 270°, albeit in different ways: in one case they served as prototypes, in the other as boundaries. The 8-cone segmentation appeared to make use of additional secondary prototypes.

Thus, our results support earlier findings by Crawford et al. (2000); Klippel and Montello (2007) and Huttenlocher et al. (1991) about the dual role of the major axes in different categorization types. However, since their research did not include any analysis of language used to describe these two category concepts, the relationship between verbalization and conceptualization had not been addressed. Our findings show for the first time how categorization relates to two fundamentally distinct types of concepts expressed in spatial language: containment vs. direction. As highlighted by Bateman et al. (2010), these two types of terms are based on ontologically distinct spatial concepts and as a consequence exhibit distinct linguistic patterns. We conclude that rather than reflecting linguistic versus non-linguistic direction categories, prototype and boundary based categorization are two separate non-linguistic strategies of dividing space, each with its own suitable verbalization strategy.

Acknowledgements. Funding by the Deutsche Forschungsgemeinschaft (DFG) for the SFB/TR 8 Spatial Cognition, project I5-[DiaSpace] and the National Science Foundation under grant number #0924534 is gratefully acknowledged.

References

Bateman, J., Tenbrink, T., Farrar, S.: The role of conceptual and linguistic ontologies in interpreting spatial discourse. Discourse Processes 44(3), 175–212 (2007)

Bateman, J.A., Hois, J., Ross, R.J., Tenbrink, T.: A linguistic ontology of space for natural language processing. Artif. Intell. 174(14), 1027–1071 (2010)

Bierwisch, M., Schreuder, R.: From concepts to lexical items. Cognition 42, 23–60 (1992)

Carlson, L.A., van der Zee, E. (eds.): Functional features in language and space: Insights from perception, categorization and development. Oxford University Press, Oxford (2005)

Crawford, L.E., Regier, T., Huttenlocher, J.: Linguistic and non-linguistic spatial categorization. Cognition 75(3), 209–235 (2000)

Gapp, K.P.: An empirically validated model for computing spatial relations. In: Wachsmuth, I., Brauer, W., Rollinger, C.-R. (eds.) KI 1995. LNCS, vol. 981, pp. 245–256. Springer, Heidelberg (1995)

Hayward, W.G., Tarr, M.J.: Spatial language and spatial representation. Cognition 55, 39–84 (1995)

Herzog, G.: Coping with static and dynamic spatial relations. In: Amsili, P., Borillo, M., Vieu, L. (eds.) Proc. of TSM 1995, Time, Space, and Movement: Meaning and Knowledge in the Sensible World, pp. 47–59 (1995)

Hickmann, M., Hendriks, H.: Static and dynamic location in French and English. First Language 26(1), 103–135 (2006)

Huttenlocher, J., Hedges, L.V., Duncan, S.: Categories and particulars: Prototype effects in estimating spatial location. Psychological Review 98(3), 352 (1991)

Klippel, A., Montello, D.R.: Linguistic and nonlinguistic turn direction concepts. In: Winter, S., Duckham, M., Kulik, L., Kuipers, B. (eds.) COSIT 2007. LNCS, vol. 4736, pp. 354–372. Springer, Heidelberg (2007)

Klippel, A., Wallgrün, J.O., Yang, J., Mason, J.S., Kim, E.-K., Mark, D.M.: Fundamental cognitive concepts of space (and time): Using cross-linguistic, crowdsourced data to cognitively calibrate modes of overlap. In: Tenbrink, T., Stell, J., Galton, A., Wood, Z. (eds.) COSIT 2013. LNCS, vol. 8116, pp. 377–396. Springer, Heidelberg (2013)

Levinson, S.C., Kita, S., Haun, D.B., Rasch, B.H.: Returning the tables: Language affects spatial reasoning. Cognition 84, 155–188 (2002)

Li, P., Gleitman, L.: Turning the tables: Language and spatial reasoning. Cognition 83, 265–294 (2002)

Logan, G.D., Sadler, D.D.: A computational analysis of the apprehension of spatial relations. In: Bloom, P., Peterson, M., Nadell, L., Garrett, M. (eds.) Language and Space, pp. 493–529. MIT Press (1996)

Medin, D.L., Wattenmaker, W.D., Hampson, S.E.: Family resemblance, conceptual cohesiveness, and category construction. Cognitive Psychology 19(2), 242–279 (1987)

Mervis, C.B., Rosch, E.: Categorization of natural objects. Annual Review of Psychology 32, 89–115 (1981)

Renz, J., Nebel, B.: Qualitative spatial reasoning using constraint calculi. In: Aiello, M., Pratt-Hartmann, I.E., van Benthem, J.F.A.K. (eds.) Handbook of Spatial Logics, pp. 161–215. Springer (2007)

Ross, J., Irani, L., Silberman, M.S., Zaldivar, A., Tomlinson, B.: Who are the crowdworkers? Shifting demographics in mechanical turk. In: CHI EA 2010 Extended Abstracts on Human Factors in Computing Systems, pp. 2863–2872 (2010)

Schober, M.F.: Different kinds of conversational perspective-taking. In: Fussell, S.R., Kreuz, R.J. (eds.) Social and Cognitive Psychological Approaches to Interpersonal Communication. Lawrence Erlbaum, Mahwah (1998)

Smith, E.E., Medin, D.L.: Categories and Concepts. Harvard University Press, Cambridge (1981)

Taylor, J.: Linguistic Categorization. Clarendon, Oxford (1989)

Tenbrink, T.: Space, time, and the use of language: An investigation of relationships. Mouton de Gruyter, Berlin (2007)

Tenbrink, T.: Reference frames of space and time in language. Journal of Pragmatics 43(3), 704–722 (2011)

Tenbrink, T.: Cognitive discourse analysis: Accessing cognitive representations and processes through language data. Language and Cognition (in press)

Vorwerg, C.: Use of reference directions in spatial encoding. In: Freksa, C., Brauer, W., Habel, C., Wender, K.F. (eds.) Spatial Cognition III. LNCS (LNAI), vol. 2685, pp. 321–347. Springer, Heidelberg (2003)

Vorwerg, C., Tenbrink, T.: Discourse factors influencing spatial descriptions in English and German. In: Barkowsky, T., Knauff, M., Ligozat, G., Montello, D.R. (eds.) Spatial Cognition 2007. LNCS (LNAI), vol. 4387, pp. 470–488. Springer, Heidelberg (2007)

Whorf, B.: Language, thought, and reality: Selected writings of Benjamin Lee Whorf. The M.I.T. Press, Cambridge (1956) (Edited by John Carrol)

Zimmer, H.D., Speiser, H.R., Baus, J., Blocher, A., Stopp, E.: The use of locative expressions in dependence of the spatial relation between target and reference object in two-dimensional layouts. In: Freksa, C., Habel, C., Wender, K.F. (eds.) Spatial Cognition 1998. LNCS (LNAI), vol. 1404, pp. 223–240. Springer, Heidelberg (1998)

Zwarts, J.: Vectors across spatial domains: from place to size, orientation, shape, and parts. In: van der Zee, E., Slack, J. (eds.) Representing Direction in Language and Space, pp. 39–68. Oxford University Press, Oxford (2003)

Spatial Language in Brazilian Portuguese as Perceived by the General Upper Model

Rodrigo de Oliveira

University of Aberdeen, UK
rodrigodeoliveira@abdn.ac.uk

Abstract. The Generalized Upper Model (GUM) is a framework used to map semantic concepts under natural languages structures. GUM has been successfully tested for expressions of spatial concepts, i.e. *spatial language*, in English and German. This paper describes an application of GUM for Brazilian Portuguese, highlighting the following findings specific for that language: GUM provided plausible semantic mappings for almost all the corpus, which also revealed spatial language in Brazilian Portuguese to be highly underspecified.

1 Introduction

We can communicate the position or movement of something, via a natural language expression of space; in other words, by producing *spatial language*. This is a trivial task for humans, but understanding this complex cognitive-linguistic process in depth, so that we may design a model for computational systems, is far from simple.

Geometric accounts have been predominant in spatial language studies [1,2,3]. In general, these theories associate a spatial marker – often a preposition – to some prototypical spatial meaning. In Herskovits' account, "X is in Y if and only if a part of X is spatially included in Y" (p. 342); this idealised description is likely the best match in case of 'the water in the glass' but a doubtful semantics for 'the bird in the tree', even though natural language is flexible enough to express different geometric situations by means of the same lexical item: *in*.

Such flexibility and the starting point in geometry to explain spatial language forced these accounts to admit overhead processes in order to fully cover the use of spatial markers: Herskovits speaks of *sense shifts* (p. 355), Kracht of semantic *approximations* (p. 37), and Francez and Steedman of *shift functions* (p. 394).

Perceiving that natural language utterances do not necessarily commit to pure geometrical truths, Bateman et al. [4] propose a two-step process to ground language on space: on one side, a conceptual ontology informs *what* idea is being conveyed, and at the natural language end, the General Upper Model (GUM) [5] – a linguistic ontology – suggests *how* or *how much* to express. This division betwen concept and utterance is paramount to help us (and computers) understand that language is not a passive medium that simply mirrors the world as it is; rather, it is an active system that construes the world in the description process [6].

C. Freksa et al. (Eds.): Spatial Cognition 2014, LNAI 8684, pp. 108–120, 2014.

Thus GUM receives an expansion devoted solely to spatial expressions: GUM-Space [6]. The most up-to-date stage of GUM was firstly tested by analysing spatial language in English and German. Aiming at verifying the applicability of the ontology also to a Romance Language, we employed GUM to analyse spatial language in Brazilian Portuguese.

2   A Linguistic Ontology

GUM has two main concepts for spatial language purposes: Configuration and SpatialModality, the former being the type of spatial fact and the latter the type of spatial relationship – often a *spatial marker* on the surface – between localised and location. Examples of configuration are SpatialLocating (*the cat is in the box*) and NonAffectingOrientationChange (*turn left*). Examples of Spatial-Modality are Proximal (*at*) and AboveProjectionInternal (*top*). The cat example may be annotated as:

```
SpatialLocating
    locatum SimpleThing 'cat' (the cat)
    processInConfiguration Process 'be' (is)
    placement GeneralizedLocation (in the box)
        hasSpatialModality Containment (in)
        relatum SimpleThing 'box' (the box)
```

Other spatial situations may differ from the cat example in geometrical arrangement considerably, but language may preserve the same semantic arrangement. This is the case of: (a) a light bulb in a socket (in the ceiling), (b) a bird in a tree, (c) a spoon in a mug (with some of its body 'sticking out'), (d) a crack in a vase or (e) a chair in the corner [1]. Is the object entirely or only partially 'inside' the location? Is the object inside the actual body of the location or in its vault? The job of GUM is to inform why *in* was used in all cases, even though geometrical dispositions vary so much.

3   A Corpus of Spatial Language in Brazilian Portuguese

In the previous section, we described the linguistic ontology GUM and what it is intended for. In this section, we describe the dataset we collected to test the suitability of GUM to map spatial semantics under Brazilian Portuguese utterances. We label this dataset the *Curitiba Corpus*.

The data for this project was extracted from the tourist guide *Guia Essencial de Curitiba* [1] (Essential Guide to Curitiba), containing many localisations and routes. This small-sized book has approximately 130 pages with few short paragraphs per page and yielded over 300 instances initially judged to carry some spatial semantics.

---

[1] http://blogdapulp.wordpress.com/guias-de-viagem/
guia-essencial-de-curitiba/

We cleaned original sentences maintaining only the information that directly reflected participants of the spatial proposition, such as localised object, event and location. The following example illustrates this process:

Original *Após a Independência do Brasil, em 1822, chegaram várias levas de imigrantes europeus, árabes e orientais, principalmente alemães, italianos, poloneses, libaneses, ucranianos e japoneses.* [After Brazil's Independence, in 1822, several waves of immigrants (European, Arab, Oriental, German mostly, Italian, Polish, Lebanese, Ukrainian, Japanese) arrived.]
Corpus Instance *várias levas chegaram* [several waves arrived]

The initial set of instances still did not correspond to the final set, the fully annotated *Curitiba Corpus*[2]. The corpus got refined in the annotation process, as we gained more understanding of the nuances of spatial language in Brazilian Portuguese and how this is anchored in the ontology.

4   Refining the Corpus

In the previous section, we described the general shape of the *Curitiba Corpus* and whence the data came. At first, it might seem a trivial task to collect spatial language examples, but as usual, borderline cases appear quickly and often. In this section, we describe how the systematicity of GUM helped us to identify borderline cases, i.e. how to tell true spatial language from apparent spatial language.

4.1   Non-spatial Attribution vs. Spatial Attribution

Utterances containing places do not always compose spatial configurations:

(1)   gato de Ipanema
       cat of Ipanema

       'Ipanema cat'

Instance 1 refers to some cat and provides further attributive information about the cat. Thereby some idea of space is conveyed by the lexical item *Ipanema*[3] but not by its lexicogrammatical structure. If the instance were *gato de brinquedo* (toy cat) or *gato de borracha* (rubber cat), instrumental or material semantics would be informed, but no spatial situation would be depicted.

GUM follows the *criterion of grammatical effect* [7], which advocates that a linguistic structure should hold only grammaticised information. Lexical items in isolation ought to be less indicative of a conceptualisation than a lexicogrammatical structure should be, which leads to the traditional distinction between

---

[2] https://docs.google.com/spreadsheet/
ccc?key=0AjjU8ITs-OqudDE1MkZoS19IQWJ2TksONE5ONFhrZEE
[3] A neighborhood in the city of Rio de Janeiro, Brazil.

closed-class words – or function words – and open-class words – or content words. Grammatical structures are much more dependent on function words such as prepositions than on nouns such as places, therefore a potential spatial semantics behind a place such as *Ipanema* is too weak of an evidence to yield a spatial conceptualisation in an isolated <de+noun-group> preposition phrase.

This leads to the conclusion that the preposition *de* is in 1 not a marker of spatial attribution as it is in motion events (*o gato saiu de Ipanema* (the cat left Ipanema)), so utterances such as 1 did not enter the final corpus.

Another borderline case of attribution happens with prepositions *com* (with) and *sem* (without):

(2) uma zona com muitas lojas
     an   area with many   shops
     'an area with many shops'

(3) as lojas ficam sem   ventiladores
     the shops are   without ventilators
     'the shops run out of ventilators'

Just like *de*, the prepositions *com* and *sem* may also conceptualise different realities. Possession and companionship, as well as space, are some of them. The problem with the examples 2 and 3, is that none of them unambiguously construe a spatial relation. Again we suffer from interference of conceptual knowledge; by knowing that areas and shops are potential locations, we quickly deduce that space is the most (perhaps the only) plausible semantics underlying the utterances. Indeed, such an analysis is plausible, but also over-committed. We could replace *shops* in 2 with *names*, and *ventilators* with *suppliers*, and suddenly a spatial configuration is no longer strictly true in either of the cases.

One way of making certain that a spatial relation is the only conceptualisation desired is by including a locative circumstance to such utterances, as in *o campanário com uma bandeira no topo* (the roof with a flag on top). We will discuss cases of alternation between localised and location in section 5.2, but for now, we may conclude that utterances with *com* or *sem* that do not accompany an explicit spatial adjunct – such as 2 or 3 – did not enter our corpus of spatial language.

4.2   Instrument Vehicles vs. Locative Vehicles

Vehicles often seem to be in a spatial relation with movers, given that actors move as vehicles also move:

(4) descer   a   serra de trem no   Serra Verde Express
     go-down the hill   by train in-the Serra Verde Express
     'go down the hill by train in the Serra Verde Express'

As we discussed above, *de* may be a marker of non-spatial concepts. One of them is instrumental function, which seems to be the case when *de* is used with vehicles, as in example 4. The use of em^4, however, strongly speaks in favour of a spatial semantics, given that *em* is vastly present in the corpus as a marker of spatial language (cf. results section 6). Our annotation classifies <de+vehicle> as instrument and <em+vehicle> as locations, so only <em+vehicle> utterances were included in the final corpus.

This reveals an interesting aspect of the lexicogrammar of expressions with vehicles. When vehicles are referred to as instruments, as in *de trem* (by train), the type of entity (train) is lexicalised and no determiner is used. On the other hand, when vehicles are made locations, as in *no Serra Verde Express*, the proper name of the entity (Serra Verde Express) and a determiner are used. This is one further piece of evidence that (spatial) concepts are not encoded in isolated lexical items, but are tightly related to the structure of natural language expressions.

4.3 Non-motion Events vs. Motion Events

Verbs seem to reside in the intersection between closed-class and open-class words. Given that most linguistic semantics is based on event semantics and verbs are reifications of events, we assume verbs to be direct conceptualisations much like prepositions are. In this sense, motion verbs will always construe spatial configurations. Nonetheless, the borderline between motion verbs and other verbs can be very subtle:

(5) para conhecer o   Madolosso
     to   check-out the Madolosso

     'to check out the Madolosso'

(6) quem gosta deve   visitar a   capela
     who   likes should visit   the chapel

     'those who like it should visit the chapel'

(7) a   festa atrai   muita gente
     the   fest   attracts many   people

     'the fest attracts many people'

(8) eles trouxeram as   receitas
     they brought   the recipes

     'they brought the recipes'

The issue is that both examples 5 and 6 inform us of some cognitive event taking place, but only 6 guarantees a motion event (as well as some cognitive event). Thus we may postulate that an uncontextualised checking-out is only a cognitive event, whereas any visiting is automatically a cognitive as well as a motion event. Likewise, *atrair* (attract) in example 7 may imply but not guarantee motion, whereas *trazer* (bring) in 8 always imply motion.

---

[4] The preposition *em* appears in example 4 as the *n-* in *no*, which is a simple morphophonological result of joining the preposition with the determiner *o*.

It should be clear by now that annotating text with GUM can be exclusive, in the sense that a final list of instances maintain only what is strictly verifiable. This is desirable for computational systems, who need to be assertive when making decisions. For this reason, utterances with verbs that only potentially convey motion such as *conhecer* or *atrair* did not enter the final corpus unless some other linguistic structure (e.g. a route preposition phrase) indicated so.

5   Broadening GUM's Coverage

In previous sections we described subtle borderlines between spatial and non-spatial language, which GUM helped to identify. In this section, we present evidence of other lexicogrammatical conceptualisations of space, to which GUM does not provide all necessary concepts to enable a fully successful mapping.

5.1   Accessibility

Currently in GUM, the concept accessibility is a boolean variable, which is enough to map the semantics underlying binary sets of accessibility markers such as those of English {*here*; *there*} or German {*hier*; *dort*}. Once we present a larger set such as that of Portuguese {*aqui*; *aí*; *ali*}, problems arise.

Accessibility semantics is a binary set in GUM, because the reference object is unitary – probably the speaker. In deciding how accessible an object is, the question is how easily reachable this object is by the speaker. Portuguese – as well as Spanish and possibly other Ibero-Romance languages – takes also the hearer into consideration, thus we arrive at three possible accessibility levels – it could have been four. This had already been perceived by Bernardo [8], when she re-defined accessibility in GUM as speaker-high or general-low, but unfortunately the proposed set still contains only two, instead of three elements. We profit from that discussion nonetheless, and suggest another reformulation of accessibility:

accessibility: **speakerHigh** high for speaker, irrelevant for hearer.
accessibility: **hearerHigh** low for speaker, high for hearer.
accessibility: **generalLow** low for both.

The semantics proposed above may be visualised in the following example (9)[5], an online interview by a journalist in Brazil with swimmer Marcelo living in another country:

(9)   Jornal: Como é a natação aí?
       Marcelo: Vou contar um pouco como é a natação daqui(...)

       Newspaper: How is swimming there?
       Marcelo: I'll tell you a little about how swimming here is (...)

---

[5] Instance extracted from *Corpus do Português*, the Portuguese language version of the Brigham Young University corpus: http://www.corpusdoportugues.org/

In 9, the interviewer and interviewee are in different locations, since the interview is carried out on-line. When the journalist refers to some place where the swimmer is at the moment, she uses *aí* to symbolize that this place is not accessible by her but easily reachable by Marcelo. In response, the swimmer uses *aqui* to confirm that the same place is indeed in his vicinity, so he may easily reach it. Note that *aqui* appears within the phonological word *daqui*, as result of contracting preposition (*de*) with adverb (*aqui*).

I order to maintain multilingual consistency, we suggest that accessibility be a parent concept of speakerHigh and speakerLow – very close to how it currently is – but that speakerLow branch to hearerHigh and generalLow, thereby enabling successful accessibility mapping across all languages tested to date.

5.2   Diathesis

The term *diathesis* relates to the possibility of thematic roles surrounding a process, i.e. its arguments, to be associated with different syntactic participants on the surface (cf. [9]). For this reason, literature on the topic of *diathesis alternation* is largely available, in order to discuss what sort of effects are caused, when similar utterances swap semantic roles under the surface[6].

For example, let us observe the following utterances:

(10)   she is cooking pasta

(11)   the pasta is cooking

The situation conceptualised in example 11 is the same conveyed by its canonical version, example 10, although underspecified. The SimpleThing *pasta*, which is the affected entity in any version, was in the first utterance a syntactic object but in the second case, when *cooking* was used as an ergative verb, *pasta* became the subject and the agent *she* disappeared. Diathetic alternations occur also when space is verbalised, as argued by ([12], p. 73):

(12)   the pumps are contained within blockhouse-type structures

(13)   blockhouse-type structures contain pumps

The problem is that we lack a configuration concept in GUM to successfully map the spatial conceptualisation in Matthiessen's example. SpatialLocating is a sub-class of Circumstantial, which by definition requires a Circumstance to fill the spatial relation of the configuration (cf. [13] for details). Recall the cat example in section 2, where *cat* and *box* are SimpleThings and *in the box* a Circumstance. In example 13, SimpleThings (*structures*; *pumps*) lie on both sides of the equation, but no circumstance – such as a preposition phrase – with a dedicated spatial marker – such as a preposition – is composed. The verb itself is the spatial marker and the location becomes the subject. Matthiessen then uses the concept *possession* to map both the above and following instances in his corpus:

---

[6] E.g. [10,9,11]

(14)   Many of the homes have paddocks.

(15)   The ornate interior houses numerous altars devoted to gods of justice.

The above type of utterances in English is what we also observe in our own data of Brazilian Portuguese, as exposed below:

(16)   o   palácio abrigava teatros
       the palace housed   theaters
       'the palace used to house theaters'

(17)   as ruas   são cheias de bares
       the streets are full   of bars
       'the streets are full of bars'

(18)   o   gramado é coberto pela   geada
       the grass   is covered by-the frost
       'the grass is covered by the frost'

Thus we suggest that GUM enables its existing Possession concept – or some other similar concept – to be used for spatial language mapping. Each of the above Brazilian Portuguese examples construcs a spatial possessive relation in the sense that one entity 'has the other somewhere in the vicinity'. In Matthiessen's illustrations, and in all other spatial-possessive examples in his work, the spatial relationship established is specifically that of *containment*, and so he is quick to associate possession and containment automatically.

Observing our data closely and making use of the powerful insight GUM provides us, we suggest moving Mathiessen's analysis one step higher. Containment is an available concept in GUM and it is disjoint with Support. Both are children of Control, which in turn is a *functional* spatial concept. This means that localised entities in containment or support configurations are controlled by their respective locations *for some contextualised purpose*.

The rationale behind not mapping all such utterances with Containment, as Matthiessen did, is so that we avoid overcommitment, since the precise spatial disposition of the relation may be explicit or not. For instance, example 16 would include the concept Containment and 18, Support, both of which are more specific sub-concepts of Control. In the case of 17, the conceptualisation is underspecified, as we cannot determine if *bars* are contained in or supported by *streets*, only that the former are controlled by the latter. Therefore the less specific concept Control seems more appropriate to underlie *full of*.

In technical terms, what GUM needs is a new configuration concept – for instance, with name SpatialPossession – which in turn spawns to other two configuration types that require spatial relations Containment and Support respectively – for instance, ContainmentPossession and SupportPossession. This is necessary because Control, Containment and Support are only the spatial relationships – or SpatialModality concepts – in GUM, not entire localised-relationship-location concepts; these are Configurations (cf. table 1).

The importance of admitting this new spatial configuration node in GUM is so that we enable diathesis to be generated or parsed in systems that use GUM as their linguistic knowledge base. Diathetic alternations are employed in natural language in order to provide more salience to one information or the other. We believe that the very role of diathesis for spatial language is to provide a mechanism with which prominence (*salience*) is swapped between localised and location. Moreover, this mechanism comprises not only passivisation (or activisation) of action clauses, but also the flexibility in constructing copula-verb spatial configurations, where passivisation may be ungrammatical.

Table 1. Annotating diathetic cases with SpatialPossession

possessor	process	possessed	Possession
the palace	*housed*	*theaters*	Containment
the grass	*is covered*	*by the frost*	Support
the streets	*are full of*	*bars*	Possession

Altogether, there were 16 cases in the data (out of 253) that displayed the diathetic configuration type. Since there is currently no concept in GUM to cope with these examples, we were forced to leave these cases outside our annotated corpus, although they inhabit a separate list of 'unmapped cases'. This is, however, surely a cross-linguistic phenomenon, since the same shown for English by Matthiessen has also been found in Brazilian Portuguese, thus one would wish to have the problem approached and resolved within the ontology.

6   A Quantitative Analysis of the *Curitiba Corpus*

In this section, we provide a short quantitative analysis of the corpus by counting lexical items (e.g. verbs) and semantic elements (e.g. configurations, modalities), in order to observe some frequencies of spatial language in Brazilian Portuguese.

Table 2 presents frequencies of lexical items, most often verbs, associated with the event constituent of configurations. Figures mean:

- What spatial configuration types were found (first column).
- How often a configuration type occurred (third column).
- How many different lexical items appeared in each configuration type found (second column).

Table 3 presents frequencies of modalities that appear in some structure (configuration or not). Figures mean:

- What spatial modalities were found (second column).
- How often each modality occurs in total (second last column).
- How often each modality occurs in each structure (middle columns).

As seen in table 2, only two configuration types – SpatialLocating and NonAffectingDirectedMotion – account for over 3/4 of all spatial configurations in the corpus. Remember that the corpus has 237 instances of spatial language but 110 of those are smaller structures such as a GeneralizedLocation("at the square"). Now we are observing only those 127 that are full configurations ("the shops are at the square").

SpatialLocating configurations, as in X is at Y, is the second most frequent spatial configuration type in the corpus. Despite being so frequent, the distribution of different lexical items that associate with the event marker – mostly the verbal group – is very low in SpatialLocatings. Only 2 in every 10 instances required a different lexical item to express the event. If compared to NonAffectingDirectedMotion (as in X goes to Y), the most frequent spatial configuration in the corpus, twice as much lexical variety occurred. This implies that the same event-related lexical items are more reused in static spatial situations (e.g. is, is located, lives, than in dynamic events (e.g. goes, crosses, turns, walks, brings).

Table 2. Occurrence count of lexical items (LI) – such as verbs – associated with the event constituent of Spatial Configurations (sic or SC)

Spatial Configuration	LI	SC	LI:SC
AffectingMotion	2	2	1.0
AffectingDirectedMotion	6	11	0.5
NonAffectingMotion	10	17	0.6
NonAffectingDirectedMotion	20	57	0.4
NonAffectingOrientationChange	1	1	1.0
SpatialLocating	9	39	0.2
Total	48	127	0.4

The fact that the speaker reuses lexical items for SpatialLocating configurations brings a second implication: that some other position of the static configuration will have to carry the burden of maintaining diversity of spatial relationships in static configurations. This hypothesis was indeed verified, since the element that reifies the spatial relationship – SpatialModality – was nearly 3 times more diverse for static configurations: out of 24, 21 distinct modalities were employed to establish grounds where something is located or some action happens, as opposed to only 9 modalities used to construct all dynamic changes of place in motion events within the corpus (cf. table 3).

The most striking finding concerns a single concept in GUM. In 50.5% of all SpatialModality values, localised and location are depicted as being in some vaguely proximal relation to one another, i.e. the concept Proximal was associated with the surface spatial marker (cf. table 3). This means that very little spatial specification is provided by the speaker (the author of the tourist guide) in communicating the location of things in the world to her interlocutor (the reader), even if the speaker is a tourist guide book, whose purpose is to help the

Table 3. Occurrence count of modalities (lines) per structure (columns). Abbreviations used for spatial modalities: APE: AboveProjectionExternal, API: Above- ProjectionInternal, BPE: BackProjectionExternal, BPI: BackProjectionInternal, Cent: Central, Cont: Containment, DOFC: DenialOfFunctionalControl, Distal: Distal, Distr: Distribution, FPE: FrontProjectionExternal, GDD: GeneralDirectionalDistancing, GDN: GeneralDirectionalNearing, MD: MultipleDirectional, NI: NorthInternal, PR: PathRepresenting, PRI: PathRepresentingInternal, Peri: Peripheral, Prox: Proximal, QnD: QuantitativeDistance, RNPA: RelativeNon- ProjectionAxial, RP: RightProjection, Sur: Surrounding, Topo: TopographicDirectional. Abbreviations used for configurations: ADM: AffectingDirectedMotion , NAM: NonAffectingMotion , NADM: NonAffectingDirectedMotion , NAOC: NonAffectingOrientationChange , SL: SpatialLocating , O: non-spatial others, -: not a configuration, just a smaller structre such as a GeneralizedLocation.

#	Spatial Modality	ADM	NAM	NADM	NAOC	SL	O	-	$\sum$	%
1	APE				1				1	0.5
2	API						3		3	1.5
3	BPE					1			1	0.5
4	BPI				1				1	0.5
5	Cent						1		1	0.5
6	Conn						2		2	1.0
7	Cont			2	2				4	2.0
8	DOFC	1					2		3	1.5
9	Distal				2			1	3	1.5
10	Distr						2	1	3	1.5
11	FPE						2		2	1.0
12	GDD	1		9	2			1	13	6.6
13	GDN	3		27	2				32	16.3
14	MD			1					1	0.5
15	NI						1		1	0.5
18	Peri						1		1	0.5
16	PR	1		10		1	1		13	6.6
17	PRI			3					3	1.5
19	Prox	5	6	4		16	46	22	99	50.5
20	QnD						2	2	4	2.0
21	RP				1				1	0.5
22	RNPA					1	1	2	4	2.0
23	Sur							2	2	1.0
24	Topo			1	1				2	1.0

reader enjoy a city and places within the city in the best way. Walking "around the park" and walking "through the park" can be two very distinct activities for a tourist to do, but this one material that is the source of the Curitiba Corpus bypasses this spatial specificity in half of the cases. This is strong evidence that the discrepancy between the physical world and the linguistically constructed picture of the same world cannot be ignored.

In the majority of cases, the preposition *em* is associated with Proximal; *em* is usually translated as *in, on* or *at*, which are the English language prototypical markers of **Containment, Support** and **Proximal**, respectively. This evidence points to the assumption that Portuguese is likely to be more underspecific than English or German in spatial language, as it enables the speaker to use one single marker (*em*) for several distinct concepts (containment; support; proximity).

7 Conclusions

In this project, we have looked at the linguistic process of conceptualising space in Brazilian Portuguese. We applied concepts of spatial language as provided by the linguistic ontology GUM to annotate a corpus of such expressions. The gains were mutual: by applying the theory proposed in the ontology, we could improve understanding of the complex architecture of spatial language, while also collecting enough evidence to improve the very definitions in the model.

GUM performed extremely well in face of a new challenge, as the model showed to be mostly applicable also for a Romance language, thus suitable for multilingual applications. Of a total of 304 utterances, only 16 (5.3%) remained unmapped, all of which being cases of diathetic alternation. For those cases, a set of new concepts has been proposed. We also proposed a reformulation of GUM's accessibility concept based on evidence found in another corpus.

The excessive use of *em* (almost 40% of all spatial markers in the corpus) shows how imprecise a spatial description in Brazilian Portuguese can be, given that this marker is less precise than the English counterparts - *in, on* and *at*. Together with other markers that blatantly express proximity, annotation with the concept **Proximal** computes half of all spatial relations in the corpus.

References

1. Herskovits, A.: Semantics and pragmatics of locative expressions. Cognitive Science 9(3), 341–378 (1985)
2. Kracht, M.: On the semantics of locatives. Linguistics and Philosophy 25(2), 157–232 (2002)
3. Francez, N., Steedman, M.: Categorial grammar and the semantics of contextual prepositional phrases. Linguistics and Philosophy 29(4), 381–417 (2006)
4. Bateman, J., Tenbrink, T., Farrar, S.: The Role of Conceptual and Linguistic Ontologies in Interpreting Spatial Discourse, vol. 44. Taylor & Francis (2007)
5. Bateman, J., Henschel, R., Rinaldi, F.: The Generalized Upper Model 2.0. In: Proceedings of the ECAI 1994 Workshop: Comparison of Implemented Ontologies (1995)
6. Bateman, J., Hois, J., Ross, R., Tenbrink, T.: A linguistic ontology of space for natural language processing. Artificial Intelligence 174(14), 1027–1071 (2010)
7. Jackendoff, R.: The architecture of the linguistic-spatial interface. In: Language and Space, pp. 1–30. MIT Press (1996)
8. Bernardo, S.: Analysis of the applicability of the Generalized Upper Model framework to Portuguese spatial language. Master's thesis, Universität Bremen (2012)
9. Korhonen, A.: Automatic extraction of subcategorization frames from corpora-Improving filtering with diathesis alternations. In: Keller, B. (ed.) Proceedings of the ESSLLI 1998 Workshop on Automated Acquisition of Syntax and Parsing, University of Sussex, pp. 1–8 (1998)

10. Franchi, C.: Predicação. Revista de Estudos da Linguagem 11(2) (2012)
11. Teich, E., Firzlaff, B., Bateman, J.: Emphatic Generation: Employing the theory of semantic emphasis for text generation. In: COLING 1994, Kyoto, Japan (1994)
12. Matthiessen, C.M.I.M.: The transitivity of space in topographic procedures. ms (1998)
13. Hois, J., Tenbrink, T., Ross, R., Bateman, J.: GUM-Space. The Generalized Upper Model spatial extension: A linguistically-motivated ontology for the semantics of spatial language. Technical Report August, Universität Bremen (2009)

Spatial References with Gaze and Pointing in Shared Space of Humans and Robots

Patrick Renner[1], Thies Pfeiffer[2], and Ipke Wachsmuth[1]

[1] Artificial Intelligence Group
[2] Cognitive Interaction Technology Center of Excellence
Bielefeld University
Universitätsstr. 25, 33615 Bielefeld, Germany

Abstract. For solving tasks cooperatively in close interaction with humans, robots need to have timely updated spatial representations. However, perceptual information about the current position of interaction partners is often late. If robots could anticipate the targets of upcoming manual actions, such as pointing gestures, they would have more time to physically react to human movements and could consider prospective space allocations in their planning.

Many findings support a close eye-hand coordination in humans which could be used to predict gestures by observing eye gaze. However, effects vary strongly with the context of the interaction. We collect evidence of eye-hand coordination in a natural route planning scenario in which two agents interact over a map on a table. In particular, we are interested if fixations can predict pointing targets and how target distances affect the interlocutor's pointing behavior. We present an automatic method combining marker tracking and 3D modeling that provides eye and gesture measurements in real-time.

Keywords: shared space, human-human experiment, gaze tracking, gesture prediction, automatic interaction analysis.

1 Motivation and Overview

The way we interact with robots changes more and more from simple task instructions to cooperative settings with a close interaction between humans and robots in a shared space. If the peripersonal spaces of the interaction partners overlap, they form an interaction space [19] in which actions need to be well coordinated to avoid harm and to ensure a successful and swift task completion. This raises completely new requirements regarding a robot's skills in interacting, especially considering the timing of actions and space allocations.

For interaction in shared space, a robot needs to be aware of its immediate surroundings. A dynamic representation of the robot's peripersonal space can be used to detect human arm movements (e.g. [12]) and thus prevent collisions by stopping the robot's movement, e.g. when both human and robot want to point to a certain target.

C. Freksa et al. (Eds.): Spatial Cognition 2014, LNAI 8684, pp. 121–136, 2014.

There are several levels on which interaction with a robot could be improved if the robot were able to follow human eye gaze and to predict upcoming human gestures: First, current action executions could be slowed down or halted if the robot notices that the human's intended movements would conflict with its current target. Second, in a more proactive manner, the robot could turn its head towards the predicted target, which would serve several functions: It would communicate the robot's interpretation of the human's movements to the human interlocutor and by this means facilitate communication robustness and increase the confidence of the human in the grounding of the current target [5]. In addition, sensors attached to the robot's head could be timely oriented towards the expected target to collect optimal data on the human gesture and its interaction with the target. Third, anticipated gesture trajectories could be considered during action planning to avoid potentially occupied areas.

So long, the focus has been on the interpretation and anticipation of human actions by the robot. For a successful interaction, the robot should also be enabled to provide signals that can in turn be used by the human interlocutor to make similar anticipations. Staudte and Crocker [27] showed that a human-like gaze behavior of a robot can positively influence human comprehension of robot speech and thus improve the interaction.

Hence, a better understanding of human skills for anticipating movements could help robots to increase robustness and smoothness of shared-space interactions. As a starting point for this idea, we investigated the coordination of gaze and gesture (see e.g. Fig. 2) in a human-human study using a complex task. In addition, we assessed the coordination of pointing gestures and upper body movements. For example, to reach far targets, humans will need to lean forward. A prediction model considering both gaze and gestures could enable the robot to have a detailed concept of a starting human pointing movement.

In the study reported in this paper, gaze and pointing directions as well as the head positions of the participants were recorded in a route planning scenario (motivated by former work of Holthaus et al. [11], see Fig. 1). Analyzing mobile eye tracking data usually requires manual annotation which would render a human-human study tedious if not unfeasible due to the needed effort in time. In addition to that, manual annotations are less precise and thus do not provide sufficient data for model generation. Therefore, an automatic method was developed combining fiducial marker tracking and 3D-modeling of stimuli in virtual reality as proxies for intersection testing between the calculated line of sight and the real objects (see also [23]). The method merely relies on the scene camera video of the mobile eye tracking device for mapping eye gaze on targets in the 3D environment. For the study, this set-up was extended with an external tracking system for recording pointing gestures. In the future target scenario of human-robot interaction, tracking of the hands could be done with the tracking sensors mounted on the robot.

The remainder of this paper is organized as follows: After discussing related work in section 2, an experiment on spatial references with gaze and pointing in a route planning scenario is reported in section 3. A novel method for auto-

Fig. 1. The route planning task of the present study is motivated by a receptionist scenario [11, p. 4].

Fig. 2. Example for a fixation (highlighted by the ring) anticipating the pointing target.

matic analysis of the acquired data is proposed in section 4. The results of the experiment are presented in section 5 and discussed in section 6.

2   Related Work

The prediction strategies investigated in this paper focus on non-verbal behavior in shared space. We will thus first discuss representations of peripersonal and shared space before we attend to different strategies making use of such representations that have already been implemented on robots. We will finally present findings on human-human interactions regarding the coordination of gaze and pointing gestures depicting insights which motivate our approach to predicting pointing targets in particular and target areas of movements in general.

2.1   Human Representation of Space

If we want to reach an object, we instinctively know if we are able to do so without moving our torso and we know how far to reach. There are different explanations for these skills. Rizzolatti et al. [26] and follow-up research on humans [25] suggest that the space immediately around oneself has an own, specific neural representation. This space is called peripersonal space. Objects in peripersonal space can be reached without moving the torso. The neural representation of peripersonal space integrates visual, tactile and even auditory signals [10][7]. It allows for constant monitoring of the position of objects in that space relative to the body. Clinical studies by Làdavas [15] show that peripersonal space can adjust with the position of the body parts. It is even possible to enlarge it by grasping objects and using them as tools [3].

For the conceptualization of shared space, Kendon [14] proposes an activity space for each partner, similar to the peripersonal space. The overlap of the partners' activity spaces then forms a common space for interacting: the O-space. Nguyen and Wachsmuth [20] combined Kendon's O-space with the peripersonal space, defining interaction space as the overlap of two peripersonal spaces. Moreover, they propose a process of spatial perspective taking for estimating the extent of the partner's peripersonal space in a virtual human.

Humans are well capable of estimating if targets are in reach, by taking into account not only the plain distance to a target, but also the surface layout on which it is located [6]. Hadjidimikratis et al. [9] found evidence for a neural process to evaluate the 3D distance between the eyes and objects: According to their findings, a neural representation of the peripersonal space related to the eye position is used to compute if objects are reachable.

Mark et al. [16] found that people do not try to reach an object without bending the torso until absolutely necessary (the absolute critical boundary), but instead have a preferred critical boundary for starting to lean forward. The preferred critical boundary is thus the point from which reaching is more comfortable when supported by bending the torso. It appears to occur from 85% of an absolute critical boundary. Leaning-forward is also an often used strategy when pointing to distant objects to increase pointing accuracy [22]. Based on these findings, Nguyen and Wachsmuth [20] introduce the lean-forward space to model the gradual transition between peripersonal and extrapersonal space.

Some of these principles have already been implemented to improve robots' capability to flawlessly interact with humans in shared space, as we discuss in the following section.

2.2 Human-Robot Interaction in Shared Space

Humanoid robots can be assumed to be anthropomorphized by humans. Thus, it is meaningful for a robot to understand and make use of human behaviors and expectations. Hüttenrauch et al. [13] compared distances participants maintained from a robot in accordance with Hall's theory of proxemics and Kendon's F-formations [14]. In a Wizard-of-Oz study where participants had to show around the robot in a home-like environment, they found that the personal distance is predominant and the vis-a-vis formation is preferred in most interactions. Mumm and Mutlu [17] observed humans' proxemic behavior when interacting with a robot. They manipulated likeability and gaze behavior of the robot. In the dislikeable condition, participants increased their distance to the robot when the robot showed increased eye contact. This suggests a coupling between those different factors for proxemic behavior. Spatial prompting is another proxemic behavior which robots may use in the gaps between two consecutive interactions [8]: By giving subtle cues, a robot can positively influence the spatial positioning of the user.

Concerning interaction in shared space, Antonelli et al. [2] propose an implicit representation of peripersonal space by experiments of gazing and reaching. This way, the robot learns a visuomotor awareness of its surrounding without making the representation explicit. An explicit approach was developed for the virtual agent Max [19]: After learning the body structure utilizing virtual touch and proprioception sensors, the dimensions of Max's peripersonal space are calculated. It is divided into a touch space, a lean-forward space and a visual attention space. The interaction space is established by spatial perspective taking, i.e. projecting the agent's own body structure onto the partner. Using the findings of an experiment conducting humans' expectations of grasping decisions of the iCub robot, Holthaus et al. [12] proposed the *active peripersonal space*, a spatial model covering handedness, distance-awareness, awareness of the interlocutor's actions and moreover accounting for attention and occupancy. The active peripersonal space is represented by a body-centered spherical coordinate system. The model allows for monitoring the overlap with the partner's peripersonal space. Thus, an interaction space can be formed.

If such a model could be extended to include predictions about human actions, the robot could include these in its own planning and thus execute actions in a foresighted way. Therefore, the use of gaze and pointing in human interaction has to be taken into consideration.

2.3 Gaze and Pointing in Human-Human Interaction

The eyes are our fastest moving body parts. Due to their dual use as sensor and communication device, they often rest on objects we are planning to use or to refer to. When conducting manual interactions, we need to have a spatial representation of the target and thus gaze is quite naturally linked to hand movements, such as pointing gestures. Once a spatial representation has been built, gaze might no longer be needed to control movements towards a target, but it is still relevant for fine controlled end positioning [1]. In our own work, we found that pointing directions can be determined most precisely when considering the dominant eye aiming over the pointing finger tip [21].

There is evidence for a temporal coordination between gaze and gestures. For example, Prablanc et al. [24] found that hand movements are initiated about 100 ms after the first saccade to the target in a pointing task. However, as for example Abrams et al. [1] argue, such findings are likely to depend on the task and the way stimuli are presented. Thus findings in laboratory conditions might not scale to situations found in natural interaction.

Neggers and Bekkering [18] report a close coupling of gaze and gesture movements. In their study, participants had to point at a first target and then as soon as possible look at a second one, which was presented a bit later. Their participants were not able to fixate the second target while still reaching towards the first and they explain that by a neural inhibition of saccades during manual pointing.

Several contextual factors may influence the interaction between gaze and gesture. Biguer and Prablanc [4] investigated latency shifts depending on target distances: With increasing distance, the first saccade to the target was produced significantly later. However, the corresponding head movement started earlier. Interestingly, the timing of arm movements was not affected by target distance.

3   An Experiment on the Interaction of Gaze and Pointing

Following our goal of improving the precision of the spatial representations of current and future actions, we conducted an experiment on eye-hand coordination. We aim at improving the prediction of pointing targets, and thereby the prediction of areas which might be entered by a pointing hand in the near future. The selection of pointing gestures is due to our scenario, but similar effects are expected and have been shown, e.g., for grasping movements. Our main hypothesis and follow-up questions are as follows:

1. Given the onset of a hand movement, the target of a pointing gesture can be predicted by looking at the location of preceding fixations.
2. How accurate and how precise can the target area be predicted?
3. How large is the advantage in timing that can be gained?
4. What influence does the distance of the target have on the performance of the pointing gesture?

As argued above, we use a relatively natural interaction scenario of two interacting, non-confederate participants, instead of a rigid experimental design with a high level of control. In our route planning scenario, the two interlocutors are sitting at a table facing each other. Placed between them is a map on which they perform several joint planning tasks. To record eye movements, we equipped one participant with a mobile eye tracker. This participant is in the following called P1, the interlocutor without the eye tracking system is called P2.

To elicit spatial references to their own peripersonal space as well as to the space shared by both participants, we use three different floor plans (Fig. 3): ground floor, first and second floor. They are placed between the participants so that there is one within each peripersonal space. The middle floor plan is placed in the interaction space. The scenario is designed to yield a lively interaction facilitating frequent pointing gestures to enable joint planning of routes. It has been verified in a small pilot study.

3.1   Setup

The three floor plans are printed on a DIN A0 format poster (84.1x118.9 cm), each plan with a size of 32x32 cm. The gap between two plans is 3.5 cm. The poster lies on a table of 130 cm length. Fig. 3 shows the distances to the ends of each floor plan, assuming participants are sitting about 25 cm away from the closest floor plan, in a comfortable position at the smaller sides of the table.

By our design, the closest floor plan and the beginning of the middle plan are located in the peripersonal space of the interaction partners. The end of the middle floor plan and the beginning of the far plan can only be reached by more or less articulately leaning forward, depending on the height of the participant. However, the end of the far floor plan cannot be reached while sitting by participants of normal height. The shared space hence comprises the middle plan and the adjacent beginnings of the other two plans.

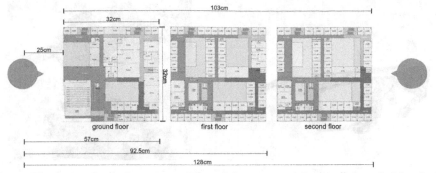

Fig. 3. The figure shows the arrangement of the two participants (left and right, facing each other, sitting) and the three floor plans of the target building on the table between them. The legend shows the relative distances of the different maps to the participants.

3.2 Task

In general, the participants' task is to plan routes from a point A to a point B distributed over the three floor plans. Instructions for individual routes are printed on cards with miniature floor plans the participants draw for each stage. Fig. 4 shows the four important steps of the first task type: (a) The task begins with P1 drawing a card where starting point and target room are marked.

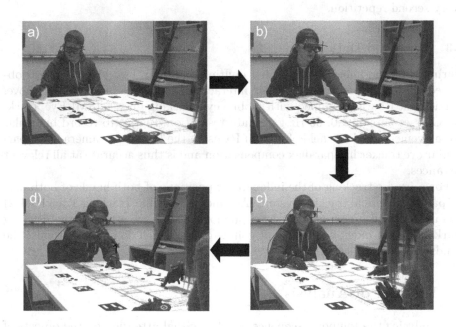

Fig. 4. The main steps of the first task type: (a) Drawing a subtask card, (b) explaining the route, (c) placing blockages and (d) jointly planning the remaining route

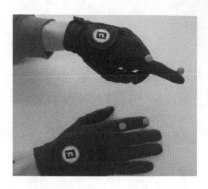

Fig. 5. SMI Eye Tracking Glasses, a binocular mobile eye tracker

Fig. 6. Gloves with tracking markers attached

(b) P1 then demonstrates these to the interlocutor and describes the fastest route. (c) The interlocutor P2 then draws a card with blockages and indicates them on the floor plans using gaming tokens. (d) Finally, P1 and P2 jointly plan the remaining route.

This basic task is followed by a second type of task in which complexity is increased: Participants have to plan the fastest route to three rooms at a time. In addition to that, the number of blockages is also increased. In total, each pair of participants had to perform eight repetitions of the first type of task and two repetitions of the second type. The roles of P1 and P2 in the tasks were switched every second repetition.

3.3 Recorded Data

During the experiments we collected multimodal data: Two video cameras observed the participants during their interactions. As already explained above, Participant P1 was equipped with mobile eye tracking glasses (SMI Eye Tracking Glasses Version 1.0, 30 Hz gaze data resolution, Fig. 5) to record binocular eye movements and the field of view of P1 using the HD scene camera. This particular eye tracker has parallax compensation and is thus accurate at all relevant distances.

For a precise tracking of the index finger positions of both hands of both participants, an optical tracking system (Advanced Realtime Tracking TrackPack 2) was used. Based on experiences from previous studies we attached the tracking markers for the index fingers to soft golfing gloves which do not compromise the hands' freedom of action (Fig. 6).

4   Method of Analysis

For analysing the temporal sequences of P1's visual attention on the objects of interest while at the same time providing as much freedom to move as possible, mobile eye tracking was used instead of remote eye tracking systems. This choice,

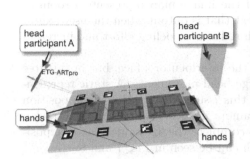

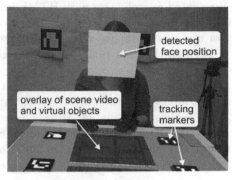

Fig. 7. The 3D representation of the scenario including three floor plans, the fiducial markers, participants' hands with highlighted pointing direction as well as the positions of the interlocutors' faces

Fig. 8. Overlay of the virtual representation over the scene camera image of the eye tracking device. The position of the participant's face is calculated by a face detection algorithm and automatically masked.

however, normally comes along with time-consuming manual annotation of gaze videos: In the present study, the duration of a recorded sessions ranged within 20-30 min, which would have to be annotated frame-by-frame.

For a different previous study, we designed the EyeSee3D approach [23]. It allows us to automatically assign fixations to stimuli based solely on the scene camera video and the 3D gaze vector provided by the eye tracker. This is done by tracking simple fiducial markers in the video. If the scene camera is calibrated, i.e. its intrinsic parameters are determined, marker positions found in the 2D images can be correctly transformed to 3D with respect to position and orientation. In other words: We can calculate the pose of the scene camera, and thus the head of participant P1, with respect to the stimuli. By re-modeling the complete scenario using virtual reality technology and representing the 3D gaze vector as a 3D ray in space, fixations can be automatically assigned to the stimuli by geometric intersection testing. The 3D model can be inspected from all perspectives (Fig. 7), or it can be aligned to the scene camera video (Fig. 8). This way, the experimenter can use EyeSee3D to monitor the recording process and validate data quality during runtime.

For the present study, we had to extend the EyeSee3D approach in several ways: In addition to using gaze directions, the external tracking system was integrated to accurately detect pointing gestures. The link between marker tracking and external tracking is established by placing a tracking target with known position and orientation relative to the fiducial markers (see Fig. 9(a), next to the middle floor plan). This way, both inputs can be fused in a multimodal 3D representation of the interaction scenario.

The floor plans contain a high number of rooms. Instead of modeling each of these separately (which normally would be necessary as each room is a stimulus) as 3D objects, a technique from web design was made use of: The plans were represented as webpages with HTML image maps mapped on the surface of the 3D table model. Each annotated area of the image map represents a room or floor and can be tagged with a specific text that is output when the user fixates the area on the floor plan. This approach reduces modeling effort and increases system performance.

We are also interested in fixations on the interlocutor's face, but in this free kind of interaction the partners show large head movements. A static representation is thus not reliable. To overcome this issue, we adapt dynamic position changes by detecting faces in the scene camera images of the mobile eye tracker using the Viola/Jones algorithm [29]. To complete the 3D model, the face position is approximated in 3D as well, which can be seen in Fig. 7 and 8.

5   Results

The study was conducted with pairs of 18 (9 male, 9 female) participants of an age between 18 and 27 (23.5 years on average; standard deviation 2.9 years). From these, seven male and two female participants took the role of P1 by wearing the eye tracker. Which participant of a pair got to wear the device was chosen with regard to visual disorders: The utilized eye tracker is difficult to calibrate with participants wearing glasses, thus usually participants without glasses were preferred for wearing the eye tracker. The arm length (measured from the head to the fingertip) of the participants P1 ranged between approximately 65 cm to 70 cm. In total, 338.8 minutes (or 5.65 hours) of interaction were recorded during the experiments.

After the first five pairs of participants, the setup was mirror-inverted to prevent possible influences of the different floor plans on the results. So, the ground floor was located in front of P1 for the pairs one to five, and in front of P2 for pairs six to nine. For abbreviation, the first pairs will be called NT, the pairs with mirrored setup MT.

In the course of the complex tasks, participants had to visit all three floor plans. Fig. 9 shows a typical course of interaction of task 2: Both participants point to locations near themselves and to the middle floor plan. Communicative fixations – fixations longer than 500 ms [28] – occur in areas near the pointing targets. In total, 642 pointing gestures were conducted by P1 and 681 by P2. In the NT, more gestures were performed by P1 which changed in the MT. Thus there is a slight shift of focus to the ground floor.

For pointing, the average coordinates (in meters) over all targets on the table were $(0.002, -0.007)$, close to the center of the plan, which testifies that our targets were well distributed over the area. As Fig. 9 shows, from the view of a participant, the x-axis describes left and right, the y-axis the distance to the middle of the table (coordinates $(0, 0)$). For placing blockage tokens the average coordinates were $(0.007, -0.009)$. Thus, regarding both, the targets of pointing and of placing tokens, interaction on the floor plans was symmetrical between interlocutors.

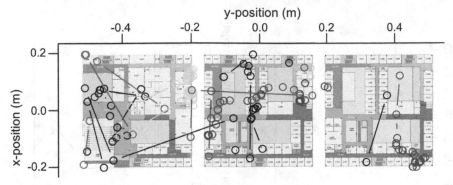

Fig. 9. A typical interaction in a route planning task: Communicative fixations are inscribed in black, pointing directions of P1 in red and yellow, those of P2 in blue and purple. The lines represent events that occurred after one another.

5.1 Gaze-Pointing Coordination

We first measured when and where fixations were made before the apex of a pointing gesture (stroke). In particular we measured whether these fixations targeted the area around the pointing target. For describing the area we used a circle with a radius of 10 cm. For each participant P1, Fig. 10 shows the percentage of pointing gestures in which at least one fixation hit the target area starting from 10 seconds before the apex onwards in bins of 1 second. As expected, fixations preceding one's own pointing gestures were likely to occur in a small area around the pointing target. For all except two participants we observed an increased percentage of fixations on the target from 2.5 s before the apex of the gesture on; one second before the apex, the percentage of fixations on the target was already higher than 50%. A similar trend can be seen for fixations of P1 on pointing targets of P2 (Fig. 11). In both cases two pairs of participants did not adhere to this scheme. As performing a pointing gesture took on average 511 ms (sd: 225 ms) from onset to stroke, gaze could be a hint for the target as soon as the hand starts moving. When averaging over the fixations during the last 200 ms before the gesture onset, at the time of the onset, the target area could be predicted in 47.7% of all pointing gestures performed; 51.1% when taking into consideration the 200 ms around (i.e. from 100 ms before to 100 ms after) the onset. Extending the target radius to 20 cm around the pointing target, 74.2% of pointing targets could be predicted about 500 ms in advance of the apex of the gesture.

Also the probability of fixating the target of a pointing gesture of the interlocutor raised when closer to the onset of the gesture. However, it is not sure whether participants actually predicted pointing targets of their interaction partner, or if this finding is due to context from e.g. the spoken conversation.

Fig. 12 illustrates the observed fixations on the pointing target of participants P1 before the stroke of the gesture. While fixations were widely spread around the target 2000 ms before the apex, 500 ms before the apex the target area was most frequently fixated.

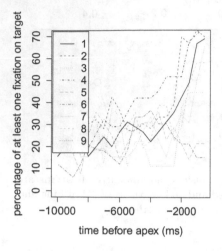

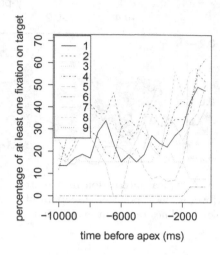

Fig. 10. The probability of fixations hitting the target area of one's pointing gesture increases the closer to the gesture's apex

Fig. 11. This also holds when observing the pointing gesture of an interlocutor but not as strongly

5.2   Characteristics of Pointing Gestures

By considering the head positions of P1 (the 3D head position of P2 was not acquired) during the stroke of the pointing gestures, body movements could be measured as well. In particular, leaning forward was investigated. Fig. 13 shows the y-position (i.e. the position in direction of the interlocutor) of the fingertip during the apex of a pointing gesture in relation to the head position in y-direction. The red curve is the approximation of the points by locally weighted polynomial regression. When the fingertip in a pointing gesture was not moved further than to the middle of the table, head movements were barely observed. Beyond that distance, leaning forward was performed for pointing. This might be due the distance of 65 cm from the edge to the middle of the table, which could mark the critical boundary from where leaning forward is preferred according to Mark et al. [16]. A trend to leaning forward was already observable from the beginning of the middle floor plan. The same trend, but less distinct, was found in the correlation of head position and the pointing targets (Fig. 14). Fig. 15 shows that, depending on how far the pointing target was away, there was a trend of not directly touching the target but rather pointing from a higher position in distance.

Summing up, most pointing gestures were performed close to the participant pointing. Thus, participants preferred pointing in their own peripersonal space, but the overall distribution of pointing targets of both interaction partners was similar over all floor plans.

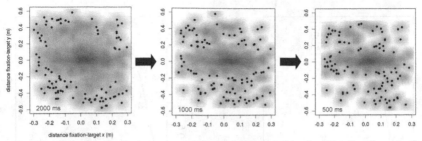

Fig. 12. Focussing the pointing target: From left to right, the distribution of all fixations (relative to the pointing target) up to the pointing gesture apex are shown for 2000 ms, 1000 ms and 500 ms (each for an interval of the next 1000 ms), averaged over all participants.

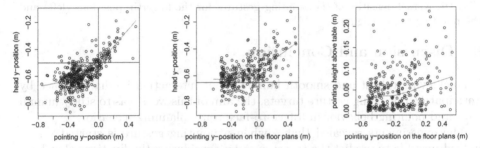

Fig. 13. Correlation between the apex position of the fingertip and the head position in pointing gestures.

Fig. 14. Correlation between the target position of pointing gestures and the head position.

Fig. 15. The height of pointing gestures dependent on the target on the floor plans.

Measuring the target position during the apex of pointing gestures, 66-73% of all gestures targeted locations in the closer half of the table, 44%-52% to the closest plan and only 10-15% to the most distant floor plan. Fig. 16 shows the estimated kernel densities for the fingertip positions at the apex of pointing gestures and the locations pointed at. The gaps between the floor plans are reflected in the graphs. There is a continuous decrease of gestures to targets beyond the middle of the table. The percentages for the position of the finger tip at the apex of pointing gestures were as well similar in all trials and conditions. Here, the NT and MT are combined. In 83% (82.5% for P1 and 82.6% for P2) of all pointing gestures, the hand remained in the own half of the table, i.e. in peripersonal space. In 64.2% (P1) and 59.2% it was within the extent of the nearest floor plan, in 96.4% (P1) and 93.7%, it was located not farther than the end of the middle floor plan.

Thus, a distribution can be observed where pointing movements were performed: A high percentage of pointing targets were located in near space, thus the first floor plan. From the middle of the table, when leaning forward had to be used, there was a continuous decrease of conducted pointing gestures.

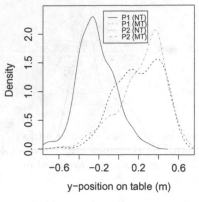 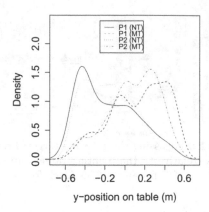

Fig. 16. Kernel densities of the pointing gestures for the fingertip positions (left) and the pointing target (right)

6   Discussion and Conclusion

For achieving robust and smooth human-robot interaction in shared space by anticipating upcoming gesture targets, the aim of this work was to study human gaze and pointing behavior in a face-to-face route planning scenario.

The experiments revealed that – when a pointing gesture is started – it is indeed possible to predict the target area by considering the fixations that happened directly before the gesture's onset. About one half of the target areas could be predicted when examining fixations 200 ms before the onset of the gestures. This provides a 500 ms (duration of common pointing gestures) advantage for interpretation, planning and reacting. With a probability of about 75%, it is possible to predict if a human hand just about starting to move will enter the robot's peripersonal space. We also examined the distribution of gesture targets: In the experiment, participants succeeded in partitioning their space equally, but for each participant, the percentage of pointing targets decreased relatively linear with distance. This suggests that the probability of conducting gestures decreases with the distance in face-to-face interactions. Reaching distant gesture targets was mostly handled by leaning forward. If the human partner starts leaning forward, it can safely be assumed that the target of the gesture will be distant (to the human). Thus, the gesture is likely to enter the robot's peripersonal space. In some cases, the pointing gesture was conducted from a higher position in some distance to the target.

Based on these findings, the robot's shared-space representation of Holthaus et al. [11] could now be extended by including such predictions. On the production side, the observed human skills can additionally be used to improve robot behavior. Fixating the target of a planned gesture shortly before conducting it could signal that the robot is going to occupy that area. Whether humans will use that information in this scenario remains to be tested.

Our method for automatically analyzing interactions facilitates follow-up studies with increased participant counts. Moreover, as our method can operate in real-time, it can also be used in the human-robot interaction to make the robot aware of the interlocutor's gaze behavior. Future work will focus on creating models based on the presented findings to improve speed and robustness of the robot's spatial interaction.

Acknowledgment. This work has been partially supported by the German Research Foundation (DFG) in the Collaborative Research Center 673 Alignment in Communication.

References

1. Abrams, R.A., Meyer, D.E., Kornblum, S.: Eye-hand coordination: Oculomotor control in rapid aimed limb movements. Journal of Experimental Psychology: Human Perception and Performance 16(2), 248–267 (1990)
2. Antonelli, M., Chinellato, E., del Pobil, A.P.: Implicit mapping of the peripersonal space of a humanoid robot. In: IEEE Symposium on Computational Intelligence, Cognitive Algorithms, Mind, and Brain, vol. 3, pp. 1–8. IEEE (2011)
3. Berti, A., Frassinetti, F.: When far becomes near: Remapping of space by tool use. Journal of Cognitive Neuroscience 12(3), 415–420 (2000)
4. Biguer, B., Jeannerod, M., Prablanc, C.: The coordination of eye, head, and arm movements during reaching at a single visual target. Experimental Brain Research 46(2), 301–304 (1982)
5. Breazeal, C., Kidd, C.D., Thomaz, A.L., Hoffman, G., Berlin, M.: Effects of nonverbal communication on efficiency and robustness in human-robot teamwork. In: International Conference on Intelligent Robots and Systems (IROS 2005), pp. 708–713. IEEE (2005)
6. Carello, C., Grosofsky, A.: Visually perceiving what is reachable. Ecological Psychology 1(1), 27–54 (1989)
7. Farnè, A., Làdavas, E.: Auditory peripersonal space in humans. Journal of Cognitive Neuroscience 14(7), 1030–1043 (2002)
8. Green, A., Hüttenrauch, H.: Making a case for spatial prompting in human-robot communication. In: Language Resources and Evaluation (Workshop on Multimodal Corpora: From Multimodal Behavior Theories to Usable Models) (2006)
9. Hadjidimitrakis, K., Breveglieri, R., Bosco, A., Fattori, P.: Three-dimensional eye position signals shape both peripersonal space and arm movement activity in the medial posterior parietal cortex. Frontiers in Integrative Neuroscience 6(37) (2012)
10. Holmes, N.P., Spence, C.: The body schema and the multisensory representation(s) of peripersonal space. Cognitive Processing 5(2), 94–105 (2004)
11. Holthaus, P., Pitsch, K., Wachsmuth, S.: How can i help? spatial attention strategies for a receptionist robot. International Journal of Social Robots 3, 383–393 (2011)
12. Holthaus, P., Wachsmuth, S.: Active peripersonal space for more intuitive hri. In: International Conference on Humanoid Robots, pp. 508–513. IEEE RAS, Osaka (2012)
13. Hüttenrauch, H., Eklundh, K., Green, A., Topp, E.: Investigating Spatial Relationships in Human-Robot Interaction. In: 2006 IEEE/RSJ International Conference on Intelligent Robots and Systems, pp. 5052–5059. IEEE, Beijing (2006)

14. Kendon, A.: Conducting interaction: Patterns of behavior in focused encounters, vol. 7. CUP Archive (1990)
15. Làdavas, E.: Functional and dynamic properties of visual peripersonal space. Trends in Cognitive Sciences 6(1), 17–22 (2002)
16. Mark, L., Nemeth, K., Gardner, D.: Postural dynamics and the preferred critical boundary for visually guided reaching. Journal of Experimental Psychology 23(5), 1365–1379 (1997)
17. Mumm, J., Mutlu, B.: Human-robot proxemics. In: Proceedings of the 6th International Conference on Human-Robot Interaction, HRI 2011, p. 331. ACM Press, New York (2011)
18. Neggers, S., Bekkering, H.: Ocular gaze is anchored to the target of an ongoing pointing movement. Journal of Neurophysiology 83(2), 639–651 (2000)
19. Nguyen, N., Wachsmuth, I.: From body space to interaction space-modeling spatial cooperation for virtual humans. In: 10th International Conference on Autonomous Agents and Multiagent Systems, pp. 1047–1054. International Foundation for Autonomous Agents and Multiagent Systems, Taipei (2011)
20. Nguyen, N., Wachsmuth, I.: A computational model of cooperative spatial behaviour for virtual humans. In: Representing Space in Cognition: Interrelations of Behaviour, Language, and Formal Models, pp. 147–168. Oxford University Press (2013)
21. Pfeiffer, T.: Understanding Multimodal Deixis with Gaze and Gesture in Conversational Interfaces. Shaker Verlag, Aachen (2011)
22. Pfeiffer, T.: Interaction between speech and gesture: Strategies for pointing to distant objects. In: Efthimiou, E., Kouroupetroglou, G., Fotinea, S.-E. (eds.) GW 2011. LNCS, vol. 7206, pp. 238–249. Springer, Heidelberg (2012)
23. Pfeiffer, T., Renner, P.: Eyesee3d: A low-cost approach for analyzing mobile 3d eye tracking data using computer vision and augmented reality technology. In: Proceedings of the Symposium on Eye Tracking Research and Applications, pp. 195–202. ACM (2014)
24. Prablanc, C., Echallier, J., Komilis, E., Jeannerod, M.: Optimal response of eye and hand motor systems in pointing at a visual target. Biological Cybernetics 124, 113–124 (1979)
25. Previc, F.H.: Functional specialization in the lower and upper visual fields in humans: Its ecological origins and neurophysiological implications. Behavioral and Brain Sciences 13, 519–542 (1990)
26. Rizzolatti, G., Scandolara, C., Matelli, M., Gentilucci, M.: Afferent properties of periarcuate neurons in macaque monkeys. Behavioural Brain Research 2(2), 147–163 (1981)
27. Staudte, M., Crocker, M.W.: Visual attention in spoken human-robot interaction. In: Proceedings of the 4th ACM/IEEE International Conference on Human Robot Interaction, HRI 2009, p. 77. ACM Press, New York (2009)
28. Velichkovsky, B., Sprenger, A., Pomplun, M.: Auf dem Weg zur Blickmaus: Die Beeinflussung der Fixationsdauer durch kognitive und kommunikative Aufgaben. In: Software-Ergonomie 1997, pp. 317–327. Springer (1997)
29. Viola, P., Jones, M.J.: Robust real-time face detection. International Journal of Computer Vision 57(2), 137–154 (2004)

Lateralization of Route Continuation and Route Order

Ineke J. M. van der Ham and Jacco van den Hoven

Heidelberglaan 1, 3584 CS, Utrecht, The Netherlands
c.j.m.vanderham@uu.nl, j.vandenhoven@students.uu.nl

Abstract. Navigation is a complex cognitive ability and its structure is still poorly understood. Memory for route continuation and route order are hypothesized to be at least partially separate components of navigation ability. In the current experiment, participants studied a route in virtual reality. The dissociation between route continuation ("what turn did you make here?") and route order ("which object did you see first?") was tested in a visual half field paradigm, to assess lateralization patterns. Route continuation showed a left visual field advantage and route order a trend for a right visual field bias. This outcome further substantiates a dissociation between spatial and spatiotemporal aspects of navigation in humans.

Keywords: Lateralization, navigation, continuation, order memory.

1 Introduction

Finding our way around is a complex ability, consisting of a range of cognitive activities. When we interact with our environment, we store various types of information about the landmarks we encounter, for example (see e.g. [1,2]). When we receive descriptions on how to find a particular location in a new city, these will commonly entail sentences like 'when you reach the train station turn left, and when you have passed the supermarket, walk straight ahead until you reach the museum'.

Landmarks are therefore linked to different types of information, not only do we process their identity, but also properties like route continuation, which turn to take at a specific location, and route order, the order of items along a route, are dealt with during navigation. Analogous to general studies on memory (e.g. [3,4,5,6]), a clear dissociation between recognition and order memory has been reported during navigation as well (e.g. [7]). Moreover, this dissociation has been extended to route continuation and route order [8]. Given the complexity of navigation ability, the attempt to identify separate elements of this ability is clearly useful. Theoretically, an overview of the separable elements is vital to better understand navigation, which in turn can explain for individual differences in navigation ability (e.g. [1,9]). Clinically, such dissociations can help in the diagnosis and even treatment of specific impairments within the navigation domain [10]. In particular, memory for order has received little attention as a potentially separate element of navigation, although several studies highlight the functional isolation from spatial forms of memory. Memory for route continuation is an explicitly spatial process, whereas route order memory comprises

C. Freksa et al. (Eds.): Spatial Cognition 2014, LNAI 8684, pp. 137–146, 2014.
© Springer International Publishing Switzerland 2014

both temporal and spatial information. The amount of studies focusing on the dissociation between these spatial and spatiotemporal aspects of route memory is limited [7,8]. With the current study we therefore aim to shed more light on the nature and extent of this dissociation with regard to its underlying processing mechanisms.

The hippocampus is the key brain structure when creating mental representations of an environment (e.g. [11,12,13]). This mental representation appears essential for answering questions concerning routes taken through an environment. Moreover, within the hippocampus a division has been made between the left and right side of the hippocampus. Igloi and colleagues [14] have studied lateralization patterns within the hippocampus and suggest that memory for places is lateralized to the right, and memory for temporal sequences to the left, which is closely related to our current research question. They interpret place memory and sequence memory as reflecting allocentric, or environment-based, processing and egocentric, or observer-based processing, respectively.

Comparing lateralization patterns is very useful for examining the distinction between route continuation and route order: if they differ in their lateralization pattern, this provides further support that there are at least partially separate underlying mechanisms to these types of memory. Therefore, in the current study we applied a visual half field design to examine potential lateralization patterns for both route continuation and route order. A visual half field design allows for a comparison of behavioral responses to stimuli presented briefly to the left visual field to responses to stimuli presented briefly in the right visual field. These responses are thought to reflect contralateral processing in the cerebral hemispheres; left visual field performance therefore reflects right hemisphere processing and vice versa (see e.g. [15]. The outcomes of the study by Igloi and colleagues provide a first suggestion that different lateralization patterns could exist. Yet, place memory as tested in [14] is explicitly allocentric. This means that for this type of memory, the external environment is consulted in order to identify locations in the environment. The spatial task of route continuation, deciding which turn to take at specific points along the route, is egocentric: the decision to go left or right is dependent on the observer's position. Moreover, there is a possibility, albeit unlikely, that the left lateralization of the sequences in their egocentric task is related to verbal coding of the turns to be taken to reach a destination, e.g. 'left, right, right, left'. Such verbalization might activate language related areas in the brain, which are typically left lateralized. In a typical route order task, participants are asked to compare specific elements of a route, based on the moment they encountered them along the route. Such comparisons are less likely to be linked to verbalization as a large number of possible combinations of elements can be presented, which cannot be labelled verbally in simple terms.

Therefore, two questions arise when translating the lateralization pattern found in [14] to route continuation and route order memory: 'Does the right hemisphere advantage for place memory generalize to the egocentric spatial task of route continuation?' and 'Does the left hemisphere advantage for sequences also emerge when verbal coding is an impossible strategy?' If memory for places is lateralized to the right, regardless of the perspective needed to perform the task, a right hemisphere bias for route continuation is expected. Alternatively, if the type of perspective used is crucial for the lateralization pattern, then route continuation should be left lateralized as it makes use of an egocentric perspective. If the left hemisphere advantage found for sequences is not based on the potential verbal nature of the task, but on the processing of order of items, then a left hemisphere advantage is expected for route order. If verbal processing is essential for the direction of lateralization, then route order memory should not show lateralization to the left. Moreover, if route continuation and route order differ in their lateralization pattern, this further supports a clear distinction between these two types of route memory.

2   Methods

2.1   Participants

In total, 35 participants (9 male) took part in the experiment, with a mean age of 22 (range 19-28). Right-handedness was ensured for all participants, as measured with a Dutch version of the Edinburgh Handedness Inventory [16], with a mean score of 77.6 (SD=34.6, range 47-100, on a scale of -100, extremely left-handed, to +100, extremely right-handed). All participants were students and participated in exchange for course credit. All participants had normal or corrected to normal vision and were unaware of the rationale of the experiment.

2.2   Task Design and Materials

The experiment consisted of a video of a virtual maze in which fifteen different objects were placed and three tasks that assessed memory of the route in different ways. First of all, participants were tested on recognition of these objects. Next, they were tested on their knowledge of route continuation, and their order memory.

A 3D virtual maze was created in Blender (Blender Foundation, the Netherlands). The objects in the maze were selected from the Bank of Standardized Stimuli (BOSS, [17]). Everyday objects were selected that were easy to identify. In the tasks, the dimensions of these objects were 300 * 450 pixels. In Figure 1A a screen shot from the video is shown, in which one these objects is visible. A path was selected in the maze consisting of thirteen turns and fifteen objects. This path was shown in the video through the virtual environment. A map of the route through the virtual environment, along with dots depicting the object positions is shown in Figure 1B.

The tasks were programmed in OpenSesame [18]. After the first instructions, participants started with the recognition task. This task consisted of three practice trials and 30 experimental trials. The trial sequence was as follows: Fixation cross (2000 ms), stimulus (150 ms), response window (until response is given). All items were presented centrally. The practice trials were inserted to expose the participants to the speed of presentation of the stimulus. Therefore, during practice, the stimuli were black squares. In the experimental trials, all fifteen objects along the route were presented, as well as fifteen distractor objects.

Fig. 1. A. Screenshot taken from the video, with a power drill as an object, after which a left turn was taken

The route continuation task also consisted of three practice trials and 30 experimental trials. The trial started with a central fixation cross (2000 ms), followed by an arrow pointing either to the left, to the right, or up (150 ms), next another fixation cross was presented (1000 ms), followed by a lateral presentation of the stimulus (150 ms), lastly the response window appeared for 3000 ms. The instruction was to indicate whether the direction of the arrow matched the direction of the route directly after the object shown. The objects were presented at a visual angle of 3 degrees, measured from the inner edge of the figure to the center of the screen. In this presentation, the objects were shown in isolation, without any informative background. Each of the fifteen objects on the route was presented twice. In the practice trials, the stimulus was a black square, instead of one of the objects.

For the order task also three practice trials and 30 experimental trials were created. The trial sequence was: central fixation cross (2000 ms), first stimulus presented centrally (150 ms), fixation cross (1000 ms), second stimulus presented laterally (150 ms), response window (3000 ms). The instruction was to decide whether the two serially presented objects were in the correct order, as encountered on the route. Again, the objects presented laterally were at a visual angle of 3 degrees, from the inner edge of the object to the center of the screen. Also, the objects were again shown in isolation, without any informative background. Each of the fifteen objects was used twice as a first object and twice as a second object. In the practice trials, the first object was a black square; the second object was a red square. The trialsequence of each of the three conditions is depicted in Figure 2.

For all three tasks, chance level was at 50% and participants responded with the arrow keys on a regular keyboard that were marked green ('correct') and red ('incorrect'). The video and tasks were presented on a 30-inch monitor, with a resolution of 1920 * 1200 pixels. Participants were seated 60 cm away from the screen and used a chin rest placed exactly in front of the center of the screen.

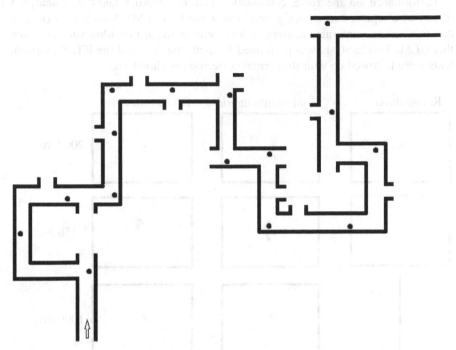

Fig. 2. B. A map of the route shown in the video. Dots represent object positions.

2.3 Procedure

Prior to participation, all participants signed an informed consent form. Next, they were orally instructed about the different parts of the experiment. The first part of the experiment was the viewing of the video. They were instructed to remember as much as they could from the video, without specific mention of the tasks that would follow. All participants viewed the same video three times.

After viewing the video, all participants were presented the recognition task. Next, either the route continuation or the route order task was presented first, followed by the other of the two tasks. The order of these two tasks was randomized across participants. Each task was preceded by an instruction on the screen, as well as an oral instruction to ensure correct understanding of the task for all participants.

2.4 Analyses

For all conditions, mean accuracy (Acc) and response time (RT) were calculated. Participants with an overall Acc at or below 50% were excluded from that particular task. At an individual trial level RT below 200 ms and above 3000 ms were excluded. The performance on the recognition task was used as an indication of how well participants had memorized the objects on the route. Sufficient recognition (at least 80% correct) was considered a prerequisite for informative performance on the route continuation and route order tasks.

Performance on the route continuation and route order tasks was analyzed by means of a repeated measures general linear model (GLM). Visual field (left, right) and task (route continuation, route order) were included as within subject factors in this GLM. This analysis was performed for both the Acc and the RT. Significant effects were followed up with Bonferroni corrected post hoc tests.

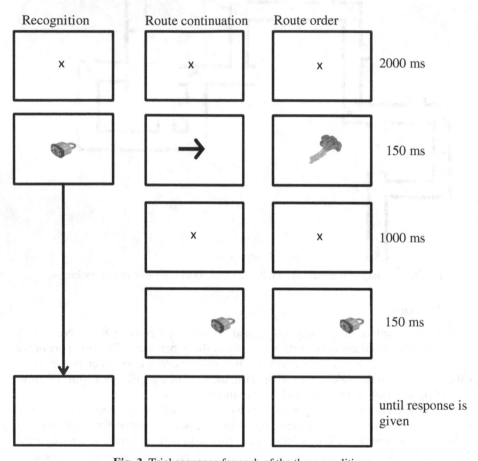

Fig. 3. Trial sequence for each of the three conditions

3   Results

First of all, the performance on the object recognition was assessed. The mean Acc of all participants was 93.3 % (SD=5.0, range 80-100%), with a mean RT of 681.3 (SD=138.8). For the route continuation task four participants had Acc values at or below chance level and were therefore excluded, for the route order task, one participant was excluded because of chance level Acc. The mean Acc and RT for both the route continuation and route order tasks are depicted in Figures 3A and B.

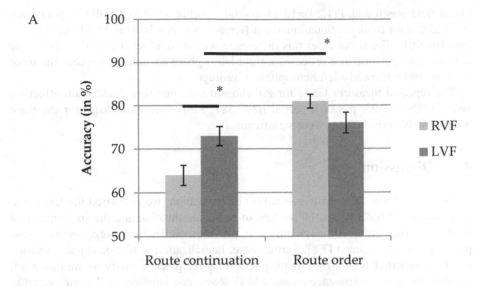

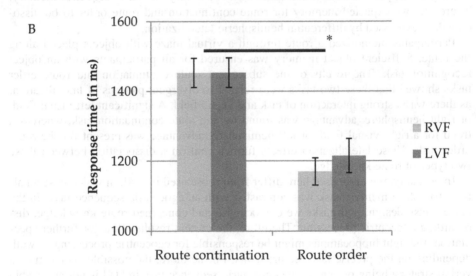

Fig. 4. Mean A) accuracy in percentage and B) response times in milliseconds for both the route continuation task and the route order tasks. Performance is split up by visual field. RVF=right visual field, LVF=left visual field. Error bars represent standard error of the mean (SEM). *p<.001

A repeated measures GLM including visual field and task was performed on Acc and showed a significant main effect of task, F(1,29)=13.55, p =.001, partial η2=0.318. Performance was significantly better for the route order task, in comparison to the route continuation task. Additionally, a significant interaction of task and visual field was found, $F(1,29)=13.23$, p =.001, partial $\eta2=0.313$. Follow up analyses showed that for route continuation, the difference between RVF and LVF was significant (p=.001). For route order this difference was at trend level (p=.077). For route continuation, performance reflected a right hemisphere advantage, whereas the trend for route order showed a left hemisphere advantage.

The repeated measures GLM for RT showed the same significant main effect for task, $F(1,29)=41.23$, p <.001, partial $\eta2=0.587$. Responses were faster for the route order task. No other effects were significant.

4   Discussion

To further unravel the cognitive structure of navigation, we compared the lateralization patterns of both the spatial process of route continuation and the spatiotemporal process of route order. Although only few, previous studies have suggested that these processes are dissociated [7,8]. Furthermore, lateralization in hippocampal activation has been reported with a right hemispheric bias for place memory as well as a left hemispheric bias for sequence memory [14]. Route continuation can be interpreted as making use of place memory, and order memory is very similar to sequence memory. Therefore, we expected memory for route continuation and route order to be dissociated, as expressed by differential hemispheric lateralization.

Participants memorized a route through a virtual maze with objects placed along the route. Sufficient object memory was ensured for all participants with an object recognition task. The results of the subsequent route continuation and route order tasks showed that these two tasks were related to divergent patterns of lateralization, as there was a strong interaction of task and visual field. A significant left visual field, or right hemisphere, advantage was found for the route continuation task, whereas a trend for a right visual field, or left hemisphere, advantage was present for the route order task. These lateralization effects further confirm a dissociation between these two types of route knowledge.

Importantly, the tasks used here differ from those used in [14], in which case an allocentric place memory task was contrasted with an egocentric sequence task. In the current task design, both tasks were egocentric and concerned route knowledge, disregarding allocentric processing. Therefore, the current results allow for further speculation; the right hippocampus might be responsible for egocentric processing as well, depending on the precise task requirements. Furthermore, the possible criticism of a verbal strategy being present in the egocentric sequence task in [14] is not applicable for the current task, as participants directly compared two objects from the route and indicated whether their order was correct. This process most likely does not rely on verbalization of the spatiotemporal information from the route, as the task design allows for many possible combinations of stimuli, for which some form of verbal coding of order would be very inefficient.

It should be noted that this type of distinction is likely not restricted to the hippocampus and that lateralization as tested with a visual half field paradigm reflects lateralization patterns of the brain as a whole. Our results indicate that there is a dissociation in terms of lateralization, at a cerebral hemisphere level.

The current outcomes further substantiate previous findings of a dissociation between the spatial and spatiotemporal aspects of route memory. Not only are they functionally dissociated as previous studies showed, but the current results reveal a clear hemispheric dissociation as well; spatial route memory is lateralized to the right, while there is a trend for a left hemispheric bias for spatiotemporal route memory. Future studies should be directed at identifying the precise areas of the brain involved in these tasks. As [14] indicates, the left and right hippocampi are primary candidates for the current lateralization pattern.

Acknowledgments. A Veni grant (451.12.004) awarded by the Netherlands Organization of Scientific Research (NWO) supported this research. The authors wish to thank Eline Koppenol for her help in collecting the data.

References

[1] Wolbers, T., Hegarty, M.: What determines our navigational abilities? Trends in Cognitive Sciences 14, 138–146 (2010)
[2] Janzen, G., Jansen, C., van Turennout, M.: Memory consolidation of landmarks in good navigators. Hippocampus 18, 40–47 (2008)
[3] Fabiani, M., Friedman, D.: Dissociations between memory for temporal order and recognition memory in aging. Neuropsychologia 35(2), 129–141 (1997)
[4] Hannesson, D.K., Howland, J.G., Phillips, A.G.: Interaction between perirhinal and medial prefrontal cortex is required for temporal order but not recognition memory for objects in rats. The Journal of Neuroscience 24(19), 4596–4604 (2004)
[5] Hannesson, D.K., Vacca, G., Howland, J.G., Phillips, A.G.: Medial prefrontal cortex is involved in spatial temporal order memory but not spatial recognition memory in tests relying on spontaneous exploration in rats. Behavioural Brain Research 153, 273–285 (2004)
[6] Hampstead, B.M., Libon, D.J., Moelter, S.T., Swirsky-Sacchetti, T., Scheffer, L., Platek, S.M., Chute, D.: Temporal order memory differences in Alzheimer's disease and vascular dementia. Journal of Clinical and Experimental Neuropsychology 32(6), 645–654 (2010)
[7] Ekstrom, A.D., Copara, M.S., Isham, E.A., Wang, W., Yonelinas, A.P.: Dissociable networks involved in spatial and temporal order source retrieval. NeurImage 56, 1803–1813 (2011)
[8] Van der Ham, I.J.M., van Zandvoort, M.J.E., Meilinger, T., Bosch, S.E., Kant, N., Postma, A.: Spatial and temporal aspects of navigation in two neurological patients. Neuroreport 21, 685–689 (2010)
[9] Chrastil, E.R.: Neural evidence supports a novel framework for spatial navigation. Psychonomic Bulletin and Review 20, 208–227 (2013)
[10] Van der Ham, I.J.M., Kant, N., Postma, A., Visser-Meily, J.M.A.: Is navigation ability a problem in mild stroke patients? Insights from self-reported navigation measures. Journal of Rehabilitation Medicine 45, 429–433 (2013)
[11] O'Keefe, J., Nadel, L.: The hippocampus as a cognitive map. Clarendon Press, Oxford (1978)
[12] Burgess, N., Maguire, E.A., O'Keefe, J.: The human hippocampus and spatial and episodic memory. Neuron 35, 625–641 (2002)

[13] Eichenbaum, H.: Hippocampus: Cognitive processes and neural representations that underlie declarative memory. Neuron 44, 109–120 (2004)

[14] Iglói, K., Doeller, C.F., Barthoz, A., Rondi-Reig, L., Burgess, N.: Lateralized human hippocampal activity predicts navigation based on sequence or place memory. Proceedings of the National Academy of Sciences 107, 14466–14471 (2010)

[15] Bourne, V.J.: The divided visual field paradigm: Methodological considerations. Laterality: Asymmetries of Body, Brain, and Cognition 11(4), 373–393 (2006)

[16] Oldfield, R.C.: The assessment and analysis of handedness: The Edinburgh inventory. Neuropsychologia 9, 97–113 (1971)

[17] Brodeur, M.B., Dionne-Dostie, E., Montreuil, T., Lepage, M.: The bank of standardized stimuli (BOSS), a new set of 480 normative photos of objects to be used as visual stimuli in cognitive research. PLoS ONE 5(5), e10773 (2010)

[18] Mathôt, S., Schreij, D., Theeuwes, J.: OpenSesame: An open-source, graphical experiment builder for the social sciences. Behavior Research Methods 44(2), 314–324 (2012)

Bayesian Cue Interaction in Human Spatial Navigation

Xiaoli Chen and Timothy P. McNamara

Department of Psychology, Vanderbilt University, Nashville, TN, USA

Abstract. We examined the manner in which people integrated visual cues and self-motion cues during spatial navigation when the two cues varied in reliability independently. Results showed that when responses were pooled across reliability levels of the manipulated cue, people integrated cues optimally or nearly optimally in a Bayesian manner. However, when responses were analyzed within reliability levels, navigation behavior often deviated from Bayesian optimal integration. These results suggest that when experiencing spatial cues changing in reliability, navigators combine cues in a way consistent with Bayesian integration theory overall, but at the cost of being non-optimal at the individual reliability levels.

Keywords: Bayesian theory, spatial cue integration, changing cue reliability.

1   Introduction

When people try to localize themselves within an environment, they typically must integrate information provided by different cues. Spatial cues can be divided into two categories. Internal self-motion cues (idiothetic cues) refer to bodily information generated by self-movement, such as vestibular cues and proprioceptive cues. Navigation using idiothetic cues alone is called dead-reckoning or path integration. External environmental cues (allothetic cues) refer to inputs from the outside world. Visual cues have been studied extensively, probably because humans rely heavily on the visual sensory system and visual cues are relatively easy to manipulate in experiments. A classic categorization of visual cues is geometric cues vs. featural cues [1,2,3]. Geometric cues are those defined by the axioms of geometry, and include extended surfaces, shapes, and angles. Featural cues refer to spatially compact objects, such as landmarks and beacons, and aspects of objects (e.g., color). Allothetic cues can also be categorized as distal cues and proximal cues, based on their relative distances to a target location [4].

Many studies have been conducted to investigate the interaction between different types of spatial cues. A majority of the studies has been devoted to investigating the competition and interference between different cues [5-11]. Fewer studies, however, directly ask the question of how different cues might be integrated and what principles might govern the integration [12,13,14]. Cue integration paradigms and cue competition paradigms might not be essentially different from each other. It is possible that cue integration might have occurred in cue competition studies.

C. Freksa et al. (Eds.): Spatial Cognition 2014, LNAI 8684, pp. 147–160, 2014.
© Springer International Publishing Switzerland 2014

In cue-competition studies, performance usually was not completely reduced to a random level when only the blocked or overshadowed cue was displayed. During the previous double-cues stage, the blocked or overshadowed cue and the blocking or overshadowing cue might have been both utilized for location representation and combined in some way. When two cues were in small conflict and a continuous response was allowed, animals usually searched for a compromise between the different dictates of the cues, suggesting both cues were used and integrated [15]. It is also possible that cue competition and integration processes might be influenced by the same set of factors relating to cue salience and prior experiences.

How are spatial cues weighted and integrated? Bayesian theory posits that people weight cues based on their relative reliability. When people combine cues with linear weights equal to cue relative reliabilities, the final combined estimate is most robust with a minimum of variance [16]. Cue reliability is inversely related to response variance, $r = 1/\sigma^2$. Based on Bayesian principles, given cue A and cue B, the weight for cue A is, $w_A = r_A/(r_A + r_B) = \sigma_B^2/(\sigma_A^2 + \sigma_B^2)$. When two cues are not congruent, the combined mean is a compromise between the two single-cue estimates and its relative distances to the two single-cue estimates are determined by the relative cue reliabilities. The combined estimate will be closer to the single-cue estimate of the more reliable cue. Response variance of the combined estimate is, $\sigma_c^2 = \sigma_A^2\sigma_B^2/(\sigma_A^2 + \sigma_B^2)$. Response variability would be reduced in double-cue conditions relative to single-cue conditions. Such a cue integration process is said to be optimal in the sense that the combined parameter estimate will have statistically minimum variability, or maximum precision.

The Bayesian approach has been employed extensively and has proven useful in many domains of investigation [17,18,19]. However, its application to spatial navigation is quite limited [20]. In this study, we investigated human spatial navigation in the framework of Bayesian theory and the interaction between visual cues and self-motion cues. Our experiments extended previous studies by manipulating the reliability of visual cues and self-motion cues independently and within-subjects. In Experiment 1, to vary reliability of visual cues, we pitted an environment rich in landmarks against an environment poor in landmarks. In Experiment 2, to vary reliability of self-motion cues, we added different levels of body rotation into the task [21]. Participants experienced all of the noise levels of the manipulated cue. This study represents the first time that the reliability of spatial cues was manipulated using a cue integration paradigm, allowing us to answer the question of whether participants could conditionalize their strategy of dealing with multiple spatial cues across cue noise levels. We also assumed that individuals would exhibit different levels of relative cue reliability, since they might have different preferences of visual cue types [22,23] and differ in path integration ability [24]. If each individual sets his or her own combination weights, we would expect to observe a correlation between cue relative reliabilities and actual weights assigned to cues.

2   Experiment 1

2.1   Method

Participants. Eighteen participants (10 males, 8 females) from the Nashville community participated in this experiment in exchange for course credit or monetary compensation. Participants ranged in age from 18 to 26 years, with a mean of 20.4. Participants had normal or corrected-to-normal vision.

Material. Virtual environments were displayed on an nVisor SX60 head-mounted display (HMD; NVIS, Reston, VA) with a 60° diagonal field of view. Stereoscopic images were presented at 1,280 × 1,024 pixel resolution, refreshed at 60 Hz. Graphics were rendered using Vizard software (WorldViz, Santa Barbara, CA) on a 3.0-GHz Pentium 4 processor with a GeForce 6800 GS graphics card. Head orientation was tracked by a 3-degrees-of-freedom orientation sensor (InertiaCube2; Intersense, Bedford, MA), and head position by a passive optical tracking system (PPTX4; WorldViz, Santa Barbara, CA). Drifting of the inertial sensor was corrected through optical tracking. Graphics were updated on the basis of sensed head movement, such that physical translations and rotations caused concomitant visual movement through the virtual world.

Each participant experienced both the rich environment and the poor environment (Figure 1b & c). The rich environment had three distinct landmarks (church, tower, & tree) positioned at different locations on a randomly textured ground plane. As shown in Figure 1a, on each trial, participants started by standing at a constant starting location, facing a constant direction (blue triangle). Next, they walked through a 3-post path, remembering the location of the first post. The posts appeared and disappeared in succession. At the end of the path, participants attempted to walk back to the location of the first post. There were four possible locations for the first post (Figure 1a, red dots) and four for the second post (green dots). The third post's location remained constant across the experiment (yellow dot). The distance from the two side landmarks to the third post was 3.4m and the distance from the middle landmark to the third post was 4.5m. The distances between the first posts and the third post were 2.15m and the distances between the second posts and the third post were 1.31m. The landmark configuration and post arrangement were symmetrical along the facing direction of the starting point. In the experiment, the location of the first red post was jittered by randomly sampling the jitter's x and y coordinates from a Gaussian distribution with mean = 0 and standard deviation = .25m. Then, an angle θ was randomly sampled from a uniform distribution between 0° and 360°. The final coordinate values of the jitter were calculated as, $x' = x *\cos(\theta)$ and $y' = y*\sin(\theta)$. Both x' and y' were truncated to .4m. In the poor environment, there was only a flag serving as the landmark, which was placed at the same location as the middle landmark in the rich environment.

Procedure. The task was to walk through a path consisting of 3 posts and then to attempt to walk back to the first post's location. Two sources of positional information were manipulated, self-motion cues and visual cues (e.g., landmarks). Participants could use both cues on some trials but only one of the two on others. The conditions were distinguished by the events that occurred at the end of the path: in the **vision** condition, participants were disoriented once they reached the last post (yellow dot in Figure 1a), so that during the response stage, self-motion information was lost and only landmarks remained; in the **self-motion** condition, the visual world was rendered invisible when participants reached the last post, so that they could only use self-motion cues; in the **combination** condition, participants were not disoriented and the world remained visible, so both landmarks and self-motion cues were available; and in the **conflict** condition, the landmark configuration was rotated clockwise by 15° so that the correct location defined by landmarks was different from the one defined by self-motion cues. The two single-cue conditions were used to estimate the cue reliabilities of visual cues and self-motion cues separately. The two double-cue conditions allowed us to examine how the two cues interacted when in agreement and when in disagreement.

In the vision condition, participants were disoriented before they attempted to make responses. The disorientation procedure was conducted as follows. The participant was guided to sit on a swivel chair once they reached the third post. Then the experimenter spun the chair for 20s while the participant counted down from a number between 100-200 in steps of 3. To match the vision condition, participants performed backward counting while standing still in the other three conditions. There were 10 blocks of trials, and each block contained 8 trials. Half of the trials were in the rich environment, and half were in the poor environment. The 10 blocks were evenly divided into 2 sessions on 2 consecutive days. The two environments alternated by segments of 4 trials, and for each 4-trial segment, each of the 4 conditions was experienced once. Hence, for each block, the first 4 trials and the last 4 trials were experienced in two environments, respectively. Half of the participants experienced the rich environment first in each block, and the other half experienced the poor environment first.

2.2   Results

The calculation of response variability and relative reliability proceeded as follows. As shown in Figure 1a, the four target locations were positioned symmetrically around the midline, with two on each side. First, for each of the four target locations, responses were transformed into a spatial coordinate system with the target location as the origin. Second, responses for the two target locations on the same side were pooled together. Outliers were defined as responses whose distance from the response centroid exceeded the 3rd quartile by 3 times the interquartile range, considering all four target locations together. Third, before pooling responses from the two sides, we corrected the bias in each side's response distribution by centering each distribution over its centroid. This was done to eliminate disparity in the centroids of the distributions on the two sides, which would increase the variability of

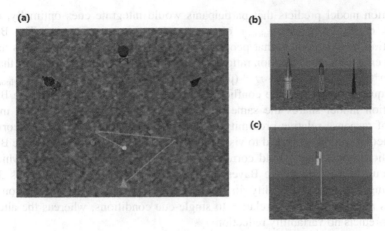

Fig. 1. Experimental environments. (a) Bird's eye view of the virtual rich environment. Red dots represent locations of the first post; green dots represent locations of the second post; yellow dot represents location of the third post. Blue triangle represents the starting point of each trial. Orange arrows represent a typical outbound path and dashed red arrow represents the correct return path. (b) & (c) Typical views in rich and poor environments, respectively.

the pooled distribution artificially. Fourth, after pooling together the two sides' response distributions, we computed the response standard deviation as,

$$\sigma = \sqrt{\sum d^2 / (n-1)},$$

where d is the distance of the response from the pooled centroid and n is the number of responses. Relative reliability of visual cues to self-motion cues was calculated as the inverse of relative variability of the two single-cue conditions, $rr = \sigma^2_{motion}/(\sigma^2_{motion} + \sigma^2_{vision})$.

The calculation of relative proximity needs to take into account any intrinsic bias in the response distribution; therefore we computed the relative proximity for each side first, then took the mean as the final estimate. For each side, we pooled together the responses on the two target locations, and then calculated the distribution centroid, μ. Euclidean distances between single-cue distributions and double-cue distributions were computed (e.g., $d_{motion-comb} = |\mu_{motion} - \mu_{comb}|$). Relative proximity to the visually defined location was calculated as the inverse of the relative distance, $rp_{comb} = d_{motion-comb}/(d_{motion-comb} + d_{vision-comb})$, and $rp_{conf} = d_{motion-conf}/(d_{motion-conf} + d_{vision-conf})$. The relative proximities computed for each side were then averaged across sides. This index reflects the actual weight assigned to visual cues relative to self-motion cues. According to Bayesian theory, response relative proximity to the visually defined location should be equal to cue relative reliability of visual cues.

Predictions for variability of double-cue conditions were calculated from variability of single-cue conditions. We tested two models, which were distinguished based on whether there was cue integration or cue alternation. The Bayesian integration model predicts that participants would integrate cues optimally, σ^2_{comb} = σ^2_{conf} = σ^2_{vision}* $\sigma^2_{motion}/(\sigma^2_{vision} + \sigma^2_{motion})$, and rp_{comb} = rp_{conf} = rr. The Bayesian alternation model predicts that people would alternate between landmarks and self-motion cues with an alternation ratio equivalent to the optimal weight, such that σ^2_{comb} = $(1-rr)$* $(\mu^2_{motion}+ \sigma^2_{motion})$+ rr * $(\mu^2_{vision}+ \sigma^2_{vision})-((1-rr)$ * $\mu_{motion}+ rr$ * $\mu_{vision})^2$. The same equation applies to the conflict condition. It is worth noting that the Bayesian alternation model shares the same predictions with Bayesian integration model in terms of response relative proximity. Response relative proximity would correspond to the actual weights assigned to visual cues in the linear combination in the Bayesian integration model, and would correspond to the percentage of trials in which only visual cues were used in the Bayesian alternation model. The two models differ in predicting response variability in double-cue conditions. The integration model predicts reduced variability relative to single-cue conditions, whereas the alternation model predicts no variability reduction.

Responses were analyzed in individual environments and across environments. For the latter, responses were pooled across the two environments based on which of the four conditions the response was in. We defined individuals as outliers when the averaged response variability across all conditions and both environments was 3 interquartile ranges above the 3rd quartile or below the 1st quartile. In correlational analyses, bivariate outliers were defined as having unstandardized residuals greater than the 3rd quartile by 3 times the interquartile range in the linear regression analysis.

Response Variability. The manipulation check shows that we successfully manipulated the reliability of visual cues without changing the reliability of self-motion cues. As shown in Figure 2a, vision variability was significantly lower in the rich environment than in the poor environment (t(17) = 5.68, p = .000), whereas there was no difference in self-motion variability (t(17) = .09, p = .926).

The second question is whether there was variability reduction in double-cue conditions compared to single-cue conditions, a hallmark of cue integration (Figure 2a). We also compared double-cue conditions to the Bayesian integration model. For the second analysis, we calculated Bayes factors (BFs) in addition to traditional inferential tests [25]. The customary cut points for Bayes factors are 3 and 1/3. A Bayes factor greater than 3 means that the null hypothesis is more than 3 times as likely as the alternative hypothesis; in the present comparisons, this means that the model fits the data. Conversely, a Bayes factor smaller than 1/3 means the model fails to fit the data.

As shown in Figure 2a, in the rich environment, the combination condition showed lower variability than vision and self-motion conditions, although only the combination-motion comparison was significant (t(17) = 1.37, p = .188; t(17) = 8.15, p = .000). The combination condition was consistent with the Bayesian integration model (t(17) = 0.51, p = .614, BF = 4.92). The conflict condition was also consistent with the Bayesian integration model (t(17) = 1.27, p = .220), even though the Bayes factor was slightly short of the cut point (BF = 2.65).

In the poor environment, the combination condition showed lower variability than vision and self-motion conditions, but neither comparison was significant (vision, $t(17) = 1.72$, $p = .103$; self-motion, $t(17) = 1.00$, $p = .332$). The combination condition seemed to differ from the Bayesian integration model ($t(17) = 2.26$, $p = .037$, BF = 0.65). The conflict condition showed reduced variability relative to both single-cue conditions (vision, $t(17) = 3.72$, $p = .002$; self-motion, $t(17) = 4.98$, $p = .000$). The conflict condition was consistent with the Bayesian integration model ($t(17) = 0.33$, $p = .748$, BF = 5.31).

When responses were pooled across both environments, both double-cue conditions showed significant variability reduction relative to the two single-cue conditions ($ps < .05$). The t-test suggested that the combination condition did not differ from the integration model ($t(17) = 1.48$, $p = .157$), although the Bayes factor fell short of the cut point (BF =2.07). The conflict condition was consistent with the Bayesian integration model ($t(17) = 0.34$, $p = .735$, BF = 5.28).

We also compared all the double-cue conditions to the Bayesian alternation model, which does not predict variability reduction. All double-cue conditions were different from this model, except the combination condition in the poor environment, which seemed to be a compromise between cue integration and alternation (combination vs. integration model, $t(17) = 2.26$, $p = .037$, BF = 0.65; combination vs. alternation model, $t(17) = 1.94$, $p = .069$, BF = 1.09).

Response Relative Proximity. We calculated response relative proximity in combination and conflict conditions separately. Because results showed that response relative proximity was very consistent between the two double-cue conditions, we took the mean of the two conditions to get a more reliable estimate of the actual weight assigned to the cues. We then compared the average response relative proximity to relative cue reliability calculated from single-cue conditions (Figure 2b). Response relative proximity measures the actual weight assigned to the visual cues relative to self-motion cues, and cue relative reliability represents the Bayesian weighting-strategy. The two indices should correspond with each other if the cues were weighted in a Bayesian manner.

In the rich environment, response relative proximity was significantly lower than cue relative reliability in both double-cue conditions and when the two conditions were averaged ($t(17) = 3.55$, $p = .002$). The two indices were consistent with each other in the poor environment ($t(17) = 0.00$, $p = .998$) and when responses were pooled across environments ($t(17) = 0.42$, $p = .678$). As shown in Figure 2c, positive correlations existed between these two indices, across participants, in both individual environments (bivariate outliers deleted) and in the pooled analysis, indicating that in general participants weighted cues based on their relative quality.

Summary. Participants' performance tended to deviate from the Bayesian integration model in individual environments. First, variability reduction was not consistently observed in double-cue conditions relative to single-cue conditions, and response variability in double-cue conditions was not consistently fit by the Bayesian integration model. Second, response relative proximity was lower than cue relative reliability in the rich environment. When responses were pooled across environments, participants' behaviors were optimal or near-optimal, both in variability reduction and response relative proximity. Across all levels of analysis, positive correlations existed across subjects between relative proximity and relative reliability, implying participants weighted visual cues and self-motion cues based on their relative quality.

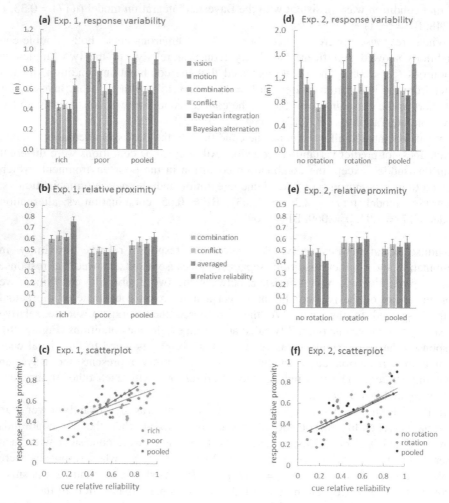

Fig. 2. Results of Experiments 1 and 2. (a) and (d) show response variability and model predictions in Exp. 1 and Exp. 2, respectively; the alternation model's prediction represents the average of the predictions for the combination and the conflict condition. (b) and (e) show response relative proximity and cue relative reliability (*rr*) in Exp. 1 and Exp. 2, respectively. (c) and (f) show correlations across participants between averaged response relative proximity and cue relative reliability in Exp. 1 and Exp. 2, respectively. Error bars represent ± SE of the mean.

3   Experiment 2

3.1   Method

Eighteen people (9 males, 9 females) from Vanderbilt University or the Nashville community participated in this experiment. They ranged in age from 18 to 32 years, with a mean of 23.7. Participants had normal or corrected-to-normal vision. Participants performed the same task as in Experiment 1. Only the poor environment was used here (Figure 1c). The reliability of self-motion cues was manipulated within-subjects by having participants either stand still or perform a body rotation while they were doing the backward counting. For body rotation, participants were instructed to rotate either to the left or to the right randomly until their facing direction was aligned with a designated marker. The body rotation was 270° on average, with jitter sampled from a Gaussian distribution with mean of 0° and standard deviation of 10°. Jitter was truncated to 10°. The layout of trials was very similar to Experiment 1, except there were only 7 types: Vision only, self-motion only with or without rotation, combination with or without rotation, conflict with or without rotation. There were 10 blocks, each with 7 trials corresponding to the 7 trial types. The 10 blocks were evenly divided over two days. In each block, participants experienced no rotation trials first, then rotation trials, and the vision-only trial with disorientation was inserted into a random position within the block.

3.2   Results

Response Variability. The manipulation check indicated that adding body rotation of 270° at the end of the outbound path successfully increased response variability (Figure 2d). Response variability in the self-motion condition was significantly greater when body rotation was added than when no body rotation was added ($t(17) = 5.88, p = .000$).

When there was no body rotation, the combination condition showed significantly smaller variability than the vision condition ($t(17) = 2.56, p = .020$) but not the self-motion condition ($t(17) = 0.99, p = .337$). The combination condition differed from the Bayesian integration model ($t(17) = 2.87, p = .011, BF = .22$). The conflict condition showed variability significantly lower than the vision condition ($t(17) = 4.65, p = .000$) and the self-motion condition ($t(17) = 2.99, p = .008$). The conflict condition was consistent with the integration model ($t(17) = 0.66, p = .515, BF = 4.53$).

When body rotation was introduced, the combination condition showed significantly lower variability than both single-cue conditions (vision, $t(17) = 3.20, p = .005$; self-motion, $t(17) = 5.70, p = .000$). The combination condition was consistent with the integration model ($t(17) = 0.01, p = .989, BF = 5.59$). The conflict condition showed significant variability reduction relative to the self-motion condition ($t(17) = 3.49, p = .002$) but not to the vision condition ($t(17) = 1.68, p = .111$). The conflict condition was consistent with the integration model, although the Bayes factor was short of the cut point ($t(17) = 1.39, p = .184, BF = 2.32$).

When responses were pooled across rotation levels, both double-cue conditions showed significantly lower variability than single-cue conditions (ps < .04). The combination condition was marginally greater than predicted by the Bayesian integration model and Bayes factor analysis suggested that the evidence was ambiguous on whether this model fit the data (t(17) = 1.92, p = .072, BF = 1.12); these results imply near-optimal mode of response. The conflict condition was consistent with the Bayesian integration model (t(17) = 1.05, p = .309, BF = 3.35).

All of the double-cue conditions differed from the alternation model, except the combination condition in the no rotation condition, which seemed to be a compromise between cue integration and alternation (combination vs. integration model, t(17) = 2.87, p = .011, BF = .22; combination vs. alternation model, t(17) = 2.54, p = .021, BF = 0.40).

Response Relative Proximity. As shown in Figure 2e, when there was no rotation, cue relative reliability did not differ from response relative proximity in the combination condition (t(17) = 1.24, p =.233). Differences between relative reliability and relative proximity were significant in the conflict condition (t(17) = 2.08, p = .053) and marginally significant when the two double-cue conditions were averaged (t(17) = 1.84, p = .083). The two indices were consistent with each other when there was rotation and when responses were pooled across rotation levels (ps > .300). At all levels of analysis, positive correlations existed between relative proximity and relative reliability, as shown in Figure 2f.

Summary. The current experiment showed a pattern of results similar to those of Experiment 1. In the current experiment, when responses were pooled across environments, participants' behaviors were optimal or near-optimal in Bayesian terms, with significant variability reduction in double-cue conditions consistent with Bayesian predictions and relative proximity consistent with relative reliability. At individual rotation levels, participants' behaviors tended to deviate from the Bayesian integration model. First, double-cue conditions did not consistently show variability reduction and were not consistently fit by the Bayesian integration model. Second, response relative proximity in the no rotation condition tended to be higher than the Bayesian weight (i.e., relative reliability).

It is worth noting that the Bayesian weight when there was rotation was higher than the Bayesian weight when there was no rotation, suggesting that the actual weights assigned to visual cues (relative proximities) were increased in the no-rotation condition to be closer to the actual visual weights in the rotation condition. The same tendency was observed in Experiment 1 as well, where the visual weights were apparently decreased in the rich environment to be closer to the visual weights in the poor environment (Figure 1b). When we analyzed this tendency across the two experiments, results showed that this bias was significant (p=.001) and no interaction was found between experiments (p=.20). This finding indicates that when subjects experienced cues changing in reliability, the actual weights were distorted at the richer level of the manipulated cue in such a direction that they would be closer to the weights at the poorer level of the same cue.

The most obvious compromise in response variability between the integration model and the alternation model occurred in the poor environment in Experiment 1 and in the no-rotation condition in Experiment 2. It is worth noting that these two conditions shared exactly the same experimental settings: The flag was the sole landmark and no extra body rotation was added. A subsequent experiment (not reported in the current paper) showed that when subjects only experienced this condition without another reliability level, variability reduction was consistently observed in both double-cue conditions and this reduction was consistent with the Bayesian integration model. This finding implies that the compromise observed in the present experiments resulted from interference caused by people alternating between different reliability levels of spatial cues; it also indicates that the better fit of the Bayesian model to the pooled data was not only caused by the doubling of the number of trials.

We also carefully compared these two conditions in other aspects. We found that response variability was significantly higher in the no-rotation condition than in the poor environment (p=.02, note that scales of ordinates differ in Figure 1a & d). In addition, as stated previously, relative proximity and relative reliability were consistent with each other in the poor environment but they tended to be different in the no-rotation condition. Finally, in the no-rotation condition, additional analyses showed that response variability in the conflict condition was not correlated across subjects with the predictions of either the integration model or the alternation model, the only double-cue condition devoid of such relationships in both experiments. These discrepancies provide additional support to the claim that even though these two conditions shared the same experimental settings, subjects behaved differently, depending on the other reliability level they experienced simultaneously.

4   General Discussion

In both experiments, we observed similar patterns of results. When responses were pooled across noise levels of the manipulated cue, people behaved in a Bayesian optimal way. Response variability reduction was evident and generally consistent with Bayesian predictions. Relative proximity was also predicted by Bayesian principles. This pattern of results is consistent with findings on cue integration of other stimulus features [17,18,19] and pioneering work in the domain of human spatial navigation [20]. However, people's behaviors deviated from Bayesian principles at individual noise levels, in that relative proximity differed from cue relative reliability and response variability was not always reduced by the amount predicted by Bayesian theory. Interference between noise levels was also evident in the apparent tendency of participants to adjust their responses at one noise level away from Bayesian predictions to be closer to that at the other noise level. These results showed that people could be non-optimal under certain circumstances.

The interference effect between noise levels might have been caused by properties shared by them. For example, the same set of physical locations was used for both noise levels, the virtual visual environments are either very similar or the same, and the navigation space was always mapped to the same real-world environment, the lab space. It is possible that Bayesian coding principles were restricted to or targeted at the target locations or the surrounding spatial context. Future research might attempt to determine which factors shared by noise levels would lead to interference. This research might shed light on how Bayesian coding principles are organized and at which level they occur in the spatial navigation system.

It was surprising that people deviated from Bayesian integration theory at individual noise levels but managed to behave in a Bayesian way when responses were pooled. A mathematical analysis suggested that when both single-cue distributions are not biased, if people behave as Bayesian integrators at individual noise levels, they would become supra-optimal at the pooled level [26]. Further simulations showed that people can compromise at individual noise levels in order to be just Bayesian optimal at the pooled level [26]. It would be worth investigating in future simulation work the forms that the interference must take in order for behavior to be optimal at the pooled level. Future simulation work should also take into account intrinsic biases in response distributions and try to incorporate the interference effect we observed in response relative proximity.

Our study is related to the recent project reported by Zhao and Warren [27]. Overall, our findings are consistent with their observations, in that we both discovered that participants could optimally or nearly optimally integrate visual landmarks and self-motion cues. However, in their conflict condition, Zhao and Warren observed a dissociation between response relative proximity and response variability. When the conflict was not greater than 90°, participants followed either landmarks or self-motion cues based on response relative proximity, but still showed optimal reduction in response variability. We only tested a 15° conflict, and found that response relative proximity seemed to be a compromise between landmarks and self-motion cues, and this compromise was predicted by cue relative reliability. We speculate that this discrepancy may be explained by different experimental procedures. In Zhao and Warren's study, both spatial cues were stable and participants practiced the task for a very long time (5 days). Participants also only experienced the conflict condition in the conflict sessions. Extensive familiarity with the experimental procedure and the blocked conditions might have encouraged the tendency to rely on one spatial cue only during the initial stage of response. It might also have allowed people to notice the landmark shift and even estimate the amount of shift. Participants then could have mentally corrected the landmark shift and been able to optimally integrate corrected landmarks with the self-motion system in a later stage of response. Familiarity with the experimental set-up was also evident when the authors found that the walked distance was not informative among different conditions, since the participants might have learned the constant distance to walk from the path end to the target location.

Our results showed that people weighted spatial cues based on cue relative reliabilities, which could have important implications for the study of spatial navigation. We speculate that cue reliability is closely related to cue salience, in that more salient cues usually correspond to higher cue reliability and result in more precise location representations [26]. Cue salience effect is a common phenomenon observed in the spatial navigation literature. Cue size, distance, and richness are three main factors affecting cue salience [5,6,8,28-31]. The Bayesian weighting-by-reliability strategy observed in our experiments thus suggests that it is as important to consider quality of cues as to consider different cue types, and that the Bayesian paradigm may be able to serve as a useful framework to study other factors influencing the cue interaction process after cue reliability has been accounted for (e.g., implicit stability, which might exert its influence as a prior information) and possible different rules for within-modal and inter-modal cue interaction [32,33].

References

1. Cheng, K., Newcombe, N.S.: Is there a geometric module for spatial orientation? Squaring theory and evidence. Psychonomic Bulletin & Review 12(1), 1–23 (2005)
2. Lew, A.R.: Looking beyond the boundaries: Time to put landmarks back on the cognitive map? Psychol. Bull. 137(3), 484–507 (2011), doi:10.1037/a0022315
3. Twyman, A.D., Newcombe, N.S.: Five reasons to doubt the existence of a geometric module. Cogn. Sci. 34(7), 1315–1356 (2010), doi:10.1111/j.1551-6709.2009.01081.x
4. Save, E., Poucet, B.: Involvement of the hippocampus and associative parietal cortex in the use of proximal and distal landmarks for navigation. Behavioural Brain Research 109(2), 195–206 (2000), doi:10.1016/s0166-4328(99)00173-4
5. Chamizo, V.D., Manteiga, R.D., Rodrigo, T., Mackintosh, N.J.: Competition between landmarks in spatial learning: The role of proximity to the goal. Behav. Processes 71(1), 59–65 (2006), doi:10.1016/j.beproc.2005.11.003
6. Goodyear, A.J., Kamil, A.C.: Clark's nutcrackers (Nucifraga columbiana) and the effects of goal–landmark distance on overshadowing. J. Comp. Psychol. 118(3), 258–264 (2004), doi:10.1037/0735-7036.118.3.258
7. Roberts, A.D., Pearce, J.M.: Blocking in the Morris swimming pool. J. Exp. Psychol. Anim. Behav. Process. 25(2), 225–235 (1999)
8. Spetch, M.L.: Overshadowing in landmark learning: touch-screen studies with pigeons and humans. J. Exp. Psychol. Anim. Behav. Process. 21(2), 166–181 (1995)
9. Wilson, P.N., Alexander, T.: Blocking of spatial learning between enclosure geometry and a local landmark. Journal of Experimental Psychology-Learning Memory and Cognition 34(6), 1369–1376 (2008), doi:10.1037/a0013011
10. Cheng, K.: A purely geometric module in the rat's spatial representation. Cognition 23(2), 149–178 (1986)
11. Doeller, C.F., Burgess, N.: Distinct error-correcting and incidental learning of location relative to landmarks and boundaries. Proc. Natl Acad. Sci. U S A 105(15), 5909–5914 (2008), doi:10.1073/pnas.0711433105
12. Kearns, M.J., Warren, W.H., Duchon, A.P., Tarr, M.J.: Path integration from optic flow and body senses in a homing task. Perception 31(3), 349–374 (2002), doi:10.1068/p3311
13. Kelly, J.W., McNamara, T.P., Bodenheimer, B., Carr, T.H., Rieser, J.J.: The shape of human navigation: How environmental geometry is used in maintenance of spatial orientation. Cognition 109(2), 281–286 (2008), doi:10.1016/j.cognition.2008.09.001
14. Nico, D., Israel, I., Berthoz, A.: Interaction of visual and idiothetic information in a path completion task. Experimental Brain Research 146(3), 379–382 (2002), doi:10.1007/s00221-002-1184-8
15. Chittka, L., Geiger, K.: Honeybee long-distance orientation in a controlled environment. Ethology 99(2), 117–126 (1995)

16. Cheng, K., Shettleworth, S.J., Huttenlocher, J., Rieser, J.J.: Bayesian integration of spatial information. Psychol. Bull. 133(4), 625–637 (2007), doi:10.1037/0033-2909.133.4.625
17. Ernst, M.O., Banks, M.S.: Humans integrate visual and haptic information in a statistically optimal fashion. Nature 415(6870), 429–433 (2002), doi:10.1038/415429a
18. Nardini, M., Bedford, R., Mareschal, D.: Fusion of visual cues is not mandatory in children. Proc. Natl Acad. Sci. U S A 107(39), 17041–17046 (2010), doi:10.1073/pnas.1001699107
19. Parise, C.V., Spence, C., Ernst, M.O.: When correlation implies causation in multisensory integration. Current Biology 22(1), 46–49 (2012)
20. Nardini, M., Jones, P., Bedford, R., Braddick, O.: Development of cue integration in human navigation. Curr. Biol. 18(9), 689–693 (2008), doi:10.1016/j.cub.2008.04.021
21. Loomis, J.M., Klatzky, R.L., Golledge, R.G., Cicinelli, J.G., Pellegrino, J.W., Fry, P.A.: Nonvisual navigation by blind and sighted: assessment of path integration ability. Journal of Experimental Psychology: General 122(1), 73 (1993)
22. Cheng, K., Spetch, M.L.: Stimulus control in the use of landmarks by pigeons in a touch-screen task. J. Exp. Anal. Behav. 63(2), 187–201 (1995)
23. Kelly, J.W., McNamara, T.P., Bodenheimer, B., Carr, T.H., Rieser, J.J.: Individual differences in using geometric and featural cues to maintain spatial orientation: Cue quantity and cue ambiguity are more important than cue type. Psychon. Bull. Rev. 16(1), 176–181 (2009), doi:10.3758/PBR.16.1.176
24. Loomis, J.M., Klatzky, R.L., Golledge, R.G., Philbeck, J.W.: Human navigation by path integration. In: Wayfinding Behavior: Cognitive Mapping and Other Spatial Processes, pp. 125–151 (1999)
25. Rouder, J.N., Speckman, P.L., Sun, D., Morey, R.D., Iverson, G.: Bayesian t tests for accepting and rejecting the null hypothesis. Psychonomic Bulletin & Review 16(2), 225–237 (2009)
26. Chen, X.: Bayesian cue interaction in human spatial navigation: mathematical demonstration, simulations, and relationship between cue salience and cue reliability. Technical Report, Department of Psychology, Vanderbilt University (2014)
27. Zhao, M., Warren, W.H.: Path integration and visual landmarks: Optimal combination or multiple systems? In: Annual Meeting of Psychonomics Society, St. Louis, MO (November 2010)
28. Bruggeman, H., Zosh, W., Warren, W.H.: Optic flow drives human visuo-locomotor adaptation. Current Biology 17(23), 2035–2040 (2007)
29. Chamizo, V., Rodrigo, T., Peris, J., Grau, M.: The influence of landmark salience in a navigation task: An additive effect between its components. Journal of Experimental Psychology: Animal Behavior Processes 32(3), 339 (2006)
30. Gouteux, S., Thinus-Blanc, C., Vauclair, J.: Rhesus monkeys use geometric and nongeometric information during a reorientation task. Journal of Experimental Psychology: General 130(3), 505 (2001)
31. Learmonth, A.E., Nadel, L., Newcombe, N.S.: Children's use of landmarks: Implications for modularity theory. Psychol. Sci. 13(4), 337–341 (2002)
32. Hillis, J.M., Ernst, M.O., Banks, M.S., Landy, M.S.: Combining sensory information: mandatory fusion within, but not between, senses. Science 298(5598), 1627–1630 (2002), doi:10.1126/science.1075396
33. Mou, W., Spetch, M.L.: Object location memory: Integration and competition between multiple context objects but not between observers' body and context objects. Cognition 126(2), 181–197 (2013)

Cognitive Values of Place Image Detected from Spatial Distribution of Building Names

Toshihiro Osaragi

Department of Mechanical and Environmental Informatics,
Graduate School of Information Science and Engineering,
Tokyo Institute of Technology,
2-12-1-W8-10 O-okayama, Meguro-ku, Tokyo, 152-8552, Japan
osaragi@mei.titech.ac.jp

Abstract. Cognitive values of place image are difficult to extract in quantitative terms, since they are dependent on various kinds of elements or activities within that places. In this paper, we focus on a phenomenon in which a part of people's cognitive values of place image can be observed in the naming behavior for building names. In the first instance, a model based on the random utility theory is constructed for describing people's naming behavior for building names. Secondly, the proposed model is calibrated using the actual data on the spatial distribution of building names in Tokyo. Third, using the model, the cognitive values of place image are quantitatively estimated and their spatial distribution is represented on a map. Finally, we demonstrate an example of its application to a land price model, and confirm that the proposed model can be applied to other urban models with ease.

Keywords: Cognitive value, Place image, Spatial distribution, Building name.

1 Introduction

The various images or impressions that people have in a certain place have an influence to no small extent on their daily activities in that place. For example, residents who will select a particular place for residence are affected by the image of that place [3]. Also, consumers' perception of the attributes of store image affects their preference for the stores [16].

Place image has traditionally been important in areas including tourism, country positioning in international relations, the protection of local producers from imports through "buy domestic" campaigns, and the export promotion of agricultural and manufactured products [6, 13]. In the field of tourism, research of the past two decades has demonstrated that place image is a valuable concept in understanding the destination selection process of tourists. Baloglu and McCleary [2] report that several studies center on the relationship between destination image (place image) and preference or visitation intentions. One other field of research where place image strongly related is in the field of marketing. The object of city marketing is the city's image, which in turn is the starting point for developing the city's brand [7], and the inception

C. Freksa et al. (Eds.): Spatial Cognition 2014, LNAI 8684, pp. 161–175, 2014.

of place branding evolved from research within various fields including place image [5]. As the previous research demonstrate, many researchers have sought to understand place image from a variety of viewpoints.

Up until now, research of place image has been conducted primarily by detailed examination of the survey results concerning the qualitative aspects of different place image [4, 10, 11, 14]. Baloglu and McCleary [2] propose a conceptual model which provides insights into how images of destinations are developed. However, it has not been easy to perform relative value appraisals for multiple places, since the place image is of complex structures derived from a wide variety of factors and the research requires covering extensive areas.

Given this background, we attempt to propose a method for extracting quantitative values of place image, which is constructed based not only on people's daily activities and elements of lives, but also on a variety of historical elements and organizational factors. In order to achieve this purpose, we focus on building names. The recent studies have shown the value of place names as environmental indicators, and Sousa et al. [15] demonstrate the possibility of using place names as a tool to study changes in different components of the landscape. In this research, we focus on a phenomenon in which a part of people's cognitive values of place image can be observed in their naming behavior for building names. More specifically, we propose a method for extracting cognitive values of place image by using the spatial distribution of building names.

The fundamental idea of our model is illustrated in Figure 1. While place names indicate the places as actual spaces, it reminds us the place image concerning actual conditions and characteristics. Therefore, by attaching the place name as one part of a building name, the impression of the building is enhanced by the place image. In other words, the probability is considered to be high that the names of buildings will include such place names as these representing favorable images of places. Taking this phenomenon into account, this research attempt to quantitatively extract cognitive values of place image (i.e., image or impressions concerning the relative preferences for a place) by examining the naming behavior for building names.

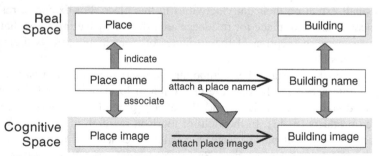

The Impressions of a building is enhanced by the place image by attaching a place name.

Fig. 1. Basics of the model: effects of attaching place name to building name

Using the actual GIS databases including building names, Masuda and Osaragi [8] and Osaragi and Ogawa [12] demonstrate the fact that the place names attached to building names do not necessarily coincide with the nearest train station nor the location of the town in which the building is located. This bias towards preferred names is a global and well-known phenomenon, which has been called 'vanity addressing' [17, 18, 19]. In this paper, our objective is to construct a model to describe this phenomena, in order to investigate the mechanism of naming behavior and values of place image. Namely, we discuss the concept of choice probability of place names in order to quantify cognitive values of place image. In addition, we evaluate the constituent factors, i.e., the kinds of place activities and place characteristics that create cognitive values of place image. The practical contribution of this paper is to discuss and demonstrate the potential of our model in application to the general statistical models previously proposed.

2   Model Describing Cognitive Values of Place Image

2.1   Place Names Used in Multiple Dwelling Residences

In this research, the term *"place name"* is used to refer to the town name and/or train station name. To be exact, the station name refers only to the facilities of the train station itself, but in everyday life and conversation it means an expansive place around the train station. Whenever pointing out the shopping areas, etc., the vicinity of the station, the train station name is used even more frequently than the town name. This is especially true in Japan. Therefore, the train station name can also be considered as being included in the collection of place names.

The study area of this research is Setagaya ward in Tokyo (Figure 2). Examining by building area, the proportion of buildings which include place names in a part of building name increases as the building area increases (Figure 3). This research makes it clear that the place name is included as part of the building name nearly 80% of the time whenever the building area is 400 m^2 or more. This suggests that place names are likely to be attached to building names as the important locality-related information, as the size of the buildings becomes larger and the buildings are located closer to the nearest train station.

Next, by examining the year of buildings' constructions, it has become clear in this research that the proportion of buildings that were built in 1980 or later that have place names included in the building names is relatively consistent at about 40% in all cases. In addition, although there is considerable variety in the building names used over a period of years, the proportion of building names that includes the place name remains consistently high.

The GIS data compiled for this area includes 60 towns and 39 train stations. The total of 8,620 residential- and commercial buildings, whose names include place names, are shown in Figure 2. There are 94 possible place names to be used for building names, since some town names and train station names are the same.

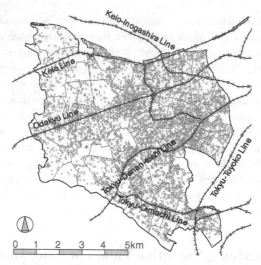

Fig. 2. Study area: boundaries of towns and the spatial distribution of buildings to be analyzed

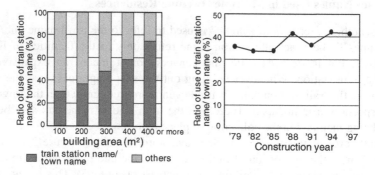

Fig. 3. Ratio of train station names/ town names used for building names

2.2   Construction of Place Image Model

There are two considerations for the evaluation of building names: (1) whether the place name is used, or whether a different name is used instead of the place name; and (2) which place name is used if a place name is used. By paying attention to the process in (2), the description below attempts to establish a model for the choice behavior in naming the buildings.

Looking at the actual spatial distribution of building names, the place name included within the name of the building does not necessarily correspond to the name of the nearest train station or the town in which the building is located. This phenomenon can be considered to manifest that there are differences for each train station and town name in the cognitive values of place image. Simple conceptual examples are shown in Figure 4.

However, an important point that should be noted here is that when attaching a town name that is outside the actual location of the building, or when using the name of a train station that is not the nearest station, psychological resistance is recognized for this unnatural naming behavior. The degree of psychological resistance can be considered to increase as the distance from the corresponding town border or train station increase.

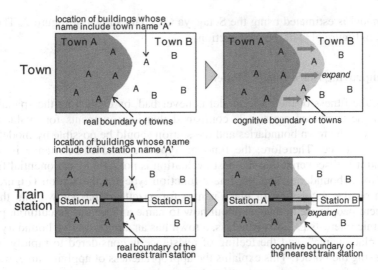

Fig. 4. Distortion of the spatial distribution of building names

Therefore, a model is constructed that describes the spatial distribution of building names. We anticipate that, within the place where a building is located, a building name that gives the most favorable impression in terms of cognitive values is selected from a collection of place names (train station names/ town names).

The probability P_{ij} for a building located in location i to use a name from place j is described by the following logit model based on the random utility theory.

$$P_{ij} = \frac{\exp[U_{ij}]}{\sum_k \exp[U_{ik}]},$$

(1)

The fixed term utility U_{ij} is considered to be made up of the cognitive value U_j of a place j and the resistance C_{ij} (negative value) for using a name from a place j. This is expressed by the following formula.

$$U_{ij} = U_j + C_{ij},$$

(2)

When the place name assigned to a building is the same as the actual location of the building, resistance is not expressed. Namely, the value of resistance C_{ii} is 0. When a train station name or town name is used that is not within the vicinity of the building location, then the resistance increases according to distance. Hence, resistance C_{ij} is expressed by the distance from town border X_{ij1}, the distance from a station X_{ij2}, and unknown parameters β_1, β_2. This model is called the *basic model*.

$$C_{ij} = \beta_1 X_{ij1} + \beta_2 X_{ij2}. \tag{3}$$

The model is estimated using the Setagaya GIS data shown in Figure 2. The result is shown in Figure 5(1) of the next section.

2.3   Improving Place Image Model

Although the fitness of the basic model is never bad, by evaluating the spatial distribution of the estimated error, it is confirmed that improvements for evaluating the distance from the town boundaries and the station should be possible by modeling the distance resistance. Therefore, the function type for distance resistance is reconsidered, and it is discovered that the best evaluation is possible by exponential function type for town boundaries and the linear function type for the station (Figure 5(2)). Research on the acquisition of place names for gazetteers has shown that there are cases where people are in dispute about how to name a place due to cultural, political or economic interests [9]. Nevertheless, a town has an administrative boundary and an "official place name", and the feeling of resistance is considered to rapidly increase after crossing the border. This explains the appropriateness of applying an exponential function type for distance from the town boundaries.

Next, because there is a possibility of differences in the function of resistance according to differences in building use, the resistance coefficients are estimated separately for residential and commercial use (Figure 5(3)). As a result, compatibility is improved, and the model is refined from the viewpoint of likelihood ratio, the value of AIC, and the fitting ratio. Observing the resistance coefficients, the value for residential use (β_1, β_2) is less than that for commercial use (β_3, β_4) respectively. This is because, in the case of multiple dwelling residences as compared to shopping areas, etc., the residents have a strong consciousness of addresses, and, accordingly, it can be inferred that, in residential use, it is harder to attach a town name or train station name to a building that is not the nearest station or that is outside the boundaries of that town.

Next, the resistance coefficient values may vary between when both a train station name and a town name are the same (hereafter referred to as *duplicate name*), and when a train station name and a town name are different (a name that is only the town name or only the train station name). Therefore, the resistance coefficients are divided into two more categories and estimated (Figure 5(4)). Looking at the estimated values of the resistance coefficients, the absolute value for duplicate names (β_1', β_2', β_3', β_4') is less than that for names that are only the town name or only the train station name (β_1, β_2, β_3, β_4) respectively. In other words, it can be understood that in cases when the train station name and town name are the same, that name is more likely attached to building names that are relatively farther away. Favorable results could be obtained by looking at the likelihood ratio, the value of AIC, or the fitting ratio, and the model is further improved. The model below uses eight resistance coefficients for resistance C_{ij}, and it is called the *place image model*. The above improvement process of models helps us understand the mechanism of our naming behavior.

(1) Basic model

Evaluation Indices	Likelihood Ratio	0.733
	AIC	19,168
	Fitting Ratio	67.0%
Estimated parameters	Distance from boundary of towns β_1	-6.76
	Distance from train stations β_2	-3.25

▼

(2) Model 1

Estimated parameters	Distance from boundary of towns	log(X+1)	log(X+1)	exp[X]	exp[X]
	Distance from train stations	log(X+1)	X	log(X+1)	X
Evaluation Indices	Likelihood Ratio	0.742	0.743	0.766	0.768
	AIC	18,568	18,474	16,845	16,659
	Fitting Ratio	67.7%	67.8%	71.0%	71.2%

▼

(3) Model 2

Evaluation Indices	Likelihood Ratio		0.770
	AIC		16,586
	Fitting Ratio		71.2%
Estimated parameters	Distance from boundary of towns	residential β_1	-2.40
		commercial β_3	-2.01
	Distance from train stations	residential β_2	-3.56
		commercial β_4	-3.33

▼

(4) Model 3 (Place Image Model)

Evaluation Indices	Likelihood Ratio			0.779
	AIC			15,943
	Fitting Ratio			71.4%
Estimated parameters	Distance from boundary of towns	residential	single β_1	-2.77
			duplicate $\beta_{1'}$	-1.84
		commercial	single β_3	-2.41
			duplicate $\beta_{3'}$	-1.44
	Distance from train stations	residential	single β_2	-5.68
			duplicate $\beta_{2'}$	-2.45
		commercial	single β_4	-5.28
			duplicate $\beta_{4'}$	-2.38

single: the building name is the same as a train station name or a town name
duplicate: the building name is the same as both a train station name and a town name

Fig. 5. Improvement of models

2.4   Cognitive Values of Place Image

Town names and train station names are considered as two different categories because a town name clearly expresses the place within the administrative borders of the town, whereas the boundary for the place indicated by the train station name is not necessarily clear. Therefore, buildings that contained the train station name are eliminated from the samples (N=7,586), and the cognitive values of place image are estimated using the town name only as a selection. These results are represented in Figure 6. From the figure, it is apparent that the cognitive values of place image are higher in places where major train stations are located.

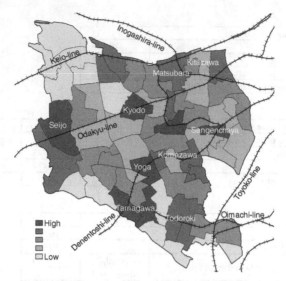

Fig. 6. Spatial distribution of cognitive values of place image

2.5   Visualizing the Highest Cognitive Values of Place Image

It can be derived that the image relating to the expanse of a particular place is influenced by our cognition of building names within that area. In other words, regions for the highest cognitive values of place image will implicitly expresses the place that is likely to be perceived as being a part of that region. Using the estimated place image model, the place names that have the highest probability of being used for building names are found (the concept is illustrated in Figure 7), and the cognitive values of place image are shown on the map for each location (Figure 8).

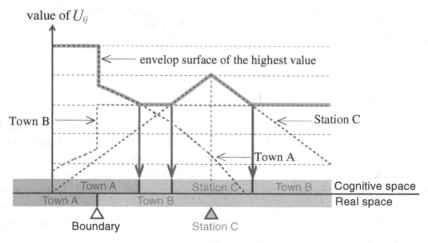

Fig. 7. Cognitive boundaries of towns and domains of train station based on the cognitive values of place image

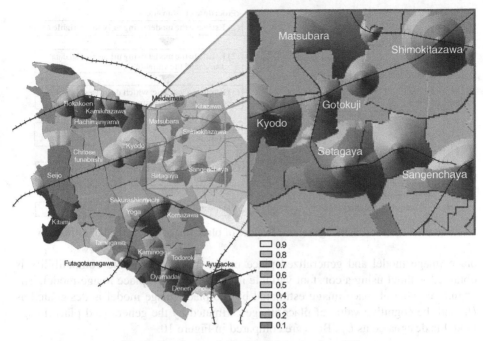

Fig. 8. Envelop surface of the highest value of U_{ij}

3 Factors Composing Cognitive Values of Place Image

3.1 Generalized Place Image Model

Whereas the previous section estimated the cognitive values of place image U_j as the constant value for each place j, this section consider factors that generate differences in cognitive value. By being rewritten, the model shown at the left of Figure 9 is a *generalized place image model*, which describes the cognitive values of place image using urban activities in that place. An estimation method of the model is shown at the right of Figure 9.

3.2 Estimation of Generalized Place Image Model

The estimation is performed by the method shown in Figure 9. Generally, the more explanatory variables, the more detailed look one can get; however, the model becomes unstable if it includes too many variables. Hence, the well-known statistic criteria, Akaike's Information Criterion (AIC) is used to incorporate variables into the model. A model showing smaller AIC value is superior to the others. As shown in Table 1, there are 37 available variables for describing the urban activities of places where buildings are located. Table 2 shows a comparison of estimation results of the

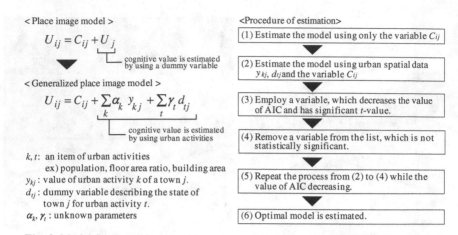

Fig. 9. Model for describing cognitive values of place image and method of estimation

place image model and generalized place image model. Favorable compatibility is obtained without using a constant variable in the generalized place image model. The cognitive value of place image estimated by the place image model is designated as U_j, and the cognitive value of place image estimated by the generalized place image model is designated as U_j^*. Both are compared in Figure 10.

Table 1. Variables of urban activities used for generalized place image model

Indicator variable		18	Number of wooden houses
1	whether the name is the same as both an existing train station name and a town name	19	Number of wooden apartment houses
Variables defined for each train station		20	Ratio of wooden apartment houses
2	Total number of passengers per day for each train station	21	Ratio of wooden structure apartment houses
3	Number of commercial buildings located within 200 m from a train station.	22	Number of buildings
Variables defined for each town		23	Density of buildings
4	Area of town	24	Average area of detached houses
5	Number of families	25	Number of detached houses
6	Population	26	Ratio of detached houses
7	Density of population	27	Ratio of housing
8	Density of families	28	Average number of stories
9	Number of distributors	29	Average building coverage ratio
10	Number of retail stores	30	Average floor area ratio
11	Number of employees of distributors/retail stores	31	Ratio of field area
12	Density of distributors	32	Ratio of housing area
13	Density of retail stores	33	Ratio of commercial area
14	Density of employees of distributors/retail stores	34	Ratio of forest area
15	Number of commercial buildings	35	Ratio of park/ground area
16	Density of commercial buildings	36	Time distance from town to train station
17	Ratio of commercial buildings	37	Time distance from town to Yama-note Line

Table 2. Results of estimationed models

	likelihood ratio	AIC	fitting ratio
Place image model	0.812	11269	78.70 %
Generalized place image model	0.792	12329	77.97 %

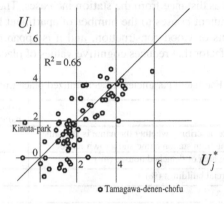

Fig. 10. Relationship between values of U_j and U_j^*

Overall, the values U_j^* agree with that of U_j. However, there are a low frequency of using the name Tamagawa-Denen-chofu in building names because the name is too long, and because it is contiguous with the famous high-class residential district Denen-chofu. For this reason, the cognitive values of place image U_j that is estimated as a constant variable is under-estimated.

3.3   Interpretation of Estimated Parameters

Values of the estimated parameters of the generalized place image model are shown in Table 3. The parameter codes express the positive and negative impacts to the cognitive values of place image, and the standardized parameter values express the level of influence on the cognitive values.

The largest positive operative force is an indicator variable expressing whether or not the same train station name exists. In other words, the existence of a train station has a strong influence on the formation of cognitive values of place image, and it is shown that the train station name plays an important role in attaching generic name to the urban activities around the train station. The average building area is also a positive operative force. In other words, high-class residential streets and their highly related premises greatly affect the cognitive values of place image. Also, the ratio of the number of commercial buildings to small shops is an important factor toward having a positive operative force. It can be considered that towns that have lively commercial activities and are often featured in the mass media contribute to the formation of favorable cognitive values of place image.

Meanwhile, the following functions concern factors that decrease the cognitive values of place image. First of all, the strongest negative operative force is the proportion of land that is agricultural or vacant because a high ratio is associated with a place still under development, and this can be considered to reduce the cognitive values. Station accessibility is expressed as the distance in traveling time from a representative point in the town to the nearest train station, and it can be verified that the cognitive value of place image decreased as distance from the station increases. The ratio of the number of wooden structure apartment houses to the number of apartment houses shows the number of rental apartments of wood construction, and it is apparent that wood fabricated apartments, etc., are a factor that reduces cognitive values of place image.

Table 3. Estimated parameters of generalized place image model

	Urban activities	Estimated parameters	Standardized values
1	Indicator variable describing whether the name is the same as both an existing train station name and a town name	1.7834	0.828
2	Average building area of detached houses (m^2)	0.0279	0.472
3	Ratio of commercial buildings (%)	0.0568	0.392
4	Ratio of field area (%)	-0.0845	-0.245
5	Time distance from town to the nearest train station (min.)	-0.0451	-0.197
6	Ratio of wooden structure apartment houses (%)	-0.0134	-0.181
7	Number of retail stores	0.0014	0.144

4   Application to Existing Urban Models

4.1   Combining Generalized Place Image Model with Land Price Model

The effectiveness of combining the place image model with existing urban models are confirmed. As for existing urban models, a model developed by Aoki et al. [1] is used. This model is based on the concept of transportation costs to express monetary burden and mental stress of transportation within the city. We describe this concept by the time distances in transportation, and thereby construct a model for expressing the structure of land pricing. Furthermore, we incorporate urban activities to express the differences of land price, which varies according to their detailed activities. Figure 11 outlines the structure of the model and also shows methods for combining the land price model with the place image model. The available variables for expressing urban activities are (1) land-use zonings, (2) floor-area ratio, and (3) actual land use types.

4.2   Comparison of Estimation Results

In the applicable area analyzed in this research, the results are shown in Table 4 for estimating a model using travel costs and a designated floor-area ratio. In the case of the estimation using the floor-area ratio, the compatibility of the real values and the estimated values are shown on the left of Figure 12. A relatively favorable result is obtained, but large residuals are apparent in locations with high real values.

Land price model (previously proposed)

$\log P = -C + A$

<Travel Cost>

$C = b_0 + b_1 M + b_2 Y + b_3 M^2 + b_4 MY + b_5 M^2$

<Urban Activities>

$A = \sum_{i=1}^{n} \sum_{j=1}^{m_i} (\log h_{ij}) d_{ij}$

P : Land price
C : Travel cost
M : Time distance from home to the nearest station
Y : Time distance from the nearest train station
to the city center (Yamanote-line)
d_{ij} : Dummy variable describing whether
urban activities of place i is j
h_{ij} : Unknown parameters

 improvement

Land price model combined with place image model

$\log P = -C + A + \theta U$

θ : Unknown parameter
U : Exponential function of cognitive values of place image

Fig. 11. Land price model combined with place image model

Table 4. Comparison of statistical values of land price models

Model	$\log P = -C + A$	$\log P = -C + A + \theta U$
Correlation coefficient	0.838	0.881
Value of AIC	-142	-197
Degree of freedom	10	11

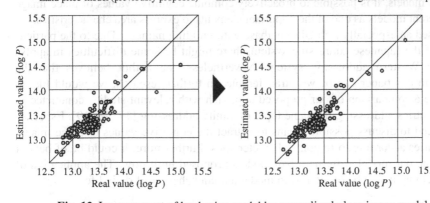

Fig. 12. Improvement of land price model by generalized place image model

Next, estimation is performed combining the cognitive values of place image with the existing land price model above. After converting cognitive values of place image into a variety of function types, it is shown that the exponential function type is the most preferable. The estimated results are shown on the right of Table 4 and on the right of Figure 12.

From the values of AIC, it is apparent that the model is improved. For confirmation purposes, the same analysis is attempted using values of U_j, but more favorable results are achieved using values U_j^* estimated from urban activities. These results also confirm the usefulness of the generalized place image model.

5   Summary and Conclusions

In this research, the place image model was constructed to describe the choice behavior for assigning building names according to the cognitive values of place image. First, one kind of choice behavior was considered for assigning building names that contain place names (train station name/ town name). Then, quantitative values were extracted for the cognitive values of place image using the actual data for the spatial distribution of building names. In order to evaluate the constituent factors of this cognitive value in detail, the generalized place image model was constructed, and in order to perform model estimation, a part of the relationships between various urban activities and the cognitive value were clarified. Finally, by combining this model with an existing urban model in order to create a model that better reflects actual conditions, the research showed the possibility and effectiveness of combining urban models with a goal to quantify cognitive values of place image.

Using the models proposed above in this research for spatial distributions of building names, quantitative values of place image can be extracted and analyzed relatively easily where as it has been conventionally difficult to grasp because of its obscurity. In conventional urban models, there has not been great discussion concerning cognitive values of place image, such as by being included in error terms, etc. However, by using the proposed models, it is possible to proactively combine cognitive values of place image into different models as one of the important elements to express area characteristics.

We used an especially rich GIS database with building names. Due to the particularities of the Japanese addressing system, there might be some difficulties in applying it to Western addressing system. Nevertheless, the author believes that the findings in this paper can be well transferable. In further research, we would like to undertake a comparison of our proposed approach with relevant studies conducted in other countries addressing the same topic of vanity addressing [17, 18, 19]. Especially, we need to discuss possible means to extract the cognitive values of place image, which varies according to regional characteristics. Furthermore, it could be of benefit to combine our model with the urban models proposed until now. The application of our model might also be of interest to model human behavior of daily life.

Acknowledgements. The author would like to acknowledge the valuable comments and useful suggestions from anonymous reviewers to improve the content and clarity of the paper. Also, he would like to give his special thanks to Mr. Ken-ichi Ogawa for computer-based numerical calculations and acknowledge the valuable comments from the audiences at the conference of the Design & Decision Support Systems in Architecture and Urban Planning (2008).

References

1. Aoki, Y., Osaragi, T., Ishizaka, K.: Interpolating model for land price data with transportation costs and urban activities. Environment and Planning B, Planning and Design 21, 53–65 (1994)
2. Baloglu, S., McCleary, K.W.: A Model of Destination Image Formation. Annals of Tourism Research 26(4), 868–897 (1999)
3. Bhat, C.B., Guo, J.: A mixed spatially correlated logit model: formulation and application to residential choice modeling. Transportation Research Part B: Methodological 38(2), 147–168 (2004)
4. Doi, T., Kiuchi, T., Mihoshi, A., Kitagawa, H., Nishii, K.: An image of railroad line area and its structure. Infrastructure Planning Review 12, 267–374 (1995)
5. Hanna, S., Rowley, J.: An analysis of terminology use in place branding. Place Branding and Public Diplomacy 4, 61–75 (2008)
6. Jenkins, O.H.: Understanding and Measuring Tourist Destination Images. Int. J. Tourism Res. 1, 1–15 (1999)
7. Kavaratzis, M.: From city marketing to city branding: Towards a theoretical framework for developing city brands. Place Branding 1(1), 58–73 (2004)
8. Masuda, K., Osaragi, T.: Spatial distribution of building names. Summaries of Technical Papers of Annual Meeting, Architectural Institute of Japan, F-1, pp. 783–784 (1996)
9. Montello, D.R., Goodchild, M.F., Gottsegen, J., Fohl, P.: Where's downtown?: Behavioral methods for determining referents of vague spatial queries. Spatial Cognition and Computation 3(2&3), 185–204 (2003)
10. Nishii, K., Tanahashi, M., Doi, T., Kiuchi, T.: The LOGMAP modelling for structural analysis of railroad line area image: An empirical study on the attribute – regression model. Infrastructure Planning Review 13, 49–56 (1996)
11. Nishii, K., Tanahashi, M., Doi, T., Kiuchi, T.: The LOGMAP model for image positioning of railroad line area: focusing on difference linguistic image between common and proper nouns. Infrastructure Planning Review 14, 107–114 (1997)
12. Osaragi, T., Ogawa, K.: Regional Images Extracted from Spatial Distribution of Building Names. Transactions of AIJ, Journal of Architecture, Planning and Environmental Engineering 592, 147–154 (2005)
13. Papadopoulos, N.: Place branding: Evolution, meaning and implications. Place Branding 1(1), 36–49 (2004)
14. Saito, K., Ishizaki, H., Tamura, T., Masuya, Y.: Analysis on the image structure of city and their relation to physical characteristics. Infrastructure Planning Review 14, 467–474 (1997)
15. Sousa, A., García-Murillo, P., Sahin, S., Morales, J., García-Barrón, L.: Wetland place names as indicators of manifestations of recent climate change in SW Spain (Doñana Natural Park). Climatic Change 100(3-4), 525–557 (2010)
16. Tan, B.L., Thang, D.C.: Linking consumer perception to preference of retail stores: An empirical assessment of the multi-attributes of store image. Journal of Retailing and Consumer Services 10(4), 193–200 (2003)
17. Winter, S., Bennett, R., Truelove, M., Rajabifard, A., Duckham, M., Kealy, A., Leach, J.: Spatially enabling 'Place' information. In: Spatially Enabling Society, ch. 4. Lueven University Press (2010)
18. Winter, S., Truelove, M.: Talking about place where it matters. In: Cognitive and Linguistic Aspects of Geographic Space. Lecture Notes in Geoinformation and Cartography, pp. 121–139 (2013)
19. Winter, S., Freksa, C.: Approaching the notion of place by contrast. Journal of Spatial Information Science 5, 31–50 (2012)

Up, Down, Turn Around: Assisted Wayfinding Involving Level Changes

Stephany Bigler, Annina Brügger, Fiona Utzinger, and Kai-Florian Richter

Department of Geography,
University of Zurich, Switzerland
{stephany.bigler,annina.bruegger,
fiona.utzinger,kai-florian.richter}@geo.uzh.ch

Abstract. Both maps and verbal descriptions have been shown to be an effective wayfinding assistance. However, most studies investigating these aids have been performed in two-dimensional spaces that ignore level changes. It seems less clear that both types of assistance work equally well in settings that involve going up some stairs or taking an elevator. In this paper, we present a study that had participants follow a route in a multi-level setting involving several level changes while being assisted by either a textual description or a sketch map. Results indicate that both types of assistance are effective and that the few differences in performance that we discovered can be attributed to differences in the employed wayfinding strategies rather than differences in the assistance types. Our findings have implications for the design of (mobile) assistance services that aim at using graphical instructions for guiding users seamlessly through indoor and outdoor environments.

Keywords: route following, description vs. depiction, sketch map, level change.

1 Introduction

Wayfinding is an everyday activity. It reflects our ability to plan a path to distal destinations and to reach those [1]. For routes that we follow regularly wayfinding becomes a simple, almost subconscious task, but if we plan to travel to places for the first time we usually require some kind of external support. Typically, such wayfinding assistance comes in the form of a verbal description or a graphical depiction, or a combination of these.

People can successfully navigate with both forms (e.g., [2,3]). However, for the most part this has been established for two-dimensional space, usually involving movement throughout an urban setting. When the routes to follow include level changes, for example, going up a staircase or taking an elevator, it is not as clear whether all forms of providing route directions are equally suited. Route following involves performing a sequence of navigation actions—essentially turning at decision points and then moving to the next. Verbal descriptions by necessity need to linearize the information they convey [4]. Thus, they seem well suited

C. Freksa et al. (Eds.): Spatial Cognition 2014, LNAI 8684, pp. 176–189, 2014.
© Springer International Publishing Switzerland 2014

to communicate the sequence of navigation actions independent of whether the space to navigate in is two- or three-dimensional. Maps, on the other hand, are two-dimensional per the medium used. It seems less clear how well it is possible to clearly communicate level changes using (sketch) maps. For example, this may become an issue in the pursuit of designing navigation services or other location-based services that offer seamless assistance between indoor and outdoor settings (e.g., [5,6]).

In this paper, we report on a study that tested wayfinding performance in a setting that involves level changes when participants are assisted by either a textual description or a sketch map. While there are some performance differences, results indicate that both forms of assistance work well. The decisions taken in designing the sketch map seem sensible, which has implications in particular for designing effective graphical aids for multilevel (indoor) wayfinding assistance.

2   Wayfinding and Wayfinding Assistance in Multi-level Settings

As stated in the introduction, both maps and verbal descriptions can success-fully convey the information necessary to reach a destination. For example, Meilinger [2] found that people mentally seem to translate route maps into propositional instructions on how to find the way. And Tversky and Lee [7] claimed that both forms have the same underlying semantics and, thus, can be seen as (nearly) equivalent in communicating route information (but see [8] for some counterarguments).

In most of the research on wayfinding assistance level changes are ignored. Largely, this research looks at how people perform with verbal descriptions or maps while navigating in an (essentially) two-dimensional space. However, there are indications that being assisted in multi-level (vertical) spaces may result in different effects. In studies performed in the Paris subway, Fontaine [9] showed that in underground (subway) environments there are differences in how people produce route directions compared to directions on (outdoor) ground level. Depending on the kind of external aid participants received, she also found differences in route following and acquired spatial knowledge [10]; different graphical aids differ in the effectiveness for different people and situations. Münzer and Stahl [11,12] demonstrated that in a complex university building participants using animated virtual walks as wayfinding assistance made fewer wayfinding errors than those using static allocentric or egocentric views.

In principle, people seem to be able to integrate spatial knowledge across different vertical levels [13]. Different factors may make this easier or harder [14]. For example, Weisman [15] identified visual access, architectural differentiation, signage, and floorplan configuration to contribute to the ease (or difficulty) of wayfinding situations. Similarly, several others have studied the effects of an environment's spatial layout on wayfinding (e.g., [16,17,18]). In particular, Soeda et al. [19] found that level changes, i.e., moving vertically, often disrupt orientation. Regaining orientation is then hindered if the layout between the two floors differs widely or if there is a misalignment of reference systems between floors [17]. Ishikawa and Yamazaki [20] demonstrated this disorientation in a study where participants had to point towards a (ground-level) destination after exiting a subway station. They found that photographs allow participants faster and more reliable reorientation than maps.

Similarly, the research presented in this paper focuses on the effect of different external aids—namely textual description vs. sketch map—on people's wayfinding success in multilevel settings.

3 An Empirical Study Comparing the Effectiveness of Textual Descriptions and Sketch Maps in Multi-level Settings

Given the research just discussed, we are interested in seeing whether maps and textual descriptions perform comparably well in wayfinding situations that involve level changes. To this end, we set up an experimental study, which has participants follow a route that involves both transitions from indoor to outdoor (and back) and multiple level changes. In their route following, they are assisted either by a sketch map or a textual description (text for short). We hypothesize that using a text in this kind of setting is easier than a map, as textual instructions are generally more straightforward to translate into wayfinding actions and, in particular, level changes are harder to communicate (well) using a map. Thus, we expect participants using the text to reach the destination faster and with fewer errors.

We also have participants rate the difficulty of the wayfinding task before and after actually performing the task. We included this test to detect possible preferences of the participants for either the map or the text and as an indication of subjective difficulty assessments. While we expect to see clear changes to occur between the two ratings, it is difficult to predict in which direction. There are good reasons to assume that afterwards the task appears easier than before (e.g., because 'the unknown' is always hard to judge), but likewise also the opposite may be the case (e.g., because both descriptions are rather short and, thus, the route may appear simpler than it actually is).

3.1 Participants

32 students (16 men, 16 women) of the University of Zurich participated in the study. Their age ranged from 19 to 37 (μ=24.9 years). Since the study was performed on the university campus, all participants have been in the general area of the study, but none ever took the study route, though parts of the route may have been known to some participants.

3.2 Study Area and Material

The study area is at the University of Zurich in Switzerland, namely at the Irchel Campus. The route chosen for the study comprises of nine direction changes and

a)   b)

Fig. 1. Example scenes from the study route: a) The first glass door the participants have to pass through to get outside; b) the second level change occurring along the route

two changes of level (see Figure 2a). The destination point cannot be seen from the starting point and vice versa. The path leads mainly through buildings, but at one point the participants had to go outside through a door and later back in again. Figure 1 shows some impressions of the study route.

A pre-test led to several adaptations to both the initially produced map and text in order to reduce confusion. The map (Figure 2a) and text (Figure 2b) contain the same elements. For both forms of assistance, design employs a route perspective. The text only uses 'left' and 'right' direction statements and references to landmarks. There are no indications of distance. Likewise, the map does not provide any information on (relative) distances; all path segments on the map have the same length. Turns are depicted using prototypical 90 degrees angles. In order to visualize landmarks, either well-known icons are used, such as the 'i' (information) sign, or icons that we believe are pictographic representations of the real-world object referred to, such as the open door or the tree icons [21] as can be seen in Figure 2a. Level changes are indicated by arrows—in the study always up—annotated by the number of floors to pass (here always '1'). These arrows either come in the shape of stairs or are placed next to an elevator icon. While distances are ignored, directions between elements are meaningful in the map, for example, the elevator is placed to the right of the route segment because it is actually located to the right when walking the route.

3.3   Experiment Design and Procedure

The experiment was conducted in German. The participants were divided into two groups of 16 participants each, with a balanced proportion of women and men. One group completed the task with the map, the other with the text. At the beginning of the experiment, each participant filled out a questionnaire with some demographic data. Afterwards each participant received their respective wayfinding assistance (map or text), printed on a DIN A5 page. Participants then had 30 seconds to study the material, after which they had to hand it back

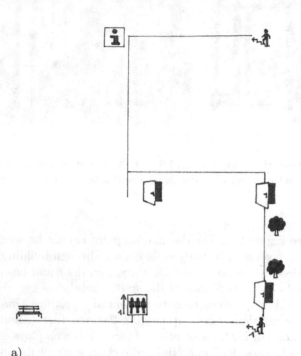

a)

Geh die Treppe hoch. Geh bei der Information links. Geh bei der
nächsten Möglichkeit links. Geh durch die zweite Tür auf der rechten
Seite. Geh rechts an den zwei Bäumen vorbei. Geh durch die Tür. Geh
die Treppe ein Stockwerk hoch. Geh links. Geh bis zum Lift auf der
rechten Seite. Geh mit dem Lift ein Stockwerk hoch. Geh rechts zur
Sitzbank.

Go upstairs. Turn left at the information desk. Turn left at
the next possible option. Go through the second door on
the right hand side. Pass to your right the two trees. Go
through the door. Go upstairs to the next floor. Turn left.
Go to the elevator to your right. Use the elevator to get
one level up. Turn right and go to the bench.

b)

Fig. 2. The map (a) and textual description (b) used as material in the study. Participants received the German text; the English translation is provided for the reader's
convenience

and then had to rate how difficult they expected the wayfinding task to be on a Likert scale from 1 (very easy) to 5 (very difficult).

Participants were then led to the starting point of the route. They were instructed to find the way described on the map or the text, respectively, and to clearly communicate when they believed they had reached the destination (the bench). They were also told that they would be followed by the experimenter, but would not receive any help from them, nor were they allowed to ask anybody else for assistance. They were given back the (same) assistance material they studied previously and started the wayfinding process taking the material with them, i.e., they were able to refer to either the map or text while following the study route. Participants were followed by one of the experimenters who did not intervene, but only recorded the time participants took and their behavior.

In particular, we recorded any errors, stops or hesitations along the way. We defined an error to be five steps in the wrong direction—any follow-up errors were ignored. During a stop, participants ceased moving forward and stood still to inspect the text or map, whereas during hesitation they only slowed down and looked at the assistance material while still moving. These variables have been previously used by Daniel et al. [22] in their studies.

Once participants indicated that they had reached the destination, the timer was stopped and they were again asked to rate the difficulty of finding their way on the same Likert scale as before. This rating was recorded, and participants were debriefed by receiving a chocolate bar as a small token of appreciation for participating in the study.

4   Results

In this section we will report on the results of the wayfinding study. In particular, we will check our hypotheses regarding potential differences in performance when assisted by text or map, respectively, and the changes in difficulty rating. The statistical evaluation is detailed below. All tests are performed against a significance level of 0.05.

A total of nine people (three using the text; six using the map) misjudged having reached the destination and stated at a wrong place that they finished route following. Still, all of these nine reached the correct floor, therefore, we included them in the analysis of error, hesitation and stop—except for finishing at the wrong place they did not make any additional errors. However, in the analysis of time they are excluded as their routes (route lengths) differ from the intended route.

4.1   Correlation of Error, Stop, and Hesitation with Time

To begin the analysis, we will check whether and how the behavioral variables error, stop, and hesitation correlate with time. We will first look at the participants overall, and then divide them according to the type of assistance (map or text) used.

Correlations without Differentiation of Assistance Type. First, in order to calculate a correlation, all variables including time were tested for normal distribution using the One-Sample Kolmogorov-Smirnov test. Time, stop, and error are normally distributed, however hesitation is not. Accordingly, a Pearson-correlation was performed for the pairs time-stop and time-error. We did not find any significant effect for stop ($p = 0.397$) or error ($p = 0.083$). For the pair time-hesitation the Spearman-correlation was used; again there is no significant effect ($p = 0.595$). That is, there seems to be no correlation between time and any of the behavioral variables when looking at the overall participants.

Correlations with Differentiation of Assistance Type. Next, we looked at the two conditions (map or text) individually. Again we tested for normal distribution. All variables except for error in the map condition are normally distributed. The Pearson-correlation showed no statistical relationship for the pairs time-stop and time-hesitation for either of the description types. The same holds for time-error in the text condition. However, in the map condition, there is a significant posititve correlation for the pair time-error ($r = 0.722$; $p = 0.018$). Table 1 summarizes these results.

Table 1. Significance of correlations at 0.05 level for the different study conditions

	Correlation Significance		
	time and stop	time and hesitation	time and error
map	0.879	0.226	0.018
text	0.902	0.251	0.367

To sum up, again there are no statistically relevant correlations between the behavioral variables and time, except for the errors that occurred in the map condition.

4.2   Difference of Description Type

The main goal of this study was to establish whether there are any performance differences between using a textual description or a sketch map as assistance when finding the way in a multi-level setting. In the following, we will test for this by comparing the behavioral variables between the two experiment conditions.

Hesitation. A t-test (without equal variances) shows no statistically significant difference between the number of hesitations when using the text or the map ($p = 0.763$).

Stop. For the number of stops, a t-test with equal variances reveals a significance of $p = 0.108$, so no significant difference can be found between using the text and using the map.

Error. The number of errors are not normally distributed. Therefore, a Mann-Whitney rank-sum test was used to establish significant differences. But, again, none were found ($p = 0.616$).

Time. Finally, we tested for any differences between the time it took participants to finish the route either with assistance by the text or by the map. A t-test with equal variances with all participants included (also those that named the wrong destination) shows no significant differences ($p = 0.215$). Still, when looking at the mean values (μ_{map} =327.47s; μ_{text} =288.35s), there is a difference of nearly 40 seconds, which seems relevant. Therefore, the nine participants who did not reach the correct destination were excluded from analysis and another t-test was performed. This test shows a significant difference of $p = 0.011$. Participants using the map ($\mu_{map_{excluded}} = 362.5s$) have been significantly slower than those using the text ($\mu_{text_{excluded}} = 269.8s$).

To sum up, there are no significant differences in the behavioral variables between the two test conditions map and text, but participants are slower when using the map than when using the text. Reasons for these differences will be discussed in Section 5.

4.3   Visualization of Behavioral Variables

In order to examine where in space errors, stops, and hesitations occurred, we marked them on the respective assistance types, i.e., text and map (Figure 3). In this figure, F, S, and Z stand for error ('Fehler'), stop ('Stopp'), and hesitation ('Zögern'), respectively. Clear clusters emerge in both assistance types. Interestingly, these are located at the same corresponding locations in the real world, i.e., these clusters do not seem to depend on the assistance types, but rather on the real-world situation. One cluster is located at the first door to get from within the building to the outside. A second cluster of recorded behavior is at the elevator. Thus, these two locations can be seen as potentially difficult spots where errors are likely to occur, which will be further discussed in Section 5. In the map condition there is a third cluster of stops and hesitations around the staircase that leads up after having entered the building again.

4.4   Changes in the Difficulty Rating

As stated in Section 3, we expect changes in the assessment of task difficulty to occur from rating it before following the route to when having finished the route following task. Rating was done using a 5-point Likert scale (1=very easy; 5=very difficult). The changes reported in the following are calculated simply by the difference between the rating after route following and before route following. Accordingly, negative values state that the task was rated easier after having performed the task compared to before the task. Positive values indicate that participants underestimated the difficulty prior to the task and had to correct this after the task.

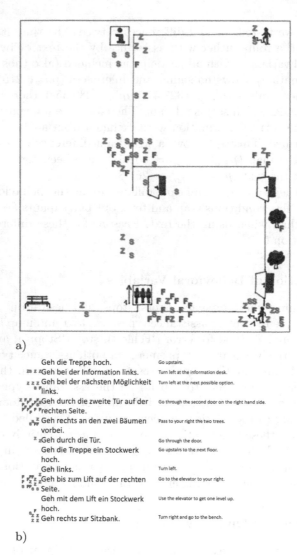

a)

	Geh die Treppe hoch.	Go upstairs.
	Geh bei der Information links.	Turn left at the information desk.
	Geh bei der nächsten Möglichkeit links.	Turn left at the next possible option.
	Geh durch die zweite Tür auf der rechten Seite.	Go through the second door on the right hand side.
	Geh rechts an den zwei Bäumen vorbei.	Pass to your right the two trees.
	Geh durch die Tür.	Go through the door.
	Geh die Treppe ein Stockwerk hoch.	Go upstairs to the next floor.
	Geh links.	Turn left.
	Geh bis zum Lift auf der rechten Seite.	Go to the elevator to your right.
	Geh mit dem Lift ein Stockwerk hoch.	Use the elevator to get one level up.
	Geh rechts zur Sitzbank.	Turn right and go to the bench.

b)

Fig. 3. Visualization of where errors, stops, and hesitations occurred along the way; a) when using the map; b) when using the textual description [F: error ('Fehler'), S: stop, Z: hesitation ('Zögern')]

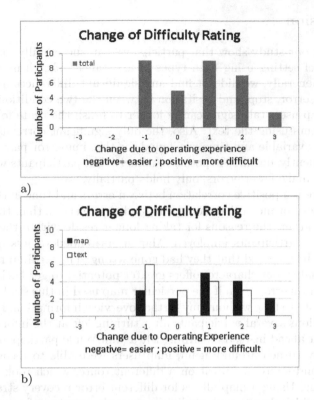

Fig. 4. Changes in difficulty rating; a) overall; b) separated between map and text

Figure 4 illustrates these changes of rating. In Figure 4a) all 32 rating changes are included, independent of assistance type. Nine participants rated the task as easier after the task, five people rated the task as equally difficult before and after route following. 18 participants stated that they underestimated the difficulty and rated the task as more difficult in their second rating.

Figure 4b) illustrates the change of difficulty rating differentiated by assistance type. Eleven out of the 18 participants that underestimated the difficulty used the map and only seven used the text. In contrast, six out of nine subjects that overestimated the difficulty used the text. No clear difference between assistance type can be found for the neutral group. Interestingly, when participants changed their difficulty rating, they only used a single point (step) if they found the task easier than previously thought, but used a broader range of ratings in case they felt it to be more difficult than initially thought.

Overall, participants rather found the wayfinding task more difficult than initially thought, and rather not easier. This is particularly true for participants using the sketch map as wayfinding assistance.

5   Discussion

The results of our study show that participants can successfully find their way in a multi-level setting using both types of assistance—sketch map or textual description. Generally, we did not find any significant differences in the behavioral variables error, stop, and hesitation between the two conditions. However, on average map users take significantly longer to finish the route following task than participants using the text. Also, the only significant correlation between any behavioral variable and time was found for the time-error pair for the map users. Consequently, our first hypothesis, namely that participants with the text are faster and make fewer errors, only holds partially.

Even if there is a positive correlation between errors and time in the map condition, this does not mean that map users made more errors than those assisted by the text. Rather, the reasons for taking longer reside within the wayfinding strategies that participants employed. Map users tended to less quickly turn around when they noticed that they had gone wrong. The medium map with its two-dimensional layout character offers greater potential to get back on the correct track after an error, even if the particular map used in this study really only showed the route to take without any further overview information. For example, in both conditions several participants after turning left at the information desk moved straight ahead instead of turning left again. While participants using the text eventually turned around again, map users were able to recover and still reach the second staircase, albeit on a different route, which took longer than the original one. Using a map allows for different error recovery strategies than using a text, which do not make a difference in the number of errors, but may make a difference in the time it takes to finish the task.

Our second hypothesis—people change their mind regarding the perceived task difficulty after actually having performed the task—overall holds true. Typically, the task was seen to be harder than expected in retrospect. In particular, when using the map, finding the route seemed easier initially than it was in the end, whereas for the text differences in rating are more even (some perceived it as harder, some are easier, some as equally difficult). The map seemed to better allow for gaining an idea of what to expect compared to the text, even if this mental image of the route possibly turned out to be inaccurate—therefore the change in rating to be more difficult. While we have not tested for this (e.g., through debriefing interviews), one reason may be that all distances are depicted as equal on the map, which would result in a heavily distorted mental image of the actual route.

We were also particularly interested to see whether sketch maps are suitable tools to instruct wayfinders in multi-level settings. Overall, we can conclude that they work well. All participants were able to understand the used icons and in particular performed the correct level changes. Still, as can be seen in Figure 3, both text and map are not without problems. Despite multiple pretests there were still confusing situations in following the route, which showed up in the behavioral data (errors, stops, hesitations). One of these issues occurred through an omission of an instruction. When coming up the stairs towards the information desk, participants actually had to turn left after the stairs to get there. The desk is clearly visible from the top of the stairs, so we omitted this instruction, which confused several participants. They clearly expected having received complete step-by-step instructions.

A second confusing situation occurred when needing to pass through the door after the information desk. The textual description states to pass through the second door ('Gehe durch die zweite Tür'). However, in the actual environment there are double-doors located there, thus, the textual instruction may be interpreted differently to the situation depicted on the map. A third issue proved to be the elevators. Both the text and the map (through positioning the elevator icon to the right of the route) clearly state to take the 'elevator on your right'. Close to where the relevant elevator is located there is a second elevator to the left of the route. Several participants took this elevator to the left, which subsequently took them off the route because when exiting the elevator they turned right (as instructed) but would have had to turn left to compensate for taking the wrong elevator. Again, map users had a better chance to compensate for this error, but overall–while technically correctly instructed–participants did not pay enough attention to the instructions at this location. It seems that more care needs to be taken to design instructions that point out and resolve such ambiguities.

Finally, our experiment was executed in a particular type of environment, namely university buildings. These buildings usually are structured along corridors–maybe to slightly lesser extent than office buildings–and these corridors offer clear affordances. Once the correct corridor is selected, there is not much choice than to follow it until it meets some other corridors or open space. In other words, corridors do not offer many opportunities for going wrong once inside them (of course it is always possible to choose a wrong corridor). Similar experiments to the one presented in this paper should be performed in other, more open space environments, such as train stations or exhibition centers, to come to more general conclusions regarding the performance of sketch maps and the use of icons in multi-level wayfinding support.

6   Conclusions

Both maps and verbal descriptions have been shown to be effective wayfinding aids in the past. However, most of those studies were performed in two-dimensional spaces where level changes (e.g., going up stairs or taking an elevator) did not occur. Some previous research indicates that there may be differences between both types of assistance in such three-dimensional settings.

In this paper, we presented a study that tested for such differences by having participants follow a route that involves several level changes while being assisted by either a textual description or a sketch map. The sketch map was designed in a way that it indicates direction changes, but not distances between decision points. Level changes as well as landmarks along the route are depicted using standard icons or pictographic representations. Results of the study show that both types of assistance work (almost) identically well. In particular, participants using the sketch maps had no difficulty in correctly executing level changes. Differences between maps and texts can be attributed to differences in wayfinding strategies, not to differences in their effectiveness.

Thus, we conclude that sketch maps and the use of stylized icons seem a suitable way of assisting people when finding their way in multi-level three-dimensional spaces. Among others, our findings have implications for the design of (mobile) assistance systems that universally guide users through both indoor and outdoor spaces (e.g. [5]).

The study presented in this paper should be seen as a first step towards using sketch maps and icon-based instructions in such scenarios. More studies are needed to systematically test their performance and the usefulness of the icons in guiding people through different settings. In particular, gender and individual differences should be investigated in follow-up studies. In our study, we balanced for gender in the different conditions, but did not find any significant differences between the genders—neither for the overall group nor in the individual conditions. A larger participant group may provide more robust results to discard such gender differences.

References

1. Montello, D.R.: Navigation. In: Shah, P., Miyake, A. (eds.) Handbook of Visuospatial Thinking, pp. 257–294. Cambridge University Press, Cambridge (2005)
2. Meilinger, T.: Wayfinding with maps and verbal directions. In: Proceedings of Twenty-Seventh Annual Conference of the Cognitive Science Society, pp. 1473–1478 (2005)
3. Tversky, B., Lee, P.U.: How space structures language. In: Freksa, C., Habel, C., Wender, K.F. (eds.) Spatial Cognition 1998. LNCS (LNAI), vol. 1404, pp. 157–175. Springer, Heidelberg (1998)
4. Daniel, M.P., Denis, M.: Spatial descriptions as navigational aids: A cognitive analysis of route directions. Kognitionswissenschaft 7, 45–52 (1998)
5. Ghafourian, M., Karimi, H.A.: Universal navigation: Concept and algorithms. In: World Congress on Computer Science and Information Engineering, vol. 2, pp. 369–373. IEEE Computer Society, Los Alamitos (2009)
6. Krüger, A., Baus, J., Heckmann, D., Kruppa, M., Wasinger, R.: Adaptive mobile guides. In: Brusilovsky, P., Kobsa, A., Nejdl, W. (eds.) Adaptive Web 2007. LNCS, vol. 4321, pp. 521–549. Springer, Heidelberg (2007)
7. Tversky, B., Lee, P.U.: Pictorial and verbal tools for conveying routes. In: Freksa, C., Mark, D.M. (eds.) COSIT 1999. LNCS, vol. 1661, pp. 51–64. Springer, Heidelberg (1999)
8. Klippel, A.: Wayfinding choremes. In: Kuhn, W., Worboys, M.F., Timpf, S. (eds.) COSIT 2003. LNCS, vol. 2825, pp. 301–315. Springer, Heidelberg (2003)
9. Fontaine, S., Denis, M.: The production of route instructions in underground and urban environments. In: Freksa, C., Mark, D.M. (eds.) COSIT 1999. LNCS, vol. 1661, pp. 83–94. Springer, Heidelberg (1999)
10. Fontaine, S.: Spatial cognition and the processing of verticality in underground environments. In: Montello, D.R. (ed.) COSIT 2001. LNCS, vol. 2205, pp. 387–399. Springer, Heidelberg (2001)

11. Münzer, S., Stahl, C.: Providing individual route instructions for indoor wayfinding in complex, multi-level buildings. In: Probst, F., Keßler, C. (eds.) GI-Days 2007 Young Researchers Forum. IfGI prints, vol. 30, pp. 241–246. Institut für Geoinformatik, Münster (2007)

12. Münzer, S., Stahl, C.: Learning of visual route instructions for indoor wayfinding. In: Hölscher, C. (ed.) Poster Proceedings of Spatial Cognition 2008, Freiburg, Germany, pp. 65–68 (2008)

13. Montello, D.R., Pick, H.L.: Integrating knowledge of vertically aligned large-scale spaces. Environment and Behavior 25(3), 457–484 (1993)

14. Carlson, L.A., Hölscher, C., Shipley, T.F., Dalton, R.C.: Getting lost in buildings. Current Directions in Psychological Science 19(5), 284–289 (2010)

15. Weisman, J.: Evaluating architectural legibility: Way-finding in the built environment. Environment and Behaviour 13(2), 189–204 (1981)

16. Dogu, U., Erkip, F.: Spatial factors affecting wayfinding and orientation — a case study in a shopping mall. Environment and Behavior 32(6), 731–755 (2000)

17. Werner, S., Long, P.: Cognition meets Le Corbusier – cognitive principles of architectural design. In: Freksa, C., Brauer, W., Habel, C., Wender, K.F. (eds.) Spatial Cognition III. LNCS (LNAI), vol. 2685, pp. 112–126. Springer, Heidelberg (2003)

18. Hölscher, C., Meilinger, T., Vrachliotis, G., Brösamle, M., Knauff, M.: Up the down staircase: Wayfinding strategies in multi-level buildings. Journal of Environmental Psychology 26(4), 284–299 (2006)

19. Soeda, M., Kushiyama, N., Ohno, R.: Wayfinding in cases with vertical motion. In: Proceedings of MERA 97: International Conference on Environment-Behavior Studies, pp. 559–564 (1997)

20. Ishikawa, T., Yamazaki, T.: Showing where to go by maps or pictures: An empirical case study at subway exits. In: Hornsby, K.S., Claramunt, C., Denis, M., Ligozat, G. (eds.) COSIT 2009. LNCS, vol. 5756, pp. 330–341. Springer, Heidelberg (2009)

21. Elias, B., Paelke, V., Kuhnt, S.: Concepts for the cartographic visualization of landmarks. In: Gartner, G. (ed.) Location Based Services & Telecartography - Proceedings of the Symposium 2005, pp. 1149–1155. Geowissenschaftliche Mitteilungen, TU Vienna (2005)

22. Daniel, M.P., Tom, A., Manghi, E., Denis, M.: Testing the value of route directions through navigational performance. Spatial Cognition and Computation 3(4), 269–289 (2003)

Effect of Simplicity and Attractiveness on Route Selection for Different Journey Types

Sarah Cook* and Roy A. Ruddle

School of Computing, University of Leeds, Leeds, LS2 9JT, UK,
sc10sc@leeds.ac.uk
http://www.personal.leeds.ac.uk/~sc10sc/

Abstract. This study investigated the effects of six attributes, associated with simplicity or attractiveness, on route preference for three
pedestrian journey types (everyday, leisure and tourist). Using stated
choice preference experiments with computer generated scenes, participants were asked to choose one of a pair of routes showing either two
levels of the same attribute (experiment 1) or different attributes (experiment 2). Contrary to predictions, vegetation was the most influential
for both everyday and leisure journeys, and land use ranked much lower
than expected in both cases. Turns ranked higher than decision points for
everyday journeys as predicted, but the positions of both were lowered
by initially unranked attributes. As anticipated, points of interest were
most important for tourist trips, with the initially unranked attributes
having less influence. This is the first time so many attributes have been
compared directly, providing new information about the importance of
the attributes for different journeys.

Keywords: Pedestrian navigation, wayfinding, simplicity, attractiveness.

1 Introduction

People plan their routes through environments every day, but what factors influence these wayfinding decisions? Although researchers have studied how humans
navigate, and particularly what affects their success and ability to do this, few
commercial solutions consider which factors are important when selecting a route
for pedestrian travel beyond the shortest path approach. However, studies have
indicated that different types of journey require different characteristics [1], and
investigated the motivations or requirements for the selection of specific routes
for a given purpose [2,3]. By considering how different attributes (eg route layout
and vegetation) influence pedestrians, it should become easier for navigational
aids to recommend more intuitive and appropriate routes for travelling on foot.

The aim of this research is to determine how different attributes affect the
selection of pedestrian routes for three wayfinding scenarios; everyday, leisure
and tourist journeys. This paper reports the results of two experiments which

---

* S Cook is funded by an EPSRC Doctoral Training Grant.

C. Freksa et al. (Eds.): Spatial Cognition 2014, LNAI 8684, pp. 190–205, 2014.
© Springer International Publishing Switzerland 2014

investigated the influence that attributes have on route choice for these different types of journey. A stated preference choice approach, using three dimensional (3D) computer generated scenes and journey scenario questions, asked participants to select routes and therefore express preferences for the characteristics illustrated. These preferences were then analysed to produce a ranked list of attributes relating to each task. As future work, these ranks will be converted into algorithms to automatically suggest more appropriate pedestrian routes.

The paper is divided into three parts. The following section briefly reviews previous work, pulling together information from research into wayfinding, walkability and route aesthetics to determine which attributes should be considered. We use this research to establish hypotheses relating to the influence that the attributes have on route preference. Two experiments were then carried out to investigate these hypotheses. Lastly, the conclusions focus on the implications of this work, its limitations and how the findings can be used for future pedestrian navigation aids.

2   Background

Research into the cognitive components of wayfinding [1] indicates that when planning a route, the decision process is dependent on the type of wayfinding task to be completed. An example of this could be the differences between the daily commute to work and the route taken when going for a stroll on a summer morning. Three of the main types of wayfinding tasks are [4,5]:

Everyday Navigation - Trips performed regularly such as the daily commute to work, or visiting the local shops.
Recreational Trips - Typically for exercise or pleasure; aesthetically pleasing.
Tourism - A typical example of this would be an individual visiting an area to see the 'sights'.

A fourth type of journey, business trips, may be considered to have many of the same characteristics as everyday journeys, and was therefore excluded from this study.

Many criteria are known to influence navigational decisions (see [2,6,7,8] for examples). The criteria associated with distance have already been investigated and are employed extensively by existing route recommendation systems, and those with a time-dependent component are difficult to represent in static virtual scenes [6,7]. The experiments in the present article will focus on the physical attributes of route attractiveness and simplicity, as described below.

Attractiveness is associated with the areas surrounding and the views visible when walking along a route, and to consider the likely influence of the attributes associated with attractiveness, we must look at the preference for them in everyday life. Aesthetics is a commonly stated criteria when choosing routes [2], and can be subdivided into a number of attributes such as vegetation, land use, cleanliness, maintenance, dwellings and points of interest [8]. Of these, cleanliness and maintenance are considered to be outside the scope of this research due to difficulties in representing them adequately in the types of graphic chosen for these experiments.

Simplicity in the context of wayfinding is associated with the layout of a route or environment, and the presence of cues such as landmarks. Turns (changes of direction at decision points) feature in a list of reasons given for choosing a route [2], as does initial leg length, and decision points with no turns have been shown to affect perceived distance and the likelihood of correctly traversing a route [9]. Additionally, the influence of landmarks on wayfinding success has been examined in depth, and it is now widely accepted that they form the basis for initial mental representations of an environment [10]. For this study, landmarks were considered to be equivalent to the attractiveness attribute 'points of interest', and the results of a pilot study (not reported here) indicated that the effects of initial leg length could not be examined using the 3D scenes used in the present study, as they showed participants the whole route not just the initial leg.

By considering all of these studies, and the experiential approach to be used, six attributes were selected. Two relate to route simplicity - number of turns and number of decision points, and four to attractiveness - vegetation, land use, points of interest and dwellings. Distance is not included in this study as it is already known to affect route choice, and was factored out in the design of the experiments. The following remainder of this section formulates hypotheses as to how each of the six attributes affect route choice for the three different journey types.

Increasing the number of turns has been shown to have a highly negative influence on the route chosen for everyday travel [2], however green space encourages walking to get to places [8] giving a positive influence. Also, as decision points increase perceived distance [11] and distance influences route choice [2], it would seem likely that these too would have a role. Combining these findings gives H1 (Table 1). However, there is very little research on how vegetation, points of interest or dwellings guide decisions for this wayfinding scenario. To determine the order of influence, the suggested ranking of a previous study was examined [2] as well as attributes that affect increases in perceived distance [11]. The number of turns ranked higher in route choice than aesthetics (assumed to be land use), and decision points affect perceived distance less than turns, but there is no comparison between land use and decision points, so we assume that the attributes will be ranked equal, leading to H2.

In contrast to everyday journeys, leisure routes seem to be wholly determined by their attractiveness. Walking for pleasure is thought to be directly associated with walkability [12] and therefore vegetation, dwellings and points of interest (all related to walkability) should be considered influential [12,13]. Also, specific land use can instigate leisure travel [8], as well as generally influence it [14]. These findings result in H3. To date, no research is available on how route simplicity affects routes chosen for leisure. Unfortunately, previous studies also do not show any significance in the order of the attributes given. What evidence there is suggests that vegetation and dwellings are less important than land use [14], and that vegetation is preferred to dwellings [12]. As points of interest are not mentioned in either of these studies, this attribute will be left unranked. These predictions are combined to give the positions indicated by H4.

Points of interest are of particular importance for tourist trips [15], as they are usually the sole basis for the journey itself; however, other aspects of attractiveness may also affect this route type. Architecture or dwellings and land use have also been alluded to as influential factors [3], and studies have indicated that vegetation may sway the directions taken during this class of travel [3,16], giving Hypothesis H5. Despite these suggestions, little indication is given about how these requirements were determined. Furthermore, as with leisure journeys, previous research has not considered how simplicity affects the choice of tourist routes. Points of interest will have the most influence on tourist routes, but only a very vague indication of the rank of the others is given in any related literature [3], and they will be considered unranked for this study leading to Hypothesis H6.

Table 1. Hypotheses of Journey Type Preference

Hypothesis	Description
H1	Everyday journeys will be affected by decision points, turns at junctions and land use.
H2	Everyday journeys will be most influenced by the number of turns, followed equally by land use and the number of decision points.
H3	Leisure journeys will be affected by land use, dwellings, vegetation and points of interest.
H4	Leisure journeys will be most influenced by land use, followed by vegetation and then dwellings. The rank position of points of interest is unknown.
H5	Tourist journeys will be affected by land use, dwellings, vegetation and points of interest.
H6	Tourist journeys will be most influenced by points of interest. The rank positions of dwellings, land use and vegetation are unknown.

The remainder of this section summarises the approaches chosen to display the attributes in virtual environments, and to test for participant preference. Computer-generated maps, scenes or virtual environments provide a controlled, safe test platform to investigate human navigation, spatial cognition and path choice in a laboratory setting [17,18,19, amongst others]. Virtual routes can be presented in one of two main ways; by traversing the route, or providing a single static snapshot of it. Static scenes based on three dimensional maps, also known as Worlds in Miniature [20] were selected for this research as they take a relatively short time to create, require little participant training [21], and can be used to test many participants at once. This approach presents pairs of routes with buildings and objects that are either mapped with photo-realistic textures, or are modelled in 3D to appear similar to real-world examples.

Stated preference choice experiments have been used to elicit responses to alternative scenarios in many different fields, including travel choice [22], bicycle route selection [23] and walkability evaluation [24]. The choice method offers participants two or more options via images or descriptions, and asks them to state which of these would be the most preferred. Although alternative approaches such as contingency ranking have also been used to test participant preference, they mostly rely on accuracy of available information and displaying an entire set of options at once [25]. Choice experiments offer a more flexible approach which relates directly to the tasks experienced in real-world situations.

3   Experiment 1: Which Attributes Affect Route Choice?

This experiment investigated whether the level of a single attribute has an effect on which route is chosen for one of three journey scenarios. A within participants design was used, with participants being shown 36 pairs of routes each showing different levels of an attribute. They were then asked to state which route in each pair they preferred, and the results analysed to give an overview of how the attributes affect route selection for different journey types.

3.1   Method

Participants. A total of 73 individuals (19 females and 53 males, 1 withheld) participated in this experiment. They were aged 18 to 25 (mean 19.3 years, SD 1.5 years, 1 withheld), and all were either university students or members of staff. The experiment was approved by the Faculty Ethics Committee, and informed consent was provided by participants returning the completed multiple choice forms.

Materials. Pairs of routes were shown side-by-side in single images connected to common start (bottom) and end (top) points as shown in Fig. 1. Each route varied by a single attribute relating to either its simplicity or attractiveness. The routes were constructed using Autodesk[R] 3ds Max[R] 2012 (14.0 student stand-alone version) [26], combined to create environments, and rendered to a 640x480 jpeg image file.

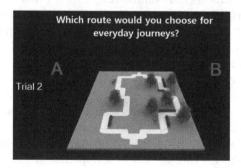

Fig. 1. Example experiment 1 environment. Journey - everday, left route - vegetation level 1, right route - vegetation level 2

All of the routes were based on one of two layouts, with features added according to the attribute being illustrated as shown in Fig. 2. For attributes which required an increase in the number of elements of this type (points of interest, turns, decision points and vegetation), a single feature was added for level one and five features were added for level two. These features were selected to be typical examples of structures or elements commonly encountered in urban areas, with churches, water features, statues and public buildings chosen as points of interest, and trees, hedges and flower beds representing vegetation. For example, Fig. 1 shows two levels of vegetation with the amount of planting being increased to raise the level of attractiveness in a route.

The type rather than amount of land use or dwellings have been shown to affect attractiveness, which is reflected in the levels of these attributes as shown in Fig. 2. Multiple occupancy housing is significantly less preferred than any other form of dwelling, whereas historic homes are more preferred [27], and these each form a level for the dwellings attribute. Land use is harder to portray in a single image of these dimensions, especially without using images of housing. To prevent confusion or misunderstanding, ground coverings showing paving (urban) and grass (parkland) were selected.

Wherever possible, overlaps between feature types were avoided. However, buildings being shown as both dwellings and points of interest, and grass (which could be considered vegetation) used for parkland were considered acceptable, as similar overlaps would exist in real world environments. A pilot study was then run on the resulting routes (results not given here) to ensure that all the selected attributes and levels were discriminable. Once this had been established, a second set of routes showing the same features, but with a slightly different route layout, were produced to increase experiment validity.

Procedure. Participants were each provided with a copy of a participant information sheet and a multiple choice form, to provide further information and collect their preferences. The form gave spaces for participants to record their gender and age, but they were instructed to not write their name anywhere on the sheet. In addition, two boxes were provided for each screen, including those in the training phase, one marked 'A' and one marked 'B'. During the experiment participants were asked to mark the letter corresponding to their preferred route in each trial on this form.

The experiment was divided into two phases; a training phase and a test phase that together took a total of approximately 10 minutes. During the training phase, instructions were provided to the participants, and six screens were displayed in succession, two for each of the three journey types. Questions were displayed above the routes relating to different types of journey (Figure 1), and they were provided with the following scenarios verbally:

Everyday Travel: 'Which route would you choose for everyday journeys? - This could be walking to work or uni, or if you were just popping out to the shops.'

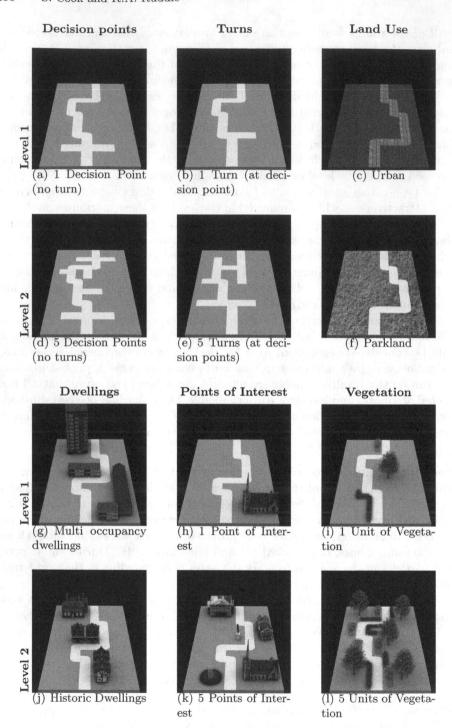

Fig. 2. Artificial environments. Each image shows a single attribute level, and the features used to represent it.

Leisure Travel: 'Which route would you choose for leisure journeys? - This
could be walking for pleasure or exercise, so say you were going for a stroll.'
Tourist Travel: 'Which route would you choose for tourist journeys? - Say you
were visiting campus for a short time and wanted to explore the area, or you
were taking a visitor on a tour of Leeds.'

Participants were asked to indicate that they had expressed a preference for
a route before moving on to the next pair. When complete, the entire sequence
of images were shown again at the same interval as those in the test, to enable
participants to acclimatise to the speed with which they would have to make a
selection. Participants were not asked to give responses during this rerunning,
only to watch the screen.

Once this phase was complete the test algorithm was run, with the question
order and sequence of the 36 images (three per attribute, for each of two route
layouts) being randomly selected. The images were each displayed for 8 seconds,
a simple sound was played indicating that the next image was being shown and
a black screen indicated that the trial was over. The completed sheets were
collected at the end and the participants were free to leave.

3.2 Results and Discussion

Of the 73 submissions the minimum percentage of completed responses was 98%,
which was considered sufficient to include all participants in the analysis. The
votes for each screen were gathered, and combined to give a single value for each
route per participant. The Friedman test for k related samples was chosen as
the most appropriate non-parametric test to analyse the data. This test ranks
k ordinal samples from a population according to their overall differences [28],
but does not require the data to have a normal distribution. This was used to
establish rank with a significance level of $p < .05$. A Wilcoxon's Signed Rank
post-hoc test with a value of $p < .01$, which gives more weight to attributes
having a large difference between their conditions, was also performed on the
outcomes of the pairwise comparisons. The results of this analysis are shown
in Fig. 3, indicating that there is a statistical significance between the different
levels of all attributes for everyday and leisure journeys, and all but turns and
decision points for tourist trips. These differences are compared to the predicted
effects in Table 2. As in earlier research, for turns and decision points there is
a negative relationship between attribute level and preference, and for all other
attributes there is a positive relationship.

For everyday journeys, the attributes predicted by H1 and previous research
[2,11,29] did have an influence on route choice, however vegetation, points of
interest and dwellings also had an effect. Previous studies [2, for example] discuss
a wayfinding criterion termed 'aesthetics', but give little or no indication of
the specific attributes being included in this category. The results found by
this experiment show that all of the tested attractiveness attributes affect route
choice for this type of journey, rather than just land use as predicted.

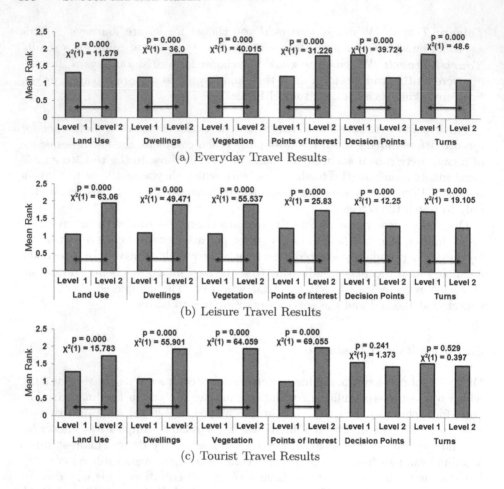

(a) Everyday Travel Results

(b) Leisure Travel Results

(c) Tourist Travel Results

Fig. 3. Experiment 1 Friedman Test Results (rank and p values) - pairwise (Wilcoxon's) statistical significance is indicated by the arrows overlaid on the plot.

In contrast to the other two journey types, for tourist trips only the attributes predicted in H5 influenced route preference. Points of interest, land use, vegetation and dwellings all affected choice as in previous studies [15,3], but turn and decision points played no part in the decisions. This indicates that simplicity plays no role in the choice of appropriate routes for tourist travel, with attractiveness being the sole source of influence. An explanation for these results is that tourists may be more likely to carry maps, reducing complexity, and that occupants of an area may want visitors to only see the more appealing areas of their environment, giving a better impression and making them more likely to return in the future.

These results indicate, that to automatically select routes for these types of pedestrian wayfinding scenario in the real world, the level of each of the tested attributes should be considered. However before an automated route selection

Table 2. Predicted (hypotheses from table 1) vs measured attribute effect for each journey type. Previously shown effects (✓), effects which are inferred from previous studies (✱), unknown effects (?) or no reported effect (✗) are compared against the effects found in experiment 1. (POIs - points of interest, DPs - decision points)

Attribute	Everyday		Leisure		Tourist	
	H1	Measured	H3	Measured	H5	Measured
Land use	✓	✓	✓	✓	✱	✓
Dwellings	?	✓	✓	✓	✱	✓
Vegetation	?	✓	✓	✓	✱	✓
POIs	?	✓	✓	✓	✱	✓
DPs	✱	✓	?	✓	?	✗
Turns	✓	✓	?	✓	?	✗

algorithm can be designed, the relative importance of each of these attributes needs to be determined.

4   Experiment 2: Order of Attributes' Influence

This experiment was designed to determine the order of influence of the attributes tested previously, on routes for the three types of journey. Stated choice experiments were again used, but this time mixed factorial design was employed; with attribute as a within participant factor and journey type as a between participant factor. Unlike the previous experiment, the two routes displayed within each of the virtual environments contained two attributes, allowing comparison between them.

4.1   Method

To make the experiment manageable a maximum of ten minutes to complete both training and test portions was given. This experiment was divided into three separate test conditions to stay within the allocated amount of time, but still investigate all of the required attributes simultaneously. The first test examined the everyday journey scenario, the second leisure journeys, and the third tourist journeys.

Participants. A total of 169 individuals (90 females and 75 males, 4 withheld) participated in this experiment. They were aged 18 to 53 (mean 23.8 years, SD 7.6 years, 4 withheld), and all were either university students or members of staff. They were divided into three groups with 55 participants for everyday journeys, 54 for leisure journeys, and 60 for tourist journeys. The experiment was approved by the Faculty Ethics Committee, and informed consent was provided by participants returning the completed multiple choice forms.

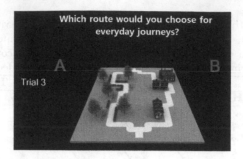

Fig. 4. Example experiment 2 environment. Journey - everyday, left route - level 2 vegetation, right route - level 2 dwellings.

Materials. The same path components, layouts and added features were used as those in the previous experiment, but in this test only the most preferred levels found in experiment 1 were included. For everyday and leisure journeys, vegetation, points of interest, land use, architecture, turns and decision points were all compared in pairs, with each route representing the most preferred level of one attribute. As the previous tests have shown that simplicity does not play a part in tourist travel, only vegetation, points of interest, dwellings and land use were considered for this type of journey. An example of the images used is shown in Fig. 4.

Procedure. As in experiment 1, participants were each provided with a copy of a participant information sheet and a multiple choice form. Each part of the experiment was broken into two phases as before; a training phase and a test phase that together took a total of approximately 10 minutes. The number of images needed for the training and test phases were determined by the number of attributes being tested - for both everyday and leisure journeys, eight training and 30 test screens were used, and for tourist journeys, there were five training and 12 test screens. The same procedure for displaying the images and collecting the participant answer sheets as in experiment 1 was followed.

The minimum percentage of completed responses was 81%, so all 169 submissions were included in the analysis. The votes for each screen were gathered, and combined to give a single value for each attribute per participant. The results from the Friedman test ($p < .05$) and Wilcoxon's tests ($p < .01$) for each part of this experiment are shown in Fig. 5.

4.2 Results and Discussion

Although the Friedman test suggests a rank for each journey type, the Wilcoxon's results indicate that the order is not as clear cut as it could be. To divide the attributes into ranked lists, we started with the Friedman rank, and then split this into groups where there was Wilcoxon's significance between adjacent attributes. Finally, these groups were subdivided at any other points of statistical significance, as shown by the dashed lines on Fig. 5. The resulting ranks compared against those predicted in H2, H4 and H6, are shown in Fig. 6, which confirms some relative rankings found in previous research (the exception being vegetation vs. land use for leisure journeys) and also highlights the previously unknown importance of other attributes.

For everyday journeys, turns were found to be more important than decision points and land use, which had equal influence, as predicted by H2. However, all three occurred lower in the ranking than expected, due to the additional

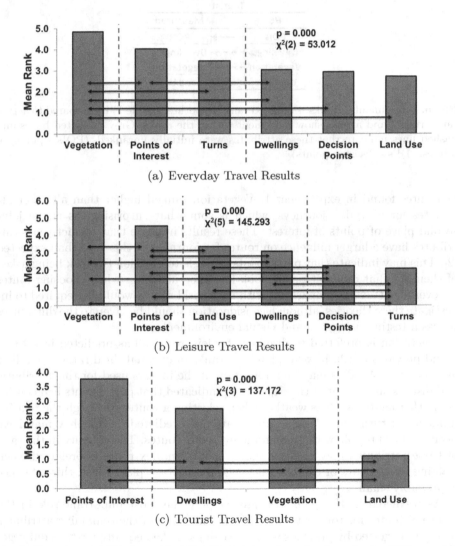

(a) Everyday Travel Results

(b) Leisure Travel Results

(c) Tourist Travel Results

Fig. 5. Experiment 2 Friedman Test Results (rank and p values) - pairwise (Wilcoxon's) statistical significance is indicated by the arrows overlaid on the plot. Dashed lines show where statistical significance divides the results into a rank order.

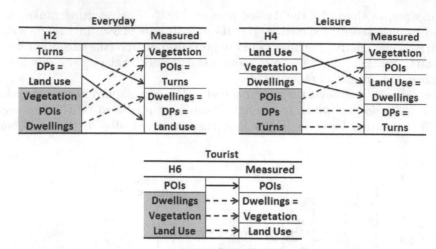

Fig. 6. Experiment 2 Ranks. Predicted rank (hypotheses table 1) is compared to actual rank (right), and arrows show movement within the ranks. Grey predicted boxes and dashed lines indicate that these attributes were initially unranked. (POIs - points of interest, DPs - decision points)

attributes found in experiment 1. Vegetation ranked higher than all other attributes for everyday journeys, which is somewhat surprising, as is the joint second place of points of interest. These results indicate that attractiveness attributes have a larger influence on routes for journeys of this type than expected [2]. This may indicate that participants struggle to envision the task being asked of them, or that different people look for different things when choosing routes for everyday travel. Comparisons with real-world routes would be required to investigate these theories, although consideration should be given to the differences between testing using real and virtual environments.

Vegetation is preferred to dwellings for leisure travel as predicted in H4 and found previously [12]; however, land use ranks only equal third rather than first as expected [14]. This may be a reflection of the images used for this attribute, and discussions held after the experiment indicated that participants had considered other factors such as weather when selecting a route. Although the relative influence of turns and decision points are not predicted in H4, they may have been assumed to follow those found in everyday routes. The equality in the rank of these attributes may indicate that a more complex route is preferred when walking for pleasure or exercise, although as they are placed last, this influence is probably small.

As predicted in H6, points of interest play the most important role in the choice of routes for tourist travel [15], but the order of the remaining attributes was not suggested by previous work. Dwellings ranked equally next, as did vegetation. As both points of interest and dwellings may actually be destinations as well as being attributes of the environment for this type of journey, this result is not that surprising. What is more unexpected is that land use ranks last for this type of journey, although this may also be explained by participants considering outside factors as in leisure trips.

5   Conclusions

The aim of this study was to determine how selected attributes affect route selection for three types of pedestrian travel; everyday, leisure and tourist journeys. Unlike previous studies, this research investigated how a number of attributes affect the preference for a route simultaneously, providing a direct comparison between them for each journey type.

Earlier research has suggested that testing in computer-generated environments may lead to different route choices to the real world [17]. However, the ecological validity of the present study is supported by the results of experiment 1, which replicated the findings of real-world research for all attributes that have previously been studied (see Table 2).

For both everyday and leisure journeys, turns, decision points, points of interest, vegetation, land use and dwellings all contribute to the preference of a route. In both cases, this was greater than the number of attributes predicted. Attractiveness was shown to affect everyday route selection more than anticipated, and leisure journeys are influenced by simplicity which had not previously been investigated. The experiments carried out also successfully produced ranks for the influence of these attributes, which unexpectedly placed vegetation as the most important for both of these journey types. Differences between the predicted and actual placings of all remaining attributes were also seen, with land use featuring much lower than anticipated in both ranks.

Despite a lack of previous data on how they were determined, the results of the experiments on tourist journeys confirm that points of interest, vegetation, land use and dwellings all influenced route preference. They also indicate that simplicity attributes have no effect, as predicted. Furthermore, it suggests a rank for the influence of vegetation, dwellings and land use, which had not been established by earlier research.

Although this study is not an exhaustive examination of all of the factors contributing to route preference, it does suggest a basis for how people choose routes. Using these results, a system which selects routes appropriate for everyday, leisure and tourist journeys is now being developed. The ranks will be converted into algorithms which use weighted equations to generate the cost of a partial route, and employ a modified version of Dijkstra's algorithm for shortest paths [30] to select the most appropriate. Although generating the weights for these algorithms will require a complex process involving machine learning techniques, once found the method for evaluating the available routes will be straightforward. It will give a system which could be used in devices to assist journeys on foot, and unlike previous approaches (such as [31]), the resulting algorithms will produce routes according to the type of journey required.

References

1. Allen, G.: Cognitive abilities in the service of wayfinding: A functional approach. RTPG 51(4), 555–561 (1999)
2. Golledge, R.: Path selection and route preference in human navigation: A progress report. In: Kuhn, W., Frank, A.U. (eds.) COSIT 1995. LNCS, vol. 988, pp. 207–222. Springer, Heidelberg (1995); 207-222 10.1007/3-540-60392-11_4
3. Vansteenwegen, P., Souffriau, W.: Trip planning functionalities: State of the art and future. Information Technology & Tourism 12(4), 305–315 (2011)
4. Federal Highway Administration, U.D.O.T.: National household travel survey (2009)
5. UK Data Archive [distributor], D.f.T.: National travel survey 2010 - statistics (2010)
6. Head, A.: 3D weather: towards a real-time 3D simulation of localised weather. In: Proceedings of the 2011 international Conference on Electronic Visualisation and the Arts, EVA 2011, pp. 35–41. British Computer Society, Swinton, UK (2011)
7. Laing, R., Miller, D., Davies, A.-M., Scott, S.: Urban green space: the incorporation of environmental values in a decision support system. ITCon 11, 177–196 (2006)
8. Pikora, T., Giles-Corti, B., Bull, F., Jamrozik, K., Donovan, R.: Developing a framework for assessment of the environmental determinants of walking and cycling. Social Science & Medicine 56(8), 1693–1703 (2003)
9. Sadalla, E.K., Staplin, L.J.: The perception of traversed distance: Intersections. Environment and Behavior 12, 167–182 (1980)
10. Siegel, A.W., White, S.H.: The development of spatial representations of large-scale environments. Advances in Child Development and Behavior 10, 9–55 (1975)
11. Staplin, L.J., Sadalla, E.K.: Distance cognition in urban environments. The Professional Geographer 33, 302–310 (1981)
12. Millington, C., Thompson, C.W., Rowe, D., Aspinall, P., Fitzsimons, C., Nelson, N., Mutrie, N.: Development of the scottish walkability assessment tool (SWAT). Health & Place 15(2), 474–481 (2009)
13. Giles-Corti, B.: Socioeconomic status differences in recreational physical activity levels and real and perceived access to a supportive physical environment. Preventive Medicine 35(6), 601–611 (2002)
14. Lee, C., Moudon, A.V.: Correlates of walking for transportation or recreation purposes. Journal of Physical Activity and Health 3(1) (2006)
15. Souffriau, W., Vansteenwegen, P.: Tourist trip planning functionalities: State–of–the–art and future. In: Daniel, F., Facca, F.M. (eds.) ICWE 2010. LNCS, vol. 6385, pp. 474–485. Springer, Heidelberg (2010)
16. Fink, J., Kobsa, A.: User modeling for personalized city tours. Artificial Intelligence Review 18(1), 33–74 (2002); 10.1023/A:1016383418977
17. Bishop, I.D., Rohrmann, B.: Subjective responses to simulated and real environments: a comparison. Landscape and Urban Planning 65(4), 261–277 (2003)
18. Loomis, J., Blascovich, J., Beall, A.: Immersive virtual environment technology as a basic research tool in psychology. Behavior Research Methods, Instruments, & Computers 31(4), 557–564 (1999)
19. Salthouse, T.A., Siedlecki, K.L.: Efficiency of route selection as a function of adult age. Brain and Cognition 63(3), 279–286 (2007)
20. Stoakley, R., Conway, M.J., Pausch, R.: Virtual reality on a WIM. In: CHI 1995 Proceedings of the SIGCHI Conference on Human Factors in Computing Systems, pp. 265–272. ACM Press (1995)

21. Davies, A.-M., Laing, R., Scott, S.: Combining visualisation and choice experiments in built environment research. In: Proceedings. Sixth International Conference on Information Visualisation 2002, pp. 785–790 (2002)
22. Louviere, J.J.: Conjoint analysis modelling of stated preferences: A review of theory, methods, recent developments and external validity. Journal of Transport Economics and Policy 22(1), 93–119 (1988)
23. Hunt, J.D., Abraham, J.E.: Influences on bicycle use. Transportation 34(4), 453–470 (2007)
24. Kelly, C.E., Tight, M.R., Hodgson, F.C., Page, M.W.: A comparison of three methods for assessing the walkability of the pedestrian environment. Journal of Transport Geography 19(6), 1500–1508 (2011); Special section on Alternative Travel futures
25. Boxall, P.C., Adamowicz, W.L., Swait, J., Williams, M., Louviere, J.: A comparison of stated preference methods for environmental valuation. Ecological Economics 18(3), 243–253 (1996)
26. Autodesk Inc: Autodesk®3ds max®2012 (2011), http://www.autodesk.co.uk
27. Kent, R.L.: Attributes, features and reasons for enjoyment of scenic routes: a comparison of experts, residents, and citizens. Landscape Research 18(2), 92–102 (1993)
28. Siegel, S., Castellan, N.J.: Nonparametric statistics for the behavioral sciences. McGraw-Hill, New York (1988)
29. Owen, N., Humpel, N., Leslie, E., Bauman, A., Sallis, J.F.: Understanding environmental influences on walking. American Journal of Preventive Medicine 27, 67–76 (2004)
30. Dijkstra, E.W.: A note on two problems in connexion with graphs. Numerische Mathematik 1(1), 269–271 (1959)
31. Akasaka, Y., Onisawa, T.: Construction of pedestrian navigation system and its evaluation. In: IEEE International Conference on Fuzzy Systems, vol. 3, pp. 1525–1530. IEEE (2004)

The Road to Direction
Assessing the Impact of Road Asymmetry on Street Network Small-Worldness

Maxime Sainte-Marie

Université du Québec à Montréal (UQAM),
Cognitive Information Analysis Lab,
P.O. Box 8888, Downtown Postal Station,
Montreal, Quebec, H3C 3P8, Canada
msaintemarie@gmail.com

Abstract. Small-world networks have proven to be optimal navigational structures, by insuring an adequate balance between local and global network efficiency. In the particular case of road networks, small-world-oriented research has led to widely diverging results, depending on modelling procedures: while traditional, geometric, road-based models fail to observe small-world properties in road networks, a new street-based modelling approach has obtained opposite results, by observing small-world properties for both named-based and angularity-based street graphs. These results are however hampered by the fact that street-based modelling has so far overlooked road asymmetry. Given this, the present research aims at evaluating the impact of road asymmetry on street network "small-worldness", by comparing symmetric and asymmetric street graphs by means of a structural indicator recently developed in brain network analysis. Results show that taking into account road asymmetry better highlights not only the small-world nature of street networks, but also the exceptional structure of name-based (odonymic) street topologies.

1   Introduction

The concept and study of small-world networks first gained popularity through a series of chains of correspondence experiments initiated by the Harvard sociologist Stanley Milgram, whose objective was to estimate the actual number of steps in a chain of acquaintances [1,2,3]. By attesting to the existence of both short-cuts and go-betweens in large-scale social networks, these studies also hinted at the existence of a new kind of network, adequately called 'small-world', which is as clustered as regular lattices, yet akin to random graphs in that any node in the network can be reached within a small number of steps [4].

It has been shown in [5] that such structures are extremely well-balanced from a dynamical point of view: by having a large number of local connections and a few long-range links connecting local clusters together, small-world networks establish an adequate balance between local and global movement efficiency, thus constituting ideal structures in terms of navigation and navigability [6,7,8].

C. Freksa et al. (Eds.): Spatial Cognition 2014, LNAI 8684, pp. 206–221, 2014.

In transportation research, where imperatives of navigability are crucial, much scholarly effort has been devoted to uncovering small-world-like patterns in various ground, air, and maritime networks [9]. In the particular case of road networks, research has led to widely diverging results, depending on the modelling procedure used: while traditional, geometric, models fail to observe small-world properties in road networks, a new street-based modelling approach, originating mainly from the Space Syntax research program, has obtained opposite results. These results are however hampered by the fact that street-based modelling has so far overlooked road asymmetry. Given this, the present research aims at evaluating the impact of road asymmetry on street network "small-worldness", by comparing symmetric and asymmetric street graphs by means of a structural indicator recently developed in brain network analysis. Both road-based and street-based models are presented in the first section, followed by a brief discussion of road asymmetry and its impact on transport-related research. The research methodology and results are then successively presented, followed by a discussion on the role of both road asymmetry and odonyms (street names) in the design of small-world-like, navigable and intelligent urban spaces.

2   Roads, Streets, and Asymmetry

Both enduring and fruitful, the investigative link between road systems analysis and network theory stretches back to Leonhard Euler's proof of the unsolvability of the Königsberg's bridges problem. Following Euler's work, early graph-based transportation research has relied on a roads-as-links approach [10,11,12]: "all graph edges are defined by two nodes (the endpoints of the arc) and, possibly, several vertices (intermediate points of linear discontinuity); intersections among edges are always located at nodes; edges follow the footprint or real streets as they appear on the source map; all distances are calculated metrically" [13, p.712].

However, representing road networks in such a metrically-faithful way excludes the possibility of finding small-world-like properties in road networks [14,8,15]. First, the number of edges (roads) that can be connected to a single node (intersection) is limited by the physical space to connect them, which prevents the occurrence of hubs or high degree nodes [16,17]. In this regard, road graph analysis of 20 German cities has shown that most nodes have four neighbours, a number of connections that rarely exceeds 5 for various other world cities [18]. Similarly, metric projection of road networks in 2-dimensional road graphs reduce the likeliness of long-range connections between nodes, given the distance dependent cost of the edges [17]. Such constraints on node degree and long-range connections exclude the possibility of small-worldness altogether, as they prevent the possibility of short average distances, akin to those of random graphs. Given the omnipresence and proven navigability of both small-world and road networks a alike, the idea that no formal matching between the two can be reached seems counter-intuitive, to say the least.

Over the last decade, a cognitively grounded alternative to these metric, road-based, models was developed, following the groundbreaking work of the Space Syntax research program [19,20]. This new representation method, here referred to as "street graphs", grew out from the realization that road-based graphs weakly represent the way people perceive, experience and deal with road networks [21]. As one author aptly pointed out, they violate "the intuitive notion that an intersection is where two roads cross, not where four roads begin" [22, p.1]. Two different but related ideas seem to be implied by this remark: (1) roads constitute the fundamental components of road networks, intersections being only the emerging result of their entanglement and crisscrossing; (2) road identity is not delimited by intersections but often extend over multiple adjacent segments. Regarding the first idea and as first suggested in [23], treating roads as fundamental topological entities suggests a new kind of network representation, in which nodes stand for roads instead of intersections, and two nodes are connected if there exists an intersection between the two corresponding roads.[1] As for the second idea, it implies that, in order to make better sense of road networks, individual segments need to be merged together, thus forming meaningful ordered sets of roads mostly referred to in urban settings as streets. Such an operation is closely related to cartographic generalization of linear objets such as hydrological networks: in order to reduce cartographic complexity in scale-reduction processes and thus facilitate global map legibility, such generalization proceeds by merging segments into longer "strokes", which are then sorted hierarchically by structural importance [25]. Here as is topological models, generalization is closely tied to cognitive factors; however, in the latter case, the main objective is not to allow for better visualization, but to build representations that better reflect the experience of road networks by its users. [26,23,27,21,28].

In order to "recover the actual streets of a city" [29, p.3], two generalization procedures have been proposed in the literature, each representing a distinct way of defining "which road segments naturally belong together" [22, p.2]. The first generalization model developed for street graphs is odonym-based: two different road segments are part of the same street if they share the same name [30,31,22]. From a cognitive standpoint, this procedure rests on the fact that through this lexicalisation process, streets become signs, which allow them to be referred to and become meaningful. Odonyms, being often the only street property that

---

[1] In transportation networks analysis, this new urban street networks modelling technique has often been referred to as the "dual approach". From a graph-theoretical point of view, such an expression is however misleading, as the "dual" of a plane graph is a graph having respectively for vertices and edges the faces of the former and their adjacency relationships. The term "dual" is used in this case because the relationship is symmetric: if one graph is the dual of another, the latter is also its dual. Street graphs are certainly not dual in this sense: a proper dual of a road graph would have its faces as nodes, faces that correspond to the city buildings, houses and parks within the gaps of urban grids. From a strictly graph-theoretical point of view, street graphs rather correspond to what has often been called line graphs [24]

is part of common knowledge, can thus be used for communicative purposes [32, p.44]:

> "When giving directions we do not describe every intersection, and do not account for every street segment through which we pass. Rather, we typically instruct people to follow linear axes, and single out only those intersections where one should make a turn, that is, cross from one axis to another. Intersections that connect two segments of the same axis or street are usually ignored. In terms of way-finding and urban orientation, then, urban linear axes can be viewed as constitutive units, which are related to each other by means of intersections" [33, p.2121].

A second generalization model was later developed, based on angular information [25]: adjacent segments meeting a specific condition relative to their incidence angle may be merged together as part of the same street. Angularity-based streets are based on a well-known cognitive principle of human wayfinding, which is the tendency to go straight at intersections [34,35,36]. In [37], path analysis of 2425 individual motorcycle trips made in London by motorcycle couriers has indeed revealed that as much as 63% of them took the minimum possible angular distance between origin and destination, while only 51% of trips followed the minimum possible block distance.

Regardless of the street recovery procedure, street graphs present structural properties that are radically different from those of straight road graphs. Distance loses its metric meaning and becomes equivalent to the number of 'steps' separating one street from street, regardless of length of those steps [13] [2]. In this sense, street networks offer " an information view of the city, where distances along each road are effectively set to zero because it does not demand any information handling to drive between the crossroads"[38, p.1]. Also, by allowing the identity of streets to span a theoretically unlimited number of intersections, nominal and angular generalization allow corresponding nodes in the street graph to be incident to a theoretically unlimited number of edges.

Regarding small-worldness, this loss of geometric constraints regarding both distance and node degree, by making street graphs analogous to complex systems not subjected to constraints related to geographical space [13,25], has led to significant results. In [30], the named-based topology of the street networks of Gävle, Munich and San Francisco have been shown to reveal small-world properties. It has also been shown in [25] that the angular topology of 1-square mile samples taken from the street networks of Ahmedabad, Venezia, Wien and Walnut Creek (CA) possess small-world properties. More recently, named street topologies as well as angular street topologies with an angular threshold value of $60°$ have shown small world properties [39]. In other words, contrary to traditional road graphs, street graphs allow for the identification of small-world-like structures in road networks. This formal matching seems to suggest that the

---

[2] However, metric information can still be derived from topological distance, given that line length can roughly correlate with the number of connections of the corresponding node [33].

navigability of road networks lies not so much in their geographical embedding, but rather in their cognitive representation by its users.

It is partly thanks to such results that street-based modelling has been said "to have sustained the by far most relevant, if not the sole, specific contribution of urban design to the study of city networks" [25]. These results are however hampered by the fact that street-based topological modelling conventionally neglect road asymmetry (Jiang, personal communication), reducing accessibility between streets the symmetrical relationships of undirected graphs [28]. Such overlooking should certainly come as a surprise, given that road networks are highly asymmetric, especially in urban settings: some streets allow vehicles to circulate in both ways while others, called 'one-ways', are strictly unidirectional. Given that recent studies in transportation research have shown that road asymmetry degree greatly impacts on algorithm performance and efficiency as well as solution quality [40,41], the overlooking of road direction by street graphs might well prove to be a significant shortcoming of these models, particularly as regards to road network small-worldness. The following research will attempt to address this specific issue through comparison of symmetric and asymmetric street graphs using the ω coefficient, a small-worldness indicator developed in brain network research.

3 Methodology

3.1 Data Collection and Preprocessing

For this research, the road networks of the London neighbourhoods of Barnsbury, Clerkenwell and Kensington have been considered. This decision is consistent with much of the research done in the Space Syntax literature, in which these neighbourhoods were often investigated [42,43,44]. GIS vector data for these neighbourhoods has been extracted from the OpenStreetMap database [45][3], which has been proven comparable to professional surveys in terms of both precision and completeness of features [46]. As for odonym completeness, it has been shown in [47] that, through analysis of 98.53 km of road in the Central London area, as few as 4.99 km (5% of total length) were unlabelled, while name accuracy for OSM maps has been shown to be above 90% [48][4].

As regards to preprocessing, only roads accessible to public, motorized transport were considered in this study. Also, due to the asymmetric nature of certain roads, neighbourhood boundaries as fixed in [39] have been slightly modified in order to be able to convert the three vector maps into strongly connected digraphs, i.e. graphs in which there is a path from each node to each other node.

---

[3] The specific dataset layer used contained a "one-way" tag which conveyed all the road direction information essential to the identification of one-ways.

[4] Since the OSM dataset used in these data quality evaluations is now old and given the fast rate of completion and updating of OSM data, we can suppose that the accuracy, completeness and overall quality of the geographical and attributive information conveyed in OSM datasets is at least as good as it was then.

These different editing operations resulted in the neighbourhood maps of figure 1, in which one-ways and "both-ways" are respectively represented in thick black and grey.

3.2   Roads, Direction and Street Membership

In order to generate street graphs, vector data was first converted into metric-preserving road graphs by converting points into graph nodes and lines between points into edges or arcs connecting the corresponding graph nodes. Two different types of road graphs were generated: undirected (symmetric) graphs, which neglect road asymmetry altogether, and mixed (asymmetric) graphs containing both arcs (unidirectional links) and edges (bidirectional links), with the former corresponding to one-ways and the latter to roads allowing traffic in both ways.

Following this, directed street graphs were generated out of the metrical and angular information carried by the undirected and mixed road graphs. In symmetric context, where road direction isn't taken into account, all directed street graphs created out of undirected road graphs are balanced (see figure 2 for symmetric examples): all arcs have their antiparallel counterparts (for each arc from node A to node B, there is another arc from node B to node A), thus making the overall relational structure similar to that of its underlying directed graph, in which each pair of symmetric arcs corresponds to a single edge.

However, such is not the case in asymmetric context, as one-ways radically alter the relational structure of road networks. On this matter and in order to better assess the impact of road asymmetry on street graphs, generation of the latter was founded on the principle of supervenience of direction on street membership. Introduced in contemporary philosophy of mind to characterize the relation between mental and physical properties [49], supervenience relations refer to asymmetric patterns of covariation in object properties. In short, supervenience can be defined in the following way: "A set of properties A supervenes upon another set B just in case no two things can differ with respect to A-properties without also differing with respect to their B-properties. In slogan form, there cannot be an A-difference without a B-difference" [50, p.1-3]. Thus, supervenience of direction on street membership means that, for any two adjacent roads, any difference regarding the former requires a difference with respect to the latter. Hence, given that there are two types of roads (one-ways and both-ways) and two different one-way orientations (for example, from A to B or from B to A), two adjacent segments of different road types or that are direction-incompatible (pointing in different directions) are also and necessarily part of different streets. Given the behavioural and cognitive impact of direction change on way-finding and navigation (suffice it to think of a urban boulevard becoming a one-way past a certain point and forcing traffic in one direction to change course), adjacent segments of different or incompatible direction types necessarily form different streets. It must be noted here the relation of covariation implied in this supervenience of direction on street membership is ontologically innocent, in that it doesn't imply any ontological priority or dependence. "Supervenience claims, by themselves, do nothing more than state that

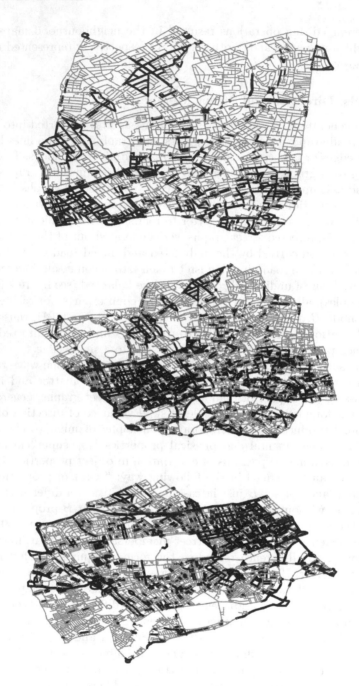

Fig. 1. Maps of Kensington (top), Clerkenwell (center) and Barnsbury (bottom)

certain patterns of property (or fact) variation hold. They are silent about why those patterns hold, and about the precise nature of the dependency involved" [50, p.20].

Street Generalization. As regards to street generalization, both nominal (odonyms or street names) and angular information was considered. Using a simple road configuration as example, figure 2 shows how the different algorithms used in this study operate.

In the case of odonymic street graphs, generalization works by merging into a single street adjacent road segments which bear the same name. In the symmetric example of figure 2, adjacent road segments 1 and 4 bear the same and are merged into a single street, while segments 2 and 4 form, which bear unique names, are thus grouped in distinct streets; also, each segment has access to all of its neighbours, thus resulting in a complete directed street digraph, with arcs from every node to every other node. If road asymmetry in taken into account, however, a very different directed digraph is formed: despite being adjacent and bearing the same name, road segments 1 and 4 are of different types, the former being a both-way and the latter a one-way. Thus, given that direction supervenes on street membership, these segments cannot be part of the same street; moreover, given that traffic on segment 4 moves away from the intersection it shares with segment 1, 2 and 3, the street it forms does not have direct access to those of the latter, an asymmetrical relationship which is expressed through single arcs.

More complex than its odonymic counterpart, angularity-based street generalization depends on two different parameters: angular fitness type and angular threshold. Regarding the former and on the basis or previous research [43], three different angular fitness types were considered : simple, mutual, and relative. According to simple angular fitness, a given segment S_1 merges with an adjacent one S_2 if the deflection angle $\angle S_1 S_2$ is 1) below a given threshold and 2) smaller than the angles formed between $S1$ and the other segments incident to the same end. Rather easy to understand and implement, simple angular fitness however generates graphs that are strongly determined by the segment order given as input to the algorithm (a different segment order will result in a different graph). Mutual angular fitness has been designed in order to avoid this kind of situation: according to this fitness type, a given segment S_1 merges with an adjacent segment S_2 if S_2 represents the best angular fit for S_1 and S_1 represents the best angular fit for S_2. Mutuality might however appear as a rather strict merging condition, preventing the extension of certain streets through other angular-compatible segments. To address this specific issue, relative angular fitness allows all the segments at a intersection to "find the best angular fit they can get", without depriving any other segment from a better fit, in order both to minimize total angle deflection and maximize the number of mergings. Finally, given that there is no definitive and objective angular value that can be used as a merging threshold, different street graphs were generated on the basis of various angular thresholds: 20^0, 30^0, 40^0, 50^0, 60^0, 70^0.

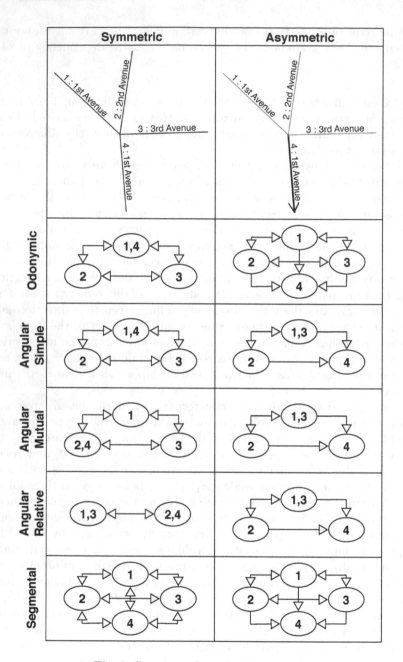

Fig. 2. Street graph generation example

The example given in figure 2 might help distinguish the different angular fitness types. Assuming that segments are processed in ascending order, simple angular fitness in symmetric context works the following way: since angle ∠14 is below threshold, segments 1 and 4 form a single street, while neither angles

∠23 and ∠32 are small enough to allow segments 2 and 3 to merge together. Of course, if the segment processing order had been different, simple angular fitness would have given a different graph; for instance, if the algorithm had started with segment 2, it would have merged segments 2 and 4 instead. Mutual angular fitness however works differently: despite the fact that ∠14 is below any given threshold and lower than ∠12 and ∠13, segments 1 and 4 can't merge, given that segment 2 represents a better angular fit for segment 4 than segment 1; as for segment 2, segment 4 constitutes its best angular fit, which means the angular fitness between 2 and 4 is mutual and thus allows for their merging in a common street; regarding segment 3, its best angular fit is segment 1, but since the latter fits better with segment 4, no merging for segments 1 and 3 is possible, despite the fact that both may very well be below the actual angular threshold. In sum, whereas street graphs generated from mutual angular fitness don't vary according to the segment order, its merging condition might prevent the identification of good angular fits between unmerged segments. Relative angular fitness takes this into consideration, by allowing next-best fits between the remaining, unmerged, segments. Thus, as the given example seems to suggest, simple, mutual or relative angular fitness can generate very different graphs. However, the impact of road asymmetry seems equally important, as its taking into account in the given example results in the creation of identical graphs, regardless of the angular fitness type.

In addition to odonymic and angular topologies, segmental street graphs, in which each road segment between two intersections in the road graphs is considered a street and transposed to a node in the corresponding street graph. Here as in other cases, however, street membership depends on direction: in the case of downtown London, many two-way roads become one-ways before their junction with other streets, in order to allow access only from one extremity. This structural peculiarity imposes important constraints on urban movement, such that its negligence in the construction of street-based topologies might prove detrimental to the validity of the results. The use of such segmental street graphs proves useful in many ways. First of all, their neutrality or non-involvement regarding street generalization should allow them to act as a kind of null hypothesis, allowing for a better assessment of the impact of road asymmetry on both nominal and angular generalization. But also, segmental graphs gives an accurate picture of the asymmetry degree of the three neighbourhoods considered in this study: by having one node for each segment, segment-based topological graphs indeed provide a comprehensive picture of the total number of one-way and both-way segments for each neighbourhood and thus of the relative importance of road asymmetry in each neighbourhood. In the case of Barnsbury, 1596 of all 5614 segments (28,43%) are directed. As for the neighbourhoods of Clerkenwell and Kensington, more than a third of road segments are one-ways (3570 of 10344 (34,5%) for Clerkenkell and 3062 of 8954 (34,2%) in Kensington). Thus, given that an intersection is made from the junction of at least three different road segments (in the case of a T junction or fork), the relatively high number of asymmetrical roads is such that, statistically speaking, there is at least one directed segment for each intersection in Clerkenwell and Kensington, and at least one directed segment for each crossroad (4-way intersection) in Barnsbury. In other words, road asymmetry awaits at every turn.

3.3   Evaluation of Network Small-Worldness: The ω Coefficient

The definition of 'small-worlds' given in [4] allowed for a more complete understanding of networks, by breaking "the continuum of network topologies into the three broad classes of lattices, random graphs and small-worlds, the latter being by far the broadest" [51, p. 1]. Despite the flurry of studies and discoveries it fostered, this definition is still rather imprecise, as it doesn't allow for a rigorous distinction between networks that are small-worlds from those that are not. To address this shortcoming, a new small-worldness coefficient, ω, is presented in [52]. Given a graph with characteristic path length L and average clustering coefficient C, the small-worldness coefficient ω is defined by comparing C to the average clustering coefficient of an "isosequential" lattice (i.e., with same number of nodes and links as well as identical degree sequence) , C_{latt}, and L to the characteristic path length of an "isosequential" random graph, L_{rand}. The value of ω is the difference between the two ratios thus established:

$$\omega = \frac{L_{rand}}{L} - \frac{C}{C_{latt}}$$

Values of ω are restricted to the interval $[-1, 1]$, and scores indicative of small-worlds span the range $-0.5 \leq \omega \leq 0.5$. The supremum and infimum correspond respectively to optimal graph orderliness (lattices) and disorderliness (random graphs) for a given degree sequence, thus placing networks "along a continuum from lattice to small-world to random" [52, p. 368]. Positive values indicate an disorderly and random network structure, satisfying $L \approx L_{rand}$ and $C \ll C_{latt}$. Negative values are indicative of ordered, regular and lattice-like graphs, with $L \gg L_{rand}$ and $C \approx C_{latt}$. Also, in accordance with the definition given in [4], the nearer a network ω score is to zero, the nearer L and C are to L_{rand} and C_{latt} respectively, and thus the higher the small-worldness of that network is. If the ω score of a given network closely approximates 0, it means the local and global structure of that network is balanced to the point that "characteristic path length is as close to random as clustering is to a lattice" [52, p. 370].

By applying this ω coefficient to many real-world networks, the authors show that "small-world networks are not as ubiquitous as reported and suggests that many systems originally thought to have small-world processing capabilities may in fact not" [52, p. 268]. To determine whether or not this conclusion also applies to street-based modelling of road networks, comparative analysis of the ω scores of symmetric and asymmetric street graphs for the neighbourhoods mentioned above was undertaken. For this to be possible, however, isosequential random graphs and isosequential lattices had to be built for each street graph. In the case of random graph generation, the algorithm works by creating a number of nodes equivalent to that of the street graph to be analyzed and by assigning to each node an in- and out-capacity number equivalent to the in- and out-degree of the corresponding node of the street graph. Then, through the generation of arcs, nodes are connected randomly according to their respective in- and out-capacity, until the graph thus created has the same degree sequence than the corresponding street graph. This graph generation procedure is executed 10 times for each street graph, after which the mean value of the characteristic path length of the isosequential random graphs thus generated is returned.

As for isosequential lattice generation, the generation algorithm starts by creating a number of nodes equivalent to that of the street graph and setting them up randomly in order to form a ring. Each node is then given an in-capacity and out-capacity number corresponding to the in-degree and out-degree of a given node of the topological graph. Starting from the nodes with the highest out-capacity, directed links towards closest available nodes with highest in-capacity are made in order to get a degree sequence identical to that of the topological graph. This ring lattice generation process is repeated 10 times for each street graph and only the graph with best initial average clustering coefficient is retained for further processing. This graph is then further "latticized" or clustered using a link-swapping procedure. "Link swaps" are carried out only if the length of both swapped links is shorter than their previous counterparts. Executed over all graph nodes, this process is repeated until no more swaps are carried out[5]. After each iteration of this link swapping algorithm, the average clustering coefficient is calculated; if the average clustering coefficient obtained is higher than the previous ones, then it is saved. At the end of the procedure, the highest average clustering coefficient of all isosequential lattices is returned.

4   Results and Interpretation

At first glance, results reported in Table 1 provide an interesting picture of the impact of road asymmetry on street-based modelling of road networks. One trend that clearly emerges is the structural distinctiveness of segmental street graphs. Whereas the ω scores of all other street graphs are positive, those of both symmetric and asymmetric segmental graphs are exclusively negative, thus indicating their strong orderly and lattice-like structure. This results from the fact that both their average clustering coefficient and characteristic path length are very high, essentially due to the powerful limitations exerted by geographical space on node degree and the existence of long-range connections. As for the effect of road asymmetry on segmental street graphs, results seems to suggest that the taking into account of road direction helps highlight the orderly nature of road geography, as ω scores for asymmetric segmental street graphs are more akin to lattice structures than their symmetric counterparts.

As regards to the different angular street graphs, symmetric ω scores are on the outer edge of the small-world range and lean strongly towards the disorderliness of random-like network structures. This is especially true in the case of the

---

[5] Isosequential lattice generation is a rather long process, which may in fact explain "why comparisons with network lattices have not been used in the literature up to this point" [52, p. 373].

Table 1. Omega scores for symmetric (S) and asymmetric (A) street graphs

		Barnsbury		Clerkenwell		Kensington	
		S	A	S	A	S	A
Segmental		−0.78	−0.81	−0.78	−0.82	−0.74	−0.75
Odonymic		0.35	0.23	0.20	0.06	0.20	0.07
Angular Simple	20	0.43	0.31	0.36	0.27	0.35	0.27
	30	0.50	0.32	0.40	0.26	0.37	0.29
	40	0.50	0.34	0.41	0.27	0.42	0.30
	50	0.51	0.35	0.41	0.27	0.41	0.30
	60	0.48	0.32	0.40	0.28	0.40	0.28
	70	0.47	0.30	0.41	0.23	0.43	0.25
Angular Mutual	20	0.43	0.32	0.32	0.26	0.33	0.27
	30	0.44	0.33	0.36	0.27	0.35	0.29
	40	0.47	0.35	0.35	0.27	0.35	0.30
	50	0.48	0.34	0.35	0.27	0.35	0.31
	60	0.47	0.34	0.37	0.28	0.34	0.28
	70	0.47	0.34	0.37	0.28	0.35	0.28
Angular Relative	20	0.43	0.31	0.33	0.26	0.33	0.28
	30	0.44	0.32	0.36	0.25	0.35	0.28
	40	0.47	0.33	0.36	0.27	0.35	0.29
	50	0.48	0.35	0.36	0.27	0.35	0.30
	60	0.48	0.34	0.37	0.27	0.35	0.29
	70	0.47	0.34	0.37	0.27	0.35	0.29

Barnsbury street graphs, as ω scores for simple angular street graphs stretch to the limit of small-worldness and even beyond. Also, while the ω scores of asymmetric graphs are markedly better than those of their symmetric counterparts, the choice of angular fitness type and threshold value has but a minor impact of ω scores, a fact which seems to put into question the relevance or appropriateness of this kind of parametrization.

As for odonymic street graphs, their ω scores are clearly the best of all models, even more so in the case of asymmetric odonymic graphs, whose scores are surprisingly close to 0 (0,06 for Clerkenwell and 0,07 for Kensington). From a cognitive point of view, these results are highly evocative. Informationally speaking, naming streets is a strategy that pertains both to chunking and tagging: it groups a set of segments together by creating a new concept, with its own unique identity, which can then be quickly referred to in any wayfinding, route planning and communication task by anyone minimally familiar with the street network. And as the excellent ω scores of asymmetric nominal topologies seem to suggest, these odonym-based and space-related activities can be performed on the basis of structural representations that are extremely efficient information-wise, thus bringing road networks, through their odonym-based representations, closer to what David Kirsch called "intelligent uses of space" [53].

Also, for all street graphs necessitating generalization (all non-segmental street graphs), the ω scores of asymmetric street graphs are closer to 0 than those of their symmetric counterparts. From an urban design perspective, the fact that an asymmetric road network has a higher small-worldness degree than if it were symmetric is very telling. Considering that the purpose of partial orientation of road networks through the creation of one-ways is to facilitate movement throughout the network, one must admit that, given the navigability of small-worlds and the high small-worldness of asymmetric graphs, it achieves its goal rather efficiently. In fact, introducing one-ways might be the best way to optimize a network in terms of costs and benefits: by installing a few traffic posts at certain intersections, the network can be substantially reconfigured in very short time, with minimal work, manpower and expenses. Once again, the concept of "intelligent use of space" comes to mind.

As for street graphs in general, results seems to indicate that the taking into account of road asymmetry and the use the ω coefficient helps make better sense of road networks: by exacerbating the orderliness of segmental graphs and the small-worldness of cognition-related street graphs, consideration of both elements have certainly proven beneficial from a street-based modelling and analysis point of view. Finally, as a matter for future research and given that studies using street-based models and various centrality measures have shown to correlate strongly with urban movement density [44], an assessment of the effect of road asymmetry on this specific correlation and on traffic flow in general might seem in order.

References

1. Milgram, S.: The small-world problem. Psychology Today 2, 60–67 (1967)
2. Travers, J., Milgram, S.: An experimental study of the small world problem. Sociometry 32(4), 425–443 (1969)
3. Korte, C., Milgram, S.: Acquaintanceship networks between racial groups: application fo the small world method. Journal of Personality and Social Psychology 15(7), 101–118 (1970)
4. Watts, D.J., Strogatz, S.H.: Collective dynamics of small-worldnetworks. Nature 393(6684), 440–442 (1998)
5. Latora, V., Marchiori, M.: Efficient behavior of small-world networks. Physical Review Letters 87(19), 198701 (2001)
6. Kleinberg, J.: Navigation in a small world. Nature 406, 845 (2000)
7. Gorman, S., Kulkarni, R.: Spatial small worlds: new geographic patterns for an information economy. Environment and Planning B: Planning and Design 31(2), 273–296 (2004)
8. Csanyi, G., Szendroi, B.: Fractal-small-world dichotomy in real-world networks. Physical Review E: Statistical, Nonlinear, and Soft Matter Physics 70, 016122 (2004)
9. Lin, J., Ban, Y.: Complex network topology of transportation systems. Transport Reviews 33(6), 658–685 (2013)
10. Kansky, K.: Structure of transportation networks: relationships between network geometry and regional characteristics. University of Chicago Press (1963)

11. Chorley, R., Haggett, P.: Models in geography. Methuen and Co., London (1967)
12. Haggett, P., Chorley, R.: Network analysis in geography. Edward Arnold, London (1969)
13. Porta, S., Crucitti, P., Latora, V.: The network analysis of urban streets: a primal approach. Environment and Planning B: Planning and Design 33, 705–725 (2006)
14. Cardillo, A., Scellato, S., Latora, V., Porta, S.: Structural properties of planar graphs of urban street patterns. Physical Review E 73(6), 066107 (2006)
15. Crucitti, P., Latora, V., Porta, S.: Centrality in networks of urban streets. Chaos: an Interdisciplinary Journal of Nonlinear Science 16, 015113 (2006)
16. Barthelemy, M.: Spatial networks. Physics Reports 499, 1–101 (2011)
17. Boccaletti, S., Latora, V., Moreno, Y., Chavez, M., Hwang, D.: Complex networks: Structure and dynamics. Physics Reports 424(4-5), 175–308 (2006)
18. Lämmer, S., Gehlsen, B., Helbing, D.: Scaling laws in the spatial structure of urban road networks. Physica A: Statistical Mechanics and its Applications 363(1), 89–95 (2006)
19. Hillier, B., Hanson, J.: The social logic of space. Cambridge University Press, Cambridge (1984)
20. Hillier, B.: Space is the machine: A configurational theory of architecture (1996)
21. Jiang, B.: Volunteered geographical information and computational geography: New perspectives. In: Sui, D., Elwood, S., Goodchild, M. (eds.) Crowdsourcing Geographic Knowledge: Volunteered Geographical Information (VGI) in Theory and Practice, pp. 125–138. Springer, Heidelberg (2013)
22. Kalapala, V., Sanwalani, V., Clauset, A., Moore, C.: Scale invariance in road networks. Physical Review E: Statistical, Nonlinear, and Soft Matter Physics 73(2), 1–6 (2006)
23. Jiang, B., Claramunt, C.: Integration of space syntax into gis: new perspectives for urban morphology. Transactions in GIS 6(3), 295–309 (2002)
24. Harary, F., Norman, R.: Some properties of line digraphs. Rendiconti del Circolo Matematico di Palermo 6(2), 161–169 (1960)
25. Porta, S., Crucitti, P., Latora, V.: The network analysis of urban streets: a dual approach. Physica A: Statistical Mechanics and its Applications 369(2), 853–866 (2006)
26. Batty, M., Rana, S.: The automatic definition and generation of axial lines and axial maps. Environment and Planning B 31(4), 615–640 (2004)
27. Jiang, B.: A topological pattern of urban street networks: Universality and peculiarity. Physica A: Statistical Mechanics and its Applications 384(2), 647–655 (2007)
28. Penn, A.: Space syntax and spatial cognition: Or why the axial line? Environment and Behavior 35(1), 30–65 (2003)
29. Courtat, T., Gloaguen, C., Douady, S.: Mathematics and morphogenesis of cities: A geometrical approach. Physical Review E 83(3), 036106 (2011)
30. Jiang, B., Claramunt, C.: Topological analysis of urban street networks. Environment and Planning B 31(1), 151–162 (2004)
31. Jiang, B., Claramunt, C.: A structural approach to the model generalization of an urban street network. Geoinformatica 8(2), 157–171 (2004)
32. Tomko, M., Winter, S., Claramunt, C.: Experiential hierarchies of streets. Computers, Environment and Urban Systems 32(1), 41–52 (2008)
33. Wagner, R.: On the metric, topological and functional structures of urban networks. Physica A: Statistical Mechanics and its Applications 387(8-9), 2120–2132 (2008)
34. Conroy Dalton, R.: The secret is to follow your nose: route path selection and angularity. Environment and Behavior 35, 107–131 (2003)

35. Dalton, N.: Fractional configurational analysis and a solution to the manhattan problem (2001), http://undertow.arch.gatech.edu/homepages/3sss
36. Dalton, N., Peponis, J., Dalton, R.: To tame a tiger one hase to know its nature: extending weighted angular integration analysis to the description of gis road-centerline data for large scale urban analysis (2003), http://www.spacesyntax.net/SSS4
37. Turner, A.: The role of angularity in route choice. In: Hornsby, K.S., Claramunt, C., Denis, M., Ligozat, G. (eds.) COSIT 2009. LNCS, vol. 5756, pp. 489–504. Springer, Heidelberg (2009)
38. Rosvall, M., Trusina, A., Minnhagen, P., Sneppen, K.: Networks and cities: An information perspective. Physical Review Letters 94(2), 28701 (2005)
39. Jiang, B., Liu, C.: Street-based topological representations and analyses for predicting traffic flow in gis. International Journal of Geographical Information Science 23(9), 1119–1137 (2009)
40. Rodríguez, A., Ruiz, R.: The effect of the asymmetry of road transportation networks on the traveling salesman problem. Computers & Operations Research 39(7), 1566–1576 (2012)
41. Rodríguez, A., Ruiz, R.: A study on the effect of the asymmetry on real capacitated vehicle routing problems. Computers & Operations Research 39(9), 2142–2151 (2012)
42. Hillier, B., Penn, A., Hanson, J., Grajewski, T., Xu, J.: Natural movement-or, configuration and attraction in urban pedestrian movement. Environment and Planning B: Planning and Design 20(1), 29–66 (1993)
43. Jiang, B.: Ranking spaces for predicting human movement in an urban environment. International Journal of Geographical Information Science 23(7), 823–837 (2009)
44. Jiang, B., Jia, T.: Agent-based simulation of human movement shaped by the underlying street structure. International Journal of Geographical Information Science 25(1), 51–64 (2011)
45. Schneider, W., Rezic, S.: Bbbike.org, the cycle route planner (March 2013), http://goo.gl/CQRziY
46. Haklay, M.: How good is volunteered geographical information? a comparative study of openstreetmap and ordnance survey datasets. Environment and Planning B: Planning and Design 37(4), 682 (2010)
47. Ather, A.: A quality analysis of openstreetmap data. ME Thesis, University College London, London, UK (2009)
48. Pitsis, N., Haklay, M.: Attribute based evaluation of openstreetmap (2010)
49. Davidson, D.: Mental events. In: Davidson, D. (ed.) Essays on Actions and Events, pp. 207–225. Clarendon Press, Oxford (1980)
50. McLaughlin, B., Bennett, K.: Supervenience. Stanford Enclyclopedia of Philosophy (2014)
51. Humphries, M., Gurney, K.: Network 'small-world-ness': A quantitative method for determining canonical network equivalence. PloS ONE 3(4), 1–10 (2008)
52. Telesford, Q., Joyce, K., Hayasaka, S., Burdette, J., Laurienti, P.: The ubiquity of small-world networks. Brain Connectivity 1(5), 367–375 (2011)
53. Kirsh, D.: The intelligent use of space. Artificial Intelligence 73, 31–68 (1995)

Spatial Planning: An ACT-R Model
for the Tower of London Task

Rebecca Albrecht and Marco Ragni

Center for Cognitive Science,
University of Freiburg,
Friedrichstr. 50, 79098 Freiburg, Germany
albrechr@informatik.uni-freiburg.de, ragni@cognition.uni-freiburg.de

Abstract. The Tower of London (ToL for short) is a disk manipulation task extensively used and well-established as a neuropsychological
diagnostic tool for assessing human planning ability in clinical and research contexts. Behavioral experiments have shown that planning in the
ToL is substantially influenced by structural, visually observable task
characteristics. This work presents an ACT-R model for three move ToL
tasks which uses a spreading activation mechanism to explain differences
in planning performance. Model evaluation is based on a task selection
that accounted for systematic variations of task demands. Based on comparisons with empirically observed planning latencies and eye-movement
patterns the explanation for human planning abilities in ToL is assessed
and discussed.

Keywords: ACT-R, spreading activation, disk manipulation tasks,
Tower of London, human planning, visuo-spatial problem solving.

1 Introduction

The Tower of London (ToL) is a disk manipulation task originally proposed
in [1] as a neuropsychological tool to measure planning deficits in patients with
frontal lobe damages. Today it is widely used as a general assessment tool to
evaluate executive and planning functions. Like any planning problem [2], ToL
can be defined by an initial configuration (or state) and a goal configuration.
Usually, each configuration consists of three pegs and a certain number of disks
with different colors which are located on pegs. The goal in ToL is to transform
the initial configuration into the goal configuration by moving disks from their
initial location to their target location. A move in ToL is constrained by (1)
only one disk may be moved at a time, (2) only the top disk on any peg may
be moved, and (3) the maximum capacity of a peg may not be exceeded. An
example ToL instance is shown in Figure 1.

ToL has been assessed in different experimental settings and with a wide
range of different task complexities (cf. [3]). Usually, the number of disks in a
ToL configuration ranges from three [4–8] to five [9, 10]. In most studies, the
maximum capacity of all pegs corresponds to the number of disks in one configuration [5, 6, 10]. However, there are also studies which use different maximum

C. Freksa et al. (Eds.): Spatial Cognition 2014, LNAI 8684, pp. 222–236, 2014.

Initial
Configuration

Goal
Configuration

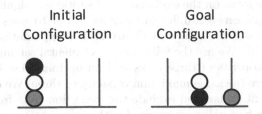

Fig. 1. Example ToL task where the initial configuration shown on the left has to be transformed into the goal configuration shown on the right. This task can be solved optimally by first moving the black disk from the left peg to the middle peg, secondly moving the white disk from the left peg to the middle peg, and thirdly moving the grey disk from the left peg to the right peg.

capacities for pegs in one configuration [1,7]. While the fact that the number of moves has an impact on planning difficulty seems obvious [4,9], the influence of several other task characteristics has been studied. One of them concerns visually observable properties of the initial and the goal configuration [5,6,11], e.g. on how many different pegs disks are located in a configuration. Another important characteristic is the search depth, i.e. the number of intermediate moves until a subgoal can be reached [5,12]. A third characteristic is the number of optimal paths to reach a solution [11].

Often participants are asked to construct a complete and optimal plan before executing the first move (e.g. [4,5]). Therefore, the impact of verbal and visuo-spatial working memory in ToL has been studied extensively to analyse the influence of executive functions usually associated with human planning. These studies reveal that the visuo-spatial working memory is an important factor in the solution process of ToL [9,13].

ToL shares structural characteristics with the Tower of Hanoi (ToH) task (cf. [3]). However, they differ in one important aspect. In ToH all disks have a different size. Therefore, an additional constraint that only smaller disks may be placed on larger disks is included. With respect to the study of human planning performance ToH has two properties that make it less interesting compared to ToL. Firstly, the goal configuration in ToH is given implicitly by the task description, which states that all disks have to be moved from one peg to another peg [14–16]. Therefore, ToH tasks usually differ in the number of disks which have to be solved and not with respect to visually observable task characteristics as studied for the ToL. Secondly, there exists a recursive algorithm to solve the ToH [17] which can be used by participants. This is not the case for ToL.

A first ACT-R model for ToL is presented in [18]. This model reproduces behavioral data reported in [5] by adapting a solution strategy from an ACT-R model for ToH reported in [14]. In this model, a goal for each disk is constructed by first attending its initial location and then attending its target location. Hence, six gaze shifts between the initial state and the goal state are necessary. As a result, this model is not able to predict eye-movement patterns as reported in [6], where most participants need less than six gaze shifts.

In this article we focus on the explanation of subtle but significant differences in planning time between eight different tasks used in [5] to asses human planning performance. The tasks are shown in Figure 2. The explanation is given by an ACT-R model [19,20]. We use the following experimental setting to evaluate the model. Each task consists of three disks and an optimal plan consists of three moves. All pegs have the same maximum capacity of three. We only analyze the time to make a mental plan and exclude the execution time from our analysis. The eight tasks can be further categorized with respect to a configuration and a search depth condition. The configuration condition includes tasks with a full-to-partial configuration where all disks are located on one peg in the initial state and on two different pegs in the goal state, and tasks with a partial-to-full configuration where disks are located on two different pegs in the initial state and on one peg in the goal state. The search depth condition includes tasks without an intermediate step and with one intermediate step. As an additional qualitative measure we use the number of gaze shifts between the initial state and the goal state with respect to these conditions reported in [6]. We will explain how the implemented solution mechanism and features from ACT-R yield an explanation for performance differences. We will also assess the quality of the presented model and discuss possible extensions in detail.

2   Cognitive Model

2.1   ACT-R

The cognitive model presented in this work is developed in the ACT-R cognitive architecture [19,20]. ACT-R is a modular cognitive architecture with an underlying production rule system operating on symbolic representations of declarative memory items – so-called chunks. The system consists of specific modules corresponding to certain aspects of human cognition. It provides a module for processing visually presented information (vision module), a module for representing goal specific information (goal module), a module for representing problem state information (imaginal module), and a module to store and retrieve declarative memory items (declarative module). Each module has at least one dedicated interface (buffer) which can hold one chunk at a time. Any buffer manipulation is a strictly serial process that is performed by the production rules. Modules may be active in parallel and consequently there may be more than one chunk that is currently processed by the model. Human performance is predicted based on the time cost associated with the processing of modules.

On the sub-symbolic side probabilistic processes direct behavior such as production selection and chunk selection from declarative memory. In example, the availability of chunks to a corresponding retrieval request depends on their activation values which are calculated on the basis of several aspects. Most notably, once a chunk has been created its initial activation starts decreasing following a fixed decay rate. However, chunks may receive additional activation determined by (a) the number of positive retrievals in the past and (b) spreading activation

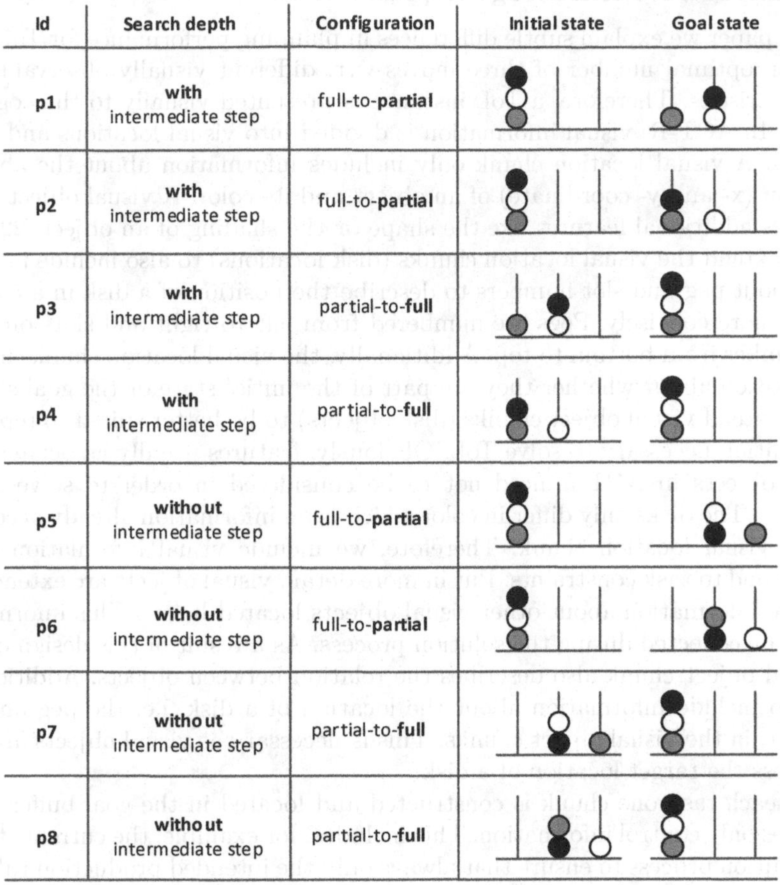

Id	Search depth	Configuration	Initial state	Goal state
p1	with intermediate step	full-to-**partial**		
p2	with intermediate step	full-to-**partial**		
p3	with intermediate step	partial-to-**full**		
p4	with intermediate step	partial-to-**full**		
p5	without intermediate step	full-to-**partial**		
p6	without intermediate step	full-to-**partial**		
p7	without intermediate step	partial-to-**full**		
p8	without intermediate step	partial-to-**full**		

Fig. 2. This figure shows eight ToL tasks adapted from [5] which are used to evaluate the cognitive model described in this work. For each task an optimal solution consists of three moves. The eight tasks can be divided into two conditions, search depth and configuration. The configuration condition is divided into tasks with a full-to-partial (p1, p2, p5, p6) and with a partial-to-full (p3, p4, p7, p8) characteristic, the search depth condition can be divided into tasks with an intermediate step (p1, p2, p3, p4) and without an intermediate step (p5, p6, p7, p8).

from the chunks located in other buffers. The time to retrieve a chunk from declarative memory depends on its activation value.

In ACT-R, the notion of working memory is defined in terms of chunk activation. Chunks can only be retrieved from declarative memory if their activation value exceeds a certain threshold. All chunks for which the designated activation value exceeds the threshold and which satisfy the constraints of the request can potentially be retrieved from declarative memory. They are, therefore, associated with working memory [21].

2.2   Declarative Knowledge Representation

In this paper we explain subtle differences in planning performance for ToL tasks with an optimal number of three moves wrt. different visually observable task characteristics. Therefore, a ToL instance is presented visually to the cognitive model. In ACT-R, visual information is divided into visual locations and visual objects. A visual location chunk only includes information about the absolute position (x- and y- coordinate) of an object and its color. A visual object chunk includes additional features like the shape or the shading of an object [22].

We extend the visual location chunks (disk locations) to also include information about peg and slot numbers to describe the position of a disk in a configuration more concisely. Pegs are numbered from left to right and slots on a peg are number from bottom to top. Additionally, the visual location chunks include information about whether they are part of the initial state or the goal state.

We extend visual object chunks (disk objects) to be better suited to represent information necessary to solve ToL. Obviously, features usually associated with visual objects in ACT-R need not to be considered in order to solve a ToL instance. The disks only differ in color which is an information already accessible in the visual location chunk. Therefore, we include visual information which correspond to task constraints. Put in more detail, visual objects are extended to capture information about other visual objects located below. This information has to be collected during the solution process. As a result of this design choice, a visual object chunk also describes the relation between objects. Additionally, we also include information about the location of a disk, i.e. the peg and slot number, in the visual object chunks. This is necessary as visual objects are used to access the target location of a disk.

For each task one chunk is constructed and located in the goal buffer which includes only control information. This includes, for example, the current state in the solution process to ensure that always only the intended production rules are enabled and information concerning the overall progress in the solution process.

In the imaginal buffer a chunk which describes the current problem state is stored. This chunk includes the following information:

- Information where disks are located with respect to already planned moves.
- The color of a disk which is currently selected to be solved.
- The initial location of a currently selected disk.
- The target location of a currently selected disk.
- The color of a disk which was blocked by the currently selected disk.
- The color of a disk which was solved before.

As this chunk also includes the initial and the target location of a disk it also incorporates goal specific information.

We do not include a mechanism to construct and retrieve goals as described in [16] for the Tower of Hanoi task. The main reason is that three move ToL tasks are relatively easy to solve, meaning that there is no need for a sophisticated goal decomposition mechanism as for the far more complex ToH instances used in [16]. Instead of a goal which includes the target position of a disk, the target position itself is retrieved. This results in a similar retrieval pattern.

We do not use chunks which represent pegs. We assume that in the solution process the peg locations where disks can be placed are much more important than the peg objects themselves. The relations between disks located on the same peg are stored in the visual objects associated with disks. There is also a practical reason for not using peg objects, concluded from experimental data reported in [6]. There are no reported differences between the full-to-partial and partial-to-full condition on the duration of the first (and second) fixation of the goal state. A model which constructs a peg chunk, for example in the imaginal buffer, would predict a longer fixation of the goal state in the full-to-partial condition. The reason is that two different peg objects would need to be constructed.

2.3   Retrieval Strategy

One core concept in ACT-R is the bottleneck of retrieving information from declarative memory. In the model presented here we decided to retrieve the disk objects located in the goal state which include information about the target positions of disks. However, as the target position is also visually accessible the model can shift between a retrieval strategy and a visual strategy to obtain that information. When a disk is selected to be checked, two different processes are started. On the one hand, the vision module is requested for the corresponding visual object in the initial state, on the other hand, the declarative module is requested for the corresponding visual object in the goal state. The time the visual module needs to respond to this request is set to the ACT-R default of 200ms. After the request to the vision module has been processed successfully, information concerning the target location of the disk is needed to continue planning. If the declarative module does not respond to the retrieval request within this time the retrieval request is aborted and the target location is attended visually. The reason is, that it seems not plausible to wait for the success of a retrieval request while no other information need to be processed, especially when the needed information is visually accessible.

When a move for a disk to its target location is planned mentally we assume that it is not necessary to retrieve the new position of that disk later on in the solution process, at least not in this simple version of the task. The reason is that this position is visually observable in the goal state and information about which disks have been solved is sufficient. However, when a disk is mentally moved to a position different from its target position it cannot be reconstructed from the environment easily. Therefore, the location of this disk has to be retrieved from declarative memory.

One important aspect in the presented model is the use of spreading activation. The main source of spreading activation is the imaginal buffer which makes problem state information as well as information about the status of the overall solution process accessible. As we will argue later, this source of spreading activation is the main factor to explain subtle differences in planning performance, especially with respect to the configuration condition.

2.4   General Solution Mechanism

The disks in the visually observable environment are always attended from top to bottom, in the initial state as well as in the goal state. For the initial state this decision is based on the constraint that only the top disk on a peg may be moved. Therefore, it makes no sense to start planning with a disk not located on top of a peg. Additionally, the model always attends disks in the goal state before it moves its attention to disks in the initial state. This decision is based on findings in [23], where it is reported that fixations are more likely to happen towards the goal state in the beginning of the task.

The general strategy implemented in the model can be divided into four main phases. Each phase corresponds to one fixation of the goal state or the initial state, respectively. In the first phase, the model attends all visual locations of disks in the goal state. This corresponds to the internalization of the goal configuration. In this phase only locations of disks are assessed, the objects itself are ignored.

In the second phase, the model attends all visual locations of disks in the initial state. Locations in the initial state are compared with target locations which were attended in phase one. For an attended initial location a visual location chunk with the same location information (peg and slot number) is requested from the declarative module. If such a visual location can be retrieved and the locations are associated with disks of the same color it is concluded that this disk is already located correctly.

In the third phase object specific information in the goal state is collected. This includes relations between disks which are located on the same peg. The visual search strategy attends disks from top to bottom. When the visual object associated with one disk is attended it is also updated with information about the disk located below.

In phase four actual planning takes place. This phase corresponds to the last fixation of the initial state reported in [6]. This phase includes several steps.

- *Select Disk.* If there is a disk which was blocked before, as indicated by the problem state chunk in the imaginal buffer, it is selected. If this is not the case, a disk is selected according to the visual search strategy.
- *Decode Disk.* The vision module is requested to shift attention to the disk object associated with the disk location. Simultaneously, a retrieval request for the disk object in the goal state which includes the needed location information is posed to the declarative module.
- *Check Constraints.* In order to check whether a disk can be moved to its target location, task constraints have to be translated into visual locations to be checked. This includes the position above a disk as only the top disk on any peg may be moved and its target position in the initial state. Additionally, as the human planner is quite aware, due to physical constraints a disk may slip down a peg. Therefore, also the positions below the target locations have to be checked. A move to a location is only possible if the position below that location is occupied. If a move is blocked, information concerning the blocking disk is stored in the problem state chunk in the imaginal buffer.

– *Recognize intermediate step.* An intermediate step is recognized when all disks have been checked and no move to a target location for any disk is possible. In this step always two disks have to be considered, a blocking disk which has to be moved to an intermediate position and a blocked disk which can then be solved. Information concerning the blocked disk is necessary to decide for an intermediate position which does not hinder future goal moves.

3 Evaluation

We tested the model with all tasks which are structurally equivalent to the tasks shown in Figure 2. To support the main contribution of this article we compared the predicted planning time to experimental data collected with the same set of tasks in [5]. The results are shown in Figure 3. The overall planning time, number of gaze shifts and last fixation duration for the tasks grouped with respect to the search depth and configuration conditions are shown in Table 2.

Concerning the search depth condition, in tasks with an intermediate step (p1, p2, p3, p4) the higher planning time compared with tasks without an inter-

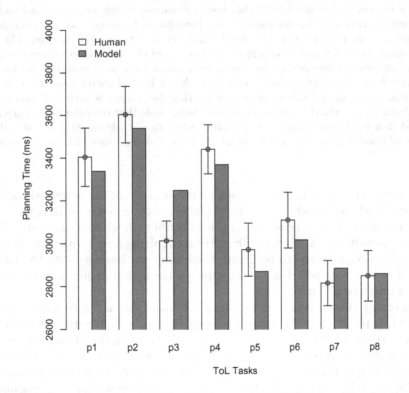

Fig. 3. This figure shows an quantitative comparison of planning time for the eight different tasks shown in Figure 2 between human data reported in [5] and data predicted by the cognitive model described in this work.

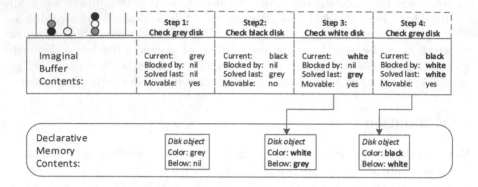

	Step 1: Check grey disk	Step2: Check black disk	Step 3: Check white disk	Step 4: Check grey disk
Imaginal Buffer Contents:	Current: grey Blocked by: nil Solved last: nil Movable: yes	Current: black Blocked by: nil Solved last: grey Movable: no	Current: white Blocked by: nil Solved last: grey Movable: yes	Current: black Blocked by: white Solved last: white Movable: yes

Declarative Memory Contents:	Disk object Color: grey Below: nil	Disk object Color: white Below: grey	Disk object Color: black Below: white

Fig. 4. This figure shows exemplary imaginal buffer and declarative memory contents for task p8 shown in Figure 2. The task is also shown in the upper left corner of this figure. Steps in the solution process are shown in boxes with dashed lines. Each step shows exactly the imaginal buffer contents in step *decode disk* of the general solution mechanism. This includes the selected disk (current), the disk which blocked a goal move for the currently selected disk (blocked by), the disk which was solved last (solved last), and information whether the disk was movable to its target location (movable). Disks are attended according to the visual search strategy from top to bottom. The box with a solid line and rounded corners on the bottom of the figure shows the declarative memory contents. Information concerning disks below have been collected in phase 2. An arrow from the imaginal buffer to a disk object in declarative memory indicates additional spreading activation received when this disk object is retrieved. Sources of spreading activation in these cases are marked bold. Note that the color of the currently selected disk is always a source of spreading activation. Only in steps 3 and 4 disks receive additional spreading activation by the grey and the white disk, respectively.

mediate step (p5, p6, p7, p8) is a result of two aspects of the described solution process. Firstly, all disks have to be attended once in order to recognize that an intermediate step is necessary. At this point, a task without an intermediate step can already be solved. Secondly, after recognizing an intermediate step, an intermediate position has to be found which may not interfere with the following goal moves. This additional effort explains the higher planning time in tasks with an intermediate step.

Concerning the configuration condition, in tasks with a full-to-partial configuration (p1, p2, p5, p6) the higher planning time compared with task instances with a partial-to-full configuration (p3, p4, p7, p8) is a direct result from the higher number of necessary gaze shifts. Additional gaze shifts are necessary if the visual object which includes the target location of a disk cannot be retrieved in time, i.e. until the attention has been shifted to the currently selected disk object in phase four, step *decode disk* in the general solution mechanism. The time to retrieve the visual object chunk depends on its activation value. In the presented model, the activation value is highly influenced by spreading activation.

The main source of spreading activation in the model is the imaginal buffer. It holds information about the current problem state and overall solution process. This includes information about (a) the currently selected disk, (b) the disk which was blocked by the currently selected disk, and (c) the last disk for which a move was planned successfully. The disk objects which are requested from declarative memory include information about disks which are located below in the goal state. They are the target of spreading activation from the imaginal buffer. Hence, two reasons for additional spreading activation from the imaginal buffer to the target visual object chunk can be observed. (1) a disk for which a move was planned successfully is also located below the currently selected disk and (2) when the disk which blocked a move of another disk before is located below the currently selected disk. Figure 4 shows exemplary imaginal buffer contents and declarative memory contents for task p8 (see Figure 2).

Table 1 shows how many disks receive additional spreading activation in the eight tasks shown in Figure 2. As a result of the described spreading activation mechanism, in tasks with a partial-to-full condition and without an intermediate step (p7, p8) 66% of disks receive additional spreading activation, in the full-to-partial condition without an intermediate step (p5, p6) only 16.5% of disks receive additional spreading activation. This would suggest that the differences in planning time should be even higher as predicted (cf. results shown in Figure 3 and Table 2). It is not, however, due to the visual search strategy. As disks are always selected from top to bottom, disks in the full-to-partial condition are already selected in the optimal ordering. In tasks with a partial-to-full condition, this is not necessarily the case. In task p8, for example, the black disk is the second one selected and cannot be solved directly. Note that information concerning disks which block the moves of other disks are a source of spreading activation later in the solution process and, therefore, a part of the explanation why no additional gaze shifts are necessary in a partial-to-full condition.

In order to evaluate the model further we also compared the predicted data qualitatively with other experimental data reported in [6]. As we did use different tasks we cannot match the predicted data with the experimental data quantitatively. In [6] the authors report that the configuration condition has an impact on the number of gaze shifts but not on the last fixation duration of the initial state. On the other hand, the search depth condition has an impact on the last fixation duration but not on the number of gaze shifts.

Table 2 shows the number of gaze shifts, overall planning time, and last fixation duration predicted by the model for conditions partial-to-full, full-to-partial, with intermediate step, and without intermediate step. The effect on gaze shifts is predicted by the model. This is a direct result of the use of spreading activation in combination with a change from a retrieval based to a vision based solution strategy described in phase 4, step *decode disk* in the general solution mechanism. The model also predicts the differences in overall planning time, which is not surprising given the quantitative fit on similar three move tasks shown in Figure 3. However, the model does not predict the effects on the last fixation duration. In the data predicted by the model the configuration condition also

Table 1. Spreading activation received by disks when the target location is retrieved for tasks shown in Figure 2. The first row gives an overview on the absolute number of disks which receive additional spreading in each task. The second row shows the percentage of disks which receive additional spreading activation, relative to the number of disks which have to be solved in a task. Note that in three move ToL tasks with an intermediate step one disk is always located on its target position. The source of the additional activation is problem state information stored in the imaginal buffer during the solution process.

Task	p1	p2	p3	p4	p5	p6	p7	p8
Number of disks	2	0	2	2	1	0	2	2
Percentage	100	0	100	100	33	0	66	66

Table 2. Absolute planning time, number of gaze shifts, and characteristics discussed. These include tasks with a full-to-partial configuration where all disks are located on one peg in the initial state and on two different pegs in the goal state, tasks with a partial-to-full configuration where disks are located on two different pegs in the initial state and on one peg in the goal state, and tasks with and without an intermediate step.

Problem class	Planning time (in ms)	Number of gaze shifts	Last fixation duration (in ms)
With intermediate step	3428.500	4.875	1577.558
Without intermediate step	2964.396	4.742	1157.688
Full to partial	3252.596	5.042	1267.704
Partial to full	3140.300	4.575	1467.542

has an influence on the last fixation duration. The reason is that while less gaze shifts are necessary, the planning time, and therefore the last fixation duration, is increased due to the visual search strategy where disks are attended from top to bottom and, therefore, disks are not attended in the optimal ordering.

4   Discussion

We present an ACT-R model which solves three move Tower of London (ToL) tasks wrt. psychological assumptions on visuo-spatial problem solving. We compare model predictions with results from two studies [5,6] which examine subtle differences in human planning performance with respect to a configuration condition, i.e. on how many pegs disks are located in each configuration, and a search depth condition, i.e. whether an intermediate step is necessary or not. The model predicts effects on eye-movement patterns and overall planning time for these conditions but not effects on the last fixation duration.

The main functioning of the model can be characterized by the following aspects. (1) A visual search strategy which attends disks always from top to bottom; (2) the extension of visual objects by relational information; (3) a retrieval strategy where target locations are requested from declarative memory;

(4) an upper bound on the time for an retrieval request because that information is visually accessible; (5) a representation of the current problem state and overall progress in the solution process; (6) a spreading activation mechanism where information from (2) and (5) influence the ability to retrieve target location information; (7) a mechanism to recognize that an intermediate steps is necessary when no goal move is possible.

Effects in the search depth condition are predicted by (7). Effects in the configuration condition can only be predicted for the overall planning time and the number of gaze shifts, not for the last fixation duration. Model predictions in this condition are explained by (1), (4), and (6).

The presented model describes one possible explanation on how three move ToL tasks are solved. While design choices are explained in this article, further possibilities should be examined in order to get more insight into human planning and executive functions.

The visual search strategy which always attends disks from top to bottom is very restrictive. Although this strategy makes sense in the initial state due to task constraints, this is not the case for disks in the goal state. In the goal state, a disk which is located on the bottom of a peg always has to be solved first. Therefore, a strategy where the disks are attended from bottom to top in the goal state should also be evaluated. As we consider the visual search strategy to be the main reason for the wrong prediction on the effect on the last fixation duration in the configuration condition, it is possible that a combination of these visual search strategies is able to predict this effect correctly.

Bottom-up processes in visual attention are not considered. The presented visual search strategy directs visual attention in a planning specific top-down fashion. There have been recent efforts to create a vision module which includes bottom-up aspects in ACT-R [24]. An ACT-R model for the ToL which includes visual search strategies could highly benefit from these findings.

A goal construction and retrieval mechanism as used in previous works which report cognitive models for disk manipulation tasks is not included. This contradicts to theories about planning in disk manipulation tasks [8, 25]. Such a mechanism is not included, as three move ToL tasks are simple to solve and a sophisticated goal decomposition mechanism is not necessary. Additionally, as target locations have to be retrieved frequently a similar retrieval pattern is predicted. For an extension of the model which solves more difficult instances of the ToL a goal decomposition mechanisms will likely be necessary.

Given the experimental data on planning time, especially the last fixation duration, it is unlikely that in three move ToL tasks more than one retrieval request per disk can be used without breaking absolute time constraints. Additionally, when using goals which include the target location of a disk it makes no sense to also retrieve the target location of a disk itself, which is then redundant information. Hence, if a goal retrieval mechanism is included, information concerning disk relations can no longer be used. As a result, the spreading activation mechanism described here cannot be implemented.

It can be questioned whether four phases which correspond to fixations of initial and goal state are necessary. Especially phases one and two do not contribute information which is essential for the solution process. Data concerning gaze shifts for the simplest one move ToL tasks presented in [4] suggest that less gaze shifts should be possible.

Although it is known that complex information is chunked to simplify problem representations [26–28] it can be argued whether utilizing visual object chunks is a plausible realization of this concept. Additionally, the use of location information in the visual object chunks contradicts to the separation between location and object information.

The list of possible and untested alternative models illustrates a fundamental problem with using cognitive architectures like ACT-R today. In order to evaluate different psychological mechanisms as discussed in this work different ACT-R models have to be defined. The reason is that production rules are explicitly expressed with respect to the chosen knowledge base, i.e. chunk types and chunks. Although different models may only deviate in certain aspects they cannot be compared easily as they use different rule sets. For example, in an implementation of a slightly different theory which proposes the construction of relations in the imaginal buffer instead of using adjusted visual location and object chunks, most rules have to be redefined. This includes rules which are structurally equivalent in both models as they, e.g. check for the existence of a relation in the declarative memory. In this example, the only difference between the models is a fixed time to construct a relation in the imaginal buffer. On the one hand, rewriting a complete model is a time consuming and error prone process, on the other hand, the impact of changing just one aspect in a model cannot be assessed by itself. As a solution, we intend to implement mechanisms to automatically evaluate partial cognitive models, e.g. ones which only make key concepts of a modeled theory explicit, in order to compare them directly wrt. experimental data. To achieve this, we intend to define a formal semantics for ACT-R and evaluate models through the application of formal methods from program analysis, like model checking and theorem proving.

To conclude, although the described cognitive model is tailored specifically to three move ToL tasks and describes exactly one solution mechanism, we believe that our findings can help narrow down theories about visuo-spatial problem solving in disk manipulation tasks in ACT-R. We show that a spreading activation mechanism based on (A) the relation of visually observable task characteristics and (B) the overall progress of the solution process can be used to explain subtle differences in planning performance. These findings can be used to guide the development of future ACT-R models in visuo-spatial environments.

Acknowledgements. This research was supported by the DFG (German National Research Foundation) in the Transregional Collaborative Research Center, SFB/TR 8 within project R8-[CSPACE].

References

1. Shallice, T.: Specific impairments of planning. Philosophical Transactions of the Royal Society of London B 298, 199–209 (1982)
2. Russell, S.J., Norvig, P.: Artificial Intelligence: A Modern Approach, 2nd edn. Prentice Hall, Englewood Cliffs (2003)
3. Kaller, C.P., Rahm, B., Köstering, L., Unterrainer, J.M.: Reviewing the impact of problem structure on planning: a software tool for analyzing tower tasks. Behavioural Brain Research 216, 1–8 (2011)
4. Kaller, C.P., Rahm, B., Bolkenius, K., Unterrainer, J.M.: Eye movements and visuospatial problem solving: Identifying separable phases of complex cognition. Psychophysiology 46, 818–830 (2009)
5. Kaller, C.P., Rahm, B., Spreer, J., Weiller, C., Unterrainer, J.M.: Dissociable contributions of left and right dorsolateral prefrontal cortex in planning. Cerebral Cortex 21, 307–317 (2011)
6. Nitschke, K., Ruh, N., Kappler, S., Stahl, C., Kaller, C.P.: Dissociable stages of problem solving (i): Temporal characteristics revealed by eye-movement analyses. Brain and Cognition 80(1), 160–169 (2012)
7. Newman, S.D., Carpenter, P.A., Varma, S., Just, M.A.: Frontal and parietal participation in problem solving in the tower of london: fmri and computational modeling of planning and high-level perception. Neuropsychologia 41(12), 1668–1682 (2003)
8. Owen, A.M.: Cognitive planning in humans: neuropsychological, neuroanatomical and neuropharmacological perspectives. Progress in Neurobiology 53(4), 431–450 (1997)
9. Phillips, L.H., Wynn, V.E., Gilhooly, K.J., Sala, S.D., Logie, R.H.: The role of memory in the Tower of London task. Memory 7, 209–231 (1999)
10. Phillips, L.H., Wynn, V.E., McPherson, S., Gilhooly, K.J.: Mental planning and the Tower of London. Quarterly Journal of Experimental Psychology 54A, 579–597 (2001)
11. Newman, S.D., Pittman, G.: The Tower of London: A study of the effect of problem structure on planning. Journal of Clinical and Experimental Neuropsychology 29, 333–342 (2007)
12. Ward, G., Allport, A.: Planning and problem-solving using the 5-disc Tower of London task. Quarterly Journal of Experimental Psychology 50, 49–78 (1997)
13. Gilhooly, K., Wynn, V., Phillips, L., Logie, R., Sala, S.D.: Visuo-spatial and verbal working memory in the five-disc tower of london task: An individual differences approach. Thinking & Reasoning 8(3), 165–178 (2002)
14. Anderson, J.R., Douglass, S.: Tower of Hanoi. Evidence for the cost of goal retrieval 27, 1331–1346 (2001)
15. Altmann, E.M., Trafton, J.G.: Memory for goals: An architectural perspective. In: Proceedings of the Twenty-First Annual Conference of the Cognitive Science Society, pp. 19–24. Erlbaum (1999)
16. Altmann, E.M., Trafton, J.G.: Memory for goals: An activation-based model. Cognitive Science 26, 63–83 (2002)
17. Hofstadter, D.R.: Metamagical themas. Scientific American 245(3), 409–415 (1981)
18. Albrecht, R., Brüssow, S., Kaller, C., Ragni, M.: Using a cognitive model for an in-depth analysis of the tower of london. In: Proceedings of the 33rd Annual Meeting of the Cognitive Science Society, Cognitive Science Society, pp. 693–698 (2011)
19. Anderson, J.R.: The Architecture of Cognition, vol. 5. Psychology Press (1983)

20. Anderson, J.R.: How can the human mind occur in the physical universe? Oxford University Press, New York (2007)
21. Anderson, J.R., Reder, L.M., Lebiere, C.: Working memory: Activation limitations on retrieval. Cognitive Psychology 30(3), 221–256 (1996)
22. Anderson, J.R., Bothell, D., Byrne, M.D., Douglass, S., Lebiere, C., Qin, Y.: An integrated theory of the mind. Psychological Review 111(4), 1036–1060 (2004)
23. Hodgson, T.L., Bajwa, A., Owen, A.M., Kennard, C.: The strategic control of gaze direction in the Tower of London task. Journal of Cognitive Neuroscience 12, 894–907 (2000)
24. Nyamsuren, E., Taatgen, N.A.: Pre-attentive and attentive vision module. Cognitive Systems Research 24, 62–71 (2013)
25. Anderson, J.: Cognitive psychology and its implications. Worth Publishers (2004)
26. Ellis, S., Siegler, R.S.: Development of problem solving. In: Thinking and Problem Solving, pp. 333–367. Academic, San Diego (1994)
27. Kotovsky, K., Hayes, J.R., Simon, H.A.: Why are some problems hard? evidence from tower of hanoi. Cognitive Psychology 17(2), 248–294 (1985)
28. Ohlsson, S.: Information-processing explanations of insight and related phenomena. In: Advances in the Psychology of Thinking, pp. 1–44 (1992)

Spatial Numerosity: A Computational Model Based on a Topological Invariant

Tobias Kluth and Christoph Zetzsche

Cognitive Neuroinformatics, University of Bremen,
Enrique-Schmidt-Straße 5, 28359 Bremen, Germany
`tkluth@math.uni-bremen.de`
`http://www.informatik.uni-bremen.de/cog_neuroinf/en`

Abstract. The estimation of the cardinality of objects in a spatial environment requires a high degree of invariance. Numerous experiments showed the immense abstraction ability of the numerical cognition system in humans and other species. It eliminates almost all structures of the objects and determines the number of objects in a scene. Based on concepts and quantities like connectedness and Gaussian curvature, we provide a general solution to this problem and apply it to the numerosity estimation from visual stimuli.

Keywords: numerosity, curvature, connectedness, Gauss-Bonnet.

1 Introduction

A fundamental ability humans and other species share is that they can interact efficiently with a spatial environment. This requires knowledge about the location of objects and their spatial arrangement. For example, the spatial distribution of food sources is an evolutionary crucial factor. To know which contains more fruits can decide on survival. The number of objects or its approximation, "numerosity" [3], thus is an important feature of spatial perception. But there is also evidence for a more extensive relation between number and space because it is assumed that the number representation of human adults is translated into corresponding spatial extensions and positions [11,15], also referred to as number-space mapping. It has also been reported that numerical processing modulates spatial representation according to a cognitive illusion [10,31]. For example, the error in the reproduction of a spatial extension is strongly dependent on the numbers delimiting the space [9], or bisecting a line flanked by two numbers is biased by the larger one [27]. Studies regarding the development of cognitive abilities in children also suggest a close relation between spatial and number sense [34]. Furthermore, with the "Theory of Magnitude" [35] exists an approach which suggests that a more general class of magnitudes, including number, are closely connected to space. This is also supported by evidence from neuroanatomical findings showing that both numerical and spatial tasks cause a similar activation in common parietal structures [13].

C. Freksa et al. (Eds.): Spatial Cognition 2014, LNAI 8684, pp. 237–252, 2014.

Qualitative spatial reasoning frameworks based on topological information, e.g. the Region Connection Calculus [26], rely on Whitehead's development of a theory of extensive abstraction based on a two-place predicate describing connection. The important point in Whitehead's theory is that formal individuals can be interpreted as spatially connected (for further information and a short historical overview we refer to [7]). Connectedness thus is not only an important concept in the description of formal individuals and in qualitative spatial reasoning but also in the estimation of numbers as we propose in this paper.

Number estimation, which includes approximate number recognition but not sequential counting, is not restricted to humans with mature cognitive abilities but has also been found in infants and animals [3,22], recently even in invertebrates [17]. Humans recognize numbers rapidly and exactly up to four, which is named subitizing [20]. They also rapidly estimate larger numbers but an error according to the Weber-Fechner law arises [16]. It is still an open question whether the two different observations rely on the same processing system [25,28]. The number is one of the most abstract properties of elements in a spatial configuration as it requires an invariance property which is not affected by spatial attributes like the orientation [1] and the shape [32] of the objects or by the modality [29]. Numerosity is an important element of a larger class of holistic properties like summary statistics [2,6], the gist of a scene [23], or just the average orientation of elements in a display [3].

The standard view of cortical organization as a local-to-global processing hierarchy [19] identifies numerosity as a high-level feature which is computed in a progression of levels. But there is evidence for a "direct visual sense for number" since number seems to be a primary visual property like color, orientation or motion, to which the visual system can be adapted by prolonged viewing [28].

Models which address the numerosity recognition in a neurobiologically plausible fashion, starting from individual pixels or neural receptors instead of an abstract type of input, are rare. A widely known model by Dehaene and Changeux [12] is based on linear Difference-Of-Gaussian filters of different sizes and an accumulation system. The linear filter operation restricts the model to number estimation from blob-like stimuli, which substantially limits the invariance property. A more recent model by Stoianov and Zorzi [30] is based on unsupervised learning in a deep recurrent network. The training images were binary and the objects presented were only rectangular areas such that moderate shape variations were investigated.

In contrary, our proposed approach starts with a general formulation of the problem of number recognition. We address the more fundamental question of how the number is interpreted as an invariance property of perceived scenes. This builds the basis to deal with the computational issues and the related neural requirements. To our knowledge, the first approach in this direction has been made in [37]. The paper is structured as follows: A clear definition of what is an object and how the number can be determined is considered in Section 2. Qualitative results for the number extraction from images are presented in Section 3. Finally, the paper ends with a discussion in Section 4.

2   Methods

As mentioned, modeling numerical cognition of humans was addressed in a few works, e.g. [12,30,37]. The majority of approaches has in common that they address the question of how numerosity within a stimulus is computed using a given algorithm. We address the same problem from a different point of view. Before we give a solution to the computational part of the problem using a specified modality, we focus on a proper formulation and its solution. We thus will begin with a characterization of the mathematical basis for the term *number*.

In set theory the definition of cardinality seems to have the same properties as what we understand as *number*. Generally spoken, the cardinality of a set describes the number of elements within the set. But if we have a closer look at this definition, the choice of what represents a number seems to be arbitrary because the numbers itself are just a formal construction to provide a label for the equivalence classes of the relation "having the same cardinality". We thus must differentiate the understanding of numbers from the definition of the natural numbers and their Arabic digits. However, set theory alone does not provide the tools and basics to properly describe how the number of objects in the real world is related to basic properties of objects. We thus address the three following issues under a topological point of view. First, we must find a formal definition of the "real world". Second, we have to specify objects and their properties. And third, the meaning of *number* in this context and its invariant properties are defined. The following considerations are based on first investigations in a similar direction in [37].

The world in which we live can be assumed to be four-dimensional if we consider the time as an additional dimension. Within the context of this paper we restrict the real world to be static such that it can be represented by a three-dimensional vector space, the real valued space $\mathbb{R}^3$. This space becomes a topological space if it is equipped with a suitable topology, e.g. the usual topology of the $\mathbb{R}^n$.

This directly leads to the second question, what is an object in the real world and how can it be specified. An object is three-dimensional which means that points, lines and planes in the common geometrical sense are no objects in the real world, rather they are theoretical constructions to describe geometrical quantities. For example a sheet of paper can be as thin as it is possible to produce, nevertheless it will always have an extension in the third dimension. We thus restrict an object to be a connected subset of the real world, which means that it cannot be represented by a union of disjoint subsets. Furthermore we make the technically caused assumption that objects are not only connected subsets but also simply connected subsets. This implies that subsets with holes, e.g. a donut or a pretzel, independent of whether they exist in nature or not, are not taken into account. This case will be considered in more detail in the discussion part. In Figure 1 the considered setup is illustrated in three examples. From a perceptional point of view, the interior of the objects is quite uninteresting, thus it is reasonable to represent the objects by their surface. As the kind of connectedness is an important feature of the objects, we need a unique relation between the connectedness of an object and its surface. It can be shown that if two objects share the same kind of connectedness, their surfaces also have the same kind of connectedness [14] (the two-dimensional invariant Euler characteristic is twice the three-dimensional one).

We now have a definition of the real world and of what is meant by an object and we thus can address the third and most important question concerning the *number* of objects. To find formal mechanisms which are suitable to measure the number of objects, we formulate the requirements for this mechanisms. The mechanism must be able to obtain the number in a one-shot manner, which means that the number should not be computed sequentially, e.g. like counting. It should be a mechanism which maps one invariant quantity to each object which is ideally the same such that it can be normalized easily in order to sum it up afterwards. The summation then results directly in the number of objects.

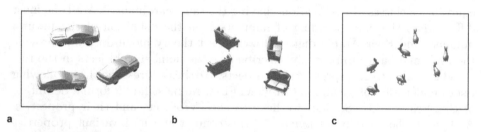

a   b   c

Fig. 1. All illustrations show a variety of three-dimensional simply connected objects which build a scene. They are all (a)-(c) differing in the spatial arrangement and the kind of objects they show.

The invariance property *number* we expect needs more clarification in the sense that an invariant is always defined on a set of elements and a set of operations. In our case the elements are the previously defined objects and the operations have yet to be defined. The set of operations which map one object to another object must be number-conserving, or the other way around the invariant property must be independent of the operation. Assuming the *number* can be represented by a topological invariant, it is obvious that the operations are restricted to homeomorphisms, i.e. continuous and bijective mappings whose inverse is also continuous. This kind of mapping is structure-conserving in the sense that the kind of connectedness does not change. Cutting, tearing and gluing of objects, for example, are no homeomorphisms in general and would cause a change of the invariant.

The additivity we expect also requires further considerations of the object properties. In order to just sum up over all surfaces without a priori knowledge we must find a feature of the surface which then results in an invariant complying with the previously described requirements. The Gauss-Bonnet theorem provides a connection between topology and differential geometry and relates the Gaussian curvature of two-dimensional surfaces to their Euler characteristic.

Theorem 1 (Gauss-Bonnet). *Let $S \subset \mathbb{R}^3$ be a regular oriented surface (of class C^3), and let R be a compact region of S. Suppose that the boundary ∂R is a simple, closed, piecewise regular, positively oriented curve. Assume ∂R consists of k regular arcs ∂R_i (of class C^2), and let θ_i be the external angles of the vertices of ∂R. Then*

$$\int_R K \, dS + \sum_{i=1}^{k} \int_{\partial R_i} \kappa_g \, ds + \sum_{i=1}^{k} \theta_i = 2\pi \chi(R) \tag{1}$$

where K is the Gaussian curvature, κ_g is the geodesic curvature, and χ is the Euler characteristic.

The presented theorem is more general as it also considers the case that the surface has a boundary. It becomes important in a later part dealing with the problems which arise from the perception via sensors. For the moment, the objects we deal with do not have a one-dimensional boundary such that we can consider the following corollary of the theorem. Proofs of the theorem and the corollary can be found in almost every differential geometry textbook.

Corollary 1. *Let S be an orientable, compact, regular surface of class C^3. Then*

$$\int_S K \, dS = 2\pi \chi(S).$$

The Euler characteristic is a topological invariant which maps a number to any subset within a topological space. This number then characterizes the kind of connectivity of the subset. For example, the surface of a sphere (no holes) has a different characteristic number than the surface of a torus (one hole). Being a topological invariant, the Euler characteristic of an object remains constant if a homeomorphism is applied to it. Given the Gauss-Bonnet theorem, the question is what that means with respect to the Gaussian curvature of the object's surface. We first give a short description of what is meant by Gaussian curvature and we then consider the influence of homeomorphisms and why the integration over this quantity is constant. Though the proof of the theorem provides a technical solution, it gives no idea of the interplay of different kinds of curvature.

The Gaussian curvature of a regular surface is defined as the product of its principal curvatures. These are the minimal and maximal normal curvatures of two orthogonal planes which are both orthogonal to the tangent plane of the surface. The local shape of a surface can be distinguished by its Gaussian curvature in elliptic ($K > 0$), hyperbolic ($K < 0$), and parabolic parts ($K = 0$). For example, the surface S of a sphere, as shown in Figure 2, is completely elliptic (blue) and has the Euler characteristic $\chi(S) = 2$. In this case, the Gaussian curvature is constant and depends only on the radius of the sphere. As increasing the radius of a sphere is a homeomorphism, Corollary 1 states that the integral over the Gaussian curvature is constant. In this example the interplay between the surface area and the Gaussian curvature is easy to conceptualize. While increasing the radius, the surface area increases and the Gaussian curvature decreases such that the surface integral, i.e. the product of Gaussian curvature and surface area in this special case, is 4π constantly. We want to emphasize that homeomorphic deformations of the sphere are exactly the objects resulting from the previously formulated assumptions. The surface integral also does not change if the sphere is dented, as can be seen in the middle row of Figure 2. Here a hyperbolic (red) curvature emerges at the boundary of the dent. Under the assumption that the curvature does not change except in the dent, curvature with a negative sign always implies the emergence of another elliptic part with a higher absolute value. We can find this elliptic part in the middle of the dent, which can be seen in Figure 2c. The Gaussian curvature of a regular surface is a continuous function and thus there exists at least a curve between hyperbolic and elliptic parts on the surface where the curvature is parabolic. The influence of a homeomorphism producing a bulge on the surface of a simply connected object and its Gaussian curvature is also shown in Figure 2. The connection of Gaussian curvature and the invariant Euler characteristic fulfills the first requirement we formulated.

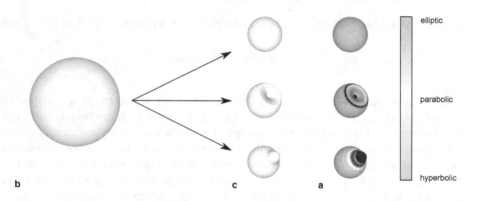

Fig. 2. In (a) the surface of a three-dimensional sphere is shown which is transformed via homeomorphisms into (b) a smaller sphere (top), a smaller sphere with a dent (middle), and a smaller sphere with a bulge (bottom). In (c) the Gaussian curvature of the 3D objects in (b) is shown qualitatively by coloring the surface respectively its kind of curvature. The elliptic parts of the surface are blue, the hyperbolic parts are red, and the parabolic parts are white. The color saturation shows the amount of curvature contributed to the integral in the Gauss-Bonnet theorem.

The second requirement, the additivity, follows directly from the linearity of the integral operator. Assume $S := \bigcup_{i=1}^{n} \partial O_i$ to be the union of surfaces of pairwise disjoint objects O_i. With $\chi(\partial O_i) = 2$, $i = 1, \ldots, n$, the integral becomes

$$\int_S K \, dS = \sum_{i=1}^{n} \int_{\partial O_i} K \, dS = 2\pi \sum_{i=1}^{n} \chi(\partial O_i) = 4\pi n.$$

In principle the problem of estimating the number of objects in a scene is hereby solved. If we assume measuring the local property, Gaussian curvature, of the surface is directly possible, the integration of local measurements over all simply connected object's surfaces results in a representation of the number.

Sensors

Estimating the number of objects requires access to the Gauss-Bonnet quantities of the surface of the object. But if we think about the modalities from which we can gather the required information, it is not obvious how an estimate of these quantities can be obtained. The abstract formulation of the problem is a comfortable starting position for further investigations. Sequential tactile scanning of the object's surface or visual sensing are imaginable sensor strategies for human number estimation. Multisensory approaches would also be possible and with additional technical sensor devices, as they are used in robots, the number of possibilities for number estimation becomes quite high. In the following we consider the human visual system as the modality to obtain an estimate of the Gaussian curvature yielding the number of objects in a perceived scene. Here we restrict the visual stimulus to be luminance only such that we have a sensory representation of the scene by the luminance function $l = l(x, y)$. An example for the luminance function of a three-dimensional sphere is illustrated in Figure 3a. But it remains unclear how this is related to the real world. The interplay between lighting and reflectance properties of the object's surface result in a mapping from the real world to the sensed luminance function. For further considerations in this directions, we refer to [21]. In the following, the real world is equipped with a binary function $g : \mathbb{R}^3 \to \{0, 1\}$ describing the physical properties at a position $x \in \mathbb{R}^3$. In the considered setup the function g is just an indicator function whether a position is occupied by an object or not. The sensor operator F maps this physical properties to the luminance function $l : \mathbb{R}^2 \to \mathbb{R}_0^+$ such that the sensory process becomes

$$F(g) = l \quad , \quad g(x) := \chi_S(x) = \begin{cases} 1 \, , & x \in S, \\ 0 \, , & \text{else,} \end{cases} \tag{2}$$

where S is a disjunction of sufficiently smooth objects according to the previous definitions and χ_S is the characteristic function. Note that χ without an index is the Euler characteristic. Assuming F is an orthogonal projection not incorporating lighting the resulting luminance level is always constant for the objects. In particular, this case for objects resulting in right-angled polygons as projections was considered in previous works [37,38]. If we assume planar surfaces to be projected this way, the resulting setup matches common visual stimuli in psychological studies, e.g. [18]. However, we assume that F takes lighting of the objects into account such that it does not result in a constant luminance level on objects. Additionally, we assume the operator F to preserve the differentiability on the objects surface. The piecewise constant function g is thus mapped to an almost everywhere sufficiently smooth function l. The background is assumed to be uniform and clearly separable from the objects. The discontinuity between objects and the environment is thus projected to the luminance function. In the following we apply similar concepts of the previously presented general solution to the luminance function in order to estimate the number of perceived objects. The different approaches all have in common that we investigate the luminance surface $\Omega \subset \mathbb{R}^3$ which is defined by the perceived luminance function l, i.e. $\Omega := \{(x, y, z) \in \mathbb{R}^3 | x, y \in \mathbb{R}, z = l(x, y)\}$. For example, in Figure 3b the luminance surface of the luminance function in Figure 3a is shown.

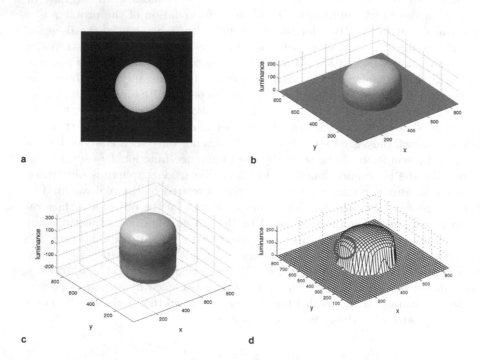

Fig. 3. In (a) the luminance function resulting from the projection of a slightly lightened three-dimensional sphere is shown. (b) shows the luminance function of the image in (a) interpreted as a two-dimensional surface embedded in the three-dimensional space. In (c) the background of the luminance surface in (b) was removed, the remaining surface was mirrored at the x-y-plane, and both surface pieces are then connected in z-direction. Thus, (c) shows a simply connected surface of a 3D object. In (d) a subsampled version of the underlying surface mesh is shown. The red circle highlights the projected discontinuity between the object and the environment. If the surface is continued in z-direction, an arc can emerge in this region, which has to be taken into account additionally while doing the curvature computation.

First, a simplified basic concept is investigated. Assume that the background, which is constantly zero, is cut off from the luminance surface. Then the rest of the surface is mirrored at the x-y-plane and it is connected in z-direction. We thus can construct closed surfaces representing three-dimensional objects from the embedded luminance surface. In Figure 3c the resulting surface corresponding to Figure 3a is illustrated. This is exactly the starting situation of the general problem in the previous section and the problem seems to be solved for luminance images. We can estimate the Gaussian curvature using the luminance function and it becomes

$$K(x,y) = \frac{l_{xx}(x,y)l_{yy}(x,y) - l_{xy}(x,y)^2}{(1 + l_x(x,y)^2 + l_y(x,y)^2)^2},\tag{3}$$

where subscript denotes the differentiation in the respective direction (e.g. $l_{xy} = \frac{\partial^2 l}{\partial x \partial y}$). Integration over this quantity should result in the number of objects times a characteristic constant. If we have a closer look at the constructed closed three-dimensional surface, there is a critical region at the boundary of the luminance surface without the background, see Figure 3d. In general we cannot guarantee the differentiability in this region. The projected discontinuity between objects and background causes errors because an additional arc at the critical region has to be taken into account. If the tangent planes in all points at the boundary region are orthogonal to the x-y-plane, this problem does not occur. For example, this is the case if the luminance function without background looks like a hemisphere. Then the differentiable extension in z-direction is possible and no error terms would occur. But this is not the general case.

The problem can be solved by only taking the boundary region into account. The boundary curve can emerge from a discontinuity detection on the luminance function. Given an appropriate detection function, possibly a linear differential operation or a threshold function, the general three-dimensional case is projected to two dimensions. The luminance is thus used for the detection only. The resulting objects are bounded two-dimensional subsets of the x-y-plane such that they can be represented by their one-dimensional boundary curve. In this case the one-dimensional counterpart of the Gauss-Bonnet theorem is the following standard corollary in differential geometry.

Corollary 2. *Let C be a closed, regular, plane curve. Then the quantity*

$$\int_C \kappa_g\, ds = 2\pi n,\tag{4}$$

where κ_g is the curvature of the plane curve and n is an integer called the rotation index of the curve.

As the rotation index is always one for the objects we consider and the integral operator is linear, the integral over the disjunction of multiple boundary curves results in their number. In Figure 4 the two-dimensional case of Figure 2 is shown. Assuming a counterclockwise parametrization, the curvature in a point is positive if the tangent is on the right side of the curve and respectively on the left side if the curvature has a negative sign. The circle in Figure 4b has always a positive curvature such that its integral becomes 2π. The second shape is a circle with a dent. Negative curvature emerges in the middle part of the dent but if we have a closer look to the positive curvature at the boundary of the dent, the absolute of this contribution to the integral increases such that it equalizes the negative contribution of the dent. Note that the curvature contribution is not mapped equivalently from the three-dimensional case to the one

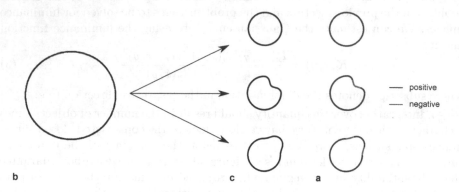

Fig. 4. The two-dimensional case of Figure 2 is illustrated. In (a) the contour of a circle is shown which is transformed into (b) a smaller circle (top), a smaller circle with a dent (middle), and a smaller circle with a bulge (bottom). In (c) the curvature of the plane boundary curves in (b) is shown qualitatively. The color shows whether the curvature has a positive or negative contribution to the curvature integral.

with lower dimensionality as the dent only produces one negative contribution and no positive contribution emerges in the middle of the dent, compare Figures 2c and 4c.

Assume a smooth boundary curve C is given by an arbitrary parametrization $c : I \rightarrow \mathbb{R}^2$ with $c(t) = (x(t), y(t))^T$, where $I \subset \mathbb{R}$. The curvature κ_g then becomes

$$\kappa_g(t) = \frac{x''(t)y'(t) - y''(t)x'(t)}{(x'(t)^2 + y'(t)^2)^{3/2}}, \tag{5}$$

where the primes denote differentiation with respect to t, e.g. $x' = \frac{\partial}{\partial t}x$ and $x'' = \frac{\partial^2}{\partial t^2}x$. This approach corresponds to the Gestalt grouping principle of connectedness [24], which assumes that points are grouped into objects based on connected regions. In this case the objects could be represented by the outlines of the connected regions. But, in order to estimate the number of objects from the one-dimensional line integral the first and second derivatives of a parametrization of a curve are necessary. Regarding a neural representation of the curve which can be interpreted as a point set, the first derivative is plausible as it can be obtained from simultaneously firing neighbored units. Second derivatives of the luminance functions are also plausible, as an neuronal approximation can be obtained via linear filtering with second derivatives of filter kernels [36,37]. But the second derivative of the parametrization seems to be an additional effort which is unnecessary. Thus it is reasonable for the system to compute a solution to the number problem using these quantities. Further investigation of curved surfaces results in another computational approach which does not contradict the Gestalt grouping principle of connectedness as both approaches are formally equivalent.

In the following we address the previously arisen question and derive a so-lution to avoid the computation of second derivatives of parametrized curves. Theorem 1 provides a solution which incorporates the luminance surface prop-erties directly. Assuming a smooth space curve C which is the boundary of a closed region S on the luminance surface Ω, i.e. $C = \partial S$, it results

$$\int_S K \, dS + \int_C \kappa_g \, ds = 2\pi\chi(S), \tag{6}$$

where κ_g denotes the geodesic curvature. Using the parametrization $\phi(x, y) := (x, y, l(x, y))^T$ of the surface and the Gaussian curvature from equation 3, the first integral can be computed by

$$\int_S K \, dS = \int_{\mathbb{R}^2} \underbrace{\frac{l_{xx}(x, y)l_{yy}(x, y) - l_{xy}(x, y)^2}{(1 + l_x(x, y)^2 + l_y(x, y)^2)^{3/2}}}_{=:\tilde{K}(x,y)} \chi_S(\phi(x, y)) \, d(x, y), \tag{7}$$

where χ_S is the characteristic function with respect to the set S. In order to calcu-late the second integral, the geodesic curvature of the boundary curve C must be estimated. Using the parametrization $c : I \to \mathbb{R}^3$ with $c(t) := (x(t), y(t), l(x(t), y(t)))^T$ of the boundary curve and the assumption $l(x(t), y(t)) = const.$, $\forall t \in I$, we can determine the geodesic curvature by

$$\kappa_g(t) = \tilde{\kappa}_g(x(t), y(t)) = \frac{l_x^2 l_{yy} + l_y^2 l_{xx} - 2l_x l_y l_{xy}}{(l_x^2 + l_y^2)^{3/2}(1 + l_x^2 + l_y^2)^{1/2}}. \tag{8}$$

The additional assumption of constant height is made to eliminate the second derivatives of the parametrization. The second integral in equation 6 thus be-comes

$$\int_C \kappa_g \, ds = \int_{\mathbb{R}} \frac{l_x^2 l_{yy} + l_y^2 l_{xx} - 2l_x l_y l_{xy}}{(l_x^2 + l_y^2)^{3/2}(1 + l_x^2 + l_y^2)^{1/2}} (x'^2 + y'^2)^{1/2} \chi_C(c(t)) \, dt, \tag{9}$$

where χ_C is the characteristic function with respect to the set C. Assuming constant height, the first derivative of the parametrization yields $x' = -(l_y/l_x)y'$. Thus the geodesic curvature depends only on differential operators applied to the luminance function and one first derivative x' or y' of the parametrization of the boundary curve. Finally, the number of objects n from a union S of pairwise disjoint regions of luminance surfaces can be determined by

$$2\pi n = \int_{\mathbb{R}^2} \tilde{K}(x, y)\tilde{\chi}_S(x, y) \, d(x, y) + \int_{\mathbb{R}} \tilde{\kappa}_g(x(t), y(t))\tilde{\chi}_C(x(t), y(t)) \, dt, \tag{10}$$

where $\tilde{\chi}_S(x, y) := \chi_S(\phi(x, y))$ and $\tilde{\chi}_C(x(t), y(t)) := (x'^2 + y'^2)^{1/2}\chi_C(c(t))$. The computation now depends on three quantities $\tilde{K}$, $\tilde{\chi}_S$, $\tilde{\kappa}_g$ depending on surface properties and the quantity $\tilde{\chi}_C$ which has to extract curve properties. All quan-tities have in common that they represent local properties of the luminance surface. Assuming a neural hardware, the characteristic functions correspond to the well known threshold functionality of neurons. The curvature operators $\tilde{K}$ and $\tilde{\kappa}_g$ depend only on derivatives of the luminance function which can be realized by neurophysiologically realistic Gabor-like filters [36,37]. The computation also requires a multiplicative "AND"-like combination of these features which can be obtained by the neural mechanism of cortical gain control [39]. A neural hardware thus is able to estimate the number of objects using the neural correlates of the operations in equation 10.

3   Results

We implemented and tested the algorithm implied by the operator defined in equation 10 to estimate the number of objects in an image. The images are represented by positive real-valued matrices. The stimuli are assumed to be sufficiently smooth which can cause high numerical errors if it is not satisfied. In order to obtain the differentiability in the discrete representation, each stimulus is lowpass filtered using a Gaussian kernel. In the following we present qualitative results for the images presented in Figure 1.

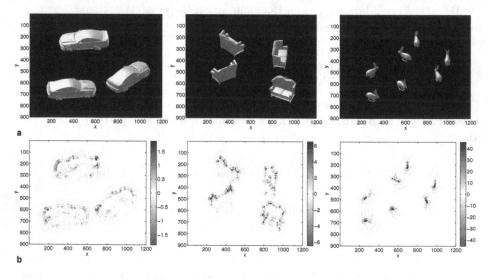

Fig. 5. In (a) the visual stimuli from Figure 1 with their original background are shown. In (b) the corresponding Gaussian curvatures (elliptic: blue, parabolic: white, hyperbolic: red) of the luminance surfaces belonging to the images in (a) are shown.

The Gaussian curvature is a prominent quantity for the extraction of the number of objects. In Figure 5 the test images and their Gaussian curvature are shown. They all show high variations in the kind of curvature over the luminance surface and especially on objects there is a noticeable interplay between

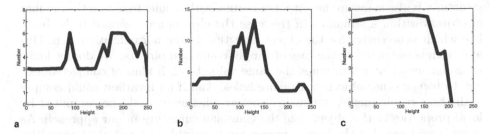

Fig. 6. In (a)-(c) the estimated number of objects from the corresponding stimuli in Figure 1a-c are shown. The number was estimated by the operator defined in equation 10.

hyperbolic and elliptic parts of curvature. Especially the boundary region of the objects has at least one change of sign in Gaussian curvature. This is caused by the zero background and the Gaussian filtering in advance which is necessary to obtain acceptable results. There is a relation between the geodesic curvature of the boundary curve and the shape of the surface if we assume the boundary curve to be a height line. The steeper the luminance surface in a point, i.e. the smaller the angle between the tangent normal vector and the x-y-plane, the less is the contribution of the geodesic curvature integral to the number. In order to get rid of the geodesic curvature integral, scaling the stimulus would be one option to control this relation but can cause numerical instability. However, the interplay of Gaussian curvature and geodesic curvature results in an estimate of the number of objects. The only parameter which must be chosen is the threshold of luminance (height) at which the boundary curves are defined. Everything above this threshold belongs to the integration domain for the Gaussian curvature. The implementation then results in a number estimate which depends on the height, as can be seen in Figure 6. The number of objects is estimated correctly for height values up to 50. Heights higher than 50 cause seemingly unsystematical errors. But it is obvious, they must have a close relation to the shape and absolute values of the luminance surface. In Figure 6b an underestimation is done for low heights. It has its origin in two objects which are close together such that the Gaussian filter operation connects both objects which means they are not separated by a background region anymore. Figure 6c has a noticeable increase of number with increased height. All graphs have in common that they suddenly descend to zero as the height is higher than the maximum value of the luminance surface.

4   Discussion

Our approach for computing the number of objects from a scene differs from other approaches in several respects.

First, our approach can deal with arbitrary simply connected objects. On a certain level the model by Dehaene et al. [12] can be seen to have a similar structure: It also sums up the output of normalization units to obtain the number of objects within a stimulus. In this case the objects are assumed to be blob-like which is necessary for the object detection in the normalization step. Our approach is restricted to the case of simply connected objects. We do not know a similar invariant which maps the same value to each kind of connectedness, e.g. to tori or other objects with more holes. And if an invariant could comply with these requirements, it remains unclear whether it could be computed by local properties of the object, like the Gaussian curvature in our approach. As there is evidence that the human perception is sensible to topological quantities [6] and as the number estimation method we proposed is based on topological concepts, the role of topology in perception should be rethought.

Second, the underlying principles to obtain the invariance are clearly defined and the system is no black box. Recent results by Stoianov et al. [30] show that an unsupervised training of a recurrent multi-layered network is able to learn a representation of number but the underlying invariance principle is not known. This raises the question, which kind of system is able to learn the full invariance principles in an unsupervised fashion and whether it extracts local properties, like the Gaussian curvature.

In digital topology there exist connected component labeling algorithms, e.g. [33], which are also able to estimate the number of labels they distribute. In contrary to our fully parallel approach these algorithms are sequentially and need multiple passes through the image which is quite unplausible for the neurobiological system. But the formulation of our approach in terms of digital topology is desirable as the neural system consists of a countable and finite set of neurons.

Other approaches [8] suggest a strong interrelation between density, covered area, and the number of objects. It is assumed that the number is obtained approximately from the product of area and density. However, the crucial properties in our view are the extraordinary invariance properties which would also be required for generally responding computations of density.

The accuracy of the proposed approach is independent of the number presented in the stimulus. The structure of the model, which includes a multiplicative gain control, is a promising basis for the emergence of a log-normally distributed output [4] if noise is taken into account. As a result the model would explain the errors in the rapid estimation for the whole range of numbers, i.e. for subitizing and for the estimation of higher numbers, but this remains a question for future research.

As we have shown, linear summation and cortical gain control, two widely accepted properties of cortical neurons, are the only requirements for the computation of the number of objects. These functions are already available at early stages of the cortex, but also in other areas [5].

Acknowledgements. This work was supported by DFG, SFB/TR8 Spatial Cognition, project A5-[ActionSpace].

References

1. Allik, J., Tuulmets, T., Vos, P.G.: Size invariance in visual number discrimination. Psychological Research 53(4), 290–295 (1991)
2. Alvarez, G.A.: Representing multiple objects as an ensemble enhances visual cognition. Trends in Cognitive Science 15(3), 122–131 (2011)
3. Brannon, E.M.: The representation of numerical magnitude. Current Opinion in Neurobiology 16(2), 222–229 (2006)
4. Buzsáki, G., Mizuseki, K.: The log-dynamic brain: how skewed distributions affect network operations. Nature Reviews Neuroscience (2014)
5. Carandini, M., Heeger, D.J.: Normalization as a canonical neural computation. Nature Reviews Neuroscience 13, 51–62 (2012)
6. Chen, L.: The topological approach to perceptual organization. Visual Cognition 12(4), 553–637 (2005)
7. Clarke, B.L.: A calculus of individuals based on "connection". Notre Dame Journal of Formal Logic 22(3), 204–218 (1981)
8. Dakin, S.C., Tibber, M.S., Greenwood, J.A., Kingdom, F.A.A., Morgan, M.J.: A common visual metric for approximate number and density. Proceedings of the National Academy of Sciences 108(49), 19552–19557 (2011)
9. De Hevia, M.-D., Girelli, L., Bricolo, E., Vallar, G.: The representational space of numerical magnitude: Illusions of length. The Quarterly Journal of Experimental Psychology 61(10), 1496–1514 (2008)
10. de Hevia, M.D., Girelli, L., Vallar, G.: Numbers and space: a cognitive illusion? Experimental Brain Research 168(1-2), 254–264 (2006)
11. Dehaene, S., Bossini, S., Giraux, P.: The mental representation of parity and number magnitude. Journal of Experimental Psychology: General 122(3), 371 (1993)
12. Dehaene, S., Changeux, J.P.: Development of elementary numerical abilities: a neuronal model. Journal of Cognitive Neuroscience 5(4), 390–407 (1993)
13. Dehaene, S., Piazza, M., Pinel, P., Cohen, L.: Three parietal circuits for number processing. Cognitive Neuropsychology 20(3-6), 487–506 (2003)
14. Dillen, F., Kühnel, W.: Total curvature of complete submanifolds of euclidean space. Tohoku Mathematical Journal 57(2), 171–200 (2005)
15. Fias, W.: The importance of magnitude information in numerical processing: Evidence from the snarc effect. Mathematical Cognition 2(1), 95–110 (1996)
16. Gallistel, C.R., Gelman, R.: Preverbal and verbal counting and computation. Cognition 44(1), 43–74 (1992)
17. Gross, H.J., Pahl, M., Si, A., Zhu, H., Tautz, J., Zhang, S.: Number-based visual generalisation in the honeybee. PloS one, 4(1), e4263 (2009)
18. He, L., Zhang, J., Zhou, T., Chen, L.: Connectedness affects dot numerosity judgment: Implications for configural processing. Psychonomic Bulletin & Review 16(3), 509–517 (2009)
19. Hegde, J., Felleman, D.: Reappraising the Functional Implications of the Primate Visual Anatomical Hierarchy. The Neuroscientist 13(5), 416–421 (2007)
20. Kaufman, E.L., Lord, M., Reese, T., Volkmann, J.: The discrimination of visual number. The American Journal of Psychology, 498–525 (1949)
21. Koenderink, J.J., van Doorn, A.: Shape and shading. The visual neurosciences, 1090–1105 (2003)
22. Nieder, A., Freedman, D.J., Miller, E.K.: Representation of the quantity of visual items in the primate prefrontal cortex. Science 297(5587), 1708–1711 (2002)

23. Oliva, A., Torralba, A.: Modeling the Shape of the Scene: A Holistic Representation of the Spatial Envelope. International Journal of Computer Vision 42(3), 145–175 (2001)
24. Palmer, S., Rock, I.: Rethinking perceptual organization: The role of uniform connectedness. Psychonomic Bulletin & Review 1(1), 29–55 (1994)
25. Piazza, M., Mechelli, A., Butterworth, B., Price, C.J.: Are subitizing and counting implemented as separate or functionally overlapping processes? Neuroimage 15(2), 435–446 (2002)
26. Randell, D.A., Cui, Z., Cohn, A.G.: A spatial logic based on regions and connection. KR 92, 165–176 (1992)
27. Ranzini, M., Girelli, L.: Exploiting illusory effects to disclose similarities in numerical and luminance processing. Attention, Perception, & Psychophysics 74(5), 1001–1008 (2012)
28. Ross, J., Burr, D.C.: Vision senses number directly. Journal of Vision 10(2), 1–8 (2010)
29. Starkey, P., Spelke, E.S., Gelman, R.: Numerical abstraction by human infants. Cognition 36(2), 97–127 (1990)
30. Stoianov, I., Zorzi, M.: Emergence of a 'visual number sense' in hierarchical generative models. Nature Neuroscience 15(2), 194–196 (2012)
31. Stöttinger, E., Anderson, B., Danckert, J., Frühholz, B., Wood, G.: Spatial biases in number line bisection tasks are due to a cognitive illusion of length. Experimental Brain Research 220(2), 147–152 (2012)
32. Strauss, M.S., Curtis, L.E.: Infant perception of numerosity. Child Development 52(4), 1146–1152 (1981)
33. Suzuki, K., Horiba, I., Sugie, N.: Linear-time connected-component labeling based on sequential local operations. Computer Vision and Image Understanding 89(1), 1–23 (2003)
34. van Nes, F., van Eerde, D.: Spatial structuring and the development of number sense: A case study of young children working with blocks. The Journal of Mathematical Behavior 29(3), 145–159 (2010)
35. Walsh, V.: A theory of magnitude: common cortical metrics of time, space and quantity. Trends in Cognitive Sciences 7(11), 483–488 (2003)
36. Zetzsche, C., Barth, E.: Fundamental limits of linear filters in the visual processing of two-dimensional signals. Vision Research 30(7), 1111–1117 (1990)
37. Zetzsche, C., Barth, E.: Image surface predicates and the neural encoding of two-dimensional signal variations. In: Rogowitz, B.E., Allebach, J.P. (eds.) Proceedings SPIE, Human, Vision and Electronic Imaging: Models, Methods, and Applications, vol. 1249, pp. 160–177 (1990)
38. Zetzsche, C., Gadzicki, K., Kluth, T.: Statistical invariants of spatial form: From local and to numerosity. In: Proc. of the 2nd Interdisciplinary Workshop The Shape of Things, pp. 163–172. CEUR-WS.org (April 2013)
39. Zetzsche, C., Nuding, U.: Nonlinear and higher-order approaches to the encoding of natural scenes. Network: Computation in Neural Systems 16(2-3), 191–221 (2005)

Qualitative Representations of Schematized and Distorted Street Segments in Sketch Maps

Sahib Jan, Angela Schwering, Malumbo Chipofya, and Jia Wang

Institute for Geoinformatics, University of Muenster, Germany
{sahib.jan,schwering,mchipofya,jia.wang}@uni-muenster.de

Abstract. Over the past years, user-generated content has gained more prominence in the area of geographic information science. In many geo-spatial applications, sketch maps are considered as an intuitive user interaction modality. As
typically only qualitative relations are persevered in sketch maps, processing
spatial information on qualitative level has been suggested. The information
represented in sketch maps are distorted, schematized, incomplete, and generalized. Particularly, streets are schematized and their angles of connectivity at
junctions are distorted. In sketch maps, streets are lineal features and each street
consists of one or more connected street segments. Straightening curved streets
and distorting angles affect the qualitative information of streets. Thus,
processing spatial information from sketch maps and making it available in information systems requires reliable formalizations which are robust against
cognitive distortions. In this paper, we proposed a set of plausible representations to formalize the qualitative information of street segments in street networks. Further, we identify suitable orientation sectors. The orientation sectors
are scrutinized and encoded with the proposed representation to capture the relative orientations of street segments. Afterwards, the representations are evaluated for the qualitative alignment of street segments from sketch maps with
geo-referenced maps. The successful alignment of street segments will allow us
to integrate spatial information from sketch maps into a Geographic Information System (GIS) as volunteered information.

Keywords: Sketch map alignment, Qualitative constraint networks, Street segments, Street network, Orientation sectors, Qualitative representation.

1 Introduction

With the advent of Volunteered Geographic Information (VGI), the amount and
accessibility of the spatial information produced by laypersons increased drastically.
Ordinary citizens have started to collect geographic information voluntarily and
publish it on websites as volunteered geographic information (VGI) [1]. In many geo-
spatial applications [2–5], sketch maps are considered as an intuitive user interaction
modality. Sketch maps contain objects which represent real world geographic
features, relations between these spatial objects, and oftentimes symbolic and textual
annotations [6]. The objects and spatial configurations between objects enable us to

C. Freksa et al. (Eds.): Spatial Cognition 2014, LNAI 8684, pp. 253–267, 2014.

use these sketch maps to communicate about our environments and to reason about our actions in those environments. In this way, sketch maps may be the key to contribute spatial information as VGI in Geographical Information Systems (GIS), without taking into account the technical barriers imposed by traditional GIS as noted by [1].

However, the information represented in sketch maps reflects the user´s spatial knowledge that is based on observations rather than on measurements. Therefore, the information in sketch maps is distorted, schematized, incomplete, and generalized [7–9]. People mentally rotate the directions of geographic entities around the axes created by themselves. Likewise, directions are commonly straightened in memory [10]: curvatures get straightened, non-perpendicular intersections are squared and nonparallel streets get aligned [11, 12]. Straightening curved streets and distorting angles affect the relative orientation of streets in street networks. Cognitive errors documented in our previous studies [13–15] are neither random nor solely due to human ignorance.

In order to allow users to contribute the spatial information using sketch maps, an automated system is required. A system must be able to process the spatial information from sketch maps and establish correct correspondences between spatial objects from sketch and geo-referenced maps. Establishing correspondences using relationships between objects is known as qualitative alignment of spatial objects if qualitative relations are involved. As typically only qualitative relations between spatial objects are persevered in sketch maps, processing spatial information on qualitative level has been suggested [2, 16]. In many geo-spatial applications [2–5], the qualitative distinctions are drawn from results in the area of Qualitative Spatial Reasoning (QSR).

In QSR, a multitude of representational systems has been developed to deal with different aspects of space and time [17]. These systems (spatial calculi) provide general and sound reasoning mechanisms based on spatial configurations in terms of qualitative relations. In [18, 19], we experimentally determine a set of qualitative sketch aspects which are not affected by cognitive distortions. In our previous studies [20, 21], we propose a set of plausible representations to formalize some of these sketch aspects qualitatively. We identified these representations being robust against cognitive distortions found in sketch maps.

This study extends our previous work on qualitative representations of spatial object. In this paper, we propose a set of plausible representations to formalize the topology and orientation information of street segments in street networks. Streets are lineal features. Each street consists of one or more street segments which are maximally connected components of a street that are not internally intersected by any other street segment. We extracted street segments from sketch maps using the segmentation procedures proposed in [22, 23]. Afterwards, the proposed representations are used to formalize the qualitative information of street segments in the form of qualitative constraint networks (QCNs). The orientation relations over points in the plane depend upon the angles formed by the points [24]. Therefore, for relative orientations, we analyze the angles between connected street segments at junctions. We extract angles between street segments from 18 sketch maps and angles from the corresponding street segments in geo-referenced map of an area about 2.10 km^2 in

Muenster, Germany. The K-means clustering technique is used to classify these angles into a set of clusters. The range of angles in each cluster defines orientation sectors. These orientation sectors are encoded with the proposed representation and the orientation information of street segments is extracted as QCNs.

We evaluate the representations by testing the accuracy of qualitative relations between street segments from 28 sketch maps with the corresponding street segments in geo-referenced maps (generated from OpenStreet Map[1]). The overall evaluation shows that the proposed representations together with identified orientation sectors are cognitively adequate to formalize the qualitative information of street segments. The representations give highly identical qualitative relations between street segments from the sketch and geo-referenced maps. This will allow us to align and integrate spatial information from sketch maps into geographic information systems (GISs) as volunteered geographic information [1].

The remainder of this paper is structured as follows: In the following section, we introduce related work on the qualitative representations of spatial configurations. In section 3, we proposed a set of plausible representations and the orientation sectors to formalize the qualitative information of street segments. The proposed representations are evaluated in section 4. Section 5 concludes the paper with an outlook on future work.

2   Related Work

Alignment of Qualitative Configurations. During the last two decades, several approaches attempt to capture spatial configurations between depicted objects qualitatively. Egenhofer [2, 3] propose *Spatial-Query-by-Sketch*, a sketch-based GIS user interface that focuses on specifying spatial relations by drawing them. The approach uses five types of spatial relations such as coarse, detail topological relations, metric refinements, and coarse and detailed cardinal directions relations to capture spatial configurations between depicted objects. Volker et al. [25] propose the visual query system— *VISCO*. It offers a sketch-based query language for defining approximate spatial constellations of the objects. *VISCO* integrates the geometrical and topological querying with deductive spatial reasoning.

Forbus et al. [26] develop a sketch understanding system—*nuSketch*. It is a battle-space search system that focuses on the qualitative topological reasoning. The system uses both qualitative topological relations and quantitative information to construct the spatial configurations between depicted entities. Nedas et al. [4] propose a similarity measure to compare two spatial scenes by identifying similarities between (i) objects in the two scenes, (ii) similarity between the binary relations among spatial objects such as buildings and lakes, and (iii) the ratio of the total number of objects to the number of objects that has been matched – or equivalently, not matched.

Similarly, Wallgrün et al. [5] propose an approach for the qualitative matching of geo-/non-georeferenced datasets using the topological and cardinal direction relations between spatial objects. In our previous study [27], we propose Tabu search [28, 29]

---

[1] http://www.openstreetmap.org

based model for matching qualitatively described spatial scenes extracted from sketch maps.

Qualitative Representation of Graph-like Structures. There are several approaches on how graph-like structures can be represented qualitatively and reason about spatial data. Lücke et al. [30] propose a qualitative approach for navigating in the street network that is described via local observations. In their approach, they use the Oriented Point Relation Algebra ($\mathcal{OPRA}$) [31] together with Klippel´s turn directions [32]. Klippel et al. [32] identify cognitively adequate representations of directions on decision points. Renz et al. [24] use the STAR calculi [33] for representing direction sectors in order to have a consistent sector arrangement for every intersection node in the route-network. The $\mathcal{OPRA}$ and STAR calculi are two types of qualitative representations that allow for defining sectors with different angles. The STAR calculi [33] supports absolute directions with same direction sectors for every point p in the plane. While the $\mathcal{OPRA}$ calculi [31] supports relative directions with different direction sectors, depending on the orientation of p.

All above cited approaches share motivation with our work and use similar methods of representing the spatial configurations with some abstract qualitative relations. However, they did not consider the influences of human spatial cognition and the effects of cognitive distortions [7, 9, 34] in the qualitative alignment of spatial objects. Since street segments´ outlines in freehand sketches are distorted, the qualitative representation of street segments leads to different relations when compare with relations in geo-referenced maps.

In this study, we propose cognitively plausible representations to capture the qualitative information of street segments in street networks. For the relative orientation, we identify suitable orientation sectors, which are encoded with the proposed representation.

3   Qualitative Representations of Street Segments

3.1   Topology of Street Segments

In sketch maps, street segments are represented as line segments and are connected to other street segments at junctions. The end-points, where street segments are not further connected to other street segments are called hanging end-points. The topology of street segments can be captured using the connectivity of street segments at junctions. For the topology of street segments, we analyze and evaluate different representations of a Dipole Relation Algebra ($\mathcal{DRA}$) [35] such as $\mathcal{DRA}_{dipolcon}$ and $\mathcal{DRA}_c$. The $\mathcal{DRA}_c$ is a coarse version of $\mathcal{DRA}$. It provides 24 base qualitative relations. The $\mathcal{DRA}_c$ captures the topology and orientation information of oriented line segments called dipoles. A dipole is an ordered pair of points in $\mathbb{R}^2$ which can be written as $A = (a_s, a_e)$, where a_s and a_e are the start- and end-point of A respectively. A basic $\mathcal{DRA}$ relation between two dipoles A and B is represented by a 4-tuple $sBeBsAeA$ where sB is the position of the start-point of dipole B with respect to dipole A and eB

is the position of the end-point of dipole B with respect to dipole A. The other two elements of the relation sA and eA are defined analogously.

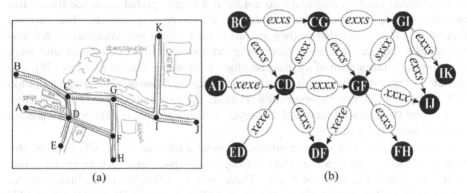

Fig. 1. (a) Street segments with start- and end-junctions in the sketch map, (b) Qualitative constraint network for the topology of street segments using $DRA_{dipolcon}$.

We use $DRA_{dipolcon}$ [5, 36] to capture the topology of street segments. $DRA_{dipolcon}$ is a coarsened version of the DRA [35], was introduced in Wallgrün et al. [5]. They use the cardinal directions [37] and $DRA_{dipolcon}$ relations to capture the connectivity and orientation information of street segments in the road-network (extracted from OpenStreet Map). The $DRA_{dipolcon}$ provides all possible topological relations between street segments at an abstract level. These abstract relations overcome the effects of street segments´ schematization and distortion in qualitative alignment. For $DRA_{dipolcon}$, the possible positions of the start-/end-point of one dipole with respect to another dipole are s (coincides with the start-point), e (coincides with the end-point), and x (coincides with neither start-point nor end-point). Using $DRA_{dipolcon}$ the connectivity of the start or end-point of one dipole with respect to another dipole is captured without taking into account their relative orientation at junctions. It provides seven base relations such as *sese, eses, xexe, sxsx, xsex, exxs* for connected and *xxxx* for non-connected street segments.

For the qualitative representation of street segments, we use the start and end-points (junctions) of street segments to define dipoles. For example, the junction B, C, G, I, D and F define the dipole BC, CG, GI, CD, DF, and GF (see Fig. 1a). The topology of street segments is represented as a set of base qualitative relations: BC *exxs* CG, CG *exxs* GI, CG *sxsx* CD, and CD *xxxx* GF. The relations with s and e represent the connectivity of street segments in the street network. Fig. 1b shows the qualitative constraint network for the topology of street segments in the sketch map.

3.2 Orientation of Street Segments

It is common to use points as basic entities in positional reasoning [17, 35]. We investigate different qualitative representations for the orientation information of street segments such as Projection- and Cone-based Cardinal Directions [37], Single Cross Calculus (SCC) [38], Double Cross Calculus (DCC) [38], and $OPRA_m$ [31]. Unlike geo-referenced maps, sketch maps do not have a single, global reference frame. Rather the sketched elements themselves act as referencing objects. The cardinal directions [37] are excluded as they are based on a global reference frame. We also exclude the DCC as it is not closed under composition and permutation and there exists no finite refinement of the base relations with such a closure property [39]. The qualitative representations with fixed granularities such as SCC [38] and FlipFlop (FFC) [40] provides precise orientation relations *front (f)* and *back (b)* corresponding to 180° and 0° angles respectively. However, street segments in sketch maps are not drawn to such high precision.

For the orientation of street segments, we need a representation with flexible granularity, which overcomes the effects of cognitive distortions such as straightening curve streets and distortions of angles. There exist two families of qualitative representations that allow for defining sectors with different angles: The STAR calculi [33] for absolute directions with same direction sectors for every point p in the plane and the $OPRA_m$ calculi [31] for relative directions with different direction sectors. However, cognitive studies indicate that human conceptualizations of space are not based on equal size sectors, not symmetric with respect to *front* and *back*, and symmetric with respect to *left* and *right* [32].

In order to capture relative orientation of street segment in street networks, we use $OPRA_m$ calculi [31]. Lücke et al. [30] propose $OPRA_m$ [31] together with Klippel's turn directions [32] as an approach for the navigation in street networks. The $OPRA_m$ considers oriented points as primitive entities and relates them with respect to their relative orientation towards each other. The granularity factor in $OPRA_m$ offers the flexibility to define orientation sectors and it is a tradeoff between the minimum size of the sectors and reasoning efficiency. The granularity factor $m \in N+$ determines the number of distinguished orientation sectors. For each of the points, m lines are used to partition the plane into $2m$ planar and $2m$ linear regions (see Fig. 2). In order to identify suitable orientation sectors for the representation of street segments, we analyze the angles between street segments from sketch and geo-referenced maps. The cluster analysis of the angles is discussed in the next section.

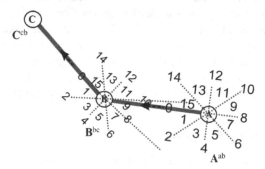

Fig. 2. Oriented junctions A^{ab}, B^{bc}, and C^{cb} of the street segments AB and BC, the junction A^{ab} represents its orientation towards junction B

In sketch maps, junctions are represented as points with their orientation given by connecting street segments. For example, the junction B with its orientation towards C is written as B^{bc} (for further information see [16]). The oriented junction A has the following relation to the oriented junction B: $A^{ab} <^9_0 B^{bc}$, which means B is in the orientation-sector (0) of A and A is in the orientation-sector (9) of B. Similarly, junction C is in the orientation-sector (0) of B. (see Fig. 2).

Cluster Analysis of Angles and Orientation Sectors. The most common qualitative orientation relations over points in the plane depend on the angles formed by the points [24]. Angles that yield the same direction relation belong to a common orientation sector bounded by different angles [24]. In order to identify plausible orientation sectors, we analyze the angles between street segments from 18 sketch maps and the angles between corresponding street segments in the geo-referenced map. The angles are measured between adjacent street segments which are directly connected at junctions (see Fig. 3a).

We use **R** (statistical[2] software) and apply K-means clustering [41] to examine the angles. The purpose is to divide the angles into homogeneous and distinct groups. The K-means clustering partitions a set of angles into a specified number of groups (k) with the help of lowest with-in the groups sum of squares. Since, the street segments are omitted and generalized in sketch maps, we find some missing angles for the street segments. The within group mean values [42] of the angles from sketch maps are used to substitute the missing angles. The within-groups sum of square values are examined to identify the number of suitable clusters, which suggests three clusters (K=3) maximum for the given dataset of angles. Using the given number of clusters, the dataset of angles is divided into three distinct groups. Subsequently, the mean, min, and max values of the angles in each cluster are used to define the ranges of angles in each cluster.

Afterwards, the range of angles in each cluster is scrutinized. The range of angles from 53° to 155°, 112° to 248°, and 205° to 305° are coded as a *left (l), front (f)*, and *right (r)* clusters respectively (see Fig. 3b). We find overlapping angles between *front/left* and *front/right*, which we called *Half-Left (HL)* and *Half-Right (HR)* sectors. The overlapping sectors indicate that during the clustering some of the highly distorted street segments are clustered into the *left* cluster, while some of the street segments within the same range of angles are clustered into the *front* cluster. For example, the street segment with angle 112° belongs to *front* cluster while the street segment with angle 155° belong to the *left* cluster using the with-in the groups sum of squares, this creates the *Half-Left (HL)* overlapping sector (analogous for *HR*).

In qualitative representation using $\mathcal{OPRA}_m$, the position of reference junction is always at 0°. Therefore, we exclude the extreme values of the *left* and *right* sectors (53° and 305°) and the *back (b)* relation is introduced at 0°. We consider the overlapping sectors *HL* and *HR* analogous to the *half-left* and *half-right* turn directions in [32]. However, their sector sizes are different from the sizes introduced in [30] (see Fig. 4). Thus, we find the new orientation sectors with the range of angles:

---

[2] http://www.r-project.org/

```
Left(l)→[1°-112°]
Half-left(HL)→[113°-154°]
Front(F)→[155°-205°]
Half-Right(HR)→[206°-247°]
Right(R)→[248°-359°]
Back(B)→[0°]
```

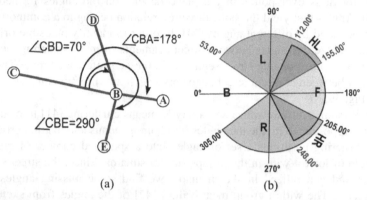

(a)   (b)

Fig. 3. (a) Measurement of the angles from sketch and geo-referenced maps, (b) range of angles in each cluster and the overlapping sectors (*HL* and *HR*)

The result indicates that the 360 degrees being divided such that, the orientation sector *half-left* is symmetric with respect to the *half-right* of having a size 41°, the orientation sector *right* is also symmetric with respect to the *left* of having a size 111°. While the orientation sector *front* is asymmetric with respect to the *back*, as we defined the *back* relation at 0° and the *front* sector has a size 50°.

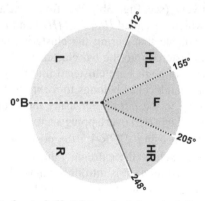

Fig. 4. The *left, half-left, front, half-right*, and *right* orientation sectors using the cluster analysis of angles and the *back (b)* relation at 0°

Encoding Orientation Sectors into $OPRA_8$. We encode aforementioned orientation sectors into $OPRA_8$ [31]. The encoded orientation sectors with the $OPRA_8$ define the *front (f)*, *half-left (hl)*, *left (l)*, *back (b)*, *right (r)*, and *half-right (hr)* orientation relations. We use the representation to formalize the orientation relations of street segments from the sketch and geo-referenced maps. The mapping of $OPRA_8$ (where m=8) with the identified orientation sectors will be as follows.

```
Front(f)→ {0,1,2,4m-1,4m-2}
Half-Left(HL)→{m-5,m-4,m-3}
Left(L)→ {m-2,m-1,m,m+1,…,m+3,m+4,m+5,2m-2,2m-1}
Right(r)→ {2m+1,…,2m+4,2m+5,3m-2,3m-1,3m,3m+1,3m+2}
Half-Right(HR)→ {3m+3,3m+4,4m-3}
Back(b)→ {2m}
```

In the situation depicted in Fig. 5a, for example, we have connected street segments AB, BC, BD, and CE with their oriented junctions A^{ab}, B^{ab}, C^{bc}, D^{bd}, and E^{ce}. The junction B with its intrinsic orientation B^{ab} represents the oriented street segment AB. The relation between a pair of oriented junctions gives the relative locations based on their intrinsic orientation. Particularly, distinguishing whether one is on the *left-* or on the *right-side* of the other. But to capture the relative orientation of an outgoing street segment requires the relative orientations with respect to both the preceding and succeeding street segments.

For example, using the junction B with its orientation B^{ab}, the junction D^{bd} (represents the connected street segment BD) is in the *half-left (hl)* orientation sector of B^{ab}. Similarly, the C^{bc} is in the *half-right (hr)* sector with respect to the reference junction B^{ab}. While the reference junction B^{ab} is at $0°$ with respect to the oriented junction D^{bd} and C^{bc}. It represents the *back (b)* relation of B^{ab} with respect to the reference junction D^{bd} and C^{bc}.

Fig. 5b shows the orientation relations of street segments which are directly connected at the junction B^{ab} and C^{bc}. The relation $A^{ab} <^f_b B^{ab}$ indicates that the junction B^{ab} in the *front (f)* sector of the junction A^{ab} and the junction A^{ab} has a linear *back (b)* relation with respect to the junction B^{ab}.

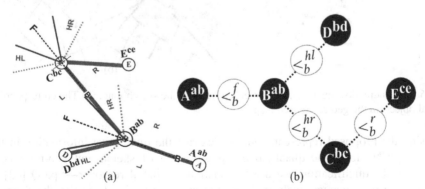

(a)   (b)

Fig. 5. (a) Orientation of street segments with respect to the oriented junctions, (b) QCN for the orientation of connected street segments at the junction B^{ab} and C^{bc}

4   Evaluation

In this section, we evaluate the proposed representations by aligning aforementioned two datasets of the sketch maps (28 in total) with the corresponding geo-referenced maps (MMs). We consider all depicted street segments and junctions from the sketch maps and the corresponding spatial object in geo-referenced maps (see Fig. 6ab).

The tested sketch maps are from two different datasets. The first dataset includes the same 18 sketch maps used to compute the angles and the second dataset includes sketch maps from a location of an area about $1.04\ km^2$ in Muenster, Germany. All the sketch maps are generated by different participants (excluding authors and colleagues) and most of them were holding an academic degree at University of Muenster, Germany. Though none of the participants were residents of the predefined locations, all of them were familiar with the locations by frequent visits by foot or vehicle. During the experiment, participants were asked to produce sketch maps of predefined locations as detailed as possible but only from memory.

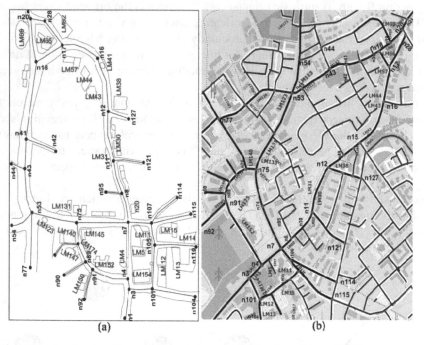

(a)   (b)

Fig. 6. (a) Landmarks, junctions, and street segments in the sketch map, (b) The corresponding spatial objects in the geo-referenced map

Using the proposed representations, we extract the qualitative information in the form of QCNs from the quantitative representation of sketch and geo-referenced maps. For the qualification, we use the qualitative spatial reasoner—SparQ [43] in combination with manual analysis. Next, the obtained QCNs from the sketch maps are compared with the QCNs derived from the geo-referenced maps to determine the degree to which qualitative information is identical[3]. If the representations are suitable, the QCNs from sketch and geo-referenced maps should be identical to a high degree and they must capture the relevant qualitative distinctions preserved in sketch maps.

To align the street segments, we identify the possible pairing of nodes from one QCN with those in the other QCN. In this part of the evaluation, the hypothesis of matching street segments are generated based on a visual analysis, where we consider each depicted street segment from the sketch maps and identify their corresponding street segments in the geo-referenced maps. In sketch maps, the spatial information is given at an aggregated level. In particular, the street segments are highly aggregated. For this evaluation, we aggregated the information in the geo-referenced maps manually. We asked our participants to indicate the corresponding street for every sketched street segment and got the information on how streets were aggregated.

4.1 Topology of Street Segments

As proposed above, the $\mathcal{DRA}_{dipolcon}$ is used to capture the topological relations between street segments. For both locations, QCNs from the sketch and geo-referenced maps are tabularized to align and compare the topological information of the street segments. From a visual analysis of the tabularized QCNs, we find that the qualitative constraints derived using $\mathcal{DRA}_{dipolcon}$ has an average accuracy rate of 98.66% for both locations (see Table 1), i.e. most of the connected street segments (with manual aggregation) are depicted correctly in the sketch maps. The result of our proposed representation is compared with $\mathcal{DRA}_c$ [35]. Note that $\mathcal{DRA}_c$ convey also the orientation information of dipoles. The accuracy rate was 91.71% for $\mathcal{DRA}_c$. Most of the conflicting constraints using $\mathcal{DRA}_c$ are caused by the orientation information between schematized and distorted street segments.

Table 1. Errors and accuracy of the topological relations between street segments in the street network using the $\mathcal{DRA}_{dipolcon}$

Sketch Maps (28)	Total # of QCNs	Mismatched QCNs	Accuracy
Location-1	832	18	98.33%
Location-II	2004	24	98.99%
Average			**98.66%**

4.2 Orientation of Street Segments

We use the orientation sectors encoded $\mathcal{OPRA}_8$ [31] to formalize the orientation information of street segments at a local level—between connected street segments at junctions. The obtained orientation information in the form of QCNs is tabularized to

---

[3] Complete QCN comparison files and images are available at
http://ifgibox.de/s_jan001/QualitativeRepresentation_
StreetSegments/

identify the suitability of proposed representation. Our evaluation shows that the representation together with the identified orientation sectors provides an average accuracy rate of 94.73% for both locations (see Table 2).

Lücke et al. [30] propose a qualitative approach for the navigation in street networks. They encoded the Klippel's eight turn directions [32] with $\mathcal{OPRA}_8$ and $\mathcal{OPRA}_{16}$ [31] to represent eight possible orientations sectors such *as left (l), sharp-left (sl), half-left (hl), right (r), sharp-right (sr), half-right (hr), front (f)*, and *back (b)*.

We compare our results with the Klippel's turn directions encoded $\mathcal{OPRA}_{16}$ [30]. Using the Klippel's turn directions, we find only 64.24% accuracy rate for the both locations. Due to the cognitive distortions, the distinction in eight sectors seems to be unsuitable for the relative orientation of street segments.

Table 2. The accuracy rate of orientation information between street segments in the street network using the orientation sectors encoded $\mathcal{OPRA}_8$

Sketch Maps (28)	Total # of QCNs	Mismatched QCNs	Accuracy
Location-1	782	20	97.37 %
Location-II	1853	146	92.10%
Average			**94.73%**

The overall evaluation shows that the proposed representation together with the identified orientation sectors seems a promising way to formalize the orientation information of distorted street segments in sketch maps.

5   Conclusion and Future Work

In this study, we identify a set of plausible representations to formalize the topology and orientation information of schematized and distorted street segments in street networks. We analyze the angles between street segments to identify the number of suitable orientation sectors. The identified orientation sectors including linear *back* relation are encoded with $\mathcal{OPRA}_8$ to formalize the orientation information of street segments.

In order to evaluate the proposed representations, the qualitative information is extracted in the form of QCNs. Next, the QCNs derived from both maps are tabularized. The suitability of proposed representations is evaluated by comparing the QCN matrices from 28 sketch maps with the corresponding geo-referenced maps. The overall evaluation shows that the representations are suitable to formalize the consistent qualitative information between street segments. The high degree of identical relations will help us to align the street networks from sketch maps with the corresponding street networks in geo-referenced maps. This way, the additional sketched information such as information on the usage of the buildings, bakeries, and completely unmapped information can be transferred into the Geographic Information System (GIS) as volunteered information.

In the present study, we evaluate the representations by aligning street segments from sketch and geo-referenced maps of an urban spatial structure. We consider street segments with minimum deviations between their start- and end-junctions. In future, we will investigate the relevance of the proposed representations for the alignment of sketch maps from rural areas, where the spatial structure is more irregular and unplanned with many curved streets. We handle the aggregations and deviations of street segments and the comparison of QCNs manually. The problem of aggregation, deviation, and QCN matching is ongoing research work and their solution will help to align street segments from sketch maps with geo-referenced map automatically.

Acknowledgements. This work is funded by the German Research Foundation (DFG) through the SketchMapia project (Grant SCHW 1372/7-1).

References

1. Goodchild, M.F.: Citizens as Sensors: The World of Volunteered Geography. Geo. Journal 49, 211–221 (2007)
2. Egenhofer, M.J.: Spatial-Query-by-Sketch. In: Burnett, M., Citrin, W. (eds.) IEEE Symposium on Visual Languages (IEEE-1996), pp. 60–67. IEEE Press, Boulder (1996)
3. Egenhofer, M.J.: Query processing in spatial-query-by-sketch. Journal of Visual Languages and Computing 8, 403–424 (1997)
4. Nedas, K.A., Egenhofer, M.J.: Spatial-Scene Similarity Queries. Transactions in GIS 12, 661–681 (2008)
5. Wallgrun Oliver, J., Wolter, D., Richter, K.-F.: Qualitative Matching of Spatial Information. In: Proceedings of the 8th SIGSPATIAL International Conference on Advances in Geographic Information Systems, pp. 300–309. ACM, New York (2010)
6. Blaser, A.: A study of people's sketching habits in GIS. Spatial Cognition and Computation 2, 393–419 (2000)
7. Huynh, N.T., Doherty, S.T.: Digital Sketch-Map Drawing as an Instrument to Collect Data about Spatial Cognition. Cartographica: The International Journal for Geographic Information and Geo-visualization 42, 285–296 (2007)
8. Tversky, B.: How to get around by mind and body: Spatial thought, spatial action. In: Zilhão, A. (ed.) Cognition, Evolution, and Rationality. A Cognitive Science for the Twenty-First Century, pp. 135–147. Routledge, London (2005)
9. Tversky, B.: Structures of Mental Spaces: How People Think About Space. Environment & Behavior 35, 66–80 (2003)
10. Tversky, B.: Navigating by Mind and by Body. In: Freksa, C., Brauer, W., Habel, C., Wender, K.F. (eds.) Spatial Cognition III. LNCS (LNAI), vol. 2685, pp. 1–10. Springer, Heidelberg (2003)
11. Appleyard, D.: Why buildings are known: A Predictive Tool for Architects and Planners. Environment and Behavior 1, 131–156 (1969)
12. Appleyard, D.: Styles and Methods of Structuring a City. Environment and Behavior 2, 100–117 (1970)
13. Wang, J., Schwering, A.: The Accuracy of Sketched Spatial Relations: How Cognitive Errors Affect Sketch Representation. presenting spatial information: Granularity, relevance, and integration. In: Workshop at COSIT 2009. AberWrac'h, France (2009)

14. Schwering, A., Wang, J.: SketchMapia – A framework for qualitative mapping of sketch maps and metric maps. In: Las Navas 20th Anniversary Meeting on Cognitive and Linguistic Aspects of Geographic Spaces, Las Navas del Marques, Avila, Spain (2011)
15. Schwering, A., Wang, J., Chipofya, M., Jan, S., Li, R., Broelemann, K.: SketchMapia: Qualitative Representations for the Alignment of Sketch and Metric Maps. In: Spatial Cognition & Computation (SCC 2014), vol. 14, pp. 1–35 (2014)
16. Chipofya, M., Wang, J., Schwering, A.: Towards cognitively plausible spatial representations for sketch map alignment. In: Egenhofer, M., Giudice, N., Moratz, R., Worboys, M. (eds.) COSIT 2011. LNCS, vol. 6899, pp. 20–39. Springer, Heidelberg (2011)
17. Freksa, C.: Dimensions of qualitative spatial reasoning. In: Carreté, N.P., Singh, M.G. (eds.) Proceeding III MACS-International Workshop on Qualitative Reasoning and Decision Technologies—QUARDET 1993, pp. 483–492. CIMNE, Barcelona (1993)
18. Wang, J., Mülligann, C., Schwering, A.: A Study on Empirically Relevant Aspects for Qualitative Alignment of Sketch Maps. In: Proceedings of the Sixth International Conference on Geographic Information Science (GIScience), Zurich, Switzerland (2010)
19. Wang, J., Muelligann, C., Schwering, A.: An Empirical Study on Relevant Aspects for Sketch Map Alignment. In: Proceedings of the 14th AGILE International Conference on Geographic Information Science (AGILE 2011), Utrecht, Netherlands (2011)
20. Jan, S., Schwering, A., Wang, J., Chipofya, M.: Ordering: A reliable qualitative information for the alignment of sketch and metric maps. In: 12th IEEE International Conference on Cognitive Informatics & Cognitive Computing (ICCI*CC 2013), pp. 203–211. IEEE Press, New York (2013)
21. Jan, S., Schwering, A., Chipofya, M., Binor, T.: Qualitative Representations of Extended Spatial Objects in Sketch Maps. In: Huerta, J., et al. (eds.) Connecting a Digital Europe Through Location and Place. Lecture Notes in Geoinformation and Cartography, pp. 37–54. Springer, Switzerland (2014)
22. Broelemann, K.: A System for Automatic Localization and Recognition of Sketch Map Objects. In: Workshop of Understanding and Processing Sketch Maps, pp. 11–20. AKA Verlag, Belfast (2011)
23. Broelemann, K., Jiang, X.: A region-based method for sketch map segmentation. In: Kwon, Y.-B., Ogier, J.-M. (eds.) GREC 2011. LNCS, vol. 7423, pp. 1–14. Springer, Heidelberg (2013)
24. Renz, J., Wölfl, S.: A qualitative representation of route networks. In: Proceeding of the 19th European Conference on Artificial Intelligence (ECAI), pp. 1091–1092. IOS Press, Amsterdam (2010)
25. Volker, H., Michael, W.: Querying GIS with Animated Spatial Sketches. In: Proceeding IEEE Symposium on Visual Languages, pp. 197–204. IEEE Press, Isle of Capri (1997)
26. Forbus, K., Usher, J., Chapman, V.: Qualitative spatial reasoning about sketch maps. AI Magazine 25, 61–72 (2003)
27. Chipofya, M., Schwering, A., Binor, T.: Matching Qualitative Spatial Scene Descriptions á la Tabu. In: Castro, F., Gelbukh, A., González, M. (eds.) MICAI 2013, Part II. LNCS, vol. 8266, pp. 388–402. Springer, Heidelberg (2013)
28. Fred Glover: Tabu Search–part 1. ORSA Journal on Computing. 1, 190–206 (1989)
29. Battiti, R., Tecchiolli, G.: The Reactive tabu search. ORSA Journal on Computing 6, 126–140 (1994)
30. Lücke, D., Mossakowski, T., Moratz, R.: Streets to the OPRA — Finding your destination with imprecise knowledge. In: Proceedings of the Workshop on Benchmarks and Applications of Spatial Reasoning at IJCAI 2011, Barcelona, Spain, pp. 25–32 (2011)

31. Moratz, R., Dylla, F., Frommberger, L.: A Relative Orientation Algebra with Adjustable Granularity. In: Proceedings of the Workshop on Agents in Real-time and Dynamic Environments (IJCAI 2005), Edinburgh, Scohtland (2005)
32. Klippel, A., Montello, D.R.: Linguistic and nonlinguistic turn direction concepts. In: Winter, S., Duckham, M., Kulik, L., Kuipers, B. (eds.) COSIT 2007. LNCS, vol. 4736, pp. 354–372. Springer, Heidelberg (2007)
33. Renz, J., Mitra, D.: Qualitative Direction Calculi with Arbitrary Granularity. In: Zhang, C., Guesgen, H.W., Yeap, W.-K. (eds.) PRICAI 2004. LNCS (LNAI), vol. 3157, pp. 65–74. Springer, Heidelberg (2004)
34. Tversky, B.: Distortions in cognitive maps. Geoforum-Interdisciplinary Journal 23, 131–138 (1992)
35. Moratz, R., Renz, J., Wolter, D.: Qualitative spatial reasoning about line segments. In: Proceedings of the 14th European Conference on Artificial Intelligence (ECAI 2000), pp. 234–238. IOS Press, Amsterdam (2000)
36. Chipofya, M.: Combining DRA and CYC into a Network Friendly Calculus. In: Proceedings of 20th European Conference on Artificial Intelligence (ECAI 2012), pp. 234–239. IOS Press, France (2012)
37. Frank, A.U.: Qualitative Spatial Reasoning about Distances and Directions in Geographic Space. Journal of Visual Languages and Computing 3, 343–371 (1992)
38. Freksa, C.: Using orientation information for qualitative spatial reasoning. In: Frank, A.U., Formentini, U., Campari, I. (eds.) Theories and Methods of Spatio-Temporal Reasoning in Geographic Space. LNCS, vol. 639, pp. 162–178. Springer, Heidelberg (1992)
39. Scivos, A., Nebel, B.: Double-crossing: Decidability and computational complexity of a qualitative calculus for navigation. In: Montello, D.R. (ed.) COSIT 2001. LNCS, vol. 2205, pp. 431–446. Springer, Heidelberg (2001)
40. Ligozat, G.: Qualitative Triangulation for Spatial Reasoning. In: Campari, I., Frank, A.U. (eds.) COSIT 1993. LNCS, vol. 716, pp. 54–68. Springer, Heidelberg (1993)
41. Everitt, B.S.: An R and S-PLUS® Companion to Multivariate Analysis, 1st edn. Springer Texts in Statistics, pp. 115–136 (2005)
42. Malarvizhi, M., Thanamani, A.: K-NN Classifier Performs Better Than K-Means Clustering in Missing Value Imputation. IOSR Journal of Computer Engineering (IOSRJCE) 6, 12–15 (2012)
43. Wolter, D.: SparQ — A Spatial Reasoning Toolbox. In: Proceedings of AAAI Spring Symposium on Benchmarking of Qualitative Spatial and Temporal Reasoning Systems, Stanford University, CA, USA (2009)

Spatial Reasoning in Comparative Analyses
of Physics Diagrams

Maria D. Chang, Jon W. Wetzel, and Kenneth D. Forbus

Qualitative Reasoning Group, Northwestern University, Evanston, IL, USA
{maria.chang,jw}@u.northwestern.edu,
forbus@northwestern.edu

Abstract. Spatial reasoning plays a critical role in STEM problem solving. Physics assessments, for example, are rich in diagrams and pictures, which help people understand concrete physical scenarios and abstract aspects of physical reasoning. In this paper we describe a system that analyzes sketched diagrams to solve qualitative physics problems from a popular physics textbook. Causal models describing each problem are formulated via visual and conceptual analyses of the sketched diagrams. We use a combination of qualitative and quantitative reasoning to solve vector addition, tension, and gravitation ranking problems in the introductory chapters of the book.

Keywords: Spatial reasoning, spatial problem solving, qualitative reasoning, conceptual physics, diagrammatic reasoning.

1 Introduction

In spatial domains like science, technology, engineering and mathematics (i.e. STEM fields), problem solving frequently requires a combination of spatial and conceptual reasoning. For this reason, spatial representations (e.g. diagrams and sketches) are pervasive in science instruction. Spatial representations act as tools of communication and, unlike photographs, may convey a mix of concrete and abstract, non-literal information [1]. Externalizing this information has the added benefit of lightening working memory load, making spatial inference easier, and promoting new ideas [2, 3]. Actively generating spatial representations through sketching has been shown to increase engagement and facilitate learning [4]. Taking advantage of these spatial representations requires considerable spatial skills. Indeed, data from over 50 years of psychological research indicate that spatial skills are a strong predictor of success in STEM fields [5].

The importance of spatial representations in physics problem solving is illustrated by the use of diagrams in assessment tools and the emphasis on drawing free-body diagrams in introductory physics courses. For example, in an analysis of advanced placement (AP) physics tests in the US, 48% of problems had diagrams and 58% of those (about 28% of the total) could not be solved without information provided by the diagram [6]. Diagrams are especially common in qualitative physics problems:

C. Freksa et al. (Eds.): Spatial Cognition 2014, LNAI 8684, pp. 268–282, 2014.

two-thirds of the problems in the force concept inventory [7] involve diagrams. The presence of diagrams in the force concept inventory is important because qualitative physics problems have been shown to be a better probe for conceptual knowledge than quantitative problem solving.

The use of drawings and diagrams in science instruction presents a challenge to researchers interested in developing intelligent tutoring systems. From a computational perspective, using spatial representations to solve problems requires domain-general spatial reasoning capabilities, domain-specific knowledge, and models for how to combine both types of information. This is especially important in the domain of conceptual physics, where problems need to be solved via spatial reasoning and often in the absence of numerical values. It is therefore important for the next generation of STEM tutoring systems to support spatial reasoning for solving both quantitative and qualitative problems.

This paper describes a system that solves conceptual physics ranking problems from a popular physics text book [8]. Each problem is represented with a sketch. The visual and conceptual information depicted in each sketch is used to formulate causal models about them. Our system uses qualitative reasoning over causal models and spatial reasoning over the sketches to make judgments about quantities even when the exact values of the quantities are unknown.

2   Background

This section describes the pre-existing systems and techniques that we use for understanding sketches and reasoning about physical systems. We use CogSketch to collect and analyze physics sketches. We use qualitative mechanics and qualitative process theory to formulate and reason about causal models of physical scenarios and we use differential qualitative analysis to determine ordinal relationships between quantities.

2.1   CogSketch

To capture the spatial and conceptual information of the diagrammatic problems, we use CogSketch [9][1], our domain-independent sketch understanding system. CogSketch provides an interface for sketching that automatically computes qualitative spatial and conceptual representations of sketches. CogSketch analyzes ink drawn by the user to generate topological relations (RCC8 [10]) and positional relations between objects (e.g. rightOf, above). Quantities from spatial computations (e.g. geometric distance) may be computed on demand. Ink may also be segmented into individual edges, which can be used to generate shape and edge level representations [11].

---

[1] CogSketch is freely available from:
www.qrg.northwestern.edu/software/cogsketch

Users manually label their sketches so that CogSketch can tie conceptual information to the spatial information from drawn ink. The labeling interface provided by CogSketch is intended to mimic the qualitative and communicative nature of open-domain sketching. When people sketch with each other, they frequently use natural language or gestures to communicate conceptual information about their drawing, rather than requiring others to interpret the ink in isolation. Similarly, CogSketch interprets users' ink with respect to the conceptual information they provide. In contrast, sketch recognition systems rely on users drawing elements from a small vocabulary of visual symbols (e.g. letters, electronic components). But symbol recognition is not enough to capture content in STEM domains because the mapping between shapes and conceptual entities is many to many. For example, in physics a circle might represent a ball, an orbit, or a disk. Thus, CogSketch's interface enables users to explicitly tell it what they mean.

In CogSketch, the basic building block of a sketch is a *glyph*. A *glyph* is a collection of ink strokes intended to represent something visually. Users define glyphs by telling CogSketch when they are done drawing something, and they can split and merge ink to edit glyphs as desired. Once the user draws a glyph, they provide it with a *conceptual label* from an OpenCyc-derived knowledge base (KB)[2], which can indicate that the glyph represents an *entity, relation,* or *annotation*. An *entity* is an instance of a concept, like a rigid object or a spring. A *relation* can be used to represent a relationship between two things, for instance, an arrow indicating that one object orbits another. An *annotation* provides additional information about another object. Annotations are of particular interest to this work because they can be used to represent quantities in diagrams. Quantitative values can be associated with annotations, but they are optional. This means that quantities can be represented at different levels of detail. For instance, in a free body diagram with two forces acting on an object, force vector annotation arrows can be drawn to represent the two forces (Figure 1). In the absence of quantitative information (i.e. force magnitude), the forces simply have some qualitative direction. This is still useful, since even without quantitative information, the qualitative direction of the net force may be estimated if the two forces are not in opposing directions. However, if force magnitudes are known, they can be entered using the same labeling interface.

Each sketch can contain multiple *subsketches*. The representations for each subsketch reside in their own logical environment, which inherits information from the sketch as a whole. Thus, subsketches can be thought of as independent states or scenarios within one sketch.

Because CogSketch generates relational representations for sketches, a sketch can be compared to other sketches using the *structure mapping engine* (SME) [12], which is a computational model of analogical comparison. SME takes two structured descriptions, a *base* and a *target,* and computes one or more mappings between them. For the purposes of this experiment, the most important aspect of the analogical mapping is the set of *correspondences,* which indicate how things in one description match up to things in another. Since subsketches may be used to represent indepen-

---

[2]   http://www.cyc.com/platform/opencyc

dent scenarios, SME is used to frame comparative analyses between sketched scenarios. For instance, in two situations with multiple objects, there may be many potential matches between objects and quantities. An SME mapping indicates how items in each subsketch should match to each other, which is used to guide comparative analyses. SME is built into CogSketch, and has been used in an educational software application to give feedback to students [13].

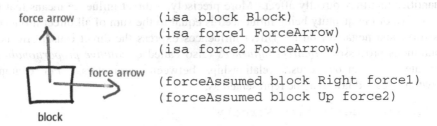

Fig. 1. An illustration of force arrow annotations. Quantitative values (e.g. force magnitude) may be included with annotations, but they are optional. A subset of the representations generated by CogSketch is shown on the right.

2.2   Qualitative and Quantitative Physical Reasoning

One of challenges of solving conceptual physics problems is combining qualitative and quantitative reasoning. Some problems may require arithmetic operations on numerical values, while others require reasoning about quantities for which no numerical values are known. Consider for example determining the net force on an object where the magnitudes of all forces are known. If all the forces are along the same axis, computing the magnitude of the net force can be reduced to addition and subtraction. Alternatively, consider a question that asks about the relative magnitude of the gravitational forces on the Moon versus Jupiter. It can be determined that the gravitational force on Jupiter is greater than on the moon because the mass of Jupiter is greater than than the mass of the moon. This inference is independent of the magnitudes of those forces and the exact masses of the Moon and Jupiter. Both types of reasoning are captured by our system.

For performing qualitative reasoning on force vectors and detecting forces between objects, we use a model of qualitative mechanics that is built into CogSketch [14]. The model is based on the work of Nielsen and Kim [15, 16] but has been adapted to capture rigid body mechanics of 2D objects in hand-drawn sketches. Vectors are represented using qualitative directions (e.g. right, left, up, down) and qualitative values (e.g. -, 0, +) to enable qualitative calculations about net force and the propagation of forces between object surfaces. While qualitative rigid body mechanics is useful for purely qualitative scenarios, there are often cases where quantities need to taken into account.

For reasoning about quantities explicitly, we use Qualitative Process Theory [17], which allows us to represent causal systems depicted in sketches. In QP theory, physical phenomena are represented with continuous processes and quantities. Quantities represent parameters of objects (e.g. mass, velocity), while processes change quantities over time (e.g. acceleration changes velocity). Under the sole mechanism assumption [17], continuous quantities may only be changed by physical processes. Importantly, quantities can be reasoned about even if their exact numerical values are unknown. Quantities may be causally influenced directly or indirectly. *Direct influences* express contributions of rates of processes to the derivatives of quantities that they directly affect. More precisely, a direct influence means that the derivative of the quantity being influenced is equal to the sum of all direct influences (positive and negative) on it. Direct influences express the direct causal effects of continuous processes. *Indirect influences* (also called *qualitative proportionalities*) indicate instantaneous causal relationships between parameters. For example, Newton's second law, may be represented as:

(qprop acceleration Force)

(qprop- acceleration mass)

These two statements indicate that changes in force and mass cause changes in acceleration. All else being equal, the qprop indicates that an increase in force causes an increase in acceleration, whereas the qprop- indicates that an increase in mass will lead to decreased acceleration.

As a representational system, QP theory can be used to capture the causal models of a wide range of phenomena [17]. Qualitative causal models can be applied to a particular scenario via *model formulation* [18, 19]. Given a domain theory containing *model fragments* for a particular domain, a scenario can be analyzed to determine which model fragments are applicable. Each model fragment can include direct and indirect influences in its consequences, which can be used to determine how quantities are changing. This propagation of causal influences among quantities is called *influence resolution*. For example, if a force is applied to an object, that provides acceleration, which causes velocity to increase, which causes position to increase. Taken together, the model fragments that are applicable to a particular scenario represent the causal model of that scenario.

In addition to characterizing quantity changes within a single scenario, it is possible to determine quantity changes between highly similar scenarios via *differential qualitative analysis (DQA)* [17, 20]. The goal of DQA is to predict how a situation would change if some of its parameters not already constrained by its causal model were changed. DQA has been explored in sketch-based physics problem solving [21, 22] but we extend previous work by using first-principles modeling strategies and by expanding the range of visual quantities that can be assessed using DQA.

3   Approach

The goal of this work is to create the domain knowledge and reasoning capabilities needed to solve conceptual diagrammatic physics problems. To evaluate our efforts, we examined ranking problems from the first five chapters of *Conceptual Physics* [8]. Each ranking problem consists of two or more scenarios depicted in diagrams that need to be ranked along a particular quantity (Figure 2, 3). For instance, a ranking problem may involve understanding how opposite forces combine to make a net force. In some cases the problems involve basic arithmetic. In others, numerical values might be left out completely. For instance, some ranking problems require ranking scenarios by a particular quantity even if no precise values are known. To solve these problems, we developed domain theories for some of the basic concepts in the first five chapters of the book, which cover Newton's Laws. We also developed strategies for conducting differential qualitative analysis that use spatial and conceptual information depicted in sketches.

3.1   Ranking Problems

The first five chapters of *Conceptual Physics* have 27 ranking problems. Out of those 27, 12 have to do with combining vectors as well as conceptual knowledge of tension and gravity. We chose these problems as a starting point, excluding exercises about Newton's third law and problems that deal with explicit calculations about time, because we think those problems will require other aspects of QP theory and vectors beyond what we discuss here.

Each ranking problem was sketched into CogSketch so that spatial and conceptual representations could be automatically generated. The scenarios within each problem were drawn as subsketches within the sketch representing the whole problem. Every object was given one or more labels using the CogSketch labeling interface. These labels were important for objects with special properties (e.g. ropes) and for vector and quantity annotations. Vector annotations could have specific numerical values associated with them, but these were only included if they were explicitly mentioned in the problem and in the diagram. Similarly, objects were given mass annotations if mass was explicitly mentioned. There were two concepts that we had to represent by adding extra information to the sketch: hanging and co-movement. To indicate that something was hanging by something else, we drew relationship arrows to explicitly include this information in the sketch. To indicate that something moved with something else (as is necessary for some net velocity calculations), we drew relationship arrows as well. In all other cases, the sketch only contained information given explicitly in the diagram. In all cases, the sketch only contained information given explicitly in the problem text.

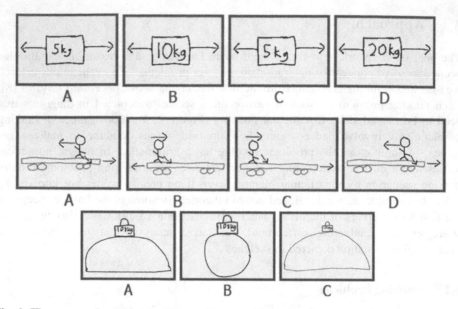

Fig. 2. Three example ranking problems with numerical values entered via CogSketch's labeling interface. The upper problem requires ranking the net forces on the objects in the four scenarios. The middle problem requires ranking the net velocity on the person in the four scenarios. The lower problem requires ranking the mass and weight of the toolbox on Jupiter, versus Earth's moon, versus Earth. The force and velocity arrows have explicit numerical values associated with them (e.g. 5 Newtons) and some of the objects have mass associated with them (e.g. 100 kg).

3.2   Model Fragments

The first five chapters of Conceptual Physics cover Newton's three laws of motion. As a starting point, we defined model fragments to express the causal relationships between tension forces in hanging systems, gravitational forces, and vectors drawn as arrows. Model fragments can be used to represent physical processes (e.g. motion) and physical situations (e.g. inclined plane). Each model fragment has participants (i.e. entities that are involved in the causal model), conditions and consequences. In order for a model fragment to be applicable to a particular scenario, its participant constraints and conditions must be satisfied. If the model fragment is applicable, it is instantiated and its consequences are inferred. Model fragment consequences can involve assertions about quantities, including causal relationships (i.e. influences) and ordinal relationships.

A simplified example of a model fragment that describes vector addition is shown in Figure 4. The participants are the things involved: the object that the vectors describe, a set of the vectors that should be summed, and the resultant vector. Each participant must belong to a particular collection in order for the model fragment to be considered. Those collections, which come from the OpenCyc KB with our own extensions, are shown in parentheses. The participant constraints provide bindings for

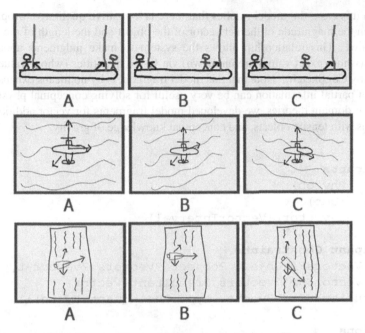

Fig. 3. Three example ranking problems without numerical values. The upper problem requires ranking the tensions in the left rope from greatest to least in the three scenarios. The middle problem requires ranking the net velocity of the airplane and the lower problem requires ranking the net velocity of the boat. No numerical values are associated with the vector arrows, so these problems must be solved visually.

potential participants of this model fragment and the conditions are criteria for instantiating the model (or considering it to be currently active). In this model, the object must be a physical object and the vectors must be represented as a set. The constraints consist of three statements. The first ensures that all the vector arrows involved in this model fragment describe the object we are interested in and that they are all the same type (to avoid summing vectors that have different meanings and different units). The second constraint calculates the sum of the vector arrows in 2D space. This operation is purely spatial and uses the *parallelogram rule* as described in the textbook: the sum of two vectors can be represented with an arrow along the diagonal of the parallelogram partially formed by the two vectors. The arrow is displayed in CogSketch and it is bound to the resultant vector variable (?resultant-vector) of the model fragment. With these two constraints satisfied, candidates are found for all three of the model fragment participants. The last constraint finds the quantity denoting function that corresponds with the vector type. For instance, if force arrows are being summed, then the net quantity function would be NetForceMagFn. Using the relationship between vector type and quantity function allows us to use one model fragment type for any kind of vector addition, rather than defining separate models for force arrows, velocity arrows, and acceleration arrows. Most importantly, the consequences of the model fragment are what give it inferential power. In this case, the model implies that there is a positive qualitative proportionality between the magnitude of the net vector of the object and the length of the resultant vector arrow. This relationship allows the system to make judgments about vector quantities (whose exact values are unknown) via visual quantities (whose values can be computed by CogSketch). Note that this model fragment is by no means exhaustive, but this type of partial information can be very useful for solving conceptual physics problems. In our domain theories, we developed model fragments for vector addition, hanging systems with tensile objects, and conceptual knowledge of gravity.

Participants
```
?object (Physob)
?vectors (Set)
?resultant-vector (VectorInterval)
```

Participant Constraints
```
(commonVectorsForObject ?object ?vectors ?vector-type)
(visualVectorSum ?vectors ?resultant-vector)
(netQuantityFnFor ?vector-type ?net-quantity-fn)))
```

Conditions
```
(hasQuantity ?object (?net-quantity-fn ?object ?axis)))
```

Consequences
```
(qEqualTo
   (?net-quantity-fn ?object ?axis)
   ((QPQuantityFn VectorMagnitude) ?resultant-vector))
(qprop
   (?net-quantity-fn ?object ?axis)
   ((QPQuantityFn Length) ?resultant-vector))
```

Fig. 4. A model fragment describing vector addition, using simplified syntax for clarity

3.3   Differential Qualitative Analysis via Causal and Spatial Reasoning

Our implementation of differential qualitative analysis (DQA) involves two main steps: (1) perform QP analysis of the scenarios, (2) compare the goal quantity across the different scenarios.

Step 1 is done using traditional model formulation and influence resolution techniques on the sketched diagrams. The domain theories are searched for applicable model fragments for each scenario in the problem. For each model fragment, the system attempts to find participants that satisfy the constraints. This usually involves conceptual reasoning about the category membership of potential participants, properties of physical scenarios, and spatial reasoning. For example, in the model fragment shown in Figure 4, the constraints involve visually computing the sum of two or more vector arrows. If the participant constraints and conditions are satisfied for a particular model fragment, it is instantiated and its consequences (which can be causal influences or ordinal relationships between quantities) are inferred. Inferences about quantities are particularly important because they can be used to determine the ordinal relationships of quantities across different scenarios. Once models have been formulated, influence resolution determines if any of the quantities are changing and propagates those changes through the causal chain of influences. The model fragments that are active for a particular scenario represent that scenario's causal model.

In step 2, the goal of DQA is to determine how a quantity changes across two scenarios. Symbolically, this is represented by the following predicate:

```
(dqValue ?quantity ?sme-mapping ?value)
```

where ?quantity is the goal quantity of the ranking problem (e.g. mass or net force magnitude), ?sme-mapping is an analogical mapping between two scenarios (i.e. a base scenario and a target scenario), and ?value is one of four possible values: -1, 0, 1, Ambig. The dqValue represents the qualitative difference between the two quantities from the base scenario to the target scenario. Therefore, a dqValue of -1 means that the quantity is lesser in the base scenario than in the target scenario. A dqValue of 1 means that the quantity is greater in the base scenario than in the target scenario. A dqValue of 0 means that the quantity is unchanged, and a dqValue of Ambig means that the difference is known to be ambiguous.

There are four strategies that are used to derive the dqValue of a quantity with respect to the analogical mapping. The dqValue may be calculated via numbers, via visual quantities, via ordinal relationships, and/or via causal influences. Calculating the dqValue via numbers is the most basic strategy and is used when numerical values for each quantity are known in advance or are derived through some other computation. Calculating the dqValue via visual quantities means that the exact quantity is retrieved from a sketched annotation (e.g. a force arrow with a numerical value) or through a spatial analysis of the sketch (e.g. a distance calculation). The exact quantities that are visually derived can then be compared directly. Calculating the dqValue via ordinal relationships means that there is an an explicit ordinal relationship between the two quantities in the logical environment. For example, the mass of Jupiter may not be known, but the mass of Jupiter relative to the mass of the Moon may be known in one of the domain theories. Lastly, calculating the dqValue via causal influences is used when there are one or more known causal antecedents to the quantity being examined. That is, when causal influences are inferred as a result of QP analysis, then a dqValue is recursively sought for the causal antecedent of the quantity. Once a dqValue is found, it is propagated back up the causal chain to determine the dqValue of the original quantity.

Using causal influences turns out to be critical for many of the problems that we analyzed and most (10 out of 12) bottom out at some kind of spatial computation. In some cases, distance was a causal antecedent of the goal quantity and calculating geometric distance between objects was required to solve the problem. In other cases, calculating the length of a resultant vector arrow was required to causally infer the dqValue of the goal quantity. Even in simple net force problems, where no spatially computed quantity was an explicit antecedent to the goal quantity, other spatial information, such as the major axis of force vectors, were needed to solve the problem. Thus, both causal and spatial information played critical roles in solving these problems.

3.4   Example

To illustrate our approach, consider the problem shown in Figure 5. The scenarios show a tree stump with two ropes pulling with equal force magnitudes but different directions. The goal of the problem is to rank the net force magnitude of the stump from greatest to least.

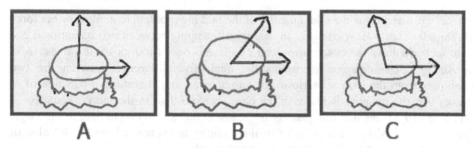

Fig. 5. An example ranking problem with three scenarios

First, the system searches for any applicable model fragments. Each of the three scenarios satisfies the constraints and conditions for the model fragment shown in Figure 4, so that model fragment is instantiated. Since one of the participants of the model fragment is a vector sum, that vector sum is calculated and represented with resultant force arrow. Once the model fragment is instantiated, its consequences are inferred and the magnitude of the net force on the stump now has a causal relationship with the length of the resultant force arrow.

Next, differential qualitative analysis begins by attempting to find differences in the net force between the three scenarios. Recall that there are four strategies for determining the dqValue of a quantity: via numerical values, visual quantities, ordinal relationships, and causal influences. The problem does not provide numerical values or ordinal relationships for the net forces, so those strategies do not succeed. Even though a resultant force arrow has been drawn, there is no numerical value associated with it, so finding a dqValue via visual quantities does not succeed either. The algorithm attempts to find differences in causal antecedents to the net force and finds one of those antecedents is the length of the resultant force arrow. DQA begins again, except this time the goal quantity is the length of the resultant force arrow. This can be measured visually, and it is found that B has the longest resultant force arrow. Since there is a positive indirect influence (qprop) between the length of the resultant arrow and the magnitude of the net force, B is consequently found to have the largest net force. This is an example of a problem that is ultimately solved using some kind of visual analysis or computation.

The problem shown in the upper portion of Figure 3, which shows a scaffold hanging by two ropes, also uses visual analysis, both in understanding the scenario before and after formulating a causal model. A model fragment describing a hanging system at mechanical equilibrium is used to solve that problem. One of the requirements of that model fragment is determining which objects are supported by the system. The fact that the scaffold hangs from the ropes is given explicitly to CogSketch via a relation arrow. Using that given information, spatial information from CogSketch, and force propagation rules in qualitative mechanics, our algorithm determines which objects are supported by the system (i.e. the two people and the scaffold itself). This characterization of the scenario enables a model fragment to be used for further inference. One of the inferences is that the tensions in the ropes are negatively influenced (via negative qualitative proportionality) by their distance to the center of mass of the whole hanging system. Using the same causal reasoning as in the previous problem, the algorithm finds that the center of mass is closest to the left rope in scenario C, and that is therefore the scenario with the greatest tension in the left rope.

4   Analysis of Problems

Using the approach described above, our system was able to solve all 12 ranking problems. Out of the 12 that were solved, 10 required spatial reasoning of some kind to solve the problem, such as a distance calculation between two objects or major axis detection.

Table 1. Summary of ranking problems and the spatial reasoning required to find a difference between the goal quantities in the scenarios

Problem Category	N	Solved	Spatial Computation Required
Vector Addition	6	6	Major axis detection
			Parallelogram rule for vector addition
			Arrow interpretation
			Arrow length
Gravity	2	2	N/A
Tension	4	4	Distance
			Approximate center of mass

In addition to the spatial computations listed in Table 1, qualitative spatial relations played an important role in the initial understanding of the sketch, before a causal model is even formulated. Surface contact detection, for example, is used by qualitative mechanics to determine how forces transfer between objects. Spatial information is also used to guide the comparison process via analogy because it shapes how items are aligned to each other.

The problems that were not analyzed in this experiment required domain models that have not yet been implemented. This includes models of friction and models that make explicit inferences over scenarios that span multiple qualitative states. For instance, problems that require estimating the velocity of an object after a certain period of time cannot be solved by our system currently. However, we plan on using other representations (e.g. encapsulated histories [19]) to capture these types of problems.

5   Related Work

Our work is very closely related to work on everyday phyiscal reasoning problems [22]. However, while Klenk and colleagues used case-based reasoning to infer causal models of physical scenarios, our work uses a first-principles approach to model formulation. It is likely that both approaches to model formulation would be needed to develop a system with robust qualtiative physics problem solving capabilities.

Many other systems have been developed to solve physics problems, but only some of them use spatial reasoning in the problem solving process. BEATRIX [23] and Figure Understanterder [24] used information from text and diagrams, but the diagrams were created with graphical diagram tools and are therefore not subject to the same qualitative spatial reasoning requirements of hand-drawn sketches. Work by Lockwood et al. [25] answered questions about information learned from a combination of text and sketches, but comparative analyses were not explored.

In the field of intelligent tutoring systems, Atlas-Andes and AutoTutor [26-28] incorporate diagrams to help students but they are not spatially analyzed by the software to solve problems. Given the integration of qualitative and quantitative information demonstrated in this paper, it is possible to accommodate both types of representations in general problem solving and models of student problem solving.

6   Conclusion and Future Work

In this paper we have shown that CogSketch's visual and spatial representations and reasoning, combined with QP theory and Differential Qualitative Analysis, can be used to solve diagrammatic ranking problems from a popular physics textbook. Out of the 12 problems examined and solved, 10 could not be solved without spatial reasoning of some kind.

One of the challenges with creating these representations is delineating spatial and conceptual knowledge. All problems assume some level of common sense knowledge. Since we are using knowledge base contents derived from OpenCyc, there is a wealth of potentially relevant material avaiable, but determining what concepts are relevant for a particular scenario is difficult. For example, there are concepts that help formalize the notion that a scaffold *hangs from* two ropes or that a plane *moves with* the wind, which we sketched as relationship arrows. However, we are currently working on models of cords and strings (and other flexible objects) that will be able to automatically infer that something hangs from something else based purely on visual and conceptual reasoning. This would reduce the amount of extra knowledge that is manually given in our sketches.

Another important consideration is the level of detail in model fragment types. Model fragment types should be as general as possible to reduce the number of new models needed for new problems. For example, all four tension problems were solved with the same model of hanging systems at equilibrium. This indicates that the model is general enough to handle different situations, yet it is likely that it will need to be extended to handle more complex hanging systems (e.g. pulleys, three or more tensile objects).

The problems that have not yet been solved by the system indicate other areas for future work. A fuller domain theory of conceptual physics is needed to model many other topics and other aspects of qualitative reasoning (i.e. encapsulated histories, limit analysis) will be needed to address problems that span multiple qualitative states [19, 29, 30].

These results add to the evidence that spatial reasoning is an important factor in physics problem solving and physics instruction. Notably, the spatial reasoning requirements appear to be greater in these qualitative, conceptual problems, which has implications for tutoring systems that aim to improve conceptual physics understanding. It is therefore important to continue to develop systems that can integrate spatial information into problem solving strategies in STEM domains.

Acknowledgements. This work was supported by the Spatial Intelligence and Learning Center (SILC), an NSF Science of Learning Center (Award Number SBE-1041707).

References

1. Tversky, B.: What do sketches say about thinking. In: 2002 AAAI Spring Symposium, Sketch Understanding Workshop, Stanford University, AAAI Technical Report SS-02-08, pp. 148–151 (2002)
2. Larkin, J.H., Simon, H.A.: Why a diagram is (sometimes) worth ten thousand words. Cognitive Science 11, 65–100 (1987)
3. Suwa, M., Tversky, B., Gero, J., Purcell, T.: Seeing into sketches: Regrouping parts encourages new interpretations. In: Gero, J., Tversky, B., Purcell, T. (eds.) Visual and Spatial Reasoning in Design II, University of Sydney, Sydney, pp. 207–219 (2001)
4. Ainsworth, S., Prain, V., Tytler, R.: Drawing to learn in science. Science 3, 5 (2011)
5. Wai, J., Lubinski, D., Benbow, C.P.: Spatial ability for STEM domains: Aligning over 50 years of cumulative psychological knowledge solidifies its importance. Journal of Educational Psychology 101, 817 (2009)
6. Chaudhri, V.K., Clark, P.E., Mishra, S., Pacheco, J., Spaulding, A.: Aura: Capturing knowledge and answering questions on science textbooks (2009),
   http://www.ai.sri.com/pubs/files/1768.pdf
7. Hestenes, D., Wells, M., Swackhamer, G.: Force concept inventory. The Physics Teacher 30, 141 (1992)
8. Hewitt, P.: Conceptual Physics. Pearson-Addison Wesley, Boston (2010)
9. Forbus, K., Usher, J., Lovett, A., Lockwood, K., Wetzel, J.: Cogsketch: Sketch understanding for cognitive science research and for education. Topics in Cognitive Science 3, 648–666 (2011)
10. Cohn, A.G., Bennett, B., Gooday, J., Gotts, N.M.: Qualitative spatial representation and reasoning with the region connection calculus. Geoinformatica 1, 275–316 (1997)

11. Lovett, A., Kandaswamy, S., McLure, M., Forbus, K.: Evaluating Qualitative Models of Shape Representation. In: 26th International Workshop on Qualitative Reasoning (2012)
12. Falkenhainer, B., Forbus, K.D., Gentner, D.: The structure-mapping engine: Algorithm and examples. Artificial intelligence 41,1–63 (1989)
13. Yin, P., Forbus, K.D., Usher, J.M., Sageman, B., Jee, B.D.: Sketch Worksheets: A Sketch-Based Educational Software System. In: Innovative Applications of Artificial Intelligence, IAAI (2010)
14. Wetzel, J., Forbus, K.: Integrating Open-Domain Sketch Understanding with Qualitative Two-Dimensional Rigid-Body Mechanics. In: Proceedings of the 22nd International Workshop on Qualitative Reasoning (2008)
15. Kim, H.: Qualitative reasoning about fluids and mechanics. Ph.D. dissertation and ILS Technical Report, Northwestern University, Evanston, IL (1993)
16. Nielson, P.E.: A qualitative approach to rigid body mechanics. Tech. Rep. No. UIUCDCS-R-88-1469; UILU-ENG-88-1775, University of Illinois at Urbana-Champaign, Department of Computer Science (1988)
17. Forbus, K.D.: Qualitative process theory. Artificial intelligence 24, 85–168 (1984)
18. Friedman, S.E., Forbus, K.D.: Repairing incorrect knowledge with model formulation and metareasoning. In: Proceedings of the Twenty-Second International Joint Conference on Artificial Intelligence, pp. 887–893 (2011)
19. Klenk, M., Forbus, K.: Analogical model formulation for transfer learning in AP Physics. Artificial intelligence 173, 1615–1638 (2009)
20. Weld, D.S.: Comparative analysis. Artificial intelligence 36, 333–373 (1988)
21. Chang, M.D., Wetzel, J., Forbus, K.D.: Qualitative and Quantitative Reasoning over Physics Textbook Diagrams. In: 25th International Workshop on Qualitative Reasoning (2011)
22. Klenk, M., Forbus, K.D., Tomai, E., Kim, H., Kyckelhahn, B.: Solving everyday physical reasoning problems by analogy using sketches. In: AAAI, p. 209 (2005)
23. Novak, G.S., Bulko, W.C.: Understanding Natural Language with Diagrams. In: AAAI, pp. 465–470 (1990)
24. Rajagopalan, R.: Picture semantics for integrating text and diagram input. Artificial intelligence Review 10, 321–344 (1996)
25. Lockwood, K., Forbus, K.: Multimodal knowledge capture from text and diagrams. In: Fifth International Conference on Knowledge Capture, pp. 65–72. ACM (2009)
26. Graesser, A.C., Chipman, P., Haynes, B.C., Olney, A.: AutoTutor: An intelligent tutoring system with mixed-initiative dialogue. IEEE Transactions on Education 48, 612–618 (2005)
27. VanLehn, K., Jordan, P.W., Penstein Rosé, C., Bhembe, D., Böttner, M., Gaydos, A., Makatchev, M., Pappuswamy, U., Ringenberg, M.A., Roque, A.C., Siler, S., Srivastava, R.: The architecture of why2-atlas: A coach for qualitative physics essay writing. In: Cerri, S.A., Gouardéres, G., Paraguaçu, F. (eds.) ITS 2002. LNCS, vol. 2363, pp. 158–167. Springer, Heidelberg (2002)
28. VanLehn, K., Lynch, C., Schulze, K., Shapiro, J.A., Shelby, R., Taylor, L., Treacy, D., Weinstein, A., Wintersgill, M.: The Andes physics tutoring system: Five years of evaluations. In: 12th International Conference on Artificial Intelligence in Education, pp. 678–685. IOS Press (2005)
29. Klenk, M., Forbus, K.: Exploiting persistent mappings in cross-domain analogical learning of physical domains. Artificial Intelligence 195, 398–417 (2013)
30. Pisan, Y.: An Integrated Architecture for Engineering Problem Solving. Doctoral Dissertation, Northwestern University, Evanston, IL. UMI No. 733042431 (1998)

Dimensions of Uncertainty
in Evidential Grid Maps

Thomas Reineking and Joachim Clemens

Cognitive Neuroinformatics, University of Bremen, Germany
{reineking,clemens}@uni-bremen.de

Abstract. We show how a SLAM algorithm based on belief function theory can produce evidential occupancy grid maps that provide a mobile robot with additional information about its environment. While uncertainty in probabilistic grid maps is usually measured by entropy, we show that for evidential grid maps, uncertainty can be expressed in a three-dimensional space and we propose appropriate measures for quantifying uncertainty in these different dimensions. We analyze these measures in a practical mapping example containing typical sources of uncertainty for SLAM. As a result of the evidential representation, the robot is able to distinguish between different sources of uncertainty (e.g., a lack of measurements vs. conflicting measurements) which are indistinguishable in the probabilistic framework.

1 Introduction

In order to generate a spatial representation of an environment, a mobile robot needs to solve the problem of simultaneous localization and mapping (SLAM) [5]. Occupancy grid maps are a popular type of spatial representation for SLAM and discretize the environment using a grid structure where each grid cell is either occupied or empty (denoted by o and e) [6]. Usually, the state of a grid cell is modeled probabilistically with a single probability $P(o)$. The problem of this approach is that different states of belief are mapped to the same probability distribution. For example, a uniform probability distribution can represent a complete lack of measurements just as it can represent conflicting measurements. In this paper, we show that the uncertainty in occupancy grid maps has multiple dimensions that cannot be uniquely captured by a probabilistic representation. Instead, we propose to model grid maps using belief functions in order to make these different dimensions explicit.

Belief function theory [19,22] (also called Dempster-Shafer theory or evidence theory) can be viewed as a generalization of Bayesian probability theory. For belief functions, probability mass is not just assigned to the singletons of a domain (here o and e) but to all subsets of the domain (including $\{o, e\}$ and $\emptyset$). While a probability function can only capture the ratio between $P(o)$ and $P(e)$, a belief function can additionally make a lack of evidence explicit by the mass assigned to the disjunction $\{o, e\}$ and it can make conflicting evidence explicit by the mass assigned to $\emptyset$. As a result, belief functions are able to represent different

C. Freksa et al. (Eds.): Spatial Cognition 2014, LNAI 8684, pp. 283–298, 2014.

types of uncertainty and therefore enable the robot to distinguish belief states that are indistinguishable using a probabilistic model.

There are a number of works in which belief functions are used to model the uncertainty in occupancy grid maps [14,17]. The additional parameters provided by evidential grid maps have been used to solve problems like assessing the quality of maps [1] and detecting moving objects [13]. However, all of these works have in common that they do not consider the joint estimation problem underlying SLAM and only consider the mapping part (by assuming perfect localization information). In this case, the localization error, which is the major source of uncertainty for SLAM, is entirely ignored. In contrast, in [16] we described how SLAM can be modeled in the belief function framework. The resulting algorithm produces evidential grid maps that reflect the full uncertainty associated with SLAM, including localization uncertainty. The major contribution in this paper is an analysis of the different types of uncertainty in the evidential grid maps produced by the algorithm, both on a theoretical as well as on an empirical level.

The remainder of this paper is structured as follows. In Sect. 2, the belief function formalism is briefly introduced. The evidential SLAM approach based on this formalism is presented in Sect. 3 along with evidential sensor models for laser scanners. The different dimensions of uncertainty are analyzed theoretically in Sect. 4 and corresponding measures are proposed. Practical examples of the different types of uncertainty in generated grid maps are presented in Sect. 5. The paper concludes with a discussion in Sect. 6.

2 Belief Function Theory

The term "belief function" is a general term which can refer to several equivalent representations. The most fundamental belief representation is a *mass function*. A mass function m is a mapping $m : \mathcal{P}(\Theta) \to [0,1]$ with

$$\sum_{X \subseteq \Theta} m(X) = 1, \tag{1}$$

where $\mathcal{P}(\Theta)$ is the power set of the (usually finite) domain Θ. The value $m(X)$ is the amount of belief strictly committed to set X. A mass assignment to a set X represents complete ignorance about the belief distribution over subsets of X. If a mass function satisfies $m(\emptyset) = 0$, it is called *normalized*. If it also satisfies $\sum_{x \in \Theta} m(x) = 1$, it is called *Bayesian* (it then simply represents a probability function).

A *plausibility function* pl expresses how much belief mass potentially supports a set X. It is therefore sometimes interpreted as an upper probability bound. The plausibility $pl(X)$ of $X \subseteq \Theta$ can be directly derived from the corresponding mass function m and is defined as

$$pl(X) = \sum_{Y \subseteq \Theta, Y \cap X \neq \emptyset} m(Y) \tag{2}$$

with $pl(\emptyset) = 0$.

Like probability functions, belief functions can be conditional. This is written as $m[Y](X)$, which means "the mass of set X given set Y" (note that the order is different from the usual conditional probability notation $P(X|Y)$).

For inference, each piece of evidence (e.g., a sensor measurement) is represented by a separate belief function and these belief functions are then successively combined in order to fuse the underlying evidence. The combination is usually performed using the *conjunctive rule* (also referred to as *Dempster's rule* if mass assignments to $\emptyset$ are not desired). Let e_1 and e_2 denote distinct pieces of evidence and let $m[e_1]$ and $m[e_2]$ denote the mass functions defined over the same domain Θ which are induced by the respective pieces of evidence. The mass function $m[e_1, e_2]$ resulting from the combination using the conjunctive rule $\textcircled{\cap}$ is defined as

$$m[e_1, e_2](X) = \sum_{Y \cap Z = X} m[e_1](Y) \, m[e_2](Z), \quad \forall X \subseteq \Theta. \tag{3}$$

3 Evidential FastSLAM

The evidential SLAM algorithm proposed in [16] uses a Rao-Blackwellized particle filter [3] to approximate the joint belief distribution of the map and the robot's path. It therefore constitutes a generalization of the well-known FastSLAM algorithm [12]. Let $x_{0:t} = x_0, \ldots, x_t$ denote the sequence of robot poses over time and let Y denote the map. The aim for evidential SLAM is to compute the joint belief distribution $m[z_{0:t}, u_{1:t}](x_{0:t}, Y)$ where $z_{0:t}$ is the sequence of measurements recorded over time and $u_{1:t}$ is the sequence of robot controls describing pose changes. In order to make computing this joint distribution feasible, it is assumed that the marginal distribution over the path is a probability density function. In this case, the joint belief distribution can be factorized into a probabilistic path component and a conditional evidential map component:

$$m[z_{0:t}, u_{1:t}](x_{0:t}, Y) = p(x_{0:t}|z_{0:t}, u_{1:t}) \, m[x_{0:t}, z_{0:t}](Y). \tag{4}$$

This factorization corresponds to a generalized version of the product rule for probabilities, a proof of which is provided in [15]. The next two subsections describe how the path distribution $p(x_{0:t}|z_{0:t}, u_{1:t})$ and the conditional map distribution $m[x_{0:t}, z_{0:t}](Y)$ can be computed. In Sect. 3.3, the resulting particle filter algorithm is presented and, in Sect. 3.4, evidential sensor models for laser scanners are presented.

3.1 Localization

Because the path distribution is modeled probabilistically, computing it is similar to classical Markov localization [27] where pose changes are modeled in a prediction step and measurements are incorporated in a correction step. In the prediction step, the motion model $p(x_t|x_{t-1}, u_t)$ is applied to the prior distribution $p(x_{0:t-1}|z_{0:t-1}, u_{1:t-1})$ from time $t-1$ in order to compute the proposal distribution $p(x_{0:t}|z_{0:t-1}, u_{1:t})$ at time t, which is given by

$$p(x_{0:t}|z_{0:t-1}, u_{1:t}) = p(x_t|x_{t-1}, u_t)\, p(x_{0:t-1}|z_{0:t-1}, u_{1:t-1}). \tag{5}$$

In the correction step, the posterior $p(x_{0:t}|z_{0:t}, u_{1:t})$ is computed from the proposal distribution and the measurement likelihood using the generalized Bayesian theorem [23]. Though the prior and posterior for the path are assumed to be probability distributions, the likelihood can be a general belief function [15], in this case the plausibility $pl[x_{0:t}, z_{0:t-1}](z_t)$:

$$p(x_{0:t}|z_{0:t}, u_{1:t}) \propto pl[x_{0:t}, z_{0:t-1}](z_t)\, p(x_{0:t}|z_{0:t-1}, u_{1:t}). \tag{6}$$

The likelihood $pl[x_{0:t}, z_{0:t-1}](z_t)$ depends on the entire history of measurements and states. In order to avoid this problem, we condition the likelihood on the estimated map Y with

$$pl[x_{0:t}, z_{0:t-1}](z_t) = \sum_{Y \subseteq \Theta_Y^M} pl[x_t, Y](z_t)\, m[x_{0:t-1}, z_{0:t-1}](Y), \tag{7}$$

where Θ_Y^M denotes the map space (defined below). Here, $pl[x_t, Y](z_t)$ represents the *forward sensor model* and $m[x_{0:t-1}, z_{0:t-1}](Y)$ represents the map belief at time $t - 1$. The sum over the power set of the map space in (7) may appear intractable but, as shown in [16], by making appropriate independence assumptions, the likelihood can be efficiently computed with time complexity proportional to the number of grid cells.

3.2   Grid Mapping

The power of the original FastSLAM algorithm lies in the fact that cells in the map become approximately independent if conditioned on the robot's path $x_{0:t}$. The same principle is exploited in the evidential FastSLAM algorithm. Let Y_i denote the evidential variable representing the i-th grid cell with $Y_i \subseteq \Theta_Y = \{o, e\}$ and $1 \leq i \leq M$ where M denotes the total number of grid cells. The entire map Y is then a subset of the product space with $Y \subseteq \Theta_Y^M$. The joint distribution over all cells can be factorized into marginal cell distributions:

$$m[x_{0:t}, z_{0:t}](Y) = \prod_{i=1}^{M} m[x_{0:t}, z_{0:t}](Y_i). \tag{8}$$

In this case, each cell can be updated independently over time. This is done by combining the prior cell belief $m[x_{0:t-1}, z_{0:t-1}](Y_i)$ at time $t - 1$ with the cell belief $m[x_t, z_t](Y_i)$ induced by the current measurement z_t using the conjunctive rule:

$$m[x_{0:t}, z_{0:t}](Y_i = \cdot) = m[x_{0:t-1}, z_{0:t-1}](Y_i = \cdot) \ⓞ\ m[x_t, z_t](Y_i = \cdot). \tag{9}$$

Here, $m[x_t, z_t](Y_i)$ represents the *inverse sensor model*. The initial belief $m(Y_i)$ at time $t = 0$ is assumed to be vacuous with $m(Y_i = \Theta_Y) = 1$, $1 \leq i \leq M$ (unless there is prior knowledge indicating otherwise). This expresses the total lack of evidence at the beginning and differs from a probabilistic model where the initial distribution is usually assumed to be uniform.

3.3   Algorithm

The algorithm for approximating the joint distribution in (4) is very similar to the original FastSLAM algorithm. It is based on a Rao-Blackwellized particle filter where each particle represents a complete path and a corresponding map belief function. This means, at time t, the k-th particle is a tuple $(x_{0:t}^{[k]}, m[x_{0:t}^{[k]}, z_{0:t}](Y))$. Like in most probabilistic particle filters, measurements are incorporated using importance sampling. The set of particles is updated recursively over time by repeatedly applying the following four steps in order to obtain the particle set at time t from the particle set at time $t-1$.

1. Prediction step: Sample a new pose $x_t^{[k]}$ from the motion model $p(x_t|x_{t-1}^{[k]}, u_t)$ for each particle in order to incorporate control u_t and update the robot's path $x_{0:t}^{[k]}$ as defined by (5).
2. Correction step: Compute importance weight $w_t^{[k]} = pl[x_{0:t}^{[k]}, z_{0:t-1}](z_t)$ for each particle using the forward sensor model $pl[x_t^{[k]}, Y](z_t)$ and the current map belief $m[x_{0:t-1}^{[k]}, z_{0:t-1}](Y)$ as defined by (7).
3. Map update: Update the current map belief $m[x_{0:t-1}^{[k]}, z_{0:t-1}](Y)$ of each particle using the inverse sensor model $m[x_t^{[k]}, z_t](Y)$ and the conjunctive rule of combination.
4. Resampling: Resample particles with probability proportional to the importance weights. This results in a particle set representing the joint path/map distribution $m[z_{0:t}, u_{1:t}](x_{0:t}, Y)$ reflecting all measurements and controls up to time t.[1]

The time complexity of the algorithm is $O(KM)$ (K denotes the number of particles) assuming the complexity of the sensor models is $O(M)$. The overall complexity is thus identical to that of classical FastSLAM aside from a constant overhead caused by the fact that, for each cell, three parameters need to be updated instead of one.

3.4   Sensor Models

For the SLAM algorithm described above, an evidential forward sensor model $pl[x_t, Y](z_t)$ and a corresponding inverse sensor model $m[x_t, z_t](Y)$ need to be specified. In this paper, we focus on laser scanners where $z_t = (z_{t;1}, \ldots, z_{t;N})^T$ is a vector of range measurements for different angles. The models considered here are adaptations of the evidential sonar models presented in [16] (the main difference is that a laser beam is much narrower than the measurement cone of a sonar sensor). Because the resulting equations are quite complex, they are omitted here and the interested reader is encouraged to refer to the original paper.

---

[1] The resampling step is only performed if the importance weights diverge too much, otherwise the importance weights are maintained over time in order to minimize sampling errors [4].

Examples of the forward and inverse sensor models for a single laser beam are shown in Fig. 1. The forward sensor model computes the plausibility of a single range measurement $z_{t;j}$ given the current state x_t and the evidential map Y. The forward model captures both noisiness and complete randomness of measurements. In order to make computing it tractable, the simplifying assumption is made that a laser beam always hits the closest occupied cell located along the beam's path. For cells representing the disjunctive state Θ_Y, the measurement plausibility is maximal but the plausibility of measuring more distant obstacles is not reduced because Θ_Y also includes the possibility that the cell is empty. The plausibility $pl[x_t, Y](z_t)$ of the entire vector z_t is simply defined as the product of the individual range measurement plausibilities $pl[x_t, Y](z_{t;j})$.

The inverse sensor model provides the robot with a belief distribution representing a "local map" obtained from a single range measurement $z_{t;j}$. A number of evidential inverse models have been proposed in the literature over time, e.g., [29,7]. All these works ignore the forward model and directly specify the inverse model, usually in a heuristic manner. In contrast, the inverse sensor model here is directly derived from the forward sensor model using the generalized Bayesian theorem. It thus reflects all the parameters of the forward sensor model. The inverse model for the entire measurement vector z_t results from combining the belief functions corresponding to the individual range measurements $z_{t;j}$ using Dempster's rule. The time complexity of evaluating both the forward and the inverse sensor model is proportional to the number of cells that intersect with the laser beams, and evaluating the models is quite fast in practice.

4   Dimensions of Uncertainty

In this section, we analyze the different dimensions of uncertainty in evidential grid maps on a theoretical level. In particular, we show how the different dimensions of uncertainty can be measured and we compare them to the Bayesian notion of uncertainty. To compare evidential and probabilistic grid maps, the question of how one representation relates to the other first needs to be addressed. In belief function theory, there is a simple operation called the "pignistic transformation" for projecting a belief function onto a probability function [24]. Usually, the pignistic transformation is applied in the context of decision making based on belief functions but, here, it is used to analyze the Bayesian uncertainty of an evidential grid map. The pignistic transformation for a cell is defined as

$$P(o) = \frac{m(o) + \frac{1}{2}m(\Theta_Y)}{1 - m(\emptyset)}. \tag{10}$$

The mass assigned to Θ_Y is split up and evenly distributed over o and e. In addition, normalization is performed to remove the mass on $\emptyset$.

In case of probabilistic grid maps, uncertainty can be measured using Shannon entropy [20], which is defined as

$$H(P) = -\sum_{x \in \Theta} P(x) \log_2 P(x). \tag{11}$$

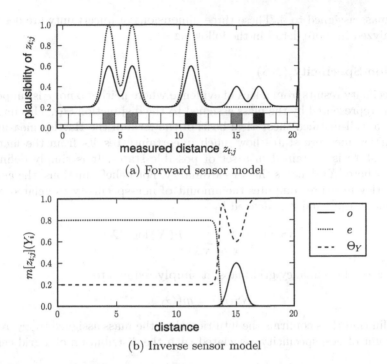

Fig. 1. Evidential sensor models for a laser scanner. The squares at the bottom in (a) represent the grid cells of a 1D map: white means e, black means o, and gray means Θ_Y. The dotted line in (a) represents the forward sensor model for a given map Y (without uncertainty) while the solid line represents the forward sensor model conditioned on an uncertain map (in the latter case, mass 0.5 is assigned to e for each of the black and gray cells). Fig. (b) shows the inverse sensor model for a measurement of $z_t = 15$. Note that the noise parameter in these examples is higher compared to the laser scanner considered in Sect. 5 in order to obtain a better visualization. (Figures adopted from [16].)

This measure of uncertainty yields 1 for a uniform cell distribution and it yields 0 if a cell is known with certainty to be either occupied or empty. In contrast, belief functions contain multiple dimensions of uncertainty and thus require multiple measures of uncertainty [10]. The two main dimensions are referred to as *non-specificity* and *conflict*. Non-specificity results from the fact that mass can be assigned to arbitrary non-singleton subsets of the domain where set cardinality represents a form of uncertainty (here, $|\Theta_Y| = 2$). Conflict corresponds more to the classical notion of entropy and reflects the uncertainty resulting from mass assigned to mutually exclusive states (o and e in this case). Because we are considering unnormalized mass functions with $m(\emptyset) \geq 0$, we further distinguish between what we call *internal conflict* and *external conflict*. While internal conflict represents the aforementioned entropy-like uncertainty associated with the masses assigned to o and e, external conflict represents how strongly the evidence underlying a belief function contradicts each other, which is represented by the mass assigned to $\emptyset$. These three dimensions of uncertainty are described and analyzed in more detail in the following.

4.1 Non-Specificity (NS)

Non-specificity results from a lack of evidence where neither o nor e is supported. It is thus represented by the mass assigned to the disjunction Θ_Y. This intuition also has a well-justified theoretical basis in the form of the Hartley measure [8]. The Hartley measure states how much uncertainty results from the fact that the true state is contained in a set of possible states. It is simply defined as $\log_2 |X|$ where $|X|$ denotes the set cardinality. For belief functions, the generalized Hartley measure computes the amount of non-specificity associated with a mass function [9], and it is defined by

$$NS(m) = \sum_{X \subseteq \Theta, X \neq \emptyset} m(X) \log_2 |X|. \tag{12}$$

For the case of occupancy grid maps, it simply reduces to

$$NS(m) = m(\Theta_Y). \tag{13}$$

This definition thus confirms the intuition that the mass assigned to Θ_Y reflects the amount of non-specificity associated with the distribution of a grid cell.

4.2 Internal Conflict (IC)

The internal conflict essentially describes the relation between $m(o)$ and $m(e)$. Like Shannon entropy, it reaches its maximum if $m(o)$ and $m(e)$ are equal and it becomes 0 in case either $m(o)$ or $m(e)$ is 0. We refer to this dimension as "internal" because, other than the external conflict which results from combining multiple belief functions, internal conflict is a property of a single belief function. In order to quantify it, we use the measure of dissonance proposed in [28].[2] It is defined as

$$Dis(m) = -\sum_{X \subseteq \Theta} m(X) \log_2 pl(X). \tag{14}$$

Because the measure of dissonance can only handle normalized belief functions, we first perform normalization before computing the measure. The result is then scaled with $1 - m(\emptyset)$, which also ensures that the measure does not exhibit a discontinuity at $m(\emptyset) = 1$:

$$IC(m) = -(1 - m(\emptyset))(m'(o) \log_2 pl'(o) + m'(e) \log_2 pl'(e)), \tag{15}$$

$$m'(X) = \begin{cases} \frac{m(X)}{1-m(\emptyset)} & \text{if } X \neq \emptyset \\ 0 & \text{if } X = \emptyset \end{cases}. \tag{16}$$

---

[2] Despite a long history of research, none of the measures proposed over time satisfy all the properties required of a general measure of internal conflict [9]. However, the limitation of the dissonance measure (violation of subadditivity for joint spaces) can be ignored here because we do not consider the internal conflict over joint spaces.

Here, m' and pl' denote the normalized mass and plausibility functions. Note that the internal conflict measure reduces to classical Shannon entropy in case of a Bayesian belief function.

4.3 External Conflict (EC)

The external conflict measures the conflict resulting from combining different measurements over time. The more these measurements contradict each other regarding the state of a cell, the higher the external conflict. The external conflict is represented by the mass assigned to $\emptyset$. Such an assignment to $\emptyset$ can also be interpreted as an open-world assumption where the true state is not captured by the set of possible states [21] (e.g., a cell is neither completely occupied nor completely empty but something in between).

Analogously to non-specificity, one possibility to measure external conflict would simply be to consider the mass assigned to $\emptyset$. However, this value quickly approaches 1 if sufficiently many measurements are combined where each measurement induces a small amount of external conflict. Instead, it is more useful to consider a logarithmic measure which makes it possible to differentiate between small differences of mass values assigned to $\emptyset$. Here, we use the *weight of conflict* proposed in [19], which is defined as

$$Con(m_1, \ldots, m_n) = -\log_2 \left(1 - \sum_{X_1 \cap \ldots \cap X_n = \emptyset} m_1(X_1) \cdot \ldots \cdot m_n(X_n) \right). \quad (17)$$

This measure states how strongly multiple belief functions $m_1, \ldots, m_n$ contradict each other if combined conjunctively. Because the conflict associated with combinations is represented by $m(\emptyset)$, the weight of conflict can be used as a measure of external conflict:

$$EC(m) = -\log_2(1 - m(\emptyset)). \quad (18)$$

4.4 Comparison

In Fig. 2, each of the proposed measures is plotted in relation to the underlying mass function. While non-specificity and internal conflict are classical dimensions of uncertainty for belief functions, the role of external conflict is a somewhat different one. A mathematical difference is obvious because NS and IC are bounded by 1 while the EC measure goes to infinity if $m(\emptyset)$ goes to 1. But the difference is also a conceptual one. Typically, belief functions representing a single piece of evidence (e.g., a single measurement) do not exhibit external conflict (i.e., $m(\emptyset) = 0$) and, only as a result of combination with other belief functions, external conflict is created. Therefore, external conflict does not describe a property of a single piece of evidence but rather describes a property of the combination process. This is also reflected by the fact that external conflict

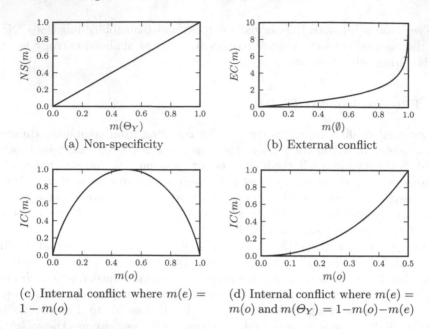

Fig. 2. Measures for different dimensions of uncertainty. The internal conflict shown in (c) and (d) is actually a function of three parameters and can therefore not be visualized in its entirety. Instead, (c) shows the IC for a Bayesian belief function, in which case it is identical to entropy. In (d), the IC is shown for the case where $m(e) = m(o)$ and where the remaining mass is assigned to Θ_Y.

grows monotonically with additional combinations. In this regard, external conflict represents a kind of "meta uncertainty" indicating whether the underlying evidence is in agreement or not.

A comparison of the evidential dimensions of uncertainty with the Bayesian notion of entropy is shown in Fig. 3. Here, several prototypical belief states are plotted in the 2D uncertainty space defined by non-specificity and internal conflict, which are then projected to the 1D uncertainty space corresponding to entropy. External conflict is ignored in these examples because entropy is invariant with respect to this dimension. It can be seen that a state of maximum non-specificity $(m(\Theta_Y) = 1)$ has the same entropy like a state of maximum internal conflict $(m(o) = m(e) = 0.5)$ when mapped to a probability function using (10). Thus, very different evidential belief states are mapped to the same entropy values, showing the ambiguity of the Bayesian representation.

5   Grid Mapping Example

This section describes a practical mapping example where different types of uncertainty are represented by an evidential grid map. The example is based on a run of a simulated mobile robot equipped with a laser scanner exploring a virtual

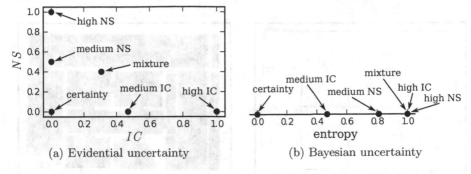

(a) Evidential uncertainty   (b) Bayesian uncertainty

Fig. 3. Comparison of 2D evidential uncertainty (without EC) and 1D Bayesian uncertainty. The 2D points from (a) are projected to 1D points in (b).

2D environment.[3] The evidential SLAM algorithm presented in Sect. 3 was used to generate an evidential grid map by selecting the particle with the highest cumulative importance weight (using $K = 100$). This map, along with the ground truth and a probabilistic grid map obtained from the pignistic transformation, is shown in Fig. 4. The corresponding uncertainty measures are shown in Fig. 5.

What is directly noticeable is that the evidential uncertainty measures are sensitive to different types of uncertainty because they are maximal in different areas of the map. NS is high for areas where no or only few measurements have been recorded. IC and EC are high in the vicinity of obstacles due to measurement noise, although EC also indicates effects like localization errors and changes in the environment. In contrast, Shannon entropy appears to represent an "aggregate" measure of uncertainty where the different maxima of the evidential measures result in high entropy. In the following, the different causes of uncertainty in this example are analyzed in more detail.

Partial Exploration: The NS measure (i.e., the mass on Θ_Y) clearly shows which parts of the environment the robot has not fully explored yet. This is visible both for the room the robot did not enter as well as for the areas on the outside. For the probabilistic representation, this belief state is represented by a uniform distribution where entropy is maximal. However, entropy is also high in other parts of the map, making the uncertainty resulting from not having explored an area indistinguishable from the uncertainty resulting from other causes.

Measurement Noise: Measurement noise in the vicinity of obstacles results from both the noisiness of the sensor and from discretization errors caused by the grid-based representation. It is reflected by high values for the IC measure as well as for the EC measure. The difference between the two measures is

---

[3] For the simulation, the "Gridmap Navigation Simulator" was used, which is part of the Mobile Robot Programming Toolkit available at www.mrpt.org.

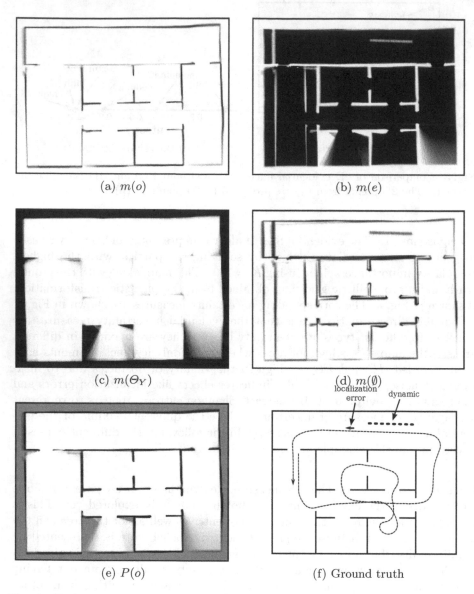

(a) $m(o)$

(b) $m(e)$

(c) $m(\Theta_Y)$

(d) $m(\emptyset)$

(e) $P(o)$

(f) Ground truth

Fig. 4. Grid map generated by the evidential FastSLAM algorithm. Plots (a) to (d) show the different mass components of the evidential grid map (black represents a mass value of one and white represents zero). The corresponding probabilistic grid map is shown in (e) while the ground truth, including the robot's path, is shown in (f). During the run, a localization error and dynamics in the environment were simulated at the indicated locations (the former by displacing the robot and the latter by simulating the presence of a moving object blocking some of the laser beams).

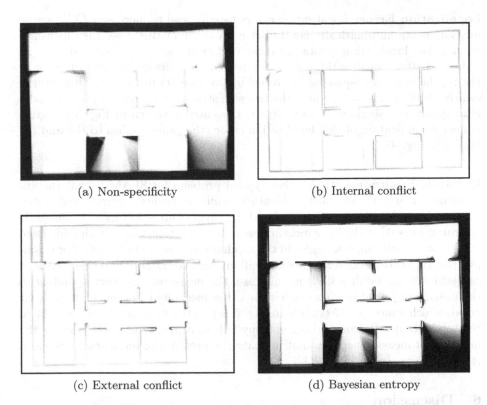

(a) Non-specificity

(b) Internal conflict

(c) External conflict

(d) Bayesian entropy

Fig. 5. Uncertainty measures corresponding to the map shown in Fig. 4. Note that the measures are scaled for improved visibility where a darker color indicates a higher value (the maximum in (a) and (d) is at 1, the maximum of (b) is at 0.34, and the maximum of (c) is at 7.58).

that IC responds most strongly if the underlying evidence is "balanced", e.g., if an equal number of measurements favors particular states (this also applies to entropy). In contrast, for a high EC value, it is sufficient that there is at least some contradictory evidence, even if the majority of evidence favors one state. In this regard, the EC measure can be interpreted as an "or-like" operation regarding the contradictory nature of the underlying evidence. In addition, both measures are sensitive to the number of measurements because EC grows with additional measurements if these contradict previous measurements at least by a small degree while the IC measure is scaled by the amount of mass assigned to $\emptyset$ (see (15)) and therefore tends to become smaller with more measurements. An example of this effect are the high EC values at the walls in the center hallway and at the lower wall of the top hallway caused by a large number of measurements where IC is relatively small. In contrast, in the lower right part of the map where few measurements were recorded, EC values are low and IC is high.

Localization Error: Localization errors usually lead to increased EC because measurements automatically contradict each other in this case. Like measurement noise, localization errors are most visible in the vicinity of obstacles. In order to better visualize this effect, we created an artificial localization error in the top hallway by displacing the robot by 2m (see (f) in Fig. 4). This error is clearly visible in Fig. 5 (c) where the two wall structures on the very left actually correspond to a single wall. In contrast, the entropy shown in Fig. 5 (d) gives almost no indication of this localization error (the same applies to (b) and (d) vs. (e) in Fig. 4).

Dynamic Environment: Another typical problem for SLAM is that the environment is usually assumed to be static while, in reality, environments often contain dynamic elements. We simulated the effect of an object moving alongside the robot by setting the laser measurements to a constant value (with additional noise) for a small range of angles in the top hallway (see (f) in Fig. 4). For example, this could correspond to a person walking next to the robot. While the robot can still reliably localize itself in this case, the measurements corresponding to the moving object clearly contradict the other measurements (current and past ones), which leads to EC (visible in Fig. 5 (c) as the gray line in the middle of the top hallway). By comparison, entropy fails to capture this effect because the majority of measurements do not indicate the presence of an obstacle (see also (b) and (d) vs. (e) in Fig. 4).

6   Discussion

In this paper, we have shown how a SLAM algorithm based on belief functions can produce evidential grid maps that provide a mobile robot with additional information about its environment. Compared to probabilistic grid maps, evidential grid maps contain multiple dimensions of uncertainty and we have proposed measures for quantifying uncertainty in these different dimensions. In a practical mapping example, we have illustrated how different causes of uncertainty can be distinguished in the multiple-dimensional uncertainty space corresponding to belief functions whereas they are indistinguishable in case of a probabilistic representation.

One interesting direction for future work would be the problem of fusing map information from different sources [11]. For probabilistic grid maps, map fusion is usually based on an absolute independence assumption [26], which can be quite problematic. In contrast, belief function theory could be of great value here due to the extensive work on different combination rules [18]. Another direction for future work that has not been considered in the context of evidential mapping is that of active information gathering. The idea of minimizing expected entropy [2,30] has been successfully applied in the past in order to make a robot drive to locations that reduce uncertainty about the environment [25], resulting in optimal exploration strategies. Using a multi-dimensional uncertainty representation, it becomes possible for the robot to discern different types of uncertainty during exploration. For example, high *NS* indicates that an area has not been explored and that moving to this area is likely to reduce overall uncertainty. High *IC* is likely to represent measurement uncertainty where the use of additional sensors may be necessary to further reduce uncertainty because previous measurements have been inconclusive. In contrast, the *EC* measure is able to capture "meta uncertainty" indicating that something is wrong (e.g., failed localization or a change in the environment). Overall, we belief that evidential representations are a valuable tool for modeling spatial uncertainty and that being able to distinguish between different types of uncertainty can provide a mobile robot with important information about its environment.

Acknowledgements. This work was supported by DFG (SFB/TR 8 Spatial Cognition, project "A5-[ActionSpace]") and DLR (projects "Enceladus Explorer" and "KaNaRiA").

References

1. Carlson, J., Murphy, R., Christopher, S., Casper, J.: Conflict metric as a measure of sensing quality. In: Proceedings of the 2005 IEEE International Conference on Robotics and Automation, pp. 2032–2039 (2005)
2. Cassandra, A.R., Kaelbling, L.P., Kurien, J.A.: Acting under uncertainty: Discrete bayesian models for mobile-robot navigation. In: Proceedings of the 1996 IEEE/RSJ International Conference on Intelligent Robots and Systems, IROS 1996, vol. 2, pp. 963–972. IEEE (1996)
3. Doucet, A., De Freitas, N., Murphy, K., Russell, S.: Rao-Blackwellised particle filtering for dynamic Bayesian networks. In: Proceedings of the Sixteenth Conference on Uncertainty in Artificial Intelligence, pp. 176–183 (2000)
4. Doucet, A., Godsill, S., Andrieu, C.: On sequential Monte Carlo sampling methods for Bayesian filtering. Statistics and Computing 10(3), 197–208 (2000)
5. Durrant-Whyte, H., Bailey, T.: Simultaneous localization and mapping: part i. IEEE Robotics & Automation Magazine 13(2), 99–110 (2006)
6. Elfes, A.: Using occupancy grids for mobile robot perception and navigation. Computer 22(6), 46–57 (1989)
7. Gambino, F., Ulivi, G., Vendittelli, M.: The transferable belief model in ultrasonic map building. In: Proceedings of the Sixth IEEE International Conference on Fuzzy Systems, vol. 1, pp. 601–608. IEEE (1997)
8. Hartley, R.V.L.: Transmission of information. The Bell Labs Technical Journal 7(3) (1928)
9. Klir, G.J.: Uncertainty and information: foundations of generalized information theory. Wiley (2005)
10. Klir, G.J., Smith, R.M.: On measuring uncertainty and uncertainty-based information: Recent developments. Annals of Mathematics and Artificial Intelligence 32(1-4), 5–33 (2001)
11. Kurdej, M., Moras, J., Cherfaoui, V., Bonnifait, P.: Controlling remanence in evidential grids using geodata for dynamic scene perception. International Journal of Approximate Reasoning 55(1, part 3), 355–375 (2014)

12. Montemerlo, M., Thrun, S., Koller, D., Wegbreit, B.: FastSLAM: A factored solution to the simultaneous localization and mapping problem. In: Proceedings of the National Conference on Artificial Intelligence, pp. 593–598 (2002)
13. Moras, J., Cherfaoui, V., Bonnifait, P.: Credibilist occupancy grids for vehicle perception in dynamic environments. In: 2011 IEEE International Conference on Robotics and Automation (ICRA), pp. 84–89 (May 2011)
14. Pagac, D., Nebot, E.M., Durrant-Whyte, H.: An evidential approach to map-building for autonomous vehicles. IEEE Transactions on Robotics and Automation 14(4), 623–629 (1998)
15. Reineking, T.: Belief Functions: Theory and Algorithms. Ph.D. thesis, University of Bremen (February 2014),
http://nbn-resolving.de/urn:nbn:de:gbv:46-00103727-16
16. Reineking, T., Clemens, J.: Evidential FastSLAM for grid mapping. In: 16th International Conference on Information Fusion (FUSION), pp. 789–796 (July 2013)
17. Ribo, M., Pinz, A.: A comparison of three uncertainty calculi for building sonar-based occupancy grids. Robotics and Autonomous Systems 35(3-4), 201–209 (2001)
18. Sentz, K., Ferson, S.: Combination of evidence in Dempster-Shafer theory. Tech. rep., Sandia National Laboratories (2002)
19. Shafer, G.: A Mathematical Theory of Evidence. Princeton University Press, Princeton (1976)
20. Shannon, C.E.: A mathematical theory of communication. The Bell System Technical Journal 27, 379–423 (1948)
21. Smets, P.: Belief functions. In: Smets, P., Mamdani, E.H., Dubois, D., Prade, H. (eds.) Non Standard Logics for Automated Reasoning, pp. 253–286. Academic Press, London (1988)
22. Smets, P., Kennes, R.: The transferable belief model. Artificial Intelligence 66, 191–234 (1994)
23. Smets, P.: Belief functions: The disjunctive rule of combination and the generalized Bayesian theorem. International Journal of Approximate Reasoning 9, 1–35 (1993)
24. Smets, P.: Decision making in the TBM: the necessity of the pignistic transformation. International Journal of Approximate Reasoning 38, 133–147 (2005)
25. Stachniss, C., Grisetti, G., Burgard, W.: Information gain-based exploration using rao-blackwellized particle filters. In: Robotics: Science and Systems, vol. 2 (2005)
26. Thrun, S., Burgard, W., Fox, D.: Probabilistic robotics. MIT Press, Cambridge (2005)
27. Thrun, S., Fox, D., Burgard, W., Dellaert, F.: Robust Monte Carlo localization for mobile robots. Artificial Intelligence 128(1-2), 99–141 (2001)
28. Yager, R.R.: Entropy and specificity in a mathematical theory of evidence. International Journal of General System 9(4), 249–260 (1983)
29. Yang, T., Aitken, V.: Evidential mapping for mobile robots with range sensors. IEEE Transactions on Instrumentation and Measurement 55(4), 1422–1429 (2006)
30. Zetzsche, C., Wolter, J., Schill, K.: Sensorimotor representation and knowledge-based reasoning for spatial exploration and localisation. Cognitive Processing 9, 283–297 (2008)

Crossing the Boundary

Two Benchmarks for Qualitative Spatial Reasoning Bridging Relative Directions and Mereotopology

André van Delden[1] and Reinhard Moratz[2]

[1] SFB/TR 8/R4 – [LogoSpace], University of Bremen, Germany
[2] University of Maine,
National Center for Geographic Information and Analysis,
School of Computing and Information Science,
Department of Spatial Information Science and Engineering,
348 Boardman Hall, Orono, 04469 Maine, USA

Abstract. A well known problem of classical Qualitative Spatial Reasoning relying on composition tables is the strict division of different spatial aspects. For example, when dealing with relative directional relations, mereotopological relations may inherently be present without being directly expressed. We discuss how mereotopological relations may arise in constraint networks over Dipole relations and how these relations may be extracted via *interdependency functions*. Having made them explicit, these relations may be used to deploy reasoning methods specific to their spatial aspect. In order to further the development of Qualitative Spatial Reasoning, we present two families of benchmark problems that are cognitively easy to solve but still cannot be decided by present qualitative reasoning methods.

Keywords: Spatial Reasoning, Relative Directions, Mereotopology, Heterogenous Constraint Networks, Interdependency Function, Consistency.

1 Introduction

A qualitative representation provides mechanisms which characterize central essential properties of objects or configurations. A quantitative representation in contrast establishes a measure in relation to a unit of measurement which has to be generally available. Qualitative spatial calculi usually deal with elementary objects (e.g., positions, directions, regions) and qualitative relations between them (e.g., *adjacent, on the left of* and *included in*). A strength of qualitative spatial relations is that they are able to express the typical relations between object classes (e.g. human concepts) in addition to the relations of specific instances of these classes. So we can say that the human heart is at the *left* side of the human body and this spatial relation typically would hold for all instances of hearts even if the metrical details differ from body to body. So often we can make relevant spatial expressions using qualitative relations where a precise metric spatial statement would not be possible. The research field about those qualitative spatial relations and the reasoning mechanisms about them is called

C. Freksa et al. (Eds.): Spatial Cognition 2014, LNAI 8684, pp. 299–311, 2014.

qualitative spatial reasoning (QSR). The main trends in QSR are topological reasoning about regions [5,22,23] and positional reasoning about point configurations [8,10,26,16], or simple oriented objects [17,15]. Typical reasoning services by QSR algorithms are checking the consistency of a set of QSR statements or deriving explicit QSR statements which are implicitly given by a set of facts. This kind of deductive QSR constraint reasoning is a classic area within QSR and attracted the most research work in this field. In the last decade there was a lot of success about designing efficient reasoning algorithms for many different calculi [24,14].

To give potential users of QSR technology an overview about the algorithms and their performance a recent trend is to develop benchmarks for qualitative spatial reasoning [21,2]. In addition to demonstrate features of individual calculi and their reasoning capabilities benchmarks also can compare the performance of competing approaches. Such comparative evaluations can show the limits of specific older approaches and strengths of new approaches. In such a setting the presentation of a new calculus or a new reasoning schema would be accompanied by demonstrations of what the new approach can achieve that older approaches are not capable of. In this paper we present two new benchmark problems for qualitative spatial reasoning about relative direction. Our benchmarks deal with expressing topological knowledge with relative direction constraints. In one setting a polyline intersects a convex polygon. Then order geometry-based calculi like LR or Dipole can represent the problem instances. Our suggested two new benchmark problems are both sets of parameterized problem instances that scale to configurations in which no solutions to decide consistency exist yet.

2   Mereotopological Constraints in Dipole Networks

2.1   Dipole Calculi

Human natural language spatial propositions often express relative spatial positions based on reference directions derived from the shape (and function) of one of the objects involved [12] (e.g., »The hill is to the left of the train«). This leads to binary relations between objects in which at least one of the objects has the feature of orientedness. For that reason, in our conception, orientedness is an important feature of natural objects. In a corresponding qualitative calculus it is necessary to use more complex basic entities than points. One option for building more complex basic entities is to use oriented line segments (see Fig. 1) as basic entities. In this abstraction we lose the specific shape of the object, but preserve the feature of orientedness.

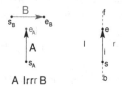

Fig. 1. Orientation between two dipoles based on four dipole-point relations

With this approach we can design relative position calculi in which directions are expressed as binary relations [18]. Oriented straight line segments (which were called *dipoles* by Moratz et al. [17]) may be specified by their start and end points. Then a dipole is a pair of different points in the Euclidean plane.

Using dipoles as basic building blocks, more complex objects can be constructed (e.g., polylines or polygons) in a straightforward manner. Therefore, dipoles can be used as basic units in numerous applications. To give an example, line segments are central to edge-based image segmentation and grouping in computer vision. In addition, GIS systems often have line segments as basic entities [9]. Polylines are particularly interesting for representing paths in cognitive robotics [20] and can serve as the geometric basis of a mobile robot when autonomously mapping its working environment [28]. To sum up, dipole calculi are qualitative calculi that abstract from metric information. They focus on directional relations, but can also be used to express certain topological relations.

To formally derive dipole-dipole relations we derive those relations from dipole-point relations. A dipole-point relation distinguishes between whether a point lies to the left, to the right, or at one of five qualitatively different locations on the straight line that passes through the corresponding dipole. The corresponding regions are shown on the right side of Fig. 1, see [10,13,26]. Using these seven possible relations between a dipole and a point, the relations between two dipoles may be specified according to the following four relationships:

$$A\ R_1\ s_B \wedge A\ R_2\ e_B \wedge B\ R_3\ s_A \wedge B\ R_4\ e_A,$$

where $R_i \in \{l, r, b, s, i, e, f\}$ with $1 \leq i \leq 4$. Theoretically, this gives us 2401 relations, out of which 72 relations are geometrically possible. These constitute the $\mathcal{DRA}_f$ calculus, see [17,18] for details. For example, in Fig. 1, the relation A lrrr B holds. The list of all 72 base relations of the $\mathcal{DRA}_f$ calculus is shown in Fig. 3.

Figure 2 presents a refinement of $\mathcal{DRA}_f$, denoted by $\mathcal{DRA}_{fp}$. This refinement has additional features in order to distinguish between *parallel* (P) and *antiparallel* (A) dipoles as well as the two states in between: (+) and (−). More precisely, the notation '+' and '−' denotes, whether the shortest rotation of the first dipole to the second dipole is in mathematically positive or negative direction, respectively. For the relations different from rrrr, llrr rrll and llll, a 'P' or 'A', '+' or '−' is already determined by the original base relation and does

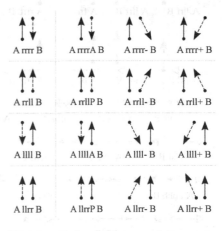

Fig. 2. Refined base relations in $\mathcal{DRA}_{fp}$

not have to be stated explicitly. These base relations then have the same relation symbol as in $\mathcal{DRA}_f$. Thus we arrive at a set of 80 base relations for $\mathcal{DRA}_{fp}$.

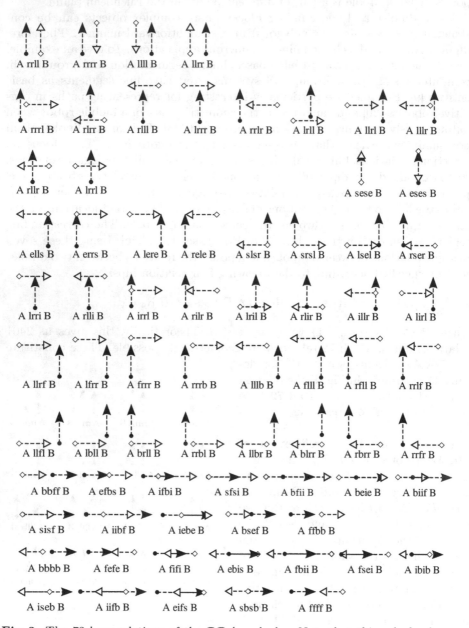

Fig. 3. The 72 base relations of the $\mathcal{DRA}_f$ calculus. Note that this calculus has no notion of orthogonality, although the graphical representation may suggest this.

2.2   How Mereotopological Constraints Arise from Dipole Networks

While the family of Dipole Calculi is meant as a tool for reasoning about relative directional relations of abstract, linear extended objects, considering intersecting dipoles or dipoles with common start or end points already yields a concept of connectedness. Extending this view to polygons described by chains of dipoles, we naturally arrive at mereotopological relations between polygonal areas, polylines and points. While it is possible to discuss more complex connection patterns between polygons and polylines, like the 16-intersection matrix described in [7], the 9-splitting measure and the 9-intersection matrix described in [6] or the Quasi-Hasse diagrams proposed in [25], according to [1] and our best knowledge there exists no composition table or other direct way of reasoning about the consistency problem for this combination of spatial objects. So for the purpose of this paper we only look at very basic relations up to the RCC-8 relations for convex polygons. In this paper we stick to *convex* polygons because for these it is relatively simple to define the relations *inside* and *outside* in terms of Dipole relations. Given a Dipole constraint network, there might be a circuit of dipoles that forms a convex polygon. Consider for example a set $D = \{d_1 \ldots d_n\}$ of dipoles such that

$$\bigwedge_{i=1}^{n-1} d_i \text{ ells } d_{i+1} \;\wedge\; d_n \text{ ells } d_1 \;\wedge\; \bigwedge_{j=3}^{n-1} d_1 \text{ disconn } d_j \;\wedge\; \bigwedge_{i=2}^{n-2} \bigwedge_{j=i+2}^{n} d_i \text{ disconn } d_j \;.$$

where *disconn(ected)* is defined by

$$d_1 \text{ disconn } d_2 \;\stackrel{\text{def}}{\Longleftrightarrow}\; \nexists rel \in \mathcal{DRA}_{fp}: d_1 \text{ rel } d_2$$
$$\wedge \left(rel \cap \{\text{lrrl, rllr}\} \neq \varnothing \;\vee\; \bigvee_{abcd \,\in\, rel} \{a,b,c,d\} \cap \{\text{i, s, e}\} \neq \varnothing \right).$$

In this example, all consecutive dipoles are connected start to end, with the tip of each successor pointing to the left as seen from its predecessor. The relation *disconnected* ensures that the polygon is simple, i.e. not self-intersecting. In general, consecutive dipoles do not have to be connected start to end; circuits of arbitrarily directed dipoles, like the triangle depicted in Fig. 4, can be identified as convex polygons as well. For this, we first have to determine the intrinsic rotation of the polygon by following the undirected linesegments given by the first two dipoles. In Fig. 4 the dipoles d_1 and d_2 determine the triangle to be rotated counterclockwise, with d_1 being directed negatively and d_2 being directed positively. The direction of d_3 then is determined by the direction of d_2 and whether it is connected to d_2 with its startpoint or with its endpoint. Here d_3 is connected to d_2 with its startpoint and d_2 is directed positively, thus d_3 is directed positively, too. Since, in this example, d_1 and d_2 determine the triangle to be a counterclockwise polygon and d_2 and d_3 are directed positively, the

Figure 4:

d_1 srsl d_2
d_2 ells d_3
d_3 lere d_1

relation between d_2 and d_3 has to be either d_2 ells d_3 or d_2 efbs d_3, otherwise the polygon would not be convex. Following this scheme, any set of dipoles can be determined to constitute a clockwise or counterclockwise convex polygon, or no convex polygon at all.

The relation *disconnected* has been defined between two dipoles, but it can be lifted naturally to be defined between dipoles and polygons as well as polygons and polygons. This, however, still allows a dipole or polygon to lie *inside* the related polygon. So, in order to extend the definition of *disconnected* to dipoles and polygons such that it complies better with its meaning in RCC-8, we have to conjunct another clause that forbids the dipole to lie inside the polygon.

We define the relation *inside* between points and polygons and lift it naturally to dipoles and polygons as well as polygons and polygons. Given the example set D from above and another dipole d_{pq} with startpoint p and endpoint q, we know that p lies *inside* the polygon $d_1 \ldots d_n$, when it is restricted to the left side of each of the dipoles d_i that constitute the polygon, i.e.

$$\bigwedge_{i=1}^{n} d_i \text{ l??? } d_{pq}$$

The whole dipole d_{pq} then lies *inside* the polygon when

$$\bigwedge_{i=1}^{n} d_i \text{ l??? } d_{pq} \ \wedge \ \bigwedge_{i=1}^{n} d_i \text{ ?l??? } d_{pq} \ \equiv \ \bigwedge_{i=1}^{n} d_i \text{ ll?? } d_{pq} \ .$$

As before, this example generalizes to polygons of arbitrarily directed dipoles, in such a way that the points have to lie either on the left or on the right side depending on the direction of the respective dipole belonging to the polygon and the rotation of the polygon itself. The natural lifting of this relation to polygons simply means that a polygon lies *inside* another polygon when all its constituent dipoles do.

Thus, a point can be identified as lying *outside* of a polygon *pol*, when there is a dipole belonging to *pol* which confines the point away from *pol*. But, as with the relation *disconnected*, this relation can not simply be lifted to dipoles or polygons as these might intersect or surround the polygon. However, intersection can be tested by lifting the relation *disconnected* as defined above naturally, and *surrounds* simply is the converse of *inside*, which we just defined.

In this manner all the relations of RCC-8 can occur between polygons in a given Dipole constraint network. But, since each of these relations depends on at least 4 dipoles, reasoning about them cannot be done using the Dipole Calculi, which are based on binary composition, alone.

3   Interdependency Functions

Formally, a connection between different sets of relations, as the one between $\mathcal{DRA}_f$ and RCC-8 described in section 2.2, can be understood through *interdependency functions* and *embeddings*. The notion of interdependency functions has been introduced by [27] in order to facilitate the development of mixed qualitative spatial calculi. Different from the approach in [27] which considers functions from the first set of relations (more precisely, the base relations of the first set of relations) to the second set of relations, we consider functions from the set of all possible constraint networks over the first set of relations to the set of all possible constraint networks over the second set of relations.

Definition 1 (Interdependency function). *Let V_1, V_2 be two infinite sets of variables and D_1, D_2 be two sets of domain values. Then, let R_1 and R_2 be two sets of relations over D_1 and D_2, respectively, and let C_1 and C_2 be the sets of all possible constraints over (V_1, R_1) and (V_2, R_2), respectively. Furthermore, let Q denote a property of constraint networks, such as consistency.*

A function $f\colon \mathcal{P}(C_1) \to \mathcal{P}(C_2)$ is called an interdependency function *for R_1 and R_2 under Q if either*

$$\forall c \in \mathcal{P}(C_1)\colon Q(c) \Rightarrow Q(f(c)) \quad or \quad \forall c \in \mathcal{P}(C_1)\colon Q(f(c)) \Rightarrow Q(c).$$

In this paper D_1 and D_2 are given by the sets of all dipoles and areas, respectively, and R_1 and R_2 are given by $\mathcal{DRA}_{fp}$ and RCC-8. While this definition gives one possible and quite general notion of interdependency, there is a more specific concept of what we call an *embedding* of one kind of objects together with their abstraction onto another kind of objects and their abstraction.

Definition 2. *Let V_i, D_i, R_i and C_1 be as in Def. 1 and let a_1 and a_2 be two abstractions from $\mathcal{P}(D_1)$ to $\mathcal{P}(C_1)$ and from $\mathcal{P}(D_2)$ to $\mathcal{P}(C_2)$, respectively.*

Given a correspondence $g\colon \mathcal{P}(D_1) \to \mathcal{P}(D_2)$ from sets of objects in D_1 to sets of objects in D_2 and a function $f\colon \mathcal{P}(C_1) \to \mathcal{P}(C_2)$ such that, for the fiber of each element $\mathcal{C} \in \mathcal{P}(C_1)$ under a_1, i.e. the set of all realizations of $\mathcal{C}$ over the domain D_1, and the corresponding fiber of $f(\mathcal{C})$ under a_2, we have

$$(a_2^{-1} \circ f)(\mathcal{C}) = \min(g \circ a_1^{-1})(\mathcal{C}) := \big\{ \mathcal{D} \in (g \circ a_1^{-1})(\mathcal{C}) \tag{1}$$
$$\mid \forall \mathcal{D}' \in (g \circ a_1^{-1})(\mathcal{C})\ |\mathcal{D}| \leq |\mathcal{D}'| \big\}$$

A pair of such functions f and g is called an embedding *of (D_1, a_1) into (D_2, a_2).*

$$
\begin{array}{ccc}
\mathcal{P}(C_1) & \xrightarrow{\ f\ } & \mathcal{P}(C_2) \\
a_1 \big\uparrow & & \big\uparrow a_2 \\
\mathcal{P}(D_1) & \xrightarrow{\ g\ } & \mathcal{P}(D_2)
\end{array}
\qquad
\begin{array}{ccc}
\mathcal{P}(C_1) & \xrightarrow{\ f\ } & \mathcal{P}(C_2) \\
a_1 \big\updownarrow a_1^{-1} & & a_2^{-1} \big\updownarrow a_2 \\
\mathcal{P}(\mathcal{P}(D_1)) & \xrightarrow{\ g\ } & \mathcal{P}(\mathcal{P}(D_2))
\end{array}
$$

Intuitively, the correspondence g simply occurs in the common spatial domain of D_1 and D_2. E.g. a set of dipoles in the $\mathbb{R}^2$ can be seen as a set of points in the $\mathbb{R}^2$, with some additional information, and this set of points might constitute a set of polygons in $\mathbb{R}^2$. The minimality restriction in (1) accounts for additional, accidental entities from D_2 that do not necessarily arise from C but still might occur depending on the actual realization of C.

So the main problem lies in finding an algorithm for the function f. Theoretically, f can be defined using a_1^{-1}, g and a_2. However, a_1^{-1} implies the realization problem over, possibly infinite, domains D_1 and D_2, which is the very problem we are trying to solve. Even with some realization function given, we would have to care for the minimality restriction, which is another big problem over infinite domains. So, practically, we have to find an algorithm for f that does not make use of the domains directly.

4 Two Benchmark Problems

The fact that Dipole constraint networks can contain mereotopological information allows for some nice benchmark problems that might further the development of QSTR. We propose two simple benchmark problems that lie at the core of the problem of reasoning about relative directions and mereotopological relations simultaneously.

The first benchmark problem we propose is a simple loop of *proper parts* represented by Dipole configurations. Consider for example the triangles A and B as defined by

$$A: \quad d_1 \text{ ells } d_2 \wedge d_2 \text{ ells } d_3 \wedge d_3 \text{ ells } d_1$$
$$B: \quad d_4 \text{ ells } d_5 \wedge d_5 \text{ ells } d_6 \wedge d_6 \text{ ells } d_4 \ .$$

With

$$\bigwedge_{\substack{i \in \{1...3\} \\ j \in \{4...6\}}} d_i \text{ ll?? } d_j \quad \wedge \quad \bigwedge_{\substack{i \in \{1...3\} \\ j \in \{4...6\}}} d_j \text{ ll?? } d_i$$

triangle A is confined inside of triangle B and vice versa; as illustrated in Fig. 5a. Thus both triangles are a *proper part* of the other, which is inconsistent. This arrangement can be extended to any number of polygons of any number of dipoles. We call this kind of arrangement, i.e. a sequence of proper parts which loops back to the first polygon such that it is a proper part of the last polygon, a *proper part loop*.

The second benchmark we propose is even simpler. Given a polygon $d_1 \ldots d_n$ in terms of Dipole relations, a further dipole d_{n+1} is given, such that its startpoint lies inside the polygon while its endpoint lies outside. Furthermore, it is required that it is *disconnected* from all dipoles $d_1 \ldots d_n$ constituent to the polygon. Since there cannot be a trail from the inside to the outside without crossing one constituent dipole of the polygon, the resulting constraint network is inconsistent. An extension of this problem would be to substitute the dipole d_{n+1} by a sequence of dipoles forming a polygonal chain that begins inside the polygon and ends outside of the polygon with all of its components being *disconnected* from the polygon. We refer to this kind of arrangement as *prison escape* problem since the arrangement is an abstraction of the situation where a path (e.g. escape route) out of a containment (e.g. prison) is searched for. Since there is no open door and no hole in the wall no escape route can be found in this scenario. When we refer to a specific instance of the prison escape problems with an n-gon modelling the prison we call the problem m-*prison escape* problem with $m = n$.

As an example, the Dipole constraint network for the quadrilateral in Fig. 5b can be given as:

$d_1\ d_2$ (ells) $d_2\ d_3$ (ells) $d_3\ d_4$ (ells) $d_4\ d_1$ (ells)

$d_1\ d_3$ (rrrrA, rrrr−, rrrr+, rrrl , rrrb , rrlr, rrllP, rrll−, rrll+, rrlf , rrfr , rrbl

, rlrr , rlll , rfll , rbrr , lrrr , lrll , llrrP, llrr−, llrr+, llrl , llrf , lllr

, llllA , llll− , llll+ , lllb , llfl , llbr, lfrr , lbll , frrr , flll , ffff , ffbb

, brll , blrr , bbff , bbbb)

$d_2\ d_4$ (rrrrA, rrrr−, rrrr+, rrrl , rrrb , rrlr, rrllP, rrll−, rrll+, rrlf , rrfr , rrbl

, rlrr , rlll , rfll , rbrr , lrrr , lrll , llrrP, llrr−, llrr+, llrl , llrf , lllr

, llllA , llll− , llll+ , lllb , llfl , llbr, lfrr , lbll , frrr , flll , ffff , ffbb

, brll , blrr , bbff , bbbb)

$d_1\ d_5$ (lrrr , lrll , lfrr , lbll)

$d_2\ d_5$ (lrrr , lrll , llrrP , llrr−, llrr+, llrl , llrf , lllr , llllA , llll−, llll+, lllb

, llfl , llbr , lfrr , lbll)

$d_3\ d_5$ (lrrr , lrll , llrrP , llrr−, llrr+, llrl , llrf , lllr , llllA , llll−, llll+, lllb

, llfl , llbr , lfrr , lbll)

$d_4\ d_5$ (lrrr , lrll , llrrP , llrr−, llrr+, llrl , llrf , lllr , llllA , llll−, llll+, lllb

, llfl , llbr , lfrr , lbll)

where the dipoles d_1 to d_4 constitute the quadrilateral. The constraints between d_5 and each of the dipoles $d_1, \ldots, d_4$ confine the startpoint of d_5 to the *left* side, i.e. towards the quadrilateral, and thus *inside* of the quadrilateral. They also require that the endpoint of d_5 does not directly lie on either of the dipoles $d_1, \ldots, d_4$ and, should it lie on the *right* side of e.g. d_i, it does so such that d_5 does not cross d_i. Additionally, the constraint between d_1 and d_5 requires the endpoint of d_5 to lie either on the *right* side or at the *front* or *back*. Thus the endpoint of d_5 cannot touch or lie inside the quadrilateral.

A pp B, B pp A

(a) A *proper part* loop.   (b) The first three m-*prison escape* problems

Fig. 5. Instances of the two benchmark problems proposed

5 First Attempts on Solving These Problems

We added these two classes of benchmark problems to Zeno [3], the qualitative spatio-temporal reasoning suite, and applied the first few instances of them on the single reasoning method directly available for dipoles, the algebraic closure procedure, which is related to path consistency [19]. As expected, algebraic closure does not detect the inconsistency of these problems. Since for bigger problem sizes the same mereotopological information is spread over more dipoles the algebraic closure algorithm cannot condense this information further than it does for smaller problem instances. Thus we know that path consistency over Dipoles does not suffice to detect the inconsistency of any of these problems regardless of their size.

As a first attempt to tackle these problems with the established qualitative spatial reasoning calculi, we implemented a proof of concept embedding that maps Dipole constraint networks onto RCC-8 constraints networks. Given a list of Dipoles, this function first compiles a list of oriented polygonal chains from which then a list of polygons is filtered. By testing each pair of polygons for the relations described in section 2.2, a list of region variables together with their respective relations is returned. Using this function a *proper part loop* is directly translated into an RCC-8 constraint network, which then is detected as inconsistent by the algebraic closure algorithm on the RCC-8 calculus. Since this function is based on a naive search for polygons and their relations over all given dipoles and constraints, it is not likely to scale on more complex constraint networks. In its current state it serves merely as a proof of concept to encourage further research in this area.

However, since the topological inconsistency underlying the *m-prison escape* problems involves unextended objects, the topological relations needed to describe it are not directly expressible in RCC-8, which is defined for extended regions only. Although [5] describes a set of relations between lines and areas based on the 9-intersection matrix (see also [11]), according to [1] and our best knowledge there exists no composition table or other direct way of reasoning about this combination of spatial objects.

In theory it is possible to decide the realizability of *m-prison escape* problems for m up to 6 by translating the Dipole constraint network into an $\mathcal{LR}$ network and testing whether this network corresponds to an oriented matroid [4]. However, for this approach we have to consider every scenario – i.e. constraint network involving base relations only – underlying the resulting $\mathcal{LR}$ constraint network. Since the constraint network of the 4-*prison escape* problem already yields 7077888 scenarios, this approach is infeasible for $m \geq 5$. In any case, this approach would only raise the bar but is not a general solution to this kind of spatial reasoning problem.

6 Conclusion and Outlook

In our contribution we demonstrated that when dealing with relative directional relations, mereotopological relations may inherently be present without being directly expressed. We extracted mereotopological relations via an *embedding* from constraint networks over dipole relations. Having made them explicit, these relations can be used to deploy reasoning methods specific to their spatial aspect.

In order to further the advancement of Qualitative Spatial Reasoning, we used this bridge between relative directional relations and mereotopological relations to develop two families of benchmark problems. The standard reasoning approach of using a composition table and the algebraic closure algorithm could not even solve the simplest instances of these parametrized problems. We demonstrated first steps for how to deal with some small instances of the benchmarks. However, bigger instances of the two benchmarks families still cannot be decided by present qualitative reasoning methods, although they are very easy to solve for humans.

In future work we will expand on the framework of using interdependency functions to design more capable reasoning algorithms for this kind of problems that are cognitively easy to solve but cannot be solved with local spatial reasoning in a single modality.

Acknowledgments. The authors would like to thank Till Mossakowski, Jae Hee Lee, Christoph Schlieder, Chris Dorr and Hari Prasath Palani for fruitful discussions. Our work was supported by the DFG Transregional Collaborative Research Center SFB/TR 8 *Spatial Cognition*, project R4 – LogoSpace, and the National Science Foundation under Grant No. CDI-1028895.   •

References

1. Chen, J., Cohn, A.G., Liu, D., Wang, S., Ouyang, J., Yu, Q.: A survey of qualitative spatial representations. The Knowledge Engineering Review, 1–31 (October 2013)
2. Cohn, A., Renz, J., Wölfl, S. (eds.): IJCAI Workshop on Benchmarks and Applications of Spatial Reasoning (2011)
3. van Delden, A.: Zeno: A Library for Qualitative Spatio-Temporal Reasoning (2011–2014), https://github.com/weltensegler/zeno
4. van Delden, A., Mossakowski, T.: Mastering Left and Right - Different Approaches to a Problem that is not Straight Forward. In: KI, pp. 248–259 (2013)
5. Egenhofer, M., Franzosa, R.: Point-Set Topological Spatial Relations. International Journal of Geographical Information Systems 5(2), 161–174 (1991)
6. Egenhofer, M.J.: Qualitative spatial-relation reasoning for design. In: NSF International Workshop on Studying Visual and Spatial Reasoning for Design Creativity, Aixen-Provence (2010)
7. Formica, A., Mazzei, M., Pourabbas, E., Rafanelli, M.: A 16-intersection matrix for the polygon-polyline topological relation for geographic pictorial query languages. In: Quirchmayr, G., Basl, J., You, I., Xu, L., Weippl, E. (eds.) CD-ARES 2012. LNCS, vol. 7465, pp. 302–316. Springer, Heidelberg (2012)
8. Freksa, C.: Using Orientation Information for Qualitative Spatial Reasoning. In: Frank, A.U., Campari, I., Formentini, U. (eds.) Theories and Methods of Spatial-Temporal Reasoning in Geographic Space, vol. 639, pp. 162–178. Springer, Heidelberg (1992)

9. Hoel, E.G., Samet, H.: Efficient processing of spatial queries in line segment databases. In: Günther, O., Schek, H.-J. (eds.) SSD 1991. LNCS, vol. 525, pp. 235–256. Springer, Heidelberg (1991)

10. Isli, A., Moratz, R.: Qualitative Spatial Representation and Reasoning: Algebraic Models for Relative Position. Tech. rep., Universität Hamburg, FB Informatik, Hamburg (1999)

11. Isli, A., Cabedo, L.M., Barkowsky, T., Moratz, R.: A topological calculus for cartographic entities. In: Habel, C., Brauer, W., Freksa, C., Wender, K.F. (eds.) Spatial Cognition 2000. LNCS (LNAI), vol. 1849, pp. 225–238. Springer, Heidelberg (2000)

12. Levinson, S.C.: Frames of Reference and Molyneux's Question: Crosslinguistic Evidence. In: Bloom, P., Peterson, M., Nadel, L., Garrett, M. (eds.) Language and Space, pp. 109–169. MIT Press (1996)

13. Ligozat, G.: Qualitative triangulation for spatial reasoning. In: Campari, I., Frank, A.U. (eds.) COSIT 1993. LNCS, vol. 716, pp. 54–68. Springer, Heidelberg (1993)

14. Ligozat, G.: Qualitative spatial and temporal reasoning. John Wiley & Sons (2013)

15. Moratz, R.: Representing Relative Direction as a Binary Relation of Oriented Points. In: Brewka, G., Coradeschi, S., Perini, A., Traverso, P. (eds.) Proc. of ECAI 2006. Frontiers in Artificial Intelligence and Applications, vol. 141, pp. 407–411. IOS Press (2006)

16. Moratz, R., Ragni, M.: Qualitative Spatial Reasoning about Relative Point Position. J. Vis. Lang. Comput. 19(1), 75–98 (2008)

17. Moratz, R., Renz, J., Wolter, D.: Qualitative Spatial Reasoning about Line Segments. In: Proc. of ECAI 2000, pp. 234–238 (2000)

18. Moratz, R., Lücke, D., Mossakowski, T.: A condensed semantics for qualitative spatial reasoning about oriented straight line segments. Artificial Intelligence 175(16), 2099–2127 (2011)

19. Mossakowski, T., Schröder, L., Wölfl, S.: A categorical perspective on qualitative constraint calculi. In: Qualitative Constraint Calculi: Application and Integration, Workshop Proceedings, pp. 28–39 (2006)

20. Musto, A., Stein, K., Eisenkolb, A., Röfer, T.: Qualitative and quantitative representations of locomotion and their application in robot navigation. In: Proc. of IJCAI 1999, pp. 1067–1072 (1999)

21. Nebel, B. (ed.): AAAI Spring Symposium: Benchmarking of Qualitative Spatial and Temporal Reasoning Systems (2009)

22. Randell, D.A., Cui, Z., Cohn, A.G.: A spatial logic based on regions and connection. In: Nebel, B., Rich, C., Swartout, W. (eds.) Proc. of KR 1992, pp. 165–176. Morgan Kaufmann (1992)

23. Renz, J., Nebel, B.: On the Complexity of Qualitative Spatial Reasoning: A Maximal Tractable Fragment of the Region Connection Calculus. Artificial Intelligence 108(1-2), 69–123 (1999)

24. Renz, J., Nebel, B.: Qualitative Spatial Reasoning Using Constraint Calculi. In: Aiello, M., Pratt-Hartmann, I., van Benthem, J. (eds.) Handbook of Spatial Logics, pp. 161–215. Springer, Heidelberg (2007)

25. Sadahiro, Y.: Spatial relations among polygons: an exploratory analysis. Tokyo, University of Tokyo, Department of Urban Engineering Discussion Paper Series (2010)

26. Scivos, A., Nebel, B.: The finest of its class: The natural point-based ternary calculus formula_image for qualitative spatial reasoning. In: Freksa, C., Knauff, M., Krieg-Brückner, B., Nebel, B., Barkowsky, T. (eds.) Spatial Cognition IV. LNCS (LNAI), vol. 3343, pp. 283–303. Springer, Heidelberg (2005)
27. Wölfl, S., Westphal, M.: On combinations of binary qualitative constraint calculi. In: IJCAI. pp. 967–973 (2009)
28. Wolter, D., Latecki, L.J.: Shape Matching for Robot Mapping. In: Zhang, C., Guesgen, H.W., Yeap, W.K. (eds.) Proc. of 8th Pacific Rim International Conference on Artificial Intelligence, pp. 693–702 (August 2004)

Active Sensorimotor Object Recognition
in Three-Dimensional Space

David Nakath, Tobias Kluth, Thomas Reineking,
Christoph Zetzsche, and Kerstin Schill

Cognitive Neuroinformatics, University of Bremen,
Enrique-Schmidt-Straße 5, 28359 Bremen, Germany
dnakath@informatik.uni-bremen.de
http://www.informatik.uni-bremen.de/cog_neuroinf/en

Abstract. Spatial interaction of biological agents with their environment is based on the cognitive processing of sensory as well as motor information. There are many models for sole sensory processing but only a few for integrating sensory and motor information into a unifying sensorimotor approach. Additionally, neither the relations shaping the integration are yet clear nor how the integrated information can be used in an underlying representation. Therefore, we propose a probabilistic model for integrated processing of sensory and motor information by combining bottom-up feature extraction and top-down action selection embedded in a Bayesian inference approach. The integration of sensory perceptions and motor information brings about two main advantages: (i) Their statistical dependencies can be exploited by representing the spatial relationships of the sensor information in the underlying joint probability distribution and (ii) a top-down process can compute the next most informative region according to an information gain strategy. We evaluated our system in two different object recognition tasks. We found that the integration of sensory and motor information significantly improves active object recognition, in particular when these movements have been chosen by an information gain strategy.

Keywords: sensorimotor, object recognition, Bayesian inference, information gain.

1 Introduction

The capabilities of artificial systems are easily exceeded by humans when it comes to perception-based interaction with the environment. With this in mind, it seems reasonable to take a closer look at the main principles of the human visual perception process. Especially the reciprocal advantageous interplay of motion and sensory information, which was early recognized by Gibson [1] and Neisser [2], should be considered here. Based on analog arguments, an "active perception" approach was proposed by [3,4,5]. The strong interrelation between movements in space and corresponding sensory perceptions can foster the even stronger concept of a *sensorimotor representation* [6,7,8,9]. In this concept, the

C. Freksa et al. (Eds.): Spatial Cognition 2014, LNAI 8684, pp. 312–324, 2014.
© Springer International Publishing Switzerland 2014

classic notion of separate cognitive processing stages for sensory and motor information does not hold. In fact, they are integrated into one sensorimotor coding. This is a precondition for a sensorimotor representation which is established from the specific pattern of alternating sensory perceptions and spatial motor actions [6,10]. The constant checking and confirmation of sensory and motor information against an internal cognitive model then constitutes a scanpath, and thus the perception of a particular object [11,12].

To be able to check such an internal sensorimotor model of an object, the next motor action has to be chosen accordingly by an object recognition system. Generally, the problem of action selection can be solved in numerous ways, but as information gathering should be the purpose of motor actions it seems reasonable to choose an information-theoretic criterion. Prior research in this area often found that the principle of *information gain* is well suited to select an appropriate next action. This has been shown by [13] in the context of decision trees, where information gain was used to decide which attributes are the most relevant ones. Robotics also proofed to be a suitable domain, as information gain can be used there to actively reduce the uncertainty of the robot regarding its position and spatial environment [14,15]. Additionally, information gain was not only used to explain human selection behavior [16,17] but also to mimic it: Both in the form of human-like expert systems [18,19] and with a modeled sensorimotor loop in a saccadic eye movement control system [20,21].

Based on the preceding considerations the basic sketch of a sensomotoric object recognition system becomes apparent. Building upon the research of Schill, Zetzsche, and coworkers [20,21], we propose a sensomotoric probabilistic reasoning system for active object recognition integrating sensory perceptions and motor actions. Our system is inspired by the human perception process and therefore should model a sequential pattern of actions controlled by a top-down and a bottom-up process. Evidence suggests that sensory perception and motor actions partly share the same cognitive processing stage which makes it reasonable to integrate them into one single sensorimotor feature (SMF) [22,23,24]. Through this integration two improvements come into effect: (i) The accuracy of the recognition process is improved through the additional motor information which encodes spatial relations and (ii) the next motor action can be chosen according to the maximum information gain principle, thus supplying the sensors with an optimized input in the next recognition step.

The basic architecture of the system we propose is outlined in Sect. 2. In Sect. 3, we describe the implementation of the system. Subsequently, Sect. 4 shows the results of the evaluation in two different scenarios: Optimized control of 3D movements of a camera mounted on a robotic arm and simulated sensor movements on images from the Caltech 256 dataset. The paper is concluded with a discussion of the specific advantages offered by the proposed sensorimotor architecture.

2   Sensomotoric Object Recognition System

The sensorimotor system described in the following is a generic architecture (see Fig. 1). In the case of visual object recognition, the senorimotor loop starts out with a particular pose of the active sensor which passes its raw sensor data to the sensory processing module. After processing, the sensory data becomes part of a new sensorimotor feature, which is then fed into the probabilistic reasoning module. The Bayesian inference module calculates the new posterior distribution based on a previously-learned sensorimotor representation. The posterior distribution constitutes the current belief of the system. This belief is used by the information gain strategy to choose an optimal next movement from the set of possible motor actions. The selected movement then also becomes part of the sensorimotor feature and is subsequently executed by the active sensor. The whole process results in a new sensor pose, which in turn delivers new raw sensory data to enter the next cycle of the sensorimotor loop.

More formally spoken, the system depends on an *active sensor* (AS), which can be controlled such that it delivers information about a specific aspect of the

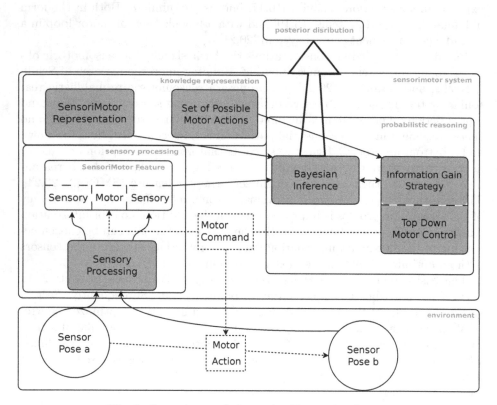

Fig. 1. Sensorimotor Information Processing System

world. In Fig. 1, the two arrows pointing from the sensor poses to the sensory processing module correspond to the mapping $A : U \times X \to R$, where U is the space of all motor actions which are currently possible, X is the state space of the active sensor, and R is the raw sensor data space.

The system has no knowledge about the actual state of the AS, instead it is only informed about the currently possible motor actions U. These are of course dependent on the state in the sense of $U : X \to \mathcal{P}(\Omega_U)$, where Ω_U is the set of all possible motor controls and $\mathcal{P}$ denotes the power set. Assuming that the output of the function U is given, we write U instead of $U(x)$, $x \in X$, for convenience. Considering the state-agnostic behavior, the formal representation of the AS can be redefined to $A_x : U \to R$ where the index x recalls the dependency on the state

$$A_x(u) := A(x, u) = r, \quad x \in X, \ u \in U(x), \ r \in R. \tag{1}$$

The only time-dependent variables are the sensor state x and the relative motor control u. In contrast, the world is assumed to be static which implies no dynamic changes in the raw sensor data $r \in R$.

This data is fed into the *sensory processing* (SP) which mainly extracts the relevant features belonging to a feature space F, i.e., $SP : R \to F$. Subsequently, the quantization operation $Q_S : F \to S$ maps the features to a specific feature class in the finite and countable space S. The possible motor actions are mapped with $Q_M : \Omega_U \to M$ to the finite countable set of actions M to yield a manageable product space of sensory and motor information. The results of these quantizations then become part of a sensorimotor feature (SMF). The single quantizations are represented in Fig. 1 by the arrows from the sensory processing and the motor command to the first-order sensorimotor feature which is defined as the triple

$$SMF_i := \{s_{i-1}, m_{i-1}, s_i\}, \tag{2}$$

where $m_{i-1} := Q_M(u_{i-1})$ is the intermediate motor action between the sensor information s_{i-1} and s_i at time step t_{i-1} and t_i (see Fig. 2). The whole chain of operations to obtain the sensor information at a time step t_i can be described by

$$s_i := (Q_S \circ SP \circ A_x)(u_{i-1}). \tag{3}$$

The *knowledge representation* is comprised of the currently available motor actions U and the learned sensorimotor representation (SMR), which is a full joint probability distribution of $SMFs$ and the classes represented by the discrete random variable Y. Every possible SMF is generated on a set of known objects in a training phase. This means that, from every possible state x, every possible motor action u is performed, resulting in

$$SMR := P(SMF, Y) = P(S_{i-1}, M_{i-1}, S_i, Y). \tag{4}$$

The *probabilistic reasoning* module consists of a Bayesian inference approach accompanied by an information gain strategy. They rely on bottom-up sensory data and top-down information from the knowledge representation. This design enables the Bayesian inference system to take into account motor actions, thus

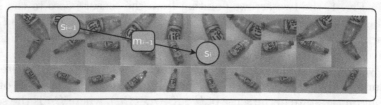

(a) Robotic arm in 3D space

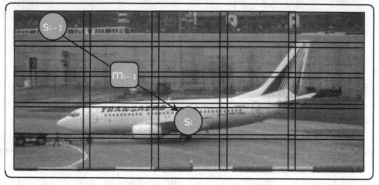

(b) Simulated active sensor in 2D space

Fig. 2. Exemplary sensorimotor features (SMF) drawn on the discretized views on an object, both for the 3D case shown in (a) and 2D case shown in (b). Here, s_{i-1} denotes the preceding sensory input, m_{i-1} denotes the preceding movement, and s_i denotes the current sensory input.

improving the posterior distribution over the object classes Y. Furthermore, the information gain strategy can choose an optimal next motor action for the active sensor, thus improving the input of the following Bayesian inference step.

3   Model Implementation

Based on the schematic outline presented above, we applied our system in the field of active object recognition. We consider both the case of an active sensor moving in 3D space and a simulated active sensor moving in 2D space (see Fig. 2).

3.1   Active Sensor Implementation

For the 3D case, we used a discrete set M of movements of a camera mounted on a robotic arm (see Fig. 2a), which resembles an observer actually moving around an object. For the 2D case, we used simulated active sensor movements on images of a reduced version of the Caltech 256 [25] dataset.[1] Here, M consists of all possible relative movements between the individual cells of a 5×5 grid (see Fig. 2b). The latter setup mimics eye movements of a stationary observer. Hence, in both cases holds $\Omega_U = M$ and the quantization Q_M is an identity operation.

Although the implemented sensors are of a fundamentally different nature, the following basic learning and recognition principles can be applied to both of them: In the learning phase, features are extracted from the training data (i.e., images from every reachable state of the active sensor), which corresponds to the mapping SP introduced above. As the robotic arm relies on views showing the entire object, GIST-features [26,27] are used, while the more local image patches of the 2D case are described by the SURF-feature [28] with the highest score on that patch. The quantization Q_S is then learned by performing a k-means clustering on the extracted features ($k = 15$).[2] In order to build the individual $SMFs$, features are extracted (see SP) and the results are assigned to clusters with the aid of the previously defined mapping Q_S. These labels are combined with the corresponding intermediate movement resulting in a set of $SMFs$. Finally, all generated $SMFs$ are stored in a Laplace-smoothed SMR.

3.2 Probabilistic Reasoning

The probabilistic reasoning is comprised of a Bayesian inference module in the form of a dynamic Bayesian network (BN) and a corresponding information gain strategy. Four of these probabilistic reasoning modules were implemented to examine the difference between *sensor networks*, which only take into account sensory information (which also implies that no information gain strategy is used), and *sensorimotor networks*, which take into account integrated sensory and motor information. The object recognition in the sense of machine vision then takes place by classification which is performed by choosing the class with the maximum posterior probability.

The first representative of the *sensor networks* is Bayesian network 1 (BN1) (see Fig. 3a), which resembles a naive Bayes model only taking into account the current sensory input s_i. Thus, the inference can be performed by

$$P(y|s_{1:n}) = \alpha P(y) \prod_{i=1}^{n} P(s_i|y),$$
(5)

where α is a normalizing constant guaranteeing that the probability function properties are satisfied and $s_{1:n}$ is a short notation for the n-tuple $(s_1, \ldots, s_n)$.

The second representative of the *sensor networks* is Bayesian network 2 (BN2) (see Fig. 3b), which assumes additional statistical dependencies between the preceding and the current sensor information, s_{i-1} and s_i, resulting in

---

[1] The reduced dataset consists in each case of 100 randomly-selected images from the object classes: *airplanes, cowboy-hat, faces, motorbikes, swan, breadmaker, diamond-ring, ketch, self-propelled-lawn-mower,* and *teapot*.

[2] We use only a small number of clusters in order to limit the number of model parameters and to prevent overfitting.

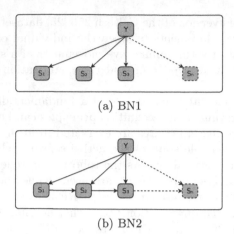

(a) BN1

(b) BN2

Fig. 3. The dynamic Bayesian sensor networks process only sensory information. BN1, which is shown in (a), represents a naive Bayes approach where the current sensory input s_i depends only on the object hypothesis Y. BN2, which is shown in (b), assumes statistical dependencies between the object hypothesis Y and the preceding sensory input s_{i-1} for every sensory input s_i.

$$P(y|s_{1:n}) = \alpha P(y)P(s_1|y) \prod_{i=2}^{n} P(s_i|s_{i-1}, y). \tag{6}$$

Bayesian network 3 (BN3) (see Fig. 4a) uses the full information of the SMF and therefore belongs to the *sensorimotor networks*. The assumption that the current sensory input s_i depends on the preceding sensory input s_{i-1} and the intermediary motor action m_{i-1} integrates motor and sensor information in the recognition process and permits the application of the information gain strategy to choose the next optimal movement. The inference can then be conducted by

$$P(y|s_{1:n}, m_{1:n-1}) = \alpha P(y)P(s_1|y) \prod_{i=2}^{n} P(s_i|s_{i-1}, m_{i-1}, y). \tag{7}$$

Bayesian network 4 (BN4) (see Fig. 4b) mainly resembles BN3, but additionally allows statistical dependencies between the preceding sensory input s_{i-1} and the motor action m_{i-1}. The inference can thus be conducted by

$$P(y|s_{1:n}, m_{1:n-1}) = \alpha P(y)P(s_1|y) \prod_{i=2}^{n} P(s_i|s_{i-1}, m_{i-1}, y)P(m_{i-1}|s_{i-1}). \tag{8}$$

3.3   Information Gain

The strategy for action selection should satisfy two main properties: (i) The strategy should adapt itself to the current belief state of the system and (ii) the

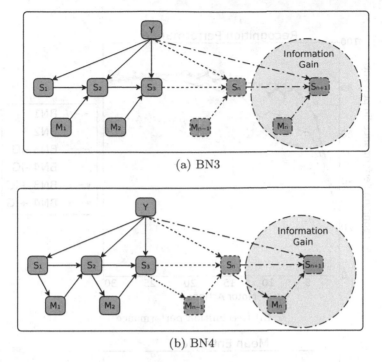

(a) BN3

(b) BN4

Fig. 4. The dynamic Bayesian sensorimotor networks process integrated sensorimotor information. As motor information is taken into account, the next movement m_n can be chosen by the information gain strategy. BN3, which is shown in (a), assumes statistical dependencies between the current visual input s_i, the preceding movement m_{i-1}, the visual input s_{i-1}, and the hypothesis y. BN4, which is shown in (b), allows for the same dependencies as BN3 and, in addition, allows for a dependency of the preceding movement m_{i-1} on the preceding visual input s_{i-1}.

strategy should not make decisions in an heuristic fashion but tightly integrated into the axiomatic framework used for reasoning. The information gain strategy presented in this paper complies with both of these properties.

The information gain IG of a possible next movement m_n is defined as the difference between the current entropy $H(Y)$ and the conditional entropy $H(Y|S_{n+1}, m_n)$, i.e.,

$$IG(m_n) := H(Y) - H(Y|S_{n+1}, m_n), \tag{9}$$

where all probabilities are conditioned by $s_{1:n}, m_{1:n-1}$. This is equivalent to the mutual information of Y and (S_{n+1}, m_n) for an arbitrary m_n. As the current entropy $H(Y)$ is independent of the next movement m_n the most promising motor action m^* can be calculated by minimizing the expected entropy with respect to S_{n+1}, i.e.,

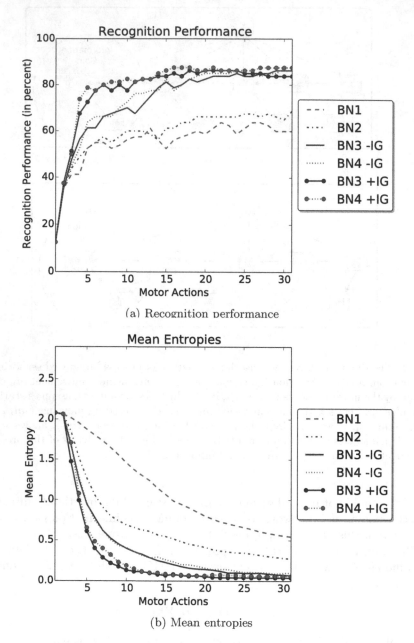

(a) Recognition performance

(b) Mean entropies

Fig. 5. Results of the robotic arm evaluation. BN 1, 2, 3 -IG, and 4 -IG executed random movements while BN 3 +IG and BN4 +IG executed information-gain-guided movements (GIST features, 15 clusters, 94 possible relative movements, inhibition of return). Recognition performance shown in (a) and mean entropy of the posterior distribution shown in (b) are both plotted against the number of performed motor actions.

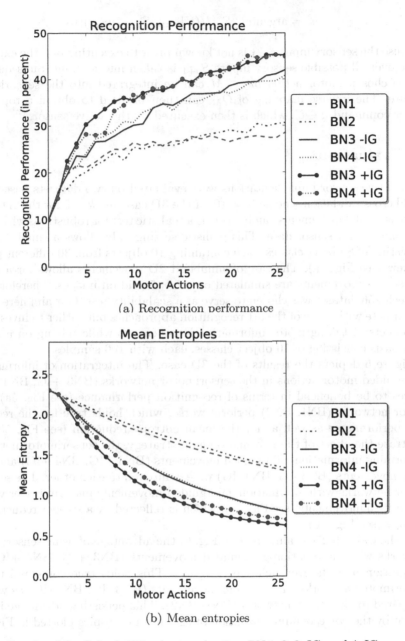

(a) Recognition performance

(b) Mean entropies

Fig. 6. Results of the Caltech 256 subset evaluation. BN 1, 2, 3 -IG, and 4 -IG executed random movements while BN 3 +IG and BN4 +IG executed information-gain-guided movements (SURF features, 15 clusters, 80 possible relative movements, inhibition of return). Recognition performance shown in (a) and mean entropy of the posterior distribution shown in (b) are both plotted against the number of performed motor actions.

$$m^* = \arg\min_{m_n}(\underset{S_{n+1}}{E}\,[H(Y|s_{1:n}, S_{n+1}, m_{1:n})]). \qquad (10)$$

Because the sensory input s_{n+1} is not known prior to executing m_n, the expected value over all possible sensory inputs S_{n+1} is taken into account. Subsequently, the so chosen motor action $m^* \in M$ can be integrated into the sensorimotor feature. The inverse mapping of Q_M can then be used to obtain a top-down motor command $u \in U$, which is then executed by the active sensor.

4   Evaluation

Both active sensor implementations were evaluated on two datasets based on a k-fold cross validation scheme ($k = 10$ for the 3D case and $k = 5$ for the 2D case). The case of 3D movements can be seen as a realistic test for robustness with noisy movements and sensor data. This realistic setting only allows a small dataset, consisting of 8 object classes, each containing 10 objects from 30 different points of view (see Fig. 2a). The case of simulated 2D movements allows for a larger dataset, as movements are simulated on a 5×5-grid on images. Therefore, the Caltech 256 dataset was chosen to serve as a scalability test. Our aim here is not to compete with state of the art recognition approaches but rather to investigate the effects of taking motor information into account while relying on a larger data basis consisting of 10 object classes, each with 100 samples.

Figure 5 depicts the results of the 3D case. The integration of information-gain-guided motor actions in the sensorimotor networks (BN3 +IG, BN4 +IG) proves to be beneficial in terms of recognition performance (see Fig. 5a). The sensor networks (BN1, BN2) perform worse, which holds true for the recognition performance as well as for the mean entropy reduction (see Fig. 5b). To illustrate the effect of the information gain strategy, the sensorimotor networks performing information-gain-guided movements (BN3 +IG, BN4 +IG) and random movements (BN3 -IG, BN4 -IG) were compared to each other. The sensorimotor networks with information-gain-guided movements perform better within the first 15 movements (see Fig. 5a), which is reflected by a steeper reduction in entropy (see Fig. 5b).

In the Caltech 256 evaluation (see Fig. 6) the advantage of using sensorimotor networks with information-gain-guided movements (BN3 +IG, BN4 +IG) for recognition persists over time (see Fig. 6a). This holds true compared to the sensorimotor networks with random movements (BN3 -IG, BN4 -IG) as well as compared to the sensor networks (BN1, BN2). This persisting advantage is also shown by the corresponding evolution of the mean entropies plotted in Fig. 6b.

5   Discussion

We have examined a sensorimotor object recognition system which chooses the next perspective on an object according to the principle of maximum information gain. The underlying sensorimotor representation improved the recognition performance and enabled the system to optimize its selective serial information intake. It could be shown that the proposed information gain strategy is well suited to control such a selection process.

In this paper, we restricted our focus to the recognition rate and the information gain strategy. However, the criteria for the optimal next step in a selective information intake process may vary in other contexts, e.g., the amount of time or energy required to perform individual actions. The system could be adapted to different contexts on the basis of multicriteria optimization approaches [29].

In principle, our system is able to cope with situations where it only has partial access to information about its environment at a given moment. To overcome this shortcoming, it can act in a sequential fashion to establish the full picture. This is often seen as a contradiction but we could show here that, by integrating sensory and motor information, the underlying sensorimotor contingencies become usable, thus improving the process of sequential information intake controlled by reasonable intermediate actions.

Acknowledgements. This work was supported by DFG, SFB/TR8 Spatial Cognition, Project A5-[ActionSpace].

References

1. Gibson, J.: The ecological approach to visual perception. Houghton Mifflin, Boston (1992)
2. Neisser, U.: Cognition and reality: Principles and implications of cognitive psychology. WH Freeman/Times Books/Henry Holt & Co. (1976)
3. Bajcsy, R.: Active perception. Proceedings of the IEEE 76(8), 966–1005 (1988)
4. Aloimonos, J., Weiss, I., Bandyopadhyay, A.: Active vision. International Journal of Computer Vision 1(4), 333–356 (1988)
5. Ballard, D.H.: Animate vision. Artificial intelligence 48(1), 57–86 (1991)
6. O'Regan, J.K., Noë, A.: A sensorimotor account of vision and visual consciousness. Behavioral and Brain Sciences 24(5), 939–972 (2001)
7. Noë, A.: Action in Perception. MIT Press (2004)
8. Prinz, W.: A common coding approach to perception and action. Springer (1990)
9. Hommel, B., Müsseler, J., Aschersleben, G., Prinz, W.: The theory of event coding (TEC): A framework for perception and action planning. Behavioral and Brain Sciences 24(05), 849–878 (2001)
10. O'Regan, J.K.: What it is like to see: A sensorimotor theory of perceptual experience. Synthese 129(1), 79–103 (2001)
11. Noton, D., Stark, L.: Scanpaths in saccadic eye movements while viewing and recognizing patterns. Vision Research 11(9), 929–IN8 (1971)
12. Stark, L.W., Choi, Y.S.: Experimental metaphysics: The scanpath as an epistemological mechanism. In: Zangemeister, W.H., Stiehl, H.S., Freksa, C. (eds.) Visual Attention and Cognition. Advances in Psychology, vol. 116, pp. 3–69. North-Holland (1996)
13. Quinlan, J.R.: Induction of decision trees. Machine Learning 1(1), 81–106 (1986)
14. Cassandra, A.R., Kaelbling, L.P., Kurien, J.A.: Acting under uncertainty: Discrete Bayesian models for mobile-robot navigation. In: Proceedings of the 1996 IEEE/RSJ International Conference on Intelligent Robots and Systems IROS 1996, vol. 2, pp. 963–972. IEEE (1996)

15. Stachniss, C., Grisetti, G., Burgard, W.: Information Gain-based Exploration Using Rao-Blackwellized Particle Filters. In: Robotics: Science and Systems, vol. 2, pp. 65–72 (2005)
16. Oaksford, M., Chater, N.: Information gain explains relevance which explains the selection task. Cognition 57(1), 97–108 (1995)
17. Friston, K., Kilner, J., Harrison, L.: A free energy principle for the brain. Journal of Physiology-Paris 100(1-3), 70–87 (2006); heoretical and Computational Neuroscience: Understanding Brain Functions
18. Schill, K., Pöppel, E., Zetzsche, C.: Completing knowledge by competing hierarchies. In: Proceedings of the Seventh Conference on Uncertainty in Artificial Intelligence, pp. 348–352. Morgan Kaufmann Publishers Inc. (1991)
19. Schill, K.: Decision support systems with adaptive reasoning strategies. In: Freksa, C., Jantzen, M., Valk, R. (eds.) Foundations of Computer Science. LNCS, vol. 1337, pp. 417–427. Springer, Heidelberg (1997)
20. Zetzsche, C., Schill, K., Deubel, H., Krieger, G., Umkehrer, E., Beinlich, S.: Investigation of a sensorimotor system for saccadic scene analysis: an integrated approach. In: Proceedings of the 5th International Conference of Simulation of Adaptive Behaviour, vol. 5, pp. 120–126 (1998)
21. Schill, K., Umkehrer, E., Beinlich, S., Krieger, G., Zetzsche, C.: Scene analysis with saccadic eye movements: top-down and bottom-up modeling. Journal of Electronic Imaging 10(1), 152–160 (2001)
22. Zetzsche, C., Wolter, J., Schill, K.: Sensorimotor representation and knowledge-based reasoning for spatial exploration and localisation. Cognitive Processing 9(4), 283–297 (2008)
23. Reineking, T., Wolter, J., Gadzicki, K., Zetzsche, C.: Bio-inspired Architecture for Active Sensorimotor Localization. In: Hölscher, C., Shipley, T.F., Olivetti Belardinelli, M., Bateman, J.A., Newcombe, N.S. (eds.) Spatial Cognition VII. LNCS, vol. 6222, pp. 163–178. Springer, Heidelberg (2010)
24. Schill, K., Zetzsche, C., Hois, J.: A belief-based architecture for scene analysis: From sensorimotor features to knowledge and ontology. Fuzzy Sets and Systems 160(10), 1507–1516 (2009)
25. Griffin, G., Holub, A., Perona, P.: Caltech-256 Object Category Dataset. Technical report, California Institute of Technology (2007)
26. Oliva, A., Torralba, A.: Building the gist of a scene: The role of global image features in recognition. Prorgess in Brain Research 155, 23–36 (2006)
27. Oliva, A., Torralba, A.: Modeling the shape of the scene: A holistic representation of the spatial envelope. International Journal of Computer Vision 42(3), 145–175 (2001)
28. Bay, H., Ess, A., Tuytelaars, T., Van Gool, L.: Speeded-up robust features (surf). Computer Vision and Image Understanding 110(3), 346–359 (2008)
29. Roy, N., Burgard, W., Fox, D., Thrun, S.: Coastal navigation-mobile robot navigation with uncertainty in dynamic environments. In: Proceedings of the 1999 IEEE International Conference on Robotics and Automation, vol. 1, pp. 35–40. IEEE (1999)

Mechanisms of Spatial Learning: Teaching Children Geometric Categories

Linsey Smith[1], Raedy M. Ping[2], Bryan J. Matlen[1], Micah B. Goldwater[3], Dedre Gentner[1], and Susan Levine[2]

[1] Northwestern University, Evanston, IL, USA
linsey@u.northwestern.edu, bryan.matlen@northwestern.edu,
gentner@northwstern.edu
[2] The University of Chicago, Chicago, IL, USA
rping@uchicago.edu, s-levine@uchicago.edu
[3] The University of Sydney, Sydney, Australia
micah.goldwater@sydney.edu.au

Abstract. Children's representations of geometric categories like triangles are often centered on a prototypical exemplar (e.g., an equilateral triangle). New cases judged based on perceptual similarity to the prototype; such a strategy leads to systematic errors in categorization. Creating correct geometric categories requires children to move beyond a reliance on perceptual similarity and learn category-defining rules (e.g., a triangle is an enclosed, three-sided shape). In this research, we test whether a brief training experience using comparison could help three- and four-year-old children learn the category of *triangle*. Further, we ask whether different types of comparisons (within-category or between-category) support learning in distinct ways. The data indicate that both types of comparison fostered category learning, but that within-category comparisons promoted generalization to new exemplars whereas between-category comparisons reduced overgeneralization to non-exemplars. Furthermore, these effects were moderated by the perceptual similarity of the compared pairs. The results indicate that comparison can foster spatial category learning.

Keywords: Spatial Learning, Analogy, Comparison, Contrast, Categorization, Geometric Categories, Education.

1   Introduction

Young children's representations of geometric shape categories like *triangle* are often centered on a prototypical category member, such as the equilateral triangle in Figure 1a; new cases are judged based on perceptual similarity to the prototype. Yet reliance on perceptual information can take the learner only so far. Such a strategy leads children to make errors such as (1) rejecting atypical exemplars (Fig. 1b) and (2) accepting non-exemplars (Fig. 1c) [1]. Geometric categories are defined by rules, e.g., "a triangle is an enclosed shape with three sides." Creating correct geometric categories requires young children to go beyond reliance on perceptual similarity as a cue for

C. Freksa et al. (Eds.): Spatial Cognition 2014, LNAI 8684, pp. 325–337, 2014.
© Springer International Publishing Switzerland 2014

membership and to instead use these rules as the basis for categorization. Of course, perceptual features of shapes are not entirely uncorrelated with the defining rules that determine membership in geometric categories, but perceptual features are not reliable bases for categorization. Thus an important problem is how learners come to construct abstract representations of categories like triangles when the exemplars are experienced perceptually [2].

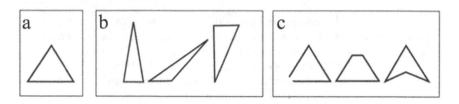

Fig. 1. Children's *triangle* category is centered on a prototype—the equilateral triangle (a). Children frequently reject (b) exemplars that are perceptually dissimilar from the prototype and accept (c) non-exemplars that are perceptually similar to the prototype.

What kinds of mechanisms enable children to go beyond compelling perceptual similarities as a basis for category membership in favor of more relevant information? A large body of literature suggests that *comparison* is a learning mechanism by which children are able to access (and prioritize) more relevant information within a categorization task [3-9].

1.1   Comparison in Children's Categorization

Gentner and Namy [7], [10] found that when children are taught a category name for an exemplar (e.g., an apple), 4-year-olds are likely to extend the name (and category membership) to a perceptually similar item (e.g., a balloon) rather than a perceptually dissimilar item (e.g., a banana) that shares significant causal and functional commonalities with the standard. But when children compared *two* perceptually similar examples from the same category (e.g., an apple and a pear) they were more likely to extend the term to the banana than to the balloon. Comparison seemed to promote focusing on category-level functional and causal commonalities. Similarly, Christie and Gentner [6] taught 3- and 4-year-old children names for novel spatial configurations and asked them to extend the name to another instance. Children given one standard chose on the basis of matching objects, disregarding the spatial configuration, but those who had compared two standards were far more likely to choose the same configuration (even with new objects).

In these studies, it appears that simultaneously presenting two category exemplars elicited a comparison process that helped children discover deeper, less obvious commonalities [7], [10-11]. These findings are consistent with Gentner's structure-mapping theory [12-14], according to which comparison involves a structural alignment process that privileges structural or relational commonalities over surface level commonalities [13], [15]. By highlighting relational structure, comparison can promote learning in at least three ways [14], [16]. First, it supports abstraction and transfer to new situations; second, it invites inferences from one case to the other; and, third, it highlights *alignable differences*—differences connected to the common structure. In this paper, we are concerned with the first and third of these.

A growing body of research indicates that category learning is supported by both within-category and between-category comparisons [3], [17]. Although these both involve structure-mapping processes, they yield different kinds of information. In *within-category comparison*, two exemplars from a single category are aligned. This type of comparison is exemplified in the Gentner and Namy [7] and Gentner and Christie [6] studies discussed above. Additional studies corroborate the positive effects of within-category comparison on children's category learning [4-5], [9], [18].

Between-category comparison—comparing a category exemplar with a non-exemplar (or a member of a different category)—is also informative in categorization. Waxman and Klibanoff [9] found an effect of between-category comparison on children's ability to infer the referent of a novel adjective. They found that 3-year-olds readily mapped an adjective to the appropriate object property (e.g., bumpy) when an object depicting the property (e.g., a bumpy frog) was contrasted with an object that was nearly identical but lacked the target property (e.g., a smooth frog). Between-category comparisons also support spatial learning; Gentner et al. [19-20] found evidence that comparison can help children learn a non-obvious spatial concept, namely that *a diagonal brace confers stability in construction*. Specifically, when children were shown two toy buildings, a stable one that contained a diagonal and a wobbly one that did not, children could use the alignment between them to identify the distinctive part (the diagonal brace) as important for stability.

It seems reasonable to suppose that within-category and between-category comparisons might serve different purposes. For example, Higgins and Ross [17] suggest that within-category comparison is particularly useful for challenging categories—those for which membership is based on nonobvious relational commonalities. In contrast, they propose that between-category comparisons should be most useful when the membership criterion is relatively transparent but category distinctions are difficult.

For children learning about triangles, both of these conditions may apply: that is, children seem not to grasp either the key relational commonalities or the category boundaries. Thus we might expect both within- and between-category comparison to help. Within-category comparisons should highlight relational commonalities that are critical for membership while de-emphasizing irrelevant surface features. For example, comparing the two triangles in Figure 2a may emphasize the relevant commonalities that both are *enclosed figures with three sides* while also revealing that relative side length is irrelevant to categorization (via highlighting the alignable difference that one exemplar has three equal sides and the other does not). Within-category comparison should therefore support generalization to further exemplars. On the other hand, between-category comparison should support learning by highlighting specific alignable differences that indicate category boundaries [17], [21]. For example, comparing the exemplar and non-exemplar in Figure 2b highlights the alignable difference that *the triangle is enclosed but the non-triangle is not*—a difference that captures a necessary condition for category membership. Between-category comparison may therefore support refinement of category boundaries, decreasing overgeneralization to non-exemplars that are perceptually similar to the prototype.

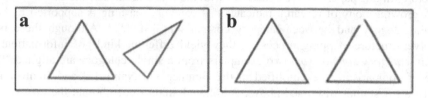

Fig. 2. (a) within-category comparison (two triangles) and (b) between-category comparison (triangle and non-triangle)

1.2   The Current Experiment

In this experiment we investigated whether comparison can support young children's learning of the geometric category of *triangle* and whether different types of comparison foster learning in distinct ways. During training, children saw a series of either within-category comparisons (two triangles) or between-category comparisons (triangle vs. non-triangle). We used a pretest-posttest design to assess changes in category knowledge due to training. We hypothesize that both within- and between-category comparisons will foster learning, but in different ways. Specifically, we expect that (1) within-category comparisons will improve categorization ability by promoting generalization to new exemplars, whereas (2) between-category comparisons will improve categorization by reducing overgeneralization to non-exemplars.

We also varied the surface (or featural) similarity of the cases being compared. Prior research shows that within-category comparison of two exemplars that share significant surface commonalities often results in a representation in which many of these irrelevant features are retained [22-23]. Comparison of dissimilar category exemplars (such as the pair in Figure 2a) is likely to lead to representations with broader generalizability. We therefore hypothesize that within-category comparisons of exemplars that are perceptually dissimilar from one another (*far* pairs) will promote generalization to a greater degree than within-category comparison of exemplars that are perceptually similar to one another (*near* pairs).

On the other hand, prior work shows that for *between*-category comparisons, pairs that are highly similar except for a crucial difference (as in Fig. 2b)—*near-miss* cases [24]—are especially effective [19-20], [25-26]. Such pairs have two advantages. First, highly similar pairs are extremely easy to align, even for children and novices. Second, once aligned, they have few or no competing differences besides the key alignable difference. We therefore hypothesize that between-category comparisons of near pairs will reduce overgeneralization to a greater degree than between-category comparison of far pairs.

2   Experiment

2.1   Method

Participants. 110 three- and four-year olds (52 Female; $M=4;0$, Range: 3;4-4;11) participated in the experiment. Children were recruited from the University of Chicago Lab School and Chicago public schools.

Materials

Triangle Classification Stimuli. Each child sorted 18 figures (9 triangles and 9 non-triangles) at pre-test and 18 figures at post-test, for 36 figures total. Four of the 18 exemplars were equilateral triangles, the remainder varied orthogonally by angle measure (acute, right, obtuse), side length (isosceles, scalene), and rotation (upright, tilted). To create the non-exemplars, we introduced a violation (non-enclosure or four sides) to each of the 18 exemplars. The 36 figures were split into two comparable sets; one set was given at pre-test and the other at post-test. The order of the sets was counterbalanced across participants.

Training Stimuli. 12 different triangles were created. The triangles varied orthogonally by angle measure (obtuse, acute, right triangles), side measure (equilateral, isosceles, scalene), and rotation (upright vs. rotated). From each exemplar, two non-exemplars were derived, one demonstrating lack of closure and the other an incorrect number of sides, for 24 non-exemplars total. For within-category comparisons, four pairs of exemplars were selected. Within a single pair, the triangles were drawn from different subcategories (e.g., an isosceles acute and scalene obtuse triangle were shown together). For near pairs, exemplars maintained the same orientation and aspect ratio. For far pairs, exemplars varied in these factors (Fig. 2a). All pairs were presented in a pseudo-randomized order.

For between-category comparisons, four exemplar/non-exemplar pairs were selected, covering the range of triangle subcategories. For all four pairs, children saw only a single violation type (non-enclosed or four-sided), not both. For near pairs, an exemplar was shown with either its non-enclosed or four-sided non-exemplar derivative (Fig. 2b). For far pairs, an exemplar was paired with a non-exemplar that varied in aspect ratio and orientation.

Procedure. The child sat at a table next to the experimenter with a video camera positioned over the child's shoulder. Children completed a triangle classification task pre-test, were given comparison training, and then completed a comparable triangle classification task at post-test.

Triangle Classification Task. We guided children through the sort task using a variant of the "picky puppet task" [27]. The child was told that Wally the Penguin (a handheld puppet) was a very picky penguin and wanted to keep only "real" instances of a triangle. The "real" instances were to be placed in the "treasure box" while others were "thrown away" in a trashcan[1]. The experimenter presented the child with one figure at a time, and told the child "Here is a shape. Is this a triangle?" The figure was then placed in the treasure box or the trashcan, contingent on the child's response. No feedback was given.

Comparison Task. Children were randomly assigned to one of four comparison conditions: within-category/near, within-category/far, between-category/near, between-category/far. Furthermore, children in the between-category groups were randomly assigned to one of the two violation types: non-enclosed or four-sided.

In the within-category comparison condition, the experimenter laid out an exemplar and labeled it: "This is a triangle." Then the experimenter placed the second exemplar next to the first one and named it with the same label as the first and encouraged the child to compare the two standards: "Can you see why they're both triangles?" (As in prior work, no answer was required; the idea was to invite children to think about it.) The experimenter repeated these statements while pointing again at each exemplar. The two exemplars were then removed from the child's view and the procedure was repeated with three more pairs of exemplars, for four total comparison pairs.

In the between-category comparison condition, the experimenter laid out an exemplar and labeled it ("This is a triangle"), then laid out a non-exemplar and told the child: "This is not a triangle" (Fig. 3). The child was then encouraged to compare the two cases: "Can you see why one is a triangle and the other is not?" These statements were reiterated then the pair was removed. The procedure was repeated for three more pairs, as in the within-category condition.

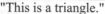

"This is a triangle."   "And this is NOT a triangle. See?"

Fig. 3. Comparison Task set-up. A Between-Category comparison is shown

---

[1] An initial sorting task using obviously different objects (dogs) confirmed that children understood the procedure.

Analysis

We assessed participants' classification ability using signal detection analysis. We examined children's sensitivity in categorization (d')—that is, how well the child was able to make correct classification decisions about triangles and avoid incorrect decisions. Furthermore, we looked more specifically at the two components that contribute to d'—hits (correctly accepting an exemplar) and false alarms (incorrectly accepting a non-exemplar). Compressing our hypotheses into the key predictions, we predict:

1. Within-category comparison will foster generalization to new exemplars; thus children who compare two exemplars will increase their hit rate from pre- to post-test.
2. Between-category comparison will reduce overgeneralization to non-exemplars; thus children who compare an exemplar and non-exemplar will decrease their false alarm rate from pre- to post-test.
3. Comparing perceptually dissimilar exemplars will promote a more abstract category representation; thus the positive effect of within-category comparison on hit rate will be more pronounced for far pairs than for near pairs.
4. Comparing a perceptually similar exemplar and non-exemplar will make diagnostic category differences more salient; thus the positive effect of between-category comparison on false alarm rate will be more pronounced for near pairs than for far pairs.

2.2   Results

We first examined children's knowledge of the triangle category at pre-test. Figure 4 shows the proportion of children who accepted each shape as a triangle. Acceptance rates are predictably high for equilateral triangles (top left), but taper off as the exemplars become perceptually dissimilar from the prototype (bottom right). Acceptance rates for non-exemplars increase as the figures become more perceptually similar to the prototype (top right). This pattern exemplifies the perceptual similarity bias demonstrated in prior work [1].

To assess changes in categorization from pre-test to post-test, we conducted a mixed MANOVA, with d', hit rate, and false alarm rate as dependent measures. Comparison Type (Within vs. Between) and Surface Similarity (Near vs. Far) were entered as between-subjects factors and Test Phase (Pre-Test vs. Post-Test) was entered as the within-subjects factor. Planned comparisons and post-hoc tests with Bonferroni-corrected alpha levels were run where appropriate. We look at each of the three dependent measures in turn.

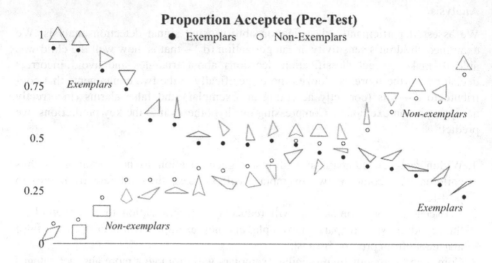

Fig. 4. Proportion of children who accepted each figure as a triangle at pre-test. A value of 1 indicates that 100% of children considered the figure a triangle, whereas a value of 0 indicates that no children considered the figure a triangle. Ideally, acceptance rates should be at 1 for exemplars and at 0 for non-exemplars, but the data reveal substantial variability by type of figure. Acceptance rates are predictably high for equilateral triangles (top left), but taper off as the exemplars become perceptually dissimilar from the prototype (bottom right). Acceptance rates for non-exemplars increase as the figures become more perceptually similar to the proto-type (top right). This pattern exemplifies the perceptual similarity bias found in prior work [1].

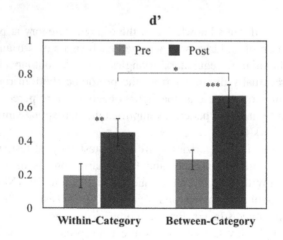

Fig. 5. Average d' at pre- and post-test, by Comparison Type

Sensitivity (d'). Figure 5 shows average d' rates at pre- and post-test for Within-Category comparison groups and Between-Category comparison groups. There was a large effect of Test Phase, $F(1,106) = 34.88$, $p<.001$; children reliably increased their sensitivity from pre- to post-test ($M_{Pre}=0.25$, SD=0.48; $M_{Post}=0.57$, SD=0.57).

No main effects of Comparison Type or Surface Similarity, nor any interactions between the factors, were found, p's>.27. Post-hoc explorations revealed that at posttest d' was higher for the Between-Category comparison group than for the Within-Category comparison group, p<.05.

Hit Rates. Figure 6 shows average hit rates at pre- and post-test for the Within-Category comparison groups and the Between-Category comparison groups. There was a main effect of Test Phase, $F(1,106) = 13.11$, p<.001—children reliably increased their hit rate from pre- to post-test (M_{Pre}=0.54, SD=0.33; M_{Post}=0.64, SD=0.30). The interaction between Test Phase and Comparison Type was marginally significant, $F(1,106) = 3.81$, p=.054. Planned comparisons revealed that the pre- to post-test improvement in hit rate was only obtained for children who made within-category comparisons (M_{Pre}=0.50, SD=0.35; M_{Post}=0.67, SD=0.31, p<.001). In contrast, there was no change in hit rate for children who made between-category comparisons (M_{Pre}=0.56, SD=0.32; M_{Post}=0.61, SD=0.29, p=.20). Thus only within-category comparisons supported generalization of the triangle category to more exemplars, in accord with our prediction. Neither Test Phase nor Comparison Type interacted with Surface Similarity (all Fs<.42, p's>.52)—similar improvements in hit rate were seen for within-category comparisons of near and far pairs (Near: M_{Pre}=0.52, SD=0.32; M_{Post}=0.69, SD=0.32; Far: M_{Pre}=0.49, SD=0.39; M_{Post}=0.65, SD=0.31; p=.66). This finding is inconsistent with our prediction that within-category comparison of far pairs would support generalization to a greater extent than comparison of near pairs; potential explanations for this finding are reserved for the general discussion.

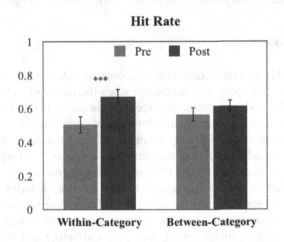

Fig. 6. Average Hit Rate at pre- and post-test, by Comparison Type

False Alarm (FA) Rates. Figure 7 shows average FA rates at pre- and post-test for the Within-Category Comparison groups and the Between-Category Comparison groups. The interaction between Test Phase and Comparison Type was highly significant, $F(1,106) = 13.20$, p<.001. Planned comparisons revealed that, for between-category comparisons, there was a significant reduction in FA rates from pre-test to post-test (M_{Pre}=0.43, SD=0.29; M_{Post}=0.31, SD=0.23, p<.001). This reduction in FA rates was only observed for between-category comparisons of near pairs (p<.001); there was no such reduction for far pairs (p=.13). There was no change in FA rate for children who saw within-category comparisons (M_{Pre}=0.42, SD=0.32; M_{Post}=0.47, SD=0.30, p=.18). These data support two of our predictions, namely that between-category comparisons would reduce overgeneralization of the triangle category to non-exemplars and that this effect would be more pronounced for near pairs than far pairs.

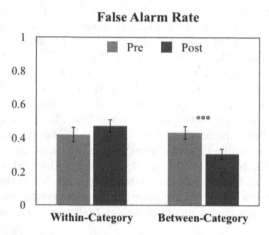

Fig. 7. Average False Alarm rate at pre-test and post-test, by Comparison Type

3   Discussion

An important problem in the acquisition of geometric categories is how learners can construct rule-based category representations when the inherently visual nature of the exemplars naturally leads to a focus on perceptual similarity [2]. Our results show that comparison processes can foster the development of such category representations in young children. Both within-category comparisons and between-category comparisons fostered better understanding of the geometric category of triangle, as evidenced by a pre-to-post-test increase in d' for all comparison conditions.

Our training method was to encourage children to make a series of comparisons. There were four groups, defined by whether children received within-category or between-category comparisons, and whether the pairs were of high or low surface similarity. Their category understanding was assessed before and after training using a classification task. We had four specific hypotheses regarding how different comparison experiences would benefit learning. All but one of these were borne out by the findings. First, we predicted that within-category comparisons would support category learning by promoting generalization to new exemplars. Indeed, children who were given within-category comparisons during training improved reliably in their hit rate. They extended the category to more exemplars at post-test than at pre-test, whereas children who saw between-category comparisons did not. Second, we predicted that between-category comparisons would support category learning by reducing overgeneralization to non-exemplars. Consistent with this, we found that children who saw between-category comparisons during training reduced their false alarm rates. They extended the category to fewer non-exemplars at post-test than at pre-test, whereas children who saw within-category comparisons did not. Our fourth hypothesis was that the positive effects of between-category comparison would be more pronounced for near (high surface similarity) pairs than for far pairs, and indeed we found that only children who compared near pairs reduced their false alarm rates. This finding is consistent with work showing that comparing two "near-miss" cases [24] improves learning [19-20], [25-26].

However, our third prediction was not borne out. For within-category comparisons, we expected to see greater improvement in hit rate for far pairs than for near pairs. In fact, we found no difference; these two kinds of pairs led to comparable increases in hit rate. These findings are consistent with recent work by Ankowski, Vlach, and Sandhofer [3], who also found that learning from within-category comparisons was less susceptible to variations in surface similarity between compared cases than learning from between-category comparisons.

This lack of difference is surprising, because normally one would expect that comparing more dissimilar pairs would lead to greater generalization. One possible explanation for why children who saw far within-category comparisons did not do better than those who saw near comparisons is that some children could have had difficulty aligning the far pairs; if so, then these children may not have succeeded in extracting the category structure. Consistent with this possibility, prior research has found that comparison between surface-similar cases is easier and less error-prone for beginning learners than comparison between surface-dissimilar pairs. For example, Kotovsky and Gentner [8] found that young children were better able to carry out relational matches when the cases were perceptually similar than when they were dissimilar.

3.1   Conclusions and Further Questions

Overall, these results show that both within-category and between-category comparisons can support children's acquisition of geometric categories. Consistent with Higgins and Ross's [17] findings, our data also reveal important differences in what learners derive from these kinds of comparison. Comparing two exemplars from a single category supports learning by encouraging the learner to create a more abstract category structure and become less reliant on perceptual similarity to the prototype. Comparing an exemplar with a non-exemplar helps learners identify critical category boundaries, therefore reducing overgeneralization to non-exemplars that violate these boundary conditions.

In future studies, we plan to pursue the question of when children can benefit from comparing near vs. far exemplars. We conjecture that children who already have some knowledge of the triangle category will benefit more from far comparison pairs. By aligning the far pairs, they will arrive at a more abstract understanding of triangles. However, learners with more impoverished knowledge may benefit from receiving near comparison pairs first, followed by far comparison. This *progressive alignment* sequence has been found to aid young children's learning in prior studies [8], [18].

Second, how might we combine within- and between-category comparisons to maximize learning? In prior work, Namy and Clepper [28] found that children benefitted more from between-category comparisons if they followed within-category comparisons. Future work should test whether this ordering is also effective for geometric category learning.

Our findings join connect with prior work in showing that the simple act of comparing two things can support category learning in children. These findings extend the range of phenomena studied to encompass children's learning of geometric categories. Perhaps most importantly, our finding of specific effects for within- and between-category comparison joins with other work that is delineating the precise effects of different kinds of comparisons.

Acknowledgements. This research was supported by NSF grant SBE-0541957 to the Spatial Intelligence and Learning Center (SILC). We thank Anna Mackinnon for help with constructing stimuli and data collection. We thank University of Chicago's Levine Lab and Northwestern University's Cognition and Language Lab for helpful comments on this work.

References

1. Satlow, E., Newcombe, N.: When is a triangle not a triangle? Young children's conceptions of geometric shapes. Cognitive Development 13, 547–559 (1998)
2. Forbus, K.D.: Qualitative modeling. WIREs Cogn. Sci. 2, 374–391 (2011)
3. Ankowski, A.A., Vlach, H.A., Sandhofer, C.M.: Comparison Versus Contrast: Task Specifics Affect Category Acquisition. Inf. Child. Dev. 22(1), 1–23 (2013)
4. Casasola, M.: Can language do the driving? The effect of linguistic input on infants' categorization of support spatial relations. Developmental Psychology 41, 183–191 (2005)
5. Childers, J.B.: Attention to multiple events helps 2½-year-olds extend new verbs. First Language 31, 3–22 (2011)
6. Christie, S., Gentner, D.: Where hypotheses come from: Learning new relations by structural alignment. J. Cognition and Development 11(3), 356–373 (2010)
7. Gentner, D., Namy, L.: Comparison in the Development of Categories. Cognitive Development 14, 487–513 (1999)
8. Kotovsky, L., Gentner, D.: Comparison and Categorization in the Development of Relational Similarity. Child Development 67, 2797–2822 (1996)
9. Waxman, S.R., Klibanoff, R.S.: The role of comparison in the extension of novel adjectives. Developmental Psychology 36(5), 571–581 (2000)
10. Namy, L.L., Gentner, D.: Making a silk purse out of two sow's ears: Young children's use of comparison in category learning. J. Experimental Psychology: General 131(1), 5–15 (2002)
11. Markman, A.B., Gentner, D.: Structure-Mapping in the Comparison Process, Amer. J. of Psychology 113(4), 501–538 (2000)
12. Falkenhainer, B., Forbus, K.D., Gentner, D.: The Structure-Mapping Engine: Algorithm and Examples. Artificial Intelligence 20(41), 1–63 (1989)

13. Gentner, D.: Structure-mapping: A theoretical framework for analogy. Cognitive Science 7(2), 155–170 (1983)
14. Gentner, D.: Bootstrapping the mind: Analogical processes and symbol systems. Cognitive Science 34(5), 752–775 (2010)
15. Markman, A.B., Gentner, D.: Structural alignment during similarity comparisons. Cognitive Psychology 25, 431–467 (1993)
16. Gentner, D., Markman, A.B.: Structure mapping in analogy and similarity. American Psychologist 52, 45–56 (1997)
17. Higgins, E.J., Ross, B.H.: Comparisons in Category Learning: How Best to Compare for What. In: Carlson, L., Hölscher, C., Shipley, T. (eds.) Proceedings of the 33rd Annual Conference of the Cognitive Science Society, pp. 1388–1393. Cognitive Science Society, Austin (2011)
18. Gentner, D., Anggoro, F.K., Klibanoff, R.S.: Structure-mapping and Relational Language Support Children's Learning of Relational Categories. Child Development 82(4), 1173–1188 (2011)
19. Gentner, D., Levine, S., Dhillon, S., Poltermann, A.: Using structural alignment to facilitate learning of spatial concepts in an informal setting. In: Kokinov, B., Holyoak, K.J., Gentner, D. (eds.) Proceedings of the Second International Conference on Analogy. NBU Press, Sofia (2009)
20. Gentner, D., Levine, S.C., Dhillon, S., Ping, R., Bradley, C., Poltermann, A., Honke, G.: Rapid learning in a children's museum via analogical comparison (submitted)
21. Goldstone, R.L., Sakamoto, Y.: The Transfer of Abstract Principles Governing Complex Adaptive Systems. Cognitive Psychology 46, 414–466 (2003)
22. Gentner, D., Rattermann, M.J.: Language and the career of similarity. In: Gelman, S.A., Byrnes, J.P. (eds.) Perspectives on Thought and Language: Interrelations in Development, pp. 225–277. Cambridge University Press, London (1991)
23. Goldstone, R.L.: Isolated and Interrelated Concepts. Memory & Cognition 24, 608–628 (1996)
24. McLure, M.D., Friedman, S.E., Forbus, K.D.: Learning concepts from sketches via analogical generalization and near-misses. Proc. Cog. Sci., 465–470 (2010)
25. Gick, M.L., Paterson, K.J.: Do contrasting examples facilitate schema acquisition and analogical transfer? Canadian Journal of Psychology 46, 539–550 (1992)
26. Kurtz, K.J., Gentner, D.: Detecting anomalous features in complex stimuli: The role of structured comparison. JEP: Applied 19(3), 219–232 (2013)
27. Waxman, S., Gelman, R.: Preschoolers' use of superordinate relations in classification and language. Cognitive Development 1, 139–156 (1986)
28. Namy, L.L., Clepper, L.E.: The differing roles of comparison and contrast in children's categorization. J. Experimental Child Psychology 107, 291–305 (2010)

Spatial Concepts: Sensitivity to Changes in Geometric Properties in Environmental and Figural Perception

Toru Ishikawa

Graduate School of Interdisciplinary Information Studies
and Center for Spatial Information Science, University of Tokyo,
7-3-1 Hongo, Bunkyo-ku, Tokyo 113-0033, Japan
ishikawa@csis.u-tokyo.ac.jp

Abstract. This study examined spatial concepts in environment perception, by looking at people's reaction to changes in shape, scale, orientation, and topology while navigating in a virtual environment, as contrasted to the case of figural perception. Although people attended to changes in shape, they were most sensitive to a topological relation and discriminated it qualitatively from other transformations. In environment perception, compared to figural perception, the property of similarity did not have great cognitive prominence. Mental-rotation ability affected spatial perception, with high-spatial people discriminating between different transformations more clearly and low-spatial people attending more to topological relations.

Keywords: Spatial thinking, Spatial cognition, Spatial ability, Scale, Environmental exploration, Geometric transformations.

1 Introduction

The fact that humans live and act in space seems rather obvious, but has profound implications for their everyday reasoning and behavior; and thus the issues of human spatial cognition and behavior have attracted theoretical and practical attention from researchers in various disciplines. In particular, the characteristics of large-scale spaces, or the *environment*, and their effects on the cognition of space (environment perception) have been discussed in the context of knowledge development, as contrasted with the perception of objects (object perception). Importantly, Ittelson (1973) contended that the environment is larger than and surrounds the human body, and thus it cannot be perceived in its entirety from a single viewpoint. To do that, a person needs to explore the environment (not simply view it as an external observer) and integrate the views at different locations into a coherent mental image of the environment. It makes the task of acquiring knowledge about the environment (or "cognitive mapping") very difficult for some people, especially people with a poor sense of direction (Hegarty et al., 2002; Kozlowski & Bryant, 1977).

In relation to the distinction between environment and object perceptions, an issue that has been extensively discussed is *scale*. Montello (1993) discussed different types of spaces in terms of spatial scale, and notably distinguished *environmental* and *figural*

C. Freksa et al. (Eds.): Spatial Cognition 2014, LNAI 8684, pp. 338–353, 2014.

spaces. The two spaces differ in the size compared to the human body (the former being larger and the latter smaller than the body) and in the requirement for the viewer to move around in the space to acquire the knowledge; thus mapping onto the environment-object distinction discussed above (also see Hegarty et al., 2006). One exception to this distinction is when a map is used: viewing a map that represents an environmental space renders the task of learning about the environment a learning about a figural space (e.g., Thorndyke & Hayes-Roth, 1982).

The issue of spatial knowledge and learning has also been recently discussed from a slightly different perspective, in terms of *spatial thinking* (National Research Council, 2006), corresponding to the recognition that spatial thinking plays critical roles in the STEM disciplines (science, technology, engineering, and mathematics) and in everyday life (e.g., Keehner et al., 2004; Kozhevnikov, Motes, & Hegarty, 2007; Newcombe, 2010; Uttal & Cohen, 2012). Particularly in the literature of geoscience learning and education, researchers have discussed the concepts of spatial thinking. For example, Golledge, Marsh, and Battersby (2008) proposed that spatial concepts can be classified into spatial primitives (identity, location, magnitude, and space-time) and derivatives at higher levels (e.g., arrangement, distribution, distance, adjacency, connectivity, scale, and projection). Similar classifications were proposed by Gersmehl and Gersmehl (2007), Janelle and Goodchild (2009), and Kuhn (2012).

The present study aims to extend the discussions of spatial concepts further, particularly by examining the perception of various spatial concepts in the scale of environmental space. Specifically, it is of interest to see, in the case of environment perception, if people perceive different spatial concepts as being different from each other and whether people perceive some concepts as more salient than others. In fact, the term spatial thinking has not been clearly defined (National Research Council, 2006) and other terms such as spatial ability are often used interchangeably to discuss its meaning (Hegarty, 2010; Ishikawa, 2013a; Lee & Bednarz, 2012).

Motivated by that interest, Ishikawa (2013b) examined spatial concepts in the case of figural perception, by extending the traditional arguments of geometric properties in the cognitive and mathematical literatures. Cognitively, an understanding of geometries has been discussed in terms of a progression of topological, projective, and Euclidean geometries (Piaget & Inhelder, 1948/1967) and scrutinized in the context of K-12 learning and education (e.g., Kidder, 1976; Mandler, 1983, 2012; Martin, 1976). Mathematically, geometries are defined in terms of properties that are preserved through a group of transformations (Gans, 1969). For example, topological transformations preserve openness, interior, order, and connectedness. In addition to these properties, projective transformations preserve collinearity and cross-ratios; similarity transformations (scaling) preserve angle-size; and Euclidean transformations (rigid motions, i.e., translation, rotation, and reflection) preserve length.

Ishikawa (2013b) presented figural configurations that were deformed (i.e., the shapes of which were changed) to different degrees and transformed through rotation, scaling, and reflection to participants, and asked them to judge the dissimilarity between the original and the deformed or transformed configurations. The results showed that participants were sensitive to the changes in shape, but their sensitivity to rotation, scaling, and reflection differed depending on the degree of deformation. Also, people with a low spatial ability were more sensitive to rotation and reflection than those with a high spatial ability, whose responses were more aligned with the mathematical classification of transformations. In sum, the study pointed to the difference in cognitive and mathematical classifications of spatial properties, and the effects of spatial ability on people's spatial conception.

The major objective of the present study is to examine the cognitive classifications of different spatial concepts in environment perception, because, as the aforementioned importance of scale in spatial cognition suggests, spatial concepts in environment perception and figural perception may differ. Therefore this study looks into the difference between cognitive and mathematical classifications of geometric properties while navigating in a virtual environment, taking differences in the level of spatial abilities into consideration. Methodologically it extends the experiment conducted by Ishikawa (2013b) for figural perception to the case of environment perception, and examines people's responses (or "sensitivity") to the changes in shape, orientation, size, and topology caused by various geometric transformations (deformation, rotation, scaling, and reflection).

2   Method

2.1   Participants

A total of 57 students (32 men and 25 women) participated in the experiment. They were undergraduate students in various disciplines including law, economics, literature, sociology, physics, chemistry, engineering, and architecture. Their ages ranged from 18 to 29, with a mean of 19.6 years.

2.2   Materials

Virtual Environments with Different Geometric Configurations. As experimental stimuli, three-dimensional views of virtual cities consisting of three "landmarks" (a traffic sign pole, a tree, and a cylindrical building) and paths connecting them, projected on a screen, were used (Figure 1). No two landmarks were visible simultaneously, being screened by the walls. The two-dimensional or configurational arrangements of the three landmarks matched the 36 geometric configurations of three dots examined in the Ishikawa (2013b) study (see Figure 2).

Fig. 1. Views from the virtual environments at the three landmarks: a traffic sigh pole (*left*), a tree (*middle*), and a cylindrical building (*right*).

The configurations varied with respect to the degree of *deformation* and the types of transformations applied. For deformation, an original configuration of an equilateral triangle was deformed into eight configurations, with the lengths and angles among the three landmarks being changed with the constraint that the scale factor was fixed at 1 (Figure 2, panels #2-9). The degree of deformation was varied on the basis of bidimensional regression coefficients computed between the coordinates for randomly generated three dots and those for the three landmarks in the original configuration (Tobler, 1994). Since bidimensional regression attempts to maximize the correspondence between two configurations to be compared through translation, rotation, and scaling, values for bidimensional regression coefficients do not become too small, for example down to 0, even when coordinates are randomly generated. In the present case of three dots, the values ranged from .73 to 1 (shown in Figure 2).

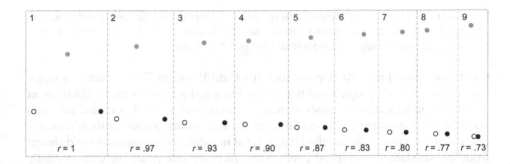

Fig. 2. Nine two-dimensional configurations (#1-9) that were deformed to different degrees. The leftmost panel shows the original configuration. Values for *r* indicate the bidimensional regression coefficients between the original (#1) and deformed (#2-9) configurations. The grey dot corresponds to the landmark of a traffic sigh pole, the white dot a tree, and the black dot a cylindrical building. In the experiment, participants looked at three-dimensional views as shown in Figure 1, not the two-dimensional plans shown in this figure. Reproduced by permission of Springer from Ishikawa 2013b, fig. 1.

To these nine configurations, three different types of transformations were applied, to yield three more sets of nine configurations: a *rotation* (half the configurations, which were chosen randomly, were rotated 90° to the right, and the other half were rotated 90° to the left), a *scaling* (half the configurations were scaled by a factor of 2, and the other half by a factor of 0.5), and a *reflection* (the nine configurations were flipped over). With the reflection, the cyclic order of the three landmarks is altered and thus it can be conceived as breaking the topology of the three landmarks (i.e., ordered clockwise vs. counterclockwise); it was included to see if the changes caused by it are perceived as qualitatively different from the other transformations.

As examples, the three transformed configurations for the original configuration are shown in Figure 3. In the virtual environment, for the deformed, scaled, and reflected configurations, participants started at the traffic sign pole (denoted by a grey dot in Figures 2 and 3) and walked counterclockwise around the paths connecting the three landmarks. For the rotated configurations, they started either at the the tree (denoted by a white dot) when the configurations were rotated to the right or at the cylindrical building (denoted by a black dot) when rotated to the left. Participants walked along the paths that connected the three landmarks at a speed of 4 km/h. The original configuration was scaled in the virtual environment so that it took 30 s to walk around the three landmarks and return to the origin.

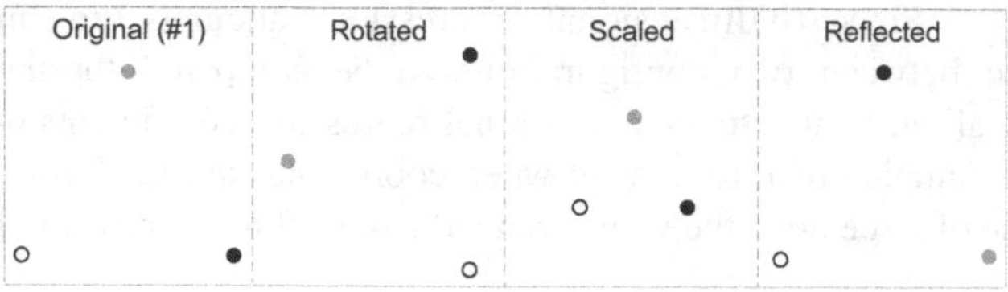

Fig. 3. Three transformations applied to the original configuration (#1, leftmost panel): rotation, scaling, and reflection (the second, third, and fourth panel from the left, respectively). Reproduced by permission of Springer from Ishikawa 2013b, fig. 2.

Card Rotations Test. Participants took the Card Rotations Test, which is a major spatial test assessing people's ability to rotate imagined pictures mentally (Ekstrom et al., 1976). In the test, participants viewed 20 items, each consisting of one card in a standard orientation and eight alternative cards, and answered whether the alternative cards were the same as the standard (i.e., rotated into different orientations) or different from the standard (i.e., flipped over). They received one point for each correctly identified card and lost one point for each wrongly identified card. Participants were allowed 6 min to complete this test. Mental-rotation ability correlates with the understanding and use of maps in the field (e.g., Liben & Downs, 1993), and so it was assessed in this study as a possible correlate with the perception of differences in geometric properties.

Sense-of-Direction Scale. Participants filled out the Santa Barbara Sense-of-Direction (SBSOD) scale, which consists of fifteen 7-point Likert-type questions about navigational abilities or preferences (Hegarty et al., 2002). It is scored so that a higher score indicates a better SOD, ranging in value from 1 to 7. People having higher SOD scores tend to do better on configurational understanding of environmental spaces, so the scale was used in this study to see whether the trait relates to the characteristics of spatial concepts in environment perception.

2.3   Design and Procedure

Participants viewed the scenes of walking through the 36 virtual environments in random order. The stimulus environments were always presented on the screen paired with the environment with the original configuration (the two-dimensional plan of panel #1 in Figure 2), which was shown half the times to the left of the screen and the other half to the right. In both of the paired environments, the navigator started at the same time. After viewing each pair of the scenes, participants answered whether they thought the configurations or arrangements of the three landmarks in the pair of cities were spatially the same or different on a 7-point scale (1 = *same*; 7 = *different*). Namely, the responses indicated a perceived degree of dissimilarity of the transformed configuration to the original configuration. This is an extension of the method used by Ishikawa (2013b) to the case of environmental exploration, which was originally based on the method used by Levinson (1996) to study the use of spatial frames of reference.

After completing all 36 scenes, participants filled out the SBSOD scale and took the Card Rotations Test. They finished all these tasks within 45 min on average.

2.4   Hypotheses and Possible Results

About the responses to changes in geometric properties in environment perception for this study, hypotheses similar to the ones examined by Ishikawa (2013b) for figural perception are constructed. Concerning the effects of the degree of deformation, participants would perceive the deformed configurations as more dissimilar to the original configuration as the degree of deformation becomes larger (i.e., the regression line of perceived dissimilarity on bidimensional regression coefficients would have a negative slope).

Concerning the effects of different types of transformations, one possibility is that participants would respond in line with the mathematical classification of geometric transformations. If participants' perception shares characteristics with Euclidean transformations, their responses would not change with rotation or reflection, because these transformations preserve Euclidean properties. Their responses to scaled configurations, however, would differ, because scaling does not preserve the Euclidean property of length. If participants' perception shares characteristics with similarity transformations, regression lines for rotated, reflected, and scaled configurations would coincide that for deformed configurations, as rotation, reflection, and scaling preserve angle-size. By contrast, if participants "live" in the world of topology, they would perceive all configurations as the same, and the regression lines would have a slope of 0; except that they would respond to reflected configurations differently as long as they regard reflection as breaking topology.

Another possibility is that participants' responses do not conform to the mathematical classification of transformations. Then, rotation, scaling, and reflection would change participants' perception, and so the regression lines for these three transformations would deviate from that for deformation. And in that case, there are two further possibilities. If the effects of rotation, scaling, and reflection are independent of the degree of deformation, the four regression lines would be parallel. Or, if the effects differ depending on the degree of deformation, the slopes for the four regression lines would be different.

As well as examining these hypotheses, this study also compares the responses in the case of environment perception (this study) to those in figural perception (Ishikawa, 2013b), particularly paying attention to the possible effects of experiencing the configurations in a horizontal perspective and not in their entirety. One issue of interest is whether the property of similarity (which is preserved by scaling) is as noticeable as in figural perception. Another issue is whether the cognitive importance of sequential or topological knowledge about the space (i.e., "route" knowledge) is greater in environment perception than in figural perception. If so, reflection, which breaks the cyclic order of the landmarks, would be perceived as qualitatively different from other transformations, and to a greater extent than in figural perception. And rotation, which preserves the topology of the landmarks, might be discriminated less sensitively than in figural perception.

With these hypotheses in mind, the present study examines the size and the equivalence of slopes for regression lines for the four sets of configurations and compares them between environment and figural perceptions.

3   Results

3.1   Effects of the Types of Transformations and the Degree of Deformation

Participants' responses were examined through a repeated measures analysis of variance (ANOVA), with the degree of deformation (the nine panels in Figure 1) and the types of transformations (deformation, rotation, scaling, and reflection) as within-subject variables. Following the general recommendation (Girden, 1992), univariate and multivariate tests were conducted at the .025 level each (when both tests are significant, statistics for the univariate test are reported).

There were significant main effects of degree of deformation and type of transformation, $F(8, 376) = 57.22, p < .001; F(3, 141) = 34.77, p < .001$, respectively; and a significant interaction between the two variables, $F(24, 1128) = 8.17, p < .001$. The existence of a significant interaction shows that although participants discriminated between the four types of transformations, their sensitivity to rotation, scaling, and reflection differed depending on the degree of deformation.

3.2   Regression for Deformation, Rotation, Scaling, and Reflection

The effects of the degree of deformation and the types of transformations were further examined through regression analysis, with participants' responses being regressed on the degree of deformation for each type of transformation separately (Figure 4A).

The slopes for regression lines are significantly different between deformation and scaling and between deformation and reflection, $t(14) = 4.41$ and 5.32, respectively, $p < .001$ (Bonferroni, $\alpha = .05/6$). All regression lines have a negative slope, showing that participants perceived the configurations as more dissimilar to the original configuration as the degree of deformation increased (or the value for r became smaller).

At the bidimensional regression value of $r = 1$ (the original configuration and its transformed images), participants' responses to the four configurations were significantly different from each other, $t(51) = 5.17, t(53) = 10.48, t(50) = 11.84, t(53) = 4.01, t(50) = 5.55, t(56) = 5.56, p$'s $< .001$. At the value of $r = .73$ (the most greatly deformed configuration and its transformed images), the perceived dissimilarity value for the reflected configuration was significantly larger than that for the deformed, rotated, and scaled configurations, $t(50) = -3.65$, $t(52) = -4.06$, $t(56) = -4.48$, respectively, p's < .001.

These findings about the differences in slopes and the distances between the regression lines along the vertical axis show that the effects of the three transformations on perceived dissimilarity differed depending both on the degree of deformation and on the types of transformations. When the degree of deformation was small, participants perceived rotated, scaled, or reflected configurations as dissimilar to the original, with the reflected configuration being most dissimilar, and then the scaled configuration, and then the rotated configuration. When the degree of deformation became large, participants did not discriminate between deformed, rotated, and scaled configurations, but still perceived reflected configurations as dissimilar to the other configurations.

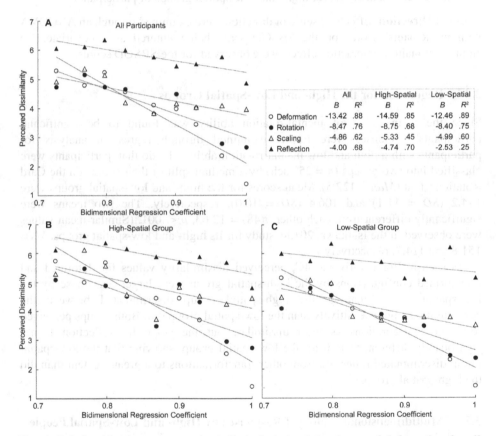

Fig. 4. Relationships between perceived dissimilarity and the degree of deformation for all participants (A), the high-spatial group (B), and the low-spatial group (C). Lines depict linear regression lines. B = unstandardized regression coefficient; R^2 = coefficient of determination.

3.3   Effects of Spatial Aptitudes

Mental-Rotation Ability. Effects of spatial ability on participants' responses were examined through an analysis of covariance (ANCOVA), with their scores on the Card Rotations Test being entered as a covariate into the repeated measures ANOVA conducted in section 3.1. A significant main effect of mental-rotation ability was observed, $F(1, 40) = 11.09$, $p < .01$, indicating that participants with a higher mental-rotation ability tended to perceive deformed and transformed configurations as more dissimilar (or to discriminate between them more sensitively). In light of the significance of spatial ability, the effects of the degree of deformation and the types of transformations on perceived dissimilarity are examined in the next section through separate regression analyses for high- and low-spatial groups of participants.

Sense of Direction. Effects of sense of direction were examined through an ANCOVA with participants' scores on the SBSOD scale being entered as a covariate. No significant main or interaction effects were observed for the SBSOD scores.

3.4   Regression for the High- and Low-Spatial Groups

Since the main effect of mental-rotation ability was found to be significant, participants' responses were further examined through regression analysis for participants with a high and low mental-rotation ability. To do that, participants were classified into two groups ($n = 25$ each) by a median split of their scores on the Card Rotations Test ($Mdn = 122.5$). Mean scores for the high- and low-spatial groups were 144.2 ($SD = 11.1$) and 106.4 ($SD = 10.0$), respectively. The two means were significantly different from each other, $t(48) = 12.63$, $p < .001$. (Similar mean values were observed in the Ishikawa, 2013b, study for its high- and low-spatial groups, $Ms = 151.8$ and 114.7, respectively.)

As seen in Figures 4B and 4C, perceived dissimilarity values for deformed and transformed configurations by the high-spatial group were larger than those by the low-spatial group; that is, the high-spatial group discriminated between the configurations more sensitively than the low-spatial group did. Both groups perceived reflected configurations as most dissimilar, but the slope for reflection is not significantly different from 0 for the low-spatial group, showing that the low-spatial group discriminated reflection from other transformations to a greater extent than did the high-spatial group.

3.5   Multidimensional Scaling of Responses by High- and Low-Spatial People

As in the Ishikawa (2013b) study, the effects of mental-rotation ability was examined in more detail through multidimensional scaling (MDS) analysis of the high- and low-spatial groups' responses. In ordinal MDS with the PROXSCAL method, a three-dimensional solution and a four-dimensional solution yielded a stress value indicating a fair fit, .09, for the high- and low-spatial groups, respectively (Kruskal, 1964). For illustration, a two-dimensional solution for each group is shown in Figure 5.

The three- and four-dimensional coordinates were further examined through cluster analysis, with three clusters being identified for each group (see Clusters I-III and the dendrogram shown in Figure 5).

For the high-spatial group, Cluster I mainly consists of the configurations to which small degrees of deformation were applied (panels #1 and #2 in Figure 2) and their rotated images. Cluster II consists of configurations to which medium degrees of deformation were applied (panels #3, #4, and #5) and scaled configurations. Cluster III consists of greatly deformed configurations and their rotated and scaled images, and the reflected configurations. For the low-spatial group, Cluster I mainly consists of configurations to which small degrees of deformation were applied (panels #1 and #2) and most of the rotated configurations. Cluster II consists of configurations to which medium to large degrees of deformation were applied (panels #3-9) and most of the scaled configurations, and Cluster III consists of the reflected configurations.

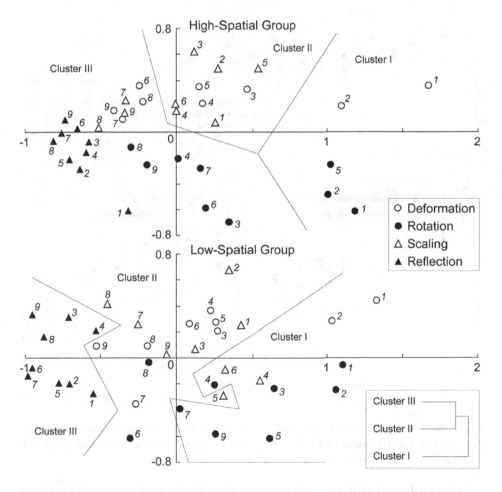

Fig. 5. MDS solutions (2D) for the high-spatial (*top*) and low-spatial (*bottom*) groups. Numbers in italics correspond to the panel numbers in Figure 2 and indicate the degree of deformation.

Compared to the low-spatial group, Clusters II and III for the high-spatial group are more tightly clustered and separated from Cluster I. Importantly, the clustering of scaling (similarity) and rotation and reflection (rigid motions) was clearer for the high-spatial group. It shows that their conception was more similar to the mathematical classification of geometries than the low-spatial group's.

3.6   Comparison between Environment and Figural Perceptions

To examine the differences in the responses to geometric properties in environment perception (this study) and figural perception (Ishikawa, 2013b), the regression lines and MDS solutions obtained in the two studies were compared. The regression and MDS results from Ishikawa (2013b) are shown in Figures 6 and 7.

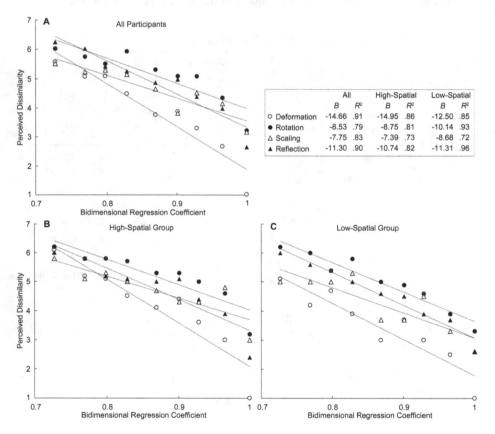

	All		High-Spatial		Low-Spatial	
	B	R²	B	R²	B	R²
○ Deformation	-14.66	.91	-14.95	.86	-12.50	.85
● Rotation	-8.53	.79	-8.75	.81	-10.14	.93
△ Scaling	-7.75	.83	-7.39	.73	-8.68	.72
▲ Reflection	-11.30	.90	-10.74	.82	-11.31	.96

Fig. 6. Relationships between perceived dissimilarity and the degree of deformation in figural perception, for all participants (A), the high-spatial group (B), and the low-spatial group (C). Reproduced by permission of Springer from Ishikawa 2013b, fig. 3.

Between the two studies, reflection has significantly different slopes, $t(14) = 4.04$, $p < .01$, with the slope for environment perception being less steeper negatively than that for figural perception ($B = -4.00$ vs. -11.30). At the bidimensional regression value of $r = 1$, perceived dissimilarity values for scaling and reflection were larger in environment perception than in figural perception, $t(105) = 2.38, p < .05$, and $t(105) = 6.37, p < .001$, respectively. At the value of $r = .73$, perceived dissimilarity values for rotation and scaling were smaller in environment perception than in figural perception, $t(105) = -4.34, p < .001$, and $t(105) = -2.13, p < .05$, respectively. Notably in environment perception, scaled configurations were perceived as more dissimilar when the degree of deformation was small, and reflection (which breaks topology) was perceived as causing a greater difference, than in figural perception.

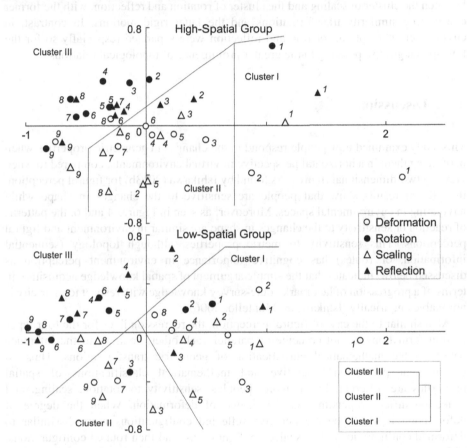

Fig. 7. MDS solutions in figural perception for the high-spatial (*top*) and low-spatial (*bottom*) groups. Reproduced by permission of Springer from Ishikawa 2013b, fig. 4.

As seen in Figures 4 and 6, perceived dissimilarity among rotation, scaling, and reflection (or the vertical distances between the three regression lines) was smaller in figural perception, suggesting that the three transformations were considered in figural perception more similar, in light of the properties of congruence and similarity. In environment perception, reflection is discriminated from the others to a greater extent, and its regression slope is less steep, than in figural perception, indicating a constant sensitivity to topological properties. Also in environment perception, the perceived dissimilarity value for rotation was smaller than in figural perception, suggesting that the fact that rotation preserves topology (or "routes") affects the judgment of configurational similarity more greatly in environment perception. By contrast, as shown above, scaled configurations were perceived as more dissimilar in environment perception, suggesting that viewing the paths horizontally, not from above, makes the property of similarity less prominent cognitively in environment perception.

As seen in Figures 5 and 7, in figural perception a clear separation was made between the cluster of scaling and the cluster of rotation and reflection, with the former constituting similarity transformations and the latter rigid motions. In contrast, in environment perception, rotation and reflection were separated (especially so for the low-spatial group), pointing to the greater prominence of topological relations.

4   Discussion

This study examined how people respond to the changes in geometric properties when perceiving them in a horizontal perspective in virtual environments, compared to when viewing two-dimensional figures. As found by Ishikawa (2013b) for figural perception, the present results show that people are sensitive to the changes in shape while navigating in environmental spaces. Moreover, as seen in Figures 4 and 6, the patterns of reaction or sensitivity to the changes in shape are similar in environment and figural perceptions. This sensitivity to metric properties, although topology (sequential information, or routes) has cognitive importance in environment perception as discussed below, indicates that the simple argument of spatial knowledge acquisition in terms of a progression of landmark-route-survey knowledge with respect to metricity is not viable empirically (Ishikawa & Montello, 2006).

Also similar to the case of figural perception, the regression lines for the four types of transformations do not coincide or parallel each other, contrary to the inference based on the mathematical classification of geometric transformations. Thus, in environment perception, cognitive and mathematical classifications of spatial properties are different. Furthermore, peoples' sensitivity to rotation, scaling, and reflection differs depending on the degree of deformation. When the degree of deformation is small, people perceive reflected configurations most dissimilar to deformed configurations, then scaled configurations, and then rotated configurations. They become less sensitive and do not discriminate rotated and scaled configurations from deformed configurations. In contrast to figural perception, in environmental perception people discriminate reflection from others constantly across different degrees of deformation, which points to the importance and qualitative distinction of topological information in environment perception.

In figural perception, the transformations of scaling, rotation, and reflection are considered relatively similar, compared to the case of environment perception, with a cognitive separation between scaling (similarity transformation) and rotation and reflection (rigid motions, resulting in congruence). By contrast, in environment perception, scaled configurations are considered dissimilar to deformed configurations, and reflection is discriminated from other transformations qualitatively. It points to the lesser cognitive prominence of similarity and the greater prominence of topology in environment perception, in which landmarks and paths need to be experienced in a horizontal perspective, not seen from above.

Concerning the effect of spatial aptitudes, people with a high mental-rotation ability discriminate between different configurations more sensitively, and in a way more aligned with the mathematical classification of geometries, than people with a low mental-rotation ability do. The extent to which reflected configurations are considered qualitatively different is greater for the low-spatial group, pointing to a greater tendency for them to attend to the property of topological relations, or to understand environments at the level of route knowledge.

In summary, the present results reveal the characteristics of spatial concepts perceived in large-scale environments, as contrasted by spatial concepts in figural perception. In particular, the results provide insights about the difference between cognitive and mathematical ways of classifying geometric properties, cognitive salience of different geometric properties and interaction among them, and the effects of spatial ability on the conception of spatial properties. Also, this study looked into the issue of environment perception from a different perspective than the existing studies, which examined the accuracy of mentally represented environments (e.g., Ishikawa & Montello, 2006) or analyzed relative positioning of landmarks in mental representations through MDS (e.g., Golledge & Hubert, 1982). Thus it exemplifies a novel attempt at investigating environmental perception and cognition from the perspective of spatial thinking.

Further issues to consider include the method for comparing the configurations of two virtual environments. In this study, participants viewed deformed and transformed configurations always paired with the original configuration, which may have been easier than comparing two environments from memory. Also, the effects of semantic or contextual factors need to be inspected, as they were found to affect the perception of spatio-temporal concepts such as topological relations represented by geometric figures (e.g., Klippel, 2012).

As a possible application of the present results, knowledge about the relationship between physical and perceived configurations may be applied to the design of city structures. As the symbol size on graduate circle maps can be varied referring to the relationship between physical and perceived dot size, the regression lines obtained in this study might be used to predict, for example, the shape of a neighborhood that is deformed to a degree that stimulates excitement of walking without disorienting the traveler. Finally, the results also provide pedagogical implications. Knowing that cognitive and mathematical classifications and environmental and figural spatial concepts differ, effective instruction of environmental learning and navigation could be developed, especially targeted to low-spatial people.

Acknowledgments. I thank HueYen Yang for his assistance in developing the virtual environments.

References

Ekstrom, R.B., French, J.W., Harman, H.H., Dermen, D.: Kit of Factor-Referenced Cognitive Tests. Educational Testing Service, Princeton (1976)

Gans, D.: Transformations and Geometries. Appleton-Century-Crofts, New York (1969)

Gersmehl, P.J., Gersmehl, C.A.: Spatial thinking by young children: Neurologic evidence for early development and "educability". Journal of Geography 106, 181–191 (2007)

Girden, E.R.: ANOVA: Repeated Measures (Sage University Paper Series on Quantitative Applications in the Social Sciences, Series No. 07–084). Sage, Newbury Park, CA (1992)

Golledge, R.G., Hubert, L.J.: Some comments on non-Euclidean mental maps. Environment and Planning A 14, 107–118 (1982)

Golledge, R.G., Marsh, M., Battersby, S.: A conceptual framework for facilitating geospatial thinking. Annals of the Association of American Geographers 98, 285–308 (2008)

Hegarty, M.: Components of spatial intelligence. Psychology of Learning and Motivation 52, 265–297 (2010)

Hegarty, M., Montello, D.R., Richardson, A.E., Ishikawa, T., Lovelace, K.: Spatial abilities at different scales: Individual differences in aptitude-test performance and spatial-layout learning. Intelligence 34, 151–176 (2006)

Hegarty, M., Richardson, A.E., Montello, D.R., Lovelace, K., Subbiah, I.: Development of a self-report measure of environmental spatial ability. Intelligence 30, 425–447 (2002)

Ishikawa, T.: Geospatial thinking and spatial ability: An empirical examination of knowledge and reasoning in geographical science. The Professional Geographer 65, 636–646 (2013a)

Ishikawa, T.: Spatial primitives from a cognitive perspective: Sensitivity to changes in various geometric properties. In: Tenbrink, T., Stell, J., Galton, A., Wood, Z. (eds.) COSIT 2013. LNCS, vol. 8116, pp. 1–13. Springer, Heidelberg (2013b)

Ishikawa, T., Montello, D.R.: Spatial knowledge acquisition from direct experience in the environment: Individual differences in the development of metric knowledge and the integration of separately learned places. Cognitive Psychology 52, 93–129 (2006)

Ittelson, W.H.: Environment perception and contemporary perceptual theory. In: Ittelson, W.H. (ed.) Environment and Cognition, pp. 1–19. Seminar Press, New York (1973)

Janelle, D.G., Goodchild, M.F.: Location across disciplines: Reflection on the CSISS experience. In: Scholten, H.J., Velde, R., van Manen, N. (eds.) Geospatial Technology and the Role of Location in Science, pp. 15–29. Springer, Dordrecht (2009)

Keehner, M.M., Tendick, F., Meng, M.V., Anwar, H.P., Hegarty, M., Stoller, M.L., Duh, Q.: Spatial ability, experience, and skill in laparoscopic surgery. American Journal of Surgery 188, 71–75 (2004)

Kidder, F.R.: Elementary and middle school children's comprehension of Euclidean transformations. Journal of Research in Mathematics Education 7, 40–52 (1976)

Klippel, A.: Spatial information theory meets spatial thinking: Is topology the Rosetta Stone of spatial cognition? Annals of the Association of American Geographers 102, 1310–1328 (2012)

Kozhevnikov, M., Motes, M., Hegarty, M.: Spatial visualization in physics problem solving. Cognitive Science 31, 549–579 (2007)

Kozlowski, L.T., Bryant, K.J.: Sense-of-direction, spatial orientation, and cognitive maps. Journal of Experimental Psychology: Human Perception and Performance 3, 590–598 (1977)

Kruskal, J.B.: Multidimensional scaling by optimizing goodness of fit to a nonmetric hypothesis. Psychometrika 29, 1–27 (1964)

Kuhn, W.: Core concepts of spatial information for transdisciplinary research. International Journal of Geographical Information Science 26, 2267–2276 (2012)

Lee, J., Bednarz, R.: Components of spatial thinking: Evidence from a spatial thinking ability test. Journal of Geography 111, 15–26 (2012)

Levinson, S.C.: Frames of reference and Molyneux's question: Cross-linguistic evidence. In: Bloom, P., Peterson, M., Nadel, L., Garrett, M. (eds.) Language and Space, pp. 109–169. MIT Press, Cambridge (1996)

Liben, L.S., Downs, R.M.: Understanding person-space-map relations: Cartographic and developmental perspectives. Developmental Psychology 29, 739–752 (1993)

Mandler, J.M.: Representation. In: Mussen, P.H. (ed.) Handbook of Child Psychology, 4th edn., pp. 420–494. Wiley, New York (1983)

Mandler, J.M.: On the spatial foundations of the conceptual system and its enrichment. Cognitive Science 36, 421–451 (2012)

Martin, J.L.: A test with selected topological properties of Piaget's hypothesis concerning the spatial representation of the young child. Journal of Research in Mathematics Education 7, 26–38 (1976)

Montello, D.R.: Scale and multiple psychologies of space. In: Campari, I., Frank, A.U. (eds.) COSIT 1993. LNCS, vol. 716, pp. 312–321. Springer, Heidelberg (1993)

National Research Council: Learning to Think Spatially. National Academies Press, Washington, DC (2006)

Newcombe, N.S.: Increasing math and science learning by improving spatial thinking. American Educator 34(2), 29–43 (2010)

Piaget, J., Inhelder, B.: The Child's Conception of Space (trans. Langdon, F.J., Lunzer, J.L.). Norton, New York (1967) (original work published 1948)

Thorndyke, P.W., Hayes-Roth, B.: Differences in spatial knowledge acquired from maps and navigation. Cognitive Psychology 14, 560–589 (1982)

Tobler, W.: Bidimensional regression. Geographical Analysis 26, 187–212 (1994)

Uttal, D.H., Cohen, C.A.: Spatial thinking and STEM education: When, why, and how? Psychology of Learning and Motivation 57, 147–181 (2012)

Virtual Distance Estimation in a CAVE

William E. Marsh, Jean-Rémy Chardonnet, and Frédéric Merienne

Arts et Métiers ParisTech – CNRS Le2i, Institut Image,
Chalon-sur-Saône, France
william@wemarsh.com, {jean-remy.chardonnet,frederic.merienne}@ensam.eu

Abstract. Past studies have shown consistent underestimation of distances in virtual reality, though the exact causes remain unclear. Many virtual distance cues have been investigated, but past work has failed to account for the possible addition of cues from the physical environment. We describe two studies that assess users' performance and strategies when judging horizontal and vertical distances in a CAVE. Results indicate that users attempt to leverage cues from the physical environment when available and, if allowed, use a locomotion interface to move the virtual viewpoint to facilitate this.

Keywords: Virtual reality, Distance perception, Spatial cognition, Scale, Architecture, CAVE.

1 Introduction

When interacting with a virtual architectural model, decision makers must accurately perceive the spatial layout of a virtual environment (VE) and make decisions, often regarding a building that has not yet been built. However, the current state of virtual reality (VR) technology presents challenges. One such challenge is that perceived spaces are routinely compressed in VR.

There are two broad categories of distance judgements: egocentric and exocentric. In egocentric tasks, distances are judged from the observer to an object. In exocentric tasks, distances are judged between two objects in the environment, neither of which is collocated with the observer. Past literature has sometimes shown different biases depending on whether a judgement is egocentric or exocentric. When movement is allowed, the distinction between egocentric and exocentric distances is less clear because a person could move in such a way that an exocentric judgement becomes egocentric, or vice-versa.

Many authors have investigated biases related to physical or virtual distance spans on, or parallel to, the ground plane. However, though they are particularly relevant to architectural decisions, there is a notable lack of studies involving vertical distances, and this dearth is even more profound in VR.

1.1 Methods to Assess Perceived Distances

In the following sections, we describe past findings regarding distance perception, and then we discuss our own studies investigating distance perception in a CAVE. This work hinges on identifying appropriate ways to measure perceived distances.

C. Freksa et al. (Eds.): Spatial Cognition 2014, LNAI 8684, pp. 354–369, 2014.

A common way of assessing perceived distances is blind walking, in which participants are asked to walk without vision to a previously viewed landmark [e.g. 11]. However, motor recalibration effects have been reported [14] by which participants learn to improve their estimates through training. These may reflect high-level cognition, as opposed to overall calibration. The effects can be avoided through triangulated blind walking or by withholding performance feedback [16].

Perceptual matching is another means of testing the accuracy of perceived distances. In this paradigm, participants are asked to reproduce a distance span, often by directing the experimenter to place a target at an equivalent distance [e.g. 9]. Due to the difficulty in blind walking a remembered vertical distance, perceptual matching was chosen for the studies described in this paper.

In the virtual architecture domain, it may be important to reproduce distances both egocentrically and exocentrically. Past researchers have often required participants to learn exocentric distance spans and then reproduce them egocentrically. This difference in orientation between learning and recall should prevent participants from using strategies relying on purely visual snapshots, though it may involve higher-level processing. In the studies described here, perceptual matching estimates are made from the same orientation as experienced during learning, but from a different distance, to prevent judgements based solely on visual angle.

1.2 Distance Perception in Real Environments

Most distance perception research has focused on horizontal distances. Real-world distance estimates on the ground are usually very accurate over short ranges, though depth spans are sometimes reportedly compressed relative to frontal spans [10]. In general, absolute distances can be calculated visually with knowledge about the size of familiar objects, the angle between an observer's eye height and an object or, when an object is on the ground, linear perspective. Some additional cues may help when judging distances shorter than approximately 2 m. Binocular disparity provides information, together with the ocular convergence required to target an object and the accommodation required for the lens to focus on an object. Motion parallax and optic flow can also help if the observer is moving.

Vertical distances viewed from the top are often overestimated. Large heights are also overestimated from the bottom, though to a lesser degree. When observing a frontal view of an object, vertical distances are often overestimated by 10–15% relative to horizontal distances [25]. Stefanucci and Proffitt [18] report evidence that these biases may be moderated by an individual's fear of heights.

When constructing the spatial model of a scene, the visual cues above are integrated with proprioceptive, efferent [22], and possibly vestibular information from movements [2]. Some researchers have implicated effort, as well as the capacity and intention to interact [24], in distance perception. For example, wearing a backpack has been shown to lead to increased distance estimates [15], though Durgin et al. [4] point to alternate explanations. If effort is indeed linked to distance perception, it follows that vertical movement requires greater effort (climbing) than movement along the horizontal plane (walking), and thus vertical distances should be perceived as greater. A related idea, *Evolved Navigation Theory*, is that biases may relate to evolutionary goals of avoiding danger [8]. In either case, there is a link to Gibson's [6] concept of affordances, in which behavioral potential impacts perception.

1.3   Distance Perception in Virtual Environments

Some of the biases described above in Sec. 1.2 also exist in VR, though they are generally greater. Distances are linearly compressed in VEs relative to corresponding estimates in the real world [13] by up to about 50% [12], with reports of rare exceptions [7]. As in the real world, depth spans are often compressed relative to frontal spans [10]. Additionally, Fink et al. [5] showed differences in trajectories between real and virtual movements, indicating greater uncertainty about object positions.

There is a shortage of literature examining vertical distance perception. However, the work referenced above in Sec. 1.2 regarding the horizontal–vertical illusion showed a greater effect in the real world (or VR) than in photos with distances controlled for optical angle, and the magnitude of this illusion increases with physical perceived height on the projection surface [25]. This shows that humans have knowledge of the display surface and that it may affect perception.

Many authors have studied these phenomena, but the causes remain unclear. The problems may be due to some combination of factors involving sensory fidelity, equipment constraints (i.e. weight), and unnatural interfaces. In principle, VE designers should aim to provide the same cues that are available in the real world. However, in practice, this is never quite possible with current technology. For example, graphics fidelity is often reduced in VR. Thompson et al. [20] showed no impact of impoverished graphics on distance estimates, but distance cues including optic flow may still be limited. In VR, accommodation and convergence cues can be in conflict, possibly also impacting virtual distance estimates [3].

Interfaces for large-scale virtual locomotion often do not allow for the types of body-based translation movements, such as walking, that may lead to construction of accurate spatial representations [17]. In fact, Sun et al. [19] showed that providing body-based proprioceptive/efferent information improved path length estimates, even if it was inconsistent with reality as experienced visually. A common class of interface for virtual locomotion is the handheld wand. There are several variations and control schemes, but because they use different muscle groups and actions involve less effort than in the real world, they may lead to non-veridical distance estimates.

Past research has indicated that the intention to interact with an environment and the expected effort associated with that interaction impact distance perception [24]. These studies have primarily focused on horizontal distances, but such theories should predict underestimation of vertical distances in VR because is often easier to travel virtually (by flying) to higher elevations than it is in the real world (by climbing).

Physical characteristics of a VR system may also serve as distance cues. For example, in a CAVE it is usually possible to see corners where the screens meet. In addition, optical accommodation can inform the user about screen position and orientation [21]. It is conceivable that a user, particularly one with a relatively low level of virtual presence [as defined by 23], may use these physical aspects when judging virtual distances. However, most studies on virtual distance estimation have been administered using a head-mounted display (HMD), likely in an attempt to limit these physical cues. For scenarios in which presence is not critical, these cues may be beneficial. Allowing movement may enable users to move into positions to make maximal use of distance cues provided by the physical system. Alternately, cues in the physical environment may introduce additional unwanted biases, so it is important to study users' abilities to use them effectively.

1.4 Architectural Decisions in Virtual Reality

The present work is motivated by the need for *scale-one* distance perception in architectural walk-throughs. The architectural domain has some key requirements that differentiate it from much of the past literature on spatial perception.

First, architectural decisions frequently involve vertical judgements. Most past work has involved only horizontal distances, but the studies in this paper include a vertical condition.

Second, virtual architectural models are often viewed by more than one person at a time. For this reason, walk-throughs often take place on a large screen or in a CAVE, as opposed to an HMD. Most past virtual distance estimation research has been conducted using an HMD, so those results may provide a good starting point, but they fail to predict the interplay between virtual and physical distance cues that are present in a CAVE. The studies reported in this paper were conducted in a four-sided CAVE. Because trials were quick, participants were not expected to achieve high levels of presence, meaning that they might use distance cues from both the VE and the physical system. This paper will not address additional distortions that arise as multiple untracked users move away from the center of projection [1].

2   Study 1: Distance Estimation and the Role of Locomotion in a CAVE

We conducted a study to investigate horizontal and vertical distance estimation in a high-fidelity, fully furnished virtual office environment displayed in a CAVE. This was intended to provide insight into the design space for VR systems used for architectural decisions. Specifically, there were two competing hypotheses in Study 1. First, the ability to locomote may help users judge distances by maneuvering to the optimal vantage point(s). If this is the case, we hoped that the experiment would provide insight into the strategies employed. Alternately, using a handheld wand may lead to greater underestimation, particularly on vertical spans, due to the ease of travel.

2.1   Method

Participants. Twelve participants (4 female, $M = 26.3$ years, $SD = 5.5$ years) were recruited through word of mouth. The only requirements were good (corrected) binocular vision and lack of expertise in the CAVE. Some were familiar with VR, but specific knowledge of the system dimensions was undesirable because it could have biased judgements. There was no compensation for participation.

Apparatus. All distances were learned in a CAVE measuring 3×3 m horizontally and 2.67 m in height, with rear projection on three walls and front projection on the floor. All walls have passive stereoscopic projection. Participants' head positions were tracked with an ARTTRACK2 optical tracking system to control the center of projection. Participants recalled distances in the same room, with their backs facing the CAVE.

Stimuli and Design. The study employed a 2 (interface) × 3 (judgement direction) within-subjects design. Every participant completed two study sessions, counterbalanced, each with a different interface condition (Flystick, none). Three judgement directions (depth, width, vertical) were each experienced three times per session, in random order, such that each participant completed 9 trials per session (18 trials total). Each trial comprised two phases: learning and recall. The learning phase for all trials took place in the same virtual office scene, rendered in Fig. 1a, but each trial in a given session was observed from a different orientation, randomly chosen from a set of nine possible. In the recall phase, exocentric perceptual matching was used to reproduce the learned distance.

The two sessions were on different days to prevent spatial learning in one condition from carrying over to the other. There were two interface conditions: Flystick and none. In the Flystick condition, participants used a Flystick2 wand to translate in the X, Y, and Z directions. The interface did not allow rotation. The hat switch on top of the Flystick2 was used to move along the virtual X–Y plane at a maximum speed of 2.0 m/s, while the trigger button was used to fly at

(a) Virtual office environment.   (b) Virtual cone.

Fig. 1. Virtual models used during the learning phase of the experimental trials

a fixed speed of 2.0 m/s. Releasing the trigger button for 2 s allowed gravity to take over, causing the participant to fall to the virtual floor. In the none interface condition, locomotion was not allowed.

In both interface conditions, participants were allowed to move their heads freely, but they were required to keep their feet in the same spot, 192 cm from the front wall of the CAVE (42 cm behind CAVE center), and equidistant from the side walls. This position was chosen in an attempt to maximize the available peripheral information. The virtual floor and the physical floor were co-planar, except when flying, though the virtual floor was larger in extent.

During the learning phase of each trial, distances were presented as a pair of virtual cones, rendered in Fig. 1b, placed at random positions in the virtual world. For depth trials, both virtual cones were placed in front of the participant, the first at a distance of 10–60 cm and the second at a distance of 245–295 cm. The range of possible observed distances was 185–285 cm, with a mean of 235 cm.

For width trials, the virtual cones were also separated by a distance of 185–285 cm, with a mean of 235 cm. The cones were placed at an equal distance to the left and right of the point 342 cm directly in front of the participant's body.

For vertical trials, the cones were also separated by a distance of 185–285 cm, with a mean of 235 cm. The first cone was placed at a distance of between 10 cm and 60 cm from the virtual floor and the second cone was placed at a distance of between 245 cm and 295 cm from the virtual floor. The vertical trials were the only ones in which the cones were not standing upright. In these trials, the tops of the cones pointed parallel to the floor, toward the participant.

During the recall phase, participants reproduced distances with exocentric perceptual matching using physical cones nearly identical to those modeled in the VE. For depth matching, the first cone was placed 105 cm from the tips of the participant's feet. The experimenter placed the second cone immediately beyond the first and slowly moved it away from the participant, until directed by the participant to stop.

For width matching, the first cone was placed 150 cm in front of and 182 cm to the right of the participant. The experimenter placed the second cone directly to the left of the first and slowly moved it leftward, along a path perpendicular to the direction the participant was facing, until directed by the participant to stop.

For vertical matching, the first cone was fixed 330 cm above the floor. The experimenter initially placed the second cone 1 m lower than the first. This avoided the need for a ladder, thus eliminating an obvious distance cue in the physical environment that may have led to biases involving anchoring or relative judgements between trials. The experimenter then moved the cone downward until directed by the participant to stop.

Procedure. When participants first arrived, they were told that they would be making a series of basic distance judgements and shown the physical cones that would be used for the perceptual matching tasks. They were given a brief explanation of how the real-world perceptual matching tasks would be used to recall the observed virtual distances.

In each trial, participants were allowed as much time as desired to learn the distances. Once they alerted the experimenter that they were ready, they moved quickly and quietly to the recall area across the room. Participants directed the experimenter to reproduce the learned distance and then a new trial began.

Before beginning the experimental trials, participants completed three practice trials (depth, width, vertical) in the real world. They were told that the tasks were intended for practice, but that the answers would be recorded. For these trials, as for the experimental trials described below, participants were allowed to view the target cones for as long as they wanted and then they were quickly and quietly led across the room to do a perceptual matching task to recall the previously seen distance.

Next, if participants were completing the Flystick session, they were trained to use the Flystick. This included a brief explanation and a practice scenario in which participants were encouraged to move around in a scene different from the experimental scene until they felt comfortable with the interface.

Next, participants completed nine experimental trials. Each of these took place in the same virtual office scenario, but viewed from a different orientation, chosen at random (without replacement) from a set of nine. There were three each of depth, width, and vertical judgements, presented in a random order. In the Flystick session, participants were instructed that they could explore as much as they wanted, but that they must also look at each cone up close.

After finishing all trials, participants were asked to complete a post-questionnaire regarding their experiences and problems when estimating the distances. They were also asked to self-report their locomotion performance for the Flystick session. Additionally, after the first session, participants completed a demographic questionnaire with questions about age, sex, height, VR experience, video game experience, and how many hours they exercised per week.

2.2 Results: Distance Estimation Error

The following preparations were made before analysis:

- Because the top cone in the vertical matching task was 330 cm from the floor and because the cones were 14 cm wide, the largest distance that could be recalled was 323 cm. For this reason, all measurements were clipped at a maximum of 323 cm. Likewise, because 323 cm is 88 cm greater than the mean cone distance of 235 cm, very low estimates were clipped at an equal distance from the mean cone distance, 147 cm. This prevented depth and width judgements from being larger than those possible for vertical judgements. This only affected four low and four high judgements.
- The raw distance estimates were converted to percent error estimates, reflecting the percent of under- or over-estimation in a trial.

A two-factor linear mixed-effects model was constructed with percent error as a response, fixed effects for interface and direction combinations (6 means), a random effect for participant, and a by-participant random slope for direction. An

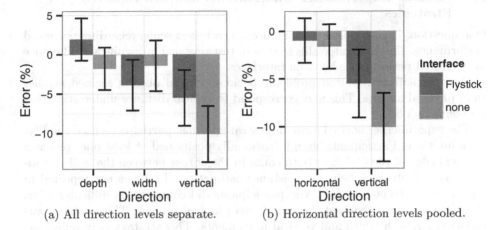

Fig. 2. Least-squares mean estimation error ± SE in Study 1 as a function of interface and direction

ANOVA using the Satterthwaite approximation for degrees of freedom showed a significant interaction between interface and direction, $F(2, 176.81) = 3.13$, $p = .046$. The least-squares means are plotted in Fig. 2a.

We were also interested in the question of whether distances were underestimated for each direction and interface. These means were compared to zero using planned t tests. This showed that vertical error was significantly less than 0 (underestimation), $t(11.0) = -2.32$, $p = .04$, while depth and width error were not significantly different than 0. Estimates in the none interface condition were less than 0, with marginal significance, $t(12.8) = -1.94$, $p = .07$. All means were compared using t tests with the Bonferroni correction for multiple comparisons, showing no additional significant differences.

When using the Flystick interface, participants were able to position themselves such that depth and width judgements may have been analogous. Additionally, there was no statistical difference between the depth and width judgements in either interface condition. Therefore, another analysis was conducted with the depth and width levels pooled into a single *horizontal* level. A two-factor linear mixed-effects model was constructed with percent error as a response, fixed effects for interface and direction combinations (4 means), a random effect for participant, and a by-participant random slope for direction. An ANOVA using the Satterthwaite approximation for degrees of freedom showed marginally significant main effects of both direction $F(1, 11.0) = 4.48$, $p = .058$, and interface, $F(1, 189.82) = 3.07$, $p = .08$. The least-squares means are plotted in Fig. 2b, showing that vertical error means are less than those for horizontal error. We can also see that the Flystick may have helped participants make better judgements.

2.3 Results: Experimenter Observations and Self-reported Strategies

One question on each post-questionnaire was a Likert scale, regarding perceived performance. The Kruskal-Wallis rank sum test revealed no significant difference in perceived performance between interfaces.

One participant reported problems because virtual objects seemed smaller than physical objects. This may correspond to typical distance underestimation problems in VR.

The experimenter noticed a common strategy when participants used the Fly-stick interface. Participants often intentionally positioned at least one cone at a physical edge of the CAVE or both cones in the corner between the walls, seemingly as a strategy to help with distance estimation. This was not reported in questionnaire responses. However, participants did comment on difficulty when the distance spans required the use of two physical screens. This problem was reported for both width and vertical judgements. This strategy may reflect attempts to use physical cues when learning the distances.

One participant noted that perceived distances were dependent on point of view, and another reported specifically that objects that were farther away appeared to be a different size when viewed up close. Another participant noted that judgements were easier when using the Flystick interface. This may be because it allows for changing the point of view or because it allows participants to position cones such that they are both on the same physical screen.

One participant reported using the number of imagined footsteps as a metric by which to remember distances. This may be considered a hybrid strategy, as the length of a footstep has meaning in both the virtual and physical environments. This same participant reported trouble on vertical estimates, because they were not easily estimable using this metric, and another stated that she did not know her own virtual height.

2.4 Discussion

Statistically, horizontal estimates were veridical. However, there was underestimation of analogous vertical spans that has not been previously explored in the literature. Note that this is not what would be predicted according to distance estimation literature in the real world, which has shown vertical distances to be overestimated relative to horizontal distances. Because estimates were actually more accurate (though not significantly so) with the Flystick interface, these results fail to support the notion that less-effortful locomotion causes underestimation of distances. However, these results do indicate that the ability to interact improves distance estimates.

While many results were not statistically significant, the patterns shown above and the subjective observations were used to motivate the next study. From the patterns we can see that the Flystick interface may have helped participants make more accurate judgements. In line with experimenter observations, this may be a result of different strategies in which the physical system boundaries are used when a participant is able to maneuver accordingly.

3   Study 2: The Role of CAVE Boundaries in Distance Estimation

We conducted a second study to further investigate the use of information from the physical environment when judging virtual distances. We hypothesized that distance judgements on the plane of the physical floor or walls of the CAVE would be more accurate than those in purely virtual space.

3.1   Method

The design and paradigm used in Study 2 closely resembled those in Study 1.

Participants. Fourteen participants (7 female, $M = 22.6$ years, $SD = 3.9$ years) were recruited through word of mouth. Participant requirements were the same as in Study 1. There was no compensation for participating.

Apparatus. As in Study 1, participants learned distances in the CAVE and recalled them in the same room, from a position with their backs to the CAVE.

Stimuli and Design. The study employed a 3 (physical position) × 2 (judgement direction) within-subjects design. Two judgement directions (width, vertical) were each experienced six times per session, in alternating order with the starting direction counterbalanced, such that each participant completed 12 trials. As in Study 1, each trial comprised two phases: learning and recall. The learning phase for all trials took place in the same virtual office scene used in Study 1, but each trial with a given judgement direction was observed from a different orientation, randomly chosen from a set of six possible. In the recall phase, exocentric perceptual matching was used to reproduce the learned distance.

There were three physical position conditions, as shown in Fig. 3: back, middle, and front. In all three conditions, participants were allowed to move their heads freely, but they were required to keep their feet in the same spot, with an equal distance from each side wall. The virtual floor and the physical floor were coplanar, though the virtual floor was larger in extent. In the middle position, participants stood 187 cm from the front CAVE wall. During the learning phase, distance spans were displayed at the front CAVE wall.

In the back condition, participants stood 50 cm behind the middle position, 237 cm from the front CAVE wall. During the learning phase, distance spans were displayed 50 cm in front of the front CAVE wall, on the physical floor (for width judgements) or right wall (for vertical judgements) of the CAVE.

In the front condition, participants stood 50 cm in front of the middle position, 137 cm from the front CAVE wall. During the learning phase, distance spans were displayed 50 cm past the front CAVE wall.

During the learning phase of each trial, participants viewed a pair of randomly positioned virtual cones, as in Study 1, though with a slightly improved cone model. The distances in Study 2 were slightly shorter than those in Study 1, because it was necessary to fit the cones for the vertical trials on the physical screen, which is 267 cm tall.

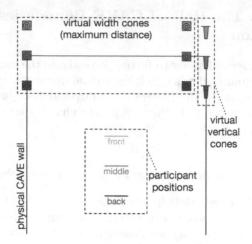

Fig. 3. Top-down diagram of the CAVE, showing the three physical participant positions together with the corresponding virtual cone positions

For width trials, the virtual cones were separated by a distance ranging from 167 cm to 267 cm, with a mean of 217 cm. The first cone was randomly placed at a position between 0 and 50 cm from the plane formed by the left CAVE wall. The second cone was randomly placed between 217 cm and 267 cm from the plane formed by the left CAVE wall.

For vertical trials, the cones were also separated by a distance ranging from 167 cm to 267 cm, with a mean of 217 cm. The first cone was placed at a distance of between 0 cm and 50 cm from the virtual floor and the second cone was placed at a distance of between 217 cm and 267 cm from the virtual floor, both on the plane formed by the right CAVE wall. As in Study 1, the cones did not stand upright in the vertical trials. Instead, the tops of the cones pointed parallel to the floor, toward the participant.

Width matching in the recall phase was identical to that in Study 1, except that the distance specifications were slightly modified. The first cone was placed 150 cm in front of and 168 cm to the right of the participant, a modification intended to expedite distance measurement between trials. The vertical-matching configuration was identical to that in Study 1.

Procedure. The procedure in Study 2 was very similar to that in Study 1, with the following differences.

Before beginning the experimental trials, participants completed only two practice trials (width, vertical) in the real world. These were counterbalanced in the same order as the experimental trials (i.e. if the first experimental trial was to be the width condition, the first practice trial was the width condition).

Participants completed 12 experimental trials. Each of these took place in the same virtual office scenario that was used in Study 1, but viewed from six different orientations chosen at random, such that there were no replacements for trials of a given judgement direction. There were six vertical and six width judgements, interleaved, with the starting direction counterbalanced.

After finishing all trials, participants were asked to complete a post-questionnaire regarding their experiences and problems when estimating the distances and a demographic questionnaire with questions about age, sex, height, VR experience, video game experience, and how many hours they exercised per week. Both questionnaires were slightly modified from Study 1, to more thoroughly investigate problems encountered and strategies employed by the participants.

3.2   Results: Distance Estimation Error

Because the mean actual distance was different, as described above, it was not necessary to clamp raw distance estimates as in Study 1. Two distance estimates were missing, due to experimenter error. As in Study 1, raw distance estimates were converted to percent error before analysis.

A two-factor linear mixed-effects model was constructed with percent error as a response, fixed effects for position and direction combinations (6 means), a random effect for participant, and a by-participant random slope for direction. An ANOVA using the Satterthwaite approximation for degrees of freedom showed main effects of both position, $F(2, 134.22) = 12.23$, $p < .01$, and direction, $F(1, 13.08) = 6.19$, $p = .03$. The least-squares means are plotted in Fig. 4.

Planned comparisons were performed for each of the three pairs of positions in the model. Significant differences were found between the middle and back positions, $t(134.4) = 3.5$, $p < .01$, as well as between the middle and front positions, $t(133.9) = 4.77$, $p < .01$.

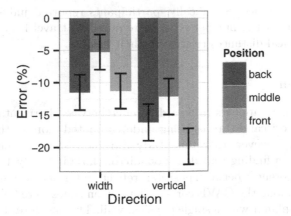

Fig. 4. Least-squares mean estimation error $\pm$ SE in Study 2, as a function of position and direction

Table 1. Comparisons between means and 0, with Bonferroni correction for multiple comparisons

Direction	Position	df	t	p	$p < .05$
vertical		13.1	-6.35	< .01	*
width		22.1	-3.81	.02	*
	back	17.8	-6.10	< .01	*
	middle	17.4	-3.86	.01	*
	front	17.4	-6.91	< .01	*
vertical	back	34.7	-5.71	< .01	*
width	back	32.9	-4.23	< .01	*
vertical	middle	32.9	-4.36	< .01	*
width	middle	32.9	-1.93	.75	
vertical	front	32.9	-7.13	< .01	*
width	front	32.9	-4.15	< .01	*

Post-hoc comparisons were performed on the model, comparing all eleven means (three positions, two directions, six position–direction combinations) to 0, with the Bonferroni correction for multiple comparisons. As shown in Table 1, all were significant except the width–middle position mean.

3.3   Results: Self-reported Strategies

Questionnaire responses provided insight into strategies employed and problems encountered during the trials. Interestingly, considering the performance results above in Sec. 3.2, no participants made any mention of using cues from the physical environment to help with distance estimation. However, many participants did report using virtual cues, including furniture and windows. Additionally, participants reported using cues that might be thought of as hybrid, in that they can be thought to exist in the physical world and the virtual world depending on the level of presence. Specifically, participants reported judging horizontal distance in terms of the number of steps required to travel between the cones and judging vertical distances relative to their heights.

3.4   Discussion

As in Study 1, there appears to be a difference between horizontal and vertical distances, with vertical distances being underestimated more so than horizontal distances. Note, however, that this study did show some underestimation of horizontal spans, a finding that does not mirror those in Study 1.

Significant differences between positions reflect better performance when cones were positioned along the CAVE corners than when cones were behind the physical screen or co-planar with a single physical wall. This indicates that users were able to make use of information from the physical environment to aid in distance estimation, and this helped equally on the vertical and horizontal judgements.

However, in contrast with our hypothesis, this only happened when cones were placed at the intersection of two CAVE walls, and not when cones were placed on a single wall or the floor.

4   General Discussion and Conclusions

We have presented the results of two studies. Together they represent an investigation into the design space for virtual architecture systems. Past studies on underestimation of virtual distances have often neglected to include vertical spans. Additionally, past research has rarely been conducted in a CAVE, which limits the extent to which findings can be applied to the virtual architecture domain.

Both studies incorporated a slightly different perceptual matching paradigm from that used in previous work. While this should allow for more direct estimates of the distance spans, it may also lead to systematic bias. The pattern of differences within a given judgement direction should still be reliable, but future work should consider possible bias particularly as it may limit the ability to measure differences between width and vertical judgements, for example.

Study 1 results indicate that vertical distances are underestimated in a CAVE. This is seemingly in contrast to findings in the real world, which show an overestimation relative to horizontal spans. Note, however, that the paradigm used here is somewhat different. Past real-world findings involved relative distances, while this study was not designed to force any sort of comparison between horizontal and vertical spans. Observations and performance patterns also indicated that participants attempted to use the physical CAVE boundaries when learning distances. This motivated Study 2.

Study 2 results indicate that users can use distance cues in the physical system to help with virtual distance estimates. Surprisingly, performance improved only when the spans were along the highly-salient CAVE corners, and not simply on a CAVE surface.

These analyses indicate that users know where the physical projection surfaces are, and these studies were interpreted under the assumption that users had a low level of subjective presence in the virtual environment. It is likely, given the above conclusions above, that increased virtual presence will cause users to neglect the physical cues in favor of purely virtual judgements. This should be explored in future work. Additionally, the CAVE used in these studies is a cube shape, with right angles and easily inferred boundaries. With a different configuration, such as a curved screen, it is likely that users will not attempt to use physical cues or that they will use them ineffectively.

Acknowledgements. This project was funded by FUI in the framework of the Callisto project.

References

[1] Banks, M.S., Held, R.T., Girshick, A.R.: Perception of 3-D layout in stereo displays. Information Display 25(1), 12–16 (2009)

[2] Chrastil, E.R., Warren, W.H.: Active and passive contributions to spatial learning. Psychonomic Bulletin & Review 19, 1–23 (2012)

[3] Drascic, D., Milgram, P.: Perceptual issues in augmented reality. In: Proceedings of SPIE, vol. 2653, pp. 123–134. SPIE, Bellingham (1996)

[4] Durgin, F.H., Baird, J.A., Greenburg, M., Russell, R., Shaughnessy, K., Waymouth, S.: Who is being deceived? the experimental demands of wearing a backpack. Psychonomic Bulletin & Review 16(5), 964–969 (2009)

[5] Fink, P.W., Foo, P.S., Warren, W.H.: Obstacle avoidance during walking in real and virtual environments. ACM Transactions on Applied Perception 4(1), 2:1–2:18 (2007)

[6] Gibson, J.J.: The Ecological Approach to Visual Perception. Psychology Press (1986)

[7] Interrante, V., Anderson, L., Ries, B.: Distance perception in immersive virtual environments, revisited. In: Proceedings of IEEE Virtual Reality (IEEE VR 2006), pp. 3–11. IEEE Computer Society, Los Alamitos (2006)

[8] Jackson, R.E., Cormack, L.K.: Evolved navigation theory and the environmental vertical illusion. Evolution and Human Behavior 29, 199–304 (2008)

[9] Jackson, R.E., Willey, C.R.: Evolved navigation theory and the plateau illusion. Cognition 128, 119–126 (2013)

[10] Li, Z., Sun, E., Strawser, C.J., Spiegel, A., Klein, B., Durgin, F.H.: On the anisotropy of perceived ground extents and the interpretation of walked distance as a measure of perception. Journal of Experimental Psychology: Human Perception and Performance 39(2), 477–493 (2013)

[11] Loomis, J.M., DaSilva, J.A., Fujita, N., Fukusima, S.S.: Visual space perception and visually directed action. Journal of Experimental Psychology 18(4), 906–921 (1992)

[12] Loomis, J.M., Knapp, J.M.: Visual perception of egocentric distance in real and virtual environments. In: Hettinger, L.J., Haas, M.W. (eds.) Virtual and Adaptive Environments: Applications, Implications, and Human Performance Issues, pp. 21–46. CRC Press, Mahwah (2003)

[13] Messing, R., Durgin, F.H.: Distance perception and the visual horizon in head-mounted displays. ACM Transactions on Applied Perception 2(3), 234–250 (2005)

[14] Mohler, B.J., Creem-Regehr, S.H., Thompson, W.B.: The influence of feedback on egocentric distance judgments in real and virtual environments. In: Proceedings of the 3rd Symposium on Applied Perception in Graphics and Visualization (APGV 2006), pp. 9–14. ACM, New York (2006)

[15] Proffitt, D.R., Stefanucci, J., Banton, T., Epstein, W.: The role of effort in perceiving distance. Psychological Science 14(2), 106–112 (2003)

[16] Richardson, A.R., Waller, D.: The effect of feedback training on distance estimation in virtual environments. Applied Cognitive Psychology 19, 1089–1108 (2005)

[17] Ruddle, R.A., Volkova, E., Bülthoff, H.H.: Walking improves your cognitive map in environments that are large-scale and large in extent. ACM Transactions on Computer-Human Interaction 18(2), 10:1–10:20 (2011)

[18] Stefanucci, J.K., Proffitt, D.R.: The roles of altitude and fear in the perception of height. Journal of Experimental Psychology: Human Perception and Performance 35(2), 424–438 (2009)

[19] Sun, H.J., Campos, J.L., Chan, G.S.W.: Multisensory integration in the estimation of relative path length. Experimental Brain Research 154, 246–254 (2004)

[20] Thompson, W.B., Willemsen, P., Gooch, A.A., Creem-Regehr, S.H., Loomis, J.M., Beall, A.C.: Does the quality of the computer graphics matter when judging distances in visually immersive environments? Presence: Teleoperators and Virtual Environments 13(5), 560–571 (2004)

[21] Todorović, D.: The effect of the observer vantage point on perceived distortions in linear perspective images. Attention, Perception, and Psychophysics 71(1), 183–193 (2009)

[22] Waller, D., Loomis, J.M., Haun, D.B.M.: Body-based senses enhance knowledge of directions in large-scale environments. Psychonomic Bulletin & Review 11(1), 157–163 (2004)

[23] Witmer, B.G., Singer, M.J.: Measuring presence in virtual environments: A presence questionnaire. Presence: Teleoperators and Virtual Environments 7(3), 225–240 (1998)

[24] Witt, J.K., Proffitt, D.R., Epstein, W.: Perceiving distance: A role of effort and intent. Perception 33, 577–590 (2004)

[25] Yang, T.L., Dixon, M.W., Proffitt, D.R.: Seeing big things: Overestimation of heights is greater for real objects than for objects in pictures. Perception 28, 445–467 (1999)

Pellet Figures, the Feminine Answer to Cube Figures? Influence of Stimulus Features and Rotational Axis on the Mental-Rotation Performance of Fourth-Grade Boys and Girls

Vera Ruthsatz[1], Sarah Neuburger[1], Petra Jansen[2], and Claudia Quaiser-Pohl[1]

[1] University of Koblenz-Landau, Institute of Psychology, Universitaetsstraße 1,
56070 Koblenz, Germany
{ruthsatz,neuburger,quaiser}@uni-koblenz.de
[2] University of Regensburg, Institute of Sports Science, Universitaetsstraße 31,
93053 Regensburg, Germany
Petra.Jansen@psk.uni-regensburg.de

Abstract. Various studies have demonstrated the male advantage in mental-rotation tests. With the Shepard and Metzler [1] "Mental Rotation Test" the largest gender effect has been found. The present study investigated if gender differences in the MRT might be due to male characteristics of the cube figures. Therefore, 136 fourth graders solved a mental-rotation test with cube-figure items (C-MRT) and 150 fourth graders solved a novel test with pellet-figure items (P-MRT) in one of two rotational-axis conditions (rotations in picture plane vs. rotations in depth), respectively. In line with hypotheses, cube figures were male-stereotyped and pellet figures were female-stereotyped. Boys significantly outperformed girls only in tasks with cube figures rotated in-depth, while there was no significant gender effect found in the picture-plane conditions and for pellet figures rotated in-depth. So, there seems to be an influence of both, stimulus content and rotational axis on mental-rotation performance.

Keywords: gender differences, mental rotation, stimulus material, rotational axis, stereotypes.

1 Introduction

1.1 Theoretical Background

Linn and Petersen [2] defined mental rotation as one subcomponent of spatial abilities, describing the fast and accurate rotation of two- or three-dimensional objects in mind. Since the 1970s, several studies found male subjects to generally outperform female subjects in mental-rotation tasks in various age groups [e.g. 3, 1, 4]. Already in studies with infants gender differences were found [e.g. 5], but these results couldn't be confirmed in all studies with age groups younger than ten years [e.g. 3]. Thus, the questions at what age performance differences emerge and which factors influence their impact, are still discussed controversially. One reason for the mixed results

C. Freksa et al. (Eds.): Spatial Cognition 2014, LNAI 8684, pp. 370–382, 2014.
© Springer International Publishing Switzerland 2014

might be due to the manifold causes of gender differences in cognitive abilities. Next to biological agents, e.g. specific genes and gender hormone levels [6-7], socio-cultural processes influence mental-rotation ability development: Gender-role sociali-zation [8], stereotypes [9], spatial activities [10] and the socio-economic status [11] are just some important examples for psycho-social factors impairing mental-rotation performance. Recent studies in different age groups emphasize the impact of task characteristics [12]: the influence of the degree of occlusion and structurally different vs. mirrored versions of the target as distractors [13] as well as influence factors on children's mental rotation performance like gender-related stimulus attributes and rotational axis [e.g. 3, 14]. Findings suggest that complexity, meaning and familiarity might contribute to gender differences in mental-rotation tasks. The large gender effect of about one standard deviation found in the Shepard and Metzler "Mental Ro-tation Test" [1] could not be confirmed in either case, e.g. gender effect decreased in mental-rotation tasks with human figures in adults [15] and was even found to be invert with female-stereotyped concrete objects in children [14]. The use of more promising holistic strategies instead of analytic strategies is partly due to differences in stimulus familiarity [16] and might lead to worse results for female subjects in the MRT, because cube figures are quite similar to LEGO® bricks or construction toys, which are more frequently part of boys' realm of experience [17]. Additionally, be-cause of the cube figures' analogy to male-stereotyped toys, they might invoke gender stereotypes of male advantage and thus lead to stereotype threat effects in female subjects [18, 9]. Furthermore, rotational axis might cause the large gender difference in mental rotation tasks like the MRT, in which target objects also have to be rotated around the Cartesian y-axis. Several studies with adults [4] and children [3, 19] found a considerably smaller male advantage in mental-rotation tests requiring the ability to solve the task by two-dimensional processing.

Administering four novel rotation tests with concrete objects rotated in the Carte-sian y-axis or in the Cartesian z-axis to 287 fourth graders, Ruthsatz, Neuburger, Jan-sen and Quaiser-Pohl [14] showed that in tasks with female-stereotyped objects, which were more familiar to girls than to boys, girls can perform as well as boys or even better, while they are disadvantaged in tests with male-stereotyped objects. Fur-thermore, they found cube figures of the MRT to be male-stereotyped. Contrary to previous results [19], they found no interaction of gender and rotational axis with concrete-object tasks. The current study is aimed at surveying these results and ex-ploring the question if fourth-grade girls can also perform as well as boys, when stimuli are female-stereotyped, but no familiar, concrete objects.

Therefore, four novel mental-rotation tests consisting of male- and female-stereotyped abstract objects (C-MRT: cube figures/ P-MRT: pellet figures) rotated either in picture-plane or in-depth were designed. Pellet figures were chosen as coun-terparts of cube figures, because they were suggested to be female-stereotyped due to their analogy to a pearl necklace and the assumption that round and soft forms are connoted as female in our cultural area [20].

1.2   Design and Hypotheses

The study had a 2 (gender) x 2 (rotational axis) x 2 (stimulus type) quasi-experimental between-subject design, in which subjects' gender stereotypes, spatial performance and the stereotyped nature of the stimulus material were assessed in four conditions: (1) the picture-plane C-MRT condition, (2) the picture-plane P-MRT condition, (3) the in-depth C-MRT condition and (4) the in-depth P-MRT condition.

To analyze if gender differences in mental-rotation tasks might be due to male characteristics of the cube figures and rotational axis, the following hypotheses were examined: First, the suggested stereotyped nature of the stimuli was expected to be confirmed by children's stimulus ratings (manipulation check). Thus, it was expected that the stimuli used in the C-MRT would be male-stereotyped, while the stimuli used in the P-MRT would be female-stereotyped (Hypothesis 1). Second, in line with Neuburger et al. (2013), male stereotypes of boys in spatial skills were anticipated, but only playing with LEGO® was expected to be male-stereotyped by girls (Hypothesis 2). The main hypotheses were that the gender effect in favor of boys in children's mental-rotation performance would be larger in tasks with in-depth rotations than in tasks with picture-plane rotations (Hypothesis 3) and larger in tasks with cube figures than in tasks with pellet figures (Hypothesis 4).

2   Material and Methods

2.1   Participants

286 students from German public schools, between 8.83 and 11.83 years (mean age = 10.12 years, SD = 0.45) solved the C-MRT (73 boys/ 63 girls) and the P-MRT (78 boys/ 72 girls). Local headmasters and teachers were invited via E-Mail or telephone call to participate in the study, and parents were informed by a letter and asked to give their written consent. The sample included children from families with low (16.4%), middle (45.8%), and high (31.8%) socio-economic status (SES), 5.9% of the participants' parents did not fill in the SES questionnaire. In terms of SES, no significant disparities between the four conditions were found. No reward was given to the participants, because the supervisory school authority did not permit rewarding in order to ensure voluntary participation.

Each class was randomly assigned to one of the four experimental conditions, i.e. to one of the four versions of the mental-rotation test; 32 boys and 30 girls solved the picture-plane C-MRT, 38 boys and 37 girls solved the picture-plane P-MRT, 41 boys and 33 girls solved the in-depth C-MRT, 40 boys and 35 girls solved the in-depth P-MRT.

2.2   Material

Mental-Rotation Tasks. The task format was the same as in the "Mental Rotations Test" of Vandenberg and Kuse [21]. The paper-pencil tasks consisted of twelve test items with one target on the left side and four comparison stimuli on the right one (see Fig. 1). Children were instructed to solve as many items as possible within five minutes. Two of the four comparisons were rotated versions of the target and had to be crossed out by the participants; the other two comparisons were rotated mirror images of the target. Differently from the VK- MRT no distractors different in structures were used. Pellet figures were constructed in the same manner as the cube figures with 3ds Max 2012 (http://www.autodesk.de). Pellet figures and cube figures had identical structures (i.e. consisted of the same number of elements arranged in the same way), they only differed in the geometrical shape of their elements, which were either pellets or cubes. Four mental-rotation tests were constructed: two versions of the C-MRT (cube figures rotated in picture-plane/ cube figures rotated in-depth) and two versions of the P-MRT (pellet figures rotated in picture-plane/ pellet figures rotated in depth). In each of the four test versions, the same rotational angles were used (45°, 90°, 135°, 180°, 225°, 270°, 315°).

Reliability analyses confirmed the internal consistency of the C-MRT rotated in picture-plane (C-MRT: α = .757), but item 3 of the P-MRT rotated in picture-plane had to be excluded from further analyses, because item-total correlation was ≤ .10. In the two in-depth rotation tests, the items 2, 4 and 5 of the C-MRT and items 4 and 12 of the P-MRT had to be excluded. The reliabilities of the shortened picture-plane and in-depth rotation scales were satisfactory (picture-plane P-MRT: α = .738; C-MRT: α = .850; P-MRT: α = .659).

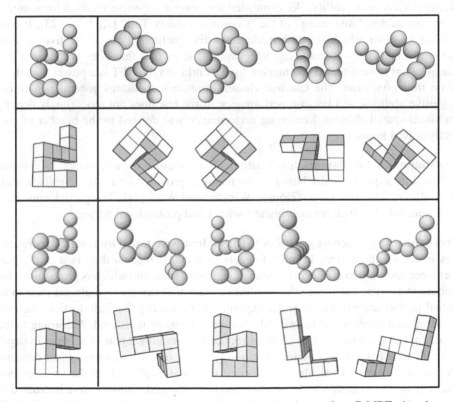

Fig. 1. Example items from the mental rotation tasks (the picture-plane P-MRT, the picture-plane C-MRT, the in-depth P-MRT, the in-depth C-MRT)

Spatial Stereotypes Questionnaire. Similar to Neuburger, Ruthsatz, Jansen, Heil and Quaiser-Pohl [8], children's spatial gender stereotypes were assessed with regard to four spatial skills: solving mental-rotation tasks, finding one's way in an unknown environment, understanding maps and road schemes, playing with LEGO®. Item formulation followed Trautner, Helbing, Sahm and Lohaus [22]: "There are children who [activity or trait]. Who [activity or trait]?" Answers were given on a picture-supported, five-point scale ("only girls", "more girls than boys", "as many girls as boys", "more boys than girls", "only boys") and coded with numbers from -2 (only girls) to +2 (only boys), so that scores above zero reflected a male stereotype and scores below zero reflected a female stereotype.

Stereotyped Nature of Stimuli Questionnaire. As manipulation check, children were shown one example item of each stimulus category and were asked to rate their gender-typicality on a five-point answering scale (1 = typical for boys / 2 = more typical for boys / 3 = neither typical for boys nor for girls / 4 = more typical for girls / 5 = typical for girls). Stereotype scores were computed by averaging the ratings of the cube and pellet stimuli, respectively, so that scores above three reflected a female stereotype and scores below three reflected a male stereotype.

General Cognitive Ability. We controlled for general cognitive abilities by administering the subtest "Reasoning" of the "Cognitive Ability Test" [KFT 1-3, 23]. It consists of 15 items which are each made up of five pictures. Four of the five pictures belong to the same category (e.g. vegetable). The picture that does not fit into this category has to be detected and marked by the child. As the KFT is a power-test, there is no time constraint. The test was chosen because it measures general non-verbal cognitive abilities, and because performance in the test does not too strongly depend on visual-spatial abilities. Reasoning performance was defined as the number of correctly solved items.

Questionnaire for Parents. Information about socio-economic status (SES) was gathered by a questionnaire based on the measure provided by Jöckel, Babitsch, Bellach, Bloomfield, Hoffmeyer-Zlotnik, Winkler and Wolf [24]. The participants' parents were asked to indicate their highest school and professional degree.

Procedure. Mixed-gender groups of 9-16 children were tested by female experimenters in school classrooms. In order to encourage children to do their best in the performance tests and to create an authentic diagnostic situation, which is prerequisite for finding stereotype threat/lift effects, children were told that they would get their individual performance results after the experiment. Following this introduction, the randomly assigned version of the mental-rotation test was administered. According to the experimental condition, the task was introduced by rotating a pair of scissors in depth or in plane in front of the children, outlining that the turnaround of an object does not change its features. Then, the paper-pencil task was explained on the basis of two example items. After task understanding had been ensured, children were instructed to work both fast and accurately on the test and solve as many items as possible within five minutes. After the mental-rotation task was finished, the three questionnaires were administered. For all questionnaires, the experimenter outlined that children should spontaneously answer according to their personal experiences and opinions and that there were no right or wrong answers. Afterwards, the KFT was administered: Before solving the test items, children were given two example items. At the end, children were thanked for their participation and dismissed. Several weeks later, when the experiment was finished, children received their individual test results, accompanied by a letter emphasizing that spatial abilities can be strongly improved through training.

3   Results

3.1   Analysis of Non-Rotators ("Guessers")

To measure the influence of rotational axis and stimulus features validly, only children with performance accuracy above guessing level (=1/6) were included in further analyses. An accuracy score was computed by dividing the number of items solved correctly, i.e. the items in which both rotated versions of the standard and none of the mirror images had been crossed out, by the number of items the child had attempted to solve.

In the picture-plane, cube-figure condition, 6 girls and 4 boys performed at or below chance level and in the picture-plane, pellet-figure condition, 4 girls and 3 boys performed at or below chance level. The gender difference in the proportion of "guessers" was not significant. In the in-depth, cube-figure condition, 12 girls, but only 6 boys performed at or below chance level; the gender difference in the proportion of "guessers" was significant, $chi^2(1)= 4.69$; $p = .030$. In the in-depth, pellet-figure condition, 16 girls, but only 9 boys performed at or below chance level; the gender difference in the proportion of "guessers" was significant, $chi^2(1)= 4.527$; $p = .033$. Overall, 60 of the 286 children, i.e. 20.98%, were excluded from the further analyses of mental-rotation performance because their performance accuracy was below chance level.

Removing subjects with performance accuracy below guessing level does not cause an exclusion of low performers. It was necessary to define the influence of the stimuli attributes, which could only lead to a stereotype-threat/-lift effect in children who understand the assignment of tasks.

3.2   Stereotyped Nature of the Stimuli

With two one-sample t-Tests computed on children's stereotype ratings of the cube and the pellet figures, Hypothesis 1 was confirmed. Ratings of both figures slightly deviated from the neutral point of the scale (=3), but significantly in the expected direction. Ratings of the cube figure (M = 2.31; SD = 1.02) significantly differed from the neutral point towards the male pole, $t (225) = -10.095$; $p < .000$, and ratings of the pellet figure (M = 3.36; SD = 1.04) significantly differed from the neutral point towards the female pole, $t (225) = 5.257$; $p < .000$.

3.3   Spatial Stereotypes

Boys' and girls' pretest ratings on the five spatial items are shown in Figure 2. Scores above zero represent a bias towards the male pole of the scale, whereas scores below zero represent a bias towards the female pole. In order to examine the degree to which the spatial items of the gender-stereotypes scale were actually stereotyped, boys' and girls' pretest ratings on these items were compared to the gender-neutral score zero by one-sample t-tests. Boys' ratings were significantly above zero on all of the spatial items (mental rotation: t (128) = 5.709; p = .000, finding one's way in an unknown environment: t (128) = 4.540; p < .000, understanding maps and road schemes: t (128) = 5.787; p = .000, playing with LEGO®: t (128) = 22.846; p = .000. Girls' ratings were significantly above zero on only one spatial item, which was playing with LEGO®: t (96) = 10.279; p = .000. Girls' ratings did not significantly diverge from zero for mental rotation and map understanding (p> .10), and they were significantly below zero for finding one's way in an unknown environment, t (96) = -2.714; p = .008.

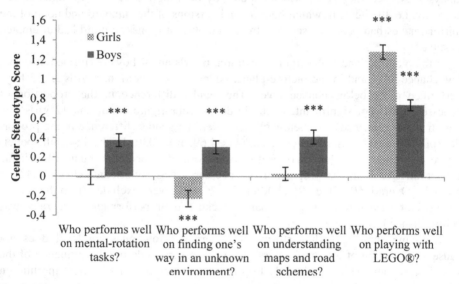

Fig. 2. Means and standard errors of boys' and girls' ratings on the spatial items of the gender-stereotype scale; possible values range from -2 ("only girls") to +2 ("only boys")

3.4   General Cognitive Ability

A 2 (gender) x 2 (rotational axis) x 2 (stimulus type) - ANOVA with standardized reasoning scores, i.e. age corrected T-values, as dependent variable revealed a signifi-cant sex difference with regard to general cognitive abilities: girls' scores (M = 55.24; SD = 7.37) were significantly higher than boys' scores (M = 51.05; SD = 9.38), F (1,218) = 11.28; p = .001; η² = .049. There was neither a main effect of stimulus material or an interaction between sex and condition, p > .10 nor a main effect of rotational axis, p > .50. Because of the sex difference, reasoning score was included as covariate in all of the subsequent analyses in which boys were compared to girls.

3.5 Mental-Rotation Performance

A 2 (gender) x 2 (rotational axis) x 2 (stimulus type) – ANCOVA with general cognitive ability as covariate was computed. Significant main effects of gender, $F = (1,217) = 12.146$; $p = .001$; $\eta^2 = .053$, and rotational axis, $F = (1,217) = 15.813$; $p = .000$; $\eta^2 = .068$ were found.

Furthermore, the ANCOVA revealed a tendency towards an interaction of rotational axis and stimulus type, $F = (1,217) = 2.988$; $p = .085$; $\eta^2 = .014$, a significant interaction of gender and rotational axis, $F = (1,217) = 4.445$; $p = .036$; $\eta^2 = .020$, and a significant three-way interaction of gender, rotational axis and stimulus type $F = (1,217) = 3.765$; $p = .054$; $\eta^2 = .017$. None of the remaining effects approached significance, all $p > .10$, all $\eta^2 < .01$. The direction of the main effects and interactions are shown in figure 3, 4 and 5 and were further analyzed by simple main effects. While participants' performance did not significantly differ in the two picture-plane conditions, $F = (1,117) = 0.000$; $p = .985$; $\eta^2 = .000$, effect analyses reflected a higher overall performance in the in-depth condition with cube figures than with pellet figures, $F = (1,103) = 7.140$; $p = .009$; $\eta^2 = .065$ (see Fig. 3). Also, simple effect analyses showed a non-significant higher performance of boys in the picture-plane condition, $F (1,117) = 1.969$; $p = .163$; $\eta^2 = .017$, and a significantly higher performance of boys in the in-depth conditions, $F = (1,103) = 10.305$; $p = .002$; $\eta^2 = .091$ (see Fig. 4.).

Analyzing the three-way interaction, only a significantly higher performance of boys in the in-depth condition for the cube-figure tasks was found, $F = (1,53) = 8.633$; $p = .005$; $\eta^2 = .140$, while there were neither significant gender differences found in the in-depth condition for the pellet-figure tasks, $F = (1,47) = 1.710$; $p = .197$; $\eta^2 = .035$, nor in the picture-plane condition for both, cube-figures, $F = (1,49) = 0.430$; $p = .515$; $\eta^2 = .009$, or pellet-figures, $F = (1,65) = 1.554$; $p = .217$; $\eta^2 = .023$ (see Fig. 5).

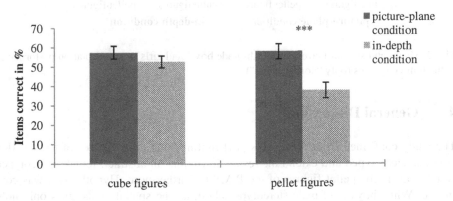

Fig. 3. Mental-rotation performance (means) as a function of rotational axis and stimulus material. Error bars represent standard errors of the mean

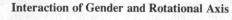

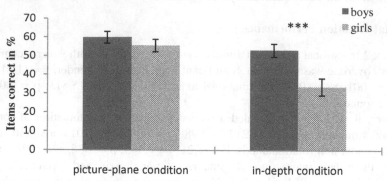

Fig. 4. Mental-rotation performance (means) as a function of gender and rotational axis. Error bars represent standard errors of the mean

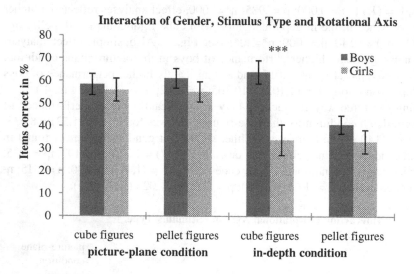

Fig. 5. Means and standard errors of fourth-grade boys' and girls' mental-rotation performance in the four conditions (only "non-guessers")

4   General Discussion

The study confirmed Ruthsatz et al.'s [14] findings that cube figures of the C-MRT are male-stereotyped and extend the results in finding an abstract, female-stereotyped counterpart in the pellet figures of the P-MRT. Furthermore, Hypothesis 2 was confirmed. While boys hold male stereotypes about all the spatial skills, girls only hold male stereotypes about the ability to play with LEGO®. These findings support results of previous research [8] and might partly explain the male advantage with cube-figure tasks. Ruthsatz et al. [14] and Alexander and Evardone [15] already revealed an advantage for own-gender congruent stimuli with concrete-objects and human-figure tasks. Present results showed that this advantage also seems to exist with abstract objects, which are constructed in the same manner as objects of the boys' realm of experience. Additionally, mental-rotation tasks themselves might induce a stereotype-lift effect in boys, because they assumed the ability to solve mental-rotation tasks to be male-stereotyped. This would extend the results of Ramirez, Gunderson, Levine and Beilock [25], who found spatial activities themselves leading to stereotype-threat effects.

In line with Neuburger et al. [19], Hypothesis 3 was confirmed. Boys significantly outperformed girls only in tasks with in-depth rotations. Furthermore, there is some evidence that gender differences in mental-rotation tasks also depend on stimulus attributes: the significant three-way interaction of gender, stimulus type and rotational axis shows that next to rotational axis the gender effect was influenced by stimulus type. In face of the highly significant simple-effect result, Hypothesis 4 was supported in the expected direction, with the constraint that performance of boys and girls did not depend on stimulus features in picture-plane tasks. Probably because of a decreased working memory load in tasks, in which the target stimuli had to be rotated only in the Cartesian z-axis, the gender effect disappeared in both picture-plane conditions [19]. A significant gender effect was only found for cube figures rotated in-depth, while performance of boys and girls did not significantly differ in pellet-figure tasks and when cube figures had to be rotated only in the Cartesian z-axis of sight. This is in line with Ruthsatz et al.'s [14] and Alexander and Evardone's [15] findings that test performance of boys could be improved by gender-congruent stimuli. It indicates that results of previous mental-rotation studies which revealed a male advantage is not simply an effect of task difficulty but might partly be explained by the often used cube-figure tasks. The implicit activation of gender stereotypes by test items which are more familiar to boys and male-stereotyped seems to cause stereotype-lift effects in boys. Contrary to Ruthsatz et al. [14], the advantage for own-gender congruent stimuli did not appear with female subjects in the pellet-figure conditions. This seems to point to the fact that an advantage for girls only occurs with concrete, female-stereotyped objects, but not with abstract pellet figures. It was proposed to induce a stereotype-lift effect for girls and thus to improve their performance by replacing the MRT cube figures by female-stereotyped pellet figures. Although pellet figures did not foster girls' performance, results showed that the male advantage disappears, when stimuli are not male-stereotyped.

In contrast to Ruthsatz et al.'s [14] and Voyer, Rodgers, and McCormick's [26] findings, the propensity to guess was not influenced by the stimulus type. The pattern of a higher proportion of male guessers combined with a simultaneously higher performance of boys in the male-stereotyped cube-figure condition was not found. Therefore, current findings did not support the assumption that gender-congruent stimuli lead to a higher propensity to guess and to more self-confidence in solving the task and consequently a higher performance. However, girls showed a significantly higher proportion to guessing in the in-depth conditions, which were accompanied by results below girls' performance in the two picture-plane conditions. This effect matches the main effect of rotational axis found in the current study and might be explained by girls' disadvantage in tasks with occluded items [27] and with in-depth rotations [e.g. 19]: the perceived higher task difficulty might induce stereotype-threat effects in girls and consequently result in lower self-confidence, while boys' low proportion to guessing reflects their higher self-confidence in this domain [28].

Limitations and Future Research. Some limitations of the study should be considered: First, although the pellet figures and the cube figures had identical structures, children in the in-depth conditions overall performed significantly higher in the cube-figure tasks than in the pellet-figure tasks. The fact that the three-dimensionality of the pellets can only be created through shading and not through lines of perspective, like they are used for the cube figures, might have caused a higher task difficulty and possibly lead to floor effects in the pellet-figure condition. Second, methods of the current study do not allow a statement about the strategy used in the administered mental-rotation tasks; hence, they provide no information whether the stereotyped nature of the stimuli influences strategy selection. In order to control this variable maybe chronometric tasks including eye-tracking methods are recommended for further studies. Future research should also consider using a manipulation check prior to conducting mental-rotation tasks in order to activate gender stereotypes more explicitly. Furthermore, because of the high percentage of guessers, sample size was severely reduced after excluding all guessers from further analyses. A larger number of participants might have led to more considerable results. At last, it would be interesting to obtain the results of adolescents and adults.

Acknowledgements. This study was supported by the German Research Foundation (DFG QU/96 4-1/JA 889/7-1).We thank Madeleine Stein, Martina Dirschka and Farida Saeed for data gathering and entry, all children, principals and teachers of the participating schools and Sebastian Pohl, Twisted Artwork, for the technical support in designing the C-MRT and P-MRT stimuli.

References

1. Shepard, S., Metzler, D.: Mental rotation of thredimensional objects. Science 171, 701–703 (1971)
2. Linn, M., Petersen, A.: Emergence and characterization of sex difference in spatial ability: A meta-analysis. Child Development 56, 1479–1498 (1985)
3. Neuburger, S., Jansen, P., Heil, M., Quaiser-Pohl, C.: Gender differences in pre-adolescents' mental-rotation performance: Do they depend on grade and stimulus type? Personality and Individual Differences 50, 1238–1242 (2011)
4. Voyer, D., Voyer, S., Bryden, M.P.: Magnitude of sex differences in spatial abilities: A meta-analysis and consideration of critical variables. Psychological Bulletin 117, 250–270 (1995)
5. Quinn, P.C., Liben, L.S.: A sex difference in mental rotation in young infants. Psychological Science 19, 1067–1070 (2008)

6. Grimshaw, G., Sitarenios, G., Finegan, J.-A.: Mental rotation at 7 years: relations with prenatal testosterone levels and spatial play experiences. Brain and Cognition 29, 85–100 (1995)
7. Pezaris, E., Casey, M.: Girls who use "masculine" problem-solving strategies on a spatial task: proposed genetic and environmental factors. Brain and Cognition 17, 1–22 (1991)
8. Neuburger, S., Ruthsatz, V., Jansen, P., Heil, M., Quaiser-Pohl, C.: Acceptance and Effects of Role Models in the Spatial Domain - A Storytelling Experiment with Fourth Graders. Frontiers in Psychological and Behavioral Science 2(3), 73–88 (2013)
9. Moé, A., Pazzaglia, F.: Following the instructions! Effects of gender beliefs in mental rotation. Learning and Individual Differences 16, 369–377 (2006)
10. Quaiser-Pohl, C., Geiser, C., Lehmann, W.: The relationship between computer-game preference, gender, and mental-rotation ability. Personality and Individual Differences 40, 609–619 (2005)
11. Levine, S., Vasilyeva, M., Lourenco, S.F., Newcombe, N.S., Huttenlocher, J.: Socioeconomic Status Modifies the Sex Difference in Spatial Skill. Psychological Science 16, 841–845 (2005)
12. Jansen-Osmann, P., Heil, M.: Suitable stimuli to obtain (no) gender differences in the speed of cognitive processes involved in mental rotation. Brain and Cognition 64(3), 217–227 (2007)
13. Bors, D.A., Vigneau, F.: Sex differences on the mental rotation test: An analysis of item types. Learning and Individual Differences 21(1), 129–132 (2011)
14. Ruthsatz, V., Neuburger, S., Jansen, P., Quaiser-Pohl, C.: Cars or dolls? Influence of gender, stereotyped stimuli and rotational axis on children's mental rotation performance (2013) (manuscript submitted for publication)
15. Alexander, G.M., Evardone, M.: Blocks and Bodies: Sex Differences in a Novel Version of the Mental Rotations Test. Hormones and Behavior 53(1), 177–184 (2008)
16. Bethell-Fox, C., Shepard, R.: Mental Rotation: Effect of Stimulus Complexity and Familiarity. Journal of Experimental Psychology: Human Perception and Performance 14, 12–23 (1988)
17. Kersh, J., Casey, B., Mercer Young, J.: Research on spatial skills and block building in boys and girls: The relationship to later mathematics learning. In: Saracho, O.N., Spodek, B. (eds.) Contemporary Perspectives on Mathematics in Early Childhood Education, pp. 233–252. Information Age Publishing Inc., Charlotte (2008)
18. Moé, A.: Are males better than females in mental rotation? Exploring a gender belief explanation. Learning and Individual Differences 19, 21–27 (2009)
19. Neuburger, S., Heuser, V., Jansen, P., Quaiser-Pohl, C.: Influence of rotational axis and gender-stereotypical nature of rotation stimuli on the mental-rotation performance of male and female fifth graders. In: Stachniss, C., Schill, K., Uttal, D. (eds.) Spatial Cognition 2012. LNCS, vol. 7463, pp. 220–229. Springer, Heidelberg (2012)
20. The Centren of Women and Job in Technics (Ed.): Gender & Design – Central Questions. Duisburg (2009)
21. Vandenberg, S.G., Kuse, A.R.: Mental rotations. A group test of three-dimensional spatial visualization. Perceptual and Motor Skills 47, 599–604 (1978)
22. Trautner, H.M., Helbing, N., Sahm, W.B., Lohaus, A.: Unkenntnis - Rigidität - Flexibilität: Ein Entwicklungsmodell der Geschlechtsrollen-Stereotypisierung. Zeitschrift für Entwicklungspsychologie und pädagogische Psychologie 19, 105–120 (1988)
23. Heller, K., Geisler, H.-J.: KFT 1-3. Kognitiver Fähigkeits-Test (Grundschulform). Beltz Test GmbH, Weinheim (1983)

24. Jöckel, K.H., Babitsch, B., Bellach, B.M., Bloomfield, K., Hoffmeyer-Zlotnik, J.H.P., Winkler, J., Wolf, C.: Messung und Quantifizierung soziodemografischer Merkmale in epidemiologischen Studien. In: Ahrens, W., Bellach, B.-M., Jöckel, K.-H. (eds.) Messung Soziodemografischer Merkmale in der Epidemiologie, pp. 7–38. MMV Münchner Medizin Verlag, München (1998)
25. Ramirez, G., Gunderson, E., Levine, S., Beilock, S.: Spatial anxiety relates to spatial abilities as a funticion of working memory in children. The Quarterly Journal of Experimental Psychology 65(3), 474–487 (2012)
26. Voyer, D., Rodgers, M., McCormick, P.: Timing conditions and the magnitude of gender differences on the Mental Rotations Test. Memory & Cognition 32(1), 72–82 (2004)
27. Voyer, D., Hou, J.: Type of items and the magnitude of gender differences on the Mental Rotations Test. Canadian Journal of Experimental Psychology 60, 91–100 (2006)
28. Cooke-Simpson, A., Voyer, D.: Confidence and gender differences on the Mental Rotations Test. Learning and Individual Differences 17, 181–186 (2007)

A Preliminary Study on the Role of Movement Imagery in Spatial Perception

Margaret R. Tarampi[1], Michael N. Geuss[2], Jeanine K. Stefanucci[2], and Sarah H. Creem-Regehr[2]

[1] Sage Center for the Study of the Mind, University of California, Santa Barbara
Santa Barbara, California, USA
margaret.tarampi@sagecenter.ucsb.edu
[2] Department of Psychology, University of Utah
Salt Lake City, Utah, USA
{m.geuss,jeanine.stefanucci,sarah.creem}@psych.utah.edu

Abstract. According to dance theory, dancers are uniquely aware of the relationship between the environment and their body, making them a type of spatial expert. Inherent in their practice are the abilities to assess the location of other people, objects and the environment relative to their body, and to use movement imagery. The current study tests if dancers perceive the world differently than non-dancers. To test this, dancers performed a battery of spatial tasks (egocentric and exocentric distance estimates, a height judgment, and affordance judgments, i.e., perceived vertical and horizontal passability, stepability, and jumpability) and completed paper-and-pencil spatial ability tests. Dancers differed from non-dancers in their movement imagery ability but superior imagery ability did not result in greater accuracy in imagined distance estimates. Height judgments were overestimated in both groups but less so in dancers. Dancers were found to be, on average, less conservative in their affordance judgments than non-dancers.

Keywords: affordances, distance perception, spatial ability, dance, individual differences, spatial expertise.

1 Introduction

People rely on their ability to represent and process spatial information when driving a car, using tools, or reading a map. Individuals can range greatly in spatial ability as demonstrated in varying aptitude to navigate a novel place, to solve geometry problems, or to dance. Even among spatial experts, such as gymnasts and surgeons, we observe differences in spatial ability specific to their talent and professional training. For example, surgeons that perform open surgery utilize different spatial skills from surgeons that perform laparoscopic surgery [1, 2]. The individual differences literature however has primarily focused on differences in spatial ability relative to cognitive processes such as mental rotation and navigation [3, 4], where individual variation on measures of spatial ability predict performance on complex

C. Freksa et al. (Eds.): Spatial Cognition 2014, LNAI 8684, pp. 383–395, 2014.
© Springer International Publishing Switzerland 2014

tasks. Previous work has not established how spatial ability relates to spatial perception. To test if individual differences in spatial ability influence spatial perception, we investigated if spatial experts differ from non-experts on perceptual tasks.

Perceptual experience is difficult to measure and must be characterized indirectly using judgments or actions. A number of different types of measures of space perception are used such as action-based and non-action-based distance judgments, judgments of height from above, and judgments about potential for action, or *affordances*. While these are effective measures, they are most often examined and compared across group performance and not for individual differences. One example is a blind walking task which involves visually directed walking to targets and spatial updating of objects in the environment [5]. In this task, observers walk without vision to a previously viewed target. Previous studies have shown that observers are, on average, accurate for egocentric distance judgments [5-7]. But under the same conditions observers make systematic errors for exocentric distance judgments [8, 9]. Further, when comparing real and imagined blind walking, absolute walking times differ with imagined walking times being faster than real walking times [10]. However, no difference in real and imagined walking times is observed in high imagery individuals [11]. Another example is judgments of height, which are generally overestimated, and even more so when the judgment of height is from above [12]. Overestimation is seen across multiple measures including verbal estimates of distance and visual matching [13]. This height overestimation may be explained by several factors, including misperception of eye height, state and trait level fear, and the evolutionary cost of falling in vertical navigation [12-14].

Affordances are defined as the perceived potential for action, given the physical limitations of the body and environment [15]. Affordance judgments require an observer to verbally indicate if a certain action can be performed in the given environment, where the capabilities of the actor (e.g. actor's height, or jumping ability) must be considered relative to the characteristics of the environment (e.g. height of a barrier, or extent of a gap). Previous research has shown that participants are cautious (indicating they are unable to perform actions that are possible) in judging perceived affordances for passage (horizontal passability), for walking under a barrier (vertical passability), for stepping up (stepability), and for jumping over an extent (jumpability) [16-18]. Physical changes to the body (e.g., changing eye height or the actor's physical width) have been shown to influence perceived affordance judgments supporting that physical aspects of the body influence action judgments [18, 19]. Additionally, the level of experience with a body change, such as wearing a helmet, may also influence action judgments [18, 20].

The variability seen in these perceptual judgments has been explained in the context of evolutionary adaptations, embodied cognition, and differences in the use of available visual information [8, 14, 19]. However, in most of the prior work conditions were averaged across people instead of defined as differences with respect to individuals. Given that other evidence suggests that perceptual judgments can be improved with practice and training [21, 22], individuals with more experience in relevant abilities may show differences in performance on perceptual tasks.

One individual difference in ability, spatial expertise, results in higher scores on traditional measures of spatial ability and can be characterized by excellence in desirable abilities or component processes. A particularly relevant group of spatial experts are dancers, who have training and practice in spatial awareness and movement imagery. Dancers rely more on an egocentric frame of reference or a body-centered reference frame [23]. Inherent in their practice is the ability to assess the location of other people, objects, and the environment relative to their body. This fundamental concept of spatial awareness of the dancer's body in relationship to the environment is captured in Rudolf Laban's modern dance theory of Space Harmony [24]. Space Harmony describes spatial awareness relative to movement and is largely body-based. Research has confirmed that motor experts including professional dancers are better able to perceive action relevant information and discriminate proprioceptive information [25-27]. Dancers are also skilled in imagery. In a study on mental imagery, experienced dancers scored significantly higher on body imagery, cognitive imagery, and visual-spatial imagery compared to novices [28]. Overby [28] attributes dancers better visual-spatial imagery to the physical manipulation of space by dancers and the constant feedback that they receive from their instructors and from mirrors.

We predict that dancers, due to their familiarity with their body's physical capabilities and superior imagery abilities, should show no difference in real and imagined blind walking times, less overestimation of perceived height due to better perception of eye height, and require a smaller margin of error when making affordance judgments. Dancers' greater experience with egocentric reference frames should result in better egocentric blind walking performance but equivalent performance with non-dancers on exocentric blind walking. We also hypothesize that dancers will score higher on the MIQ-R (Movement Imagery Questionnaire-Revised) and the Perspective Taking/Spatial Orientation Test (SOT) compared to non-dancers. The MIQ-R assesses movement imagery through two subscales of visual and kinesthetic imagery [29], both of which are essential in dance practice [30-32]. The SOT is a measure of spatial orientation ability, which is the ability to mentally transform one's perspective relative to others, objects, or the environment. Perspective taking is necessary in learning dance choreography from instructors, other dancers, or mirrors [28, 33]. Finally, we predicted no differences in spatial visualization ability and environmental spatial ability. Spatial visualization is the ability to mentally transform objects. Environmental spatial ability is large-scale spatial ability related to navigation and learning the layout of a space.

2   Method

2.1   Participants

Twenty University of Utah students participated as part of a course requirement or for monetary compensation. All participants had normal or corrected-to-normal vision. The experimental group included 10 dancers (9 females and 1 male), with a mean age of 21.9 years, mean dance experience of 16.3 years, and mean frequency of practice per week of 28.4 hours. Dancers were trained in ballet, jazz, or modern dance. The dancer population at University of Utah is majority female, so recruitment was biased towards females. Non-dancers were gendered matched. The control group consisted of 10 participants (9 females and 1 male), with a mean age of 26.3 years, mean dance experience of 1.5 years, and mean frequency of practice per week of 0.0 hours.

2.2   Materials

The materials included a battery of pencil-and-paper measures - Perspective Taking/Spatial Orientation Test [SOT; 34], Santa Barbara Sense of Direction [SBSOD; 35], Movement Imagery Questionnaire-Revised [MIQ-R; 29], and Vandenberg Mental Rotation Task [MRT; 36]. In the SOT, participants were shown a 2D drawing of seven objects. They were asked to imagine themselves standing at one of the objects while facing another object and then asked to indicate the location of a third object relative to the imagined position. In the SBSOD, participants self-reported their environmental spatial ability based on responses to fifteen questions on a 7-point Likert scale. In the MIQ-R, participants were asked to perform a movement and then imagine performing the movement using either visual or kinesthetic imagery. In the MRT, participants were presented with a series of five 2D line drawings of 3D objects where one image was a reference image and the participants were asked to choose two of the four remaining drawings that were the same as the reference image but just rotated.

2.3   Apparatus

In each egocentric distance estimate trial, two poles (2.43 m tall and 20 cm wide) placed at an exocentric distance of 3 m on the ground-plane were located so that the center point between the two poles was at the egocentric distances of 3, 4, or 5 meters. In each exocentric distance estimate trial, two poles placed at an egocentric distance of 3 m were located away from each other at exocentric distances of 3, 4, or 5 meters. For the blind walking task, participants saw the same two black vertical poles and were asked to estimate walking to their location.

For the passing through affordance judgment, the same vertical poles were set up 2 m away from the participant. The poles were set up randomly between 30 and 55 cm apart at 5 cm intervals and were centered at the participant. For the stepping up affordance judgment, an adjustable workout step platform was set up 1.5 m away from the participant. The whole apparatus was covered with a blanket to hide the number of blocks holding up the platform. The platform sat on top of stackable blocks allowing for random presentation of the step at 54 cm to 89 cm tall at 5 cm intervals. For the jumping over affordance judgment (standing long jump), two wood sticks indicated the extent. Participants stood with their toes touching one board while the position of the other board was varied. The extent was presented in random intervals between 90 cm and 250 cm at 20 cm intervals. For the walking under affordance judgment, a horizontal barrier was set up 3 m away from the participant. The barrier was a 1.9 cm × 14 cm x 244 cm wood board oriented so that the smallest dimension faced the participant. The barrier could be raised and lowered via a pulley system. The barrier was initially placed (in randomized order) at the top and was lowered or at the bottom and was raised.

2.4   Procedure

Participants gave informed consent in a hallway outside of the experiment room. First, they were trained for the various tasks, including 1) walking without vision while being guided by the experimenter, 2) blind walking independently, and 3) practicing with egocentric and exocentric distance judgments. None of the training involved feedback about accuracy. Then the experimenter guided participants to a starting location in the experiment room, from which they performed two practice trials without feedback to ensure that they understood each task. Following the practice, the participant performed 24 additional trials (a total of 2 trials at each distance for each task).

In the same room and using the same black poles, participants indicated whether they could pass through an opening without touching the inside of the two poles and without rotating their shoulders. Then, they judged the size of the opening, by instructing the experimenter to retract or extend a tape measure (number facing away from the participant) until the length of the tape measure was perceptually equal to the presented aperture.

Following the aperture judgments, participants were taken to a second floor balcony and asked to make a height judgment from the top of the balcony railing to the ground. The judgment was made using a visual matching measure where the experimenter moved away from the participant until the participant judged that the distance between themselves and the experimenter was equal to distance from the top of the railing to the ground plane.

Participants were then brought to another experiment room where they completed a battery of spatial abilities tests. The order of presentation for the psychometric tests was counter-balanced and pseudo-randomized across participants.

Participants were then asked to judge what they could walk under. A barrier was moved continuously up or down until the participant judged that they could pass safely underneath the barrier without needing to duck. Following the affordance judgments perceptual judgments were made of the height of the board presented randomly at 141 cm, 166 cm, 191 cm and 262 cm. The same visual matching measure from the height judgment was used. Next participants were asked to judge what they could step on using only one foot on the top of the step and without any assistance to remain balanced such as the use of hands to grasp another object or person while stepping. They also estimated the height of the step. The experimenter would pull out the blank side of a tape measure which was affixed to the top of a door and the participant would indicate when they thought the tape measure was equal to the height of the step. Finally, participants judged (yes or no) what they could jump over without a running start. They also estimated the extent using the visual matching measure previously described.

Participants' vision was checked using a Snellen eye chart and anthropometric measures were taken. The participants were also asked to physically jump as far as they could using the same parameters as the jumping over task and the distance of their jump was measured from the toes at their starting position to their back heel at their landing position. Participants were also asked to physically step onto a platform as tall as their highest affirmative stepping up judgment using the same parameters as the stepping up task. If they were not able to step on the platform successfully, blocks were removed until they were able to step on the platform. If they could step on the platform, blocks were added until they were no longer able to step on the platform successfully. Participants were then debriefed. The study took a total of two hours to complete.

3   Results

3.1   Spatial Ability Measures

Independent-samples t-tests were conducted to compare psychometric test scores between dancers and non-dancer controls. Dancers' scored significantly higher on the visual ($M = 27.300$, $SD = 0.823$) section of the MIQ-R than non-dancers ($M = 22.400$, $SD = 6.851$; $t(18) = 2.246$, $p = 0.038$). A higher score on the visual section of the

Table 1. Mean and Standard Deviation for Psychometric Tests According to Expertise

Variable	n	M	SD	t	p
SBSOD					
Controls	10	4.514	0.865	-0.277	0.785
Dancers	10	4.409	0.827		
SOT					
Controls	10	54.443	55.508	0.445	0.662
Dancers	10	64.796	48.298		
MRT					
Controls	10	36.000	20.656	0.312	0.759
Dancers	10	38.800	19.510		
MIQ-R VIS					
Controls	10	22.400	6.851	2.246*	0.038
Dancers	10	27.300	0.823		
MIQ-R KIN					
Controls	10	21.300	6.219	1.99	0.062
Dancers	10	25.700	3.199		

Note. M = mean. SD = standard deviation. *$p < .05$.

MIQ-R indicates better visual imagery ability, which is associated with how effective the use of imagery will be in the performance of movement. Dancers' scores on the kinesthetic (M = 25.700, SD = 3.199) section of the MIQ-R was trending in the predicted direction compared to non-dancers (M = 21.300, SD = 6.219); $t(18)$ = -1.990, p = 0.062). There were no other differences between dancers and non-dancers on measures of spatial ability (*see* Table 1). These results confirm previous studies that have demonstrated that dancers have higher imagery abilities than non-dancers but are no different in other spatial skills [28, 37]. No age or gender differences were found in spatial ability.

3.2   Egocentric and Exocentric Distance Estimates

A 2 (task: ego, exo) x 3 (distance: 3, 4, 5m) x 2 (expertise: dancer, non-dancer) mixed-measures ANOVA was performed on mean absolute distance walked with task and distance as within-subjects variables and expertise as a between-subjects variable. There was no effect of task (p = 0.140) or expertise (p = .453). There was a significant effect only of distance [$F(2,36)$ = 192.952, p < .001, η^2 = .958] indicating that distance walked increased with increasing absolute distance. A 2 (task: ego, exo) x 2 (condition: real, imagined) x 3 (distance: 3, 4, 5m) x 2 (expertise: dancer, non-dancer) mixed-measures ANOVA was performed on mean walking time with task, condition and distance as within-subjects variables and expertise as a between-subjects variable. There was a significant effect of distance [$F(2,36)$ = 236.841, p < .001, η^2 = .929] and of task [$F(1,18)$ = 8.265, p = .010, η^2 = .315]. There was also a significant effect of condition [$F(1,18)$ = 28.847, p < .001, η^2 = .616] where imagined walking times were underestimated compared to real walking times. There was no effect of expertise (p = .620).

3.3   Height Judgment

We regressed height ratios (judged height/actual height) onto expertise (0 – non-dancers, 1 – dancers). There was a trend toward a significant effect of expertise (B = -.161, p = .075) where dancers (M = 1.504; SD = .166) were more accurate than non-dancers (M = 1.665; SD = .213) but both groups overestimated the height.

3.4   Affordance Judgments

Passing through Affordance Judgment. We regressed passing through ratios (judged height/actual shoulder weight) onto expertise (0 – non-dancers, 1 – dancers). There was a significant effect of expertise (B = -.122, p = .010). On average, dancers judged that they could pass through aperture sizes that were .122 smaller relative to their own shoulder width (dancers: M = .877; SD = .062; non-dancers: M = .999; SD = .118). A 2 (order: first judgment, second) x 6 (aperture size: 30, 35, 40, 45, 50, 55) x 2 (expertise: dancer, non-dancer) mixed-measures ANOVAs were performed on ratios of aperture estimates (estimate/actual aperture size) with order and aperture size as within-subjects variables and expertise as a between-subjects variable. There was no effect of aperture size ($p = 0.270$). There was a trend toward a significant effect of order [$F(1,18) = 4.348$, $p = 0.052$, $\eta^2 = .195$]. There was a significant effect of expertise [$F(1,18) = 6.052$, $p = .024$, $\eta^2 = .252$] where dancers ($M = .954$; $SD = .033$) perceived apertures as smaller than they actual are compared to non-dancers ($M = 1.070$; $SD = .033$).

Walking under Affordance Judgment. We regressed walking-under ratios onto expertise (0 – non-dancers, 1 – dancers). There was not a significant effect of expertise ($B = .0004$, $p = .981$) suggesting that expertise does not influence judgments of when one has to duck to walk under a barrier (dancers: $M = 1.020$; $SD = .028$; non-dancers: $M = 1.019$; $SD = .039$). A 4 (height: 141, 166, 191, 262) x 2 (expertise: dancer, non-dancer) mixed-measures ANOVAs were performed on ratios of barrier height estimates (estimate/actual barrier height) with height as a within-subjects variable and expertise as a between-subjects variable. There was a significant effect of height [$F(1,18) = 2.992$, $p = .039$, $\eta^2 = .143$]. There was no effect of expertise ($p = .702$).

Stepping Up Affordance Judgment. We regressed stepping-up ratios onto expertise (0 – non-dancers, 1 – dancers). There was not a significant effect of expertise ($B = .045$, $p = .326$) suggesting that expertise does not influence judgments of stepping up (dancers: $M = .925$; $SD = .048$; non-dancers: $M = .880$; $SD = .133$). A 2 (order: first judgment, second) x 8 (height: 54, 59, 64, 69, 74, 79, 84, 89) x 2 (expertise: dancer, non-dancer) mixed-measures ANOVAs were performed on ratios of step estimates (estimate/actual step height) with order and height as within-subjects variables and expertise as a between-subjects variable. There was a significant effect of height [$F(1,18) = 12.021$, $p < 0.001$, $\eta^2 = .400$] where smaller steps are seen as shorter than actual and larger steps are seen as taller than actual. There was no effect of order ($p = 0.193$). There was no effect of expertise ($p = .175$).

Jumping Over Affordance Judgment. We regressed jumping-over ratios onto expertise (0 – non-dancers, 1 – dancers). There was not a significant effect of expertise ($B = .081$, $p = .228$) suggesting that expertise does not influence judgments of jumping over extents (dancers: $M = 1.163$; $SD = .172$; non-dancers: $M = 1.082$; $SD = .112$). A 2 (order: first judgment, second) x 9 (extent: 90, 110, 130, 150, 170, 190, 210, 230, 250) x 2 (expertise: dancer, non-dancer) mixed-measures ANOVAs were performed on ratios of extent estimates (estimate/actual extent) with order and extent as within-subjects variables and expertise as a between-subjects variable. There was a significant effect of extent [$F(1,18) = 4.457$, $p < 0.001$, $\eta^2 = .198$] where in general shorter extents are seen as longer and longer extents are seen more accurately. There was also a significant effect of order [$F(1,18) = 5.471$, $p = 0.031$, $\eta^2 = .233$] where second judgments ($M = 1.043$; $SD = .018$) were more accurate than first judgments ($M = 1.078$; $SD = .024$). There was trend toward a significant effect of expertise [$F(1,18) = 4.338$, $p = .052$, $\eta^2 = .194$] where dancers ($M = 1.020$; $SD = .028$) perceived extents more accurately than non-dancers ($M = 1.102$; $SD = .028$).

4   Discussion

Our investigation provides insight into whether certain populations of spatial experts, such as dancers, may perceive space differently as a function of their training (i.e., greater body awareness and better movement imagery compared to the non-dancers). Dancers differed from non-dancers in their movement imagery ability but superior imagery ability did not result in greater accuracy in real or imagined distance estimates. Height judgments were overestimated in both groups but less so in dancers. On average, dancers were found to be less conservative in their affordance judgments than non-dancers.

Body awareness of dancers may be complicated by their motor expertise [27, 33]. This is a reasonable assertion given Keinänen, Hetland and Winner's [38] argument that dance is multifaceted, making use of many cognitive skills. Dancers use an egocentric frame of reference when performing motor movements in space. Thus, dancers may have a greater egocentric awareness that is specific to their moving bodies in personal space and reflective of their greater movement imagery.

Dancers might not have been as effective in using their exceptional body awareness because they were asked to make affordance judgments relative to their bodies but *outside* of their personal space. Cutting and Vishton [39] defined three regions of space – personal space, action space, and vista space. Personal or near space is roughly the region of space within arm's reach and includes a 2 meter area extending from the observer. Personal space is the space that is reachable by a stationary observer. Action or intermediate space is the area just beyond personal space from 2 to 30 meters. Action space is easily accessible through locomotion or other actions. Vista or distant space extends beyond 30 meters. Objects in vista space are generally not immediately actionable by the observer. The affordance tasks in our study were perceptual tasks requiring egocentric judgments beyond personal space but within action space. Again in dance theory, Laban [40, 41] refers to the space directly around the body within reach of the body's limbs as the Kinesphere. The Kinesphere defines zones of possible movement and is consistent conceptually with personal space. A dancer's intensive experience of egocentric awareness may therefore be constrained by a dynamic rather than a static understanding of space. Another possibility is that dancers' egocentric experience relies more on an intrinsic egocentric representation (i.e., body-part representations) rather than an extrinsic egocentric representation (i.e., body representation) [42]. The affordance judgments used in this study could be adapted to involve actual movement, or dynamic rather than static judgments. Affordances involving judgments relative to an actor's body parts may also be interesting to test.

Dancers did not differ from non-experts on measures of egocentric and exocentric distance perception but were least variable on egocentric blind walking compared to non-dancers. This may be due to dancers' reliance on an egocentric frame of reference for their dance practice. Surprisingly, dancers also did not differ on imagined blinding walking even though they have greater movement imagery ability. Kunz, Creem-Regehr and Thompson [10] argue that imagined walking requires both motor imagery and the presence of biomechanical information to calibrate mental timing. While dancers excel at movement imagery it is possible that for experimental tasks that limit actual movement, imagery ability alone does not help.

Past research of the MIQ-R has suggested that movement imagery ability is implicated in predicting motor task performance [29]. Additionally, Taylor & Taylor [43] indicated that there is a relationship between dancers' use of imagery and increases in self-confidence. Interestingly, we found dancers to be, on average, less conservative in their affordance judgments than non-dancers. Their overconfidence sometimes even led to judging that they could perform tasks that they could not physically perform. It is also possible that the greater self-confidence resulted in greater accuracy on some affordance judgments. Dancers were actually more accurate in their judgments of stepping up. But greater confidence can also run the risk of overestimation of ability. This may have been the case when dancers indicated that they could pass through apertures that they physically could not pass through. This is further complicated by the incongruence of dancers' perceptual judgments relative to their affordance judgments. There is some data to suggest that the position of the hands may influence perceptual judgments of aperture size, where apertures appear smaller when hands are positioned further away from each other [19]. But little is known about how hand position influences affordance judgments. While all participants were asked to keep their hands at their sides, there may have been variation in how participants complied.

The disparity in our results of no significant differences between dancers and non-dancers for walking under a barrier, jumping over an extent, and stepping up compared to significant differences in passage, may be explained as a matter of experience. Of the four affordances, dancers judge passage frequently in their daily practice when negotiating between other dancers whose position changes dynamically while level changes, head height barriers, and jumping over a critical extent rarely occurs. Measures of confidence and body image should be included in future studies as they may help explain more of the variance in affordance judgments.

The perceptual tasks in this study were chosen as the potentially most indicative measures of individual differences in spatial perception. In general, small sample sizes in perceptual tasks are common and found to be sufficient in revealing significant group effects. However, caution should be given to the specific body of results obtained in the present study. Larger sample sizes may be necessary to support these findings and to investigate further differences in spatial perception as a function of individual differences in spatial ability. As a preliminary study, the variety of perceptual tasks and psychometric tests were included to allow for future comparisons with other spatial expert groups, such as athletes and architects, where different predictions may be expected. For example, architects may be predicted to be better at exocentric distance estimates and affordance judgments based on reliance on an allocentric reference frame [44]. Using the effect sizes in the present study, a prospective power analysis could be used to estimate an adequate sample size for future between-subjects studies. As a starting point, this battery of measures also indicates future research directions, such as investigating dynamic spatial thinking in dancers. Dynamic spatial thinking refers to the ability to deal with moving objects and relative motion. The literature suggests that there are robust individual differences in dynamic spatial ability that are partially mediated by experience [45]. Individual differences in spatial perception should also be explored in other spatial perception tasks such as size perception or dynamic spatial orientation.

Acknowledgements. We would like to thank Aaron Haskell, Chuanjian Wang, and Shilo Platts for laboratory assistance in running participants, and Ellen Bromberg for help in recruiting dancers. This work was supported by NSF grant 0914488.

References

1. Klatzky, R., Wu, B.: The embodied actor in multiple frames of reference. In: Klatzky, R.L., MacWhinney, B., Behrmann, M. (eds.) Embodiment, Ego-Space and Action, pp. 145–176. Psychology Press, Philadelphia (2008)
2. Keehner, M., Lippa, Y., Montello, D.R., Tendick, F., Hegarty, M.: Learning a spatial skill for surgery: How the contributions of abilities change with practice. Applied Cognitive Psychology 20, 487–503 (2006)
3. Hegarty, M., Montello, D., Richardson, A., Ishikawa, T., Lovelace, K.: Spatial abilities at different scales: Individual differences in aptitude-test performance and spatial-layout learning. Intelligence 34, 151–176 (2006)
4. Wolbers, T., Hegarty, M.: What determines our navigational abilities? Trends in Cognitive Sciences 14, 138-146 (2010)
5. Loomis, J.M., Da Silva, J.A., Fujita, N., Fukusima, S.S.: Visual space perception and visually directed action. Journal of Experimental Psychology. Human Perception and Performance 18, 906–921 (1992)
6. Philbeck, J.W., Loomis, J.M.: Comparison of two indicators of perceived egocentric distance under full-cue and reduced-cue conditions. Journal of Experimental Psychology. Human Perception and Performance 23, 72–85 (1997)
7. Rieser, J.J., Ashmead, D.H., Talor, C.R., Youngquist, G.A.: Visual perception and the guidance of locomotion without vision to previously seen targets. Perception 19, 675–689 (1990)
8. Loomis, J.M., Philbeck, J.W., Zahorik, P.: Dissociation between location and shape in visual space. Journal of Experimental Psychology: Human Perception and Performance 28, 1202–1212 (2002)
9. Foley, J.M., Ribeiro-Filho, N.P., Da Silva, J.A.: Visual perception of extent and the geometry of visual space. Vision Research 44, 147–156 (2004)
10. Kunz, B.R., Creem-Regehr, S.H., Thompson, W.B.: Evidence for motor simulation in imagined locomotion. Journal of Experimental Psychology: Human Perception and Performance 35, 1458–1471 (2009)
11. Decety, J., Jeannerod, M., Prablanc, C.: The timing of mentally represented actions. Behavioural Brain Research 34, 35–42 (1989)
12. Stefanucci, J.K., Proffitt, D.R.: The roles of altitude and fear in the perception of heights. Journal of Experimental Psychology: Human Perception & Performance 35, 424–438 (2009)
13. Sinai, M.J., Ooi, T.L., He, Z.J.: Terrain influences the accurate judgement of distance. Nature 395, 497–500 (1998)
14. Jackson, R.E., Cormack, L.K.: Evolved navigation theory and the descent illusion. Perception & Psychophysics 69, 353–362 (2007)

15. Gibson, J.J.: The ecological approach to visual perception. Houghton Mifflin, Boston (1979)
16. Warren, W.H.: Perceiving affordances: The visual guidance of stair climbing. Journal of Experimental Psychology: Human Perception and Performance 10, 683–703 (1984)
17. Warren, W.H., Whang, S.: Visual guidance of walking through apertures: Body-scaled information for affordances. Journal of Experimental Psychology: Human Perception & Performance 13, 371–383 (1987)
18. Stefanucci, J.K., Geuss, M.N.: Duck! Scaling the height of a horizontal barrier to body height. Attention, Perception, & Psychophysics 72, 1338–1349 (2010)
19. Stefanucci, J.K., Geuss, M.N.: Big people, little world: The body influences size perception. Perception 38, 1782–1795 (2009)
20. Franchak, J.M., Adolph, K.E.: Gut estimates: Pregnant women adapt to changing possibilities for squeezing through doorways. Attention, Perception, & Psychophysics, 1–13 (2013)
21. Gibson, E.J.: Improvement in perceptual judgments as a function of controlled practice or training. Psychological Bulletin 50, 401–431 (1953)
22. Ahissar, M., Hochstein, S.: Task difficulty and the specificity of perceptual learning. Nature 387, 401–406 (1997)
23. Leman, M., Naveda, L.: Basic gestures as spatiotemporal reference frames for repetitive dance/music patterns in Samba and Charleston. Music Perception 28, 71–91 (2010)
24. Laban, R.: Mastery of movement on the stage. MacDonald & Evans, London (1950)
25. Jansen, P., Lehmann, J.: Mental rotation performance in soccer players and gymnasts in an object-based mental rotation task. Advances in Cognitive Psychology 9, 92 (2013)
26. Barrack, R., Skinner, H., Cook, S.: Proprioception of the knee joint: paradoxical effect of training. American Journal of Physical Medicine & Rehabilitation 63, 175–181 (1984)
27. Steggemann, Y., Engbert, K., Weigelt, M.: Selective effects of motor expertise in mental body rotation tasks: Comparing object-based and perspective transformations. Brain and Cognition 76, 97–105 (2011)
28. Overby, L.Y.: A comparison of novice and experienced dancers' imagery ability. Journal of Mental Imagery 14, 173–184 (1990)
29. Hall, C.R., Martin, K.A.: Measuring movement imagery abilities: A revision of the Movement Imagery Questionnaire. Journal of Mental Imagery 21, 143–154 (1997)
30. Fish, L., Hall, C., Cumming, J.: Investigating the use of imagery by elite ballet dancers. Avante 10, 26–39 (2004)
31. Hanrahan, C., Tétreau, B., Sarrazin, C.: Use of imagery while performing dance movement. International Journal of Sport Psychology 26, 413–430 (1995)
32. Hanrahan, C., Vergeer, I.: Multiple uses of mental imagery by professional modern dancers. Imagination, Cognition and Personality 20, 231–255 (2000)
33. Jola, C., Mast, F.W.: Mental object rotation and egocentric body transformation: Two dissociable processes? Spatial Cognition & Computation 5, 217–237 (2005)
34. Hegarty, M., Waller, D.: A dissociation between mental rotation and perspective-taking spatial abilities. Intelligence 32, 175–191 (2004)
35. Hegarty, M., Richardson, A., Montello, D., Lovelace, K., Subbiah, I.: Development of a self-report measure of environmental spatial ability. Intelligence 30, 425–447 (2002)
36. Vandenberg, S., Kuse, A.: Mental rotations, a group test of three-dimensional spatial visualization. Perceptual and Motor Skills 47, 599 (1978)
37. Corsi-Cabrera, M., Gutierrez, L.: Spatial ability in classic dancers and their perceptual style. Perceptual and Motor Skills 72, 399–402 (1991)

38. Keinänen, M., Hetland, L., Winner, E.: Teaching cognitive skill through dance: Evidence for near but not far transfer. Journal of Aesthetic Education 34, 295–306 (2000)
39. Cutting, J.E., Vishton, P.M.: Perceiving layout and knowing distances: The integration, relative potency, and contextual use of different information about depth. In: Epstein, W., Rogers, S. (eds.) Handbook of Perception and Cognition: Perception of Space and Motion, vol. 5, pp. 69–117. Academic Press, San Diego (1995)
40. Laban, R.: Modern educational dance. Macdonald & Evans, London (1975)
41. Laban, R., Ullmann, L.: Choreutics. Macdonald & Evans, London (1966)
42. Creem-Regehr, S.H., Neil, J.A., Yeh, H.J.: Neural correlates of two imagined egocentric transformations. Neuroimage 35, 916–927 (2007)
43. Taylor, J., Taylor, C.: Psychology of dance. Human Kinetics Publishers, Champaign (1995)
44. Hölscher, C., Brösamle, M., Conroy Dalton, R.: On the role of spatial analysis in design synthesis: the case of wayfinding. In: NSF International Workshop on Studying Visual and Spatial Reasoning for Design Creativity, SDC 2010 (2010)
45. Law, D.J., Pellegrino, J.W., Hunt, E.B.: Comparing the tortoise and the hare: Gender differences and experience in dynamic spatial reasoning tasks. Psychological Science 4, 35 (1993)

Author Index